Edward Terry
SANFORD

Edward Terry SANFORD

A Tennessean on the US Supreme Court

STEPHANIE L. SLATER

THE UNIVERSITY OF TENNESSEE PRESS

Knoxville

Copyright © 2018 by The University of Tennessee Press / Knoxville.
All Rights Reserved.
Hardcover: 1st printing, 2018.
Paperback: 1st printing, 2018.

LIBRARY OF CONGRESS CATALOGING-IN-PUBLICATION DATA
Names: Slater, Stephanie L., author.
Title: Edward Terry Sanford: a Tennessean on the US Supreme Court /
Stephanie L. Slater.
Description: First edition. | Knoxville: The University of Tennessee Press,
[2018] | Includes bibliographical references and index. |
Identifiers: LCCN 2017027915 (print) | LCCN 2017028125 (ebook) |
ISBN 9781621903703 (pdf) | ISBN 9781621903697 (hardcover) |
ISBN 9781621905172 (paperback)
Subjects: LCSH: Sanford, Edward Terry, 1865–1930. |
Judges—United States—Biography. | United States. Supreme Court—
Officials and employees—Biography. | Judges—Tennessee—Biography.
Classification: LCC KF8745.S25 (ebook) | LCC KF8745.S25 S53 2018 (print) |
DDC 324.73/2634 [B] —dc23
LC record available at https://lccn.loc.gov/2017027915

To the memory of Sandra G. Slater (1942–2008).
She lit the light of learning for me and continues to keep the lamp well oiled.
In me and her countless students, her soul exists—she is a part of us.

To live in hearts we leave behind is not to die.
—Thomas Campbell (1777–1844)

CONTENTS

	Preface	xi
	Acknowledgments	xiii
CHAPTER ONE	The End Came Swiftly	1
CHAPTER TWO	"A Distinct and Peculiar People"	5
CHAPTER THREE	Sanford's Early Years	29
CHAPTER FOUR	Private Practice and Family	55
CHAPTER FIVE	Civic and Professional Pursuits and Political Activities	89
CHAPTER SIX	Department of Justice	125
CHAPTER SEVEN	District Judge	145
CHAPTER EIGHT	US Supreme Court Justice	183
CHAPTER NINE	The Taft Court	225
CHAPTER TEN	Sanford's Tenure	237
CHAPTER ELEVEN	*Gitlow v. New York*	281
CHAPTER TWELVE	Forgotten	305
	Appendix: Sanford's Decisions	315
	Notes	323
	Bibliography	427
	Index	455

ILLUSTRATIONS

following page 208

Knoxville's Post Office and Custom House, Completed in 1874
Knoxville as Seen from Summit Hill, ca. 1877
Albert Chavannes
Anna Francillion Chavannes
Colonel E. J. Sanford
Emma Chavannes Sanford
Sanford Family Photo
Edward J. Sanford Mansion, Maplehurst
View of Gay Street's 400 Block, Early Twentieth Century
Woodruff House, Knoxville, Tennessee
Edward Terry Sanford as a Student at Harvard University
Lutie M. Sanford
The First Official Photograph of Associate Justice
   Edward Terry Sanford
Formal Group Photograph of the 1923 Taft Court
Formal Group Photograph of the 1925 Taft Court
Supreme Court Justices Standing Behind a Model of the
   Proposed Building to House the US Supreme Court,
   May 17, 1929
Supreme Court Justices Leaving the White House after Paying
   Their Annual Courtesy Call on President Calvin Coolidge
Edward and Lutie Sanford Seated in the Grandstand for
   an Event
Justice Edward Terry Sanford and Alice Roosevelt Longworth
   Attending a New Year's Day Reception at the White House
Congressman Hubert F. Fisher and Wife Louise Sanford Fisher
   Standing with Sanford on the Platform at Union Station

Chief Justice Taft and Associate Justice Sanford outside the White House

Justices Harlan Fiske Stone, Pierce Butler, James Clark McReynolds, and Chief Justice Charles Evans Hughes at the Rites for Edward Terry Sanford, March 10, 1930

Mounted Photograph of Associate Justice Edward Terry Sanford Seated in His Robes

Half-Length Portrait of Justice Edward Terry Sanford

PREFACE

In the early 1990s, I was a law clerk at the United States District Court for the Eastern District of Tennessee in Knoxville. The court then was housed in the old US Courthouse and Post Office on Main Avenue. Any time we had a hearing in the main courtroom, I would glance up at a huge portrait that hung behind the bench. Intrigued, I investigated and learned that the person depicted was Edward Terry Sanford, a Knoxville native who once sat on the United States Supreme Court. I was absolutely dumbfounded that I had never heard his name mentioned during my time at the University of Tennessee in Knoxville and shocked that no local memorials to him existed. I would stare at that portrait and ask, "What was your life like?" and "Why are you overlooked?" This project seeks to answer these questions and to enlighten readers regarding Sanford's background and career.

STEPHANIE L. SLATER
Knoxville, Tennessee

ACKNOWLEDGMENTS

Many people have given me encouragement and assistance with this project. First, I wish to acknowledge and thank Don Ferguson, Historical Society of the US District Court, Eastern District of Tennessee, who pushed me to believe that I could find the time and energy to even begin this endeavor. Don has been a wonderful friend since my days with that court, and one could not find a better mentor for this effort or for life in general.

Another major supporter of this project and everything else I do is the Honorable Sharon G. Lee, Chief Justice of the Tennessee Supreme Court. Sharon provided me access to her personal library of books on Tennessee history, a gift card to purchase additional books, and, most importantly, constant encouragement. Similarly, Judy Cornett, Ph.D., J.D., Professor with the University of Tennessee College of Law, gave me much needed inspiration and necessary prodding, along with top-notch editing assistance. Without Judy's help, this work would never have been completed.

Many thanks to Sally Goade, D.A., J.D., Attorney for the Tennessee Court of Appeals, for her proofreading and suggestions. I am indebted to Harolda Bryson, LaToyia Trotter, and Mary Halliburton Dyer, University of Tennessee College of Law, for their research assistance. The mother/daughter team of Bernie and Janet Buzzelli served as excellent proofreaders, as did John Price, a law student at Ohio State University; Vickie Valentine, J.D., a former colleague at the US District Court for the Eastern District of Tennessee; Julee Tate Flood, Ph.D., J.D., a Professor of Law at Elon University; my sister-in-law, Barbara M. Slater; and my co-worker, Amy Paul, J.D., Attorney with the Tennessee Court of Criminal Appeals.

Additional appreciation goes to Sandy Selvage for typing, technical, and research assistance; Shelley Ward for scanning help; Stanley Cook and John Maguire for their prior research on Sanford; and David Babelay for his work on the French-Swiss of Knoxville. It has been my good fortune to secure the editing services of my dear childhood friend, Lee S. Ward. Further, I must mention the assistance of Sally Polhemus, Archivist, McClung Historical Collection at the Knox County Public Library, and Michael Frost, Library Service Assistant, at the Sterling Memorial Library, Yale University.

Special thanks to my co-worker, Carlotta Lewis, and the Honorable John W. McClarty, Judge of the Tennessee Court of Appeals, for being so enthusiastic and supportive of this undertaking. In a reversal of roles, Judge McClarty was so kind as to help proofread!

 CHAPTER ONE

The End Came Swiftly

The paths of glory lead but to the grave.
—Thomas Gray, "Elegy Written in a Country Churchyard" (1751)

March 8, 1930, a Saturday, marked the eighty-ninth birthday of Justice Oliver Wendell Holmes, and his colleagues planned to convene at noon at the Supreme Court's chambers in the Capitol for a celebration. When Justice Edward Terry Sanford, then sixty-four years old, left his Washington, D.C., home that morning, his wife believed him to be in good health. However, he was suffering from a toothache.[1] He stopped at the office of his dentist, Dr. Arthur B. Crane, at 10 a.m.[2] The dentist found an infected molar and pulled it. Following the extraction, Sanford became dizzy as he left the dental chair. He subsequently fell to the floor in an adjoining room. He was found limp and rubbing his forehead.[3]

Bleeding profusely from the site of the extracted tooth, Sanford was carried into a nearby restroom where he became "violently nauseated."[4] Alarmed by Sanford's condition, the dentist called Dr. J. Lawn Thompson, a physician, who administered a heart stimulant. Sanford, despite being "in a hazy, semi-conscious condition," was able to inform the physician that he previously had suffered similar attacks of nausea.[5] His condition this time, however, failed to improve. Nearly unconscious, Sanford was carried to his home at 2029 Connecticut Avenue. Along the way he mumbled "at twelve o'clock, at twelve o'clock," evidently having on his mind the birthday celebration for Holmes.[6]

Sanford died at 12:20 p.m., soon after reaching his home.[7] His wife of thirty-nine years, Lutie, was at his side, as was the wife of Justice George Sutherland, who had rushed to the Sanford home upon hearing of the collapse of her husband's colleague.[8] Mrs. Sutherland observed that Sanford's death appeared to have been caused by a heart attack.[9] His hometown newspaper reported that his death resulted from a stroke.[10] The official determination was that his passing resulted from uremic poisoning, the result of waste products building up in the blood due to malfunctioning kidneys.[11] Uremia occurs when a person reaches the final stages of chronic kidney disease, a condition that may not reveal itself until the kidneys are severely damaged. Usually, by the time symptoms develop, the kidney failure has progressed to the point that dialysis or a transplant is needed. Neither would have been an option during Sanford's lifetime. A 1921 newspaper article reveals what little could be done for the condition at that time:

> No matter what may be the symptoms, if uremic poisoning is suspected, immediate efforts should be made to cause the skin to do what the kidneys are neglecting. Profuse sweating will carry the poisons out of the system.
>
> To this end, put the patient to bed and cover him with blankets or, better still, wrap him in a blanket wrung out of hot water. Hot water baths, hot flat irons wrapped in cloth, or any other method of applying heat without burning the skin, may be employed. In the country, when they may be had, ears of field corn may be immersed in boiling water, fished out, wrapped in layers of cloth and packed about the patient. Free action of the bowels from the use of salts will do good. Hot drinks, if the patient can swallow, are to be given.[12]

Just the day prior, Sanford had sat on the bench with his colleagues, "seemingly normal in every respect, participating actively" and "frequently interrupting with questions."[13] According to one account, close friends asserted that despite the appearance of robust health, Sanford, a smoker, long had been suffering from diabetes,[14] which perhaps damaged his kidneys and led to the uremic poisoning. His physician acknowledged that Sanford had suffered "a less severe attack" of uremic poisoning "during the Christmas season, but that recently his health had been fairly good."[15] While known to be suffering from uremic poisoning "for some time," he had "not been considered critically ill."[16] His wife later related that Sanford had experienced two previous attacks of dizziness of which she knew, one the previous autumn and another one at Christmas, but that he had appeared in unusually good health that morning as he left for the dentist.[17] In his correspondence, Supreme Court Justice Willis Van Devanter related that the members of the Court "were quite unprepared" and "shocked by the sudden death of Mr. Justice Sanford," but had "thought heretofore that [Sanford] was not well and that his color was bad."[18] According to Van Devanter, as Sanford "said he was well there was nothing which I could do.... In all probability his kidneys had not been functioning properly."[19]

Because death came quickly, no other members of Sanford's family were with him at his death. Sanford's 37-year-old daughter Anna Magee was in Florida with her family when her father died.[20] His sister Mary, married to Frederick A. Ault, a national officer of the American Red Cross and herself a well-known figure in service club circles in her hometown of Knoxville, Tennessee, read of her brother's death in a newspaper.[21] Both of Sanford's brothers, Alfred and Hugh, were away from their homes in Knoxville at the time.[22] His sister Emma was at her home in Canada.[23] His sister Louise, the wife of US Representative Hubert F. Fisher from Tennessee's Tenth District, was in Washington but did not reach Sanford's residence before he expired.

In an incredible coincidence, on the same day Sanford died, William Howard Taft, the only man in the history of the United States to have filled both the offices of president and chief justice of the United States, died at age seventy-three. It had been said that Sanford's "sweet and compliant personality made him a satellite of the affable chief justice Taft."[24] According to some observers, Sanford and Taft became so close that Taft, in effect, had two votes at the Court.[25] Sanford also participated in the chief justice's "inner club" of conservative justices who met at Taft's home on Sunday afternoons.[26] A Taft biographer described the Sunday meetings as "extra-curricular conferences at which...plans were made to block the liberal machinations."[27] Some contended that Taft had been instrumental in obtaining Sanford's selection to the Court, and Sanford seemed to believe that Taft had secured his appointment. During the former chief justice's illness, Sanford was an almost daily caller at the Taft home.[28] As a result of Taft dying on the same day, Sanford's death was overshadowed.

Sanford's body left Washington the day after his passing and was brought back to Knoxville by train for burial on Monday. His sister Louise and her husband joined Mrs. Sanford on the journey.[29] Chief Justice Charles Evans Hughes[30] and Associate Justices James Clark McReynolds, Pierce Butler, and Harlan F. Stone escorted the body to Knoxville and attended the funeral service at Greenwood Cemetery.[31] They were designated honorary pallbearers. Other notables serving in that capacity included Grafton Green, chief justice of the Tennessee Supreme Court; James A. Fowler, Sanford's former law partner and former US Department of Justice official; Judge Xenophon Hicks of the United States Sixth Circuit Court of Appeals;[32] Dr. Harcourt A. Morgan, president of the University of Tennessee; and Newell Sanders, former US senator from Tennessee.[33]

Hundreds gathered at Knoxville's Southern Railway station to meet the train carrying Sanford's body. Hundreds more traveled to the cemetery. Knoxville's mayor issued a proclamation of mourning, and city hall was closed for officials to attend the funeral. The courts also were closed.[34] The body was carried directly to the cemetery, where the rector of St. John's Episcopal Church conducted the brief graveside service over a casket covered with red roses and carnations.[35] Chief Justice Hughes, in a later note to Sanford's wife, stated, "It was a beautiful and impressive service, most dignified and appropriate.... I could not but feel that our dear friend would have approved all that was done."[36] Sanford was interred near members of his wife's family and beside his daughter Dorothy, who had died on August 8, 1915, at age twenty-three from eclampsia shortly after the birth of her only child, Edward Sanford Metcalfe.[37] Just a little over an hour after arriving in Knoxville, the justices rushed to board a train for the return trip to Washington for Taft's services the following day.[38] By the time a monument was erected on his grave in Greenwood Cemetery in September 1940, Sanford was descending into obscurity.[39]

CHAPTER TWO

"A Distinct and Peculiar People"[1]

There was a South of slavery and secession—that South, thank God, is dead. There is a South of union and freedom—that South, thank God, is living, breathing, growing every hour.[2]

—Henry Grady, 1886

Edward Terry Sanford was born on July 23, 1865, in Knoxville, Tennessee, to Emma Chavannes Sanford and Edward Jackson ("E.J.") Sanford. Sanford's parents had married on August 21, 1860, E.J. about ten years older than Emma. Four of their children died in infancy or as toddlers: Anna, 1861–64; John Adrian, 1862–64; Louis Chavannes, 1868; and George William, 1871–72.[3] Sanford, born a few months after the end of the Civil War, was the eldest of six children who lived to maturity.

Nearly thirty years after his birth, Sanford observed:

> There is, I believe, nothing more conducive to good citizenship, more stimulating to patriotic love of country and a high sense of civic duty, and more inspiring to true ambition, than the study of that history which teaches us what manner of men our forefathers were; in what high emprises they engaged; what they suffered, dared and achieved; and what was their rugged virtue and strength of character.[4]

Sanford was undeniably influenced by the region and the times in which he was reared, and by his family and other individuals important in the development of his career. The history of his family must be examined. The impact of the region in which he was reared must be considered. The influence of individuals important in the development of his career must be assessed.

The State of Tennessee is "a narrow strip of real estate running from mountainous East Tennessee to the flat cotton land of West Tennessee along the Mississippi River. In between are the rolling hills of Middle Tennessee."[5] The three distinct regions of the state are known as the grand divisions. The Tennessee in which Sanford was born and raised had been greatly impacted by the Civil War.

At its most elementary, the conflict resulted when the northern and southern states were unable to agree on the issue of slavery. Both the North and the South were concerned about the balance of power between the free and slave states in the US Congress, as the side controlling the votes controlled what happened with the rest of the country.[6]

From its inception, Tennessee was a slave state, although fewer than twenty percent of small landholders in the state owned or could afford to own slaves.[7] Tennessee's state constitution of 1796 did not address slavery but implicitly accepted the institution by referring to "slaves" for purposes of taxation. By statute, slaves in Tennessee were considered personal property, and their activities and labor were subject to the wills of their masters.[8] Many in Tennessee objected to slavery on moral or religious grounds, but by the late 1830s, there were very few outright abolitionists. Delegates to a state constitutional convention in 1834 debated around thirty petitions seeking the abolition of slavery in the state.[9] To most whites, however, "law and order, economic progress, and white supremacy seemed best secured through the perpetuation of slavery."[10] By 1860, approximately one-fourth of Tennessee's total population consisted of slaves, ranging from approximately eight percent in East Tennessee to thirty-three percent in Middle Tennessee to sixty percent in West Tennessee.[11]

In the early 1860s, Tennessee's grand divisions were divided like the country, with West Tennessee favoring the Confederacy and East Tennessee loyal to the Union. Middle Tennessee itself was split, with some portions heavily favoring secession while other counties were ambivalent.[12] It is often opined that East Tennessee's loyalty to the Union came from its terrain and its traditions. The area was isolated by mountain barriers. It developed "a diversified farming and small manufacturing economy" different from that of the more "'Southern' slave-owning and staple-raising Middle and West Tennessee."[13] East Tennessee crops were not labor intensive, so farmers did not rely on slaves. The East Tennessee region also had a strong anti-slavery tradition.[14]

From the late 1830s until the early 1850s, Tennessee was divided in political matters between the Democrats and the Whigs, with much of the support for the Whigs drawn from East Tennessee. In the mid-1850s, the Whig Party collapsed over the issue of slavery. While most Northern Whigs joined the new Republican Party, Southern Whigs were troubled by the abolitionist sentiments of the Republicans. Accordingly, during the 1860 presidential election, East Tennessee's former Whigs supported the Constitutional Union Party, a third party that rejected both secession and abolition. Constitutional Unionists disliked the idea of dissolution of the Union, but they were equally opposed to the federal government's attempts to "coerce" the states.[15] Tennessean John Bell, often considered the "creator" of the Whig Party in the state,[16] ran for president on the Constitutional Union ticket.[17]

The 1860 election in Knoxville, East Tennessee's largest city, "was never a battle between North and South but rather a struggle within the South between Constitutional Unionists and Democrats. The Jacksonian party system [Democrats] had fragmented nationally, but not locally. Lincoln, the Republican candidate, was not even on the ballot. Except for the five percent of voters who cast their ballots for Stephen Douglas, the Northern Democrat, the men in Knoxville evidently believed that they had only two choices—Kentucky Senator John C. Breckenridge (Democrat) or Tennessee's John Bell (Constitutional Unionist)."[18]

Following Lincoln's election on November 6, 1860, South Carolina immediately seceded from the Union, joined quickly by Mississippi, Florida, Alabama, Georgia, Louisiana, and Texas.[19] These states formed the Confederate States of

America with a provisional government in Montgomery, Alabama.[20] Most Tennesseans clearly had hoped for Lincoln's defeat, yet they were not ready to secede.

Knoxville was home to a strong pro-Union element during the secession crisis of the early 1860s, and it remained bitterly divided throughout the Civil War.[21] The population of the city at this time was around 5,000, with almost one-tenth being slaves.[22] Although the surrounding countryside was predominantly Unionist, Knoxville itself was split down the middle. When Knoxville voters first cast their ballots on the question of secession, forty-nine percent supported it, and fifty-one percent opposed it.[23] Many Knoxville residents—including a great many who did not own slaves—were firm believers in the principle of states' rights: that the powers delegated by the Constitution to the federal government should be few and defined, and those remaining with the state governments should be numerous and indefinite.[24] These individuals were advocates of secession,[25] contending that the sovereign state of Tennessee had voluntarily joined the federal Union and was at liberty to withdraw from it at any time.[26] Knox County and East Tennessee overall, in contrast to Knoxville, overwhelmingly voted against secession.[27] A vote taken in February 1861 showed that East Tennesseans voted 33,299 to 7,070 to remain in the Union.[28]

Like the city, Sanford's family was divided. Although Sanford's father E.J. was a Unionist originally from Connecticut, his mother's family supported the Confederacy. Sanford's maternal uncle, Albert Chavannes, was part of the citizens-guard that defended then-Confederate-occupied Knoxville from a raid by Union Colonel (later General) William P. Sanders in June 1863.[29]

Prior to the firing on Fort Sumter, Unionist sentiment predominated in Tennessee. After the fort's fall in April 1861 and President Lincoln's subsequent call for troops, however, Virginia, Arkansas, and North Carolina seceded. The president was informed by Tennessee's governor Isham Harris, a secessionist, that "Tennessee will not furnish a single man for purposes of coercion. . . ."[30] Governor Harris began efforts to align Tennessee with the Confederacy, and sentiments in Middle and West Tennessee began to shift in favor of secession. As Oliver Perry Temple, a leading citizen of the Knoxville area at the time, noted, the question for each Tennessean was: "What shall I, as an individual, do? Shall I go with my state into secession, or shall I remain true to the old government?"[31] In May, the legislature, controlled by Democrats in both chambers, passed legislation establishing a military alliance with the Confederacy and issued a "Declaration of Independence" from the United States. On June 8, 1861, citizens considered whether to adopt the new declaration and leave the Union. In the final vote on secession, the citizens of Tennessee voted 105,000 to 47,000 to secede.[32] While many may have been opposed to secession, the thought of using force against fellow Southerners was unacceptable to citizens of West and Middle Tennessee.[33] Nearly 20,000 more votes were cast than in any previous election, lending credence to the contention of Unionists that Rebel troops from other states voted.[34] The final June 1861 vote in Knoxville was more than two to one in favor of secession, while Knox County voted three to one against it. Interest in Knoxville was so high that nearly every qualified voter cast a ballot.[35] East Tennessee as a region voted to stay in the Union,[36] 32,205 to 14,095.[37] On July 22, 1861, Tennessee formally became the eleventh and final state to join the Confederate States of America.[38]

In East Tennessee, ironically almost all of the area's leading anti-secessionists were slave holders.[39] They "never whole heartedly embraced Northern Radicalism as their political faith," and they did not fully abandon Southern cultural values.[40] They believed, however, that "preservation of the Union, rather than the perpetuation of slavery, was the issue now at stake."[41] The unconditional Unionists of East Tennessee viewed the Confederacy as slave-holding exploiters who dragged poor whites unwillingly into rebellion.[42] They "warn[ed] that a government led by a wealthy, Southern aristocracy 'endangered their status as free white men.'" and would "infringe upon their rights." The Unionists of East Tennessee "invoked the image of slavery to depict their future status in the Confederacy."[43] An example of the "class warfare" between the opponents is revealed in the following passage:

> We belong to the "low flung" party of Unionists, and don't aspire to any higher class of associates. We have always despised in our heart of hearts, a hateful aristocracy in the country, based on the ownership of a few ashy negroes, and arrogating to themselves all the decency, all the talents, and all the respectability of the social circle.
>
> The "low flung," aye, the "mudsills" of society, the hard-fisted yeomanry of this country are going to govern it, and the respectability of the land may prepare to meet their humiliation. Educated Labor is to take the place of your slave-ocracy, and it will not be long until it will be looked upon as no disgrace for a man to eat his bread by the sweat of his brow.[44]

Leading Unionists in the Knoxville area included Congressmen Horace Maynard and Thomas A.R. Nelson, and attorneys Oliver P. Temple, John Baxter, and Connally F. Trigg. With the exception of Baxter, these men had limited wealth when compared to East Tennessee's prominent Confederates, who were wealthy businessmen and merchants economically dependent on Southern markets.[45] Secessionists and slave holders, on the other hand, regarded Unionists as "elements desirous of upsetting sacred property relations, as levellers, the equivalent of Socialists and Communists."[46]

Knoxville, East Tennessee's center of population, commerce, government, and culture since its first settlement, had seen slow growth prior to the Civil War, handicapped by its lack of good transportation to the outside world. Growth had to await the arrival of the railroads in the 1850s.[47] Just prior to the Civil War, two railroads—the East Tennessee & Virginia (ET&V) and the East Tennessee & Georgia (ET&G)[48]—joined at Knoxville to link the city to Bristol, Tennessee, and Bristol, Virginia, and to Dalton, Georgia. From these cities, connecting railroads ran to Washington, D.C., and New York City and to Atlanta, Memphis, and New Orleans.[49] Once the conflict began, however, Knoxville's new role as an important transportation hub made it a target of both Union and Confederate forces. Because the state legislature was aware of East Tennessee's anti-secession sentiments—it had been presented a petition by East Tennesseans to form a separate state aligned with the Union—six Confederate regiments were sent to the region in the summer of 1861 to secure the ET&V and ET&G Railroads, considered to be the principal rail transport route between the new Confederate capital of Richmond and the lower South.[50] For the Confederacy, therefore, Knoxville's railroads were vital for moving men and supplies to the Virginia theater.[51] Thereafter, the city remained occupied by Confederate forces until September 1863. No other section of the country would experience military occupation by the Confederacy "for so long or to such an extent."[52]

The best known champion of the pro-Unionists in East Tennessee was William G. Brownlow, known as the "Fighting Parson" because he was a former Methodist circuit rider.[53] In the late 1840s, Brownlow, by that time a newspaper editor, had moved his radical Whig (anti-Andrew Jackson) newspaper, the *Whig*, to Knoxville. The city was recognized as a Whig stronghold because former President Jackson often advocated policies and diverted funds to shortchange or ignore East Tennessee interests.[54] Jackson further alienated many East Tennesseans when he supported Martin Van Buren for president instead of Knoxvillian Hugh Lawson White, son of Knoxville's founder. The election of 1836, therefore, began an enduring tradition in East Tennessee of Whig (later Republican) opposition to the Democratic party.[55] During this period, state legislators from East Tennessee continuously bickered with those from Middle and West Tennessee over funding for road and navigational improvements.[56]

Despite being a loyalist to the Union, Brownlow was not a Lincoln supporter. He also was a strong believer in slavery.[57] In 1861, Brownlow stated that "if we were once convinced in the border slave states that the Administration at Washington . . . contemplated . . . the abolishing of slavery, there would not be a Union man among us in twenty-four hours."[58] He disliked, however, the plantation aristocrats, and he sincerely loved the Union.[59] Brownlow's advocacy for the Union was displayed in an editorial style often involving vicious personal attacks; "[h]e reveled in a fight, and he filled his paper with vituperation, abuse, and denunciation. . . ."[60]

By April 1862, three years before Sanford's birth, Brownlow had left Knoxville, embarking on an extensive speaking tour of the North.[61] He described Knoxville of that period as a city of destitution, telling an audience in Cincinnati: "In Knoxville there is not a bolt of bleached domestic or calico to be had, nor a spool of Coates's thread. . . . Sewing-needles and pins are not to be had. . . . It has been remarked on the streets of Knoxville that no such thing as a fine-toothed comb was to be had. . . ."[62] East Tennessee communities lacked the labor and resources to produce sufficient food for survival; the grain and livestock raised was seized by Confederate troops or guerrillas.[63]

Thirty-one thousand Tennesseans, mostly from East Tennessee, joined the Union Army. Eventually, 8,777 would die fighting for the North, the highest percentage of casualties of any state.[64] By the fall of 1862, however, the loyalists to the Union in East Tennessee were despondent. During the Confederate occupation from 1861 to 1863, Unionists were harassed without mercy.[65] A Tennessean later recounted that Unionists "were driven from their homes . . . persecuted like wild beasts by the rebel authorities, and hunted down in the mountains; they were hanged on the gallows, shot down and robbed. . . . Perhaps no people on the face of the earth were ever more persecuted than were the loyal people of East Tennessee."[66] Horace Maynard, East Tennessee Unionist and congressman, wrote directly to President Lincoln: "Having provided for the freedom of the slaves can you not, I beg you, in God's name, do something for the freedom of the white people of East Tennessee?"[67] The situation for the region grew more desperate after the Emancipation Proclamation of 1863, which came as a great shock to East Tennesseans who were true to the Union. Some denounced Lincoln, stating that they did not go to war for the purpose of freeing the slaves.[68] They recalled that Lincoln, in his inaugural address, had declared, "I have no purpose, directly or indirectly, to interfere, with the institution of slavery in the states where it exists."[69] The proclamation put an end to slavery for 3.5 million blacks located in Confederate states, but not for the 425,000 within the states that had not rebelled, as President Lincoln's war powers authority did not extend to blacks in the Union-controlled or neutral states.[70] Tennessee is the only Confederate state not mentioned in the Emancipation Proclamation because most of the state (Middle and West Tennessee) was considered under Union control when it was issued.[71]

The despair of East Tennessee loyalists turned to jubilation when Union General Ambrose Burnside and the Army of the Ohio[72] took Knoxville from the Confederates in September 1863. Northern newspapers rejoiced in the liberation of the "downtrodden" residents of the "renowned Union stronghold."[73] Sanford's father returned to the city, having previously fled Knoxville in April 1862 to avoid the "Rebel Conscript Law"[74] that declared "every man between the ages of eighteen and forty-five" must become a "soldier of the Southern Confederacy."[75]

E.J. had joined with Union men from Knox and Blount counties "for the purpose of running through the rebel lines and joining the federal army in Kentucky."[76] The trip in a pouring rain over the Cumberland Mountains to the Union Army Camp at Boston, Kentucky took six nights. Ill with pneumonia after his escape, E.J. traveled to his family home in Connecticut to recover.[77] He had left behind in Knoxville his pregnant wife and daughter Anna, who had been born in June 1861. Sanford's mother approached the Confederate authorities and "made several applications for a passport but had been always refused."[78] Because his family "had not been able to get a pass ... to come north" to Connecticut, E.J.'s son John Adrian was born in Knoxville in November 1862 in his absence.[79]

E.J. went on to defend Knoxville against the forces of Confederate General James Longstreet in the Battle of Fort Sanders on November 29, 1863.[80] The battle lasted only twenty bloody minutes, with the Confederates losing a total of 813 men—killed, wounded, or taken prisoner—in that time.[81] When General Burnside subsequently repulsed an attempt by General Longstreet to retake Knoxville for the Confederacy, President Lincoln proclaimed the outcome of the fighting in East Tennessee a "great advancement of the national cause" and urged loyal citizens to "assemble at their places of worship and tender special homage and gratitude to Almighty God."[82]

After the battle, one observer noted, "I hardly knew our poor Knoxville."[83] The city's shade trees were cut down, one by one, to warm the wounded in the hospitals. All the timber on the surrounding hills had been cut down prior to the conflict to construct numerous forts and countless trenches. Scarcely a fence remained standing. The sidewalks were like stable yards. Nauseating odors emanated from the churches and schools serving as hospitals, and dead horses and mules lay rotting in the streets. A great many houses had been burned to the ground. Countless persons were suddenly homeless and hungry.[84] As cold weather approached, freed slaves and the starving converged on Knoxville, expecting the federal authorities headquartered there to provide for them. They roamed the streets, begging.[85] During the winter of 1864, ten thousand army animals died in East Tennessee for lack of feed and forage. Many civilians were forced to let their horses and cattle die for the same reason. Travelers in the spring of 1864 commented on the scarcity of the stock and the emaciated condition of the few animals seen. Barns looked empty; hogs and poultry were rare sights.[86]

In late January 1864, the *Knoxville Whig* reported:

> We doubt most seriously if there is a more superlatively filthy town than this. Filthy basements, filthy upper stories, filthy streets, dead mules, horses, hogs, and dogs meet the eye at every point. Filthy clothes and filthy sleeping apartments are the order of the day.
>
> The insides of beeves, and hogs are strewn all over town, and spoiled meat and bones are thrown out without any regard to where they fall. The Small Pox is all over the place, and is daily on the increase. The approach of warm weather will slay us all in this state of affairs.[87]

During these wartime conditions, including actual famine,[88] the deaths of Sanford's two elder siblings occurred due to measles. Three-year-old Anna died on July 13, 1864 and twenty-month-old John Adrian died on August 9, 1864.[89] Sickness and diseases of all types spread with alarming ease due to the increased number of soldiers and civilian refugees in the city.[90]

The Tennessee of Sanford's youth had experienced suffering, deprivations, and dislocations related to the Civil War.[91] As one author observed, "[i]n the annals of American wars no more tragic history exists than that of East Tennessee during the Civil War[;] East Tennesseans, unlike other Southerners who briefly found themselves, . . . in the path of Sherman . . . and Sheridan, . . . suffered throughout the conflict from the bitter reality of military occupation, contending armies, devastating raids, internecine conflict, and social dislocation."[92]

Knoxville had endured perpetual military occupation, hosting Confederate troops during the first half of the war and Union forces throughout the remainder.[93] Destruction and upheaval reigned throughout both occupations, with the Union control nearly "as onerous, and almost as obnoxious, as that of the Confederates."[94] "Shops when still open had little on their shelves. Many articles of common use disappeared from the market. Honey and sorghum molasses replaced sugar, while citizens made do with ground-up okra seeds and dried sassafras for coffee. During the war, the cost of living rose dramatically."[95] The price of coffee rose from fourteen cents to over $1.00 per pound; salt from two and one-half cents to thirty cents; and brown sugar from twelve and one-half cents to seventy cents. The price of calico cloth rose 800 percent, and all clothing rose in proportion.[96] Barter became a common mode of trade.[97]

Post-War Knoxville

After the Civil War, material conditions slowly improved, but personal animosities lingered. As the former soldiers and political foes began returning to their homes, bloody violence broke out on Knoxville's streets. Residents wondered if true peace would ever return. On May 24, 1865, ex-Union soldier Shadrick Harris attacked Confederate veteran William Beard in downtown Knoxville, seeking retribution for the abuse he suffered as a prisoner of war under Beard. Two days later, Unionist D. Foster killed former Confederate W. M. Cox in a downtown store. Shortly after Sanford's birth in July, Abner Baker was lynched by Union troops for the killing of Unionist William Hall.[98] During this period, secessionist Ellen Renshaw House confided to her diary: "We certainly live in horrible times. Scarcely a day passes someone is not killed."[99] House embellished the facts, but two years later in 1867, Knoxville resident Louis Gratz observed: "In reality the war is terminated but we are still far from peace."[100]

Post-war Knoxville saw other misfortunes. Periodic epidemics ensued; a smallpox outbreak in 1866 was especially brutal. A great flood occurred the following year.[101] Lightning during a thunderstorm caused a fire in 1869 that left a large part of the city's main business district in ashes.[102]

By the spring of 1865, however, shortly before Sanford's birth, things had begun to improve in the Knoxville region.[103] There were about 4,000 inhabitants in the city.[104] Farmers began planting normal crops, and trade was on the upswing.[105] Retail prices of food began to decline in 1865 and, by late 1866, had reached pre-war levels. Variety was on the increase. Raisins, tea, lemons, and spices were available by February 1866. Furs were obtainable. Eggs, chickens, turkeys, and ducks were plentiful and inexpensive after 1866. Sugar, candy, and coal oil, however, remained costly. An ice cream parlor had opened on Market Square at this time, and a number of saloons and billiard parlors were to be found.[106] By 1867, a building boom saw 400 houses erected in the city,[107] and street lights were installed in September of that year.[108] A modern fire department began operations a few months later.[109] The city purchased a steam fire engine, 1200 feet of hose, and a hose carriage. A firehouse was constructed at the head of Market Square.[110] Members of the leading families of Knoxville, including Sanford's father, were involved in the fire department.[111] E.J. served as captain of the Hook and Ladder Company stationed on Prince (now Market) Street near Union Avenue.[112]

By the end of 1868, Knoxville was home to two wholesale dry goods houses and approximately twenty-two retail dry goods stores.[113] Several of the streets were graded and had curbs; a few were macadamized.[114] Knoxville's economy was beginning to recover. An opponent of now-Governor Brownlow observed: "Knoxville seems to be a wonderful exception to the general rule. In all directions, as if by magic, factories, machine shops, storehouses, dwelling houses, and buildings of every description are springing up. Business, in all its varieties, seems to be thriving. The people, generally, seem to have remunerative occupations—at least they dress well, look well, and appear to be healthy."[115]

A visitor from Virginia in 1868 called Knoxville "perhaps the widest awake and livelist [sic] town of its population, not only in Tennessee, but in the Southern States."[116] The Knoxville of Sanford's youth witnessed the organization of a dancing club that year, with dances held regularly. Circuses passed through town frequently. Baseball was very popular, with Knoxville having at least five white teams at one time, in addition to several black teams.[117] The city had "an elaborate opera house, a German brewery, a local literary weekly, and a thriving and diverse urban lifestyle of streetcars and late-night coffee houses."[118] "The Great New York Grocery" advertised "English breakfast tea, 'Old Governor' Java Coffee, dried herring, 'New York cheese' and Havana cigars," and the St. Nicholas Saloon was known for its Norfolk oysters.[119]

The post-war period saw newly rebuilt railroads, the availability of new consumer goods from factories in the North, and growing markets to assist the region's residents in discovering consumerism. The railroad network, the largest generator of post-war economic growth,[120] transformed Knoxville into the center of a wholesale industry that distributed goods to the entire Appalachian region. In 1871, when Sanford turned six years old, a Richmond, Virginia, newspaper announced, "[N]o city of the South except Atlanta had improved more rapidly since the war than had Knoxville, Tennessee."[121] By 1882, when Sanford was seventeen, Knoxville was home to forty-four wholesalers, half of whom began operation after the Civil War. Three years later, the Tennessee Agricultural Commission proclaimed Knoxville the South's fourth-leading wholesale center (behind New Orleans, Nashville, and Atlanta) and reported an annual volume of trade passing through the city in the $15–20 million range. By 1887, a historian noted: "It is universally conceded that no other city of equal size in America has so large a wholesale trade as Knoxville. . . . Nearly all the firms are backed by abundant capital, and are controlled by competent, progressive and practical men."[122] Other improvements to the city between 1883 and 1890 included the establishment of the first permanent public library, an annual opera festival, a symphonic group, and a French restaurant.[123]

As the city grew, entrepreneurs—including E.J. Sanford—reinvested their burgeoning profits from Knoxville's wholesale trade into other manufacturing pursuits. Extractive industries, primarily timber and coal, were popular among the city's investors.[124] Through the last half of the nineteenth century, the marble quarries expanded, as did the textile and clothing trade. Other major concerns in post–Civil War Knoxville included furniture makers, grain mills, nurseries, and the brick industry.[125] In 1898, the Traveler's Protective Association moved Knoxville up to the South's number three wholesale center, estimating annual trade through the city at $50 million. By around 1900, when Knoxville "was at its industrial height, [it was] a compact metropolis of about thirty-five thousand, growing perhaps a little too fast. . . . A pragmatic city, a beehive of factory workers, lawyers and salesmen. . . ."[126] A third of Knoxville's total work force was employed in manufacturing or mechanical jobs. At that time, Knoxville employed a larger percentage of its population in manufacturing than did Atlanta, Birmingham, Memphis, Nashville, or New Orleans.[127] During the postbellum period of prosperity, ninety-seven new factories were built in and around Knoxville.[128] Merchants like Sanford's father occupied leadership positions within business and commerce and established themselves as the community's postwar economic leaders. Such capitalists provided the resources to finance industrial projects.[129] E.J. played a major role in many of the city's jobbing and wholesaling businesses. As noted by *The New York Times*, "Col. Sanford's impress is all over Knoxville. He is fairly the representative businessman of East Tennessee."[130]

However, "[d]uring the same period ... Knoxville also had cattle, pigs, and gunfighters roaming the streets, a few log cabins still standing downtown, and a farmer's market with a rural character that sometimes astonished visitors."[131] A council meeting recorded a petition signed by a large number of citizens requesting an ordinance to prohibit "hogs running loose in the streets."[132] Street fights and shootings were common. Outlaw Harvey Logan, known as "Kid Curry," shot and seriously wounded two Knoxville policemen.[133] There were plenty of executions of felons, and "[b]arbarous public hangings were common."[134] Perhaps partly because death from tuberculosis, diphtheria, smallpox, and numerous other maladies was common, and there was no city hospital until 1883, it was estimated that the city's twenty-five saloons served five thousand drinks a day in 1879.[135] Accordingly, the Knoxville of young Sanford's days "was still a country town in which boys frequently chased rabbits through the streets and gardens, and a gentleman caught a large opossum under his house in the heart of the city as late as the fall of 1868."[136] Attempts to regulate unfenced livestock resulted in extensive city council debate, and it was not until 1890, when Sanford was twenty-five years old, that the council voted to outlaw cattle on Knoxville's streets: "No one question has ever caused more different attempts to frame it into a law in this city than the cow ordinance."[137]

On the political scene, Knoxville and East Tennessee became important as a result of the Civil War and its aftermath. The Union victory brought "the Fighting Parson" William G. Brownlow and other loyalists back to Knoxville. Technically, Tennessee had been under federal military rule since March 1862, when Union troops had forced the Confederate forces out of Nashville and Middle Tennessee. The state was "the first one to succumb to federal arms–only eight months intervening between the [secession] and the appointment of Governor [Andrew] Johnson,"[138] who was at that time the United States senator from East Tennessee. Johnson, the only southern senator to remain in Congress during the Civil War,[139] served as military governor until early 1865, when he became vice president. President Lincoln, to give a "facade of national unity to the Republican Party, which had renamed itself in 1864 the 'National Union Party,'" had selected Johnson, a Southerner and lifelong Democrat, to share the ticket. Despite being a slave owner and supporter of slavery, Johnson despised the "'Slave Power'—the aristocrats in the plantation regions—as much as any Northerner, and sought throughout his career to do away with the political bonus these slave masters received through extra legislative representation, in both the state and federal legislatures, for their slaves."[140]

Johnson's last official act as Tennessee's military governor was the authorization of a convention of unconditional Unionists to select officials for a civil state government. In January 1865, more than 500 Unionist delegates convened in Nashville with the aim of improvising a civil government for the state.[141] The delegates nullified Tennessee's ordinance of secession, provided for the abolition of slavery, and arranged for two elections: one to ratify the acts of the convention, another to elect the state officers proposed by the convention.[142] In early 1865, the state's constitution was amended to prohibit slavery, and the ratification of the Thirteenth Amendment in December 1865 formally abolished the institution.[143] With dissident Unionists taking control of the state government, it was a militant oligarchy that selected Brownlow as governor on March 4, 1865, and inaugurated him shortly before Confederate General Robert E. Lee's surrender at Appomattox.[144] The improvised government, probably unconstitutional, was all the civil government Tennessee had.[145]

Many of the wartime Unionists, mainly former Whigs, joined Sanford's father as Republicans.[146] The Republican party had only been established for a short period, with its first official party meeting not occurring until 1854.[147] When it first appeared, the party was "associated with abolitionists and feared as a radical movement."[148] After the war, the party of Lincoln was the dominant party in the Union. Further, the Democrats were discredited and in shambles. With the Democrats out of power, the Republican party thereafter dominated Tennessee politics from 1864 to 1869, and Knoxville was the party's stronghold.[149] The strength of the Republican party in Knox County and East Tennessee has not waned since that period.[150] The party was never popular in Middle or West Tennessee, however, because its dominance during Brownlow's time as governor was based on disfranchisement and intimidation by the militia authorized by the legislature. Governor Brownlow, described by the *Public Ledger* of Memphis as able to "express more vituperativeness and a scorching hate than any half a dozen men that ever appeared in American politics,"[151] set out to punish former Confederates and to restrict the right to vote to Union men only.[152] At Brownlow's urging, the legislature enacted proscriptive measures to deny the vote to all former Confederates.[153] Accordingly, the Democratic party in Middle and West Tennessee was disfranchised. Secessionists and former Rebels were zealously excluded from official posts.[154] Statutes were enacted to concentrate considerable police power in the hands of Brownlow.[155] His "rigorous policy of white disfranchisement, albeit aimed at 'rebels,' and the simultaneous advancement in the legal status" of blacks, doomed any growth for the GOP in the rest of the state for more than a century.[156] After Brownlow left Knoxville to become governor, some of the city's inhabitants became disgusted by Brownlow's policies, and his more Radical Republicanism lost favor.[157] For the most part, however, East Tennesseans found little about which to complain during Brownlow's tenure.

After Lincoln's assassination, Andrew Johnson became president. Johnson's stance was that southern state governments should reject the Fourteenth Amendment, which gave constitutional authority to the Civil Rights Act of 1866. Tennessee, the first state to consider it, ratified it in 1866.[158] The amendment was ratified so quickly in Tennessee because Governor Brownlow, aligned with the Radical Republicans in Congress, was President Johnson's mortal enemy.[159] Pro-Johnson legislators had gone into hiding to prevent a quorum, but the Brownlow forces had "the fugitives arrested and held them under guard while the House passed the measure."[160] Brownlow later cabled John W. Forney, the clerk of the United States Senate, with the following details: "We have fought the battle and won it. We have ratified the Constitutional amendment in the house—43 to 11 against it, two of Andrew Johnson's tools not voting. Give my respects to the dead dog of the White House."[161]

Pursuant to the amendment, freedmen were granted civil rights, including citizenship, but excluding the right to vote. Former Confederates who had previously sworn to uphold the Constitution as prior federal office holders were disqualified from state and federal positions. Federal debts were guaranteed while all Confederate debts were repudiated.[162] Upon Tennessee's ratification of the Fourteenth Amendment, Congress immediately voted to seat Tennessee's members, and the state was readmitted to the Union that same year, thus avoiding formal Military Reconstruction.[163] Tennessee was the first former Confederate state readmitted to the Union. The remaining states had to rewrite their constitutions, guarantee suffrage of black males, and ratify the Fourteenth Amendment. The last states readmitted to the Union also were required to ratify the Fifteenth Amendment, which extended, constitutionally, suffrage to adult black men.[164]

Despite the division between opposing sides, in East Tennessee many Unionists took an oath not to seek retribution against Confederate sympathizers. E.J. Sanford became active in Reconstruction matters and in May 1865, shortly before Edward Terry's birth, signed a "Petition for a Proclamation to Save East Tennessee Rebels."[165] According to the petition, Rebels who returned under the parole agreement at the end of the war had been greeted by violence and threats. The petitioners, worried about impending lawlessness if the situation were allowed to continue, asked Governor Brownlow to issue a proclamation instructing those with grievances against the former Rebels to use peaceful and legal means to seek redress through the courts. Prominent Knoxville citizens such as Thomas W. Humes, Episcopal clergyman and later president of the University of Tennessee, were among other petitioners who asked Brownlow to protect those who sympathized with the "late Rebellion." The petition had more than two pages of signatures, with more than one hundred Unionists pledged to refrain from violence against ex-Rebels.[166]

Governor Brownlow, viewing the petition as a politically motivated move to embarrass him, was unsympathetic to it. On May 29, 1865, he issued an official proclamation directing "all aggrieved citizens to apply for redress of their wrongs … to the civil courts." However, "he urged those confederates who had driven Union men from their homes early in the war 'to quietly and forever withdraw from the country.'"[167] Brownlow declared that the Confederates had "forfeited all rights to citizenship, and to life itself."[168] A war-time diarist noted that Brownlow "encourages the people to kill their rebel neighbors wherever they find them, to do it without noise, secretly, but do it, and bury them in the woods like brutes."[169]

Eventually, many former Confederate sympathizers were able to return to Knoxville, regain their property after wartime confiscations, and even cooperate with Union men in business dealings and civic affairs.[170] This lenient attitude helped the area recover more quickly than other parts of the South and brought in new investors, particularly former Union officers who had been stationed in Knoxville during the war. One such Union officer was W.W. Woodruff, the father of the future Mrs. Edward Terry Sanford.[171]

The Civil War left the South with a shortage of investment capital and a surplus of unskilled labor. Republicans in Tennessee sought to encourage business, and Governor Brownlow began to actively seek capital investment from outsiders to develop state resources.[172] Brownlow had long sought a statewide railroad system "at whatever cost its completion may require" along with infusions of Northern capital.[173] There was "a significant push" for industrialization and the exploration of resources in the area.[174]

In 1867, Tennessee established a state Board of Immigration, charged with encouraging immigration from northern states and Europe.[175] Brownlow supported a pro-industrial Reconstruction government, and "[t]he theory ... was that changing from a predominantly agrarian to a diversified economy" required "the help of immigrants, skilled in machine labor and attuned to the factory system."[176] The preface to Tennessee's immigration handbook stated: "Instead of an almost exclusive attention to agriculture, which has prevailed in the South for so many years, there is now a general desire that there should be a harmonious development of its resources. In consequence of it, immigration which was regarded with indifference or dislike, is now greatly desired."[177] Although Brownlow saw immigration as buttressing Radical Republican control, Conservatives and Democrats, bristling at black independence, also supported "schemes to replace black laborers with Northern immigrants or imported foreigners." Some believed that "white immigrants could not only solve the labor problem but also help redeem the state from Radical rule."[178] Prudent businessmen, like Sanford's father, flourished in this new business environment and soon made a fortune. In Knoxville, peace and prosperity reigned, for the most part, because the economy grew strong.

As opposition to Brownlow's administration grew, leading Radicals in the state pushed for black suffrage to bolster the party's strength. Despite Brownlow's reluctance to confer the right to vote on blacks, he declared in January 1867 that "[w]ithout their votes, the state will pass into disloyal hands, and a reign of terror ... will be the result."[179] Radical legislators responded by passing the suffrage bill and enfranchising forty thousand black men. Tennessee became the first southern state "to establish biracial democracy in the aftermath of slavery."[180] Violence erupted soon thereafter at the hands of the Ku Klux Klan. Opponents of Brownlow saw the Ku Klux Klan as a "necessary political expedient justified by the Radical disfranchisement policy, the high taxes imposed by Brownlow's administration, and the threat black voting posed to white supremacy."[181] The

Klan violence, along with other concerns, resulted in increasing dissatisfaction with Brownlow's administration. "Growing opposition to the administration's economic policies, traditional sectional animosities in the state, incompetence and corruption within the Brownlow government, and widespread sympathy for disfranchised whites" weakened Brownlow's power and undermined the Republican party.[182] In an effort to curb the actions of the Ku Klux Klan, Brownlow called up the militia and issued a proclamation putting Tennessee under martial law.[183] With this move, whites deserted the administration in large numbers.[184] One Knoxville newspaper denounced Brownlow's deployment decision "as the wild utterance of an insane man."[185]

The return of Andrew Johnson to the state became a symbol around which opponents of Brownlow could rally.[186] Johnson, aiming bitter criticism "at the declaration of martial law and the deployment of the militia,"[187] accused Brownlow's administration of "mishandling state funds and driving the state into debt." Johnson drew on popular discontent "to whip his audiences into a frenzy."[188] When a vacancy occurred in one of Tennessee's US Senate positions, the opportunity was seized by the legislature to elect Brownlow to the seat in order to remove him from the state. He resigned as Tennessee's governor on February 25, 1869, and departed for Washington. The speaker of the state senate, DeWitt C. Senter, assumed the governor's chair.[189]

Brownlow was under the impression that Senter would adhere to the Radical agenda, but Senter, like other wartime Unionists, had grown weary of the harsh measures enacted by Brownlow's administration. One of his first acts as governor was to disband the state militia that had been used primarily to protect black voters.[190] Voting privileges soon were returned to all Tennesseans, and the ex-Confederates who had been abused by Brownlow began to regain power. In the August 1869 election, the Radical Republicans lost control of the General Assembly. Over the course of approximately five months—from October 1869 to early March 1870—the "destruction of Radical Reconstruction ensued one law at a time."[191] Afterwards, the Conservatives and Democrats used the device of gerrymandering to punish the Republicans. Regarding a redistricting bill introduced shortly after the overthrow of Radical rule, a Tennessee senator observed: "One main object was to redistrict the state [so] that for the next ten years not a Republican can be elected to the Legislature. . . . I believe in the law of revenge. The Radicals disfranchised us, and now we intend to disfranchise them."[192] The Radical Republicans were swept from power, and the lasting resentment toward them spoiled chances for future state government service by Republicans like E.J. and his sons, especially Edward Terry. The so-called Reconstruction after the Civil War caused Tennesseans only more wounds and casualties.

The influx of over four thousand blacks to Knox County after the Civil War brought dramatic change to Knoxville.[193] In 1860, only a small number of Knoxville's citizens were blacks. When Union soldiers took the city in 1863, blacks began arriving in large numbers. Their numbers in the city quadrupled between 1860 and 1880, growing to around thirty percent of the city's total population. Eventually, the influx of whites from rural areas struck the balance in existence today.[194]

In Tennessee, as in the rest of the South, "pro-Union" did not necessarily mean "pro-black." Governor Brownlow expressed that "[i]f there is anything a loyal Tennessean hates more than a rebel, it is a nigger."[195] During the Civil War, *Brownlow's Knoxville Whig* frequently contained references to "nigger," and it would appear that postbellum blacks found Knoxville "only slightly less hostile than ... the South as a whole."[196] According to the editor of the *Whig*, during Sanford's youth, racial disturbances occurred daily on the city's streets.[197] One official of the Freedmen's Bureau noted: "It is a melancholy fact that among the bitterest opponents of the Negro in Tennessee are the intensely radical loyalists of the mountain district—the men who have been in our armies...."[198] Whitelaw Reid, a northern journalist traveling through Knoxville in November 1865, opined that "[t]he freedmen have more hope from Virginia Rebels than from East Tennessee Loyalists, if the public sentiment of Knoxville may be accepted as a test."[199] Historian Charles Faulkner Bryan, Jr., observed that most East Tennesseans, despite their wartime loyalties, refused to embrace freedmen as equals. He noted that "although East Tennessee was a locus of Southern Unionism, it is evident that this Unionism was marred by racial attitudes little different from [those] of the most devoted Confederates."[200]

Although racial violence and bigotry did exist in Knoxville during Sanford's youth, they were the exception and not the rule. Blacks in Knoxville "lived a relatively good life."[201] "They moved about freely in patronizing various businesses, traveled unimpeded throughout the region, [and] voted as they pleased in elections."[202] In November 1866, the Freedmen's Bureau Superintendent for Knox County, reported that "freedmen are quiet and peaceable, and generally industrious; with few exceptions the whites treat them kindly and deal with them honestly. The civil authorities particularly of this city are disposed to extend to them all the rights and privileges to which they are entitled by existing laws."²⁰³ In 1867, an official with the Freedmen's Bureau observed that black Knoxvillians "were bargaining shrewdly with their white employers, and in many cases had managed to buy their own homes. Two black churches were active, both under the supervision of black preachers. Three schools for blacks were in operation...." Further, blacks in Knoxville did not experience organized brutality as in other parts of the South because terrorist groups such as the Ku Klux Klan did not gain a foothold in Knoxville.²⁰⁴ In nearby Maryville, Tennessee, interracial harmony was evidenced by the May 1869 election of William B. Scott, Sr., a free-born black, as the city's mayor.²⁰⁵

In 1870, the Fifteenth Amendment to the Constitution was ratified, giving black men the right to vote. The Tennessee legislature had extended the vote to black men in 1867, but in 1870, with the Republicans out of power, the new state constitution instituted a poll tax, which reduced the number of poor blacks who could vote.²⁰⁶ Additional restrictions on the rights of blacks began around 1875, when state law gave proprietors the right to discriminate against blacks in hotels, restaurants, and theaters.²⁰⁷ An act of 1881 prohibited blacks and whites from riding in the same train cars.²⁰⁸ Knoxville, however, "was slow in adhering to the 1875 law." One source observed: "Blacks like Frederick Douglass stayed at the city's finest hotel ... in 1881. As late as 1898, 25 years after the law's initial passage, blacks were still served at the soda fountain at Kuhlman's drugstore on Gay Street, at Peter Kern's swank bakery and ice cream parlor on Market Square, and other places...."²⁰⁹ Indeed, until after the turn of the twentieth century, Knoxville "prided itself on its peaceful race relations, said by some to be the best in the South."²¹⁰ For the most part, the state's "Jim Crow" laws arose from the demands of lower-class whites. "The best people of the South do not demand this separate car business.... [It is] ... but a pandering to the lower instincts of the worst class of whites in the South."²¹¹ Segregation in state public schools, however, remained continuous until the 1950s. Both the public school law passed by the Radical Republicans in 1867 and that of the Democratic Redeemers in 1873 had required racial segregation in public education.²¹²

Despite setbacks and challenges, Knoxville's black community attained a measure of success after the Civil War.²¹³ Blacks in Knoxville advanced the cause of their education and achieved statewide and national influence. A reporter for the *The Army Mail Bag*, a military publication, described an 1864 visit to the school for blacks operated by Robert Creswell in the basement of Knoxville's First Baptist Church.[214] With the permission of Union General Burnside, Laura Cansler, a free black, opened "the Burnside School" around the same time to teach former slaves.[215] In 1875, the United Presbyterian Church opened Knoxville College as a normal school offering classes for blacks from first grade through college level.[216] Free public education was first offered to black children in 1876,[217] and Austin School, funded by donations from citizens in northern cities, was opened for blacks in 1879.[218] With a gift of $10,000 from the Carnegie Corporation, a library was secured for blacks in the city in 1917.[219]

Knoxvillian William F. Yardley, a successful criminal defense lawyer active in public affairs as a volunteer fireman, justice of the peace, and member of the city's government, became the first black to campaign for governor of Tennessee in 1876.[220] Samuel R. Maples and William Francis were other noted black attorneys in the city. In 1869, Isaac Gammon and David Brown became the first blacks to be elected to Knoxville's governing body, then known as the Board of Alderman.[221] Former slave Cal Johnson became one of Knox County's wealthiest citizens and also served as an alderman.[222] Dr. J.B. Young, probably the first black physician in Knoxville, had an office on Market Square[223] and ran for the legislature as a floater for Knox and Sevier counties in 1869.[224] Of course, not all the news was positive, as when a black won election to the Knoxville School Board in 1888 and the white members of the board held secret meetings at a private residence in order to exclude him.[225] By the 1880s, however, Knoxville had black policemen and businessmen.[226] William Henry Hastie, born in Knoxville just after the turn of the century, became the first black federal trial judge in 1937 serving the District Court for the Virgin Islands, and the first black appointed to the United States Court of Appeals when he joined the Third Circuit bench in 1949.[227] President John F. Kennedy reportedly "gave serious consideration" to appointing Hastie to the United States Supreme Court in 1962.[228]

The City of Knoxville appeared to retain a somewhat liberal attitude toward race despite friction over job opportunities arising between immigrating rural whites and the city's black population.[229] Most blacks in Knoxville during Sanford's lifetime were laborers for the Knoxville Iron Company, the marble-finishing plants, railroad companies, or local mines,[230] and "[t]here was resentment of and prejudice against blacks among the white working class.... Despite the lip service given to black achievement by white leaders, neither political party was above using crude appeals to racial prejudice when it suited election politics.

If blacks were happier, more secure, and better liked by whites in Knoxville than in the rest of the South, it may have been because blacks composed a relatively small proportion of the population."[231] Indeed, Knoxville always had the smallest black population among the major cities in Tennessee because there had been no plantation system in the area and no industries using large numbers of slave laborers.[232] In East Tennessee, the Republican party generally benefitted from the support of the black community for Republican candidates, despite the party's failure to promote blacks for office.[233] Furthermore, the black labor pool resulted in profits for the business elites like Sanford's father. Accordingly, most citizens of Knoxville, particularly the elite and middle-class whites, considered blacks a greater economic advantage than a social or political threat.[234] Thus, while discrimination on the basis of race characterized community life in Tennessee during Sanford's lifetime, the small black population, the dominance of the Republican Party in East Tennessee, and the abundance of good jobs and economic prosperity contributed to more peaceful racial coexistence.

After the lynching of a black soldier who had shot a white soldier in 1866, a year after Sanford's birth, another lynching did not occur in Knoxville until 1890, when Sanford was a young lawyer in the city. No further racial violence of this magnitude occurred until the Knoxville Race Riot of 1919.[235]

Knoxville in 1919 was a city of about 80,000. It was "one of the cities in the South whose black citizens could not only vote (upon payment of the state poll tax) but hold public office, serve as policemen, and sit on juries." The region's largest black newspaper, the *East Tennessee News*, was published there. One of its most distinguished citizens was Charles W. Cansler, principal of Knoxville Colored High School, who was a personal friend of Booker T. Washington. Cansler boasted in 1918, "In no place in the world can there be found better relations existing between the races than here in our own county of Knox. No race riots have ever disgraced our city and no mob has ever vented its fury here upon any Negro victim."[237]

The end of World War I threw the national economy into disarray. Returning soldiers flooded the job market at a time when government contracts were being cancelled. Unemployment and strikes increased, breaking down the nation's wartime unity, particularly along racial lines. Black veterans returned to a country that still denied them full citizenship.[236]

Hostility finally broke out in Knoxville in 1919 when a black man was accused of killing a white woman. Despite the removal of the accused to Chattanooga, a white mob gathered and stormed the Knoxville city jail. They confiscated the whiskey stored there from prohibition raids and destroyed both the jail and the sheriff's house adjoining it. The mob then headed for Vine Avenue, where blacks were reportedly gathering. Along the way, the mob broke into stores in search of guns. The Tennessee Fourth Infantry was called out. When the mob reached the corner of Vine (now Summit Hill Drive) and Central, the mob and the guardsmen fired at the blacks, who returned fire. One black citizen and one guardsman were killed. Thirty-six whites were arrested, but no convictions resulted.[238] The incident occurred not far from the childhood home of the then fifty-four-year-old Sanford.

The Knoxville of Sanford's time clearly impacted his development and his views of people and events. Sanford's inquiring mind, desire to serve, and thoughtfulness were formed and shaped by his environment, along with the influence of his family and the myriad of friends and acquaintances in the region. These East Tennessee roots cultivated "one of the ablest lawyers in the country," a man of "finest integrity" and "the highest type of American."[239]

Sanford's Early Years

One thing is forever good: That one thing is Success.
—Ralph Waldo Emerson

Though Sanford was born and reared in a region ravaged by the Civil War, the financial position of his family clearly softened its effects on him.[1] Sanford's father's career was "symbolic of Knoxville's great era of growth."[2] E.J. was described as "the architect of his own fortune; endowed by nature with great strength of mind and body, coupled with great business sagacity," who had "by dint of hard work, won his way from comparative poverty to great affluence...."[3] E.J. had arrived in Knoxville from Connecticut essentially destitute. "With little except a set of carpenter's tools, which he knew how to use, and an indomitable will, a resolute purpose and integrity of character,"[4] E.J. began a meteoric rise in East Tennessee business circles in the postwar economy of Knoxville.[5] He became active in commercial pursuits such as wholesale drugs, banking, railroads, textiles, mining, and newspaper publishing[6] and served as president or vice president of two banks and more than a half-dozen companies. As a driving force behind Knoxville's late nineteenth-century industrial boom, in which the city became a nexus between rural towns in Southern Appalachia and the nation's great manufacturing centers, Sanford's father was involved in nearly every major industry operating in the area during this period.[7] The Sanfords became one of the richest and most prominent families in Knoxville[8] as E.J. amassed a fortune by the standards of the time.[9] An article from *The New York Times* in 1887 described E.J. as follows:

> Mr. E.J. Sanford, who has large New York interests, and is almost well enough known in the business district there to be a native, is President of the [Knoxville] [W]oolen [C]ompany, having a good deal of money in it, as, indeed, he seems to have in pretty generally everything else in Eastern Tennessee. . . . He was a farmer's boy up in Fairfield County, Conn., before he drifted down to Dixie to make a way for himself. He is a millionaire now, and every penny of his fortune is the outcome of enterprise undertaken and pushed to success on Southern soil. He came to Tennessee before the war, won a wife of the South, and was prospering when the war drums sounded. But he didn't falter. His business he put aside; money sacrifice was uncounted; he shouldered a rifle for the Union's sake. And the Southern bride—she was as loyal as ever the husband was. When the war was over he was again "at the old stand" and one long unceasing line of prosperity has marked his goings and comings ever since. With him every man of capital and brain is interested in Knoxville's development. . . .[10]

At the time of his death, one of the local newspapers reported: "No man of his time has left his impress upon the commercial, industrial and social life of the city in a higher degree or in more indelible characters than Col. Edward Jackson Sanford."[11]

Young Sanford also benefitted from the fact that Tennessee was the only state of the Confederacy not required to undergo the Military Reconstruction imposed by Congress in 1867.[12] With the state under Radical Republican rule until 1869, the East Tennessee region rebounded rather quickly from the effects of the war. Sanford's family prospered in this environment. When support for the Republican agenda retreated to East Tennessee, the Sanford family was less affected than Unionists in other parts of the state and the rest of the South. Further, Sanford's father embraced the view that cooperation with respectable former Confederates would ensure the most successful and profitable outcomes. "[W]hat some would call Reconstruction in Tennessee [the time Brownlow was governor] ended early, with no lasting shift of political power away from the older, more affluent white families."[13]

The Civil War and the fact that his father and a large segment of East Tennessee had favored the Union side in the conflict influenced Sanford. E.J., a Republican from the North, assisted in the defense of Knoxville at the Battle of Fort Sanders.[14] Earlier in the war, however, to escape conscription into the Confederate Army, E.J. left his pregnant wife and young daughter and fled Knoxville in April 1862. After becoming ill on that journey, he returned to Connecticut to recuperate. There he remained until General Burnside took Knoxville in September 1863, due to his wife's "earnest entreaties for me to not join the army . . . to postpone it & see if I could possibly avoid it consistent with duty."[15] These entreaties from Sanford's mother, whose family supported the Confederate cause, were due not only to her fear for the life of her husband but also because of the sympathy she felt for the Rebels. Thus as noted by Sanford's Harvard Law classmate, Chauncey G. Parker, the son "was nurtured during his adolescent years in a community" and a family "that was divided in its aspirations and efforts by [the war]," and "[h]e could not have failed to be influenced by . . . these conflicting currents."[16] Indeed, the Reverend E.E. Hoss observed in an 1872 speech, when Sanford was seven years old, that the antagonism between North and South had not yet subsided and that Knoxvillians remained deeply divided.[17] Parker, therefore, correctly concluded that "the loyalist to the North and the loyalist to the South both contributed to the atmosphere in which Sanford grew up."[18]

We know little about Sanford's early years. According to the 1870 Census, the family lived in Knoxville's Sixth Ward, which in 1870 was described as follows: "Beginning at the northeast corner of Gay and Clinch Streets; thence on Gay Street to Vine and Academy Streets to the East Tennessee and Georgia railroad; thence with the railroad to Second Creek; thence down Second Creek to Clinch Street, and thence with Clinch Street to the beginning."[19] The Sanford family "lived in a stately old home on the northwest corner of Prince [now Market] and Commerce,"[20] in the downtown area on Summit Hill, then Knoxville's elite neighborhood.[21] Nearby was the "beautiful home of Col. Adrian Terry of the Burr & Terry Lumber Mill."[22] Little Ed's middle name, "Terry," reportedly was meant to honor Col. Terry, his godfather.[23] Terry was from Connecticut, like E.J., but the two men became best friends in Knoxville prior to the war.[24] Terry served in the Union Army on the staff of his brother, Major General Alfred Howe Terry, and gained the rank of Lieutenant Colonel.[25] After 1866, Terry was living in Knoxville and working as chief engineer on a railroad project with E.J.[26]

At the time of the 1870 Census, Sanford, then four years old, spent his days with his mother; his father's sister, Georgiana, then age twenty-six; and his one-year-old sister Emma (1869–1940). His sibling Louis Chavannes had passed away two years earlier after living about seven months. His grandmother, Anna F. Chavannes, had been a presence in the Sanford home since 1860.[27] Other members of the household included Andrew Shetals, forty, the driver; Emily Shetals, twenty-three, the chambermaid; and Cynthia Shetals, twenty-four, the cook.[28]

In July 1872, shortly after the death of yet another sibling, George William, in March of that year from pneumonia, one of his father's business interests, the drug firm of Sanford, Chamberlain, and Albers, erected a soda fountain. Sanford appeared at the store, and his father gave him a soda. Soon, Capt. W.P. Chamberlain, another member of the firm, treated Sanford to another soda, unaware that the youngster had already had one. A little later, A.J. Albers, the third member of the firm, treated Sanford to yet another soda! Soon young Ed had "an ache in the stomach" that he never forgot, but he fondly remembered the event as a "banner day!"[29]

In June 1873, when "Little Ed" Sanford was almost eight, *The Knoxville Daily Chronicle* reported that he had "attracted considerable attention" riding "his velocipede" in the city "down towards the depot."[30] Two years later, when Sanford was nearly ten years old, the velocipede was "carried from the front porch" of his home by a thief.[31] By the 1880 Census, Sanford was fourteen and listed as "Eddie T." The address was noted as 252 Prince Street. Sanford, along with his eleven-year-old sister Emma and five-year-old brother Alfred (1875–1946), were noted as "at school." Also living in the household at that time were two-year-old sister Mary (1877–1970), one-year-old brother Hugh (1879–1961), and Sanford's grandmother, Anna F. Chavannes, then seventy years old. Eventually, another sister, Louise (1882–1964), would join the family. In 1888, E.J. sold "his splendid residence property" at the "northwest corner of Prince and Reservoir [now Commerce] streets" to Jacob W. Borches.[32]

A friend of Sanford's brother Hugh, William Cary Ross, described the activities of his childhood in Knoxville as

> making kites of all sizes and flying them; of having had a taxidermy outfit and stuffing birds we hadn't any business killing; of doing amateur photography and developing our own films; of collecting birds' eggs, climbing trees to get them all over the surrounding country; of selling flowers to merchants on Gay Street to get money to order rare eggs that could not be found in this part of the country; still later, of playing baseball and football with the boys of the neighborhood, and of spending a lot of time on the Tennessee River in rowboats and canoes and swimming in the river. . . .[33]

Ross was fourteen years younger than Sanford, but one would assume Sanford's youth was similar. Sanford clearly had a familiarity with baseball, playing in a charity game in 1892.[34]

No record exists of Sanford's early schooling, and "very little seems to be known of him during this period."[35] James A. Fowler, Sanford's future law partner, stated that Sanford "graduat[ed] from the City Schools of Knoxville" but provided no information as to Sanford's early education.[36] It is unlikely that Sanford attended a public school. No workable public schools existed in Tennessee prior to the Civil War, and after the conflict they were further hindered by an attitude of indifference. As one historian characterized,

> Typical were the words of one bombastic state representative who, after observing "booklearning" was "not the only source of information," asserted, in many cases "booklearning" was "cramping and stupefying." He boasted the people of Tennessee "are amongst the best observers in the world." He lambasted the colleges of the East and brazenly asserted "the boys of eighteen in Tennessee, without knowing a letter in the book, are really more shrewd than many who have gone through the course of a common school. . . ."[37]

Further, at the outset of the Civil War, Governor Isham Harris had forced the Bank of Tennessee, where the state's "school fund" was deposited, to purchase state bonds to finance war expenses. These bonds became worthless with the defeat of the Confederacy, and with the failure of the Bank of Tennessee, the "school fund" was lost.[38]

After the war, decades elapsed before a satisfactory school system became a reality across the state.[39] Knox County, Tennessee, began opening public schools in 1868. A year later, however, the Tennessee legislature, now controlled by Democrats, repealed the school law passed during Brownlow's tenure as governor, which had provided schooling for black as well as white children. It further appears that the Republican "school fund" had been plundered by corrupt politicians during the Brownlow administration. The result was that any public schools in existence quickly deteriorated.[40] In an effort to reduce taxes and debt, responsibility for educating the state's youth was placed solely in the hands of county authorities with no mandate that the counties provide any public schools.[41] "The year after the Tennessee Redeemers [Democrats] had all but destroyed the public school system ... it was realized that while the white population had increased only 13 percent during the preceding ten years, white illiteracy had increased 50 percent."[42]

It was not until 1871 that the citizens of Knoxville voted to establish free schools.[43] *The Knoxville Chronicle* published an article on May 21, 1872, touting Knoxville's brand new school system affording children "good free schools."[44] Sanford himself noted in his book, *Blount College and the University of Tennessee*, that there was no efficient public school system in Tennessee until 1873, eight years after his birth.[45]

Before that time, the only educational opportunities for children in Knoxville were in private subscription schools and academies, such as Hampden-Sydney Academy, which had begun operation in 1817 and was named for the noted Virginia college.[46] A contemporary of Sanford's in Knoxville, Adolph S. Ochs—the future publisher of *The New York Times*—"got the beginnings of his school education at Bradford's Hampden-Sydney Academy, a Knoxville day school" and at "the preparatory department of the East Tennessee University (now the University of Tennessee)."[47] Ochs was older than Sanford, however, and after January 1868, when Sanford was two, Hampden-Sydney's property was leased to the university for the use of the preparatory department.[48] As the 1870 Knoxville Census listed the occupation of Sanford's aunt Georgiana as "Teacher," if he did not attend a private school, perhaps she served as his early tutor, along with his mother.[49]

Sanford's father pushed for the establishment of a public school system in the city, served as the president of the Knoxville Board of Education from 1881 to 1885, and was a presence on the board for several terms.[50] Despite "the ingrained prejudice of Tennesseans against public schools," E.J. was one of the strongest advocates for a tax levy to maintain Knoxville's school system.[51]

William Rule, two-time mayor of Knoxville and a local newspaper editor for more than sixty years,[52] was a family friend and knew Sanford from boyhood. In November 1861, after Union sympathizers burned railroad bridges and the Confederates placed Knoxville under martial law, Sanford's father had helped Rule sneak out of the city to carry messages to Rule's employer, newspaper editor and future governor Brownlow, who was then hiding in the mountains of Sevier County, a strongly Unionist area.[53] Rule, who went on to serve with distinction in the Union Army,[54] was the founder of *The Knoxville Chronicle* in 1870, which later consolidated with *Brownlow's Knoxville Whig*. In 1885, he founded *The Knoxville Journal*.[55] As to Sanford, he observed: "[E]ven in his youth he showed a determination to know things and to know them well, an outstanding characteristic Sanford maintained throughout his life."[56] As Sanford matured, his parents discovered that he had an unusual concentration upon his studies, excelling particularly in history and politics.[57] He was "[a]lways first in his studies, or in any contest he entered, [but] he aroused no jealousy on the part of other contestants."[58] Indeed, Sanford was known for his inquiring mind and a predilection for comprehensive treatment of a subject.[59] While most often an asset, the last characteristic "would come to negatively impact him when speed and deadlines were important, as in trial court work, especially when coupled with a self-doubt that frequently troubled him."[60]

Although Sanford's father took great interest in all his children, and both parents stressed education and achievement, Sanford's cultural outlook and love of learning were fostered by his mother, Emma, who "carefully directed her children's education."[61] Having lost two children to the measles the year prior to Sanford's birth, Emma was especially attached and attentive to her young son. Under the supervision of his mother, who was bilingual, Sanford acquired a cultured cosmopolitan education.[62]

Emma Chavannes Sanford was born in 1841 in Aigle, Vaud, Switzerland. She was the daughter of Charles Adrien Chavannes, a fifth-generation pastor who had been educated at the Academy of Lausanne, where he also studied forestry, and Anna Francoise Albertine Charlotte Francillon, a member of a Swiss family of "prominence and of wealth."[63] Emma had five siblings who lived to adulthood: Leon (1834–1862), Marc Samuel Albert (1836–1903), Louisa Marie (1839–1878), Adele (Chavannes) Ogden (1847–1917), and Emile (1850–1905).[64] The Chavannes family identified themselves with the Open Brethren, a Fundamentalist Christian group that had withdrawn from the National Protestant Church of Switzerland in 1824. The group had a simple, scripture-based, laity-oriented practice of faith. Their worship service was characterized by spontaneous Bible reading, prayer, and hymn singing without musical instruments as they sat in a circle facing one another.[65] Assemblies of the Open Brethren, however, were not permitted by the Swiss government. Members found holding Bible studies in their homes were dragged into the streets and beaten by authorities.[66] To escape the persecution for their religious beliefs, the Chavannes family, originally from Charmoisy, France, left Switzerland via the port at Le Havre, France, in 1848.[67] They arrived in the United States on June 12, 1848, aboard the ship *Hector*.[68] A travel account of the family's emigration from Switzerland to Tennessee kept by Sanford's grandmother, Anna, was later translated by his sister, Emma, and published in *The Knoxville News-Sentinel* in installments on June 22, June 29, and July 9, 1930, shortly after Sanford's death.[69] The story recounts almost incessant motion sickness caused by the extremely rough seas encountered during the voyage of forty-one days. Periods upright were spent singing hymns, praying, and studying English.[70]

Sanford's grandmother, Anna, like most of the French-Swiss in the Knoxville area, was a Confederate sympathizer. Before the war, she had owned a slave named Hannah.[71] In 1860, however, five years after her husband Adrien's death in 1855 from "a malady of the larynx," Anna and her daughter, Louisa, moved in with newlyweds Emma and her Unionist husband, E.J. Sanford. Thirty years later, Anna moved with the family to Maplehurst at 816 West Hill Avenue, after E.J. and Emma purchased the home in 1890 from the daughter of Knoxville businessman and politician James Hervey Cowan.[72] The property, originally called "River Lawn," was renamed "Maplehurst" by the Sanfords because maple trees grew on the property.[73] The house was "a gorgeous Italianate brick thing with tall, narrow windows and a central three-story tower."[74] At Maplehurst, Presidents Benjamin Harrison and Theodore Roosevelt, along with presidential candidate William McKinley, would be among the Sanfords' guests.[75] President Harrison visited when he gave a major speech in Knoxville on April 14, 1891, during a nationwide whistlestop tour.[76] E.J. held a reception for then Ohio Governor McKinley in September 1895.[77] Sanford's sister Mary, in her later years, recalled that Governor McKinley had a "charming manner" and showed "constant solicitousness" for his invalid wife, who "delight[ed] in the little girls of my brother, Edward."[78] President Roosevelt visited Maplehurst in the fall of 1902, shortly before E.J.'s death.[79] A decade after E.J. passed away in the house on October 27, 1902, his estate sold the property in 1912 to Alex McMillan & Company for development.[80] In the 1920s, the residence served as the Kappa Sigma fraternity house at the University of Tennessee, and during that time, Monroe Countian Estes Kefauver, a future US senator and presidential candidate, lived there.[81] The house was damaged by fire in 1932, and the remnants eventually were razed.[82]

Sanford's grandmother, Anna Chavannes, despite never learning to speak English, became a US citizen on June 20, 1859. She kept track of family births, marriages, and deaths in the old Chavannes family Bible her husband Adrien had received from his father upon being ordained a minister. When Anna died of bronchitis on September 25, 1891, at the age of eighty-one, her will named her son-in-law, E.J., and her grandson, Edward Terry, as the "Trustees and Executors" of her estate.[83] Buried in Old Gray Cemetery in Knoxville, Anna was memorialized as a woman whose "rare sweetness and gentleness of ... character brought her the warmest love and devotion of all those who did know her."[84] "She was charitable in thought, word and deed."[85] The future would see similarly phrased expressions delivered regarding her grandson, a man "beloved by the laymen and citizens generally."[86]

Sanford's mother, Emma, with long curly dark brown hair, blue eyes, and rosy dimpled cheeks, was known for her beauty and sweet disposition.[87] During the journey to America, her mother had written in her journal: "It is a very good thing for Emma that we are going into a retired place, for everyone looks at her. She would soon be filled with vanity."[88] A cousin described Emma as "compassionate, affectionate, and good-humored."[89] A Civil War diarist recalled that Emma "carried flowers for the graves of her two little children" at Old Gray Cemetery.[90]

The Sanfords were active members of St. John's Episcopal Church, and in her adult years, Emma was known in Knoxville as a major supporter of the parish's orphanage, serving on the Executive Board of Lady Managers as secretary.[91] In 1892, within a year of her mother Anna's death, Emma was stricken by a mysterious illness. She was taken to the Battle Creek Sanitarium in Michigan, founded by Dr. John Harvey Kellogg, the cereal pioneer, with the hope of restoring her mental and physical condition.[92] At Battle Creek, she "had every attention that the affection and care of a devoted husband could suggest, or the skill of physicians and trained nurses could bestow."[93] Sanford, then thirty years old, and his father were on a train traveling to visit Emma when she passed away on October 1, 1895, at the age of 54. She had died young like her father, Adrien, whose death involved "mental suffering as well as physical illness."[94] Emma's cause of death was described as "simply a sudden giving away of the physical and nervous system which proved too much for her strength. Nature simply yielded and was unable to rally and to prolong life."[95] The circumstances of Emma's illness, as well as those of her father's, probably contributed to a later claim by a detractor of Sanford's that "Judge Sanford, like the other members of his family and his mother's family, has a peculiar and not a well balanced mind."[96]

An excerpt from Emma's obituary describes her well:

> She was a friend to all mankind. To those who enjoy plenty of luxury she was a pleasant companion. With those of our citizens who like her came from historic old Switzerland she was always a prime favorite. She was a friend to the poor and many a time and often has her purse been opened to drive away want from the doors of the distressed. If the sick or poor needed medicine or food or raiment she was always ready to furnish what might be needed, and so unostentatious was she in her benefactions that only those of her own immediate family knew their extent. It was not strange therefore that among the mourners at her bier were not the rich only but orphan children from the charitable institution which she has fostered so liberally. Domestic in her tastes and habits, a model of womanly modesty, sweet spirited and gentle, all Knoxville mourns over her death.[97]

East Tennessee University and The University of Tennessee

> [A]s our University shall train her youth in those pursuits that make for wealth, so too, as wealth shall be developed in the community, bringing with it, as it always does, well earned rest and more at-

tention to the polite arts, to the graces and luxuries of life, to those things that lift life above mere money-getting and make it a thing of joy and beauty, it shall be that those arts which make for culture and refinement shall also keep their homes within the walls of our University, which shall ever be the abiding place, not only of that which is practical, but also of that which is ideal.[98]

—Edward T. Sanford

At eleven years old in 1876, Sanford entered the Preparatory Department of East Tennessee University as a junior.[99] Due to his age, his admission required a waiver of the stated requirements ("age 14, able to read, write and spell well, grounded in arithmetic, English, grammar and geography").[100] He chose the Classical course option rather than the Agricultural or Mechanical option.[101] The record kept in his junior year revealed that Sanford "was a conscientious student, was neither absent nor tardy for the entire year, accumulated no demerits, and earned perfect or near perfect scores in all his academic subjects."[102] In March 1879, by legislative act, "East Tennessee University," the school originally chartered as Blount College in 1794,[103] became the University of Tennessee.[104] When Sanford enrolled at the University of Tennessee in the fall of 1879, he was fourteen years old.[105] The school's entrance requirements included a minimum age of sixteen for enrollment, so he again needed a waiver. Getting these waivers posed no difficulty for Sanford, however, as his father had been appointed a trustee of the East Tennessee University in 1870 and remained on the board after the school became the University of Tennessee.[106]

In 1869, E.J. had been appointed as agent for the East Tennessee University by President Thomas W. Humes[107] and had helped secure for the school the state's Morrill Act (land-grant) funds.[108] To E.J. "must be assigned the lion's share of the credit for the endowment of East Tennessee University with the Morrill Act land fund."[109] The school, destitute after the war, desperately needed the designation. President Lincoln had approved the donation of "public lands to the several states and territories ... [to] provide colleges for the benefit of agriculture and the mechanic arts." Under the provisions of the 1862 Morrill Act, each state received federal land based on its population, and the income generated from the sale of that land supported the designated land-grant schools.[110] The Civil War, however, prevented Tennessee from accepting this gift until 1865, which, according to the provisions of the Act, was too late. Fortunately, with Tennessee the first state readmitted to the Union in 1866, a Congress sympathetic to the Republican-controlled state passed special legislation in 1867 extending the time specified in the original act so that Tennessee might avail itself of its provisions. In 1869, the legislature appropriated the fund to East Tennessee University, making it the duty of the school's trustees to establish an agricultural college.[111]

In a footnote to his remarks on the history of the University, Sanford recalled that the board of trustees in February 1869 passed a resolution commending his father "for his faithful and very efficient service as our agent in securing the location of the Agricultural College at Knoxville, as a branch of the East Tennessee University."[112] In 1903, shortly after E.J.'s death, a memorial in *The University of Tennessee Record* stated:

> The Trustees record with great sorrow the loss of the useful and respected member of the Board, Colonel Edward Jackson Sanford, of Knoxville, who died on the 27th of October, 1902. Colonel Sanford had been a trustee of the University since 1870, and had always taken a most active and influential part in its business. From the beginning he was deeply devoted to it, and throughout the whole of this period he never failed to respond to any call which the University made upon his time and energies. The successful management of the financial affairs of the University during these years was due more to his sagacity as a public man and his energy as a trustee than to that of any one else.
>
> Colonel Sanford was a liberal friend and supporter of education in all its departments ... [H]e did as much as any man of his time in this state to promote the interests of science and literature.[113]

At the University of Tennessee, Sanford excelled at his studies. He was awarded a Class Certificate of Distinction and an honorary scholarship in his freshman year.[114] Under the terms of the Morrill Act, instruction in military tactics was compulsory, and, as a sophomore, Sanford achieved the rank of 3rd Sergeant and was listed as a Distinguished Undergraduate.[115] In his junior year, he was promoted to 2nd Lieutenant of "C" Company. He also earned Certificates of Distinction in Mathematics, Surveying, Chemistry, Physiology, Zoology, and Philology, and Certificates of Distinction with Proficiency in Pure Mathematics and Ancient Languages.[116] In his senior year, Sanford became a Captain and Adjutant of the Cadet Corps.[117] He received Certificates of Distinction in Mechanics, Astronomy, Political Economy, Mental and Moral Science, History, Biology, and Geology.[118] He was a member of the Chi Delta Literary Society, serving as the business manager of its *Monthly Crescent* publication as a junior. At the graduation exercises held in Staub's Opera House in Knoxville on June 20, 1883, Sanford received two bachelor's degrees from the University of Tennessee, a B.A. and a Ph.B. (Bachelor of Philosophy).[119] He graduated at the head of his class and delivered the valedictory oration, "Danger Ahead," a "warning against the dangers of Communism in America."[120]

Throughout his lifetime, Sanford always maintained close ties with the University of Tennessee, a place he described as "a venerable and dignified institution, upon whose future, more than any other of the state, hangs the welfare of generations yet unborn."[121] He compiled a history of the school entitled *Blount College and the University of Tennessee*, published in 1894. In a speech concerning this history, one matter he addressed was coeducation, noting that women had recently been admitted to the university.[122] Sanford recalled that Blount College, a predecessor of the University of Tennessee, had permitted women to attend, one such young lady being Barbara Blount, the daughter of Governor William Blount.[123] Sanford, who during his senior year at the University of Tennessee had penned a letter to then-US Senator Howell E. Jackson of Tennessee inquiring about congressional action on women's suffrage,[124] issued remarks revealing that he supported equal educational opportunities for women:

> It would be inappropriate for me to fail to-day to make some reference to that formidable enterprise which was undertaken with such fear and trembling and reluctance one year ago: the admission of blue eyes and rosy cheeks within the academic halls. We have had one year's experiment. The reports of the professors, if they have not been bewitched by the brightness of those eyes, indicate not only that Tennessee yet has daughters as bright and fair as charming Barbara Blount, and who, like her, are entitled to be classed as not only attentive, but also diligent, and also ingenious, but they, furthermore, indicate that the experiment has been most successful, and are full of encouragement to those who believe that the daughters of the state

are entitled to be educated as thoroughly as her sons, and that the giving to them of this education, side by side with their brothers and the brothers of the other girls, will not detract from their feminine charms, nor deprive them of their graces, but will, on the contrary, in the generous rivalry of the schools, stimulate both the young men and women to higher excellence."[125]

Sanford, by that time the father of two young daughters, was pleased to see women come to share in the opportunities given to young men. The change by the university was overdue, because by the turn of the century, women were an increasing presence in the workforce. With war deaths affecting a significant portion of the population, the Civil War resulted in many young women's giving up hope of marriage or remarriage. Many war widows had to go to work. Their plight helped establish the right of women to earn a living by their own labor.[126] By the 1890s, almost half of the applicants who passed the US Civil Service examination were women, and by 1900, 6,000 women were working in federal offices. The growth of the nation's public schools resulted in more than 70 percent of teachers being female by 1900.[127] Progress occurred for women despite the medical advice of experts like Dr. Edmund Clarke, who "warned that too much education would channel young women's energies into their brains instead of their ovaries, leading to infertility, sickly babies, and the 'decline of the race.'"[128]

After obtaining his law degree from Harvard, Sanford returned to the University of Tennessee to serve as a part-time lecturer in the law department from 1897 to at least 1907,[129] teaching courses in corporation law and federal jurisdiction and procedure.[130] He also lectured outside the law department in the general academic department of the university, teaching the History of Tennessee.[131] Sanford was known to donate books to the university's library.[132] A catalogue of record noted that Sanford had donated some "marine shells"[133] to the school.[134] Further, he could be called upon to serve on a reception committee for a dance honoring new graduates or to judge a debate.[135] Demonstrating his well-rounded nature, during a College of Agriculture program in 1908, Sanford offered a prize of "$10 for proficiency in judging light horses."[136] He also actively supported his alma mater as a member of the University of Tennessee Alumni Association, serving as its president in 1892 through 1893 and again from 1909 to 1912.[137] In 1894, as the Alumni and University orator, he gave the Centennial Address,[138] "Blount College and the University of Tennessee," which traced the school's evolution.[139] Officials at the university were so impressed with the speech that they ordered it to be published, and it became a major source of information on the early years of the school.[140]

Sanford's oratorical abilities were well recognized by the university's alumni. The year 1896 saw him serving as toastmaster for an alumni event honoring United States Secretary of Agriculture J. Sterling Morton, the founder of Arbor Day.[141] During the alumni event, Sanford reflected on the improvements seen at the university since the arrival of President Charles W. Dabney and observed that "with the rise of the institution the Alumni Association cannot but rise."[142] Sanford and Dabney remained friends even after Dabney assumed the presidency of the University of Cincinnati in 1903.[143]

During Dabney's time as president of the University of Tennessee, the school joined with the University of Maine in 1899 to establish a new national honor society, Phi Kappa Phi. In 1901, the university's chapter elected Sanford as an alumnus member. Upon Sanford's selection to the Supreme Court years later, a *Phi Kappa Phi Journal* editor noted, "Judge Sanford is recognized as a man of great legal ability and of unimpeachable character. He is widely known as a writer and public speaker upon legal, historical, and educational subjects. . . ." The journal entry further stated: "[B]oth Republican and Democratic editors agree in saying the president could have made no wiser selection to the Supreme Court."[144]

In 1903, Sanford delivered the alumni address at the University of Tennessee commencement, speaking on "Ralph Waldo Emerson." *The University of Tennessee Record* related that "[f]rom the opening to the close of his address [Sanford] delighted the large and cultured audience with his eloquent and interesting account of the life and work of this American man of letters."[145] In the speech, Sanford noted that Harvard, his other alma mater as well as Emerson's, had missed out on the opportunity to have Emerson serve as a professor, in part, "on account of his bravely-spoken opposition to slavery at a time when such opposition was as distasteful to good society in Boston as in Charleston. . . ." Interestingly, Sanford's speech, given not long after his father's death, condemned "the arrogance of wealth" and "our national absorption in things material rather than things spiritual; our consuming desire for wealth as an end in itself rather than as a means of worthier ends." In Sanford's words: "Instead of being the owners of wealth for nobler uses, we are fast becoming its diggers merely, its watch dogs and its slaves."[146]

Sanford gained a seat on the University of Tennessee's Board of Trustees in July 1897 and served until July 1923.[147] From 1897 until his father's death in 1902, he sat alongside E.J., who had served as a trustee for over thirty years.[148] Sanford was an exemplary trustee who exercised substantial influence.[149] During his time on the board, Sanford took a leading role in the financial and policy-making decisions of the university. He "carefully scrutinized any expenditure which caused an account to overdraw its appropriation."[150] He was involved with efforts to control indebtedness and to secure money from the state for the university.[151] The school's difficulties in obtaining financing from the Tennessee General Assembly stemmed, in part, from the perception that the composition of the board of trustees was not representative of the state. The board of trustees had previously largely represented East Tennessee.[152] Sanford was instrumental in the reorganization of the board to make it more representative of the state and reduced its numbers from thirty to twelve. The reorganization provided gubernatorial appointed members from the entire state.[153] In 1903, the university finally received its first direct appropriation from the state. Six years later legislation was enacted providing for annual appropriations.[154] Sanford's last public act as a trustee involved procuring needed financing for the university.[155]

While on the board of trustees, Sanford served as chairman of the law department committee. The law department had been established in February 1890. It was a two-year program that led to a Bachelor of Laws degree. No other law school in the region required two years of study.[156] Dr. John R. Neal, who served at the University of Tennessee in the law department from 1909 to 1923, observed that "Sanford was the trustee who took most interest in the law department, and it was due to his efforts that we succeeded in bringing up the standard of the law school, which led to its admission into the Association of American Law Schools. . . ."[157] Neal gained fame in 1925 when he undertook the defense of John T. Scopes in Dayton, Tennessee's "Monkey Trial" and enlisted famed attorney Clarence Darrow as his co-counsel.[158] According to James D. Hoskins, a former president of the University of Tennessee, when the law school became a charter member of the association in 1900, it was the only such school south of the Ohio River.[159]

An interesting story regarding Sanford as a trustee occurred in 1904, upon the decision of Tennessee's president Charles Dabney to become president of the University of Cincinnati. Sanford was chairman of the committee charged with filling the presidential vacancy. Among those nominated was Howard Ayers, incumbent-president of the University of Cincinnati, whom Dabney was succeeding. Ayers was supported by Judge Horace Lurton, a former justice of the Tennessee Supreme Court and then a member of the Sixth Circuit Court of Appeals based in Cincinnati. Another backer of Ayers was William Howard Taft, at that time secretary of war in President Theodore Roosevelt's cabinet. In a response to Taft's letter of April 2, 1904, nominating "Dr. Ayers of Cincinnati," Sanford instead acknowledged receipt of the nomination of Dr. Ayres. Indeed, Dr. Brown Ayres, the acting president of Tulane, had become a candidate to fill the vacancy at Tennessee. As noted by the former historian for the University of Tennessee: "Whether this represented a typographical error or whether Sanford confused the two candidates with similar names will never be known. There are no extant trustee records on the subject. That Howard Ayers should not have been given consideration by the trustees after such strong recommendations from Lurton and Taft seems incredible. In any case, on July 20, 1904, a member of the board of trustees proposed Brown Ayres for the presidency, and a few weeks later, he was elected unanimously."[160] Others contend that Dr. Ayers of Cincinnati simply was not selected; rather, Alphonso C. Smith of the University of North Carolina was chosen initially. Smith, however, declined the office on July 13, 1904.[161] Historians speculate that Sanford had received a letter from former President Dabney proposing and endorsing Brown Ayres.[162]

In 1923, when Sanford was elevated to the Supreme Court, he had hoped to continue as a university trustee; however, he was disqualified because of his non-resident status.[163] At an alumni event in 1894, prior to taking his seat on the board of trustees, Sanford had issued a call for an alumni voice in the management of the University of Tennessee.[164] Humorously, he had noted, "It is a difficult thing to inspire alumni enthusiastically to come to annual conclaves under the stimulus merely of dry speeches and equally dry dining."[165] In a more serious tone, Sanford further elaborated:

> Let them feel that at their annual meetings they shall have some voice in the affairs of the University. We do not ask to control the University, but we respectfully urge that consent be given to some provision by which at least a certain portion of future Trustees shall be selected from the Alumni and elected by them.[166]

In 1909, Sanford spearheaded the alumni association's successful campaign to revamp the board of trustees to require the selection of alumni as members. The board was reconstituted to require that "at least one-third of the Trustees shall be members of the principal minority political party of the state, and at least one-third shall be alumni of the University," thus ensuring a continuation of the board's "non-partisan character" and providing for beneficial alumni representation. To Sanford's detriment, however, the 1909 language also contained a residency requirement. Therefore, because Sanford was principally residing in Washington, D.C., in 1923, he was not eligible for reappointment.[167]

The board of trustees and the university faculty passed the following resolutions commending Sanford's service:[168]

Resolution of the Board of Trustees

Resolved, that the Board regrets that conditions arising in the life of Judge Sanford and the necessity of his removing from the State for the time, at least, make it impossible for him to accept reappointment by Governor Peay as a Trustee. Judge Sanford had been a member of the Board for many years, always greatly interested in the University, faithful and earnest in his work on the Board, wise and just in all his positions and actions.

Resolved, further, that we part with him in this relation with regret, and wish for him a continuation of the good fortune that has always followed his earnest and worthy life.

Resolution of the University Faculty

Whereas Justice Sanford has long and faithfully served his Alma Mater as student, alumnus and trustee; and

Whereas his devotion to the institution has been further signalized by a meritorious history of its origin and progress; and

Whereas his removal from the State renders his tenure of the honorable office of Trustee impracticable;

> *Be it therefore resolved* that we felicitate ourselves upon his enlightened interest in education, and regret the loss of his wise counsel; that we, however, congratulate him, his Commonwealth, and his Nation upon the high honor of his elevation to the Supreme Court of the United States as an Associate Justice; that the University takes enduring pride in the distinction of its alumni in all the fields of endeavor, and is the more illustrious from the reflection of their glory; that we confidently expect in his new relations, as in those of the Federal Court, the unimpeachable sense of justice, the conspicuous legal erudition, and the irreproachable integrity which characterize him as an exemplary citizen and as a knightly gentleman; and that this resolution be a part of the record of 15 September, 1923.[169]

The *Tennessee Law Review*, with Howard H. Baker, Sr., a future US Congressman from Tennessee serving as editor-in-chief, observed that "[t]he College of Law, in particular, has reason to regret this departure, for Judge Sanford was a member of the Board's Committee, which had direct supervision of the College of Law, and as such he gave constantly of his best efforts for the development and upbuilding of this college."[170] The law review tribute continued: "Tennesseans know Judge Sanford well enough to enable them to feel confident that [his] elevation to the Supreme Court will not cause any loss of interest on his part in the forward movement of the State and this institution. Likewise, he will never be forgotten here. . . ."[171] Alas, Sanford was soon as forgotten as those words. Ironically, until just recently, the University of Tennessee College of Law's chapter of the legal fraternity Phi Alpha Delta was named for US Supreme Court Justice James C. McReynolds, a Kentucky-born graduate of Vanderbilt University and the University of Virginia School of Law, rather than for Sanford. In an effort to honor Sanford's contributions to the school, a name change was requested from the International Executive Board of Phi Alpha Delta. In January 2016, the name "Edward Terry Sanford Chapter" was approved for the Phi Alpha Delta chapter at the University of Tennessee College of Law.[172]

Perhaps the residency requirement was not the only reason Sanford left the board of trustees, as his departure from the body took place shortly before the dismissal of six professors from the university, an act which came to be known as the "Slaughter of the PhDs." Newspapers across the country announced that a "fight for academic freedom" was occurring at the University of Tennessee and that the matter of the firings had been placed before the board, of which Sanford was a member.[173] Upon the dismissal of Professor John R. Neal, who later defended John Scopes, thirty-two students in the law department announced "that they would quit in a body and go to another school" unless Neal was reinstated.[174] Professor Jesse W. Sprowls noted that the turmoil arose as follows:

> I was professor of sociology, holding the chair furnished by the John D. Rockefeller Educational Board. I taught evolution. I believe in it. I gave the students Robinson's *Mind in the Making* for research reading. They took the book home and people began to write in.
>
> The president called me to his office and asked if I couldn't change the phrasing from evolution to something else. He said he didn't want to have a "monkey-legislature on his hands."

> President Morgan said to me, "You're not dismissed. You're just not rehired. If you don't tell this, I'll travel to any place in the country at my own expense to get you a job."[175]

> The matter went to the board of trustees on July 17, 1923. The chairman, Edward T. Sanford, resigned when the hearing began, saying he must decline to sit because he had been appointed a justice of the United States supreme court. The six professors were dropped that day after a hearing on charges . . . [that] the American Association of University Professors held after investigation to have been unsubstantiated.[176]

Thus it was, perhaps, the anti-evolution movement in Tennessee that led to the dismissal of the professors and ultimately to the Scopes "Monkey Trial" at Dayton, Tennessee, rather than the strict adherence to the residency requirement that precipitated the departure of Sanford from the board of trustees.[177] The Scopes case "dramatized one of the most momentous struggles of the age—the conflict between religion and science."[178] Professor Sprowls noted that the state was stirred "to religious fervor." He recalled: "Revival meetings sprang up in every town in the state." Evangelist Billy Sunday "went to Nashville and fought a live, red devil on the stage." Additionally, Kiwanis, Rotary, and trade clubs adopted resolutions "demanding protection from 'German infidels who teach that man sprung from a lower order of things.'" According to Sprowls, "tracts were circulated declaring that the teachers of the theory are a cross between a human being, an imp of hell and the serpent." Politicians who campaigned on an anti-evolution platform were elected.[179]

The Tennessee legislature passed the anti-evolution bill in 1925.[180] The new law provided that "it shall be unlawful for any teacher in any of the Universities, Normals and all other public schools of the State, which are supported in whole or in part by the public school funds of the State, to teach any theory that denies the Story of the Divine Creation of man as taught in the Bible, and to teach instead that man has descended from a lower order of animals."[181] John W. Butler, the state representative who introduced the bill in the House, justified his proposal as follows: "If we are to exist as a nation the principles upon which our Government is founded must not be destroyed, which they surely would be if . . . we set the Bible aside as being untrue and put evolution in its place."[182] For teaching evolution at the University of Tennessee, Sprowls "was branded as apostate, infidel and atheist."[183] Harcourt A. Morgan, the president of the university, who privately opposed the anti-evolution bill, "held his tongue so long as [Governor] Peay's proposal for expanding the University still awaited action in the State legislature—and admonished his faculty to do likewise."[184] As a member of the board of trustees, Sanford, now an associate justice on the United States Supreme Court, clearly did not desire any involvement in the controversy and adroitly avoided it by his timely resignation.

Harvard University

Following his graduation from the University of Tennessee in 1883, with his father's encouragement, Sanford enrolled as a junior at Harvard University in the literary department.[185] Letters Sanford wrote during his time as a student at Harvard were published in a Knoxville newspaper. According to a later article, one letter "caught the hearts of the native East Tennesseans by a reference to an old box car of the [East Tennessee, Virginia, and Georgia Railway Company,

ETV&G] road sidetracked away up in bleak New England."[186] A Harvard classmate noted that Sanford's "earnest, companionable enthusiastic nature, and his ability speedily gained him recognition and friends," despite the fact that he was "a stranger coming to us at a time when many of our college intimacies were formed."[187] While at Harvard, Sanford earned a Bachelor of Arts in political science (1885) (magna cum laude); a Master of Arts (1889); and a Bachelor of Laws (1889) (cum laude).[188]

Sanford's well-rounded education—including five earned degrees—was summed up in a 1930 Nashville newspaper editorial: "While the law was always his favorite study, his education was of the broadest and most liberal type. He was at home in the fields of literature. He was a patron of the arts. He had a true understanding and a genuine grasp of the essential facts of life. There was a breadth and a catholicism about his learning that enabled him, as a jurist, to avoid many of the pitfalls into which the narrow technical, precedent-bound judge is too often likely to fall."[189] According to Lewis L. Laska, a Tennessee attorney, Sanford might be the most educated justice ever appointed to the United States Supreme Court.[190] The justice closest to Sanford in regard to education is William Rehnquist, with four earned degrees.[191]

At his 1885 graduation from Harvard, Sanford was selected Class Day Orator. A portion of the oration noted as follows:

> The essence of the spirit of liberal investigation is an unprejudiced mind which compels every opinion to appear before the bar of reason and stand the test of an impartial investigation.... [H]e who can see fairly both sides of the questions often remains for a time entangled in a maze of doubt.
>
> ... A liberal spirit is beneficial in so far as it enables us to form sound judgments as a basis for action; but that liberality which causes us to see so clearly both sides of the question, that we are left with no definite belief as a motive force is only a paralysis of vital power. We must decide upon some belief, and then carry it into action.[192]

Sanford's words seem to acknowledge that he was aware of his tendency to be slow in making up his mind. Later in the oration, Sanford expressed his goal to serve others:

> The desire to make the world brighter and better is the hope of hopes, which ever grows as man develops his nobler nature, which leads him, as an earnest man has said, to turn his back upon the feast and place of power, to toil for those he can never see or for a scant justice that can come only long after the clods have rattled upon his coffin lid. Amid the scoffs of the present and the sneers that stab like knives, he builds for the future, he cuts the trail that progressive humanity may hereafter broaden into a highway.[193]

The goal of service to mankind remained constant throughout his lifetime. Sanford's civic involvement, pro bono legal work, and reform efforts while on the bench reflect his commitment.

Following completion of his Harvard undergraduate degree, Sanford and four classmates studied languages and economics abroad and traveled the European countryside,[194] visiting France and Germany. Sanford attended L'École des Sciences Politiques in Paris,[195] where Leon Say and Paul Leroy-Beaulieu, distinguished French statesmen, were in attendance.[196] The McClung Historical Collection at the Lawson McGhee Library in Knoxville contains a letter dated January 13, 1886, written by Sanford while he was in Paris to his younger brothers, Alfred and Hugh, regarding his European trip.[197] Sanford also traveled to Lausanne, Switzerland, to meet members of his mother's family.[198]

While at Harvard, Sanford participated in extra-curricular activities, including the Historical Society, Consolidated Signet Society (president), and the Southern Club (founder and first president).[199] The Southern Club's purpose was to promote fellowship among the southerners attending Harvard. A clubhouse was located in a Cambridge building on Brattle Square.[200] Sanford also participated in rowing.[201] Additionally, Sanford was a member of the Pow Wow Law Club, founded in 1870 and the oldest of the law clubs at Harvard. The object of the club was to hold moot courts; it was not a social club.[202] The members pursued a demanding schedule of formally arguing and adjudging cases, including the preparation and presentation of extensive written pleadings, briefs, and decisions.[203] Primary criteria for election to Pow Wow were academic achievement and commitment.[204] Further, Sanford was a member of the legal fraternity of Phi Delta Phi.[205] Once Sanford became a federal judge in the Middle District of Tennessee, he affiliated with the Malone Chapter of Phi Delta Phi at Vanderbilt Law School.[206]

In 1910, Sanford became an honorary member of Phi Beta Kappa at Harvard.[207] He was also an associate member of the Vanderbilt University Phi Beta Kappa Chapter.[208] The University of Tennessee did not have a chapter until 1965.[209] Almost a year prior to the day of his death, he was awarded honorary membership in the "Sanford Law Club" at Harvard, an organization apparently created in his honor.[210]

During Sanford's time at Harvard Law, he was a member of the *Harvard Law Review*. From November 15, 1887, through March 15, 1889, he served as one its first editors, as the *Review* was established while Sanford was a law student.[211] Sanford "valued his experience as editor, was throughout his life a friend of each successive board, and followed with interest the success of the magazine."[212]

As in all his educational endeavors, Sanford was successful at Harvard Law. He led his class at the end of his first year and at the completion of his course.[213] He was twenty-three years old when he received his law degree in 1889.

Law school as an educational entity only began to gain traction in the latter third of the nineteenth century.[214] Previously, even for a significant part of the twentieth century, "reading law" with an attorney already a member of the bar was the far more common way of entering the legal profession.[215] The consensus among legal historians is that the Harvard Law School of Sanford's time "intellectually, socially, and numerically overwhelmed all the others."[216] The impact of its dean, Christopher Columbus Langdell, was enormous, and his contributions—in both legal doctrine and teaching methodology—were impressive.[217] Langdell's case study method "combined the detailed study of case opinions issued by appellate judges with a vigorous Socratic dialogue between professor and student on the facts, holding, and rationale of each decision."[218] This tool for developing critical thinking skills by using probing questions to get at the heart of the subject matter became standard in most American university law schools by 1910.[219]

Once his studies were over, Sanford remained active in Harvard affairs, as he did with the University of Tennessee. He served on Harvard's Committee on Alumni Relations[220] and served as vice president of the Harvard Law School Association and later as director of its executive committee.[221] In 1924, he served as Harvard's alumni president, chaired the annual association meeting, and gave the address of welcome.[222] At the June commencement that year, Harvard awarded Sanford an honorary Doctor of Laws degree,[223] and the class dinner was a testimonial to him.[224] In his speech at the commencement, Sanford reflected on the significance of service in the aftermath of the First World War:

> ... [t]he spirit of Harvard is the spirit of service. In the World War almost one-third of her sons, it is recorded, were enrolled in the service of the Nation and her Allies, in various capacities; and of those who entered the armed forces nearly four hundred gave up their lives in the defense of Freedom.
>
> Again our Mother summons us to service as citizens of the Republic. Never had the Nation, in time of peace, greater need of faithful, valiant service than in these troubled and bewildered days, when, as the aftermath of war, so many evil passions have been turned loose that plague the children of men and seek to undermine the foundations of Liberty itself. . . .[225]

Sanford constantly addressed the themes of service and patriotism. In his 1885 Class Day oration, Sanford observed that "they who have received ten talents must make larger returns than they who have received five," and "'[t]is not by your thinking alone the world will be made better, but by your thinking made living in action. The age demands men of heart, head and hand alike."[226]

After Sanford was named a district judge in 1908, he was honored with an L.L.D. from the University of Cincinnati, whose president was his friend and former University of Tennessee president Charles W. Dabney. The honor was presented in the following manner by Dean William Perry Rogers:

> I have the honor of presenting ... for the degree of Doctor of Laws in this University one already trusted and honored by the men of his native hills and leaders of his country; Bachelor of Arts of Tennessee and Master of Arts and Bachelor of Laws of Harvard; long a trustee of the University of Tennessee, elected by his legal colleagues to high offices in their associations; a true scholar, more than able in interpreting law, a patriotic citizen; now Assistant Attorney General of the United States, and by the nomination of the President and with the consent of the Senate, about to sit on the Federal bench—Judge for the Eastern and Middle Districts of Tennessee. . . .[227]

In his acceptance speech, Sanford spoke about "the double nature of our legal system; its continuity . . . and its diversity. It is a constant process of adaptation, having permanence and stability upon the one hand and progress and adaption upon the other."[228] This view that the law must be adapted to changing times would later find expression in Sanford's greatest contribution to American jurisprudence.

 CHAPTER FOUR

Private Practice and Family

The purpose of life is not to be happy. It is to be useful, to be honorable, to be compassionate, to have it make some difference that you have lived and lived well.

—Ralph Waldo Emerson

Sanford's legal career covered the end of the nineteenth century and the early years of the twentieth century, a period that, like Sanford himself, is sometimes overlooked. During the time he served as an attorney, Sanford was a witness to or participant in many of the historical and otherwise significant events in Tennessee after the conclusion of the Civil War.

Sanford's admission to the Tennessee Bar was acknowledged by a license dated September 24, 1888, at Knoxville.[1] He passed the bar exam while still in law school at Harvard.[2] Justices William C. Folkes and Horace H. Lurton of the Tennessee Supreme Court were his examiners. Folkes was a Confederate veteran who was severely wounded at the first battle of Manassas and lost a foot in the skirmish at Malvern Hill.[3] Eighteen years old when the war started, Lurton joined the Fifth Tennessee Regular Infantry of the Confederate Army but was captured in 1862 when Fort Donelson was surrendered. He later escaped from the Union prison at Camp Chase in Ohio and joined the guerilla forces of General John Morgan ("Morgan's Raiders"). Lurton was captured again in July 1863 on a raid in Ohio.[4] In 1865, after an appeal by Lurton's mother, President Lincoln, in a longhand order, wrote: "Let the boy go home with his mother."[5]

Lurton, a member of the Tennessee Supreme Court from 1886 to 1893, later was elevated to the Sixth Circuit Court of Appeals, where he served from 1893 to 1909 and for a time with future president and future chief justice William Howard Taft. When Taft became president, his close friend Lurton, despite Lurton's age (65) and his party (Democrat), was his first appointee to the US Supreme Court in 1909. Lurton was one of the last persons appointed to the Supreme Court to have served in the Civil War.

Years later, upon congratulating Sanford on his appointment to the district court bench, Lurton remarked: "Having admitted you to the bar through the severest examination any man ever went through, I now welcome you to the judiciary."[6] According to Sanford, however, the examination proceedings were rather cursory, consisting of oral comments about a case that Lurton had recently decided. Sanford gave the following account at the 1923 annual meeting of the Tennessee Bar Association:

> Judge Lurton began by asking me my age, and then he said: "Young man, what would you say if a stock company, a corporation—I think he said a mining company?—should buy a controlling interest in another like mining company?" I thought a moment, and I ventured the suggestion that it would be ultra vires, that the statutes of Tennessee did not give any such authority, a corporation was a thing of limited power, a statutory corporation; and I had hardly got the words out of my mouth, when he said: "Young man, you are exactly right; I decided that thing, I decided it about one month ago." He then proceeded to tell me about *Harvey v. Marble Company*, and for about half an hour, I should say, in my recollection, he gave me the details of that case in which he had been tremendously interested, and of course I listened with the greatest interest. After he got through, in about half an hour, he said: "Young man, you are splendidly equipped; I

am not going to ask you another question," and he never asked me another question, not one.[7]

While on the US Supreme Court, Lurton had respect for precedent, and his opinions tended to trace earlier case law in detail. He subscribed to liberty of contract, yet he was sympathetic to federal economic regulation. He was conservative in civil rights matters. Biographer James F. Watts, Jr., described Lurton as an "experienced jurist, 'a courteous southern gentleman,' even-tempered, fair-minded, kind, gentle, a person of integrity, reasonable, and charmingly collegial—a person who seemed the very 'reincarnation of an ancient lawgiver.' He was no radical wild-eyed result-oriented lawmaker, but a safe, middle-of-the-road technical jurist with a mildly pragmatic nationalist streak."[8] What stands out in Lurton's record is moderation. According to historian Paul Kens, not even Lurton's most significant opinions broke new legal ground.[9] Sanford, with a personality similar to Lurton's, became fast friends with the judge.

Around the time Sanford started private practice, the Gilded Age, the period of industrial growth that produced a great deal of wealth for businessmen like Sanford's father, was ending. That label, borrowed from the title of an 1873 novel by Mark Twain and Charles Dudley Warner, "suggested that America glittered on the outside while it rotted at the core."[10] Nevertheless, many great fortunes were created during this period supporting an impressive way of life.[11] Although the Gilded Age was ending, the "New South" was beginning, as declared by Henry Grady, the editor of *The Atlanta Constitution*, in 1886. In a monumental speech to the New England Society of New York, Grady declared that the South was on the verge of greatness. He asserted that a new era was at hand in which a "New South" would emerge from the ashes of the Civil War and the turmoil of Reconstruction. Many adopted Grady's belief and felt that the South was destined for prosperity.[12] Sanford and his father worked to make Grady's belief a reality.

Upon Sanford's return to Knoxville from Harvard, he began a career as an attorney that lasted for eighteen years. He was first employed during the summer of 1889 as an assistant in the office of the general solicitor of the ETV&G, a company his father served as a director.[13] Following the summer position with the railroad, Sanford joined the reputable Knoxville firm of Andrews and Thornburgh on August 1, 1889. George Andrews, born in Vermont, had arrived in Tennessee in 1865 after practicing law in Detroit, Michigan. He initially became a law partner of O.P. Temple but soon was appointed to the Tennessee Supreme Court by Governor Brownlow, serving from 1868 to 1870.[14] Upon retirement from the bench, Andrews served as United States attorney for the Eastern District of Tennessee until 1877.[15] Jacob Montgomery Thornburgh was born in Jefferson County, Tennessee. Like Sanford's father, he had crossed over the mountains into Kentucky to escape conscription into the Confederate Army.[16] In 1861, he was commissioned a lieutenant colonel of the Fourth Tennessee Cavalry and eventually served as commander of that regiment, as well as a brigade consisting of the Second, Third, and Fourth Tennessee Cavalry, and the First Brigade of the Tennessee Cavalry.[17] After the war, Thornburgh served as district attorney of Tennessee's Third Judicial District from 1866 to 1871.[18] He served two terms in Congress after his election from the Second District in 1872.[19]

The firm had an extensive practice in Knox County and the surrounding area and represented the various business interests of Sanford's father, E.J.[20] However, twenty-two days after Sanford joined the firm, Andrews died as a result of a railroad accident that occurred during an excursion tour of the Knoxville, Cumberland Gap & Louisville Railroad. The newly-built railroad extended from Knoxville to Middlesboro, Kentucky. Andrews was among the prominent Knoxvillians invited to make the first trip over it. Less than twenty-three miles out of Knoxville, the coach carrying most of the passengers detached and plunged from a high trestle into a creek.[21] Sanford's future father-in-law, W.W. Woodruff, was among those injured in the wreck. An account of the accident noted, "Capt. Woodruff, lying on two cushions, his left leg and left arm broken, was as cheerful as any man could be under the circumstances. He assisted materially in the removing of others by his timely suggestions."[22] After Andrews's death Thornburgh and Sanford formed a new partnership under the name, Thornburgh & Sanford.[23]

Sanford, despite his inexperience, was forced to bear the burden of a number of cases pending before the Tennessee Supreme Court.[24] As observed by his future law partner and friend James A. Fowler, "[h]owever highly a young man may be educated in the schools, yet he is more or less groping in uncertainty when he enters upon the active practice. And because of young Sanford's unwillingness to do anything imperfectly, the extensive and important business thus thrust upon him was very burdensome." Sanford, however, was "industrious in the prosecution of the firm's business, applied himself to the task with great diligence, and within a remarkably short time he acquired the habits of a well-trained practitioner."[25]

Sanford's status as a Harvard Law graduate made him something of an oddity in the Knoxville of those days, and individuals would crowd into the courtroom to see how he would perform.[26] In one case, he was hired to prosecute a man who, after enjoying "too much Christmas cheer . . . had shot up" the Hattie House in downtown Knoxville.[27] Sanford succeeded in obtaining a judgment.[28] As a rule, however, Sanford avoided criminal cases and seldom appeared in criminal court.[29] "His inclination and training were such that he cared nothing for the practice of criminal law."[30]

Cornelius E. Lucky,[31] a Jonesborough, Tennessee, native, ex-Confederate major, and Phi Beta Kappa graduate of Hamilton College in New York, became Sanford's next partner on September 1, 1890.[32] Lucky gained his legal training by reading law with Thomas A.R. Nelson, a distinguished Tennessee lawyer who was one of the counsel who defended President Andrew Johnson in his impeachment trial and also served as a Tennessee Supreme Court justice.[33] Nineteen days after Lucky joined the firm, however, Thornburgh passed away from natural causes.[34] A contemporary book on Knoxville relates the following on the resulting firm:

> Lucky & Sanford, attorneys, at 123 and 125 Prince [S]treet, are largely engaged in corporation practice—sometimes for and sometimes against those embodied creations of the law. They are general counsel for the East Tennessee National Bank, the Knoxville Southern Railroad, and the Coal Creek Mining and Manufacturing Company (which, with 50,000 acres of coal lands, is one of the great corporations of the State), and for other such concerns besides.
>
> But they have also distinguished themselves as opponents of corporations at the bar. They have won, but lately, a celebrated case of this character, that of McDonald, Shea & Co., et al[.], railroad contractors, against the Chicago, Cincinnati & Charleston Railway; a case involving $581,528, the full amount of which they recovered for their clients. Able counsel were opposed to them, and powerful interests antagonistic, but they succeeded nevertheless.[35]

In other railroad work, Sanford represented the Marietta & North Georgia Railway Company (M&NG), "which became part of a through route from Marietta, Georgia, to Knoxville when the Knoxville Southern Railroad, a M&NG subsidiary, completed its tracks from Knoxville to Blue Ridge, Georgia, in

August 1890."³⁶ The line was "built in the obsessive drive to reach Ducktown," Tennessee, and the copper industry located there.³⁷ The Knoxville Southern and M&NG eventually merged to form the Atlanta, Knoxville, and Northern Railroad, a company absorbed in 1902 by the Louisville and Nashville Railroad Company.³⁸

Railroads brought "a large volume of legal business with them into any locality: title work, right-of-way negotiation, casework for claims." Lawyers, as small businessmen, welcomed the new clients. Attorneys for railroads "became a powerful group of pro-growth advocates, and many became the most articulate and effective proponents of the new business economy in the region." During Sanford's time in practice, "the most important litigant in the courts was the corporation, and the most lucrative field in legal attainments was the study of corporation law."³⁹ Sanford, while engaging in general practice, "ma[de], however, a specialty of corporation law, often involving railroads."⁴⁰

Sanford represented the M&NG in an interesting case involving the death of a Mrs. Peck at the Grady Depot in Georgia. As the evening passenger train was pulling into the station, a terrible storm arose. A flash of lightning occurred, after which the telegraph poles were scattered all about. Shortly thereafter, the operator at the Grady station found his wife dead on the floor of the office, having been struck by the lightning. The husband brought suit against the M&NG for $50,000 in damages. The evidence revealed that Mrs. Peck had hastened over to the depot in the rain from the post office, getting drenched in the process. She proceeded to sit down at a table beneath which two wires were hooked together. Mrs. Peck's feet probably were on the ground wire under the table, and her wet clothes made her "an exceptionally good conductor for the overcharged current on the wires over-head." M&NG won the suit, with Sanford convincing the judge that the company was not legally responsible for Mrs. Peck's death.⁴¹

In addition to representing railroads, Sanford paid careful attention to the affairs of the East Tennessee National Bank, where his father and his wife's father, W.W. Woodruff, both served as officers and on the board of directors.⁴² Representation of E.J. Sanford's many interests, particularly Coal Creek Mining and Manufacturing Company, consumed a considerable portion of his son's practice. Coal Creek Mining and Manufacturing Company owned more than 90,000 acres of land in the coal-rich Coal Creek Valley of western Anderson County, Tennessee.⁴³ Sanford's father was president and a director of the company;[44] Sanford also served as a director along with E.J.'s friend and business partner, Charles McClung McGhee.

Many of the ventures of Sanford's father involved McGhee, a native of Monroe County, Tennessee, who was a descendant of James White, Knoxville's founder, and Charles McClung, a prominent early Knoxvillian.[45] McGhee served as a banker, railroad man, and financier. He was a principal stockholder, vice president, and general manager of the ETV&G. As a trustee of the University of Tennessee, McGhee used his influence to reopen the school soon after the Civil War. He was a member of the Tennessee legislature from 1870 to 1871.[46] McGhee established the Lawson McGhee library, then at 128 South Gay Street in Knoxville, as a memorial to his daughter, May Lawson McGhee, who died in 1883.[47] The downtown library still retains the name.

McGhee had been a loyal Confederate, with a cavalry company called the "McGhee Invincibles" formed in his honor in 1861 in his native Monroe County.[48] The post-war collaboration of E.J. Sanford and McGhee demonstrates, again, both the divided loyalties of Knoxvillians during the Civil War, and the success achieved by the ability to put aside those differences after the war. In this regard, E.J.'s son modeled his father's behavior, as Sanford maintained close friendships with former Rebels Judge Horace H. Lurton and his law partner, Cornelius E. Lucky. Sanford's ability to overlook differences and advocate trust and unity ultimately resulted in a groundswell of supporters in his future pursuits.

In a letter to McGhee about Coal Creek, E.J. revealed his hope that their East Tennessee properties would yield great wealth, securing their children's future in the upper echelons of Tennessee's business world. "Coal Creek was even worth more than Tennessee Coal, Iron, and Railroad Company," he stated. "[I]t was going to be good ... for our children as long as any thing is good."[49] Coal Creek Mining and Manufacturing Company leased land to various mining firms, most notably the Knoxville Iron Company,[50] Knoxville's first major post-Civil War manufacturing firm.

E.J. was a stockholder, director, and from 1892 to 1895, vice president[51] of Knoxville Iron Company. The company had been started on Second Creek in Knoxville by Hiram Chamberlain, a former Union officer from Ohio who had been Chief Quartermaster in the city during the Union occupation.[52] Knoxville Iron Company's plant eventually covered more than three acres in Knoxville and included mills manufacturing nails, bars, railroad spikes, and components for railroad cars.[53] It eventually became the city's largest employer[54] and played a key role in bringing heavy industry and railroad facilities to Knoxville.[55]

It was Knoxville Iron Company that shipped out Coal Creek's first rail car of coal in October 1867 and, by 1871, had opened a mine there. In its first year, the mine shipped some 2,000 tons of coal to Knoxville for the iron company's rolling mill and related processes. By 1873, Knoxville Iron Company leased land at Coal Creek and was shipping about ten cars a day out of the mines, each car containing ten tons of coal.[56] In the decades 1880 to 1900, Anderson County led the state in coal production, with the mines in the Coal Creek area served by the Knoxville & Ohio Railroad (K&O).[57]

The K&O, previously known as the Knoxville & Kentucky Railroad (K&K) when the road was first chartered in 1855, was built to provide access to Anderson County's coalfield. Knoxville was utilizing around 10,000 tons of coal annually. In view of the demand for coal, Knox County as well as Knoxville signed up for stock to back the venture.[58] After the Civil War, the road came under the management of Charles McClung McGhee, who was president in 1866.[59] McGhee hired E.J.'s friend, Col. Adrian Terry, a Yale-educated Union veteran, as chief engineer. McGhee also conferred with the president of the Louisville and Nashville Railroad about establishing a connection with the K&K at the Kentucky state line.[60] The State of Tennessee provided bonds for the K&K's construction,[61] but a firestorm eventually erupted over Governor Brownlow's state support of railroads, funding for which had essentially bankrupted the state.[62] Before the storm hit, McGhee resigned from the K&K's presidency and board. Sanford's father, however, remained on the board and rode out the tempest.

Some believe that E.J. and McGhee foresaw the ultimate collapse of the K&K and devised a plan to benefit from the event.[63] A period of economic depression in the 1870s soon decreased the viability of local railroads.[64] With E.J. still a director, McGhee came back as president of the railroad in 1870.[65] The K&K filed for bankruptcy, and the pair subsequently moved in to reorganize and control it.[66] McGhee and E.J. ultimately sold the railroad to a group of capitalists, including McGhee,[67] for $350,000, resulting in a loss of $2 million to the State of Tennessee.[68] The name was changed to the K&O because the new owners did "not propose to stop at Kentucky or in Kentucky, but will push forward their great work to Ohio...."[69] Ultimately, the K&O ran sixty-six miles from Knoxville to Jellico, Tennessee.[70] In 1893, Sanford successfully represented the K&O in a lawsuit to enjoin the collection of over $100,000 in taxes assessed against the railroad during Governor John P. Buchanan's administration.[71]

During this time period, E.J. also helped McGhee put together a regional rail network—with Knoxville as its headquarters—that became one of the most important systems in the South.[72] McGhee formed a syndicate of northern capitalists that acquired a majority of the stock in the ETV&G, and E.J. served as a director.[73] In 1881, prior to Sanford's graduation from the University of Tennessee, McGhee and his associates sold the K&O that they had purchased for $350,000 to the ETV&G for over $1.8 million, a more than 400-percent profit. At the time of the transaction, McGhee was serving as the president of the K&O and vice president of the ETV&G, with E.J. on the boards of both entities, but the conflicting interests apparently were ignored.[74]

E.J. and McGhee masterminded a similar deal with the purchase and sale of the Tennessee & Ohio (T&O) to the ETV&G. The T&O started out as the Rogersville and Jefferson prior to the Civil War.[75] It ran only sixteen miles from the ET&V line to Rogersville, Tennessee.[76] During the war, the railroad was wrecked, and the State of Tennessee issued bonds for its rebuilding, but, like the K&K, the company defaulted. In 1871, the Rogersville and Jefferson, which had cost the state $385,000, was sold to the ETV&G for $23,000. In 1877, the company was conveyed to Horace M. Aiken, who reorganized it as the T&O.[77] With the coal boom in the 1880s, McGhee requested that E.J. sound out Aiken about selling the road. McGhee told E.J., "If I bought, it would all have to be done in your name." McGhee was aware that he and the other New York directors would have to avoid any public involvement in the purchase in order to keep the price down. Presumably, he also wanted to escape a conflict of interest charge when the road was sold later to the ETV&G. The asking price was $150,000, but E.J. bargained it down and closed the deal at $100,000.[78]

At McGhee's direction, E.J. reorganized the T&O with a dummy board of Knoxville directors and himself as president.[79] McGhee advised E.J. to continue the management of the road as it had been in the past, "spending no more money than is absolutely necessary and take as large net earnings as you can. We will lay no more rails than required to keep the road in a safe condition...."[80] George S. Scott, president of the Richmond and Danville Railroad, met with E.J. concerning extension of the T&O from Rogersville to Big Stone Gap, Virginia, asserting that "[w]henever Mr. Sanford sees that the extension is a necessity he will build it" and "[t]hen Knoxville will be the mistress of the coal and coke business of the south, just like Pittsburgh is to the north."[81] No extension was ever built, however, and in July 1889, the T&O was sold to the ETV&G for $320,000 in ETV&G extension bonds.[82] The purchase of the T&O at an exorbitant profit of 220 percent to E.J.'s group loaded the ETV&G with debt and significantly contributed to its ultimate bankruptcy.[83] Ironically, in 1892, McGhee was appointed as the ETV&G's receiver.[84] The ETV&G existed for twenty-five years until August 1894, when the Southern Railway assumed its operation.[85] Sanford was involved in the final disposition of the ETV&G,[86] and the firm of Lucky & Sanford was awarded a portion of $30,000 in attorney's fees to be paid out of the proceeds of the sale.[87]

Greater scrutiny of such conflicts of interest would begin in the 1890s, when the public started viewing railroads with suspicion and skepticism. In the early part of the decade, a major depression "exposed the railroads' visions of economic growth and prosperity as false dreams and cursed hopes." The Populists gained widespread support during this time period by calling for government intervention to "remedy the inequities of the new industrial system."[88] The Populist Party described the nation as on "the verge of moral, political, and material ruin." They called for a graduated income tax; currency expansion; government ownership of railroads, telephone, and telegraph; and a farm–labor coalition. Populists urged greater protection against immigrant labor, which "crowds out our wage-earners."[89] They became an active political movement in the South and "challenged the way business and government worked in the Gilded Age South." Everything about the interstate railroads offended Populists.[90] Farmers vented anger at railroads, and every southern state passed legislation to create a railroad commission. Southerners played leading roles in writing and passing the Interstate Commerce Act of 1887, which created the first federal regulatory agency.[91]

With most mines in the Coal Creek Valley established by companies leasing land from Coal Creek Mining and Manufacturing Company, the area of Anderson, Campbell, and Morgan counties became a lucrative mining region. In the lawsuit *Cullen v. Coal Creek Mining &Manufacturing Co.*,[92] the complainants alleged that E.J., McGhee, and the directors of the ETV&G were determined to dominate the coal fields along the line of the K&O and had used their control of the railroad to force their way into and to dominate Coal Creek Mining and Manufacturing.

The company initially was organized in March 1872 by Charles H. Bulkley, William S. McEwen, and Henry H. Wiley, who were the owners of the mountain lands under different and often conflicting titles. On December 25, 1871, they agreed to procure a charter of incorporation for mining and manufacturing purposes. All the lands became 25,000 shares of corporate stock held as follows: Bulkley one-half, and McEwen and Wiley each one-fourth.[93] The *Cullen* complaint asserted that the defendants—the owners and bondholders of the K&O, which hauled the coal from the more than twenty-five mines located on the land—had coerced Bulkley to sell them all the stock he held, which was 12,500 shares.[94] Reportedly, these defendants, which included E.J. and Charles McClung McGhee, threatened to divert the railroad facilities away from Coal Creek's property, which would leave the mines isolated and unable to operate.[95] Added to assets already owned, the stock transfer gave the defendants actual dominant control of the company. E.J. and McGhee were, thereafter, elected to serve as company officers and on the board of directors.[96] According to the lawsuit, the defendants further deceptively manipulated the purchase of the Poplar Creek Coal and Iron Company and other property, owned by the Wiley estate, through a third person.[97] The complainants, Curtis Cullen and Charles S. Newman, owners of 1,500 shares of Coal Creek Mining and Manufacturing stock, contended that "since 1885 there has been no accounting of the property to the minority stockholders, the defendants controlling affairs"; the defendants "have become immensely wealthy, while the minority stockholders of the Coal Creek company have secured dividends only"; and Poplar Creek Coal and Iron Company,[98] organized from 30,000 acres of the Coal Creek company, had "been obtained by fraud."[99] According to the complaint, the directors, with the sanction of the majority stockholders, had consummated a purchase of the stock of another corporation.

The minority stockholders had taken some nine years to request an accounting and to pray that the defendant directors be held personally liable for the sums spent in the unauthorized purchase of stock. Further, they sought to set aside, as ultra vires,[100] the corporation's deed, executed nine years before. Sanford, then a young attorney, represented the interests of Coal Creek Mining and Manufacturing Company, in which he was also a director. E.J. and McGhee justified their actions by arguing that the high royalties of the prior management were retarding development of mining in the area and adversely impacting the freight revenues of the K&O. In their view, that fact necessitated "capitalists with enlarged views" to acquire the Bulkley stock.[101] Their activities have been described as "a case of the unscrupulous use of raw power" and "virtual fraud."[102]

Despite the allegations of misconduct, Sanford won the *Cullen* lawsuit. The court acknowledged that the transactions by Coal Creek Mining and Manufacturing were probably ultra vires but provided no relief to the complainants due to the lapse of time. After the passage of nine years, the court determined that the defendants were protected by the statute of limitations.[103]

After the Southern Railway[104] gained control of the ETV&G in 1895, it inherited a majority holding in the K&O. The remaining shares were owned by the City of Knoxville, Knox County, and various individuals, including Sanford's father, who owned a large number of the outstanding shares.[105] At the time E.J. was selling his K&O stock to Southern, he and McGhee were "assisting" the railway company in the acquisition of the shares held by the city and the county. "With the development of a large coal hauling business, the K&O had become a profitable little railroad."[106] Sharing the view of the directors of the ETV&G, the Southern Railway "had no desire to pay out this surplus in dividends." Attempts were made "to disguise the profits by spending heavily on equipment; in this way they hoped to persuade the minority holders," especially the City of Knoxville and Knox County, "that their stock was of little value and might be sold at a low price."[107]

E.J. devised a plan to obtain the sought-after stock. An individual named Col. Albert E. Boone proposed to build a railroad known as the Ohio River, Jellico, Knoxville, and Tidewater ("the Black Diamond Line") from Columbus, Ohio, to the coalfields on the Tennessee–Kentucky border through Knoxville and into the Carolinas to Port Royal, South Carolina.[108] Boone declared that the road, projected as a rival of the Southern, would "relieve Knoxville and Knox County from the death grip the Southern Railway has upon [their] future prosperity" and "strike a death blow to the coal barons."[109] On behalf of Southern, E.J. proposed that the city and county should swap their K&O stock for shares in the Black Diamond Line. E.J. acknowledged that the proposal was a "dead fraud."[110] He made alliances with some of the local men who were promoting Boone's railroad. "Money spent in the right places secured a referendum on the question of making an exchange of the stocks, and a campaign of picnics and speeches by Boone persuaded the voters to approve the swap."[111] A few weeks after the Boone group obtained the stock, E.J., who remained president of the K&O until his death in 1902,[112] succeeded in buying it at $30 a share.[113]

E.J. sent a letter to McGhee explaining how he had accomplished the stock purchase:

> Had it not been for a couple of pools being formed by citizens here to buy up this stock and hold it as a matter of speculation for the future, I could have gotten it at quite a sum less, but these combinations had to be broken up and it has cost money to do it. I have not appeared in the matter at all myself, having worked entirely through others, as one of the great "bugaboos" was that it should not be sold to you, I or the Southern and at present, no one here knows who the purchaser is. Of course there are many rumors associating us all with it, but they know nothing.[114]

Thus did the citizens of Knoxville and Knox County give up their valuable K&O stock to the Southern Railway. In exchange, the two governments received shares in the Black Diamond Line, a railroad never built.[115] A 1902 letter from then-Knoxville Mayor S.G. Heiskell reflected on the fact that Col. Boone "got from our local suckers $40,000 as a promoting fund to promote 'the Black Diamond.'"[116] E.J.'s actions caused resentment with citizens, and the financial moves of both E.J. and McGhee were scrutinized in the future. A journalist observed in 1893 that many thought the pair were again "endeavoring to take an unfair advantage of the city" and that "they must be watched, as what would be in their interest cannot be the interest of the city."[117] E.J. noted to McGhee: "[O]ur connection with any city improvement seems to have the same effect upon the citizens here as a red rag does to a bull."[118]

An acknowledgment of E.J.'s stature in railroading occurred in February 1891, when the private train of Jay Gould, a leading American railroad developer and financier, stopped in Knoxville; the party went to E.J.'s home for lunch.[119] Almost a year later, Sanford and his wife Lutie, along with E.J. and Emma, were Gould's guests at a party in New York City.[120] Gould was reputed to have built a fortune of at least $75 million by manipulating railway stocks and bonds and by being indifferent to sound construction, regular maintenance, and good service of the companies he controlled.[121] Ranked in the top ten of an inflation-adjusted listing of the all-time richest Americans,[122] Gould is acknowledged as one of the nation's leading and most unscrupulous "robber barons" of the period.[123] E.J. likewise grew rich through ruthless business deals. From 1890 until his father's death in 1902, Sanford was intimately involved with E.J.'s business concerns as legal counsel, director, and stockholder.

The land leased by Coal Creek Mining and Manufacturing was the scene of the "Coal Creek Rebellion."[124] The conflict is "undoubtedly the best known labor story of nineteenth century Tennessee and one of the most dramatic and significant episodes in all American labor history."[125]

Coal Creek Rebellion

> *"My song is founded on the truth,*
> *In poverty we stand.*
> *How hard the millionaire will crush*
> *Upon the laboring man.*
> *The miner's toiling underground*
> *To earn his daily bread;*
> *To clothe his wife and children*
> *And see that they are fed.*
> *I am in sympathy with the miners,*
> *As everyone should be.*
> *In other states they work free labor,*
> *And why not Tennessee? . . ."*
>
> —"Coal Creek Troubles" ballad[126]

By 1870, Tennessee's debt stood at $40 million—the second largest in the nation.[127] After four years of war and Governor Brownlow's underwriting of railroad construction, Tennessee was in deep debt, with its infrastructure in ruins.[128] Starving and displaced Tennesseans, both whites and blacks, ran afoul of the law and were incarcerated, swelling the prison population. Blacks, who before the Civil War seldom comprised more than five percent of those incarcerated in the state's jails, made up over half of the inmates after the conflict, as "stiff penalties for petty crime were enforced rigidly" against them.[129] With the state treasury empty, a proposal to erect two additional prisons failed because of the expense involved.[130]

Legislators viewed leasing convicts to private business as a way of saving the state the expense of housing, clothing, and feeding prisoners, thus eliminating the need for a new central prison.[131] Under the program, convicts were rented to the highest bidder. The state (in theory) retained enough control to ensure that the prisoners were well guarded and properly treated. Governor John P. Buchanan, elected as the candidate of the populist Tennessee Farmers Alliance, modestly praised the leasing scheme as "successful," "relieving [the state] of all business risk and expense, and paying a surplus into the treasury." Admittedly, between 1870 and 1890, lessees paid more than $1 million into state coffers, four-fifths of which constituted a net surplus.[132]

In 1877, when Sanford was around twelve years old, Knoxville Iron Company, of which E.J. was a director and stockholder, brought in the first convict laborers to Coal Creek[133] to resolve a labor dispute.[134] Around 1885, about one hundred fifty convicts worked at Knoxville Iron Company's Coal Creek mines, and the company was the only one that continued using primarily convict labor into the late 1880s.[135] By the time of the Coal Creek Rebellion of 1891-92, Knoxville Iron Company had been using convict labor for nearly fifteen years.[136] Sanford's father supported the use of convict labor as a means to keep East Tennessee coal companies competitive with interests in Middle Tennessee and to maintain a cheap and dependable workforce.[137] The company had initially used free labor at its Coal Creek mine, but production was continuously interrupted by strikes and other labor disputes.[138] E.J. also reiterated conventional wisdom of the day that the presence of convict laborers curbed the demands of the free miners for unionization.[139] The coal interests and parties like E.J. had "their eyes clearly focused on corporate profits ... adamant in opposition to labor reform." Likewise, state lawmakers "had a substantial interest in the system as well" and "[c]los[ed] their eyes to the injustice done to free laborers. . . ."[140]

In 1889, after the state leased the entire penitentiary and all its inmates for six years to the Tennessee Coal, Iron, and Railroad Company in return for $100,000 per year and maintenance of the convicts, many of the men were used at mines in Anderson County. In multiple insurrections from 1891 to 1892, hundreds of free miners attacked the convict labor camps, overpowered the guards, burned prison stockades and company buildings, and released hundreds of inmates. The violence primarily centered on the communities of Briceville and Coal Creek. Three times in one year, the free miners sent a trainload of convicts—including Knoxville Iron Company miners—out of Coal Creek toward Knoxville.[141] In talks with the governor, the free miners declared that their actions were taken to defend their property and wages.[142] The convicts, however, were escorted back by Tennessee state militia companies and returned to work.[143] Eventually, during the fourth and final insurrection, Governor Buchanan sent trainloads of soldiers to Coal Creek bearing Gatling guns and heavy artillery to maintain order. The free miners, severely outnumbered, were forced to surrender and allow the convict miners to stay.[144] Although the free miners lost the war, Governor Buchanan lost the next election, remembered for his "indecision, imbecility and general incompetency."[145] As noted by a historian, the governor was hurt by a crisis not of his own making. He was caught between businessmen who considered a strike "a crime without parallel" and "laws he felt duty-bound to enforce, on the one hand, and, on the other, the strong feeling of labor and reformers that the lease system was a disgraceful injustice." He was unable to satisfy those who blamed him for negotiating with law-breakers, and the miners resented him for sending in the militia.[146]

Sanford's father, as lessor of the mine properties and a shareholder in Knoxville Iron Company, opposed the Knights of Labor organizers who represented the free miners.[147] He further maintained that much of the blame for the revolt lay with stipulations in the leases allowing the state to appoint prison wardens and guards, even though the companies paid their salaries: "The result of this [arrangement]," E.J. argued, "has been that every guard employed and deputy warden employed by [Governor] Buchanan, are Knight[s] of Labor."[148] He complained bitterly that the government appointees exhibited sympathy with the free miners and encouraged a general state of defiance in East Tennessee.

With the issue of convict leasing brought to public view, the negative publicity eventually forced the state to reconsider the system. When the convict lease contracts expired in 1896, Tennessee did not renew them, becoming one of the first southern states to end the practice.[149] However, legislation was enacted to build Brushy Mountain State Penitentiary in Morgan County, and land was purchased nearby where convicts would mine coal directly for the state rather than compete with free labor.[150] Coke ovens were built to increase the value of the coal mined there. While convicts were able to benefit by reducing their sentences based on how much coal they mined, the state garnered substantial profits until the mine closed in 1938.[151]

Fraterville Mine Disaster

Sanford was on the board of directors of Coal Creek Mining and Manufacturing Company when the Fraterville mine, the oldest in the Coal Creek section, exploded on May 19, 1902, resulting in the deaths of two hundred sixteen men and boys and nineteen mules.[152] At the time of the disaster, E.J. was president of the company, with McGhee joining Sanford, then thirty-six years old, on the board.[153] The explosion is acknowledged as the worst mine disaster in Tennessee history.[154] At about 7:20 in the morning, nearly an hour after the miners started working, a horrendous methane gas and coal dust explosion erupted, sending debris and smoke billowing from the ventilation shaft and the mouth of the mine.[155] Many miners were killed instantly by the heat and impact of the blast. Some who survived moved into side passages and deeper into the mine trying to escape the build-up of toxic gases. They built barricades in an attempt to shield themselves from the gases and heat. The bodies of twenty-six men were found in one such side passage. Some had stayed alive until as late as 2:30 in the afternoon, as evidenced by notes they left with their bodies.[156] A statement from George M. Camp, the mine's superintendent, described the disaster:

> [B]odies [were] found lying in every conceivable posture. A young boy of the number had his head blown completely off, both arms torn off and otherwise horribly mutilated. That the explosion had not killed most of the men, however, was apparent for some of them in their desperate agony to escape had furrowed their faces into the earth. Others had torn off their shirts and wrapped them around their nostrils in their efforts to keep out the [noxious] vapors which finally killed them.[157]

The precise cause of the explosion was never determined or disclosed. A mine inspector noted that the mine had recently installed a sixteen-foot fan for better ventilation and had remedied most deficiencies identified in a 1900 inspection report:

> I have just completed official inspection of Fraterville mine, and called your attention to ventilation and condition of this mine; ventilation is far below requirements. The volume of air entering mine was only 8,000 cubic feet per minute, just half of what it should be. This current is laden with black damp[158] from the Knoxville Iron Company's mine. I must insist that you get ventilation up to legal requirements as rapidly as possible. You must reduce the force in

this mine to eighty men, until you can provide the legal amount of air for these men...."[159]

The mine had been operated for over thirty years without a mishap and had the reputation of being one of the safest in Tennessee. It was reputed to be generally free of methane, an extremely explosive gas that can build up in poorly ventilated coal mines. At the time of the explosion, however, some suggested that the mine's ventilation fan had been negligently shut down all weekend, which could have accounted for the methane accumulation. The report of the Tennessee Commissioner of Labor revealed that the ventilation "furnace was not fired from Saturday night until Monday morning, and ventilation was stagnated."[160] When the ventilation operator was later put on trial, however, he was acquitted of any wrongdoing.

The methane may have leaked from a nearby abandoned, unventilated mine belonging to Knoxville Iron Company, into which the Fraterville miners had tunneled. The Knoxville Iron Company mine had been worked by convict laborers, who apparently mined beyond the lease of Knoxville Iron and onto the lease of Coal Creek Coal Company, owner of the Fraterville mine.[161] Whatever the source of the gas, it was probably ignited by the open flames of the miners' oil lamps atop their hats.[162] The explosion ignited the coal dust blown into the air, spreading fire throughout the mine and adding even more force to the explosion.[163]

The owner of the Fraterville mine was Eldad Cicero ("E.C.") Camp, a former major in the Union Army, United States attorney for the Eastern District of Tennessee, and Knoxville businessman, who treated his employees fairly and ran the mining operation as safely as possible.[164] Major Camp had refused to utilize the convict leasing system. He instead hired expert miners, mostly Welsh immigrants, and paid his workers in cash per tonnage rather than company scrip. The miners at Fraterville were members of the United Mine Workers of America within years of the organization's creation in 1890.[165] That such a disaster would strike what was a model mine for the times is a great irony.

As lessor of the land on which the Fraterville mine sat, Coal Creek Mining and Manufacturing Company seemingly bore no legal responsibility for the disaster. However, the company, along with Knoxville Iron, was brought into numerous resulting lawsuits.[166] Lawyers "hightailed" it to Fraterville to "engage widows and other kin," and lawsuits were filed a week after the incident. By the time the case of *Slover v. Coal Creek Coal Company*[167] reached the Tennessee Supreme Court, more than one hundred fifty lawsuits had been filed and were pending in the circuit courts of Knox and Anderson counties. In the *Ingersoll v. Coal Creek Coal Company* case,[168] the Tennessee Supreme Court outlawed lawyer solicitation of clients. The Court noted: "When a case is presented of attorneys rushing to the scene of a disaster in hot haste and competing with each other in soliciting the bereaved ones to allow them to sue for their losses, we feel that we are called upon to say in no uncertain terms that such conduct is an act of impropriety and inconsistent with the character of the profession."[169]

The Knoxville Journal and Tribune, established by Sanford's father in 1898 by merging *The Knoxville Journal* and *The Knoxville Daily Tribune*, opened a relief fund for the families of the miners. Sanford's brother Alfred Fanton Sanford served at the time as manager and president of the newspaper. With William Rule as the editor, the paper was viewed as the legitimate successor to *Brownlow's Knoxville Whig*.[170] As a Republican paper, it was the only such daily south of the Ohio River at that time.[171] Coal Creek Mining and Manufacturing Company, with E.J. and Sanford as local directors, contributed $5,000 to the relief fund.[172]

Like his older brother, Alfred was educated at the University of Tennessee (1891–93). After a world tour with a cousin, E.W. Ogden, Alfred worked as the bookkeeper at the Knoxville Brick Company, organized in 1888 on a 750-acre farm at Powell Station, and ultimately became its manager.[173] During his lifetime, Alfred was associated with his father and brothers in numerous businesses: Sanford-Day Iron Works (vice president); Knoxville Printing and Box Company (vice president); Knoxville Iron Company; Coal Creek Mining and Manufacturing Company; East Tennessee National Bank (director); Knoxville Woolen Mills; Manufacturers Acceptance Corporation; Sanford Realty Company; Empire Building Corporation; Sanford, Chamberlain and Albers Co. (vice president); Knoxville Office Company (secretary and treasurer); Lenoir City Company; Poplar Creek Coal and Iron Company; and others. He was a director of the Knoxville Board of Commerce, Rotary Club, and Advertising Club.[174]

Alfred later served as a member of Tennessee Governor Ben Hooper's military staff. In 1918, with Sanford serving in a federal district court judge position he was unwilling to relinquish, Alfred was encouraged to run for the governorship of the state. An article from *The Atlanta Constitution* noted the endorsement:

> General Sanford is a straight-out republican, and the political policies of the *Journal and Tribune* under his direction have been distinctly

> partisan.... [H]is paper stands unique among southern newspapers, for it is the only dyed-in-the-wool republican daily journal in the south. But General Sanford's republicanism is of the unwavering, in-season-and-out-of-season consistency and obduracy that cannot be changed. Though the heavens fall, he would stick to the G.O.P. There is nothing of the mugwump, nothing of the time-server about General Sanford....
>
> If any republican is to be elected governor of Tennessee, no more competent or faithful member of that party could be chosen than Mr. Sanford....[175]

Alfred was an accomplished musician and owner of what was characterized as the most complete arboretum in the United States, extending from the rear of his home to the shoreline of the Tennessee River.[176] He was also the president of the Chattanooga and Cincinnati Division of the eastern route of the Dixie Highway.[177] The Dixie Highway "became the most successful and consequential of the so-called marked trails of the 1910s and 1920s," linking "existing local roads into the first long-distance highways in the nation."[178] Supporters of the campaign believed that the Dixie Highway would benefit everyone: "Northerners and Southerners, city people and farmers, and governors and county commissioners—all rallied behind the campaign to build the highway."[179] Alfred passed away in 1946 at age seventy-one, after falling from a hospital window in Philadelphia, Pennsylvania. He had suffered for several years with a "throat malady," reminiscent of the health issues of his grandfather Adrien Chavannes.[180]

In the mid-1890s, Lucky and Sanford were joined at the law firm for a short period of time by Lawrence D. Tyson,[181] Charles McClung McGhee's son-in-law.[182] Tyson, born in North Carolina, was a graduate of West Point and had fought with the Ninth Infantry in Wyoming in the western Indian campaigns before coming to the University of Tennessee in 1891 as a professor of military science and tactics.[183] He had studied law while in the military, received a law degree from the University of Tennessee in 1894, and began practicing with Sanford in 1895.[184] That same year, Sanford and Tyson invested in a half-interest in a mineral artesian well that produced "Dixie" water. According to Sanford, he and Tyson had thoroughly investigated the product and "had satisfied themselves that it was one of the finest mineral waters ever brought into the market of the world."[185] A report in 1899 described the water as having extensive sales in Tennessee and adjoining states, but no mention of the continuing involvement of the two men.[186] Upon the outbreak of the Spanish-American War in 1898, Tyson left the firm to take command of a regiment of the United States Volunteers.[187] Later in 1898, he was appointed military governor of the northern portion of Puerto Rico. Upon his return to Knoxville, Tyson engaged in textile manufacturing, real estate, and mining. He became a partner with E.J. in Knoxville Woolen Mills and served as president of Poplar Creek Coal and Iron Company and vice president of Coal Creek Mining and Manufacturing Company. He served in the Tennessee House of Representatives from 1903 to 1908 and later served as US Senator from Tennessee from 1925 until his death in 1929.[188]

In 1916, during World War I, Tyson sought the office of assistant secretary of war. Sanford, by that point a United States district court judge, wrote President Woodrow Wilson on Tyson's behalf. In his letter, Sanford extolled Tyson's "strength of character and intellect" and "painstaking attention to everything which he takes in hand." Sanford ended the recommendation by stating that Tyson's appointment would "serve both the Government and the War Department in this high and honorable office with fidelity, unswerving loyalty and the highest efficiency."[189] Wilson did not select Tyson for the position, but he named him a brigadier general in May 1918.[190]

Around the turn of the century, James Alexander Fowler entered Sanford's firm, and it operated under the name Lucky, Sanford, and Fowler until 1907, when Sanford became assistant United States attorney general.[191] A native of Knox County, Tennessee, Fowler was born at Bull Run Crossing near Heiskell Station and was a graduate of East Tennessee Wesleyan College.[192] Prior to joining the firm, Fowler had been the unsuccessful Republican candidate for governor in 1898.[193] During his time in private practice, Fowler served as a special prosecutor in the high profile trial of James Fulton, an attorney accused of killing fellow attorney and former University of Tennessee football standout, Sam Parker.[194]

Sanford and Fowler had originally met as opposing counsel in *Pearne v. Coal Creek Mining & Manufacturing Co.*, a dispute over ownership of mineral interests and rights-of-way.[195] After the favorable judgment Fowler obtained was affirmed on appeal, he was employed thereafter as a local representative of Coal Creek Mining and Manufacturing Company.[196] Reflecting on joining the firm with Sanford, Fowler related that "the most important thing to me was the relationship that it brought about between me and Sanford. . . . Sanford and I became closely attached to each other. . . ." According to Fowler, "[f]or about eight years nothing unusual occurred in carrying on the firm's business." He noted that they "looked after the rather numerous questions that arose in regard to land titles vested in the Coal Creek Mining & Mfg. Co.," but claimed that this "was but a small fraction of the business of the firm which was divided between all the members."[197]

As Sanford's legal career continued, he earned a reputation as a capable attorney, aggressive on behalf of clients, yet a fair and gracious adversary.[198] A gifted speaker, mentally quick, always prepared in his cases, and knowledgeable in the law, Sanford possessed all the qualities of a good trial lawyer.[199] Words such as "industrious, thorough, honest and courteous" were used to describe him.[200] He impressed both courts and juries with his fairness and sincerity. Sanford had, however, what has been described as "an unusually cautious disposition, which made it very unpleasant to him to be compelled to act upon the spur of the moment in emergencies that from time to time arise in the course of a trial. . . ."[201] "[H]e attempted to avoid juries and the concomitant periodic need for quick, undeliberative decisions. If when before a jury he elicited from a witness an unfavorable response or used an argument or illustration that negatively influenced a juror, he would be disturbed for days. . . ."[202] According to his fellow practitioners, "[t]he practice which [Sanford] preferred, and in which he excelled, was the preparation and presentation of arguments in chancery causes and before appellate courts,"[203] and "few lawyers possessed equal ability with him in that line of work; unquestionably, cases were won by the skill and force with which he presented them to the courts."[204]

Fowler observed that Sanford had "confidence in his own ability, yet he was always anxious to have his judgment confirmed by the judgments of others; and he therefore rarely regarded a paper as complete until he had submitted it for criticism to those with whom he was associated." He was known to "examine[] issues and cases exhaustively and devote[] much attention to the preparation of briefs and other legal documents."[205]

Sanford's legal work was not limited to the courts of East Tennessee. In 1896, he represented the Southern Railway in an Interstate Commerce Commission matter concerning the freight rates for peaches after the State of Georgia filed a complaint asserting that the fees needed to be reduced.[206] He appeared as counsel for the Southern Railway before the US Supreme Court in *R.H. Sanson v. Southern Railway Company* in 1902.[207] Sanford also made an appearance before the Supreme Court in *Knoxville Iron Company v. Harbison*,[208] a lawsuit challenging an 1899 Tennessee law barring companies from paying employees in scrip, a case considered significant in Tennessee labor history.

Knoxville Iron Company v. Harbison

Knoxville Iron Company paid its employees in cash, but it allowed workers to accept payday advances in store or coal orders at twelve cents per bushel. About 75 percent of all the wages earned by the laborers was paid in coal orders. The company's coal orders were in the following form: "Let the bearer have_____ bushels of coal, and charge to my account. [Signed]_____Accepted_____1899. Knoxville Iron Company." In 1899, Tennessee passed a law declaring that companies "shall, if demanded, redeem [scrip and other evidences of indebtedness] in the hands of such laborer, employee, or bona fide holder, in lawful money of the United States."[209] Scrip, usually tokens coined by the company, could either be used at company-owned stores with marked-up prices or redeemed for cash at a percentage of its value.[210] Shortly after the law was passed, a securities dealer named Samuel Harbison purchased 614 coal orders from Knoxville Iron employees for 85 cents on the dollar.[211] When he attempted to redeem these credits for cash, the company refused to pay, arguing that Harbison was not a bona fide holder of the credits. Knoxville Iron Company asserted that only its workers were a party to the agreement to accept coal in payment—now cash as a result of the new state law. Harbison sued. After a Knox County Chancery Court ruled in favor of Harbison, the company filed an appeal in which it argued that the state law violated the right to contract. The Tennessee Supreme Court upheld the chancery court's ruling.[212] Upon appeal to the United States Supreme Court, the earlier rulings again were upheld, dealing Sanford and his client the ultimate defeat. By a seven-to-two vote, the Court acknowledged the abridgment of contract rights, but it found that the law was a legitimate exercise of the state's power.[213] The Court held:

> Under the act, the present defendant may issue weekly orders for coal, as formerly, and may pay them in that commodity when desired

by the holder, but, instead of being able, as formerly, to compel the holder to accept payment of such orders in coal, the holder may, under the act, compel defendant to pay them in money.[214]

Thus, the Supreme Court upheld the rights of states to ban scrip and other forms of non-cash payments.[215]

Maloney v. Collier

A significant pro bono case taken by Sanford, *Maloney v. Collier*,[216] alleged corruption in the Knox County, Tennessee, Election Commission. In a 1902 election, a group of disgruntled reform-minded Democrats and Republicans had sponsored a bipartisan, fusion slate of well-known and respected citizens. No one on the ticket was elected. Suspecting the continued fraudulent manipulation of elections, the defeated candidates challenged the results. Maloney was a candidate for county judge. He contended that massive fraud occurred in a great many precincts.[217]

Pursuant to the applicable statute, if a contestant alleged in his complaint and proved that more legal votes were cast for him than for his opponent, the court was required to declare him the winner. Should the contestant "feel that he might be unable to verify that he actually received the greater number of votes, he could, in the alternative or in addition, allege and demonstrate that the voting was so steeped in fraud that the contestee's victory was uncertain and consequently the election should be voided." Of the attorneys involved in the several cases, only Sanford chose to employ both of the above provisions in his complaint, asking either that his client be determined elected or that the election be nullified.[218]

At the trial court level, the contestants lost in all cases. The Tennessee Supreme Court affirmed the action of the lower court in all the cases except *Maloney*, in which Sanford was the lawyer. The Court concluded that the facts did not prove that the challenger obtained the majority of the votes. However, in *Maloney*, where Sanford alleged that the election should be voided, the Court decided that there was enough possibility of fraud to remand the case. The Court agreed with Sanford that the election had failed to afford the voters an opportunity for the free expression of their will. In further proceedings, the trial court found adequate evidence of corruption to overturn the election.[219]

To this case, which illustrated his legal skills and foresight to plead alternative theories, Sanford perhaps gave more of his time gratuitously than to any other while an attorney.[220]

Wife and Children

After Sanford finished law school at Harvard, returned to Knoxville, and began practicing law, he started spending time with twenty-four-year-old Lutie Mallory Woodruff. Born September 26, 1866, Lutie was the daughter of wealthy Knoxville merchant William Wallace ("W.W.") Woodruff and Ella T. (Connelly) Woodruff.[221] Lutie was five feet, five inches tall, with blue eyes.[222] Society columns in a Knoxville newspaper reveal the young couple's attendance at local receptions.[223]

Sanford married Lutie on January 6, 1891.[224] The wedding, described in newspapers as "[t]he leading event in Knoxville society circles for years" and "[o]ne of the most beautiful and impressive marriage ceremonies ever witnessed in Knoxville," was held at the First Baptist Church.[225] Lutie's father had matched every dollar donated by members to build the church, then located on Gay Street.[226] The sanctuary was decorated in "one grand array of beautiful plants and flowers. Roses of all colors, lilies, palms, ferns . . . had been tastefully arranged by the designers." Back of these "were strings of ferns and smilax interwoven" along with "a huge row of cedar, which completely hid from view the members of the church choir."[227] A large diamond pin, a gift from E.J., adorned Lutie's wedding dress.[228] Newspaper accounts noted that "[t]he wedding was followed by a brilliant reception at the bride's home, in which a number of prominent people from different sections of the country participated." The residence "had been decorated in a profusion of holly, while white hyacinths, smilax and white roses" completed the view.[229] "The presents amounted to over $25,000, including two $10,000 checks from the parents of the bride and the groom."[230] The couple spent a month in Florida on their honeymoon.[231] Upon their return, E.J. hosted another reception in their honor for 400 persons at his Maplehurst home.[232]

Lutie's father, W.W. Woodruff, was born in Bardstown, Kentucky. Before the Civil War, he worked in the shop of a Louisville book publisher binding books for $4 a week. A co-worker related that "Woodruff did not have a cent more than what he earned" and that "he worked like a beaver there until the war broke out."²³³ Woodruff attained the rank of captain in the Union Army during the Civil War, serving as a member of the 13th Kentucky Volunteer Infantry, which became part of General Burnside's troops for the campaign in East Tennessee. After leaving Knoxville, the 13th Kentucky joined General William T. Sherman for the campaign through Georgia. After the war, Woodruff decided to return to Knoxville.²³⁴

Like Sanford's father, Woodruff was active in civic affairs and played a prominent role in Knoxville's commercial development.²³⁵ Woodruff recognized Knoxville's "potential and moved to take advantage of it."²³⁶ He was president of the wholesale hardware firm of W.W. Woodruff & Company, an enterprise he developed into one of the largest and most profitable commercial enterprises in East Tennessee.²³⁷ His first store opened in February 1865 on Gay Street. It closed its doors for the last time one hundred twenty-seven years later in July 1992. Woodruff was so successful in Knoxville "that within fifteen years of his arrival he had built one of the city's most magnificent mansions set on an entire block across Cumberland Avenue from the university campus."²³⁸ After her father died on January 31, 1926, Lutie and the other Woodruff heirs deeded the property to the University of Tennessee for $80,000. Lutie received $12,000 as her share. When the university first acquired the property, the huge Woodruff Mansion was used as a women's dormitory until it was razed for the construction of the Hoskins Library, which still stands today.²³⁹

Lutie's father, in addition to being a Mason and a member of the Cherokee Country Club, served as the official scorer for local baseball games, as he had "a keen appreciation of the national game."²⁴⁰ He was an original subscriber of the Knoxville Fire Company, served as president of the Knoxville Community Chest, and sat on the Knoxville Board of Education in the 1874–75 academic year. Woodruff was vice president of the Knoxville Public Library in 1879 and a trustee of the Lawson McGhee Library. He also was a trustee of the Knoxville Deaf and Dumb School, president of the board of trustees of Carson-Newman College,²⁴¹ an officer with the Tennessee State Baptist Convention,²⁴² and on the board of directors of Standard Coal and Coke.²⁴³ Woodruff served as president of the Knoxville Real Estate Company, an entity noted for doing "much to build up the growing metropolis of the south by the addition of its vast property interests to the city and the development thereof."²⁴⁴

Like E.J. Sanford, Woodruff was also active in the Republican Party.²⁴⁵ In 1891, Woodruff announced that he would run as a candidate for the United

States Congress in the Second Congressional District.²⁴⁶ In a speech at Coal Creek, Woodruff "expressed his hearty sympathy" with the miners. He told them that he knew "full well the trials and hardships of poverty, having started [as] a poor boy at the age of thirteen to work at the bench at one dollar a week."²⁴⁷ In contrast to his son-in-law's father, he denounced convict labor in his speeches.²⁴⁸ Further, Woodruff always "show[ed] a cordial spirit to trade unions."²⁴⁹ Despite Woodruff's going "to the extreme of purchasing all the carriages in Knoxville so that [his opponent] could not rent any transportation to take his supporters to the polls," he lost the election to John C. Houk by more than seventy percent of the vote.²⁵⁰

Prior to her marriage to Sanford, Lutie was socially active. April 1886 found her cast as the beauty in a performance of "The Sleeping Beauty" given at Staub's Theater.²⁵¹ In 1888, a journalist addressed her involvement in the Knoxville Lawn Tennis Club.²⁵² Around that same time, she hosted a reception at her father's mansion for "an assemblage of young society people." An account of the evening noted that an "orchestra rendered the choicest music," and "the refreshments were elegant." It was observed that "there are few homes adorned by a daughter who can do the honors of such an occasion with the easy grace and hospitality of Miss Lutie."²⁵³

Like the New South women of her time, Lutie hosted elaborate dinners, often in support of her husband's work and ambitions.²⁵⁴ One newspaper account described a nine-course luncheon with the home "lit with waxen tapers" and decorated with "the choicest cut flowers."²⁵⁵ A newspaper reporter once noted that "Mrs. Edward Terry Sanford's the most charming hostess that I have ever seen, and her rare beauty and grace won warm places in the hearts of every correspondent."²⁵⁶ Additionally, Lutie served as a hostess for E.J. after the death of Sanford's mother.²⁵⁷ She also worked in local clubs and organizations designed to uplift society.²⁵⁸ A newspaper article in 1923 noted the following about Lutie: "Mrs. Sanford is of the quiet, home-loving type, but with a deep interest in the worthier and more intellectual sort of feminine activities. . . . She also is concerned in all civic activities and in the local clubs which aim to advance study or to promote civic responsibility."²⁵⁹ One year found Lutie in charge of the flower parade of the Knoxville Fall Carnival.²⁶⁰ Lutie's father was a member of the local chapter of the Sons of the American Revolution,²⁶¹ and she was an active member of the Bonny Kate Chapter of the Daughters of the American Revolution (DAR).²⁶² At a DAR event in 1897, Lutie presented conversations on "James

White and His Descendants," and "How Tennessee Entered the Union."²⁶³ She also was named to the organization's board of directors around that time.²⁶⁴ In 1913, Mrs. William C. Story, the president general of the DAR, stayed with the Sanfords as Lutie's guest during a Knoxville visit.²⁶⁵ At a University of Tennessee alumni event, Lutie showed that she could play a shrewd game of cards, winning a contest of six-hand euchre and gaining a jeweled salts box for her efforts.²⁶⁶ The year 1919 found Lutie serving on a committee of women seeking the assistance of Tennessee's senators and congressmen to obtain a two-cent piece bearing the likeness of Theodore Roosevelt.²⁶⁷ Just prior to Sanford's being elevated to the Supreme Court, she was active on the executive committee of a health clinic for the needy, which was located at Clinch Avenue and Locust Street.²⁶⁸

Sanford and Lutie had visited the World's Fair in Chicago in 1893,²⁶⁹ and she was very active in the movement to organize expositions in Knoxville. Designed to show outsiders that the region was progressive, the fairs displayed the New South's advances in agriculture, industry, and commerce.²⁷⁰ Lutie was first vice president of the women's department at the first month-long Appalachian Exposition, held in Knoxville's Chilhowee Park in October 1910.²⁷¹ The arts and crafts and floral arts sections of the woman's department held contests for home products as a demonstration of "the kind of work that ... will make the home more attractive."²⁷² The woman's department also established an "Appalachian library" exhibit to raise the status of southern literature. Prohibition was preached through the Women's Christian Temperance Union display.²⁷³ For that fair, President William Howard Taft symbolically pressed a telegraph button in Massachusetts that rang a bell at Chilhowee Park and turned on the lights. Former President Theodore Roosevelt attended the fair and addressed a huge crowd with a speech on "progressive reform, morality, and conservation."²⁷⁴ Charlotte Perkins Gilman, a renowned feminist, suffragist, and socialist, also spoke to the exposition crowd.²⁷⁵ So successful was the 1910 fair that another equally successful one was held in 1911.²⁷⁶ President Taft attended the 1911 exposition and, upon viewing the exhibits, expressed that "he did not see why all the people of the section were not millionaires."²⁷⁷ After the exposition visit and a parade through Knoxville's business district, the president, introduced by Sanford, addressed a throng of 5,000 people at the city's auditorium.²⁷⁸

The 1913 fair—the National Conservation Exposition—displayed "conservation-themed exhibitions that 'looked forward, pointing the way to better conditions ...

in line with the advanced thought of the day.'" President Roosevelt had introduced the goal of conservation to the national conscience and, in 1908, established the National Conservation Commission. The Knoxville exposition was proposed "to celebrate the new idea." It opened on September 1, 1913, with eleven large white buildings, similar to the World's Fair in Chicago, around the expanded fair grounds.[279] Governor Ben Hooper participated in the opening ceremonies. Gifford Pinchot, the National Conservation Association's president and chairman of the Knoxville exposition's advisory board, remarked concerning the city's efforts: "Unquestionably the best exhibition I have seen of the needs, possibilities and accomplishments of the movement for the conservation of our natural resources... was to be found at the Conservation Exhibition of Knoxville." He observed that for a city its size, "Knoxville accomplished the task, accomplished it successfully...."[280] United States Secretary of Labor W.B. Wilson deemed it "a great exposition in every sense of the word. Not only the best by far ever held in the South, but, in many respects, one of the greatest expositions ever held anywhere."[281] Knoxville historian Jack Neely related that the following events were held: "A mock coal-mine explosion; a man sliding 75 miles an hour down a cable across a lake; motor-cycle races, balloon ascensions, hot tamales, fireworks every night for two months; portraits of President Wilson's face glowing in mid-air; elephants cavorting; a woman, known as Mozelle of the Mist, dancing in the water. And music all the time, brass horns and strings and men singing in Italian...." Additionally, there were phonograph demonstrations and "moving pictures."[282]

Lutie's duties at the exposition in 1913 included service on the reception and entertainment committee and the executive committee.[283] Sanford's two daughters served on the young ladies' reception committee.[284] When United States Supreme Court Justice Horace Lurton attended the exposition, Sanford and Lutie "entertained brilliantly" the honored guest and his wife at dinner on the Van-Wright houseboat in Exposition Park. Among others in attendance were Tennessee Senator and Mrs. John K. Shields, Mr. and Mrs. Horace Van Deventer, Col. Robert J. Lowry of Atlanta, and T.A. Wright.[285] Mrs. Van Deventer, Justice Lurton's daughter, was the chair of the women's board of the exposition.[286] Within the year, Sanford's dear friend Justice Lurton would pass away.[287]

The 1913 exposition featured a spirited debate over suffrage for women between Lizzie Crozier French, founder of the Knoxville Equal Suffrage League, and Annie Riley Hale, an anti-suffragist. Mrs. Hale appealed to the New South role of women as moral guardians, arguing that females could be more useful at home than in a voting booth.[288] It is unknown where Lutie stood on the issue of women's suffrage, but Sanford's sister Louise was an active supporter of the movement.[289] Further, Julia S. Lucky, the wife of Sanford's former law partner, Cornelius E. Lucky, was the president of the Knoxville Equal Suffrage League.[290]

One noted visitor to Knoxville for the 1913 exposition was "the Great Commoner," William Jennings Bryan, congressman from Nebraska, secretary of state, famous orator, and three-time Democratic presidential candidate (1896, 1900, and 1908). Bryan is said to have given his greatest speech at the 1896 Democratic National Convention, where he defied his party's incumbent president, Grover Cleveland, "and the eastern establishment that dominated both political parties by demanding an alternative silver-based currency to help debtors cope with the crippling deflation caused by exclusive reliance on limited gold-backed money." In the speech, Bryan exclaimed: "You shall not press down upon the brow of labor this crown of thorns, you shall not crucify mankind upon a cross of gold."[291] In a speech given at Lenoir City, Tennessee, in October 1896, Sanford decried the economic radicalism of Bryan, describing Bryan's speech as an effort "to force the nation into bankruptcy."[292] Excited about Bryan's visit to Knoxville, however, was a sixteen-year-old Maryville, Tennessee, youth, Wiley Blount Rutledge, whose father brought him to join "some five or six thousand people" to hear Bryan.[293] Rutledge "listened spellbound for more than two hours" and "[w]hen Bryan then waited to shake hands with the hundreds who filed by, Rutledge and his father stood in line." According to Rutledge, "[j]ust to touch his hand was a thrill for me." In fact, he was so in awe of Bryan that young Wiley "stood in line again and shook hands with Bryan a second time."[294] Rutledge went on to become, like Sanford, an associate justice on the United States Supreme Court, serving from 1943 to 1949, his tenure also cut short by ill health.

Not long after the conclusion of the 1913 exposition, the murder in June 1914 of Archduke Franz Ferdinand, heir to the Austro-Hungarian throne, led to the outbreak of World War I. The United States stayed out of the conflict until Congress declared war on Germany on April 6, 1917.[295] After the United States entered the fray, Sanford, a ready patriot of his country with a high sense of public duty, worked on the Liberty Bond drives conducted between 1917 and 1919. Liberty Loans were one of the primary means by which the government financed US participation in the war. Sanford's papers include notes from a speech he delivered at Sevierville, Tennessee, on October 6, 1918, during the

Fourth Liberty Bond campaign.[296] Lutie joined her husband in supporting the war effort as one of the "Minute Women"—an offshoot of the "Four Minute Men"—to sell Liberty Bonds.[297] As one of the "Minute Women," Lutie would give one-minute speeches daily on Gay Street and at public meetings.[298] Lutie also is listed as a member of the teams of women who fed the troops arriving in Knoxville by train.[299]

Lutie's efforts on behalf of Sanford and his career were acknowledged when her husband was being considered for elevation to the United States Supreme Court. Judge Arthur C. Denison of the Sixth Circuit Court of Appeals remarked to US Attorney General Harry M. Daugherty that "[i]t is not wholly without importance that Mrs. Sanford is admirably and unusually fitted to take the place in Washington which the wife of a Justice of the Supreme Court might naturally take."[300] Once in Washington, the Sanfords were regulars in the society pages, attending numerous receptions and teas at embassies and hotels.[301] They attended White House parties and dinners with Presidents Coolidge and Hoover.[302] Lutie remained an avid bridge player as well.[303] During her time in Washington, she was active in the Monticello Memorial Fund for furnishing the home of Thomas Jefferson.[304]

A Knoxville writer once noted that "no story of [Sanford's] life nor any tribute to his character would be complete which did not take into consideration the wisdom and sweetness of his wife's companionship, and what her presence meant to him."[305] Sanford's district court secretary recalled:

> He was the most devoted man to his family I ever saw. He always kept a picture of Mrs. Sanford on his desk at Knoxville, and had one for each of the offices at Chattanooga and Nashville, which was the first thing placed on his desk on arrival at those places for a term of court. If Mrs. Sanford's letters were not promptly received, I was kept busy finding out about train schedules from Knoxville, and investigating the efficiency of the postal system.[306]

Upon Sanford's death, he left virtually his entire estate to his "beloved wife." The will was executed on June 8, 1927, and gave no indication of the value of the estate.[307] Later newspaper accounts noted that Sanford owned securities and personal property worth $217,000 and 1,000 acres of land in Chicot County, Arkansas.[308]

Sanford and his family had started a tradition of spending summers in Nantucket in the 1920s, and he had purchased a home there in 1928 valued at $48,000.[309] Charles N. Burch of Memphis, in his remarks after Sanford's death, recalled sitting in the gallery of the Nantucket summer home, talking and "looking out to sea."[310] Upon closing up the Washington, D.C., home shortly after Sanford's death, Lutie fled to Nantucket for the summer with her sister Daisy Meek.[311] She thereafter traveled to Europe, arriving abroad in September 1930.[312] By April 1937, when Lutie was honored with a reception held in Knoxville by her sister-in-law, Mrs. Alfred Sanford, Lutie had "been living for a number of years with her daughter, Anna Magee Cameron, in Canada." She remained in Knoxville until June with her sister, Daisy, then sailed for Europe with her niece, Kitty Sanford (Hugh Sanford's daughter), and her grandson, Edward Sanford Metcalfe.[313] In August 1937, at the age of seventy, she arrived back in Quebec, Canada, aboard the *Empress of Britain* on the return trip from Europe. She passed away nearly two years later on July 6, 1939, at her daughter's home in Toronto, Ontario, Canada.[314] She died nine years after losing Sanford.[315] Her remains were returned to Knoxville for burial, and after a brief graveside service conducted by the pastor of the First Baptist Church, Lutie was interred beside her husband and daughter Dorothy at Greenwood Cemetery.[316]

Sanford and Lutie had two children: Dorothy, born December 5, 1891, and Anna Magee, born a year later on December 19, 1892.[317] In the early 1890s, the couple built a home at "Hill Street,"[318] a block to the east of Maplehurst, Sanford's father's home.[319] A Knoxville paper observed: "The beautiful part of Hill Street near the residence of Col. Sanford and Col. Mead is now being made still more attractive by the addition of four elegant new homes, each one a model of architectural skill and in a style so different as to be in striking contrast to each other in many essential points." One of those described was Sanford's.[320] A society column noted that the couple was moving into their new home in February 1892.[321] Shortly after Anna Magee's birth later that year, however, Sanford, twenty-seven years old, suffered an attack of typhoid fever. He traveled to Florida and Cuba "with the hope of recuperating his strength."[322] The following year, on October 31, 1893, Sanford hosted "ye ancient Games of Hallow E'en" at "ye earlie candle light" at his home. This was one of the first local observances of Halloween of which there is an explicit record.[323]

While Sanford was with the Department of Justice in Washington, D.C., reports indicated that the children were attending school in Philadelphia, Pennsylvania.[324] By 1910, when Sanford returned to Tennessee to serve as federal district judge, the family had moved to the home of his father-in-law, W.W. Woodruff, now a widower, at 1401 Cumberland Avenue.[325] There, despite his demanding schedule, Sanford was a devoted parent, and the family enjoyed great popularity socially, entertaining visitors from all over the United States.

Sanford's twenty-two-year-old daughter Dorothy married James Garrison Metcalfe, thirty-three, of Paris, Kentucky, in November 1914.[326] Originally from Louisville, Kentucky, Metcalfe had moved to Morristown, New Jersey, with his parents and attended Yale and "Boston Tech."[327] Metcalfe was Master of Trains on the division of the Louisville & Nashville Railroad Company with headquarters in Paris.[328] The wedding at the Woodruff home in Knoxville was described as "elegant" and "palatial" in newspaper accounts.[329] The bride had been born in the house, and "many years of her childhood and young ladyhood [had] been happily passed beneath th[e] hospitable roof."[330] The joy of the couple was fleeting, however, as Dorothy died less than a year later, on August 8, 1915, from eclampsia.[331] She left an infant son named Edward Sanford Metcalfe, born July 25, 1915, who became a great favorite of her father's.[332] Metcalfe spent his early years with Sanford and Lutie until his father remarried, after which time he spent summers with his grandparents in Nantucket.[333] The 1920 United States Federal Census shows Metcalfe, age four, residing in Knoxville with the Sanfords. A young black woman named Delia Mason, twenty-six, resided with the family as a nurse.[334] At the time of Sanford's death in 1930, Metcalfe was a student at Deerfield Academy in Massachusetts, a boy's preparatory school.[335] He remained close to his Sanford cousins, serving as best man at the wedding of Alfred F. Sanford II (Hugh Sanford's son).[336] By 1940, Metcalfe was living in Knoxville and working at a local bank.[337] He later married Frances Hill Arnold, who was one of the first volunteers with "Gray Ladies" at Eastern State Hospital in Knoxville and a long-time volunteer with the American Red Cross, Knox County Chapter. Edward Sanford Metcalfe died on August 18, 1999.[338] According to Metcalfe's daughter, Lutie Metcalfe Culver, her father told her that he had "worshipped the ground [Sanford] walked on."[339]

Shortly after spending nearly a year in France performing canteen service for the American Red Cross,[340] Sanford's younger daughter, Anna Magee,[341] married a young doctor whom she met there, Dr. George Milne Cameron of Kirkland Lake, Ontario, Canada. The wedding was held on January 22, 1920, at St. Paul's Church in London, England, where Dr. Cameron was attending graduate school.[342] The

Camerons became parents of two daughters they named Dorothy and Anna Sanford.[343] Dorothy, born in 1924, was six when her grandfather Sanford passed away; she later accompanied her grandmother Lutie on a trip to Knoxville in 1937.[344] Dorothy married Charles F. Moes and had a daughter, Shari Cameron Moes. Anna Sanford, born in 1927, was only two years old when Sanford died. In 1958, she was an actress who had played professionally in Toronto and New York, but who "[t]wice a week" went "home to mother for a roast or other hearty dinner unsuitable cooking for one." At the time of the article, she was serving as the co-host of an afternoon television program, "Open House," on the Canadian Broadcasting Corporation in Toronto.[345] Anna noted in the article that her father had been a physician-surgeon with Lake Shore Mines in Kirkland Lake until she was six or seven. After schooling in Toronto, she joined the St. John Ambulance Brigade and spent a year as a nurse's aide in the Christie Street Veterans' Hospital. When she was eighteen, she went to school in New York. Reminiscent of comments made regarding her grandfather, her co-workers on the television show described her as "the nicest person I think I've ever met. ... She's so natural-just the same with everyone, from ... the show's organizer, right to the lowliest member of the stage crew."

In 1960, *The Ottawa Journal* published a piece in which Anna spoke of helping at her sister Dorothy's art gallery in Toronto.[346] A 1963 newspaper article discussed Anna's two-year sabbatical from "Open House," her new show "Take 30," and her time working in Britain. At that time, Anna related that "[h]er ailing parents drew her back to Canada."[347] Her mother, Anna Magee, died on October 8, 1973, in Toronto, Ontario, Canada. Sanford's granddaughter subsequently moved to England until 1982, working for a publishing firm and in television drama. Recalling fond memories of spending summers in Nantucket, when she returned to Canada, Anna found a house by the sea in Nova Scotia. She observed at that time: "There's no road between me and the ocean, and that is my balm, it refreshes me. ... If I didn't go back at nights and look at that ocean, I think I would fall apart."[348] She died in January 2014, at the age of 87.

 CHAPTER FIVE

Civic and Professional Pursuits and Political Activities

Like the turning of the seasons, Knoxville's changing every day, she's reaching for tomorrow, Holding on to yesterday. . . .[1]

Edward Terry Sanford epitomized the best aspects of the New South vision: shedding the stigmas of slavery, poverty, and cultural backwardness. He believed that "the best resource of the South is its people," and "the best way to develop its wealth is to develop the capacities of its people."[2] Throughout his lifetime, Sanford gave much of his time to the cause of education and was a booster for improving education across the South. Sanford sought "to train and educate our own youth" and find in "our own chosen youth those who shall lead in our industrial future."[3] He has been described as "one of the more prominent and personable Tennesseans of his time"[4] and Knoxville's "most illustrious son."[5] Acclaimed for his public speaking, he was one of Tennessee's most popular platform speakers.[6] According to one commentator, "[Sanford's] ability as a speaker was recognized far and wide, and he was often called upon."[7] One of his "eloquent tributes" was to the memory of the "Spokesman of the New South," Henry W. Grady.[8] Grady advocated unity and trust between the North and South, a view likewise held by Sanford and his family.

The topics addressed by Sanford in his speeches covered a broad spectrum. Not long after returning to Knoxville from law school, in January 1890, Sanford gave a lecture at the YMCA on the author Robert Louis Stevenson.[9] Two years later, Sanford was the graduation speaker at the Tennessee Medical College in Knoxville in March 1892.[10] April 1894 found him participating in another lecture series at the YMCA, where he spoke on "Studies on the Constitution: Its Origin, Letter and Spirit."[11] The following year, in March 1895, Sanford delivered a lecture at the Knoxville library on the settlement of Tennessee.[12] A newspaper reporter reviewing the lecture observed that Sanford, in an exceptionalist manner, opined that "a few wild Indians had no right to hold all these fair lands to the exclusion of civilization, simply because they were found roving over portions of it."[13]

Later in 1895, Sanford gave a welcome address to members of the Washington Press Club on their visit to Knoxville.[14] A speech he gave to another group of newspaper correspondents traveling back to the North after a trip through the South garnered praise in *The New York Times* as "a graceful and complimentary address."[15] At the Independence Day celebration[16] in 1895, Sanford spoke on citizenship and concluded his address with the reading of "America the Beautiful."[17] His speech at a reception for then-Governor William McKinley of Ohio, held at E.J.'s Maplehurst home in September 1895, covered the Battle of Fort Sanders and the suffering of East Tennessee in the Civil War, John Sevier and the Overmountain Men at the Battle of Kings Mountain, and the East Tennesseans at the Battle of New Orleans.[18]

In April 1896, in a series of lectures on events and literature of the Elizabethan era, Sanford spoke on the statesmanship of Queen Elizabeth I.[19] By October 1896, Sanford was a popular speaker at the local McKinley and Hobart Club sound money meetings.[20] The question of whether to use paper, silver, or gold for money was receiving attention because farmers and others carrying a lot of debt "wanted more money in circulation, believing that would enable them to earn more for their products and to afford life's necessities."[21] Free silver supporters desired that the Treasury mint large volumes of silver dollars to expand the money supply and make cheaper money widely available.[22] Sanford opposed free silver and favored a currency based on gold and a shrinkage of the money supply to strengthen the dollar's value.[23] In a nativist speech to the Sound Money Club of West Knoxville, Sanford noted that "[t]he question that looks every honest American in the face today is whether or not we will give up the present currency system of the United States for that of the pig-tail Chinaman, or the half-breed Mexican."[24] Sanford contended that "the present hard times" and "the fall in the prices of agricultural products ... had nothing to do with" the "money question" and "were not caused by our system of currency."[25]

At the 1897 Tennessee Centennial Exposition in Nashville on "Knoxville Day," June 17, Sanford was honored to deliver a key address.[26] He also provided the "Address of Welcome" to Governor Robert L. Taylor on "Governor's Day" at the Knoxville Street Fair and Trade Carnival on October 13, 1897. Praising the city of his birth and recognizing the natural resources that drove the local economy, Sanford stated in his speech: "Our city, our greater Knoxville, lies in the center of the beautiful valley of East Tennessee, the richest area in resources of any territory of like extent in the civilized world. ... In the center of this matchless valley our Knoxville reigns, sitting queenlike on her marble throne."

The turn of the century found Sanford speaking in Chicago to Harvard alumni in the presence of the school's beloved president, Dr. Charles W. Eliot.[27] By May of 1900, Sanford was back in Knoxville to deliver an address at a banquet honoring Admiral George Dewey, who had traveled to the city to dedicate the memorial to Knoxville area native Admiral David Farragut.[28] The following year, Sanford was the orator at Knoxville's Memorial Day ceremonies at the national cemetery.[29] In February 1902, he spoke on "John Paul Jones: The Founder of Our Navy," at a Knoxville banquet honoring Admiral Winfield Scott Schley, a hero of the Spanish-American War.[30] November 1907 found Sanford, now working with the Department of Justice, delivering a speech in Washington, D.C., on "the equality of the law" before the British Ambassador at the annual dinner of the Society of Mayflower Descendants.[31]

Back in Tennessee in June 1918 as a federal judge, Sanford gave a rousing address detailing the career as a soldier, judge, and politician of the state's second governor, Archibald Roane, at a monument dedication.[32] In October of the following year, Sanford forcefully spoke to delegates at an American Legion Convention in Nashville on the principles motivating Germany to enter the war, in contrast to those of the United States. According to Sanford, "the American soldier entered the conflict in defense of the Christian precepts set forth in the Sermon on the Mount." He observed "that the German policy of 'might is right' should not be relied upon by either capital or labor," and that "a continued adherence to Christian principles of brotherhood and co-operation was the only solution to the present labor difficulties."[33] Sanford clearly was cognizant of the writings of Vernon Kellogg and Benjamin Kidd, which described "the link between German militarism and Darwinian thinking."[34]

In 1922, Sanford joined in a movement championed by the Lions Clubs throughout the United States to "teach better citizenship to young Americans and to give patriotic instruction to the foreign born."[35] Sanford noted that good citizenship required "four big constructive forces—the church, school, state and home." Fighting against the four constructive forces are four destructive ones: "sin, ignorance, disease and poverty." To be good citizens, he stressed that we must "have in our hearts the conception of the Constitution and a knowledge of our government's affairs." Sanford stated that obedience to federal and state laws was the foundation of better citizenship and better government: "Law sometimes interferes with our personal privilege, but it serves to the best advantage . . . [;] I know of no greater destructive influence than disobedience of the law."[36] Around this same time period, Sanford complained about the lack of any regular "Americanization school" in Knoxville wherein persons "desiring to take out citizenship papers might receive proper instruction in regard to the examination and laws of the United States."[37] Sanford's "patriotism was most sincere." His talks to those seeking naturalization papers are reported to have been phrased in clear, simple, but beautiful English.[38]

In June 15, 1923, after taking his seat on the US Supreme Court, Sanford delivered an Optimist Club speech that revealed his nostalgia for the ways of yesteryear and a disdain for the "Roaring Twenties":

> We are in an age of excitement; no matter how we get it we must have a thrill. To some people life seems to be a continual vaudeville or movie show, dancing to the jazz band which is symbolical of the discord of today. Many of the old landmarks and institutions which in times past we have accepted are now questioned today with the exception of the multiplication table, and I am not sure Einstein does not question that.

> We believe in the sound sense and judgment of our government. We believe that God is on His throne and all things are well. As optimists our optimism would be a vain useless thing without hope and action. Our optimism must be a vital thing; it must be organized; must be effective. That includes in the first place work without which it is idle and useless. An optimist is a Columbus who has vision and courage to bring his dreams to a realization.[39]

In other activities while a Supreme Court justice, Sanford gave a speech on the establishment of the federal judiciary to the Michigan State Bar Association during its meeting in Grand Rapids in September 1923.[40] In June 1926, he joined Chief Justice William H. Taft and Associate Justices Willis Van Devanter, George Sutherland, and Pierce Butler in judging a national oratory contest on the Constitution.[41]

Throughout his legal career, Sanford was constantly asked to give talks and was very entertaining, although long winded at times. His favorite topic was the federal constitutional convention of 1787, and he gave that particular speech many times over the 30-year period from 1893 to 1923.[42] At the request of the Tennessee Bar Association (TBA), he reduced this address to writing, and it was published as part of the *Proceedings of the Annual Session of the Bar Association of Tennessee.*[43]

Many of Sanford's speeches reveal that he was a passionate amateur historian. He was well versed in the history and spirit of American institutions. Throughout his lifetime, Sanford also engaged in research on the history of Tennessee.[44] He kept scrapbooks of historical articles from newspapers and other publications, one of which can be examined at the East Tennessee Historical Society of Knoxville. In his publication *The Constitutional Convention of 1796*, Sanford described the proceedings of Tennessee's first constitutional convention, held in Knoxville in January 1796.[45] He was a member of the Tennessee Historical Society, serving as its vice president from 1915 until his death.[46] Sanford was later acknowledged to be among forty people who had "lent dignity, strength, and stability" to the organization and contributed to its life by membership, holding office, and participating as a guest speaker.[47] In 1911, as a result of Sanford's knowledge of Tennessee history, he was "elected by the Tennessee legislature [as] a member of the committee to select names of two sons of Tennessee for the statues in

Statuary Hall in Washington."[48] J.B. Henneman's 1896 article, "Recent Tennessee History by Tennesseans," discussed the historical work done by Sanford: "Mr. Sanford has established his claim to being both an accurate lawyer and a faithful historian. All his university culture and legal training have come to his assistance, and have cleared and pointed the way to original work for Tennesseans along paths almost as untrodden and untraversed as the original dense forests of their State."[49]

Like his father, Sanford was a member of several social clubs. When in New York, E.J. held memberships in the Manhattan Club and the New York Club.[50] Sanford was a member of the Century Association of New York City and the Cosmos Club of Washington, D.C.[51] The Century Association was founded in 1847 by a group of artists, writers, and "amateurs of the arts" to cultivate the arts and letters in New York City. Throughout the course of the Century's existence, an extraordinary number of members have found themselves in federal public service. Theodore Roosevelt and William Howard Taft were fellow Centurions. From 1923 to 1930, during Sanford's time on the nation's highest bench, Centurions constituted a third of the sitting Supreme Court justices.[52] Other Centurions included Presidents Grover Cleveland, Chester A. Arthur, Woodrow Wilson, Herbert Hoover, Franklin D. Roosevelt and Dwight D. Eisenhower.[53]

The Cosmos Club was founded in 1878 by John Wesley Powell and other early members of the National Geographic Society. Its stated goal is the "advancement of its members in science, literature, and art,"[54] and members are expected to publish significantly in their fields of expertise.[55] William Howard Taft also was a member of this organization.

A 1923 article stated that Sanford also was a member of the Chevy Chase Club of Washington, D.C., founded in 1892.[56] Golfing opportunities probably brought Sanford to Chevy Chase, where fellow Justices McReynolds, Butler, and Van Devanter were also members. Butler and Van Devanter eventually transferred from Chevy Chase to Burning Tree Club in Bethesda, Maryland, because McReynolds "got disagreeable even beyond their endurance."[57] Another organization in which Sanford was active while in the nation's capital was the Southern Society of Washington. He was chosen as its vice president in 1924.[58]

In his hometown, Sanford was a member of the Irving Club of Knoxville, a group founded in 1886 by Knoxville attorney Joshua William Caldwell as a private club that met to discuss literature and current events.[59] Individual members were assigned topics or literary works that they were then required to research and present to the rest of the group.⁶⁰ A newspaper column dated June 1890 noted that Sanford was scheduled to present to the membership a paper on author Robert Louis Stevenson, probably adapted from his speech given on this topic earlier in the year at the YMCA.⁶¹

The Chilhowee Club of Knoxville, to which his father belonged, also claimed Sanford as a member. During the time Sanford was being mentioned for a seat on the United States Supreme Court, S.B. Dow, grand commander of the local Knoxville Knights Templar Chapter and a Chilhowee Club member, wrote the following letter to President Warren G. Harding regarding Sanford's membership:

> Many years ago, Chauncey Depew of New York was a visitor here in Knoxville and a guest of the Chilhowee Club. Young Sanford was just home from college and the last member elected by the club. One of the club members addressed Mr. Depew telling him that the "Baby" member of the club would welcome him. Young Sanford's talk was a gem. When he finished Mr. Depew clapped his hands and said, "Bravo, Bravo." In answer said, he was surely glad the "Baby" member of the club had welcomed him for if it had been ma[d]e by a Full grown member it would have been beyond his power to have found fitting words to reply.⁶²

Sanford also was a member of the Cumberland Club of Knoxville. A charity ball hosted by the organization in 1893 saw Sanford and his wife serving on the reception committee.⁶³ A year later, Lutie, as "a wi[fe] of [a] member[] of the club," served on the refreshment committee of a reception given for "Knoxville's Four Hundred leading citizens." A reporter for *The Knoxville Journal* noted in 1894 that the club was "about two years old and numbers about 100 members, representative men of the city of the younger class."⁶⁴

Sanford additionally was a member of several service clubs. He supported the Benevolent and Protective Order of the Elks, an organization whose members undertake projects to address unmet needs, such as those of disabled veterans and impoverished children.⁶⁵ In 1890, Sanford, at age twenty-five, was elected the First Exalted Ruler of Lodge No. 160.⁶⁶ Further, Sanford was affiliated with the honor court of the Boy Scouts and administered the tests and officiated at the investiture ceremonies of that organization.⁶⁷ He also was an active member of

Civitan International,[68] a club which focuses on providing aid to handicapped and mentally challenged children, among other projects. Even with all these activities and demands on his time, Sanford was never too busy to join his wife in chaperoning a group of young people, such as on a boating party complete with an orchestra and dancing.[69]

An avid golfer, Sanford was a member of the Cherokee Country Club of Knoxville.[70] A 1922 article in *The Knoxville News-Sentinel* notes that he participated in the Kiwanis–Rotary Golf Tournament as a member of the Kiwanis Club team.[71] In 1923, upon his elevation to the Supreme Court, he was named an honorary member of the Kiwanis Club and "presented with a gold life membership card."[72] He also was a bicycle enthusiast and a member of a local cycling club.[73] All of these memberships revealed the extent of his love for the company of his fellow men and his desire to serve the community. His commitment to service never diminished.

Tennessee Bar Association

According to Sanford, he joined the TBA "the very first year [he] was admitted to the Bar."[74] By the middle of the 1890s, Sanford was a member of the TBA committee on Jurisprudence and Law Reform.[75] At the annual meeting in 1896, Sanford delivered his well-documented address on Tennessee's first constitutional convention.[76] By 1898, he served on the central council[77] and was named one of three vice presidents.[78] Over the years, he continued to hold various offices and memberships on TBA committees.[79] While serving on the committee on Legal Education and Admission to the Bar, he submitted recommendations suggesting upgrades to the intellectual and ethical standards of the profession.[80]

Sanford was selected to preside at the TBA's annual meeting and assume the presidency for the 1903–4 term, filling a vacancy caused by the death of the sitting president.[81] In his presidential speech to the membership, he decried the proliferation of special interest legislation, "especially in general matters relating to contracts, commerce and the like. . . ." He observed that "there are no local reasons requiring difference," and that the lack of uniform laws is "a matter of constantly increasing inconvenience, annoyance and expense." Sanford noted that he had a keen interest in uniform legislation because it "facilitat[ed] the business interests of the country, remov[ed] the inconveniences and petty annoyances that harass its interstate trade, [and] promot[ed] a large community of interests, a mutuality of benefits throughout the country, and a comity among the states binding them yet more closely in fraternal union...."[82]

As president of the TBA again during the 1905–6 term,[83] Sanford presided over the twenty-fifth anniversary meeting in Chattanooga.[84] He also served as chairman of the organization's Jurisprudence and Law Reform committee during that year. In 1905, three years prior to Sanford's selection as a federal judge, the TBA passed a resolution urging appointment of an additional United States District Judge for Tennessee:

> Resolved, That in the opinion of this Association, the business in the courts of the United States for the Eastern and Middle Districts of Tennessee has grown to such an extent and has reached such proportions that an additional United States District Judge should be appointed and the work fairly and justly divided between two separate courts and two separate districts. The proper method of dividing the entire work can be best determined by Congress through proper committee work and inquiry, and this Association only desires to express the view that such division should be made and to recommend accordingly to Congress and to our Senators and Representatives in Congress.[88]

Once Sanford assumed the federal judgeship for the two districts, the enormity of the workload became even more apparent to all concerned, especially Sanford. Following his second term as president of the TBA, Sanford's involvement with the organization decreased when he became a district judge. In 1913, however, he presented an address on the "New Federal Equity Rules" at the annual meeting in Nashville.[85] When Sanford was introduced to the lawyers assembled, the president commented that "there is no member of the Tennessee Bar Association who has contributed more to its success and to the success of its annual meeting."[86] Even after becoming a judge, Sanford remained an active contributor to the published proceedings of the organization.[87]

At the annual meeting of the TBA in 1911, Sanford observed that "[l]awyers are born, not made," and possess the characteristics of "integrity, intellect, courage, and industry."[89] An attorney with integrity is "a person who does not engage in deception or give corrupt advice; whose unwritten word can be relied upon;

and who is faithful to his client and to the courts." Acceptable intellect "should allow for distinguishing between appearances and realities and between things which are non-essential and those that are vital." Courage is demonstrated by "a willingness to support unpopular causes when justice demands; to maintain at all hazards the rights of a client; and to speak in the defense of liberty whenever it calls." Faced with "a multiplicity of cases and statutes," industry is shown by "unremitting study and unceasing toil."[90] In the TBA speech, as in his Class Day oration at Harvard, Sanford stressed the idea of service: "[T]he lawyer must look upon the pursuit of law not merely as a trade or money-making avocation, but as ranking with the noblest of earth's professions. He must look across the fields of gold to the snowy heights of honor, seeking his reward not so much in dollars made, as in honorable reputation, the esteem of his fellow men, and upright and courageous service in the administration of justice."[91] In these words the influence of Sanford's grandmother, Anna Chavannes, can be detected. As a presence in his life from the time of his birth to her death in the 1890s, she undoubtedly shaped his spiritual development, as did his mother. His grandmother exemplified internal fortitude and strength of belief, while exuding sweetness and charity. In his chosen profession and throughout all the pursuits of his life, Sanford exemplified many of these same qualities and strove to live up to the noble ideals he professed.

American Bar Association

Sanford joined the American Bar Association (ABA) in 1896 and thereafter represented Tennessee in several positions.[92] He served initially as one of three members of the Tennessee Local Council and held the office occasionally into 1909. In 1899, he served as vice president for Tennessee; he later became a member of the General Council and Executive Committee of the ABA.[93]

Sanford was chosen as Tennessee's delegate to the Universal Congress of Lawyers and Jurists in St. Louis, Missouri, in September 1904.[94] The intent of the Congress, conducted under the auspices of the Universal Exposition and the ABA,[95] was to bring together delegates from bar associations and kindred organizations all over the world to consider "the history and efficacy of the various systems of jurisprudence" and to discuss "those questions of international, municipal and maritime law which concern the welfare of all civilized nations."[96]

As noted by the ABA, "[i]f not the first, this is certainly one of the earliest efforts of the members of the American Bar Association to join with their brothers in other lands in the promotion of a world legal order."[97] The cosmopolitan outlook instilled in him by his mother made Sanford the perfect delegate to represent Tennessee at this gathering.

At times, Sanford served on special ABA committees concerning litigation issues.[98] For instance, in 1905, he was on a state committee interacting with the ABA's Federal Procedure Committee.[99] In 1908, Sanford was involved with a committee advocating changes to the federal courts.[100] In a 1909 report signed by Sanford, the committee recommended the establishment of official stenographers in US courts, creation of state bodies to supervise the administration of courts, abolition of fee systems in the administration of justice, and ending the separation of law and equity in federal courts.[101] The following year, the committee, with Sanford's endorsement, recommended the adoption of legislation to provide that issues of fact be found specifically by a jury, with questions of law reserved for consideration by judges; that expenses of proceedings on appeal and writ of error be diminished; that judgments be rendered on the merits without respect to technical errors; and that no matter be dismissed solely on account of being brought in the wrong court or venue.[102] At the 1910 national convention of the ABA, held in Chattanooga, Sanford spoke on "The Beginning of the Federal Judiciary."[103] One biography lists Sanford as "Mngr." of the Corporation Law Bureau of the ABA;[104] his true position was on the Comparative Law Bureau.[105]

In 1924, while a member of the Supreme Court, Sanford joined the ABA on a trip to Europe. At the reception given by the Bar of the City of Paris in the Palais de Justice, he delivered his remarks in fluent French, which he had learned from his French-Swiss mother and grandmother.[106] While in London, Sanford was invited to speak at the Harvard Law School dinner in Lincoln's Inn and at the Lord Mayor's banquet in Guild Hall.[107] As the keynote speaker at the latter, Sanford related in part:

> The memories of these days will be fadeless. But they will fail of their ultimate purpose if these happy memories are not vitalized in our lives and do not become an active force. Of deep and far-reaching significance may they be—this sense of kinship and unity—a lasting influence for law and for justice abiding in our hearts. May, in the days that are to come, the different English-speaking races, side by side,

shoulder to shoulder, stand in the defense of the ancient liberties of men, helping by such actions as they may take, to bring it about that justice shall be enthroned the sovereign of the world.[108]

Expressing the gratitude of the Americans for the welcome they had received, Sanford responded:

> Gathered as we are in the historic Guildhall, with memories of ancient glories all around us, we feel that we are indeed at the heart of Great Britain and the British Empire. In the warmth of the welcome which has been extended to us we see the best tribute to our kinship. It has brought home to our hearts and our dearest feelings the fact that we are part of the great Anglo-Saxon race. History tells us that about three hundred years ago the first band of Pilgrims went across the seas to establish a new altar of liberty in the New World. They went, cabined and confined in one little boat. On the present memorable journey, which has been termed the belated return of the Pilgrims to the land of the Magna Charta, we have not come in one little boat, but in a fleet, the number of which rivals the list of the ships in the Iliad. There is nothing which could have met the requirements of the situation other than the inexhaustible, splendid hospitality of the English Bench and Bar.[109]

Chief Justice Hughes later recalled Sanford's participation in this trip, stating: "The members of the Bar cannot fail to remember with special pleasure his address in London at the Lord Mayor's dinner at Guild Hall . . . and his graceful response to the welcome of the French bench and bar in the Palais de Justice in Paris. The lawyers and judges of France had the unusual and welcome opportunity of listening to an eminent member of the American judiciary paying a beautiful tribute in their own tongue to their achievements and aspirations."[110] During a visit to Italy, Sanford led an ABA delegation to meet with Prime Minister Benito Mussolini.[111] Sanford shared with "Il Duce" that the lawyers had come to Italy to "pay a visit to the country which was the mother of law."[112]

Probably Sanford's last ABA event was the annual convention in October 1929, ironically held in Tennessee, in Memphis, the first meeting held in the South since the association had met in Chattanooga nineteen years earlier.[113]

At that event, Sanford acted as chairman of a special committee to award a medal annually to a member "for conspicuous service in the cause of American jurisprudence."[114] Sanford's career-long participation in the ABA, like his involvement with the TBA, revealed his commitment to the legal profession as well as to justice throughout the nation and the world.

Southern Education

In addition to striving to improve and promote the legal profession, Sanford, like his father, maintained a deep and abiding interest in education and its improvement.[115] He worked to ensure that good educational opportunities were available not only for his children but for all young people in Tennessee.[116] He observed that the "manifest destiny of the University [of Tennessee] [was] to give an education to every industrious youth within [the state's] borders who shall deserve it and desire it."[117] The 1905 *Annual Report of the State Superintendent of Public Instruction of Tennessee*[118] cited Sanford for assisting with a series of rallies involving discussions of educational topics. As a young lawyer, he was never too busy to present "a handsome gold medal" to a top scholar in a local classroom.[119] His endeavors on behalf of education, however, were not limited to Tennessee. Sanford was on the executive committee of the Conference on Education in the South, a body formed at the turn of the century to sponsor annual open meetings to arouse interest in and support for public education throughout the region.[120] He served as chairman of the proceedings held by the conference in April 1903 in Richmond, Virginia.[121] The conference's work was performed by its executive arm, the Southern Education Board, a private organization supported partially by John D. Rockefeller's money. The conference's efforts were highly successful throughout the South.[122]

Sanford's support for these Southern public education goals was once forced to yield to his fidelity to the University of Tennessee. His friend, Charles W. Dabney, then-president of the University of Tennessee, was a leader in the effort to raise Southern educational standards.[123] Dabney viewed the education of "*all* southern children in free public schools as the South's only salvation."[124] Dabney suggested a summer school for the in-service training of teachers, and he persuaded the university's trustees, Sanford among them, to allow use of the university campus for the sessions. The success of the program—known as the

"Summer School of the South"— exceeded expectations. Organizers planned for about 300 teachers to enroll in the first summer; instead, more than two thousand individuals from thirty-one states attended. In 1902, the American psychologist G. Stanley Hall called the program "the greatest summer school the world has ever known." The following year, the school garnered the praise of President Roosevelt, who described it as "the greatest event since the Civil War."[125] Ambrose L. Suhrie, then a professor at New York University, further observed regarding the program: "Judged by its immediate and long-term practical results, I do not think that we have ever had an educational movement launched in any one of our colleges or universities in any part of the country or in any period of our history, which accomplished so much as did the Summer School of the South...."[126] Until its demise in 1918, the Summer School of the South, initially run by President Dabney and Philander Priestly Claxton, the head of the university's department of education, brought advanced instruction to some 32,000 teachers.[127] The program also gave the University of Tennessee national prestige as a center for education reform.[128] The success of the school led to Claxton's appointment as US Commissioner of Education by President Taft.[129]

Certain trustees at the university, however, expressed concern over Dabney's zealous advocacy of increased expenditures for public education, his support for the schooling of black children, and his involvement in educational concerns beyond the limits of the university's presidency.[130] Some professors and administrators complained "that the large number of women interfered with regular summer activities."[131] In 1902, women accounted for only about 50 of the 350 registered full-time students at the University of Tennessee, but women accounted for nearly seventy percent of the total attendees at the summer school. Other critics agreed with a journalist in a 1909 *Nation* article who opined that "women's participation in summer programs turned campuses of higher learning into mere normal schools."[132] Some historians claim that Sanford, as a trustee of the university, objected to Dabney's connection of the campus with these public school efforts.[133] Regarding the trustees' concerns, Sanford received a letter from William H. Baldwin, Southern Education Board member, a portion of which noted as follows: "I have learned that some of the trustees of the University of Tennessee have been disturbed because Dr. Dabney is undertaking work in connection with the Southern Education Board. I assume that the cause of the criticism is that race prejudice will be excited." Sanford responded: "I think there is some misunderstanding as to the attitude of the Trustees of the University.

They are not in any wise opposed to the work of the [Southern Education Board] but on the contrary . . . believe that it will do splendid work and heartily favor its plans."

Addressing the university's yearly concerns with obtaining funding from the Tennessee General Assembly, Sanford further remarked:

> The upward path of the University of Tennessee, however, has been difficult. It has encountered much opposition among politicians especially, and the Board does feel that it is outside of the real function of the university, and especially where the real purpose of the movement has been misunderstood and antagonism aroused, which would inevitably be visited to a certain extent upon the university. In short, the Trustees feel that they have troubles enough of their own without assuming others not within the scope of their own Educational Department.[134]

Dabney's dissatisfaction with the trustees led to his departure from the University of Tennessee to become the president of the University of Cincinnati.[135] According to Dabney, some of the trustees indeed disapproved of the university's collaboration with the Southern Education Board and believed that elementary and secondary school reform was not a concern of the school. He informed George Peabody in January 1904 "that the new position [at Cincinnati] freed him from the miserable prejudice, narrowness, and this political and (so called) religious machination that pervaded his last years at" the University of Tennessee. Dabney further noted his disappointment that little financial assistance was provided for the summer school.[136]

When Brown Ayres became the next president of the University of Tennessee, Sanford and the other trustees voted to make school facilities available to the summer school for an additional three-year period, with the stipulation that the program would pay for lights and water.[137] As the three-year period was ending, considerable opposition developed to further renewals of the summer school in its existing form. Four disadvantages to continuing the program were cited by President Ayres. First, misuse and abuse of equipment and buildings, especially scientific laboratories, resulted in university staff having a hard time repairing and replacing materials for the regular session. Second, the "Chautauqua" or adult education features of the summer school, with public lectures and concerts, tended to discourage serious study. Third, emphasis on kindergarten and primary school teaching methods and other work "not falling within the scope of college or even secondary work has filled up the school mainly with elementary teachers, mostly women." The result, according to Ayres, was that serious-minded students, instead of enrolling at the University of Tennessee, traveled instead to northern universities. Fourth, Ayres believed that Jefferson Hall, a large temporary pavilion used by the summer school, disfigured the campus and needed to be removed at once. Ayres further declared that the indirect advertising the Summer School was supposed to deliver was not promoting the university as a center of higher learning, but was having "no marked effect upon the recruitment of regular students." After Claxton resigned to become US Commissioner of Education, the trustees continued the summer school under the direction of Ayres until World War I.[138]

George Peabody College for Teachers

Sanford's support for public school education in the South was also demonstrated through his involvement with the George Peabody College for Teachers at Nashville.[139] Founded in 1875, the State Normal College, later known as Peabody Normal College, was the first and leading school for training teachers in the South.[140] In 1909, the George Peabody College for Teachers was chartered as a legally independent and free corporation, with Sanford a founding member and first president of the board of trustees.[141] Sanford was selected by the Peabody Fund to head the board from 1910 to 1929.[142] In a *New York Times* article announcing plans for the college, Sanford was quoted as follows:

> [A] college for the training of teachers is the crying need of the South today. Much as the South needs money for the support of common schools, the prime need is of trained educational leaders. The lack of money for school purposes is temporary. A new era of agricultural, industrial, and commercial activity is already at hand, and throughout the Southern states there is a sense of coming prosperity. The South will soon be able to support an adequate system of common schools. The securing of such [a] system is less a question of money than of

ideals. Men are needed to organize and teach the schools, which [the] rural South will soon be able to support."[143]

According to a Peabody historian, Sanford "lent prestige to the board" but was "rarely able to attend executive committee meetings."[144]

The Peabody Education Fund was created in 1867[145] by George Peabody, an upstanding Massachusetts merchant and financier whose gift was motivated by a desire for sectional reconciliation after the Civil War.[146] Admiral David G. Farragut, who was born in Knox County, Tennessee, was a trustee of the fund. Presidents Rutherford B. Hayes,[147] Grover Cleveland, William McKinley, and Theodore Roosevelt also participated as trustees over the years. J.P. Morgan, the son of Peabody's partner, Junius Spencer Morgan, would later serve on the board of the fund and contribute to the first endowment of the college.[148]

When Peabody was granted its charter by the Tennessee Secretary of State in 1909, Sanford was listed on the document as an incorporator, having been "chosen for the first directorate of the school."[149] In that year, all the major decisions about the new college confronted the newly appointed board, such as "what to do with the $1.8 million in funds and property granted it by the Peabody Education Fund." While a new campus was purchased, the board also "had to supervise the continued operation[s] of Peabody Normal College on the old campus." "The board had to find a president, . . . raise an additional million dollars, work out a complex relationship with Vanderbilt University, clarify its academic goals, and design a curriculum."[150] Classes opened in the summer of 1914.[151]

Until his death in 1930, Sanford was a frequent graduation speaker at Peabody.[152] At the first commencement on June 2, 1915, he commented on the school's benefactor: "George Peabody, realizing the needs of the South and what would be of most service in the building up of the South, made his memorable gift, his priceless gift, to the cause of Southern education—the greatest and most helpful single gift ever given to the South."[153] This statement was uttered in all sincerity, as Sanford had stressed since his Class Day speech at Harvard in 1885 the view that "education can no longer be a mere thing of fashion and appearance; it must fit men to live as active helpers in the world's progress."[154]

At the 1916 commencement exercises, Sanford further stressed the importance of education embodying not only intellectual growth but also moral guidance both for the nation and for individuals. In Sanford's view, education was the means of transmission of the tenets of a civil society, thereby ensuring the preservation of the country. Explaining this notion, Sanford averred:

> [T]he one, sure preparation for the future, which can alone prevent final calamity, is the training of its youth; training in righteousness, in wisdom and in truth; in the strength of an unhesitating courage and in the power of calmness and of self-control; in the standards of life that give to it worth and beauty, dignity and nobility, and bring sure and abiding happiness; in the firm and deep-seated convictions of duty and patriotism that, whatever the future may have in store, shall not only inspire them with the idea that America means equality of opportunity, but shall engrave, deep in their souls, the knowledge that this, of necessity, carries with it equality of responsibility, and shall nobly fit them to discharge the duties that may come upon them as true, loyal and courageous citizens of the Republic....[155]

"'[S]ervice' and 'democracy' defined the spirit of the new Peabody," ideals held dear by Sanford and espoused by him throughout his lifetime.[156]

The topic of war dominated Sanford's 1917 graduation speech, in which he endorsed President Woodrow Wilson's decision to enter World War I. Sanford observed that the United States

> did not enter [the war] from the desire of conquest or dominion, or from rancor or passion, but because there were no other means to defend its violated rights and to array itself against wrongs that cut to the very roots of human life. The peace of the world and the freedom of its peoples were menaced by the organized force of autocratic governments, and civilization itself seemed in the balance. In such circumstances, we had seen the last of neutrality; we could, God helping, do no other than join the forces that were fighting for freedom in the world, for justice and for peace.[157]

Sanford warned of the difficulties to come in the post-war era—the resultant economic and social changes; the shattering of precedents; and the intensified demands of a democracy for the greater socialization of its institutions, the lessening of inequality, the regulation of wealth, and the control of markets and prices. He voiced the hope that these problems could be addressed in an equitable fashion, "settled by reason and not by passion; in a spirit of righteousness, justice, mutual fair dealing, and the common good; and neither by blind reaction nor by revolution."[158]

In a commencement address at the dawn of the Roaring Twenties, Sanford revealed his attitude toward economic excess by "prais[ing] the unselfish cooperation and the concomitant diminishing of individual greed shown by the citizenry during the war." He criticized, however, "the inevitable psychological reaction of excess that had followed the conflict." In Sanford's view, the individual discipline and respect for the common interest shown by the citizenry "had been replaced by a riot of extravagance, a seeking of luxury, a love of display, and a yearning for idleness." He believed that "[t]ime was being wasted on frivolous things. The desire for materialistic gain was resulting in an increase of hatred, jealousy, and suspicion among the population." Sanford asked: "Are we to have in our national life the German theory of the survival of the strongest, that might makes right; the jungle theory of the strongest tooth and claw? Is that to be our civilization?"[159] Sanford's references to the theory of Social Darwinism reveal how different his world view was from that of his father, who tirelessly pursued business success and financial gain.

Sanford further commented:

> The sound mental and moral strength of the American people, we believe, will reassert itself after this feverish interlude, this hysterical period in our lives; and we will come back. We must do it, if our nation is to be safe. The war that made the world safe for democracy must not undermine the foundations of democracy itself. We must settle the problems that insistently press for solution in a spirit of law and order, of obedience to law which is the only sure foundation upon which civilization can rest. We must settle them, not in a spirit of avarice and greed, but of justice; that justice whose handmaid, it has been said, is freedom, whose child is liberty and whose companion is peace; whose favorite attitude is stooping in compassion to the lowly and the unfortunate. We must settle them, not in a spirit of hatred, not in a spirit of trifling, not in a spirit of selfishness, but in

a spirit of sympathy, a spirit that will recognize the rights of others, in a spirit of love instead of hatred, through which the Sermon on the Mount will be made manifest, not merely upon the Sabbath Day, but in our daily lives.[160]

Sanford argued that "if our civilization is to be a success," our nation must be "a thing worth living for, the abiding place of truth, and peace, and love for one another, and sympathy for one another, and not of clashing and conflict." Of the current state of the country, Sanford observed:

Life is losing its old time peacefulness and serenity, its beauty and its holiness. We are wasting time on things that count for nothing, on the joys that are alluring but that lead nowhere that we should be led. Greed is with us, instead of unselfishness; avarice, the making of money at the expense of one's fellows; the feverish desire of people not to cooperate with their neighbors, but get ahead of them, the dividing into camps of hatred, of jealousy, of suspicion, between men and classes of men.[161]

Sanford's criticisms of greed and his attitude toward seeking wealth were not unique. His views were characteristic of other critiques of economic excess that were touted in works like *The Gilded Age* of Mark Twain and Charles Dudley Warner. The work satirized the political corruption, materialism, and greed in post–Civil War America, the time of Sanford's youth. To Sanford, the post–World War I period in America seemed similarly corrupted by avarice, self-gratification, and immorality. President William Howard Taft had observed in 1910 that "for thirty years we had an enormous material expansion in this country, in which we all forgot ourselves in the enthusiasm of expanding our natural resources and in making ourselves the richest nation on earth."[162] President Warren G. Harding now called for "thrift and economy, for denial and sacrifice, if need be, for a nation-wide drive against extravagance and luxury. . . ."[163] Sanford agreed with the views of these leaders. Thus, unlike his father, he was displeased that the nation was increasingly driven by commerce and expressed hope that Peabody would be a "sanctuar[y] from what the novelist Henry James called 'the poison plant of the money-passion.'"[164]

Returning to the education theme in the 1920 commencement address, Sanford expressed his view that Peabody's goal was "not merely to train" the students "that they may gain some advantage over their fellows in the race of life," but to "strengthen their character." He declared:

> Teach these children ... Teach them the real and true things of life; train them in righteousness; train them in the sense of justice; train them in simple living, in honest worth, in manly virtues. Teach them the things that are worthwhile, that make life not a camp of contending forces, not a battleground of hate, but a place of joy, of beauty, of love, a place where justice abides. Teach them not merely to get and grasp and spend all they can; but the duty and joy of service and helpfulness to their fellows. Teach them what a human life rightly lived means in its joy, in its power, in its serene satisfaction. Train them to be brave, true-hearted citizens of the Republic. These children are our hope.[165]

At the 1925 graduation, with the British ambassador in the audience, Sanford stressed the school's mission, the importance of developing good teachers:

> In the hearts of all here present is the same faith in the gospel of education, the "beautiful key that gives access to the realities of life"; the same belief that education is essential to the higher life of the nation and the permanency of its institutions of freedom; the same conviction that to make education effective the teacher must be trained for the responsibility of his high calling.
>
> We believe, as did George Peabody, that education is a "debt which the present owes to future generations"; we have hearkened unto the admonition of the Wise Man: "Lay fast hold of instruction; let her not go; for she is thy life." This is the unswerving faith of America— the very bedrock of its security—that the one sure preparation for the future is the training of its youth....
>
> The sacred responsibility of thus training the children of the nation for citizenship rests upon the teacher; weightier responsibility or greater privilege no man could have....

Outside of the home and church his is the strongest and most enduring influence in the life of the child.

[W]e exalt and reverence the teacher, and the beauty, the dignity, and the holiness of his calling; we honor his devoted heroism as he leads the children in the battle against ignorance and the powers of darkness; and we hold him in an affection granted only to the true and brave leaders of the nation's higher life.[166]

Political Activities

Republican in name and sympathy, Sanford was not a highly partisan individual.[167] While quite well connected politically, it appears he took little true interest in politics.[168] James A. Fowler described their political views as follows: "Both Ed Sanford and myself had rather exalted political ideals. We thought that political honesty ought to be on parity with honesty in business, and further that the principles of a party ought to conform to the real public needs; and not to consist of merely sonorous sentences designed solely to catch votes."[169] The Republicans controlled East Tennessee, but they remained a minority party statewide. Throughout Sanford's adult life, Middle and West Tennessee were dominated by Democrats. Nationally, the Republicans were still a sectional party because the GOP had not found reliable ways to develop a significant Southern following.[170] Sanford actively campaigned on behalf of the Republican national tickets in 1896, 1900, and 1904.[171] In 1896, he gave a number of campaign speeches throughout the state supporting presidential candidate William McKinley.[172] His father, as one of the preeminent Republicans in Tennessee, held receptions for McKinley and Presidents Benjamin Harrison and Theodore Roosevelt.[173]

The political environment in Knoxville, Tennessee, that impacted Sanford had been created just after his birth. Governor Brownlow established in the city a powerful political organization fueled by federal patronage at the post office and Custom House. Brownlow's support for local Second District Congressman Horace Maynard was known as the "Custom House Ring."[174] When Maynard ran for governor in 1874, the Custom House Ring backed Jacob M. Thornburgh for Congress. When Thornburgh, eventually Sanford's law partner, ultimately left the House seat in 1878, Leonidas Houk beat out William Rule, the Custom

House Ring's candidate and Sanford family friend, for the position.[175] Houk remained the unchallenged boss of the Republicans in Tennessee's Second District until his death in 1891.[176] After Houk's death, his son, John, beat out W.W. Woodruff, Sanford's father-in-law, for the Second District seat in a special election. After defeating Woodruff, the younger Houk lost the seat to Henry R. Gibson in 1894.[177]

Even before Leonidas Houk's death, the seat of Republican power in Tennessee had moved to Chattanooga when Henry Clay Evans and Newell Sanders seized control in the Third District in 1884. After the loss of his seat in Congress in 1890, Evans was named Commissioner of Pensions and distributed most of the patronage in the state because he had become a personal and political friend of President William McKinley. It was not until Walter P. Brownlow, Governor Brownlow's nephew, challenged Evans in 1900 that Evans faced any opposition to his control of the Republican party in Tennessee.[178]

Another factor affecting Sanford's career goals was the growth in the late 1880s and early 1890s of the Farmers' Alliance in Tennessee. This organization formed as a result of falling farm product prices.[179] Contrary to the economic vision of the Republicans, the Alliance attempted to "lift the economic and psychological burdens of the farmers by striking at those who obviously held power, and who seemed to be responsible for the[ir] helplessness...."[180] Farmer cooperatives and a grain subtreasury—warehouses where farmers could store their crops to wait for higher prices than those available if everyone sold produce at the same time—were emphasized. Under the theory of the Alliance, "[w]hile farmers waited to sell their crops, they could borrow from the government as much as 80 percent of the value of the crops, paying interest at the rate of 2 percent per year and a small fee for grading, storage, and insurance."[181] The Alliance also called for regulation of railroads and control of inflation.[182] In the late 1880s, in view of falling farm prices, the Farmers' Alliance demanded "the most rigid, honest, and just state and national control and supervision of public ... transportation." If that did not work, the Alliance called for public ownership of railroads.[183] Southern merchants, bankers, and lawyers were explicitly banned from membership in the Farmers' Alliance, as members believed that capitalists should not be accorded special privileges. They demonized "monopolists" and denounced government intervention on behalf of the "aristocrats" of capital.[184] With the election of John P. Buchanan, members of the Alliance won the governor's chair in Tennessee. They also won a plurality of seats in the legislature in 1890.[185] Fourteen of the thirty-three state senators and forty of the ninety members of the state house were Alliance members, making Tennessee decisionmakers "distinctly agrarian in character."[186] For someone with Sanford's political pedigree and professional and family background, achieving statewide political success was extremely difficult.

Sanford's father attempted to secure a political office in 1895 when he ran for United States senator. At that time, senators were elected by the state legislatures.[187] The senator who placed E.J.'s name in nomination described him as follows:

> It gives me pleasure to put in nomination for United States senator a citizen of East Tennessee, who, by his energy, integrity, sobriety, and patriotism, has endeared himself to the people who know and associate with him; one who has been instrumental in bringing a large amount of capital, immigration and business to our state; one who believes in protection to American industries; one who believes in protecting our marble, our coal, our iron ore and lumber; who is opposed to reducing the wages of American workmen to compete with foreign pauper labor; one who believes in honest money and is opposed to wildcat banks; one who is a friend to the union soldier, his widow and orphan, and who never turns them away empty handed when they call on him for help; one who never was a candidate for any office but who on account of his business qualities, energies and integrity, was asked to become president of the Knoxville & Ohio Railroad Company, in which capacity, he has fully demonstrated these high traits of character, fitting him so well for the position.
>
> He has always taken much interest in electing men to office who he believed would represent the best interests of Tennessee and the South. A man with a strong native intellect, and experience in business, with broad and liberal views on all questions. He would make a senator that Tennessee would be proud of.... That man is the Hon. E.J. Sanford, of the City of Knoxville, East Tennessee.[188]

E.J. won the entire Republican vote in the Tennessee legislature for senator that year, but he could not defeat the Democratic incumbent, former Governor Isham G. Harris, the same man who had led the state into the Confederacy.[189]

E.J.'s failed attempt at public office did not besmirch the Sanford name. Despite the obstacles in the state for Republicans, *The Atlanta Constitution* soon described E.J.'s eldest son as "one of the most prominent politicians in Tennessee."[190] Sanford made what has been called the "best speech of his career" when he nominated James Fowler for governor at the 1898 Republican State Convention. According to a reporter, Sanford was called upon without warning to make the nomination, a request that was surely unsettling to him. Any nervousness on Sanford's part went unnoticed, as the speech was "declared to have been a determining factor in landing the nomination" for Fowler.[191] However, 1898 was a year when Democrats were united, and with no split within that party, Fowler received only 39.8 percent of the vote. Democrat Benton McMillin was elected governor. In 1900, the *Columbia Herald* touted Sanford as a potential Republican candidate for governor, but John E. McCall became the eventual candidate of the Republican Party.[192] Democrat McMillin was reelected and served as governor until 1903.[193]

In 1902, Sanford's name was discussed in connection with a position on the Tennessee Supreme Court.[194] Democrat James B. Frazier was easily elected governor. Two years later, in 1904, Sanford made his only try for elective office, seeking the Republican nomination for governor.[195] According to Fowler, "they had discussed the possibility of Sanford being a candidate for governor and had decided such service for the party might 'put him in line for preferment if an occasion should arise of which he might desire to take advantage.'"[196] A newspaper reporter from the period noted as follows:

> For the first time in a great many years in Republican politics there is a real fight over the gubernatorial nomination. Jesse M. Littleton and Edward T. Sanford, the chief candidates for the empty honor, are both in Nashville, and both have opened headquarters at a prominent hotel. Conferences have been in progress between Littleton and Sanford and their respective partisans thoughout the day.... [E]ach man declares he will surely win [so] there is no hope of an agreement short of the convention.... Both of the aspirants are seeking to get control of the vote of D.A. Nunn, a third aspirant, as upon this vote depends the fate of each.
>
> Congressman [Walter P.] Brownlow ... is straining every nerve to secure the nomination of Littleton. This fact, however, does not

disconcert the Sanford crowd. They claim Littleton is the representative of the whisky interests, and that his nomination in the face of the strong Republican temperance vote in the state will be suicidal.

The fight is becoming more bitter every hour.[197]

Ultimately, Sanford lost the nomination to Jesse M. Littleton, the Mayor of Winchester, Tennessee, the candidate with the support of the Republican Party's boss, Congressman Walter P. Brownlow from northeastern Tennessee's First District. Brownlow, who first won the First Congressional District seat in 1896, had dominated the state Republican Party since 1900.[198] In the gubernatorial race, observers had "hinted that Sanford's candidacy was the beginning of a movement to clip the high soaring wings of Brownlow and to prevent him from controlling federal patronage in the state," so Brownlow had no incentive to support Sanford.[199] Democratic Governor Frazier was easily reelected by a 38,000 vote plurality.[200]

Despite the political setback for Sanford, he continued to be "mentioned frequently as a candidate for governor," and there was little doubt he could secure the nomination if he wanted it, because Congressman Brownlow had been ousted from control in 1906, and Second District Congressman Nathan W. Hale of Knoxville and Newell Sanders of Chattanooga had gained control of the Tennessee Republican Party after the ouster.[201] Sanford was a supporter of Hale, on whose behalf he had written the following letter to US Representative Joseph G. Cannon, Speaker of the House of Representatives:

> The Republicans of this, the Second Congressional District, which has elected a Republican member for 54 consecutive years, would, I am sure, most deeply appreciate their recognition in the appointment of their representative, Mr. Hale, to responsible committee work.
>
> Mr. Hale was elected last time by a very large majority and has the respect and confidence of the entire community. He has made his way to the forefront as a business man, by a combination of integrity, intellect and industry, and is one of the most successful businessmen in this community, being a Director in our oldest National Bank, the organizer and President of various corporations and a member and Director in others. His character and experience are such as to

preeminently fit him for the discharge of committee work requiring business knowledge and executive and administrative ability.²⁰²

A 1908 political column noted: "Tennessee Republicans profess to see in the Democratic split in that state, a chance to elect a Republican governor. E.T. Sanford of Knoxville, now assistant attorney general of the United States, is talked of as the Republican standard bearer."²⁰³ Again in 1910, Sanford, by that time a federal judge, was "being talked of for the nomination" for governor.²⁰⁴ Sanford, however, chose to retain his lifetime appointment as a federal judge and not try again. As fate would have it, a split arose that year in the Democratic party, and an East Tennessee Republican, Ben W. Hooper—who had at one time lived in Knoxville's St. John's Orphanage to which Sanford's mother Emma had dedicated so much time—won the governor's chair.²⁰⁵

After he became a jurist, Sanford engaged in civic activities to the extent allowed by his judicial position.²⁰⁶ In addition to Liberty Bond drives during World War I, he spoke to audiences regarding the need for development of close international relations, and he served as a strong advocate of international efforts to secure peace. May 1919 found Sanford speaking on the League of Nations at the Tennessee Bankers' Association Convention held in Knoxville.²⁰⁷ His papers reveal speech notes describing the League's Covenant as "[t]he most important international document ever published" and "the most momentous single document ever presented for the consideration of mankind." Sanford observed that the League of Nations was "the first definite, united, concrete effort that has ever been made by the nations of the world, since the birth of Christ, to secure peace on earth and good-will among men, and to relieve the world from the scourge of war that has been a foul blot upon Christian civilization."²⁰⁸

In regard to international peace efforts, Sanford recognized the contributions of William Howard Taft as "the chief founder and president of the League to Enforce Peace, which was organized soon after the war began, and which ha[d] done so much to educate public opinion on this question and to show the necessity of the organized union of the nations of the world to suppress war."²⁰⁹ After Taft lost the presidency in 1912, he had assumed the leadership of the League to Enforce Peace in 1915, an organization established to resolve disputes short of war.²¹⁰ When President Wilson sought to convince the Senate to approve the League of Nations, Taft was one of the very few Republicans willing to defend him publicly.[211] As noted by historian Henry F. Pringle, "[Taft's] appearance on the same platform with President Wilson indicates that there is at least one of our public men who recognizes other motives than selfishness and partisanship. It is one of those spectacles which the American spirit admires above all else. . . ."[212] "It took real courage for Taft to speak 'kind words of President Wilson when speaking anything except defamation and condemnation of the president was considered treason by the old guard in the senate. Taft was for peace when peace was looked upon as a crime by some of the leaders of his party.'"[213] When Sanford's consideration for the Supreme Court became public knowledge, some sources contended that his support of America's involvement in international relations had made a favorable impression on Chief Justice Taft and Attorney General Harry Daugherty, an old-school Ohio politician who had close ties to the chief justice going back to Taft's presidential campaigns.[214]

In March 1920, while a professor at Yale Law School, Taft visited Knoxville at the invitation of the local Kiwanis Club. During his time in the area, Taft, as president of the national league, attended a meeting of the Knox County Chapter of the League to Enforce Peace. Taft spoke at the First Methodist Episcopal Church to a capacity crowd on "Americanism as Compared to Bolshevism." He exhorted listeners to not allow Knoxville "to degenerate into a hotbed of discontent and radicalism."[215]

Opposition to the League of Nations increased, however, with the election of Warren G. Harding. Leading Republicans wanted the United States to avoid further intervention in European affairs. No "entangling alliances" were desired by the majority of the population.[216] The Harding administration made it clear that the United States would not join a "super government" such as the League of Nations.[217] Harding opposed the league because he felt that such a "super state" would "deal with international disputes on grounds of political expediency and in accord with the selfish designs of the principal powers." He advocated a "voluntary association of sovereign nations, on a basis of equality, to settle disputes on the basis of international law, in a permanent international court of justice."[218] With idealism on the ebb, and in view of Republican opposition, Sanford abandoned his public advocacy of the league.[219]

Sanford had a "high sense of public duty" and involved himself in numerous civic activities. He became a leading member of the community and the state.[220] One of the enterprises in which he shared involvement with his father was the Lenoir City Company.[221]

Lenoir City Company

> Lenoir City will be ... where the two streams of immigration and capital flowing southward—from the Eastern and Middle states ... and from the valleys of the Ohio and Upper Mississippi rivers—will unite and build up a great industrial center.
> —Prospectus of the Lenoir City Company, 1890

In the late 1880s, E.J., then "at the apex of his business career,"[222] became enamored with social theories regarding the development of planned cities where company workers could live free from vices that plagued large cities. An opportunity to create such a city arose in 1889, when the Lenoir family sold the entire Lenoir estate—ceded to General William Lenoir by the state of North Carolina for service in the Revolutionary War—including property and buildings, to a syndicate of New York and Knoxville businessmen, including E.J. and his long-time associate, Charles McClung McGhee.[223] The Lenoir City Company's proposed town site, approximately thirty miles west of Knoxville, consisted of a 2,700-acre tract on the north shore of the Tennessee River, near its confluence with the Little Tennessee River.[224] Part of present-day Lenoir City still follows the Lenoir City Company's early 1890s grid.[225]

The company's growth strategy was to become "one of the healthiest, most attractive and prosperous manufacturing and commercial cities in the entire South." Its expectations of industrial development were based "largely on the proximity of its land holdings to the mineral resources of the Upper Tennessee River Valley,"[226] because the "same syndicate that was involved in the Lenoir City Company had a controlling interest in the Coal Creek Mining & Manufacturing Company, an enterprise principally involved in coal extraction ... in Anderson County, Tennessee. The Lenoir City Company planned to use the coal from this property to promote industry in its Lenoir City urban development."[227] To ensure that the new city would be free from vices, the Lenoir City Company had a temperance policy:

> The promoters of this company, as a matter of business, and for the protection and general welfare of the people already living on this property, and of those who will soon make the city the home of their

families, and to prevent disorders and lawlessness, have determined to put into each deed executed by the Company a clause forfeiting the title if liquor shall ever be manufactured or sold on the premises conveyed. All manufacturers know that it is the convenient dram shop which does the most to demoralize workmen and impair their usefulness.[228]

Employers had come to realize "how drink plays havoc with production." As workers "became machine tenders, the damage from the liquor habit in impairment of efficiency and in injury to delicate and costly machinery became ever more unmistakable. More and more employers came to look upon prohibition as a labor-efficiency policy...."[229]

The Lenoir City Company was incorporated in April 1890, and its stock and land sale was held in September 1890. Sanford sat on the board of directors, and his law firm served as general counsel.[230] By June 1892, however, the company was experiencing problems paying on debt it had accrued earlier. By November 1892, only 144 of the 3,448 lots platted in Lenoir City had been sold.[231] In 1893, a national economic crisis occurred, "the worst economic crisis in American history, save for the Great Depression."[232] Unemployment soared and wages sunk.[233] Banks failed, depositors lost their savings, and the Treasury's gold reserve plunged. It took the help of private financiers J.P. Morgan and August Belmont to stabilize the situation.[234]

Lenoir City survived the economic depression of the 1890s because of the work and dedication of E.J. and McGhee. As the originator of the project, Sanford's father took responsibility for overseeing many of the early activities of the company and worked tirelessly to ensure the development's success in the uncertain economic times. In a letter to McGhee in 1891, E.J. reflected, "I have not yet lost faith in Lenoir, and I feel it will all work out yet, although as I stated before I have had more disappointments in it than in any other business attempt in my life."[235]

Another matter of public interest in which Sanford became involved was securing adequate water for Knoxville. Not long after returning from Harvard, he served as secretary of the Knoxville Water Company.[236] An 1890 article describes a Chamber of Commerce meeting at which Sanford responded to inquiries about the scarcity of water. He reported to those assembled that the president of the water company was making arrangements for $250,000 in improvements.[237] His father may have influenced his son's involvement with the water plant; in 1879 E.J. served on a special committee regarding the construction of a reservoir and establishment of a system of waterworks in Knoxville.[238] Sanford's involvement with the Chamber of Commerce around that same time period included delivering a speech on "The New South" at a chamber banquet.[239]

Sanford also was a charter member of the board of governors of the Knoxville General Hospital.[240] When the new city hospital was formally opened on April 14, 1902, he spoke as a representative of the governing board. Sanford observed that in France, the greatest hospital was known as the "House of God" and noted that next to the churches, such a term could not more fittingly apply than to hospitals. In his remarks, Sanford expressed gratitude to the women who started the hospital project and labored to accomplish their dream. He related that the hospital was a new undertaking, and he asked for the help and cooperation of all the people of the city. Sanford encouraged a group touring the facility to note the empty places and to think of how the spaces might be filled so "that there might be joy and comfort brought to many for years to come."[241] Knoxville General Hospital, located on Cleveland Place near Dameron Avenue, served as the city's primary hospital until August 1956, when the University of Tennessee Memorial Hospital opened.[242]

The year 1886 had seen the Public Library of Knoxville converted into the Lawson McGhee Library, so named in memory of Charles McClung McGhee's deceased daughter, May Lawson McGhee.[243] Sanford served as a trustee of that library from 1921 until his death in 1930.[244] Additionally, Sanford took over his father's position as trustee of the East Tennessee Female Institute in June 1900 and served until it closed in 1911. The institute had been established in 1827 as the Knoxville Female Academy.[245] It offered classes in arithmetic, orthography, reading, music, penmanship, astronomy, chemistry, and Latin.[246] Sanford's sister Mary was a student there, serving as president of her junior class.[247] It closed because of declining enrollment in the face of competition from public schools. The property was ultimately deeded to the University of Tennessee and was occupied for a time by the law school.[248]

After E.J.'s death in 1902, Sanford remained vice president of the drug firm Sanford, Chamberlain, and Albers.[249] The company was created in 1872, when the Chamberlain and Albers drug company of William P. Chamberlain and Andrew Jackson "A.J." Albers[250] consolidated with the firm owned by Sanford's father, E.J. Sanford and Company.[251] The business occupied a three-story building, forty feet by one hundred fifty feet, with a double basement, at 430 Gay Street in Knoxville.[252] Sanford, Chamberlain, and Albers eventually grew to become one of the largest pharmaceutical companies in the South.[253] Extremely diversified, the company was known for such products as the "three-heart" brands of patent medicine, as well as lubricating oil that was sold to the local railroads. The business delivered products throughout the region and even had a steamboat at one time to serve its clients.[254]

The period after the Civil War saw exponential growth in the drug industry, in part because many wounded veterans had become addicted to opiates after having received them in wartime hospitals.[255] Cheap patent medicines also often provided a safer alternative than doctors of the era, particularly in rural areas where physicians were few in number. "[P]atent medicines were often taken to relieve the symptoms of overeating and poor diet, which went hand in hand in that period. Remedies for upset stomachs were the most common class of medication during the late nineteenth century."[256] The substantial quantities of alcohol, cocaine, and opium in these nostrums undoubtedly helped sales.[257] Tennessee Congressman Leonidas C. Houk is credited with saying that "old E.J. Sanford . . . made a fortune selling Pokeberry juice to the people."[258] The company operated in Knoxville as Albers, Inc., until 1994.[259]

Additionally, Sanford was elected to succeed his father as a director of the East Tennessee National Bank, with his father-in-law W.W. Woodruff succeeding E.J. as vice president of the bank.[260] Sanford also stayed on as a principal stockholder in the Knoxville Woolen Mills, along with Charles McClung McGhee, Oliver P. Temple, William P. Chamberlain, James Van Deventer, Lawrence D. Tyson, C.M. McClung, L.M. Cowen, and A.J. Albers.[261] A description of the company from 1891 read as follows: "The Knoxville Woolen Mills have an equipment of 600 looms, and it is said, the largest production of Kentucky jeans and doeskins, which are its specialties, of any concern of the kind in the country, viz.: $1,000,000 worth annually. They employ 600 hands; the cost, the machinery included, $475,000, and $500,000 of local capital is embarked in them."[262]

During the 1880s and 1890s, Sanford's father had been one of the incorporators, organizers, and stockholders of the company, and, under his leadership as its president, it grew to become Knoxville's largest textile firm by 1900.[263] It was proclaimed by the Traveler's Protective Association in 1896 as "the largest producing woolen mill in the world."[264] With an initial capital outlay of $180,000, the firm's assets had increased to $1.3 million by 1903, the year following E.J.'s death. By 1905, the company employed 900 people.[265] Soon, however, the company was producing more goods than could be sold, resulting in losses.[266]

Knoxville had been a part of the New South movement, as the city's "close-knit civic-commercial elite," men like E.J. Sanford, had been ideal converts to the New South creed after the Civil War. "For these men the great dream was that the fortuitous combination of natural resources, outside capital, good rail connections, and the heretofore virtually untapped labor pool of the surrounding hinterland would make of Knoxville a major commercial and industrial center."[267] As an example of their efforts, E.J. and a number of leading capitalists in Knoxville formed a syndicate and organized a company known as the "Central Market Company." The object of the company was outlined as follows: "The encouragement of immigration; the locating, establishing and building of towns and cities; the purchase, improvement, and sale of property and encouragement of industries."[268] Ultimately, however, the "[b]ankers and businessmen who had been the original architects of the New South credo...found themselves resisting some changes...."[269] Among the elite like Sanford, "there appeared a growing conservatism, a loss of dynamism, and an unwillingness to provide top-down direction for the city."[270] "[I]t was as if their political conservatism (so typical of New South elites) had infected their economic and social ideas as well."[271]

One industrialist of the early 1900s, William J. Oliver, opined that the only thing holding Knoxville back during that period "was an attitude of greed and conservatism which afflicted many in the city."[272] In a speech, Oliver charged that "many actually discouraged growth and new businesses, preferring the city as it was rather than as it could become."[273] One historian observed, "Whether the old 'establishment' of monied families actually conspired to keep Knoxville from growing is impossible to prove."[274] However, a growing number of the elite like Sanford were resisting change, often for fear taxes would have to be raised.[275] The historical record reveals that Sanford, who served as the secretary of the Knoxville Water Company, indeed was reluctant to address Knoxville's need for a modern municipal waterworks and, in 1904, opposed the sale of bonds to raise funds to construct a modern water plant. The bond issue was approved in a popular referendum, but Sanford charged that the vote had been fraudulently conducted and that numerous "no" ballots had not been counted by election officials.[276]

There were exceptions to this mindset. The members of "The Three Musketeers" or "One Hundred Percent Club," an extremely influential group of financiers, included Sanford's brother, Hugh Wheeler Sanford; his brother-in-law, Benjamin Andrew Morton,[277] and William Cary Ross. Hugh had been educated at the University (Baker-Himel) School of Knoxville, established in 1889, and graduated from Harvard in 1900. Upon returning to Knoxville, he acquired a half-interest in an iron foundry, which became Sanford-Day Iron Works. He was its first secretary and treasurer, later president, and from 1938 to 1947, board chairman. In 1921, the Day interests were acquired by the company, which merged with coal and mining interests. Over one hundred US Patents were granted to Hugh and his associates.[278] One of the products developed by the Sanford-Day Company was a highly valuable automatic mine car coupler, built in coordination with W.F. Deaderick.[279] In 1911, Hugh also founded the Knoxville Stove Works, which later became the Knoxville Metal Products Company. Like his brother, he served as a director of Sanford, Chamberlain, and Albers and held interests in the Knoxville Woolen Mills, the Lenoir City Company, and his father-in-law's business, the W.W. Woodruff Hardware Co. His other business interests included the Myers-Whaley Company; Knoxville Office Company (vice president); Journal & Tribune Company; Sanford Realty Company; Empire Building Corporation; Sanford Investment Company; Manufacturers Acceptance Corporation; Kimball's, Inc.; Automatic Sprinkler Company; and Fidelity-Bankers Trust Company. During World War I, he served on the Council of National Defense and on the War Industries Board. Frequently described as aloof, Hugh was an author of works in economics and philosophy and a member of several foreign scientific and cultural academies. His first wife was Margaret Woodruff, the sister of Lutie Sanford, with whom he had five children: Edward Jackson, Hugh W., Alfred F., Margaret, and Katherine.[280] When he passed away in 1961 at the age of eighty-two, a reporter noted that Hugh was a "multi-millionaire" and "probably Knoxville's wealthiest man."[281]

Ben Morton, who was married to Pauline Woodruff, another sister of Lutie Sanford, was president of the wholesale grocery firm H.T. Hackney Company and served as Mayor of Knoxville from 1923 to 1927. Other business interests of his included banking, flour milling, and automobile dealerships.[282] William C. Ross was a Yale graduate who left an informative record that "reveals much about the financial practices of his day and explains what was happening to the city's businesses and industries."[283] For example, Ross commented that when the group attempted to secure investors for a new hotel, "[a]ll we got was discouragement and statements that it couldn't be done. That stimulated us so, we went out and did it ourselves." In 1908 however, after Ross was elected vice president and treasurer of the Knoxville Woolen Mills, he "saw other mills of like kind going into receivership all over the country so we decided to liquidate while we could still pay our debts and have a little something left for the stockholders." The investors, Sanford among them, had been receiving large dividends for years, usually twelve percent, but sometimes as high as forty percent. Layoffs occurred in 1908, followed by strikes in 1909. The year 1910 found the company in bankruptcy. Ross did try to adapt the woolen mill to meet the changing market, but the lack of modern equipment limited his options.[284]

One likely explanation for the "growing conservatism" and exchange of "long-term growth and vitality for short-term profits" by Knoxville's elite was the recognition that the city was "finding it increasingly difficult to compete in the emerging consolidating national economy."[285] In Sanford's case, he had observed his father over the years opt for maximizing personal profits. Further, he apparently was in debt. His law partner, James A. Fowler, acknowledged financial issues with the law firm and bad investments. According to Fowler, Sanford's indebtedness was not fully satisfied until after he joined the Supreme Court, at which time he received a significant amount of money from the sale of stock from his father's estate.[286] Whatever the reasons, Knoxville's "greatest economic assets had lost their vitality."[287] The elite of Knoxville became increasingly conservative and turned away from the economic, social, and political issues facing the area at that time.[288] Resistance to the taxes and investments needed to promote further growth took hold.[289] By the time of Sanford's death, the progressive Knoxville of his time had also passed away.

Sanford's uncle, Albert Chavannes,[290] a sociologist and Utopist, observed as early as 1883 that Social Darwinism, with its emphasis on "survival of the fittest," had been rendered obsolete in the age of Standard Oil, the Goulds, and the Vanderbilts. He concluded that the growth of trusts and monopolies, and a few individual fortunes, made the search for success in America an "unequal struggle." Chavannes indicted the "individualistic system" for creating a "race for wealth" in which "individual greed [was] encouraged." He denounced the nation's maldistribution of wealth, where the rich had "all the wealth and power and leisure while the poor toiled for a subsistence." Chavannes, who attacked "private capitalism" and "laissez-faire individualism," deplored the contradiction presented in the simultaneous existence in America of "millionaires and paupers."[291]

Chavannes ran for the state legislature as a Populist in 1892. At a campaign address to the Knox County Populite Central Club in September 1892, he stated that a few had become rich at the expense of the people and that "[t]hirty-one thousand men owned half of the wealth of the United States." In line with Populist thinking, he attacked the ETV&G Railroad, of which his brother-in-law E.J. was a director, as an example of an entity by which a few "made great scads of wealth."[292] Considered by some as "one hundred years ahead of his time" and by others as "a visionary fool,"[293] Chavannes lost the election. Years later, however, Sanford expressed in his speeches ideals surprisingly similar to the themes addressed by Chavannes. To be successful in business during that time, a certain amount of ruthlessness was required. It seems that Sanford did not have the appetite for seeking wealth that his father had possessed. He also did not possess the business acumen of his father and his brothers. Sanford, with his sense of ethics, was uncomfortable going to any extreme to make money. Once out of the shadow of E.J.'s dominating personality following his father's death in 1902, Sanford instead pursued a career in public service.[294] Living out his "desire to make the world brighter and better,"[295] Sanford joined his Uncle Albert Chavannes in targeting the trusts and monopolies of the wealthiest class.

 CHAPTER SIX

Department of Justice

The White House
January 3, 1907
To the Senate of the United States:

I nominate Edward T. Sanford, of Tennessee, to be Assistant Attorney-General in place of James C. McReynolds, resigned.
—Theodore Roosevelt

Theodore Roosevelt entered the presidency in 1901 amidst rapidly growing public concern over the vast power that corporations had amassed in preceding decades. The great American obsession of the late nineteenth century was money, and, in the post-Civil War decades, large corporations exploited the nation's natural resources, thereby accumulating enormous wealth.[1] In the 1880s, major corporations turned to the trust, a legal invention through which multiple firms deposited stock in an umbrella entity. The Standard Oil Trust led the way in 1882. Within five years, trusts in linseed oil, sugar, whiskey, salt, and many other products were created. These trusts enabled large corporations to dominate key sectors of the economy,[2] leading Congress to pass the Sherman Antitrust Act of

1890. The act prohibited combinations "in restraint of trade or commerce among the several states, or with foreign nations."[3] As the twentieth century began, the public started to suspect the worst of the impersonal, powerful corporations and came to view them as the enemy.[4] Roosevelt dedicated himself to "trust-busting" and enforcing the Sherman Antitrust Act.[5] Roosevelt's antitrust policies were considered "radical" for a Republican. The president was accused of lacking respect for the Constitution: "Roosevelt's all right, but he's got no more use for the Constitution than a tomcat has for a marriage license."[6]

Roosevelt's presidency came at a time when Progressivism was developing in response to the rapid industrialization and urbanization in the late nineteenth century. Progressives sought to remedy such problems as the exploitation of female and child factory workers, unsafe and unsanitary working conditions, urban poverty, political corruption, and abusive practices of giant corporations.[7] The movement pushed for labor and business regulation and education reform. Progressives believed in the administrative state, the idea that administrative bureaucracies, staffed by unelected professionals, could find solutions to economic and social problems. This required a strong central government. Roosevelt was convinced that the times called for "far more active governmental interference with social and economic conditions in this country."[8] He had initially opposed legislation limiting the rights of businessmen as long as they conducted their affairs honestly. As a legislator early in his career, Roosevelt declined to support a bill reducing the working hours of street car conductors, calling it "socialistic." Eventually, however, he became a reformer concerned with social justice and human welfare.[9] As a Roosevelt supporter, Sanford shared many of these progressive ideas.

In 1905, Sanford was called upon to act as special assistant to the United States attorney general to prosecute under the Sherman Antitrust Act what was known as the Fertilizer Trust.[10] Sanford, then forty years old, left private practice to become a special prosecutor under then-Assistant United States Attorney General and future Supreme Court Justice James Clark McReynolds.[11] As noted in *The New York Times*, "[i]t is alleged by the Government that this [fertilizer] trust, embracing manufactories all over the South, is conducting a business in restraint of trade.... The Government is said to contend that the entire fertilizer interests of the South are embraced in one vast combine to control prices, and the fight will take the nature of the one recently waged against the Beef Trust." The article further related that Sanford was "a well-known Southern attorney" who had "been selected by the attorney general as special counsel owing to his familiarity with the details of the proposed prosecution."[12] Many of the activities of this alleged combination were in the South, partly in Tennessee.[13]

McReynolds, who had become assistant United States attorney general in 1903 under then-Attorney General William H. Moody, had been a practicing attorney in Nashville[14] and a law professor at Vanderbilt University, his undergraduate alma mater. In 1896, McReynolds had lost as a Democratic candidate for Congress in Middle Tennessee.[15] He and Sanford were "rather particular friends," having come into contact over the years.[16] According to Fowler, Sanford received a letter from McReynolds "suggesting that the government would like to employ him to participate in prosecuting a case which it contemplated bringing." Sanford asked Fowler his thoughts regarding the position and expressed a belief that he should not accept it. In response, Fowler remarked: "You have been saying that you would like to be a Federal judge and you are offered a fine opportunity to obtain that appointment because we know that the present [US District] Judge Clark cannot live but a short time, and there will be a vacancy and you will be in the Department and it should be an easy matter to obtain such appointment."[17] Fowler recognized that working with members of the Department of Justice would give Sanford a distinct advantage over other possible contenders for selection to the district bench.[18] Sanford took the suggestion and accepted the office from McReynolds. His commission provided as follows: "You are hereby appointed a special assistant to the United States attorney for the Middle district of Tennessee to assist in the investigation before the grand jury in that district of the so-called 'Fertilizer Trust,' and in the trial of any suits and prosecutions on behalf of the United States, against the Virginia-Carolina Chemical Company, a corporation, and other corporations and individuals arising from such investigation."[19]

According to the government, an illegal combination of manufacturers was formed through a corporation organized in Canada, resulting in an increase in the price of fertilizer by about $2 a ton. As a consequence, farmers of the southern states were overcharged approximately five to seven million dollars.[20] The charter for the "Canada Improvement Company" was obtained by one of the leading attorneys involved in the interests of Armour & Company, a meat packing entity, which at the time sold every product that could be produced from animals, including fertilizer.[21] Stock in the Canadian company was held by all the fertilizer companies whose products were sold in the Southern states east of the Mississippi River, and, through it, the factories' output and the fertilizer prices were regulated.[22]

Sanford prosecuted fertilizer manufacturers from Chicago, Baltimore, Norfolk, Richmond, Charleston, Atlanta, and Nashville.[23] Among the companies targeted were Tennessee Chemical Company, Read Phosphate Company, the National Fertilizer Works, the Federal Chemical Company, Swift, and Armour.[24] The grand jury in Nashville was charged by Sixth Circuit Court of Appeals Judge Lurton, who defined the nature of a trust and interpreted the sections of the Sherman Antitrust law upon which indictments might be found if the grand jury concluded that there had been a restraint of trade by the fertilizer entities.[25] After a large number of witnesses appeared before the grand jury, Sanford eventually succeeded in securing indictments against thirty-one corporations and twenty-five individuals for price fixing and suppressing competition in the manufacture and sale of fertilizer.[26] Prior to the time of Sanford's involvement, the Department of Justice had not been particularly successful in its efforts to enforce the antitrust law.[27]

McReynolds also achieved great success in President Roosevelt's "trust-busting" campaign.[28] He reportedly prosecuted the Tobacco Trust "with a zeal worthy of Carrie Nation," the famous temperance advocate. He described the trust as "illegal, its methods wicked and oppressive, and its effect destructive of competition and detrimental to the public."[29] Once, when he was arguing that the government ought to appoint a receiver to sell the tobacco combine out, one of the lawyers for a corporation suggested that such a procedure would involve a destruction of property rights of the individual defendants and would amount to confiscation. McReynolds remarked, "What if it is? . . . Since when has property illegally and criminally acquired come to have any rights?"[30] Indeed, an investigator of the tobacco cases noted: "In no other industry has there been developed so complete and so splendid an organization as the Tobacco Trust."[31] Despite his success, in January 1907, McReynolds resigned as assistant United States attorney general in protest over compromises made in his prosecution of that trust.[32] He moved to New York and became a partner in the leading Wall Street firm of Cravath, Henderson, and de Gersdorff.[33] While in private practice in New York, however, McReynolds continued to serve as a special assistant to the attorney general in the tobacco litigation until the Supreme Court directed that the Tobacco Trust be dismantled in May 1911.[34] He did not formally resign as special assistant to the attorney general until December 31, 1911.[35]

After a few years of private practice, McReynolds became attorney general from 1913 to 1914 under President Woodrow Wilson. McReynolds soon made enemies in Congress and President Wilson's administration. His time at the head of the Department of Justice has been described as "a cavalcade of controversy." According to reports: "Department building projects went grossly over budget, and there were allegations that the department spied on federal judges. McReynolds was even accused of hindering the prosecution of the son-in-law of a politically prominent official charged with taking a woman across state lines for 'immoral purposes' in violation of the Mann Act. McReynolds's explosive reaction to criticism alienated Congress and mortified the president."[36]

When Justice Lurton died in 1914, President Wilson nominated McReynolds to a seat on the Supreme Court, a move many considered "a ploy to get him out of the cabinet."[37] As a Supreme Court justice, McReynolds later became best known as one of the "Four Horsemen"—the four conservative justices famous for opposing President Franklin D. Roosevelt and the New Deal.[38] His critics described him as "intolerably rude" and the "crustiest of the conservatives."[39] Taft characterized him as "reactionary on the subject of the constitution."[40]

When McReynolds resigned from the assistant attorney general slot, Department of Justice special agent Victor N. Roadstrum encouraged Sanford to seek the position. It was Roadstrum's job to investigate and collect evidence relative to the antitrust violations of the fertilizer manufacturers. In the course of his work, Roadstrum had taken a liking to Sanford.[41] With Nathan V. Hale, congressman from the Second Congressional District of Tennessee, supporting his candidacy for the job, Sanford decided to apply.[42] Sanford also gained the endorsement of two members of the Tennessee Supreme Court, then-Chief Justice W.D. Beard and Justice John K. Shields. Beard, who served as chief justice from 1902 to 1910, was a former Confederate, like many Sanford supporters.[43] Shields later became chief justice of the Tennessee Supreme Court and eventually a United States senator.[44] William Rule, Sanford's long-time advocate, also lent his support and traveled to Washington to speak to President Roosevelt on Sanford's behalf. According to Rule, after he described Sanford's qualities and abilities, Roosevelt replied that he was aware of Sanford. Rule then reminded the president that Sanford was, like Roosevelt, a Harvard man, at which point Roosevelt showed more interest and asked additional questions. The president then sent a note to his soon-to-be attorney general, Charles J. Bonaparte,[45] in which he remarked: "I would not attempt to dictate any of your appointments, but I would be pleased to see a southern man of the Sanford type named as one of your assistants."[46] Within two weeks, the appointment as assistant attorney general was Sanford's.[47]

Sanford was confirmed by the Senate, in executive session, on January 9, 1907.[48] He served in this role until May 1908.[49] According to future Attorney General William D. Mitchell, "[t]he marked ability disclosed in [the Fertilizer Trust] case secured [Sanford] immediate recognition and resulted in his appointment in 1907, to the position of Assistant Attorney General. While occupying that post, he appeared before [the Supreme] Court on several occasions and made a favorable impression, by the skill and force with which he presented the cases entrusted to him."[50]

One interesting matter that Sanford addressed while serving as assistant attorney general related to the Freedman's Savings and Trust Company in Washington, D.C. In March 1865, Congress had chartered the bank to help newly freed blacks become more financially stable by expanding their access to capital.[51] As noted by Sanford in a comprehensive memorandum prepared for the attorney general, all deposits received "were to be invested in United States securities, except that not exceeding one-third of the total amount might be kept in other available form as a fund to meet current payments." The profits of the company "were to be paid to the depositors as interest on their deposits," and any unclaimed funds of deceased or missing depositors could "be held by the company as a separate trust fund for the education and improvement of former slaves or their descendants." Quoting from congressional reports, Sanford observed that "the honor of the government became engaged in this undertaking when . . . Congress . . . held out to the lately emancipated slaves inducements to entrust their earnings to this institution. . . ." He noted that the freedmen were urged to bring their savings to be taken care of "by these their friends and protectors."[52] During the bank's existence, it had over $57 million in deposits and more than 70,000 depositors. However, Congress allowed the bank's charter to be amended without the knowledge or consent of those who had deposited their savings there. Quoting a report from a House Committee on Banking and Currency, Sanford related that the amendment

> embodied a radical change in the investment of these deposits, by providing instead of the safe, conservative, and prudent provision in the original charter "that two-thirds of all the deposits should be

invested exclusively in government securities," the dangerous privilege of allowing the irresponsible officers to loan one-half of its assets in bonds and mortgages and other securities, and invest in and improve real estate without inspection, without examination, or responsibility on the part of its officers. The institution could only go on to certain bankruptcy.[53]

The bank declined rapidly during the Panic of 1873. The economic contraction pushed down the yield on government securities, which formed a primary component of the bank's investment portfolio and which reduced the return to depositors.[54] It closed its doors in June 1874.[55] Among the deposits lost was $10,000 belonging to Frederick Douglass.[56]

According to Sanford's comprehensive memorandum on the failure of the Freedman's Savings and Trust Company, the evidence showed that Congress's amendment of the bank's charter was "not in the interest of the depositors, not according to any conceivable principle of justice, good faith, or public policy." He observed that a congressional investigation in 1879 revealed that "nearly every man of position and means had withdrawn prior to the collapse in 1874," and that "only $400 in United States securities were found among the assets in 1874, when the bank failed."[57] According to Sanford, at the time of the failure, there were 61,131 depositors, to whom was owing $2,939,925.22. Five dividends were declared as follows: 20 percent, November 1, 1875; 10 percent, March 20, 1878; 10 percent, September 1, 1881; 15 percent, June 1, 1882; and a final dividend of 7 percent on May 12, 1883. The dividends of 62 percent amounted to $1,822,753.62. Sanford noted that legislation had been recommended by each president since 1886 to pay the depositors of the failed bank the remainder of the amount owed in full. President Taft, in his message to Congress on December 7, 1909, followed the precedent set by the presidents who came before him by renewing the recommendation that Congress appropriate sufficient funds to pay "about thirty-eight percent of the amount due the depositors."[58] Despite Sanford's acknowledgment that "the honor of the government" was at issue, the depositors and their descendants were never fully reimbursed.

Sanford's papers housed at the University of Tennessee include notes revealing that during his tenure in the Department of Justice, he also dealt with the subjects of conspiracy, negligence, incompetency of witnesses, and habeas corpus.[59] In 1908, a reporter related that Sanford had "been engaged for the most part . . . on customs cases and questions involving international law."[60] For example, Sanford argued *Goat & Sheepskin Import Company v. United States* before the US Supreme Court. In that case,[61] a duty was assessed on the growth upon certain skins of Mocha sheep imported from Arabia. This growth was classified as "wool on the skin of the third class" and assessed for duty at three cents per pound. The importer protested the classification, insisting that the merchandise should be free of duty. The evidence revealed that the hair on this breed of sheep was not bought or sold in the United States as wool but as hair, and that there was no substantial use of any portion of the growth on the skins for the purposes for which wool is generally used. Mocha hair did not have the appearance, feel, or qualities of wool. The chief use of the substance was for stuffing, for the saddlery trade, and by bed manufacturers. Sanford's protestations that the Mocha hair should be treated as wool did not sway the Court, and the justices found in favor of the importer and assessed no duty.[62]

In *United States v. Cerecedo Hermanos y Compania*,[63] the importer had obtained from France thirty cases of red wine, twenty-four bottles to the case. The wine was classified by appraisers as being dutiable at $1.25 per dozen bottles, for a total of $75. Sanford convinced the Court to adopt another construction of the applicable tariff statute, raising the duty to $1.60 per case.[64] In yet another lawsuit, *Henry E. Frankenberg Company v. United States*,[65] the question was whether certain metal beads were dutiable at 35 percent, ad valorem, or 45 percent, ad valorem. These metal beads were strung on cotton cords or strings. The importer argued that the true issue depended on the use to which the beads were to be put and contended that the beads had been strung together merely for the purpose of facilitating transportation. The Court determined that the threaded item could not be considered loose beads and adopted Sanford's position.[66]

In July 1907, Sanford was sent to North Carolina, purportedly as President Roosevelt's emissary, to meet with Governor Robert Brodnax Glenn about a pending, volatile railway rate dispute between the state and the Southern Railway Company.[67] Governor Glenn's wife was the former Nina Deaderick of Knoxville, although there is no indication that Sanford was acquainted with her or that this is the reason he was chosen for the task;[68] rather, Sanford's past experience as an attorney for the Southern Railway probably had more influence on his selection.

Around the turn of the century, railroads began raising their rates. The State of North Carolina passed a law reducing both passenger and freight rates on the railroad lines within the state. The Southern Railway and other railroad corporations obtained an injunction in federal court to enjoin the North Carolina Corporation Commission from enforcing the lower rates. The federal judge declared the penalty clause of the North Carolina rate bill unconstitutional and void. In an address to North Carolina authorities, Governor Glenn responded that the railroads, their agents, and employees should be indicted for violating the new state law. Glenn noted that he was prepared to enforce the law if it took "every dollar in the treasury and put arms in the hands of every available man in the state."[69] Two agents of the Southern Railway were actually sentenced to thirty days on a chain gang for selling passenger tickets in disregard of the new state law. Intimidation became so great that it threatened to interfere with the operation of the railroads. An observer noted that "never before has so sharp a conflict between the state and the United States Courts been presented."[70] Sanford was directed to persuade the Southern Railway to secure a stay of execution and to take appeals through the state courts until the matter could be addressed by the United States Supreme Court, because President Roosevelt was said to be embarrassed by the appearance of interference by a federal judge.[71] The railroads eventually put the lower rate into effect to break the impasse.[72] They agreed to appeal the case to the North Carolina Supreme Court and, if necessary, take the case on writ of error to the United States Supreme Court.[73] The Southern and other railroads began adopting a more conciliatory policy toward state commissions and legislatures, and the Hepburn Act of 1906, a Progressive-backed bill, reined in railroad abuses by regulating the rate increases instituted by the railroads.[74]

In *Winters v. United States*,[75] Sanford represented the government on appeal in an action to restrain individuals from constructing or maintaining dams or reservoirs on the Milk River in Montana. In 1905, public-land settlers upstream of the Fort Belknap Indian Reservation diverted all the water in the drought-reduced Milk River to irrigate their hay and other crops, a right they believed they had under Montana law.[76] The non-Indian settlers claimed that they had appropriated the water before the Indians on the reservation had put it to beneficial use. Such actions by the plaintiffs prevented the river's water from flowing to the Indians at the reservation. Sanford, representing the government, asserted the rights of the Fort Belknap Indians to reserve the waters from appropriation, arguing that all waters of the Milk River were essential to fulfilling the implied intent of the treaty creating the reservation. The government contended that water rights were appurtenant to the Indian lands under the Agreement of 1888, as ratified by Congress, and subsequent state legislation could not divest those rights. In his opinion for the Court, US Supreme Court Justice Joseph McKenna observed that "it would be extreme to believe ... Congress destroyed the reservation and took from the Indians the consideration of their grant, leaving them a barren waste...."[77] The Court determined that the federal government had the power to reserve and exempt waters from appropriation under state law. According to the Court, the measure of the reserved right was whatever water was now needed or might become necessary in the future to allow the Indians to lead successful lives on these lands as "pastoral and civilized people," at least to make the lands "productive and suitable for agricultural, stock raising and domestic purposes."[78] Pursuant to this view, the Court held that the Agreement of May 1, 1888, by implication reserved from appropriation under state law an amount of water sufficient for irrigation purposes, "which would be necessarily continued through the years." The Court rejected the notion that admission of Montana to statehood in 1889 abrogated the reservation of waters made the prior year. Thus, the decision made clear that the Indians' water rights were not limited to amounts then needed or then in use on the reserved lands, in contrast to water rights established under the western state law system of prior appropriation, which provided that the first user to put the water to a beneficial use has the right to continue using it in the same quantity as long as the use is beneficial. The principle of protecting present and future Indian water needs has since become known as the *Winters* doctrine.[79] The decision and doctrine have become central to modern Native American efforts to retain and control their natural resources.

Another issue Sanford addressed during his time in the Department of Justice was a request for the transfer of an inmate from federal prison at Leavenworth, Kansas, to Minot, North Dakota, for the purpose of giving testimony in a state court proceeding. On the matter, Sanford observed: "While there is no authority for it, it seems to me that if a person charged with a crime in a state court is desirous of obtaining the testimony of a federal prisoner in his behalf, it is not a matter of judicial comity for the federal court to grant the writ but a matter of law and necessity. Otherwise, what becomes of the provision of the Sixth Article that in all criminal prosecutions the accused shall have compulsory process for obtaining witnesses in his favor?"[80] Sanford's comment revealed his belief that the Sixth Amendment's guarantee of compulsory process to ensure witnesses in one's favor should apply to the states. Approximately eighteen years later, as a member of the Supreme Court, Sanford authored the opinion, *Gitlow v. New York*,[81] in which the Court first applied the First Amendment to a state. Interestingly, however, it was not until 1967 that a defendant's right to secure witnesses on his behalf was applied to the states in *Washington v. Texas*.[82]

Sanford's thinking was similar to that of the Supreme Court justice he purportedly most admired, John Marshall Harlan, who advocated for the total incorporation of the Bill of Rights by the Fourteenth Amendment.[83] Harlan, the last Whig justice, was the first justice to voice the idea that the due process clause of the Fourteenth Amendment applied or "incorporated" all the protections found in the first eight amendments to the Constitution, an idea he expressed in his dissent in *Hurtado v. California*.[84] Best known for two dissents—in the *Civil Rights Cases*[85] and *Plessy v. Ferguson*[86]—Harlan argued as follows in *Plessy*:

> [I]n the view of the Constitution, in the eye of the law, there is in this country no superior, dominant ruling class of citizens. There is no caste here. Our Constitution is color-blind and neither knows nor tolerates classes among citizens. In respect of civil rights, all citizens are equal before the law. The humblest is the peer of the most powerful. The law regards man as man and takes no account of his surroundings or of his color when his civil rights as guaranteed by the supreme law of the land are involved.[87]

Harlan further warned that "[t]he destinies of the two races, in this country, are indissolubly linked together, and the interests of both require that the common government of all shall not permit the seeds of race hate to be planted under the sanction of law."[88] In both the *Civil Rights Cases* and *Plessy*, Harlan argued that segregation in public accommodations was a badge of slavery.[89]

Sanford was considered "a firm believer in equal rights, who understood the Southern mentality, but aligned himself with the more liberal views of the North."[90] For that reason, he was believed to be a perfect choice to serve as lead prosecutor for the federal government in the trial of Joseph Shipp, sheriff of Hamilton County, Tennessee, and others accused of lynching Ed Johnson, a black prisoner who was the subject of a writ of habeas corpus issued by the United States Supreme Court.

United States v. Shipp[91]

On January 23, 1906, a twenty-one-year-old white woman, Nevada Taylor, was raped in Chattanooga on her way home from work. Ms. Taylor told the sheriff that she did not see her assailant. The newspaper reported, however, that the crime had been committed by a "Negro brute."[92]

Sheriff Shipp and Hamilton County Judge Samuel D. McReynolds[93] were both up for reelection soon and were desperate to make an arrest. When some days passed without finding the attacker, a reward was announced. Inspired by the reward, a white man implicated Ed Johnson, a nineteen-year-old black youth who could neither read nor write. Despite three hours of interrogation, Johnson maintained his innocence and provided the names of a dozen men who could vouch for his whereabouts at the time of the crime.[94]

Judge McReynolds appointed two lawyers to represent Johnson, neither of whom had previously handled a criminal case.[95] The judge told the attorneys that they were taking the case pro bono, a hint that he did not expect them to invest a lot of time or effort in their representation of Johnson.[96] A third lawyer stepped forward to help: Lewis Shepherd, a former judge who was widely regarded as one of the best lawyers in Tennessee. He was also known for representing the poor and blacks charged with crimes against whites. A former Confederate, Shepherd had twice been elected to the legislature, but he reportedly resigned each time because he did not enjoy "serving with men with less intelligence than my wife's mule."[97] When he died in 1917 while trying a lawsuit, Shepherd fulfilled his last wish "to go to his reward straight from the courtroom."[98]

When Judge McReynolds ordered that the trial would commence in ten days in Chattanooga, Shepherd argued that Johnson's attorneys could not put together an adequate defense in such a short time. McReynolds warned the attorney against filing any motion to delay, stating, "I won't grant it and it will only make me angry." When Shepherd requested that the judge move the trial to anywhere but Chattanooga because the pool of jurors would be biased, McReynolds replied, "Don't file a motion for a change of venue ... I won't grant it, either."[99] Johnson was convicted on February 11, 1906, and sentenced to be "hung by the neck until dead" on March 13.[100] Governor John Cox changed the execution date to March 20.

No appeal to the Tennessee Supreme Court was taken by the court-appointed lawyers. One of them told *The Chattanooga Times*:

> We discussed the recent mob uprising [in relation to Johnson] and the state of unrest in the community. It was the judgment of all present that the life of the defendant, even if the wrong man, could not be saved; that an appeal would so inflame the public that the jail would be attacked and perhaps other prisoners executed by violence. In the view of all of us a case was presented where the defendant, now that he had been convicted by a jury, must die by the judgment of the law, or else, if his case were appealed, he would die by the act of the uprising of the people.[101]

Noah W. Parden and his law partner, Styles Linton Hutchins, black attorneys in Chattanooga, agreed to Johnson's father's request to appeal the rape conviction. When Parden and Hutchins visited Judge McReynolds in his courtroom to inform him of their intention to file an appeal, the judge, stunned by this development, told the two attorneys to return the next day to formally file their motion. Upon their arrival the following day, Judge McReynolds laughed out loud at them, scolded them, and told them that they had missed the filing date.[102] The judge denied them help in obtaining a transcript, describing their efforts as a waste of time and a personal rebuke of him and the three prior attorneys.[103]

Despite numerous obstacles, Parden and Hutchins filed the appeal with the Tennessee Supreme Court, but it was denied without a single dissenting vote. Refusing to give up, Parden took the train to Knoxville to file a petition for a writ of habeas corpus in the United States District Court for the Eastern District of Tennessee.[104] Filed on March 3, 1906, the petition alleged that Johnson's constitutional rights had been violated. Specifically, it asserted that all blacks had been systematically excluded from both the grand jury considering the original indictment and the trial jury. Further, the petition asserted that Johnson had been substantively denied the right to counsel because his lawyers had been too intimidated by the threats of mob violence to file motions for a change of venue, a continuance, or a new trial, all of which could be reasonably expected under the circumstances. The document outlined that Johnson was, in effect, about to be deprived of his life without due process.[105] Johnson's attorney,

Shepherd, observed that the threat of mob violence had caused a violation of Johnson's Fourteenth Amendment rights.[106]

The petition was heard on March 10, 1906, by District Court Judge Charles Dickens Clark, a Confederate veteran and himself a resident of Chattanooga.[107] After listening to arguments and witnesses on both sides for eight hours on a Saturday, Judge Clark agreed that there might have been serious flaws in Johnson's trial but concluded that the Sixth Amendment's guarantee of a fair and impartial trial did not apply in state court. He rejected as well the claims that the panels of grand and trial jurors were illegally drawn, despite a witness's testimony that he had not seen a single black on a Hamilton County jury since the jury law of 1899 became effective.[108] Judge Clark did allow ten days to file further appeals.[109] An outraged Judge McReynolds considered the federal judge's delay of the execution to be a personal insult. In his view, the action demonstrated contempt by the federal courts for the authority and jurisdiction of the state court system.[110]

With Johnson just days from execution, Parden raced to Washington, D.C., to file an appeal with the United States Supreme Court. On March 17, Parden entered the waiting room of the Supreme Court in the Old Senate Chamber,[111] at that point becoming the first black to be designated as lead counsel in a Supreme Court matter.[112] He was seen by the circuit justice for the Sixth Circuit, none other than Justice Harlan, who inquired "why the United States Supreme Court should care about this case?"[113] Due to precedent, the chances of success seemed slim. Despite the fact that the trial was a mockery in terms of due process, none of the procedural rights in the Fourth,[114] Fifth,[115] or Sixth[116] Amendments had yet been held applicable to state court proceedings.

When Parden's train returned to the Chattanooga station two days later, he saw Hutchins waving a telegram from Justice Harlan: "Have allowed appeal to accused in habeas corpus case of Ed Johnson." At Justice Harlan's request, a majority of the justices had gathered on Sunday morning at the home of Chief Justice Melville Fuller to consider federal intervention in the case. After debating the issue, the justices had agreed upon staying the execution and granting Johnson's appeal. Telegrams were sent to Judge Clark, the defense lawyers, Judge McReynolds, District Attorney Matt Whitaker, and Sheriff Shipp, informing them of the Supreme Court's action.[117] The ruling was given full coverage by Chattanooga's newspapers, with one running the headline: "An Appeal is Allowed. Ed Johnson Will Not Hang Tomorrow." The article provided in part: "The gallows in the Hamilton County jail has again been disappointed in the case of Ed Johnson, convicted by the state courts of rape, and sentenced to death. The hanging will not take place to-morrow morning, as scheduled."[118] Importantly, *The Chattanooga Times* noted that "the granting of an appeal in a case like this acted to supersede all process in the state courts. . . . Pending a decision of the appeal there can be no execution by any state authority."[119]

The Clerk of the Supreme Court advised Sheriff Shipp that the prisoner was "to be held at the instance of the United States, to whom the sheriff could look for the expense of the prisoner's maintenance. . . ."[120] This meant that Johnson had become a federal prisoner. Upon news of this development, a mob gathered at the jail, demanding that Johnson be turned over. From the moment the mob first entered the jail, no policemen appeared, and there was no attempt to stop the attack.[121] Shipp and his chief jailer allowed the mob to carry Johnson from the jail and lynch him on Chattanooga's Walnut Street Bridge.[122] Moments before he was hanged, Johnson made one last declaration of his innocence: "I am ready to die. But I never done it. I am going to tell the truth. I am not guilty. I am not guilty. I have said all the time that I did not do it and it is true. I was not there. I know I am going to die and I have no fear to die and I have no fear at all. . . . God bless you all. I am innocent."[123]

Soon, Johnson's body was swaying more than one hundred feet above the Tennessee River, still jerking with life. The crowd grew impatient and opened fire. When a bullet severed the rope, Johnson's body dropped to the floor of the bridge. Johnson's head seemed to move and his body twitched, and another barrage of bullets ended his life. Scores of bullets had ripped the youth's body apart. A leader of the mob pinned a sheet of paper to Johnson's body that read: "To Justice Harlan. Come and get your Nigger now."[124]

The next morning, when the news of the brutal lynching reached the Supreme Court, the justices were stunned.[125] Justice Harlan observed that "the mandate of the Supreme Court has for the first time in the history of the country been openly defied by a community."[126] President Roosevelt announced that the incident was "an affront to the highest tribunal in the land that cannot go by without the proper action being taken." He ordered an extensive federal preliminary investigation. Attorney General William Moody sent undercover Secret Service agents into Chattanooga, who discovered that both Judge McReynolds and District Attorney Whitaker knew about the attack on the jail from the moment it began and had watched the events from the courtroom window. It was also learned that Sheriff Shipp did nothing to stop the lynching and claimed to be unable to identify a single conspirator despite spending considerable time near them while the mob was in the jail.[127] On March 27, seven days after the lynching, Sheriff Shipp was reelected by a sizeable margin.[128]

On May 28, 1906, the Department of Justice filed charges against twenty-seven Chattanooga residents, including Sheriff Shipp and eight of his deputies. The defendants were charged with criminal contempt of the Supreme Court, a charge never previously brought. The attorney general filed the charges against the defendants directly with the Supreme Court, giving the Court original jurisdiction in the matter. The information alleged that Sheriff Shipp, his deputies, and other citizens engaged in actions "with the intent to show their contempt and disregard for the orders of this Honorable Court ... and for the purpose of preventing Ed Johnson from exercising and enjoying a right secured to him by the Constitution and laws of the United States."[129]

The proceedings began with the Court first hearing oral arguments on the issue of whether it had jurisdiction to try the conspirators for criminal contempt.[130] Solicitor General Henry Hoyt contended that Johnson's right to be heard on his application for habeas corpus was protected by the Constitution and that the Court acted appropriately in staying his execution. "This proceeding is about nothing less than establishing and protecting the rule of law," Hoyt told the justices. Judson Harmon, a Cincinnati lawyer and former US attorney general representing Sheriff Shipp, asserted that none of Johnson's federally protected rights had been violated and that the Supreme Court had improperly granted the stay. According to Harmon, since the stay was improperly issued, no one who violated it should be found in contempt. Justice Holmes then asked, "But you would agree that this Court has the authority to determine that the Sixth Amendment [with its guarantee of a fair trial] is binding on the state courts, do you not?" In a unanimous decision written by Holmes, the Court ruled that it had jurisdiction to try the conspirators.[131] Holmes concluded that "[a] state officer having prisoners committed to his custody by a court of the United States is an officer of the United States."[132]

The members of the Court had neither the time nor the inclination to travel to Tennessee to hear weeks of testimony. Further, they concluded that witnesses could be more easily gathered locally than in Washington, D.C. Accordingly, on February 12, 1907, the trial opened in the United States Custom House in

Chattanooga, with James D. Maher, deputy clerk of the Supreme Court, presiding as a special commissioner and preparing an evidentiary record for the Court's review.[133]

Sanford, then forty-one years old, served as lead prosecutor for the United States. He prepared the case for trial and took the primary role in examining and cross-examining witnesses in Chattanooga.[134] For five days, testimony was taken from thirty-one government witnesses. The trial then recessed until June 1907, at which time the defense presented its case.[135] It was Sanford who spent the better part of two days cross-examining Shipp concerning his alleged role in the lynching.[136] In an interesting turn of events, Lewis Shepherd, one of Ed Johnson's defense attorneys, represented nine of the accused members of the lynch mob in the contempt trial before the US Supreme Court.[137]

Although at least two witnesses claimed to have seen three deputies participate as members of the mob,[138] Sanford observed that some witnesses the government had relied upon to testify were too afraid to come forward and say what they had seen or heard.[139] These reluctant witnesses had heard about Reverend Howard Jones of the First Baptist Church in Chattanooga. After he told Secret Service detectives that he had called the police to report the lynching but found them unwilling to act, his home was set on fire.[140] Following the evidentiary phase of the trial, however, Sanford told observers that he thought he had proved the case against Shipp, some of his deputies, and a handful of members of the lynch mob.[141] He acknowledged that other defendants had not been shown to be guilty beyond a reasonable doubt.[142]

When the trial shifted to Washington for final arguments before the Supreme Court, Attorney General Charles Bonaparte, who had replaced Moody, took it upon himself to offer the government's summation.[143] Charges had been dismissed against seventeen defendants, leaving nine, including Shipp. By the time the Court announced its decision on May 24, 1909, Sanford had left Washington to become the United States district judge for the Middle and Eastern Districts of Tennessee, replacing Judge Clark.

The Supreme Court concluded that the sheriff, fully knowledgeable of the Court's order, nonetheless willfully ignored his duty to protect a prisoner in his care. "Shipp not only made the work of the mob easy, but in effect aided and abetted it."[144] The Court determined that the conspirators "did not attempt to resist the mob, to protect the prisoner, or to identify the persons involved in the mob."[145] Shipp, jailer Jeremiah Gibson, and four members of the lynch mob were found guilty. He and most of his codefendants were sentenced to terms from two to three months in federal prison in Washington, D.C.[146]

When Johnson's attorney, Noah W. Parden, was asked to comment on the Court's action, he declared: "The very rule of law upon which our country was founded and on which the future of this nation rests has been enforced with the might of our highest tribunal. We are at a time when many of our people have abandoned the respect for the rule of law due to the racial hatred deep in their hearts and souls, and nothing less than our civilized society is at stake."[147]

After the *Shipp* verdict, angry citizens set the law offices of defense attorneys Hutchins and Parden ablaze, threw rocks at their homes, and threatened their lives. Both left Chattanooga and never returned.[148] On January 30, 1910, after completing his three-month sentence, Shipp returned to Chattanooga, greeted by a crowd of more than 10,000 people singing "Dixie."[149]

The *Shipp* case took on special significance as the first and only criminal trial conducted by the Supreme Court,[150] acknowledged by many as a source of federal habeas corpus actions in state criminal cases.[151] It stands for the principle that the Supreme Court has the power to intervene in state capital cases when there is an alleged violation of a criminal defendant's right to due process contained in the United States Constitution. Sanford's participation thus found him aligned with federal progressive principles rather than the states' rights view still prevalent in the South.

Sanford's tenure in the Department of Justice "made quite a record for industry and efficiency."[152] "A number of cases pending in the Supreme Court were assigned to him by Solicitor General Hoyt for preparation and argument," and Sanford distinguished himself and "made a very favorable impression upon the Court."[153] Newspapers reported that Attorney General Bonaparte was considering Sanford's promotion from assistant attorney general to assistant to the attorney general, the second highest office in the federal legal branch.[154] However, he never served in the post because he was soon elevated to the district court bench.

In the fall of 1902, President Roosevelt had made a brief visit to Knoxville, stopping by two homes. The first was that of Governor Brownlow's widow,[155] as every president who visited Knoxville while Mrs. Brownlow was alive, from Johnson to Taft, paid his respects to her.[156] The second was the residence of Sanford's father.[157] E.J. was considered a Republican party leader in the state.[158] He had been chosen as chairman of the Tennessee delegation to the 1896 Republican Convention[159] after having been a Tennessee delegate to the GOP National Convention of 1880 and serving as the Tennessee Republican caucus nominee for United States senator in 1895.[160] Roosevelt's visit acknowledged that the Sanfords were a major force in the community and in the East Tennessee region.[161]

Young Sanford, then a practicing attorney in Knoxville, was in the middle of arranging the activities for President Roosevelt's visit.[162] He was a member of the invitation, reception, and entertainment committees; traveled to Chattanooga to meet the presidential train and accompanied the party to Knoxville;[163] rode with Roosevelt on his brief tour of Knoxville; and shared the speakers' platform.[164] During his time in Washington with the Department of Justice, Sanford became much better acquainted with Roosevelt. Indeed, "the President acquired quite a liking for him"[165] and soon rewarded Sanford with an appointment to the federal bench.

 CHAPTER SEVEN

District Judge

The White House
May 14, 1908
To the Senate:

I nominate Edward Sanford, of Tennessee, to be United States district judge for the eastern and middle districts of Tennessee, in place of Charles D. Clark, deceased.

—Theodore Roosevelt

Prior to his time in the Department of Justice, Sanford had expressed interest in becoming an appellate judge. On January 30, 1903, the president of the University of Tennessee, Charles W. Dabney, wrote to President Roosevelt on Sanford's behalf:

> Is there still time to present the claims of a candidate for the position made vacant on the bench of the Sixth [Circuit] by the appointment of Judge Day to the Supreme Court? You will do me a great kindness if you will send me word whether it is worthwhile for us

to make up the case for a very dear friend of mine, a distinguished lawyer of this city.

Let me tell you briefly who the man is. Edward Terry Sanford is a native of Tennessee, thirty-eight years of age, the son of Colonel E.J. Sanford, a lifelong Republican who did more than any other man to hold his party in this section together, and never, as far as I know, asked any recognition for his services. Mr. Sanford is a graduate of the University of Tennessee and of the law department of Harvard University, whose faculty I know, think very highly of him. The dean of the law faculty of Harvard recommended him recently for a law professorship in Washington and Lee University, which he declined. Mr. Sanford is known as one of the ablest and most scholarly lawyers in the South, and will undoubtedly receive the highest endorsement of the Supreme Court of Tennessee, of Judge Lurton, and other eminent jurists in this section. He has been a consistent Republican, but has never sought office. Mr. Sanford and his brother own the Knoxville Journal and Tribune, which is, I believe, the most influential Republican newspaper in the South. President Eliot and the law faculty of Harvard can testify to his scholarship and legal learning. The bar of Tennessee will, I am sure, be a unit in approving the appointment in addition to his high social standing and noble character as a man.[1]

President Roosevelt quickly responded with a disappointing message:

My dear Mr. Dabney:
I should rather doubt if it were possible for me to appoint a Tennessean to that vacancy. If I go outside of Ohio it will be a little difficult to skip Kentucky. At the same time, it is possible I might go to Tennessee. If so, I will let you know. From what you say, Mr. Sanford is exactly the man I should want.[2]

As noted in the letter, the vacancy had arisen when William R. Day was elevated to the Supreme Court. Ultimately, President Roosevelt replaced Day of Ohio with another Ohioan, US Solicitor General John K. Richards.[3]

In mid-March 1908, upon the death of Judge Charles Dickens Clark of Chattanooga, the district judgeship for the Eastern and Middle Districts of Tennessee became vacant.[4] Because the deceased Judge Clark had been a resident of Chattanooga, most decision makers believed that the new appointee should come from elsewhere in the district.[5] United States Supreme Court Justice John Marshall Harlan suggested that Sanford be nominated for the post, the aging justice writing President Roosevelt, "Could you do better than to put in Sanford?"[6]

At the time the vacancy arose, the Tennessee Republican Party was divided into two factions quarreling over the distribution of federal patronage: the forces of First District Congressman Walter P. Brownlow and the rival supporters of Second District Congressman Nathan W. Hale of Knoxville and Newell Sanders of Chattanooga. The Hale-Sanders wing had ousted Brownlow from control in 1906, when Sanders replaced Brownlow as chairman of the state GOP Executive Committee.[7] This faction now enjoyed superior influence with the president. Sanford was allied with the Hale-Sanders group mainly because he had been defeated by Brownlow's candidate in his unsuccessful attempt to win the Republican nomination for governor in 1904. However, Sanford's good nature and low-partisan profile enabled him to maintain relatively amicable relations with both factions.[8] Further, Brownlow, who had previously urged the appointment of Sanford to a vacant federal judgeship,[9] had been supported by Sanford's father.[10] Sanford, therefore, had the right geographical and political credentials for the job.

Correspondence from William H. Taft, then in Roosevelt's War Department, to Judge Horace Lurton acknowledged "the warring elements with respect to this nomination, for which the aspirants are myriad."[11] In March 1908, Taft related to Lurton: "I don't know about Sanford at all. He seems a very excellent man, and professes to be strongly for me, and I suppose he is. . . ."[12] The following month, however, Taft observed to Lurton that "H.B. Lindsay of Knoxville, ha[d] been recommended" to him "as an excellent candidate for judge to fill Clark's vacancy."[13]

William Rule, a lifelong friend of the Sanford family, once again visited with President Roosevelt to advocate for Sanford. Roosevelt appeared convinced that Sanford should be the appointee but indicated that he desired to discuss the matter with Newell Sanders before reaching a final decision.[14] When Sanders arrived at the White House, Roosevelt gushed: "Well Mr. Sanders, I have just about made up my mind to appoint Mr. Sanford: He is rich; is a graduate of Harvard; has made a most enviable record in the Department of Justice; and I think I'll just appoint him."[15] Fowler's version of the story had the president telling Sanders: "Well, I have reached the conclusion that I will appoint Sanford judge and Fowler asst. attorney general; and Sanders says, 'Well, go ahead and do it.'"[16] William Frierson, a former mayor of Chattanooga, recalled that he was in a delegation of lawyers who called upon Roosevelt to urge the appointment of another Tennessean. The president finally said to them: "I tell you, gentlemen, the man I want to appoint is Ed Sanford, but he won't take it."[17]

Indeed, despite having initially stated that he would like to have the position, Sanford was unwilling to accept the appointment.[18] A Washington newspaper reporter on May 14, 1908, noted that Roosevelt "had offered the judgeship to Mr. Sanford six or seven weeks ago, but the offer was declined."[19] Sanford had decided that he would prefer to stay in Washington[20] because both he and Lutie were pleased with Washington's cultural, intellectual, and social environment. Upon reflection, Sanford, then forty-three years old, had become somewhat uncomfortable with the prospect of what he considered to be the associated isolation of a judge, a condition that he felt would impinge on friendships from which he derived so much satisfaction.[21] Further, he was more content in the practice of law on the appellate level.[22] In an address he gave in later years to the Nashville Bar Association, Sanford related:

> I did not want to go on the bench, for I loved the profession of the lawyer. I remember that one of the saddest days of my whole life was when I made my last argument before the Supreme Court in Washington when I knew that I would never have again that most delightful of intellectual exercises. I love it [the practice of law] still and hope that I shall always be called a lawyer, in a profession that defends the weak and gives justice among men.[23]

Additionally, Sanford was interested in being appointed solicitor general. According to William Frierson, Sanford "had come to think that, for a lawyer of his age, the position of all positions was that of Solicitor General, and entertained the hope that, if he remained in the Department of Justice, that office might, in time, be his."²⁴ Over a decade later, Sanford congratulated Frierson on his attainment of the solicitor general position, writing as follows: "As I view it, the office of Solicitor General is the finest and most desirable office that a practicing lawyer can hold in the entire Government service. I can think of no privilege more highly to be valued by a lawyer than that of appearing as the chief representative of the Government in the argument of cases before the Supreme Court of the United States."²⁵

Fowler, with the backing of Hale and Sanders, was also under consideration for the judicial position, although he made his availability contingent on Sanford's declining the post.²⁶ Sanford even accompanied Fowler on a visit to the White House in an effort to persuade the president to appoint his former law partner to the judgeship.²⁷ According to Fowler, Sanford agreed to accompany him to visit with the president because Roosevelt would not appoint someone that he had not seen first. Fowler traveled to Washington and was introduced to Roosevelt.²⁸ When Fowler's name appeared as a candidate for the judgeship, however, organized labor attempted to block his appointment because of Fowler's prosecution of the Coal Creek miners involved in the 1891–92 rebellion.²⁹

Despite Sanford's proposal of an alternative candidate, the "Rough Rider" persuaded Sanford to take the post. The president announced that Sanford, following seventeen months with the Department of Justice, was appointed "United States Judge for the middle and eastern districts of Tennessee."³⁰ When Sanford finally accepted the nomination, it "settle[d] a somewhat troublesome proposition for the President" as "[w]ith twenty or thirty candidates for the judgeship, some republicans and some democrats, the President was having his hands full in deciding what to do."³¹

Before Sanford left Washington, then-Associate Justice Edward D. White told him that the district judgeship "in some respects was the most important in the Federal Judiciary System, that there the first and real hearing of a case was had, and upon that hearing depended very largely whether justice would be administered in the cause."³² White, elevated to chief justice by President Taft in 1910,³³ also predicted that Sanford would someday return to Washington as a Supreme Court appointee.³⁴ Future justice James C. McReynolds, at this time in private practice in New York, wrote in a telegram: "Accept my felicitations and sincere good wishes. The District will surely have a judge of high ideals and I hope you will find great satisfaction in the new work."³⁵

Sixth Circuit Judge Horace Lurton administered Sanford's oath as a district judge in Nashville.[36] Lurton read Moses' instructions to the judges:

> And I charged your judges at that time, saying, Hear the causes between your brethren, and judge righteously between every man and his brother, and the stranger that is with him.
>
> Ye shall not respect persons in judgment; but ye shall hear the small as well as the great; ye shall not be afraid of the face of man; for the judgment is God's: and the cause that is too hard for you, bring it unto me, and I will hear it.[37]

According to Sanford, this was "[a]n oath that just burns itself into the conscience of every man who sits upon the bench."[38]

In a letter congratulating Sanford on his promotion to the federal bench, Lurton stated: "Having admitted you to the bar through the severest examination any man ever went through, I now welcome you to the judiciary."[39] Lurton further noted: "I have always held you in high esteem as a lawyer, a gentleman and a friend and it is not necessary for me to assure you of my very warm feeling toward you and my pleasure in receiving you into the ranks of the judiciary. I hope this will be the beginning of a long judicial career and that you have not been so long in politics as to be unable to give yourself entirely to the work of the courts."[40]

Upon assuming the district court bench, Sanford inherited a full docket and found it impossible to work quickly enough to decrease his caseload. By January 15, 1909, a letter from Sanford was submitted to the House of Representatives in support of a bill to change the time of the terms of court in his districts. According to Sanford, the changes would "greatly facilitate the due and orderly dispatch of the work of these courts."[41] Sanford observed:

> Under the present arrangement the first spring term commences in Knoxville on the first Monday in March and the last at Greeneville on the first Monday in June, with both the Chattanooga and Nashville terms between; while the first fall term commences at Knoxville on the second Monday in September and the last at Chattanooga on the first Monday in December, with both the Nashville and Greene-

ville terms between. This puts all of the spring terms practically in the three months of March, April, and May and the early part of June, and all of the fall terms practically in the four months of September, October, November and December, leaving no term whatever in July, August, and the greater part of June in the summer."[42]

Sanford noted that this schedule denied him the chance to promptly decide the matters "while clear in the memory" and required that they frequently be postponed until after the ends of the terms held elsewhere.[43] He observed that the fall term at Knoxville "is especially inconvenient, being held in September, which is the hottest, and, I think, the most trying month of the year in this section, and also commencing on the same date that the [Tennessee] Supreme Court begins its sessions there, thus making it very inconvenient for the attorneys, who are just returning from their vacations and have considerable office work on hand, as well as the preparation of cases for hearing in the Supreme Court."[44]

Sanford was an assiduous researcher who paid careful attention to details and preferred ample time for contemplation and reflection.[45] These characteristics contributed to one of the few criticisms of him: his deliberative personality resulted in his often being too slow in rendering a decision.[46] Initially overwhelmed by the workload, he started seeking an appellate court appointment soon after becoming a district court judge.[47] Just as he had preferred appellate work as an attorney, Sanford thought that the appellate courts would better suit him as a judge.[48] As noted by Fowler, Sanford "was anxious for an appointment to an Appellate Court" because "he disliked the necessity of imposing punishment upon the many tried and convicted before him," as well as "the necessity of ruling immediately upon the many questions arising in the progress of a trial." Sanford "preferred to give mature consideration to every question that he had to pass upon."[49] Sanford had long desired an appointment to the Sixth Circuit.[50] Three vacancies occurred on that court after he came a district judge, and his "name was presented by his friends to the President in connection with the appointment to fill each vacancy."[51] When Judge Lurton was elevated to the Supreme Court and his chair on the Sixth Circuit became open, a reporter with *The Cincinnati Enquirer* related, "The entire Bristol [Tennessee] bar to-day joined in a telegram to President Taft urging him to name Judge Edward T. Sanford, of Knoxville, to succeed Judge Horace H. Lurton as Judge of the United States Court of

Appeals."⁵² A 1910 *New York Tribune* reporter noted that "[t]he friends of Judge E.T. Sanford are making almost daily calls on the President to urge his appointment to the vacancy in the 6th Circuit. Senators [Robert Love] Taylor and [James Beriah] Frazier, accompanied by the entire delegation from Tennessee, called in the interests of Judge Sanford this morning."⁵³ Another journalist related: "The Tennessee democrats have united with the republicans in asking that the vacancy be given to Judge Sanford, who stands high throughout the state."⁵⁴ As Fowler had observed, however, "Tennessee had already had far more than its quota of Circuit Judges.... Baxter, Jackson and Lurton ... had been appointed in succession...."⁵⁵

Sanford also considered a seat on the Court of Customs Appeals in 1909. An article in the *Utica Herald-Dispatch* of November 4, 1909, reveals this interest:

> Edward T. Sanford and James A. Fowler, the first being a former assistant attorney general, and the latter his successor in the same office, are being mentioned as probable appointees as members of the proposed Customs Court of Appeals. In their work at the Department of Justice each became familiar with customs matters because all legal questions arising in that branch of the treasury service were referred to them for decision. It is understood that the President is favorably impressed with their qualifications for membership in the new court.⁵⁶

After giving the matter more thought, Sanford decided not to pursue the post.⁵⁷ He told Secretary of War Jacob Dickinson, a fellow Tennessean and former ABA president, that he could not "with any feeling of permanent satisfaction, give up my present position, with its opportunities of formative and constructive work in the development of the law, and of aiding in the general administration of justice as it affects the life of the community in vital matters, for a field of work which would be practically narrowed to the construction and enforcement of a single revenue act."⁵⁸ Lurton later responded to this news: "I received with much pleasure your letter stating that you had concluded not to apply for appointment on the Customs Court. I have many reasons for believing that you would have received the appointment, but I think you would have made the greatest mistake of your life, and I am heartily delighted on your account, as well as my own, that you have concluded to give up the aspiration."[59]

Part of the reason for Sanford's large workload and his resulting desire to leave the district court bench was the extent of his districts. According to the 1910 Census, the total population of the two large judicial districts was just over 1.5 million. The districts together embraced seventy-four counties of the then ninety-six in the state. Of the largest cities in Tennessee, only Memphis was not in his districts.[60]

The Judiciary Act of 1789 created the basic organizational structure of the federal judiciary.[61] It divided the nation into thirteen districts, for which district court judgeships were created. The court Sanford joined in 1908 had originally encompassed the entire State of Tennessee. It was established in 1797, less than one year after Tennessee became a state on June 1, 1796. One judge was authorized to hold court, having both district and circuit court jurisdiction, alternatively at Nashville and Knoxville. Congress provided for four court terms per year—two in Nashville and two in Knoxville.[62] In 1802, the Tennessee District was divided into the Eastern and Western Districts, with the same judge presiding over both districts. The Middle District was created in 1839, but the three districts continued to be presided over by one judge. In 1878, a second judgeship was created, encompassing only the Western District.

Pursuant to the Judiciary Act, district courts exercised original jurisdiction over admiralty and maritime cases, as well as some minor civil and criminal cases. Circuit courts served as trial courts for "most criminal cases, for suits between citizens of different states (diversity cases), and for civil suits initiated by the United States." Accordingly, some decisions from Sanford designate the trial court as "Circuit Court, M.D. Tennessee" (or "E.D. Tennessee"), while others state "District Court, E.D. Tennessee" (or "M.D. Tennessee"). Circuit courts also "exercised appellate jurisdiction over all but the smallest admiralty cases and other civil suits that originated in the US district court."[63] In order to exercise this appellate jurisdiction, however, a Supreme Court justice was required to preside over the proceedings.[64] The appointed district judge would sit with a Supreme Court justice to constitute the circuit court for the district.[65] In 1869, Congress created separate circuit court judgeships for each of the circuits. These new judges, unlike the district court judges in the circuit, were authorized to conduct appellate business with the district judge in the absence of a Supreme Court justice.

In 1891, with the creation of the modern courts of appeals, the circuit courts were stripped of their appellate jurisdiction.[66] They retained their original jurisdiction and served as trial courts for certain federal cases. In January 1912, the circuit courts were abolished.[67] Throughout these changes, the courts of the Middle and Eastern Districts of Tennessee continued to be served by one district judge until 1922, around the time Sanford prepared to leave for the Supreme Court, when Congress authorized a judgeship exclusively for the Middle District.[68]

Sanford served as district judge of the Eastern District of Tennessee and Middle District of Tennessee from 1908 to 1923.[69] For fifteen years, he sat regularly at Greeneville, Knoxville, Nashville, and Chattanooga.[70] Sessions were also held in Cookeville.[71] The work was described as "arduous and exacting," but it was "performed with diligence and ability."[72] Sanford also was called periodically to Cincinnati to sit with the United States Sixth Circuit Court of Appeals.[73] The chief judge of a circuit is permitted to designate and assign a district judge to sit on the court of appeals "whenever the business of that court so requires."[74] When sitting with judges of higher rank, however, Sanford reached his own decisions and did not allow himself to be unduly influenced by the thinking of the other members of the panel.[75]

As district judge, Sanford was entitled to clerical help. The stenographic clerk of Sanford's day performed mostly clerical tasks, including typing and paying personal bills. The position differed significantly from that of the modern law clerk, whose duties focus mainly on legal research and drafting of judicial opinions. The first stenographer Sanford hired was Ashton Fox Embry,[76] a 1906 graduate of the Tampa Business College. Embry left a position at the Department of Justice in Washington, D.C., to accept the post with the newly appointed federal judge in 1908.[77] Embry accompanied Sanford "whenever necessary in terms of court at various cities."[78] Originally from Hopkinsville, Kentucky, Embry seemed to appreciate the time with Sanford, informing a friend that he "like[d] the change [to working for Sanford] very much."[79] He did not find pleasant, however, the criminal cases heard by Sanford. "The Judge and I have just returned from Greeneville, where he held court for four days last week. Most of the cases were criminal, illicit distilling and so forth, and the defendants presented on the whole a pitiable spectacle, ignorant, low-browed cusses, who undoubtedly will be better off in jail than at large."[80] By October 1909, Embry had returned to employment as a stenographer with Solicitor General Frederick W. Lehmann in Washington, D.C. A few years later, Embry, a 1912 graduate of National University Law School, became US Supreme Court Justice Joseph McKenna's sole stenographic clerk.[81]

On the district bench, Sanford left an impeccable record and gained a reputation as a lenient, thorough, and impartial judge.[82] If the testimony of those who knew Sanford as a federal district judge can be accepted, he possessed many of the characteristics of an ideal judge.[83] He was "open-minded" and "scrupulously fair"; at times he even reversed his own decisions.[84]

Sanford was uncompromising in the standards he set for himself. He was industrious and meticulous in the performance of his duties. He intensely researched the law applicable to cases before him and kept abreast of new legal developments.[85] He annotated the Supreme Court and Federal Court reports and prepared a book containing his opinions in bankruptcy matters. These materials were arranged in alphabetical subject matter order.[86] Sanford was highly driven and nervously energetic. His secretary of fourteen years, A.C. Dore, stated:

> He was a man of highly nervous temperament, and the moment he started dictating he arose to his feet and started walking around the office, always smoking. He smoked cigars of a small size that could be consumed during a five or ten minute recess of court, but during the latter part of his tenure as District Judge, he got to smoking my cigarettes, which he always borrowed by the fives and tens, and would light one from the other.
>
> In my fourteen years' association with Judge Sanford while he was United States District Judge, I think his outstanding characteristic was his intense interest in his work as District Judge, and his untiring efforts in the investigation of the law applicable to cases before him for decision, together with a desire to have his written opinions as nearly perfect as possible in the way of correct diction and punctuation.
>
> This latter habit of attempting to secure perfection in diction often led him to change again and again his way of stating a proposition, which of course made endless work for me as his secretary. While always working intensely and nervously, and at times abrupt in his manner, when he would finish his work he would always have some complimentary remark to make. Sometimes he jokingly called me "the fastest secretary he had ever seen, but not morally fast."

> He was very orderly and systematic in the office, and kept close check on everything that came under his supervision.[87]

Sanford's opinions were described as "brief and pithy, easily read and understood. His sentences [were] short, sometimes beginning with 'and' and 'nor' that punctuation may not break the sequence of ideas or continuity of thought."[88] In preparing opinions, Sanford sought a flawless product.[89] It was common knowledge among the lawyers who practiced before him that Sanford "was never satisfied with his opinions until he got them exactly the way he wanted them and that he would tear up and rewrite them time and time again, as long as any word or phrase did not convey the precise shade of meaning he intended it to convey."[90] Occasionally, he would become so dissatisfied that he would utter profane language.[91]

Likewise, "[i]n the drawing up of legal documents [to be presented to him,] Sanford was most exacting in his requirements." A member of the Greeneville Bar observed that Sanford once requested an attorney to revise a document five times before it was accepted.[92] He was "never stampeded into hasty action."[93]

According to James Fowler, Sanford would not permit a case to pass through his court without the most careful consideration:

> He was just as careful in trying and disposing of an accusation against the most humble mountaineer as in considering the most important litigation pending in his court. Never did a Judge have a keener sense of Justice, or was inspired with a greater determination to see that equal and exact justice was administered to everyone. If he deviated in any respect from that cause, it was on the side of mercy towards the many poor defendants who were arraigned before him. Anyone entering a court room where he was presiding at once realized that he was in the presence of one who represented the dignity and power of the United States Government.[94]

Fowler further described Sanford's management of his courtroom:

> In the trial of a cause he would permit no wrangling between counsel, and required the trial to proceed in a dignified and orderly way. He

was always alert to the proceedings before him, and kept along with the course of the testimony. From time to time he would propound questions to both counsel and witnesses, so as to direct the proceedings to the real points in controversy and eliminate unimportant issues. If he saw that counsel either purposely or by oversight failed to elicit from a witness material facts he apparently knew, he did not hesitate to question the witness himself upon the subject evaded. He always ruled promptly upon objections to testimony. But if during the progress of a trial he concluded that he had ruled improperly, on his own motion he would reverse his ruling. He would not permit himself to be influenced by pride of opinion, and gave the most careful consideration to arguments of counsel.[95]

Tennessee attorney Charles N. Burch noted that he had "never known a Judge to display the patience which [Sanford] did or to indicate a greater desire to arrive at the exact truth of a controversy."[96] A Knoxville lawyer, John W. Green, further recalled that Sanford was "[a]lways patient, courteous, and impartial, [and that] it was a delight to try lawsuits before him."[97]

As a district court judge, Sanford was known for his consideration and compassion for people:

> [H]e was gentle and courteous but firm. . . . It was not his way to be theatrical or dogmatic. The atmosphere of his court was orderly and even grave. . . . Attorneys who practiced in his court seem to have agreed that he was the most impartial judge in the South. It was no easy matter for employers to secure injunctions from him in labor disputes, and despite the fact that he was born and reared in wealth, he had a deep appreciation of the struggles of those who labored for a living as well as for unfortunate persons brought before him. Sanford's voice was full and firm but he never used harsh or overbearing language in his courtroom.[98]

Sanford's decisions were often lenient and always sympathetic.[99] Sanford "gave no preferential treatment to the influential, privileged, and wealthy. In fact, he held them to a higher standard than the disadvantaged, poor, and weak."

He was "a friend of the mountain men who had violated the law."[100] In 1930, a newspaper reporter recalled Sanford's exchange with a poor mountain boy charged with working a moonshine still. After the youth's attorney entered a guilty plea, Sanford began to deliver the sentence. During the explanation of the charge, the boy declared, "I am not guilty of that." "How is that?" inquired Sanford. "Why, I'm just not guilty," the lad stated. Sanford turned to the lawyer and inquired, "How is this? Your client says that he is not guilty, yet you are offering to plead guilty." The attorney responded, "Your honor, he is ignorant and doesn't understand." Sanford replied, "That doesn't make any difference. Ignorant or not, he says that he is not guilty; and I am not going to sentence any man who says that he is not guilty without giving him a trial." Another lawyer in attendance was appointed to represent the youth. At the trial, the boy was acquitted.[101]

Described as "intensely human," Sanford showed compassion for the "frailties of human nature and tempered justice with mercy."[102] He would postpone execution of a sentence if the prisoner's wife was sick or expecting a child.[103] One such case involved Mansfield Herring, a moonshiner, who was allowed to return home to care for his sick wife on the promise to return at a later date. Herring reported at the designated time, and Sanford, in appreciation for the man's honesty, shortened to three months what would have been a year in the penitentiary.[104] Sometimes he decreased sentences to time served so that a violator might accept an offer of employment.[105] He many times delayed or removed a sentence so that the defendant could return home and make a crop.[106]

One humorous example of Sanford's leniency was related by Sanford's secretary:

> His tender regard for women and children was well known throughout both districts; and if a defendant's wife with one or two or more children got in his private office to beg for her husband's liberty, she was pretty sure to get a reduction in the sentence, and quite often would take her husband home with her. In one case tried by him at Nashville, the defendant, a broker, was charged with using the mails to defraud, and during the trial, which lasted several days, his wife sat by him in the court room. A jury found him guilty. After hearing a motion for a new trial, Judge Sanford imposed a sentence of eighteen months in the Atlanta penitentiary. He had barely got

the words out of his mouth when the defendant's wife fainted in the court room. Judge Sanford was very pale and shocked. A physician was called, who reported that she had heart trouble, and had had it for some time. She would rally in a few minutes, and Judge Sanford would tell the marshal to tell her that he had taken three months off the sentence. Then she would faint again and Judge Sanford was afraid the shock might prove fatal. On the way to lunch, the Judge told me to tell the marshal to advise her he had taken another three months off the sentence. The next morning the Judge called me at home, and said he had taken off all the sentence, and let the man go on a fine. I agreed with him that was the best thing to do.[107]

A 1923 article gave a comprehensive description of Sanford as a district judge:

> There is about him, on the bench, an impressive dignity. Federal courts usually give an air of sternness, from the judge's robes, the unhurried proceedings, the quaint forms. But under Judge Sanford this has been crowned with a sense of poise and detachment. As presiding officer of the court he offers a picture worthy [of] the pencil of an artist. There is none of the lackadaisical inattention to proceedings too frequently noticed. The Judge sits easily, listening alertly to testimony or argument. He guards the rights of defendants scrupulously, no matter what public sentiment on the case is. He conforms to the quaint old injunction to judges to "administer equal and indifferent justice to all," indifferent being used in the sense of impartial.
>
> Even a casual visitor to his court is impressed with the atmosphere of solemnity; it isn't an air of mourning, nor of grief, but you feel that grave things are under consideration, which are requiring the full thought of the judge, and the jury, the lawyers, and the witnesses, so that the United States of America will not be offended against, and so the Nation will not commit an injustice against the defendant. Judge Sanford is far from pompous. He has the natural courtesy and gentility of one to the manor born. His accents are full and firm, but

neither harsh nor overbearing. He is conscious that in him is vested the judicial power of the Nation; and is properly determined that proper respect and gravity shall be observed.

His character is a positive rather than a negative one. He is a liberal rather than a conservative.... His sympathies are keen for the sufferings of men. He feels the woes of the offenders who are brought before [him] very deeply. He has a humanity, and a love for men and women, which more than counterbalance any capitalistic environment.

One of his intense interests is Americanism.... He feels the rights of free speech, free press, free assemblage, with the other parts of fundamental law....

Open-mindedness is one of Judge Sanford's distinguishing characteristics. He does not prejudge his cases. He listens to the evidence, and then makes up his mind from what has been presented. His desire to be scrupulously fair is always patent. He is not hasty at decisions; he is not stampeded or bullied, or the victim of sudden emotionalism.[108]

Partisan politics had little effect on the decisions Sanford made. A newspaper editor in Chattanooga acknowledged that fact in an editorial: "Judge Sanford used to be a Republican before he went on the bench, and he may still vote the Republican ticket—perhaps does in national elections—but there are very few people who know what his politics is. He has a more sensitive appreciation of the nonpartisan functions of the judiciary than most men occupying judicial positions...."[109] Although Sanford had been "rocked in a Republican cradle and ha[d] remained steadfast in that political faith," he exhibited no partisan behavior on the bench. There were never any accusations of political bias in his many judicial decisions or in the appointments that he made while he was a district judge.[110]

According to Fowler, "Sanford was the greatest stickler about ethical conduct of all the Judges I have known."[111] In a 1974 interview, Sanford's nephews described him as a "very strait-laced individual, perhaps super idealistic" and as "highly ethical, [a man] who lived strictly within the law."[112] The nephews noted that during Prohibition, bootleggers visiting the home of Sanford's brother Hugh entered by the back door to avoid possibly running into Sanford.[113] Upon the adoption of Prohibition, Sanford completely stopped drinking alcohol and would not knowingly attend gatherings at which alcohol was served.[114]

When confronted with possible conflicts of interest, Sanford rigidly pursued the policy of recusing himself if an obvious direct connection with a party revealed itself. He would decline to sit on cases in which he was related to one of the litigants or was a stockholder in a corporate party to the suit. He would not sit on cases with parties represented by his former firm. Generally, if any question regarding his impartiality arose, he recused himself.[115] Unlike his father, he avoided conflicts of interest, removing himself from any circumstance in which it might be perceived that he had a concern.

Sanford further had a rule of never discussing cases with lawyers; to avoid allegations of partiality, he curtailed most social contact with other members of the bar.[116] Upon leaving the district court bench, he remarked, "It is one of the penalties—and a great penalty—of the judicial life, that it is so largely an isolated life; and to one who loves his fellow men, it is a great deprivation that his work from day to day, has to be done in solitude, and alone, out of touch, in a large measure."[117] Sanford's comments throughout his time on the bench reveal that his judicial career brought him loneliness and isolation.[118]

Some observers considered Sanford to be somewhat liberal. "Judge Sanford was in sympathy with the enforcement of moral and social legislation, and if not a thorough-going liberal, at least he may be classified as a liberal conservative. Perhaps he might be better characterized as a conservative with progressive tendencies."[119] A liberal editor and historian observed that "as a judge [Sanford] has been both progressive and conservative; he aims to keep abreast of the times and the changing conditions of society, but desires to do so without losing hold on fundamentals."[120] Philosophically, he leaned toward a restricted use of judicial power. He preferred generally to narrowly interpret statutes and to defer to regulatory authorities.[121] Where legislation was obviously remedial and humanitarian in nature, Sanford appeared to have been more generous in his interpretation of congressional intent.[122]

The district court decision in *Cumberland Telephone and Telegraph Co. v. Railroad and Public Utilities Commission of Tennessee* reflects Sanford's judicial mindset.[123] In that case, the state was attempting to make the company provide a valuation of its property for rate-fixing purposes. The company sought an injunction, which would have prevented the state from gaining the information, on the grounds that such disclosure amounted to a taking of property without due process. In a liberal-leaning move, Sanford refused to grant the injunction because he believed that the state should have considerable authority to regulate private property in the public interest.

In another telephone company case, *Postal Cable Telegraph Company v. Cumberland Telephone and Telegraph Company*,[124] Sanford demonstrated his progressive tendencies by enforcing equality of access to relatively new communications technology. The telephone company refused to furnish telephones to Postal for the same rate charged to other subscribers. Postal was also required to pay fifteen percent of the tolls taken in on telegram messages received over the telephone and two cents on messages delivered by the telegraph company over the telephone. When Postal refused to pay the commission and the two cents per message, Cumberland began removing the telephones from the telegraph offices, and Postal sought an injunction. Sanford sustained the contention of the telegraph company, holding that the rates chargeable by the telephone company depended on the character of the service rendered, not on the value of the service to the customer. Sanford found that Postal was entitled to telephone service at the same rate charged to other business subscribers. The telephone company was enjoined from removing the telephones or otherwise depriving Postal of telephone service.[125]

In a matter attracting national attention, Sanford's courtroom was the scene for *United States v. Forty Barrels and Twenty Kegs of Coca-Cola*,[126] the second lawsuit brought under the Pure Food and Drug Act. Coca-Cola was invented in May 1886 by John Styth Pemberton, originally as a patent medicine. It evolved from an earlier Pemberton proprietary, French Wine of Coca.[127] The beverage was a blend of two stimulants: the kola nuts provided caffeine, and cocaine was derived from the coca leaves. The drink was originally billed as a cure for numerous ailments, including morphine addiction and impotence.[128] By June 1886, several drugstores in Atlanta, Georgia, featured the new Coca-Cola, hailed as an "Intellectual Beverage and Temperance Drink." Packaged in recycled beer bottles, the syrup sold at soda counters for 25 cents.[129] Despite the image of Coca-Cola as a temperance drink, however, over time it became known as "coke," "dope," "cold dope," and a "shot in the arm."[130] By 1904, the pure coca leaf extract (containing an estimated nine milligrams of cocaine per glass) was replaced by "spent" leaves with the cocaine content removed. The remaining stimulant came from the caffeine provided by the kola nuts, amounting to 46 milligrams of caffeine per twelve fluid ounces of Coca-Cola.[131]

During this time period, powerful, impersonal corporations were incurring the public's wrath. Upton Sinclair's *The Jungle* had been published in February 1906, revealing the revolting conditions in Chicago's meat-packing houses. When the Pure Food and Drug Act was passed in June 1906, Coca-Cola became a target.[132] The chief chemist with the government, Harvey Washington Wiley, contended that because children were the greatest consumers of Coca-Cola, they needed special protection from the negative effects of caffeine.[133] According to Wiley, "no more serious menace" existed "to the health of children ... than drinking caffeine in soft drinks."[134] Wiley believed that the caffeine in soft drinks also posed "a great danger to the public."[135] He termed caffeine a poison "exactly similar in its chemical relations to strychnine and morphia."[136]

On October 20, 1909, Coca-Cola syrup was seized by federal officers in Chattanooga after it crossed the state line from Georgia, and specimens were sent to the Bureau of Chemistry, the forerunner of the Food and Drug Administration, for analysis.[137] In 1911, the United States brought two criminal charges against the Coca-Cola Company: misbranding and adulteration of the product by adding caffeine.[138] According to the Pure Food and Drug Act, a product was adulterated if it had a deleterious added ingredient. The government, therefore, sought to prove that caffeine was both harmful and an "added" ingredient under the law. Ironically, the government charged that Coca-Cola was misbranded because it did not, in fact, have the whole coca leaf in it (i.e., cocaine was removed), and it had only an infinitesimal amount of kola nut.[139] Although the beverage did not contain coca or cola, the Coca-Cola Company contended that it did include "certain elements or substances derived from coca leaves and cola nuts." The company asserted that the "small portion of caffeine" in the drink was an ingredient in the recipe and not an adulterant.[140]

The matter was tried in Chattanooga, home to a major Coca-Cola bottling facility.[141] The trial explored whether Coca-Cola was "detrimental and menacing to the health of those who use it." The government's case was premised on several issues:

> whether the caffeine in the drink was "poisonous" or "deleterious" and might prove "injurious to health"; whether the beverage was stained to conceal inferiority of the product; whether or not substances such

as "coca" and "cola" were known by their particular names, and if the design of the packaging actually represented the essence of "coca" and "cola," which were derived from kola nuts and coca leaves found in the product; whether or not Coca-Cola imitated other products or was sold under another name; and if the name "Coca-Cola," the "distinctive name of the product," maintained the same formula which the company had known and sold for twenty years.[142]

The lawsuit additionally examined the conditions in the bottling facility in Atlanta where the seized product had been produced.[143]

The government had hoped to use as its star witness George R. Stuart, a Methodist evangelist who had observed "dope" use at soda fountains. Stuart claimed that Coca-Cola "kept boys awake" and "tempt[ed] them with the evils of masturbation" and that "excessive use of Coca-Cola at a girls' school [had] led to wild nocturnal freaks ... and ... immoralities."[144] Those seeking entertaining testimony were disappointed, however, when the prosecution had to withdraw Stuart in the face of defense objections.[145] The trial proceeded with more mundane testimony.

Sanford issued his opinion from the bench, directing a verdict in favor of Coca-Cola. He ruled that the product was not misbranded because it did contain coca and cola, even though in small amounts. He concluded that whether the product contained coca leaves was immaterial. According to Sanford, under the Pure Food and Drug Act, a compound shall not be deemed to be misbranded if it is "known as an article of food under its own distinctive name," it is "not an imitation of or offered for sale under the distinctive name of another article," it is "properly labeled with the place of manufacture," and it "does not contain[] any added poisonous or deleterious ingredients."[146] Without deciding whether caffeine was a poison, Sanford said that it was not an added ingredient under the law but had been an integral part of the formula since the drink was invented.[147] He observed "that the caffeine ... in ... 'Coca Cola' is one of its regular, habitual and essential constituents and that without its presence ... the product would lack one of its essential elements and fail to produce upon the consumers a characteristic if not the most characteristic effect which is obtained from its use. In short Coca-Cola without caffeine would not be Coca-Cola...."[148] Despite his long family connection to patent medications, Sanford apparently felt no need to recuse himself from this matter.

The Atlanta Constitution declared that "[t]he Coca-Cola case has been one of the most important ever heard in the federal courts of the south, and the cost of the litigation has been enormous. Both sides have had experts from all sections of the country, the most eminent scientists. . . . The government has spared no expense in the effort to prove its contentions, and the Coca-Cola people have been equally liberal in securing expert testimony." Exposing the still-sensitive feelings of Southerners, the newspaper's editorial board later asserted that the government "disregards the man-slaying whisky whose manufacture and sale it licenses" yet "picks out the producers of a southern soda fountain drink for persecution in a way that might have blasted their reputations, had they not been men of unassailable integrity in their own community."[149]

On June 13, 1914, the Sixth Circuit affirmed Sanford's ruling,[150] but on May 22, 1916, the United States Supreme Court overturned it, in an opinion by Justice Charles Evans Hughes.[151] In his last opinion before leaving the Supreme Court to run for president against Woodrow Wilson,[152] Hughes ruled that the word "Coca-Cola" was not a distinctive name but simply the conjunction of two common words. He also ruled that caffeine was indeed an added ingredient and remanded the case for a retrial to determine whether the caffeine in the product was harmful.[153] The case was settled out of court on November 12, 1917, after the Coca-Cola Company, on its own initiative, changed its formula, thus reducing the amount of caffeine by half.[154] Having taken this step, Coca-Cola asserted to the district court that retrying the case would not be warranted. Sanford and the government attorneys agreed on the condition that Coca-Cola forfeit all claims to the product seized and pay all the court costs.[155]

Another interesting case over which Sanford presided while a district court judge involved Callie D. House and the National Ex-Slave Mutual Relief, Bounty and Pension Association. House, a black laundress from Nashville, Tennessee, became the leader of a poor people's movement seeking pensions from the federal government as compensation for slavery.[156] The seat of the activities of the association, organized in 1894, was Nashville.[157] The group collected dues and solicited contributions to support its efforts. It "issued literature, held annual meetings, prepared lists of ex-slaves, and lobbied in Washington for passage of pension bills."[158] A Senate report dated January 16, 1900, noted that "[t]he charge for charters for local associations is $2.50 each, for membership certificates 25 cents each, and each member agrees to pay 10 cents per month to the local association to aid the movement."[159] The federal government kept the organization under tight surveillance for several years.[160] Based upon investigations by the Department of Interior's Bureau of Pensions, a Senate report speculated that "almost $100,000.00 had been taken from the poor."[161] In May 1916, House was indicted in the United States District Court for the Middle District of Tennessee.[162] She was charged, along with other alleged black co-conspirators, with violating the postal laws of the United States by obtaining money through the mails from a number of ex-slaves "by means of false and fraudulent pretenses."[163]

To prove conspiracy, it was necessary to show that at least one co-conspirator had committed one overt act in furtherance of the conspiracy. The indictment charged that House had mailed a letter on December 21, 1914, from Nashville to a black woman, Alice Williams, at the Hotel Imperial in Knoxville, containing a printed circular announcing the results of the association's November national meeting.[164] The circular, containing an eagle in the upper left-hand corner, as did all the association's literature, said nothing about forthcoming pension payments, but it did "indicate the national convention was represented from every section of the government by delegates and many proxies."[165] This statement was interpreted by the government as a promise or guarantee of a pension or a false assertion that Congress had passed the pension law.

When the case came to trial in 1917, the media interest was high.[166] Sanford "seemed to believe that [House] was puzzled about the actual stages of congressional action." Since House denied any guilt, Sanford "rejected the attorneys' statements that [House] wished to plead guilty and ordered her placed on trial."[167] For three days, Sanford heard testimony from federal agents and from blacks from "every section of the South."[168]

In her book on the case, historian Mary Berry opined that Sanford "gloried in being called the most impartial judge in the South" and "saw himself as a benevolent judge who overtly tried to act with scrupulous fairness no matter the status of the client." According to Berry, in the government's eagerness to convict House, it "did not reckon on her independence or Judge Sanford's predilections." Recalling Sanford's Department of Justice role in *United States v. Shipp,* Berry noted that "Sanford was certainly not a civil rights activist, but he opposed lynching and demonstrated as a prosecutor a conscious interest in avoiding racial bias."[169] A 1909 article in *The Tennessean* confirms Sanford's unbiased approach to his role as a judge: "The visitor to the federal court notes with a feeling of satisfaction that its presiding officer looks well and quite as closely to the rights of the black man who appears before him, deprived by poverty of the benefit of counsel, as to the rights of litigants more fortunate as far as this world's goods are concerned."[170] Sanford's actions in the *House* case were consistent with how he approached all his trials. He showed no partiality to the government. Sanford concluded that House's letters "might mean nothing more than the association needed to keep working until passage of the legislation."[171] His interpretation of House's testimony was that she "knew bills had been introduced repeatedly, hoped eventually one would pass, and organized ex-slaves to support the effort in their own interest."[172] His past sympathy with the plight of the depositors of the Freedman's Bank may have caused him to view House's cause with compassion. Sanford certainly recalled his time as assistant attorney general and his comprehensive memorandum regarding the bank. The document had detailed how passbooks issued to depositors bore "likenesses of President Lincoln and Generals Grant and Howard, and others whom the Freedmen had learned to reverence as special benefactors of their race; the flag of the Union ... depicted as sheltering and binding together the persons thus portrayed, while the remaining space was occupied with other pictorial devices ... designed to assure ... that the Government sanctioned the enterprise and would protect their interests."[173] In contrast, the circular in the *House* case bore none of these images.

Despite Sanford's view of the facts, however, House was convicted by the all-white, male jury. At sentencing, Sanford ordered "only one year in prison, apparently no more persuaded of her criminality [after three days of trial] than at the failed plea-bargain proceedings."[174] Cornelius Jones, a black lawyer connected to House, was similarly charged in Memphis with violation of the Postal Code.[175] The United States Attorney for the Western District of Tennessee at that time was none other than Hubert Fisher, Sanford's brother-in-law.[176] Upon reviewing the facts, Fisher became uneasy with prosecuting the case and ultimately dropped the charges.

A similar case on Sanford's docket involved a black man named J.W. Harding. Known to blacks as "Doctor Harding, the United States pension attorney," and to whites as "Uncle Wash," Harding also was accused of running a scheme promising government pensions to former slaves.[177] Described as "one of the shrewdest negro crooks in the state," Harding worked "to gain the complete confidence of any colored person from whom it was possible to filch a few dollars ... to carry out 'investigations' which would soon–but never did–result in securing a mythical government claim." His "specialty was government pensions for the widows and descendants of slaves." The postal authorities nabbed him when he signed money order receipts for an elderly black woman and appropriated a portion of the money for his "services."[178] He was found guilty on a charge of forging a money order and was sentenced to one year and a day in the federal penitentiary in Atlanta.[179] In an example of his compassion for the less fortunate among the convicted, Sanford gave Harding "a minimum sentence" because the defendant was old and "in a bad physical condition."[180]

In 1911, Sanford heard *Thomas Menees v. T.J. Matthews*, a matter involving the "Night Riders of the Black Patch." The so-called "Black Patch" region of southwestern Kentucky and northwestern Tennessee took its name from the dark, fire-cured tobacco grown in the area. This type of tobacco is used primarily in snuff and in chewing and pipe tobacco. At the time the crop became a dominant source of income in the Black Patch area, prices began to decline because of the monopolistic power held by James Buchanan "Buck" Duke and his American Tobacco Company. Duke "had pioneered the industrialization and monopolization of the tobacco industry" and had eliminated most of his competitors. Growers in the area blamed "The Trust," as Duke's monopoly was known, for the decline in prices. On September 24, 1904, many of the local growers formed the "Dark Tobacco District Planters' Protection Association of Kentucky and Tennessee," the goal of which was to raise tobacco prices by the cooperative marketing of the crop. The association urged its member growers to boycott Duke's American Tobacco Company. Initially, seventy to ninety-five percent of the growers signed contracts to have their crops delivered to the association. In an attempt to destroy the association, however, the Trust began paying ten to twelve cents a pound for the tobacco while association members were receiving less than eight cents.[181] Consequently, many non-member producers and association members chose personal profit and sold their crops to the Trust. When the association failed to force tobacco prices up, some of its more radical members formed a second organization, the Night Riders. Over the next few years, these Night Riders, also known as the Silent Brigade, "[used] intimidation, threats, terrorism, and sometimes murder to force farmers into the Association and to coerce tobacco buyers to purchase only from the cooperative."[182] To those who refused to become members of the association, the Night Riders "committed depredations and did great damage."[183] The Black Patch War raged in the tobacco belt from 1904 until 1914,[184] with the violence peaking from 1907 to 1909.[185]

Thomas Menees, a merchant and farmer, lived in Cedar Hill, Tennessee. In addition to a small store there, he owned a threshing machine, which he took from farm to farm harvesting wheat. Despite "threats, ostracism, and a boycott of his store," Menees refused to join the association.[186] In July 1907, the Night Riders retaliated against Menees by destroying his threshing machine, engine, water wagon, and sacker.[187] Menees was forced to move from the area due to these attacks. He brought a civil suit for $25,000 in damages for the loss of his threshing machine and other valuable property and for being forced to move.[188] At trial before Sanford, the defendants were shown to be "twenty-five of the most prominent farmers of Robertson and Montgomery Counties." The prosecution's chief witness, Robert Warfield, who had extensive knowledge of the association, helped secure the only verdict against the Night Riders in Tennessee.[189] The jury awarded Menees $1,500 in actual damages but $13,500 in punitive damages, reflecting their judgment that the conduct of the defendants was exceptionally blameworthy.[190] However, Sanford, apparently not as convinced by the testimony as the jury, cut the total award in half to $7,500 ($1,500 actual damages plus $6,000 punitives), advising Menees "that should he not care to accept this as final settlement," a new trial would be granted to the defendants.[191]

In 1911, Sanford presided over a lawsuit brought against the Nashville, Chattanooga and St. Louis Railroad, which became popularly known as the "Jim Crow Case." Four years earlier, in 1907, the Interstate Commerce Commission had decided that segregation of white and black passengers on interstate journeys was a reasonable regulation of interstate traffic but that the carriers must furnish blacks who paid the same fare as white passengers with equal accommodations.[192] The case before Sanford arose from complaints that the accommodations furnished blacks on many roads in the South had been much inferior to those given white passengers, although both paid the same fare.

Interstate railroad companies had opposed the Jim Crow legislation that swept across the South in the 1890s because segregation of the races was costly and encroached on business operations. In the view of the companies, "it was inefficient to run extra cars for Black passengers if there was no demand to fill them." The railroads in the South, therefore, delayed complying with segregation as long as possible.[193]

Southern trains of the time period traditionally had a "smoking" car for men and a "ladies" car for white families and non-smoking men as well as for women. Blacks customarily rode in the smoking car.[194] In the typical smoking car, "the floors were thick with spit and tobacco juice" and "the air thick with smoke and vulgarities." Smoking cars had hard seats, low ceilings, and no water; frequently, the smoking car was merely a part of the baggage car set off by a partition.[195]

Having complied with laws requiring segregation, the railroads resisted the Interstate Commerce Commission's regulation requiring equal accommodations. Officials with the ICC, however, stated that if the railroads did not afford the same accommodations for both white and black passengers, they would have no alternative but to direct the southern railroads to pay extremely heavy fines or to discontinue the use of the "Jim Crow" cars and allow blacks to ride in the same coaches with whites.[196] The railroads believed that the Interstate Commerce Commission lacked the power to require equal accommodations, but the courts consistently ruled in favor of the government agency.[197] Sanford likewise ruled that the railroad had to treat all passengers alike regardless of race. Newspapers with headlines like "Negroes Win Victory" and "Must Be No Discrimination" announced "a big triumph for the Negroes of the South who have been fighting for equal accommodations."[198]

Sanford's ruling in the Jim Crow case was not radical, since other judges before him had upheld the ICC regulation, but it did illustrate his tendency to uphold government regulations that were remedial and humanitarian. His acceptance of the "separate, but equal" doctrine is reminiscent of the position espoused by David McKendree Key, who served as a United States district judge over the Eastern and Middle Districts of Tennessee prior to Sanford's tenure. Key, born in Greene County, Tennessee in 1824, attended Hiwassee College and the forerunner of the University of Tennessee. After service in the Confederate Army, he rose to become a US senator from Tennessee and US postmaster general. He was nominated to the federal bench by President Rutherford B. Hayes in May 1880.[199]

Although he did not advocate separate but equal facilities for blacks, Key accepted it "as a solution to what he judged to be the popular racial antipathies of lower-class whites; to him, however, the system of making distinctions in public facilities on the basis of color had a ludicrous aspect."[200] In a speech to the Tennessee Bar Association, Key told the assembled lawyers "that if separate facilities were required, the law should not tolerate inequality in their character."[201] Key viewed "discriminations unjustly made on the part of public common carriers" as the "detestation of the law," and declared that if they were "tolerated anywhere," they presented dangers "to the public everywhere."[202]

When the United States finally became involved in World War I, a provocative matter of purported espionage landed on Sanford's docket. In 1917 and 1918, Congress passed the Espionage and Sedition Acts, hoping to target radicals and to silence opposition to American involvement in the war. In addition to criminalizing the expression of opposition to the war, the two acts also provided stiff penalties for anyone found guilty of aiding the Germans. Anti-German passions were strong in Tennessee.[203]

On December 5, 1917, the Baroness Iona Wilhelmina Pickhardt Sutton Shope Zollner, age forty-four, the spouse of a captain in the German army, stepped off the train in Chattanooga and registered at a local hotel.[204] Soon thereafter, Lieutenant John William Spaulding, age twenty-two, stationed at nearby Fort Oglethorpe[205] and assigned to the Sixth United States Infantry, checked into the same hotel. He became a frequent visitor to the Baroness and even took her to Fort Oglethorpe, the largest cavalry post in the country and a major Army induction and training center.[206]

The Baroness was well known to federal authorities. She was considered a dangerous enemy alien required to inform intelligence services of her whereabouts, and although she had received permission to travel to Chattanooga, she did not have authorization to visit Fort Oglethorpe. Around midnight on December 13, 1917, the Baroness and Spaulding were arrested in her room. Both found partially clad, they were taken to police headquarters and charged with indecent and immoral behavior. The couple was subsequently released on bond, and the Baroness registered at another hotel intending to continue her relationship with Spaulding. Shortly thereafter, she was arrested again by United States Marshals. She was charged with being a dangerous alien who had visited Fort Oglethorpe for an undisclosed but dangerous purpose and denied bond. The government argued that the Baroness's friendship with military and government officials was for the purpose of furthering her "activities as a servant of the German government." A probable cause hearing lasting two days was conducted in Chattanooga before United States Commissioner Sam McAlester. The commissioner refused to grant bail because the Baroness traveled extensively, was the daughter of an eccentric German millionaire, owned real estate all over the world, had been married five times, and knew high-level officials in Germany, England, and the United States.[207] He found probable cause to hold the Baroness under section two of the Espionage Act.[208]

Spaulding's acquaintance with the Baroness had begun two years earlier when her oldest son, Beresford Shope, became a cadet at the Naval Academy in the fall of 1915. Because he had not done well on his entrance examinations, Beresford had great difficulty getting an appointment to the academy. On his behalf, the Baroness traveled to the Department of the Navy and apparently met with Assistant Secretary Franklin D. Roosevelt to use her "Roosevelt family relation" to secure her son's appointment.[209] The Baroness's brother, Ernest, had married Maude Fortescue, Theodore Roosevelt's first cousin. While Franklin was only distantly related to Theodore, Franklin's wife Eleanor was Theodore's niece.[210]

After Beresford's appointment was obtained, the Baroness would visit the Naval Academy and board at a house nearby. One of the cadets who befriended Beresford was John Spaulding, who had been at the Naval Academy since December 1913. Beresford, who had since flunked out and re-entered, introduced Spaulding to the family. When Spaulding was expelled from the Naval Academy in February 1917 for debts and failed exams, he moved into the boarding house with the Baroness and her younger son, Bedford. The Baroness, Bedford, and Spaulding soon moved to a house just outside the gates of the academy, but her presence caught the attention of the authorities because she was the former wife of a German baron and was currently married to a German army officer.[211] The Baroness was visited by Navy Secret Service, who informed her that she had been watched for months and that her mail had been opened and read. She was urged to leave Annapolis, which she shortly thereafter did.[212] She subsequently helped Spaulding obtain an officer's commission in the Army.

The Baroness's attorney applied for release on bond, and prior to the hearing before Sanford, she was moved to Knoxville.[213] A crowd of spectators—mostly women—had gathered for the hearing in anticipation of salacious testimony, even bringing their knitting in order to combine a productive form of entertainment with one more titillating, but they became annoyed when Sanford cleared the courtroom.[214] Before Sanford, the Baroness admitted having been in touch with her husband, German Army Captain Zollner, at least fifteen times since he rejoined the German army in 1914, and she acknowledged receipt of thirty-six letters from him during the period. However, the Baroness proclaimed her complete loyalty to the United States and maintained that she was innocent of any violation of the Espionage Act. Sanford released her on a $2,500 bond and ruled that the personal letters introduced as evidence were provocative but immaterial.[215] The Baroness agreed that she "would stay in her home in New York, refrain from communicating with American military personnel and anyone in Austria or Germany, and report in ... twice a week regarding her whereabouts."[216] For reasons that are unclear, she was never tried.[217]

In *The Harding Affair: Love and Espionage During the Great War*, James David Robenalt opined that Sanford perhaps swept the matter aside as a favor to the Roosevelts because the anti-German Theodore Roosevelt was planning to run again for president in 1920 and would not want any publicity connecting him to Germans. However, absolutely no evidence exists to show that Sanford handled this matter any differently from others on his docket. Sanford's disposition of this matter was consistent with his generally merciful attitude. Indeed, the failure to follow through with the prosecution is likely attributable to the federal prosecutor, not to Sanford. Robenalt further noted that the Baroness, in addition to being tied to the Roosevelts, was the first cousin of the fiancé of the daughter of Carrie Phillips, better known as a mistress of future president Warren G. Harding. Phillips, an avowed supporter of Germany, is often mentioned as "the only woman known to have successfully blackmailed a US president."[218] It was Harding who would soon elevate Sanford to a seat on the Supreme Court. Again, however, there is no evidence of any relationship between Harding's mistress's pro-German views and Sanford's handling of the Baroness's case.

Another espionage case Sanford presided over in his courtroom in Greeneville revealed the limitations on speech during World War I. William E. Martin was charged with slandering the Red Cross, President Wilson, and the United States Government. Martin declared that "the Red Cross was merely a scheme to support a lot of women" and that "several hundred Red Cross nurses had been sent back from France because of their conduct in that country." He further asserted that the president "was sending all the men of the United States to France to be killed and that he would 'see the President in hell before he would go to France to fight.'" Martin additionally charged that the government was misapplying money for war purposes.[219] Although Sanford's daughter Anna Magee served with the Red Cross in France, Sanford uncharacteristically ignored any perceived conflict, conducted the trial, and denied the motion for a new trial on all grounds except that of insanity. He postponed the final disposition of the case to enable the defense attorneys to address Martin's mental condition.[220]

An additional war-related matter brought before Sanford's court involved J.I. Graham, a "Holy Roller preacher" from Loudon County, Tennessee. During the course of a Sunday night sermon, Graham advised the men of the congregation not to fight. He contended that he did not believe it to be God's will that men should fight each other. Graham was convicted on a charge of advising registered men not to report for military service if called and "to resist to death, if necessary."[221]

A noted big league baseball player of the day found himself before Sanford instead of rabid fans. Fred Toney, a resident of Davidson County, Tennessee, was a star pitcher with the Cincinnati Reds. He had originally been tried on a charge of evading the Selective Service Act, the government contending that Toney swore falsely when he stated that he was supporting his wife, mother, father, and other members of the Toney family. The facts established that Toney was holding out a woman known as Gladys Strange to be his wife and that he transported her to Cincinnati during the baseball season. When the prosecution tried to show that Toney was supporting Strange rather than his family, Sanford ruled that the government had no legal right to question Toney as to his relations with the woman because he was specifically being tried for evasion of the Selective Service Act. The prosecution immediately procured a Mann Act White Slave Traffic indictment.[222] The Selective Service matter eventually ended in acquittal.[223] Toney entered a guilty plea to a violation of the Mann Act and was sentenced to four months in the Davidson County jail.[224]

Sanford heard numerous "smoke" cases against Ducktown Sulphur, Copper & Iron Company and Tennessee Copper Company, located in southeastern Tennessee along its borders with Georgia and North Carolina. In the cases before Sanford, the plaintiffs sought to enjoin the companies from operating their copper smelters on the grounds that the fumes were destroying the forest and vegetation.[225] Pleas for injunction were filed by J.H. Vestal, Shippen Brothers Lumber Company of Ellijay, Georgia, and others.[226] The smoke from the copper smelters was "a dark, bluish 'color' with the rotten-egg stench of sulfur."[227] A witness at a 1914 trial testified regarding the smoke: "It come right through this county and scattered every way.... When we have had a shower of rain and the smoke comes in, it settles down heavy and looks like a fog, and when that dries off you can see the damage."[228] A landscape architect noted that Ducktown, Tennessee, was "variously described as: a hellhole, a blister, a desecration, something out of Dante's *Inferno*, the Tennessee Badlands, the ugliest place in the South, [and] a ravaged wonder."[229] In Ducktown, "[a] new environment of naked red hills and gullies replaced the green hardwood forests typical of the region."[230] Hundreds of lawsuits were filed over the years in federal and state courts seeking damages for crop and timber losses and injunctions to abate the smoke.

Volstead Act

In a 1918 case prior to federal Prohibition, Sanford handed down an opinion in which he held that the government had no right to seize and confiscate automobiles captured in connection with transporting intoxicating liquor. Sanford, strictly construing the statute cited by the government, found that the seizure language was appended to legislation concerning "Indian" affairs and could not be generally extended beyond matters related to the Indians.[231] The decision was seen to "have a far-reaching effect because it ha[d] been the practice of the federal authorities in their raids to seize the vehicles used in the transportation of the liquor."[232] To address this gap in the law, the Prohibition statute, the Volstead Act, specifically provided for forfeiture of a vehicle after conviction of the person in charge of it, subject to all bona fide liens.[233]

Cases involving homemade liquor, called moonshine because it was made and moved at night by the light of the moon, had always crowded Sanford's dockets.[234] During the Civil War, the United States government authorized a liquor tax of twenty cents per proof gallon to help fund the war effort and, to collect the tax, established the Office of Internal Revenue. After the war, Congress retained the tax and increased it to two dollars per proof gallon. Moonshiners in Sanford's districts resented the tax and the government agents, disdainfully called "Revenuers," hired to collect it.[235] By 1919, the moonshine industry had grown to such dangerous proportions that authorities "could no longer control the situation."[236] Even women were under indictment in federal court for distilling liquor and brewing beer.[237] An even greater mass of litigation soon grew out of the Volstead Act and the Eighteenth Amendment.

During World War I, alcohol had been viewed as a menace to the efficiency of the war effort, leading to the passage of the War-time Prohibition Act. As recalled by Frederick Lewis Allen, a historian of the period:

> The entrance of the United States into the war gave the dry leaders their great opportunity. The war diverted the attention of those who might have objected to the bone-dry program: with the very existence of the nation at stake, the future status of alcohol seemed a trifling matter. The war accustomed the country to drastic legislation conferring new and wide powers upon the Federal Government. It

necessitated the saving of food and thus commended prohibition to the patriotic as a grain-saving measure. It turned public opinion against everything German—and many of the big brewers and distillers were of German origin. The war also brought with it a mood of Spartan idealism of which the Eighteenth Amendment was a natural expression. Everything was sacrificed to efficiency, production, and health. If a sober soldier was a good soldier and a sober factory hand was a productive factory hand, the argument for prohibition was for the moment unanswerable. Meanwhile, the American people were seeing Utopian visions; if it seemed possible to them that the war should end all wars and that victory should bring a new and shining world order, how much easier to imagine that America might enter an endless era of efficient sobriety! And finally, the war made them impatient for immediate results. In 1917 and 1918, whatever was worth doing at all was worth doing at once, regardless of red tape, counter-arguments, comfort, or convenience. The combination of these various forces was irresistible. Fervently and with headlong haste the nation took the short cut to a dry Utopia.[238]

Thus, "[t]he frenzied emotions of war mobilization carried over into the drive for national constitutional prohibition."[239] Prohibition "went through on the tide of the war spirit of 'no compromise.'"[240] The movement seemed to have a united country behind it. With amazing speed, the Eighteenth Amendment was ratified on January 16, 1919. It prohibited "[t]he manufacture, sale, or transportation of intoxicating liquors." The Volstead Act[241] was enacted to implement the amendment. It defined liquor as intoxicating whenever it contained more than 0.5 percent alcohol. The act was upheld in the *National Prohibition Cases*.[242] However, evasion of the law began immediately, and opposition to it appeared just as rapidly. As a result, drinking became "the thing to do." A new spirit of deliberate revolt ensued, which lasted until the Volstead Act was repealed by the Liquor Law Repeal and Enforcement Act in 1933.[243]

The government's efforts to enforce national Prohibition after the Eighteenth Amendment took effect on January 17, 1920, alone accounted for an 8-percent increase in the number of federal cases.[244] The criminal dockets of Sanford's district court overflowed with Prohibition infractions in addition to the usual ration of moonshining cases.[245] *The Tennessean*, in a 1914 article prior to federal

Prohibition, quoted Sanford regarding untaxed liquor and bootlegging: "The retailing of liquor is not only in defiance of the federal statutes, but also the state laws.... There is nothing that spreads a greater spirit of disregard for the law than this business, which makes desolate homes and broken hearts." Sanford observed that some defendants "provoke[d] a sympathetic feeling," but that "[i]ndividuals shall not take the law in their own hands, nor shall they decide for themselves what laws they think just or unjust and act accordingly."[246]

A 1920 article quoted Sanford's thoughts on the burden on the courts resulting from Prohibition:

> Judge Edward T. Sanford in a charge to the federal grand jury here yesterday announced a more drastic policy in dealing with violators of the prohibition laws, declaring those convicted would be given a year and a day in the federal prison at Atlanta, in addition to heavy fines.
>
> Judge Sanford said the growth of "moonshining" was due to the excessive profits gathered from the illicit traffic and that unless the courts took action immediately the industry would continue to become a still greater menace.
>
> Judge Sanford deplored the lack of sufficient men in the internal revenue department to enforce the laws, declaring the force was entirely inadequate to cope with the situation. He excoriated the bootlegger, saying that he was worse than the moonshiner, who is courageous, while the bootlegger is a "dirty coward."[247]

A year later, Sanford declared that it was an unfortunate circumstance that the purchasers of liquor were not "punished in a like manner as the man who sells it."[248] The federal judicial system was completely unprepared to deal with the huge influx of cases generated by Prohibition. Legendary journalist H.L. Mencken once observed that "[p]erhaps the chief victims of Prohibition, in the long run, will turn out to be the federal judges...."[249]

A contemporary of Sanford's from his youth in Knoxville, William Cary Ross, made the following observation regarding Prohibition:

> We have tried every way possible to prohibit the manufacture and sale of alcohol by law, but it seems to me all attempts have been failures.

...[A] neighbor had a gardener named Sims. He was a hard worker and a good man except for the fact that he would go to town every Saturday night, get drunk, come home, beat his wife and raise the very old Harry generally. So when we had the opportunity to vote dry, I was glad to do it with the thought that I would give up the little use I ever had for alcohol for the benefit of Sims and those like him. We drys carried the election, but what happened? Sims got just as drunk every Saturday night and had to spend more of his wages on rotten whisky that made him wilder than ever and might even have killed him, while my temperate friends couldn't have a highball without condoning the violation of the law.

It soon developed that all of the best element of our citizenship was either violating the law or condoning it. Racketeers, high jackers, gun men and grafters were reaping fortunes out of illegal traffic in alcoholic beverages and were writing the pages of the most lawless age of American history. The decent people couldn't conscientiously do anything about it because they were violating the law too.

After years of experience trying to force prohibition on our people, I for one, was glad to vote for the repeal of the prohibition amendment to our constitution. Without doubt we should preach temperance and hope that each individual can develop strength enough to look out for himself, but we have very definitely proven that we can't force him to do it by law.[250]

With Sanford's workload ever increasing, a plea was made for another district judge to handle Middle Tennessee.[251] Sanford and the attorney general for the Middle District both wrote letters that were transmitted to the Senate Committee on the Judiciary. They each noted "that, due to recent federal legislation, conferring additional jurisdiction upon the federal courts in criminal matters ... and [the] notable increase of litigation by reason of the many condemnation suits brought under the forest reserve act ... the work of the present district judge has so increased that it is a physical impossibility for him to long cope with the situation without impairing his health."[252] Sanford, "[b]y extraordinary application to his duties," had been "able to keep up the work until 1913. At the commencement of the fall term of 1913, there was not a single undisposed of matter pending in the court."[253] Sanford, however, was "feel[ing] increasingly the strain of work and the difficulty of keeping it up satisfactorily with the constant pressure due to holding live courts at widely separated places."[254] He remarked that "the business of the courts is increasing so rapidly that it is really impossible for one judge to adequately keep up the work in the two districts."[255] In the spring of 1914, when requested to sit with the Sixth Circuit Court of Appeals in Cincinnati, Sanford advised that he was "getting considerably behind."[256] In a subsequent letter to District Judge John McCall, Sanford explained that he had been under a doctor's care for an "over-worked condition."[257] A reporter noted in 1916, however, that Sanford had been required "to sit in cases in other districts than [his] own."[258] In the fall of 1917, he spoke of "unusually heavy dockets" and the fear he would be "badly in arrears."[259] Sanford expressed worry about "[t]he great hardship . . . to the public in the inevitable delay of the trial of cases, and some times in their determination after they are heard."[260] In December 1919, the Tennessee Congressional delegation pushed a measure to secure another judgeship for Tennessee. One congressman observed that there was "only one other instance in the country where a judicial district of this size has no separate judge."[261] Another House member related that Sanford "has been straining heaven and earth to take care of these two districts. . . . Almost every night, every day and Sunday he has been engaged in open court or in chambers, or in hearing extraordinary processes or some other matter." He further stated that "Judge Sanford holds court early and late. I never knew a more industrious man, and he really can't get time scarcely to sit down to his meals."[262] Sanford wrote a letter in support of the legislation in which he noted: "At Greeneville in the old days, only two or three days were required to clear the docket. Now it consumes three weeks or more."[263] Everyone with knowledge of the situation agreed that it was "a physical impossibility for one judge to take care of the volume of work in both Middle and East Tennessee."[264]

When Sanford later was being considered for appointment to the Supreme Court, his case backlog was the primary complaint raised with respect to his qualifications.[265] In a letter to Arthur C. Denison of the Sixth Circuit, Chief Justice Taft requested Denison's confidential appraisal "as to the criticism of Sanford that he is slow in making up his mind and has delayed business in his

Court on that account."[266] Denison replied that "[t]here is some complaint of delay and some basis for the theory that he has a tendency to be hesitant; but I think they are rather negligible as to justification."[267]

In 1920, approaching the conclusion of his time on the district court bench, Sanford wrote to his class secretary at Harvard:

> My life has varied little since 1915, except for the stress of the Great War. My judicial labors were greatly increased by the many enlarged responsibilities placed upon the Federal Courts by Congressional legislation relating to the war-time activities of the Government. As far as the discharge of these duties permitted, I served upon local committees in the campaigns for Liberty Loans and other funds for patriotic purposes, and made frequent speeches in behalf of these and like objects.
>
> My dockets are now crowded, and my work very heavy and done under constant pressure, but, with a bit of vacation now and then and a little golf by the way, [I] have kept in excellent health and continue to find enduring satisfaction and contentment in my work.[268]

At this point in time, despite previous protestations of being under a doctor's care for an over-worked condition, Sanford, in his mid-fifties, claimed to be in excellent health. If Sanford was aware of any issue with his kidneys, he kept it to himself. In June 1922, he learned that Congress had finally agreed to provide a judge for the Middle District of Tennessee.[269] Shortly thereafter, however, Sanford was elevated to the United States Supreme Court.

According to Sanford's records, out of several thousands of cases heard over a fifteen-year period in two districts, a total of one hundred four of his court decisions were appealed, with seventy-two affirmed, twenty-five reversed, and seven modified.[270] Not surprisingly, because his dockets were full of Prohibition cases, one of the last reversals involved an interpretation of the Volstead Act. Sanford rendered a judgment of condemnation of an automobile which had been used for the purpose of "concealing or removing whiskey upon which the internal revenue tax had not been paid and for the purpose of defrauding the United States of such tax." In *Lewis v. United States*,[271] the Sixth Circuit reversed Sanford's judgment based on the authority of *United States v. Yuginovitch*,[272] which held that the statute applied by Sanford had been repealed by implication due to its inconsistency with the National Prohibition Act. With taxes on liquor no longer payable, the Sixth Circuit ruled that there could be no intent to defraud in not paying them.

On January 30, 1923, upon the familiar cry of "Hear ye, hear ye, this honorable court has adjourned," Sanford stepped down from the district court bench.[273] After his death, United States Attorney General William D. Mitchell remarked: "[Sanford's] duties as a District Judge were not entirely congenial to him, since he was constantly faced with the necessity of passing immediately upon questions to which he would have preferred to give more mature consideration. Nevertheless his preferences in no way influenced his achievements, and his record was an enviable one."[274]

US Supreme Court Justice

The White House
January 24, 1923

To the Senate of the United States:
I nominate Edward T. Sanford, of Tennessee, to be Associate Justice of the United States, Mahlon Pitney, resigned.
                                        —Warren G. Harding

Tennessee has produced far more United States Supreme justices than its population or political significance would seem to warrant. By the early 1920s, the state could claim four Justices: (1) John Catron, appointed by President Martin Van Buren; (2) Howell Jackson, appointed by President Benjamin Harrison; (3) Horace Lurton, appointed by President William H. Taft; and (4) James McReynolds, appointed by President Woodrow Wilson. Sanford's time finally arrived in 1923, when the fourth vacancy in two years opened on the Court with Mahlon Pitney's retirement. Justice Pitney had suffered a stroke, and legislation was passed to allow him to retire with full benefits because he had not reached the age required for full retirement.[1]

By the time he had served as president for two and a half years, President Warren G. Harding had named four justices to the Supreme Court. The selection of William H. Taft to succeed Edward Douglass White as chief justice in 1921 was followed by three additional appointments in the next two years. George Sutherland, born in England, was appointed in 1922 to the seat unexpectedly vacated by Justice John H. Clarke, reportedly in large part due to the baleful influence of Justice McReynolds.[2] The selection of Pierce Butler, a life-long conservative Democrat and railroad attorney, followed in 1923 to replace Justice William R. Day,[3] who had been ill for most of the previous term. Day retired on November 13, 1922, and accepted an appointment to serve on the Mixed Claims Commission, an entity set up to settle claims remaining from World War I.[4] Sanford's elevation likewise occurred in 1923. Harding's appointees, like Taft, tended to be conservatives who cast their votes with Willis Van Devanter, McReynolds, and Joseph McKenna, who had been frequent dissenters before 1921. A vocal minority, therefore, became the majority.[5]

Once confirmed in 1921, Taft exercised great influence over Harding and was the principal adviser on matters relating to the Supreme Court.[6] After Taft's selection, Harding's general criteria for candidacy on the Court were those of his chief justice: "their 'real' politics were 'right'; they were all experienced public figures; and they were all conservative, property-minded, business-oriented attorneys."[7] Harding's attorney general, Harry M. Daugherty, told Taft's brother Henry that the president "would not approve of anybody for appointment who was not approved by [the chief justice]."[8] For the most part, Taft was not only able to succeed in getting those he preferred nominated by Harding, but he also was able to block potential nominees with whom he disagreed. He was determined to sink any prospective candidate who might side with that "dangerous twosome," Justices Oliver W. Holmes and Louis D. Brandeis.[9]

Warren G. Harding

The 1920 presidential election was a referendum on Wilsonian progressivism. Warren Gamaliel Harding pitched himself to voters who were tired of the reform politics of the Progressive era. He declared that "America should return to 'business as usual'; the federal government, which had grown fat and powerful during World War I, should be cut back; and the free enterprise system should be restored to its prior prominence."[10] In a campaign speech, Harding noted that "America's present need is not heroics, but healing; not nostrums, but normalcy; not revolution, but restoration; not agitation, but adjustment; not surgery, but serenity; not the dramatic, but the dispassionate; not experiment, but equipoise; not submergence in internationality, but sustainment in triumphant nationality."[11] Harding sought "diminished governmental presence, nineteenth-century values, and economic prosperity resulting from minimal governmental regulation of business."[12] He looked longingly to "the good old days when the government didn't bother businessmen with unnecessary regulations, but provided them with fat tariffs and instructed the Department of Justice not to have them on its mind."[13]

Harding's election ushered in a conservative tone. His call for a "return to normalcy," which sought a return to the policies of President William McKinley,[14] signaled a move away from Theodore Roosevelt's "Square Deal" and Woodrow Wilson's "New Freedom."[15] With Harding's election, American voters "rejected both the tone and substance of the political movement Roosevelt had galvanized," and the public declared itself "weary of crusades and of charismatic leaders who constantly demanded that [Americans] live a political life of great deeds and heroic sacrifice at home and abroad."[16] As one leading historian of the day put it, "Harding was shunted into the White House as a passionate protest.... For the first time in twenty years, we were tired of men with burning convictions, curative or palliative panaceas or reforms; ideas that might develop into causes.... The land was more or less afflicted with moral shell-shock...."[17]

Harding began his political career by winning a seat in the Ohio Senate in 1898, serving there until 1903. He was the lieutenant governor of Ohio from 1904 to 1906, but lost his race for governor in 1910. At the 1912 Republican National Convention, Harding gained greater exposure by giving a speech nominating fellow Ohioan William H. Taft for a second term as president. After a four-year hiatus from politics, he was elected to the US Senate in 1914 and remained there until becoming president in 1921.[18]

While in the Senate, Harding rarely took a strong position. A Harding biographer noted:

> During Harding's five Senate years he introduced 134 bills, of which 122 were local Ohio affairs, bills to change the name of a lake steamer, secure a Civil War veteran's back pension, and such. None of his

twelve public bills were of a national significance but concerned such ephemeral matters as encouraging the teaching of Spanish, celebrating the anniversary of the landing of the Pilgrims, authoriz[ing] the loan of tents to relieve the 1920 housing shortage, providing for the investigation of influenza and other diseases, amending the McKinley Memorial Birthplace Act, and giving discarded army rifles to the duly-accredited camps of the Sons of Veterans Reserve. On roll calls ... he usually managed to be somewhere else when a vote was taken on any measure that might antagonize a minority group in Ohio. With bills affecting labor, for instance, he voted seven times in favor of labor, eleven times against, while ten times he was not present to vote.[19]

According to his congressional voting record, Harding missed two-thirds of the votes held during his tenure as senator, including the vote on women's suffrage, a cause he purportedly strongly supported.[20]

After ten rounds of voting at the 1920 Republican National Convention, the delegates were deadlocked over the choice for a presidential nominee. Through the political maneuvering of Harry M. Daugherty, his campaign manager, Harding was pushed as the compromise candidate. According to Daugherty, Harding "looked like a president." He further stated, "His upbringing was classically homegrown American; he was well-known by Republican leaders; he had no major political enemies; he was 'right' on all the issues; and he represented the critically important state of Ohio." On the eleventh round of voting, Harding emerged as the nominee.[21] In the first presidential election in which women could vote—the Nineteenth Amendment had been ratified in August 1920—Harding won the presidency with a pro-business, conservative Republican agenda.[22]

Harding has been described as a man "patently unqualified to serve as president."[23] He once remarked to editor William Allen White: "This is a hell of a job. ... My God-damn friends ... they're the ones that keep me walking the floors nights.... This White House is a prison. I can't get away from the men who dog my footsteps. I am in jail."[24] He admitted to President Nicholas Murray Butler of Columbia University: "I am not fit for this office and should never have been here."[25] When Harding began his administration, *The Nation* suggested that it was the "most material, the most sightless Administration ever to begin its rule in America."[26]

Harry M. Daugherty

Harry M. Daugherty, Harding's campaign manager, was an ambitious and resourceful lobbyist whose relationships with Taft and Harding stretched back to their days in Ohio politics.[27] Daugherty was a member of the "Ohio Gang" and has been described as Harding's "political mentor."[28] According to Francis Russell, however, Daugherty exaggerated the closeness of his relationship with Harding.[29] Russell claimed that "[i]n spite of the legend, Harding was neither a fool nor a tool, but an astute and able Ohio politician ... who knew how to get what he wanted.... Harding was not a creation of Daugherty's."[30] The two men experienced "strained relations at times." In a letter to Daugherty, Harding stated: "The trouble with you, my dear Daugherty, in your political relations with me, is that you appraise my political sense so far below par that you have no confidence in me or my judgment. Pray do not think because I can and do listen in politeness to much that is said to me that I am always being 'strung.'" Harding also acknowledged to others regarding Daugherty: "I do not always think him a trustworthy adviser."[31] But Daugherty was responsible for making Harding a viable candidate for president.[32] In a campaign that was run on a shoestring budget, Daugherty spent $50,000 of his own money on Harding's behalf.[33]

After Harding became president, Southern Republicans sought to obtain a reward from the Republican party "for the break in the Democratic Solid South in the recent election." The prize they desired was a place in the Harding cabinet. Sanford was being urged for attorney general;[34] however, Daugherty was the leading candidate. Despite being urged more than once to pick anyone other than Daugherty as his attorney general, Harding finally exclaimed: "Harry Daugherty has been my best friend from the beginning of this whole thing. I have told him that he can have any place in my Cabinet he wants, outside of Secretary of State. He tells me that he wants to be Attorney General and by God he will be Attorney General!"[35] Just as Harding was an inadequate choice for president, Daugherty likewise was a man "totally unprepared for such an office" as attorney general.[36]

Daugherty was instrumental in the appointment of Taft as chief justice, a selection that enraged Progressives. Harold Ickes, who would become President Franklin D. Roosevelt's Secretary of the Interior, wrote: "I regard Taft as utterly unfit to be a member of the Supreme Court." Senator Hiram Johnson of

California thought the nomination was "the most sinister thing that has come to us thus far in the administration." He further remarked, "When you think that many of the most grave policies of the country have been decided by the United States Supreme Court by a single vote, the possibility of Taft casting that vote makes your heart sink."[37] Idaho Senator William Borah described Taft's selection as chief justice as "almost sacrilegious." He lamented, "[T]o take a man who has dedicated his life to politics and who has at best only seven or eight years of service left and make him the head of that great tribunal" was tantamount to "prostituting the Court . . . to the mere call of expediency in politics."[38] In *The Nation*, Oswald Villard and the editors called the choice of the "intellectually indolent" Taft "a grave mistake."[39] Harding, for his part, thought he should consider other candidates for the position of chief justice, but Daugherty persistently suggested Taft to him, arguing that the appointment must come immediately because of the congested courts, the inadequate number of judges, and the need for judicial reform. Daugherty also claimed that he needed Taft to advise and guide him in his role as attorney general.[40] Likewise, no one had a greater positive influence on Daugherty than Taft. With the chief justice's guiding hand, Daugherty generally recommended well-qualified judges for the federal courts.[41]

How did Sanford, an individual who had not been very prominently connected with either party politics or national corporate interests[42] accomplish the feat of being appointed to the United States Supreme Court? Although his appointment was ultimately due to Daugherty, Sanford's former law partner, James A. Fowler of Knoxville, played an important role at the outset. According to historian Harold M. Hollingsworth: "When Harding did not find a place for a Southerner in his cabinet, a campaign was launched by . . . Fowler . . . to place a Southerner, preferably Edward T. Sanford, on the Supreme Court."[43]

As early as 1921, the Tennessee Bar Association suggested Sanford as an ideal appointee to the United States Supreme Court, a body Sanford once described as an "[a]ugust tribunal which constitutes the sure bulwark of law and order and liberty under the Constitution, administering justice between the Nation, the state and the citizen with equal and exact regard for the rights of each."[44] Speaking before the association's 1921 annual meeting held in Knoxville, United States Senator Kenneth D. McKellar of Tennessee, a Memphis Democrat, backed Sanford for elevation to the Court, noting that he had known Sanford for a number of years and that "a more delightful gentleman never lived on the face of the earth." McKellar observed that Sanford "is a great judge. He is an honor to this State and to the Nation. He will make a great Justice of the Supreme Court, if the President shall appoint him."[45] The TBA then passed a resolution urging the promotion of Sanford, noting that he

> is a citizen of unblemished character, having lived an exemplary life among the people where he was born and reared. In his social relations with his fellows he is a Prince, he is loved by all with whom he is acquainted, and his name as a citizen and a Judge is honored and respected wherever known. For many years Edward T. Sanford was recognized as one of the ablest lawyers of Tennessee.... He always exemplified the highest ideals in his profession.
>
> He has made a faithful, industrious, able, fearless and just Judge; and we confidently assert that no more capable or efficient District Judge ever sat on the Bench.
>
> While Judge Sanford is profoundly learned in the science of the law, he has by no means lost himself in dogmas and theories; he is distinctly practical and human; he has a sense of sympathy for all those in distress. He gives equally careful consideration to the great and the small. He possesses the fine combination of a clear head and a good heart. In him are the elements of true greatness.[46]

Judge S. F. Wilson, who described himself as "an old hide-bound, old fashioned States' Rights Democrat," seconded the resolution.[47]

The push for Sanford, an East Tennessee Republican, by Southern Democrats is significant. When the States' Rights supporters accomplished secession from the Union in 1860, the constitution of the Confederacy began, "We, the people of the Confederate States, each State acting in its own Sovereign and independent character...." Support for Sanford, the son of a Unionist, was symbolic of a reconciliation of sorts. He represented the party of the victor but the geographic region of the loser.

As the movement to place Sanford on the Supreme Court grew, Democratic support increased as well. An eminent Democratic attorney in Tennessee wrote the following letter to the Department of Justice:

> Without the slightest regard to party affiliations, the people of this State are behind Judge Sanford's application. The Democrats will be as well satisfied with his appointment as if he were one of them. In fact his brand of Republicanism, as manifested in his loyalty to the Constitution and constant efforts to elevate the manhood of this State by an even-handed enforcement of the law, has tended largely to wipe out that prejudice which has kept the Southerner in the Democratic ranks. Every citizen who has served as a juror, every litigant and every lawyer who has been in any of his numerous terms of Court, is a better American citizen today than he was before for this experience. Judge Sanford, as everybody must admit, is qualified by his legal attainments and experience, and by his character for this high position—why should he not be appointed?
>
> It seems as if his residence as far South as Tennessee is the only thing against him. If so, the South will not be to blame for getting solid again and remaining so. A great many Democrats rejoiced when Mr. Harding carried this State. We thought it better for us in every way....
>
> We want to have Judge Sanford appointed, and that is our consideration. If he is not, then it should be candidly understood that the South has no place in the Republican party because of political conditions that the President must recognize. In other words the Solid South is a political and not a sectional evil as is constantly being charged. You will see from this that it is not conducive to good humor when a man like Judge Sanford must be sacrificed to the policies of his own party....[48]

Accordingly, nonpartisan Sanford was backed by a highly partisan movement.

In later discussing the support for Sanford's elevation to the Supreme Court, Fowler observed: "Sanford had the earnest support of every lawyer and every prominent citizen in the Districts in which he held Courts. In addition to this he was well and favorably known to many influential citizens in the South outside his Districts, and to many prominent men throughout the United States."[49] Fowler's observation is supported by a 1922 editorial in *The Atlanta Constitution*. The piece expressed the South's right to a seat on the High Bench and Sanford's being the perfect choice to fill it:

> Having filled the last vacancy by the appointment of a northern democrat... it is generally accepted that the next appointment will go to a republican, and the name of Judge Edward T. Sanford of the federal court of the eastern district of Tennessee, is said to be under serious consideration. Judge Sanford is held in universal esteem, regardless of politics, and his appointment would be entirely acceptable to democrats as well as republicans of this section. The situation is such that we do not see how the president can afford to ignore the just claim of the south for recognition in this appointment.
>
> The time has passed when a southern republican cannot proclaim himself as such and at the same time enjoy the confidence and esteem of his fellow citizens. Judge Sanford has always been a republican, and being a southerner, and in every way identified with the welfare and the best interests of his people, and he has always held their confidence and merited their good will, this being true not only of the state in which he lives, but of this section.
>
> And so, if a republican is to be chosen for this vacancy on the supreme bench, the president can in the choice of Judge Sanford meet at the same time the demand of this section for the consideration to which it is justly entitled.[50]

In support of Sanford's candidacy, the attorney general and the White House received a large number of letters of recommendation for Sanford from across the South.

Sanford enjoyed bipartisan support from southern legislators, journalists, and the American Bar Association.[51] Tennessee Governor Austin Peay wrote President Harding as follows: "No one of all our citizenship ... stands higher than Judge Edward T. Sanford of Knoxville whose scholarly attainments, judicial temperament, experience and character render him preeminently qualified for this high trust."[52] Former Tennessee Governor Ben Hooper likewise contacted Harding to voice his support.[53] Former Kentucky Governor Augustus E. Willson submitted a letter, as did then-Governor Edwin P. Morrow.[54] The justices of the Tennessee Supreme Court, Colin P. McKinney, Nathan L. Bachman, Grafton Green, Thomas H. Malone, and Hugh G. Morrison, each informed Attorney General Daugherty of their support of Sanford.[55] US Representative J. Will Taylor of Knoxville traveled to Washington with a delegation of Knoxville lawyers to urge Sanford's appointment.[56] Perhaps in part because Sanford was frequently named as a viable Republican candidate for governor, the predominantly Democratic Tennessee General Assembly unanimously passed a resolution in support of Sanford's nomination.[57] It was in the best interest of Tennessee Democrats to see the popular Republican leave the state.

Sanford further was supported by retired US Supreme Court Justice William Day, before whom he had practiced while with the Department of Justice. Day recommended Sanford to the attorney general: "I became acquainted with Judge Sanford when he was Assistant Attorney General, and heard his arguments as such before the Supreme Court. I think it was the general impression, and I know it was mine, that he presented cases very well indeed.... I believe Judge Sanford has the qualities which would make him an excellent Judge should the honor suggested be conferred upon him."[58] Judge Loyal E. Knappen of the Sixth Circuit Court of Appeals also related that he was impressed with Sanford's knowledge of the law, his industry, his scholarly habits, and his culture and personality. He observed: "I regard him not only as one of the very best of our district judges, but as unusually adapted to appellate work. I cannot doubt that he would make a most excellent Justice of the Supreme Court."[59] Supporters touted the fact that at an ABA meeting in late 1921, Chief Justice Taft had called Sanford "one of the ablest District Judges in the United States."[60]

Sanford enjoyed the support of *The New York Times*, which National Republican Party Finance Chairman Charles D. Hilles attributed to the fact that "Mr. Ochs, who owns the *Times*, is a Tennessean."[61] Hilles, Taft's private secretary during his presidency, further noted that Boston journalist Jimmie Wilson was supporting Sanford because Wilson had been born in North Carolina and "always had a soft spot for promising men from the South."[62] Rotary Club, Optimist Club, and Civitan Club members urged Sanford's elevation. Bar associations across the State of Tennessee chimed in. The representative of a Chattanooga labor union sent a telegram to President Harding noting Sanford's "absolute freedom from bias."[63] Sanford was "a man of great modesty and was astonished when a movement began to make him Justice."[64] Opposition arose to Sanford's nomination on the part of many Northerners who felt that Tennessee already was represented on the Court by Justice McReynolds.[65] In spite of the fact that Brandeis and Holmes were both credited to Massachusetts, critics argued that it was a mistake to place two justices from one state on the Court.[66] An example of the criticism is as follows: "Though there is no necessity for the Executive to be geographically limited in making his selections for membership on the supreme bench[,] it would seem fairer to the country as a whole—all other things being equal—if he would scatter his favors around a little more. It is perfectly patent that a State which already has a member of the Court is fully represented. This might be different if a few of the States had a monopoly of judicial timber but no one believes that to be the case."[67] McReynolds had been born on the family plantation in Elkton, Kentucky. His connections to Tennessee were that he graduated as valedictorian of his undergraduate class at Vanderbilt University in Nashville and practiced law in that city from 1884 to 1903 after receiving his law degree from the University of Virginia and prior to taking a position with the Department of Justice. After leaving law school, McReynolds worked for US Senator and future Supreme Court Justice Howell Jackson of Tennessee. From 1900 to 1903, he taught commercial law at Vanderbilt with Judge Lurton of Tennessee.[68] After 1907, McReynolds lived in New York. The perception of McReynolds as a Tennessean was a significant obstacle for Sanford.[69]

When it became clear that Sanford would secure the nomination, Taft sent him a letter, dated January 23, 1923: "Do Come, Your seat on the Bench is waiting for you." Taft informed Sanford that there would be little delay in his confirmation.[70] The next day, on January 24, 1923, Sanford was formally nominated, and the Senate Judiciary Committee unanimously voted in favor of the nomination. In a telegram three days later, Taft announced that Sanford had been confirmed as the 72nd Justice of the United States Supreme Court by voice vote without opposition.[71] Sanford received his commission on January 29, 1923.[72] Justice Willis Van Devanter wrote him a congratulatory note: "I congratulate you on your nomination and confirmation as a member of our court and extend to you a most cordial welcome. The work in which we are engaged is of the greatest importance and is both interesting and exacting. You are splendidly fitted for it, and I am sure your participation in it will be helpful to all of us and also acceptable to you. I anticipate a high degree of satisfaction and pleasure from the approaching association."[73]

On February 5, 1923, in the presence of approximately 200 lawyers, officials, and citizens, Sanford took his statutory oath in the federal courtroom at the Custom House in Knoxville, where he had presided for fifteen years. The clerk of the court, Horace Van Deventer, Justice Lurton's son-in-law, used the same Bible from Sanford's district court ceremony and read the same passages from Deuteronomy that Lurton had read.[74] Two weeks later, on February 19, 1923, Sanford took his seat on the High Court bench in Washington, sworn in by Taft and then escorted to his chair at the far left of the chief justice.[75] Sanford was fifty-seven years old.

Sanford's confirmation might have been complicated had senators supportive of Prohibition viewed a message on the press wires the day following his nomination. It read: "Chattanooga bartenders banquet Judge Sanford." Upon verification, the big story turned out to be misleading. The correct message should have read: "Chattanooga bar tenders banquet to Judge Sanford."[76]

In *The Story of the Supreme Court*, Ernest Bates related that Sanford's appointment, for the most part, aroused little criticism.[77] Clearly the South was pleased with the pick. Senator William J. Harris of Georgia observed: "I am glad the president has appointed from the south a member of the highest court in our country. While I would have preferred a democrat, Judge Sanford is a man of fine character and excellent legal ability and many people in Georgia have spoken highly of him. I am gratified to see that the president feels that our section should have representation on the important courts, commissions, and boards of the government."[78] The Democratic *Courier-Journal* of Louisville, Kentucky observed that "the President could not have made a better choice." A Chattanooga editor, George Fort Milton, noted: "Edward Terry Sanford is not a [George Weston] Anderson[[79]] nor a [Kenesaw Mountain] Landis,[[80]] nor is he a Sutherland or a Butler. The fears of liberals on this point may as well be stilled. He is more of the mental stripe of Mr. Justice Holmes than of Mr. Justice Brandeis; yet his openness of mind, breadth of culture, and innate liberalism of thought class him, in my mind, as a distinctly, valuable addition to the Supreme bench. He possesses what I would call a justiciable mind."[81]

Milton observed further:

> The fact that [Sanford] is a Republican is the least important thing about him. The unanimity with which the members of the Democratic party in Tennessee and elsewhere in the South have [e]ndorsed

him and sought to aid his appointment indicates in a measure the esteem in which he is held where known. Labor leaders, capitalists, Democratic Congressmen, Republican Governor, Democratic Legislature, urged his choice.... Democratic editors were as zealous for Judge Sanford as if he were of their own party.

Milton proceeded to announce Sanford as exemplifying the "New South":

> The South is proud of the new Justice, and presents him to the Nation as a true representative of that spirit of idealism and common sense which has distinguished our material and ethical advance in the two past decades....
>
> Unlike many of his party in the South, he is not a Republican for revenue only. He is an East Tennessean, and to those who know the South this is an illuminating political classification.
>
> The man himself is neither businessman nor politician. He is as gentle as a woman and as brave as a lion.... Americanism is dear to his heart—the true type of Americanism, of love for the Constitution, including the Bill of Rights. He is an ideal judicial officer of the Federal Government; conscientious, kindly, precise, and open-minded.[82]

In another article, Milton labeled Sanford "a liberal–conservative" and, in an examination of Sanford's cases in *The Evening Star* of Washington, D.C., asserted that he "never allows conservative views ... to have the slightest weight when the future is to be considered in connection with rights dependent upon progressive future ideas."[83]

At this point in the history of the nation, a little over a half-century beyond the Civil War, Sanford's appointment was viewed by Southerners as acknowledgment of "the legitimacy and importance of the South as a region."[84] The northern press was also pleased with Sanford's selection. A *Philadelphia Public Ledger* reporter wrote that Sanford was "a man of great legal ability and of unimpeachable character." Other Pennsylvania newspapers proclaimed that Sanford "has a record of judicial fitness behind him" and opined that "[t]he standard of our highest court will be maintained."[85] The *Springfield* (Mass.) *Republican* declared: "Sanford has practiced law, taught law, administered the law and interpreted the law."[86]

For President Harding, a man described as preferring "instinctively the middle way," Sanford was a comfortable choice.[87] Harding has been described as "one of the most agreeable men with whom [one] ever came into contact, courteous and cordial.... With Democrats [Harding] was as genial as with Republicans...." Democrat Franklin Delano Roosevelt, when he was assistant secretary of the Navy and prior to his crippling illness, occasionally played golf with Harding.[88] Like Harding, Sanford did not antagonize any group.

The appointment of Sanford can be traced to several factors. First, Sanford was a southern Republican and received support from both parties. Second, Sanford had the backing of Harry M. Daugherty due to the influence of James A. Fowler. Third, Taft acquiesced in Daugherty's choice. Fourth, Sanford had experience as a district court judge. Additionally, the large number of court vacancies occurring within a short period of time worked to Sanford's advantage.[89]

Sanford was a southern Republican acceptable to Harding, who had won election to the presidency through the Southern vote.[90] The president had received all of Tennessee's twelve Electoral College votes, the only state in the South to support Harding, and Tennessee Republicans believed that they deserved a reward for that support.[91] Further, legislators in Tennessee passed a resolution in support of Sanford's candidacy.[92] The dean of the Vanderbilt Law School, the president of George Peabody College, the president of the University of Tennessee, the Episcopal bishop of Knoxville, the Catholic bishop of Atlanta, Tennessee's outgoing Republican governor, and the incoming Democratic governor all recommended Sanford.[93] Although Sanford's "selection was generally regarded as a move to restore the numerical representation of the South on the high court bench as it was when Chief Justice White died," he "was brought onto the Court to represent ... not the usual Democratic, Confederate South, but rather the atypical Republican South of his native East Tennessee."[94]

As to the theory that Sanford's nomination to the United States Supreme Court was secured largely by the lobbying efforts of Taft[95] and Attorney General Harry M. Daugherty,[96] more credit is due Daugherty than Taft. Although it has been argued that Taft was instrumental in obtaining Sanford's appointment to the Court, the evidence does not support that conclusion.

Fowler described a short delay in the appointment process occasioned by critics of Chief Justice Taft:

> The names of many other prominent Judges and Attorneys had been pressed upon the President[,] and when the announcement [regarding Sanford's potential appointment] appeared many protests were made to the President by the friends of the other applicants. The appointment was withheld for some time, a sufficient length of time to create uneasiness among Judge Sanford's friends. Apparently the appointment was withheld because of rather strong criticism by some Senators, who had endorsed other applicants, directed at the Chief Justice, who they asserted was dictating appointments. This was denied by the Chief Justice; and a few days later Judge Sanford's name was transmitted to the Senate; and the appointment was confirmed without question.[97]

Taft had resigned from the Sixth Circuit bench before Sanford became a district court judge, so the pair did not have a chance to sit together during Sanford's visits to that court as a judge. As a practicing Knoxville attorney, Sanford did argue cases before Circuit Judge Taft. They may have crossed paths when Taft campaigned for president in Tennessee in 1908, speaking first in Chattanooga on October 16, 1908, then traveling to Knoxville.[98] They may have interacted when Taft attended the 1911 Exposition in Knoxville. During World War I, Sanford had been active in Taft's League to Enforce Peace, and when the League of Nations was first being advocated, he made speeches in its support.[99] They were both active in the ABA and warm friends with Horace Lurton. The two men knew each other and were acquaintances, but they were not close. It appears that Daugherty guided Taft, because Sanford clearly was not Taft's first choice; he was adamant that Sanford was Daugherty's choice. Taft wrote to his brother Henry as follows: "I don't think Sanford is the strongest man, and he isn't my original suggestion, but I would now be glad to have him appointed."[100] Taft reported to Charles D. Hilles: "Sanford is not my candidate. He is really the candidate of the Attorney General, who suggested him to me, and took him up vigorously at the insistence of Fowler...."[101] In a communication from Hilles to Taft, Hilles remarked that "Fowler of Tennessee has done some effective work on behalf of his Candidate [Sanford]."[102] Hilles seemed wary of Fowler and cautioned Taft about supporting the appointment of Sanford on the recommendation of Fowler: "I know nothing of Sanford," he wrote, "except that the fact that Fowler presses him would put me on my guard."[103] Taft continued to recommend several other candidates to President Harding, including Governor Nathan Miller of New York; Cuthbert Pound, former dean of the Cornell Law School and a judge on the New York Court of Appeals; US Circuit Judge Charles M. Hough; Marshall Bullitt from Kentucky, solicitor general under Taft; and Henry Anderson, a prominent Virginia attorney.[104]

Daugherty suggested Sanford to Taft, supplying background information provided by Fowler, Sanford's former law partner and long-time friend.[105] Fowler, who was serving as Daugherty's special assistant, came into frequent contact with the attorney general. A letter from Daugherty to Fowler reveals the close working relationship between the two:

> [Y]our relations and mine were among the most pleasant of my experiences. You always told me what you thought and I gave your opinions consideration. Perhaps I did not always do what you wanted me to do, but I did the best I could in all situations and under the circumstances.... I would enjoy seeing you looking far away, as was your habit, then coming back, looking me in the eye and telling me straight out what you thought. That kind of man is not easy to get in the public service.[106]

In a letter to Fowler after Sanford's death, Daugherty reminisced on his role in Sanford's elevation to the Supreme Court:

> I suppose you know that I had more to do with the appointment of Judge Sanford than anybody else, and you might sometime when talking to Mrs. Sanford, if she is still alive, tell her a little story about his appointment. I knew Sanford's capabilities; I wanted to please Tennessee, and I was always glad to please you and other men like you who would not allow me on their advice to make a mistake. Taft had little to do with the appointment of Sanford and had not

considered him when he came to me in a special conference about the appointment of judges. I told him that I was friendly to Sanford of Knoxville, that I knew all about him, but had never talked to him on the subject and was not committed. Taft said, "Let's look him up," and I said it was not necessary as I knew all about him and if he wanted to pick him to pieces to do it in my presence and I would discuss it with him. At the conclusion he said he thought Sanford's appointment would be a fine one, adding, "You are lucky and you strike some good ones." I talked to the President about it the day I went to the W[hite] House. . . . I said to the President, "I want to see this vacancy filled before I leave the White House." He asked me who I was going to recommend and I said I wanted to recommend Sanford. He said, "All right." I said, "Well, let's send for a blank, the vacancy should be filled and I would [want] to send Sanford's name in immediately." He had his secretary bring in a blank which we prepared and sent in promptly. I suppose Sanford was surprised and pleased. Poor fellow, he has gone to his reward, but he served long enough to make a good record and to justify my recommendation. Afterwards, Taft saw fit to write me a letter in which he said, "Of course, you are the one person responsible for Sanford's appointment which is an excellent one.". . . I was proud of that appointment, as I was of every other appointment to the judiciary.[107]

In acknowledging that he "knew Sanford's capabilities" and that he "wanted to please Tennessee [for supporting Harding]," Daugherty possibly also backed Sanford for the Supreme Court seat to make amends for depriving him of the position of attorney general, the cabinet position the Southern Republicans had urged for him.

In a letter to President Harding, Taft acknowledged that he had "discussed the matter with the Attorney General, who had suggested Judge Edward T. Sanford of the Eastern District of Tennessee, 'a man whose appointment to the Supreme Bench would be on the whole a very satisfactory one. . . . He is a man of high culture . . . and most highly respected at the Bar in the community where he is known.'"[108] In a letter to Hilles, Taft indicated that Daugherty was convinced Sanford was the man for the job, and he agreed that Sanford would make "a good member of our court."[109] A subsequent letter to Hilles reiterated Taft's view that

"Harry [Daugherty] is strongly for Sanford." Taft stated, "I am bound to say that I think Sanford would be a good accession to our Bench."[110] Taft then told his brother Henry that he "so much prefer[red Sanford] to Pound or Crane or the Chief Justice of Pennsylvania that I would now be glad to have him appointed."[111]

Another Court scholar, William G. Ross, agrees that the idea of appointing Sanford originated with Daugherty and appealed to Taft "because he believed that the appointment of a federal district judge would raise the prestige of the lower federal courts."[112] Historian Henry Abraham concurs in this view: "Taft was not wild about Sanford, but he was aware of the virtue of the candidate's lengthy judicial experience on lower federal courts."[113] Taft valued prior judicial experience, believing it to enhance such desirable qualities as judicial temperament, personal integrity, collegiality, and proper philosophy of law. Prior experience as a judge meant that one knew how to behave as a judge rather than as a legislator, which "would only enhance the Court's reputation as an impartial body doing its best to apply the Constitution it had inherited."[114]

Ross further observed: "Even *The Nation* hailed Sanford's appointment, contending that Harding's selection of the Tennessean was 'the best of his several judicial appointments' since Sanford was 'a man of moderate instincts, had not served as a corporation attorney, and was not a friend of the president's.'"[115] According to Ross: "Although Sanford was conservative, his reputation as an urbane and open-minded man helped to make him palatable to progressives. In contrast to Butler, Sanford had no notable ties to large corporations, and his record as a judge did not reveal any anti-labor or corporate bias...." A Tennessee editor reported that Sanford lacked "the dogmatism of a Butler. He is not a professional patrioteer, 'hundred per center,' nor labor-baiter."[116] "Taft merely acquiesced" in the choice of Sanford because he was satisfied that Sanford was a "sound economic conservative with proved antagonism toward contemporary 'liberal progressive elements.'"[117]

Sanford's past as a railroad attorney for the Southern Railway, along with his work for his father's business interests and other corporate clients, was apparently overlooked. Sanford, described as "an oft-mentioned also-ran" for a position on the Court—"everybody's second choice"—was much like Harding in that he was the "available man."[118]

Sanford did appear to believe that Taft had been instrumental in his appointment.[119] The day after his Senate confirmation, he wrote to Taft: "I cannot adequately thank you. I can only endeavor, by steadfast and earnest effort, to prove worthy of your confidence and to aid, in every way within my powers, in the work of the Court and the faithful discharge of the high and sacred duty to our country which is its precious privilege." Taft's passive role in Sanford's nomination, however, sharply contrasted with his active role in the nomination of Pierce Butler. As noted by Walter F. Murphy, Taft "opened an intense campaign to bring off . . . [Butler's] nomination." On Butler's behalf, Taft then called on Harding and "wrote him several letters lavishly praising Butler and criticizing other candidates." After Butler was nominated, Taft gave Butler "detailed advice on which senators were important" and "arranged a quick judiciary committee meeting to approve the nomination."[120] Taft was quite frank in admitting to friends his limited part in Sanford's nomination.[121] As one source has observed:

> [T]here was no cordial exchange of pre-nomination letters between Taft and Sanford as there had been between Taft and Butler. On Jan. 6, 1923, the Chief Justice wrote Sanford a rather formal note, stating merely: "The newspapers report that you are to be appointed to succeed Justice Pitney. I only write to say that if this happens, I shall be delighted to welcome you as a colleague." Sanford's reply was effusive: "I cannot tell you how deeply I feel the kind expression in your letter. . . . If this good fortune should come to me, it would be the highest privilege to serve under your chieftainship." On Jan. 14, Taft wrote that he did not know what was holding up the nomination. Perhaps, he warned, the Senators from Pennsylvania, who resented his influence with the President, were pressuring Harding for their own candidate. On Jan. 29, 1923, Taft wired Sanford: "I congratulate you that the Senate has just confirmed your nomination. When may we expect you?"[122]

Harold M. Hollingsworth in "Tennessee and the Supreme Court of the United States" commented on the "exaggerate[d] role of Taft":

> When Sanford was elevated to the Supreme Court, the *Literary Digest* and several other leading periodicals attributed the appointment to the influence of Chief Justice Taft. In fact, Taft, who had enthusiastically campaigned for George Sutherland and Pierce Butler to join him on the high bench, felt Sanford was not the strongest man for the place.

However, since Sutherland and Butler had had no prior judicial experience, Taft believed that Sanford had the "very important" advantage of giving needed recognition to the inferior federal judiciary. If the Chief Justice was not enthusiastic, between three and four hundred people were, including the overwhelmingly Democratic Tennessee Legislature. However, Jerome P. Frank has observed that Sanford's support came "from the most nondescript group of unimportant little people ever organized to impress the President of the United States with the Supreme Court caliber of a candidate."[123]

It is surprising that Sanford's Century Club connections did not seem to help him attain the nomination. "As members of the small social club started to become presidents and cabinet members, a self-perpetuating network came into being that continued to place Centurions in high federal positions.... This network did not just benefit job applicants; it also enabled Centurions to recruit qualified assistants from a pool of able and motivated people with whose qualifications they were familiar."[124] The biographer of a noted Centurion has observed:

> Centurion mentors, role models, and people whom [Centurion] Charles C. Burlingham called "meddlers" were major factors in the ascent of Centurions to high federal office. In Burlingham's lexicon, "meddlers" were persons like himself who believed that one way to achieve good government was to mentor able people and then help secure their election or appointment by "meddling" in the political process. It was typical of Burlingham's mischievous side that he turned the usual meaning of "meddling" on its head and made it a noble political technique—at least when employed to place highly qualified mentees (or other good people) in important government positions. He considered "meddling" the final step in successful mentoring.[125]

Burlingham had joined the Century Club in 1893 and was a member for sixty-six years. He never held public office, but his influence exceeded that of many individuals who did. "Presidents, chief justices, cabinet members, governors, and mayors took his phone calls and responded promptly to his letters."[126] Burlingham was not sold on Sanford; rather, he supported US Circuit Judge Charles M. Hough, whom Burlingham described as "a horse for work and a very fast horse at that" and "one of the finest judges I have ever encountered."[127] In response to a charge made by Burlingham that Sanford was "vacillating and fussy," "would be overwhelmed," would be "swept along" on the bench, and would not be "the tower of strength you need," Centurian Taft declared: "I think I know more about Sanford than you. I have talked with his colleagues on the Bench who have sat with him in the Court of Appeals, and who have had to consider his opinions in review." Taft here refers to his inquiry to Judge Arthur C. Denison of the Sixth Circuit concerning the criticism of Sanford as being slow.[128] Stating that he had known Sanford for many years and had "always regarded him as a good judge,"[129] Taft proceeded to chastise Burlingham as follows:

> It is not so easy to select a Judge as you reformers think when you are really up against the responsibility. There are a good many side lights that don't strike you when you are sitting up in an apple tree and view the procession from there. If you people in New York were not so eager for money and would be content to live on a reasonable salary (and the same thing is true of Pennsylvania), you might have some representatives on the bench, but you are all after the almighty dollar. Now put that in your pipe and smoke it.[130]

Sanford did fit the mold of the majority of individuals elevated to the United States Supreme Court during that time-frame. He was, of course, a white male and a Protestant.[131] He came from a very prominent family of above-average financial means. He and his father had been involved in politics and public service.[132] Additionally, the economic circumstances of his family had provided Sanford cultural and educational advantages, although the Ivy League law degree was not an essential requirement then as it now appears to be for a seat on the Court.[133]

In contrast to all the support of his candidacy, only one enemy emerged, a purported attorney by the name of "J.D. Connel" of Knoxville. The first letter from this individual to President Harding, dated December 26, 1922, read as follows:

> The local papers in this city are daily announcing that you will, in a few days, promote Judge Edward T. Sanford from the judgeship of this Federal District to a place on the Supreme Court bench.
>
> I take it for granted that you have, or will fully investigate, Judge Sanford's judicial record.

I wish to call your attention to a few facts in his judicial career, to which you are entitled. It is very natural for the lawyers in his judicial district to commend him to you, most of whom feel he will not be appointed, but know that they will have to continue to practice their profession before him.

Judge Sanford is a gentleman of fine character and many excellent qualities as a man and with considerable literary attainments, but was never a successful practitioner at the bar before he entered public life. It is said of him that during his practice at the local bar he never had the satisfaction of winning an important lawsuit.

Judge Sanford is a very timid man and has little or no confidence in his judicial judgme[n]t.

Among the first important cases that came before him when he went on the bench was a lawsuit involving considerable money originating at Johnson City, Tennessee. After having heard this case argued, Judge Sanford was unable to decide it for three years, and when he did deliver an opinion in the case, it was three hundred pages long and was so full of errors, his decision was reversed by the higher courts, but, in the meantime, the delay proved disasterous [*sic*] to the litigants and the property involved was depreciated and dissipated to the ruin of the complainants.

This is only one of numerous instances of Judge Sanford's failures to come to conclusions in lawsuits, and of being too timid and without confidence in himself to make decisions.

A case was argued before him last June in Nashville to dissolve or sustain an injunction in some telephone litigation. I am informed that he has not yet sustained or dissolved the injunction, but is holding the case under advisement to the embarrassment and financial loss of the telephone company.

I am also reliably informed that he has several other cases under advisement which he has held six, twelve, twenty four and thirty months, and is yet unable to make up his m[i]nd in these cases.

During the recent labor troubles in Tennessee where it required courage, firmness and prompt judicial action, Judge Sanford desserted [*sic*] his court and left the state and Judge Ross of the western district had to come to Nashville and Knoxville and protect the interests of railroads and other property which was assailed by striking labor unions.

Some two or three years ago in the case of the United States government against the W.J. Oliver Manufacturing Company of Knoxville, in which much violence was in evidence, Judge Sanford left the state and the judge from the western district was called upon to come to Knoxville and try this most sensational case.

Judge Sanford lacks firmness [of] decision and would be the most incompetant [sic] man ever placed on the Supreme Court bench in its history.

I have no prejudice against him personally or judicially. I admire him as a high class man, but Judge Sanford, like the other members of his family and of his mother's family, has a peculiar and not a well balanced mind.

I submit these facts to you and if his appointment is seriously considered, you have only to summon leading members of the Tennessee bar before you to sustain these facts.

Having to practice my profession before Judge Sanford, I am submitting these facts in the interest of a competant [sic] and fearless judiciary in the great court of last resort, and I hope this information can be used confidentially and without prejudice to my business, but, if necessary, you can disclose the facts contained in this letter and the author of it.[134]

"Connel" followed up the first letter with another the following day. The second letter pertained to Sanford's financial record:

Some years ago, Judge Sanford became involved for more than he was worth in the East Tennessee National Bank of Knoxville, of which his father was vice president. Mr. Sanford paid the Judge's indebtedness to that bank, charging the amount against his son's interest in his estate. After the death of his father, Judge Sanford again became seriously involved in debt, and was forced to sell his home on West Hill Avenue, which his father gave him, to his brother, Alfred F. Sanford. He then moved his family into the home of his father-in-law, Capt. W.W. Woodruff, on West Cumberland Avenue, and has since and is now living in his wife's fathers' [sic] home. It is understood that her father is largely supporting their family.

Judge Sanford, since he went on the bench, became involved in business transactions, the tree nursery business, the quarrying of marble and dealing in real estate, in which he met with very heavy losses, and became deeply involved for borrowed money to banks, money sharks and pawn brokers, and had it not been for his two prosperous brothers, Alfred F. and Hugh W. Sanford, it is more than probable that Judge Sanford would have faced bankruptcy proceedings, a humiliating proceeding to the federal judiciary.

It is understood that these brothers paid for him and are still carrying, an indebtedness amounting to $75[,]000 to $100[,]000[135] and possibly more.

If Judge Sanford's indebtedness, principal and interest, were liquidated, he would be utterly insolvent.

I do not know that Judge Sanford has been guilty of anything dishonest in these disasterous [sic] business transactions, but has conducted them without business ability and always with losses, both to himself and his associates in these transactions.

As stated in my former letter, personally, he is a high class gentleman, but judicially, financially and in business transactions, is visionary, without balanced judgment, firmness or decision of mind.

I do not believe you want to put a man of this type, whose only qualification is courteous and gentlemanly manner, in the high position of a member of the Supreme Court of the United States.[136]

Harding sent an acknowledgment of the December 26th letter on January 3, 1923, but it was returned as undeliverable.[137] As word of the protest spread, attorneys involved in several of the cases mentioned in the first letter wrote to defend Sanford, stating that he was not to blame for the delays. The prosecution of millionaire manufacturer W.J. Oliver on charges of conspiracy, fraud, and sabotage in the manufacture of defective shells for the US Army occurred around the time Sanford traveled to England for his daughter Anna Magee's wedding.[138] Other judicial issues mentioned in the letter essentially correspond with Sanford's difficulties with the district court backlog. As to the financial matters outlined in the second letter, Fowler acknowledged that Sanford had difficulty financially managing the law practice when he was an attorney, inadequately billing and collecting fees.[139] This lack of diligence on Sanford's part apparently only manifested itself in his personal business matters because he was acknowledged as a strict keeper of the books for the University of Tennessee while a trustee.[140] Fowler further admitted that he and Sanford suffered some major investment losses.[141] Some of Sanford's bad investments involved deals concerning a nursery, peach orchards, and a marble quarry.[142] Sanford's father's will, executed in April 1902 approximately six months prior to E.J.'s death, did not reference any prior payments made on behalf of Sanford to be charged against his share of the estate. The document named Sanford, along with his brothers Alfred and Hugh, as executors and trustees of their father's estate.[143] E.J. specifically stated that he had "every confidence in the[] integrity" of his sons.[144]

As Sanford ultimately gained the $20,000 a year judicial appointment, it appears that any concerns of the Harding administration regarding the Connel letters were put to rest.[145] Whoever wrote the letters was knowledgeable of Sanford's affairs, but the author was never identified. The name "J.D. Connel" was undoubtedly a pseudonym. The bar membership rolls for Knox County, Tennessee, and the TBA for that time-frame contained no name similar to it. Sanford's indebtedness was not fully satisfied until after he joined the Supreme Court, at which time he received a significant amount of money from the sale of stock from his father's estate.[146] Ironically, E.J. had once written his partner Charles McClung McGhee that "[w]ith the start we will be able to give our children, if they can't take care of themselves, they could not keep what we give them no matter how much it might be."[147] Although he was less than successful in achieving his father's goals and ambitions for his business and financial future, Sanford did fulfill E.J.'s wish "to see him on the Supreme Court Bench."[148]

Knoxville's Post Office and Custom House, completed in 1874. Photographs of Tennessee Cities Collection, MS. 0951, University of Tennessee Knoxville—Libraries.

Knoxville as seen from the Sanfords' back yard on Summit Hill, ca. 1877. The cow in the foreground was owned by the Sanford family. Thompson Photograph Collection, C.M. McClung Historical Collection, Knox County Public Library.

Albert Chavannes. Knox County Two Centuries Project, C.M. McClung Historical Collection, Knox County Public Library.

Anna Francillion Chavannes. Knox County Two Centuries Project, C.M. McClung Historical Collection, Knox County Public Library.

Colonel E. J. Sanford. Knox County Two Centuries Project, C.M. McClung Historical Collection, Knox County Public Library.

Emma Chavannes Sanford. Knox County Two Centuries Project, C.M. McClung Historical Collection, Knox County Public Library.

Sanford Family Photo. Knox County Two Centuries Project, C.M. McClung Historical Collection, Knox County Public Library.

Edward J. Sanford Mansion, Maplehurst. Photographs of Tennessee Cities Collection, MS. 0951, University of Tennessee Knoxville—Libraries.

View of Gay Street's 400 block, early twentieth century. Photographs of Tennessee Cities Collection, MS. 0951, University of Tennessee Knoxville—Libraries.

Woodruff House, Knoxville, Tennessee. Thompson Photograph Collection, C.M. McClung Historical Collection, Knox County Public Library.

Edward Terry Sanford as a student at Harvard University.

Lutie M. Sanford.

The first official photograph of Associate Justice Edward Terry Sanford.

Formal group photograph of the 1923 Taft Court. Collection of the Supreme Court of the United States. Left to right: Front row: Willis Van Devanter, Joseph McKenna, William H. Taft, Oliver W. Holmes, James C. McReynolds. Back row: Pierce Butler, Louis D. Brandeis, George Sutherland, and Edward T. Sanford.

Formal group photograph of the 1925 Taft Court. Collection of the Supreme Court of the United States. Left to right: Front row: James C. McReynolds, Oliver W. Holmes, William H. Taft, Willis Van Devanter, Louis D. Brandeis. Back row: Edward T. Sanford, George Sutherland, Pierce Butler, Harlan F. Stone.

Seven Supreme Court Justices stand behind a model of the proposed building to house the United States Supreme Court, unveiled at the U.S. Capitol on May 17, 1929. Left to right: Louis D. Brandeis, Willis Van Devanter, Chief Justice William Howard Taft, Oliver Wendell Holmes, Pierce Butler, Edward Terry Sanford, and Harlan Fiske Stone. Collection of the Supreme Court of the United States.

The Supreme Court leaving the White House after paying their annual courtesy call on President Calvin Coolidge. Collection of the Supreme Court of the United States.

Edward and Lutie Sanford seated in the grandstand for an event.
Collection of the Supreme Court of the United States.

Justice Edward Terry Sanford and Alice Roosevelt Longworth
attending a New Year's Day reception at the White House.

Congressman Hubert F. Fisher and wife Louise Sanford Fisher (sister of Edward Terry Sanford) stand with the associate justice on the platform at Union Station.

Chief Justice Taft and Associate Justice Sanford outside the White House.

Left to right: Justices Stone, Butler, James Clark McReynolds, and Chief Justice Charles Evans Hughes at the rites for Edward Terry Sanford, Monday, March 10, 1930.

Mounted photograph of Associate Justice Edward Terry Sanford seated in his robes. Collection of the Supreme Court of the United States.

Half-length portrait of Justice Edward Terry Sanford. By Eben F. Comins, Collection of the Supreme Court of the United States.

CHAPTER NINE

The Taft Court

The Taft Court
Chief Justice William Howard Taft (1921–30)
1923–25: J. McKenna, O. W. Holmes, W. Van Devanter, J. C. McReynolds,
L. D. Brandeis, Geo. Sutherland, P. Butler, and E. T. Sanford.
1925–30: O. W. Holmes, W. Van Devanter, J. C. McReynolds, L. D.
Brandeis, Geo. Sutherland, P. Butler, E. T. Sanford, and H. F. Stone.

The office of chief justice carries scant inherent powers. The chief justice manages the docket, presents the cases in conference, and guides the discussion. When in the majority, the chief justice assigns the writing of opinions. The influence exerted in the exercise of these powers depends on the personality of the chief justice.[1] Former President William Howard Taft was well suited for the position.

Like Sanford, Taft capitalized on his Republican connections to move from one prominent position to the next. He was the son of a powerful Ohio lawyer, Alphonso Taft, who had been attorney general and secretary of war during the administration of President Ulysses S. Grant.[2] Taft's public service began in his home state of Ohio with positions as assistant prosecutor and assistant solicitor for Hamilton County and as a Superior Court judge. He served as the youngest-ever Solicitor General of the United States for two years, until he resigned in 1892 to become a judge on the Sixth Circuit Court of Appeals.[3] Taft served eight years on the federal appellate bench until 1900, when President William McKinley appointed him as chairman of the Philippine Commission. In this role, he was tasked with overseeing the transition of the Philippines from military to civilian rule.[4] After McKinley's assassination, President Theodore Roosevelt named Taft the first governor of the Philippines. From 1904 to 1908, Taft served as President Roosevelt's Secretary of War.[5] He served as president of the United States from 1909 to 1913.[6] After his presidency concluded, Taft spent time at Yale Law School as the Kent Professor of Constitutional Law.[7] President Harding nominated Taft to succeed Chief Justice Edward D. White in 1921.

In Taft's mind, property, including the right of contract and the right of labor, was the "keystone of our society," and any impairment of property rights threatened the "social fabric by undercutting the motive of enlightened activity."[8] In a 1907 speech to a group of Boston businessmen, he expressed his view forthrightly: "I believe that in connection with personal liberty, the right of personal property is the basis of all our material progress in the development of mankind, and that any change in our social and political system which impairs the rights of private property and materially diminishes the motive for the accumulation of capital by the individual, is a blow at our whole civilization."[9] Taft believed that the United States Constitution "rests on personal liberty and the right of property."[10] According to Taft, there was a minimum level of protection to which property was entitled and of which it may not be deprived without exceeding the Constitution. The due process clause guaranteed this minimum, and the equal protection guarantee spelled it out.[11] The due process clause, according to Taft, is a means to "enshrine liberty of contract and to preserve a laissez faire economy free from governmental control."[12]

In Taft's view, property rights were the benchmark against which other claims on government must be weighed.[13] Yet his experiences during World War I gave him a growing awareness that the rights of property might well have to be balanced against the interest of the community, especially the rights of labor.[14] Taft wrestled with the often-conflicting demands of property and natural human rights.[15] After his term as president, Taft served as co-chairman of the National War Labor Board, created by his successor President Wilson to mediate labor disputes during World War I. The board explicitly recognized "[t]he right of workers to organize in trade-unions and to bargain collectively, through chosen representatives," and it affirmed that this "right shall not be denied, abridged, or interfered with by the employers in any manner whatsoever."[16] While on the board, Taft went into the South to apprise himself of working conditions in the mills and factories. He was appalled by the grim realities of industrial labor. As a result of the trip, Taft secured an immediate increase in pay for the workers so that they could enjoy a decent standard of living.[17] The board shocked industrial leaders by declaring official support for the right of employees to receive a "living wage" to "[e]nsure the subsistence of the worker and his family in health and reasonable comfort."[18] Taft also supported the eight-hour workday.[19] He further backed the use of the Sherman Antitrust Act to curb the abuses of the public interest by the trusts.[20]

Although a conservative, Taft was aware "of the needs of the people in the throes of living and the abuses perpetrated by the wealthy."[21] He was to the right of center but not so far right as to ignore the social and economic inequities common to the nation. Indeed, he sought to alleviate them, insofar as it was constitutionally possible.[22] He was a conservative jurist who could, in given circumstances, render liberal decisions.[23] Before taking over the Court's center chair, Taft expressed the progressive view that courts must look beyond the law. Taft considered it both proper and necessary for a judge to adapt the law to new social conditions,[24] and he viewed the shaping of law to meet new situations as the Court's "highest and most useful function." The notion that "judges should interpret the exact intention of those who established the constitution" was thought by Taft to be the "theory of one who does not understand the proper administration of justice."[25] He recognized that the law was a living phenomenon, not something inert held fast by the past.

Taft the judge, however, was "known among labor men everywhere as the father of the offensive injunction rule of procedure in labor disputes."[26] As a judge prior to serving as president, Taft had issued injunctions frequently and was called the "Injunction Judge" during the 1908 presidential campaign. In Taft's view, judges had the power to protect property rights "against the depredations of the mob," and such rights were "'preferred freedoms' to be protected by the judiciary against have-not majorities that were always inclined to assault and redistribute the resources of the wealthy few."[27] Because he believed that the influence of organized labor threatened private property rights,[28] Taft's Court gave its blessing to the use of the labor injunction to crush union organizing efforts and rejected federal and state efforts to prevent courts from interfering with collective action by union members.[29] The period of the Taft Court was "a decade of the most intensive use of the labor injunction the country had ever seen."[30] The Court also applied the antitrust laws more aggressively to unions, which were viewed with suspicion by Taft.[31] A statement by Taft reflects his anti-labor bias: "The only class which is distinctly arrayed against the court is a class that does not like the courts at any rate, and that is organized labor. That faction we have to hit every little while, because they are continually violating the law and depending on threats and violence to accomplish their purpose."[32]

Taft's jurisprudence otherwise was dominated by a few other major ideas: the importance of nationalism, the necessity for intelligent social management, and the enforcement of law and order.[33] Taft's concern with lawlessness also accounted for a good deal of his well-known hostility to pro-labor legislation. In the wake of World War I, the country was experiencing sharply rising costs and a shortage of jobs with the return of American servicemen. In 1919, one-fifth of the nation's labor force was on strike. Race riots erupted in nearly two dozen cities, fueled by inflation, unemployment, and racial discrimination in employment. The unrest was blamed on "Reds, the Industrial Workers of the World (the Wobblies), radicals, and undesirable immigrants, especially those from southern and eastern Europe who were seen as carriers of the potentially deadly and highly infectious Bolshevism virus."[34] Taft, like millions of otherwise reasonable citizens, feared the impact of a Communist revolution in the United States.

The overwhelming majority of the Taft Court's decisions involved issues of regulation of the economy.[35] Because the Taft Court gave high priority to protection of private property, it supported freeing American businesses from most forms of governmental regulation.[36] The Supreme Court under Taft generally frowned on regulations that "excessively interfered with the liberty of contract and the free play of the capitalist system." The Court held economic regulations unconstitutional and substituted its views for those of Congress and state legislatures. The Court further viewed any necessary regulation of businesses and private property as the domain of the states, not the federal government.[37] Federal regulatory agencies found their power greatly restricted.[38] To keep the federal government off the back of business, the Taft Court adopted a restrictive interpretation of federal power based on the concept of dual federalism under the Tenth Amendment: the "separate jurisdictions of federal and state authority were clearly established and jealously defended."[39] Under Taft's leadership, the Court was regarded as "a reign of terror for state and federal legislation."[40] Taft's Court wielded the authority of a "super legislature."[41] Senator George Norris noted, "We have, in reality, another legislative body, called the Supreme Court, of 9 men; and they are more powerful than all the other [branches of government] put together."[42]

Taft believed in teamwork. Commentators observe that during Taft's time in President Roosevelt's service, "[o]ne can look in vain for any significant legal or political issue on which Taft and Roosevelt differed publicly."[43] Taft was "a loyal lieutenant, a team player, and it would have been out of character for him to go out of his way to confront [Roosevelt] directly on any issue." He "had made his way up the political ladder by working loyally within the party and winning the confidence of his peers—ingratiating himself along the way with those who had won political power through election."[44] Once Sanford joined Taft's Court, he acceded, for the most part, to Taft's desire for him to be a team player.

On the bench Taft did not appreciate dissents, especially those involving long explanatory footnotes.[45] He noted in a letter to then Justice John H. Clarke that "I don't approve of dissents generally, for I think that in many cases, where I differ from the majority, it is more important to stand by the Court and give its judgment weight than merely to record my individual dissent where it is better to have the law certain than to have it settled either way."[46] Taft was prone to attribute improper, even evil, motives to those who differed with him on constitutional issues.[47] He believed that most dissents were "displays of egotism that weakened the Court's prestige and contributed little of value."[48] Norms against dissent were prominent in the 1920s and were explicitly embraced in Canon 19 of the ABA's 1924 edition of the Canons of Judicial Ethics drafted by a committee chaired by Taft:[49] "It is of high importance that judges constituting a court of last resort should use effort and self-restraint to promote solidarity of conclusion and the consequent influence of judicial decision."[50] Taft especially hated "an exactly divided Court," which merely affirmed the judgment below.[51] According to Taft, "[t]he chief duty of a court of last resort is not to dispose of the case but to elaborate the principles, the importance of which justify the bringing of the case here at all, to make the discussion of those principles and the conclusion reached useful to the country and to the Bar in clarifying doubtful questions of constitutional law and fundamental law."[52]

Sanford wrote the Court's majority opinion in about eight percent of the cases in which he participated.[53] Sharing the views of Taft, Van Devanter, Butler,

McReynolds, and Sutherland that public displays of discord were distasteful, Sanford generally suppressed any disagreement with his colleagues.[54] He wrote only seven dissents or joined twenty-three dissenting opinions and seven concurring opinions.[55] In an effort to be a team player and to assist the Court to speak with one voice, Sanford changed his vote to join the Court opinion ninety-three times.[56] Although Taft was often at odds with Brandeis over footnotes, Sanford used more footnotes in his majority opinions than any other justice on the Taft Court, averaging 3.41 footnotes per opinion.[57]

Motivated by his passion for teamwork, Taft "persuaded by example," "exploited personal courtesy and charm, maximized the assignment and reassignment powers, [and] relied on the expertise of his associates."[58] He made it a point "to encourage his colleagues ... especially the narrow-minded Justice James C. McReynolds, to adopt a tolerant attitude toward Brandeis, the first Jewish member of the Supreme Court."[59] McReynolds, due to his "astonishingly mean and bigoted character," is "commonly regarded as one of the *worst* justices ever to sit on the Supreme Court."[60] Throughout his judicial tenure, McReynolds, openly anti-Semitic and racist, demonstrated prejudice against Jews, African Americans, and female professionals. He declined to appear at functions or ride in cars with Justice Brandeis[61] and would stalk from the conference table when Brandeis spoke, listen at the outside door until Brandeis finished, and then return to his seat.[62] Taft described McReynolds as "selfish to the last degree ... fuller of prejudice than any man I have ever known ... one who delights in making others uncomfortable. He has no sense of duty. He is a continual grouch; and ... really seems to have less of a loyal spirit to the Court than anybody."[63]

McReynolds's personality contributed, at least in part, to the resignation of Justice Clarke after only five years on the bench. Clarke wrote to President Wilson:

> McReynolds, as you know, is the most reactionary judge on the Court. There were many ... things which had better not be set down in black and white which made the situation to me deplorable and harassing to such a degree that I thought myself not called on to sacrifice what of health and strength I may have left in a futile struggle against increasing odds.... It was in some respects as disillusioning a chapter as Washington could afford....[64]

McReynolds also disliked Justice Harlan Stone, who had replaced Justice McKenna on the Court in 1924; he complained about almost every opinion Stone wrote. "When, on one occasion, Stone observed to McReynolds that a particular attorney's brief had been 'the dullest argument' he had ever heard, McReynolds, in typically abrasive and tactless fashion, replied, 'The only thing duller I can think of is to hear you read one of your opinions.'"[65] The so-called "rudest man in Washington" would also write comments such as "This makes me sick" on circulating opinions.[66] McReynolds "appeared to consider those who disagreed with him to be either stupid or evil."[67]

McReynolds was not alone in his unhappiness at having Justice Brandeis on the Court. Taft was serving as a Yale law professor when President Wilson appointed Brandeis to the Supreme Court, and it was a "fearful shock" to him. He considered Brandeis to be a socialist. Taft noted at that time, "It is one of the deepest wounds that I have had as an American ... that such a man as Brandeis could be put in the court."[68] Upon Brandeis's nomination, Taft joined the current and former ABA presidents in sending a petition to the Senate Judiciary Committee to question the personal and professional fitness of the nominee to sit on the Court. They urged the Senate to reject the nomination, which was delayed but ultimately approved by a margin of forty-seven to twenty-two.[69]

Prior to gaining a seat on the Court, Brandeis had been involved in movements for social justice: legalization of unions, women's suffrage, maximum hours and minimum wage legislation, and use of natural resources for the public rather than the private good. He criticized government and corporate corruption. Once on the Court, his opinions and dissents expressed "his views about the nature of the democratic state and the proper role of the individual within it."[70] The Constitution, in Brandeis's eyes, was designed to be flexible, as amenable to legislative experimentation as to judicial imagination. Dissenting in *New State Ice Company v. Liebmann*,[71] Brandeis stated: "There must be power in the States and the Nation to remould, through experimentation, our economic practices and institutions to meet changing social and economic needs."[72] Although Taft believed in a living Constitution, Brandeis was much more radical in his view.

In regard to the Court's caseload, Taft insisted that members stay current. During his tenure, Congress provided each justice one law clerk (at a salary of $3,600 per year) and one stenographic clerk (at an annual salary of $2,000)[73] to facilitate review of certiorari petitions and to assist with legal research and the drafting of opinions.⁷⁴ In the 1920s, the law clerks provided largely technical assistance.⁷⁵ Taft described the work of his law clerk as follows:

> The work which I would expect him to do would be to prepare for me a succinct statement of the briefs and record in every application for a certiorari, and to prepare, under my direction of course, the per curiams, which include nothing but references to authorities upon which the case is disposed of. There will be of course other things I shall need him for in the running down of a list of authorities and the finding of authorities where the briefs are insufficient in this regard. Then I would wish him to correct the proofs of my opinions and to keep track of my docket and keep it up to date.⁷⁶

Although each current justice of the US Supreme Court is entitled to four clerks, two secretaries, and a messenger, the contemporary Court publishes far fewer opinions than did the Taft Court.⁷⁷

During Sanford's time on the Court, he employed only one assistant, William R. Loney, a native of Baltimore.⁷⁸ Loney, fifty-four years old when he was hired by Sanford in 1923, had previously worked in the Office of the Attorney General and as a stenographer to Solicitor General Henry M. Hoyt.⁷⁹ In 1907, Loney graduated from National University School of Law, which he had attended at night.⁸⁰

Despite Loney's assistance, Sanford found it increasingly difficult to compose his opinions in a timely manner, as measured by the Court's pace of production. He considered this situation a personal failure. In the 1924 term, the Court as a whole averaged 70 days from oral argument to the announcement of a full opinion; but in that same term it took Sanford 121 days on average to produce his opinions. At the beginning of the 1925 term, Sanford, devoted to excellence, expressed his chagrin to Taft: "[I] hope I can do my full share of the labor. I believe I have gotten into better methods of work, and can successfully lay aside some of my besetting meticulosity–But verily the writing of an opinion worthy of perpetual type is a task of the highest difficulty that takes every ounce of the best that one may have."⁸¹

By May 1926, Taft asked Holmes to take some cases from "brother Van Devanter and brother Sanford" because they were "loaded down with cases which have been hanging over them for a long time and ought to have been disposed of." Taft related that "[t]hey are both nervous, they are both opinion shy, and they really need encouragement."[82]

Van Devanter, born and raised in Indiana, rose to prominence as a lawyer, politician, and judge from Wyoming. Prior to reaching the Supreme Court, he served as chief justice of the Wyoming Territorial Supreme Court, as a federal judge on the Eighth Circuit Court of Appeals, and, like Sanford, as an assistant attorney general with the Department of Justice. Van Devanter was considered to be well versed on issues of western land claims, Indian affairs, and jurisdictional matters. He was, however, criticized for his close connection with railroad interests.[83] It appears that Sanford's past legal work for the railroads and his father's involvement with their development escaped the scrutiny of Court watchers.

Considering his case backlog, why Sanford failed to take advantage of the government funding and hire a second assistant is an interesting question. So many years as a district court judge utilizing only one stenographer perhaps explains Sanford's comfort in working with only one person. His desire for excellence in his work product also may have made him reluctant to delegate any part of his duties. Sanford's workload struggles probably fueled Brandeis's criticism of him as a weak justice. Brandeis described Sanford as "nice, but no spark of greatness; thoroughly bourgeois."[84] He noted that "Sanford's mind gives one blurs; it does not clearly register."[85] He further opined that "Sanford ought never to have been above [district judge]—a dull bourgeois mind—terribly tiresome."[86] It was quite unusual for Brandeis to accept revisions suggested by Sanford.[87] Further, Sanford was not viewed as a justice able to "attract" votes to join his opinions.[88]

Taft's most significant contribution to the Court was as a leader and reformer. He laid the foundation for the institution of the Supreme Court as we know it today. Taft lobbied informally for passage of the Judges Act of 1922 and the Judiciary Act of 1925.[89] The 1922 act established a conference of senior circuit judges composed of the chief justice and the nine senior circuit judges (now called chief judges). The conference is the direct ancestor of the present Judicial Conference, which is the national policy-making body for the federal courts.[90] The law implemented the managerial task of compiling an annual "comprehensive survey of the condition of business in the courts of the United States" and recommending such changes as might be necessary or advisable.[91] This legislation empowered Taft, with certain limitations, to geographically reassign district court judges to meet the needs of judicial business. Taft's new statutory authority to transfer judges enabled him to oil "the judiciary machinery" and "to mass the force of the judiciary where the arrears are the greatest."[92] As a result, the situation in which Sanford found himself on the district court could now be addressed and the overcrowded dockets alleviated.

The 1925 act gave the Justices the ability to choose their own docket and decide which cases would be heard.[93] This statute abolished writs of error, restricted the cases in which appeals "as of right" were allowed to proceed to the Supreme Court, and provided that most cases be reviewed only when four of the nine Justices voted to issue a writ of certiorari.[94] The act drastically reduced the mandatory appellate jurisdiction of the Supreme Court to four classes of cases: (1) cases in which a state court has upheld a state statute against claims that the statute is invalid under federal law, or in which a state court has held invalid a federal statute or treaty; (2) cases in which a circuit court of appeals has held a state statute invalid under federal law; (3) cases coming by way of direct appeal from specially constituted federal district courts; and (4) cases certified by circuit courts of appeals, the District of Columbia Court of Appeals, or the Court of Claims.[95] Underlying the act was a reconceptualization of the function of the Supreme Court. According to Taft: "No man ought to have, as a matter of right, a review of his case by the Supreme Court. He should be satisfied by one hearing before a court of first instance and one review by a court of appeals." In Taft's view, the primary function of the Supreme Court was to supervise and administer the development of federal law.[96] Today, with only minor exceptions, the Supreme Court essentially is an "all-certiorari tribunal."[97] In the words of Peter Fish, the 1925 act "transformed" the Court "from a forum that primarily corrected errors arising in ordinary private litigation to a constitutional tribunal that resolved public policy issues of national importance."[98]

Taft also advocated for a new building for the Supreme Court, which during the Taft Court era held its sessions in the former Senate chamber of the US Capitol.[99] The courtroom in the Senate chamber was "visually impressive," having "columns of native Potomac marble, gray, painted walls, and mahogany furnishings with red draperies and carpeting."[100] The "intimate, elegant surroundings echoed with the debates of Webster, Clay, and Calhoun."[101] However, it had physical limitations: "The courtroom was badly ventilated and ill-lit. The Clerk's quarters were inadequate. There was no room provided for the bar. The library and conference room, in the basement, was small, cluttered, and extremely ill-ventilated...."[102] Because space was such a problem for the Court while it was housed in the Capitol, not all of the justices had offices in the building. Sanford had an office adjoining Sutherland's on the Capitol's the top floor.[103] Loney, his clerk, worked out of Sanford's home.[104]

Taft was appalled at the inadequate space and resources available to the Court within the Capitol building. Its administrative staff and offices were "scattered haphazardly and inefficiently" throughout the facility.[105] Taft lobbied for and obtained Congressional authorization and monies for a new Supreme Court building. The current site of the Court owes its existence to his efforts.[106] At the cornerstone ceremony in October 1932, Chief Justice Hughes stated: "For this enterprise now progressing to completion, we are indebted to the late Chief Justice William Howard Taft more than anyone else. The building is the result of his intelligent persistence."[107]

By July 1929, Taft began relieving himself of his workload. He turned over a patent case to Sanford that month, commenting in his letter, "I thought I ought to take it myself; but the truth is that I have been sick for nearly a month and I haven't been able to do any work."[108] Disabled by illness, Taft ceased participating on December 9, 1929. He resigned effective February 3, 1930.[109] To the end, however, he remained firm in the belief that the Court must hold the line; it must protect property and liberty of contract from "troublemakers who stimulate popular passion and threaten encroachment."[110]

# CHAPTER TEN

Sanford's Tenure

[There are justices] who have served the country . . . usually with honor, but whom history has all but forgotten. . . . Each was shaped by, and shaped, his times and circumstances. And each reveals that the judge is more than his jurisprudence. Underneath their robes, so to speak, the Justices of the Supreme Court are real, often quite unique, people. With all the current focus on judges' so-called ideologies, it is worth remembering that a judge's personal history and character also matter. . . .[1]

—Sandra Day O'Connor

Once Sanford joined the Taft Court in 1923, he was described as "urbane" and a "genial southerner"[2] who brought to the Court "a quiet moderation, a respect for precedent, and considerable erudition."[3] Future Chief Justice Hughes observed of Sanford: "In addition to sound technical training as a lawyer and broad experience as a judge, Mr. Justice Sanford had resources of culture, developed by travel and liberal studies both here and abroad. He was interested in literature, music and art, and those who enjoyed companionship with him were not disappointed because of limitations in his horizon. While the learning of the law was his supreme interest, it neither monopolized nor narrowed him." A lawyer from Tennessee noted that Sanford's opinions disclosed

> his scholarly training; for not only was he equipped with technical knowledge, but he also had that culture and breadth of vision which is so valuable in high judicial position. His professional learning was supplemented by an intimate familiarity which gave to his judicial opinions an unusual clarity and attractive style. He had the rare gift of felicitous expression, which he used to good advantage at the Bar, and could not be satisfied with any judicial utterance that did not clearly show his views and disclose the reasons upon which he based his decisions.[4]

Most of the opinions authored by Sanford "were the ordinary cases that ground their way through the courts in the 1920s, including judicial review of economic regulations, war-related cases, and prohibition cases."[5] Regarding Sanford's opinions that addressed procedural issues and generated little public interest, Hughes further remarked: "[W]ith philosophic bent and conscientious application, he was faithful to the judicial tradition devoting the same care to every case which came before the Court, without regard to its rating in public opinion. He was ever intent upon the intrinsic quality of his work rather than upon adventitious circumstance."[6] After Sanford's death, the resolution adopted by the Supreme Court Bar and spread upon the minutes of that tribunal read as follows: "His work upon the Supreme Court was thorough, conscientious and exacting, and he had the high commendation of his associates and of the Bar."[7]

Sanford's 130 published Supreme Court opinions are found in volumes 261 to 281 of the United States Reports. By the liberal press, Sanford is considered a conservative. In his voting, he was found most often with the conservative majority, particularly on economic issues.[8] The majority on the Taft Court typically used the judicial power to enforce their commitment to laissez faire economic policies,[9] opposing government regulation of business and economic practices. A reporter observed in a 1925 article that the majority on the Court desired to relieve business "from restraints imposed during the administrations of Presidents Roosevelt, Taft, and Wilson."[10] Sanford was co-opted into Chief Justice Taft's conservative economic group, and his opinions usually were written for the solid majority of Justices Van Devanter, Butler, Sutherland, and McReynolds. From

Taft's viewpoint, he led this group against "radicals," "Progressives," "Bolsheviks," "Socialists," and others who favored "breaking down the Constitution" whether on or off the bench.[11]

Nevertheless, Sanford had "progressive tendencies" and voted with the liberals to sustain the validity of the federal gift tax and state regulation of ticket scalpers.[12] He exhibited at times a "pre-New Deal liberalism" and felt that "courts ought to defer to democratic lawmaking."[13] "On civil libertarian matters, too, Sanford's record betrays some mercurial behavior."[14] He was not rigid in his interpretation of the Constitution and felt that interpretation of it should "be adjusted by the times."[15] A view of Sanford's tenure on the Supreme Court reveals that as one of the justices "closest to the Court's statistical center," he often "leaned toward the Brandeis-Holmes [liberal] pole rather than toward the McReynolds-Sutherland [conservative] pole."[16]

By 1928, Sanford was "leaning to the right, but only slightly."[17] This fact validated the 1923 observation of Court watchers: "Liberal opinion is quite as much pleased over the appointment of Edward Terry Sanford to the Supreme Court as it was distressed over that of Pierce Butler. Liberals in fact are claiming Judge Sanford as one of themselves just as they have claimed Justices Holmes and Brandeis."[18] It was Van Devanter, rather than Sanford, who served as Taft's closest Court ally. Taft claimed that his "mainstay in the Court is Van Devanter"[19] and observed to a friend: "Mr. Justice Van Devanter is far and away the most valuable man in our court" and he "exercises more influence, a good deal, than any other member...."[20] Outside the Court, Taft referred to Van Devanter as "my chancellor."[21] Brandeis noted in 1922 that Van Devanter "runs Court now" and "is like a jesuit general...."[22]

Opinions on Technical Matters

Sanford was known for his opinions involving the interpretation of difficult procedural or statutory matters.[23] The vast bulk of decisions he authored addressed issues relating to war claims, tax matters, government, admiralty, business, patents, and especially bankruptcy.[24] Additionally, Sanford was requested by Chief Justice Taft to write quite a number of opinions addressing federal jurisdiction.[25] His clear and precise writing style resulted in few dissents by the other justices to these technical and jurisdictional opinions.[26]

As once noted by the late Justice Antonin Scalia of the US Supreme Court, patent cases tend to be the "hardest."[27] In *I. T.S. Rubber Company v. Essex Rubber Company*,[28] Sanford, writing for the Court, addressed the scope of a patent for a rubber heel. The claims in the suit were limited to "the specific form of a three-point contact lift" style of heel. Sanford determined that the plaintiff's patent was not infringed by the heels made by the defendant because the defendant's heels were not "three-point contact lifts, their upper side edges having no vertical curve and lying entirely in the same horizontal plane as the rear edge and breast corners."[29] He concluded:

> It is well settled that where an applicant for a patent to cover a new combination is compelled by the rejection of his application by the Patent Office to narrow his claim by the introduction of a new element, he cannot after the issue of the patent broaden his claim by dropping the element which he was compelled to include in order to secure his patent. . . . The applicant having limited his claim by amendment and accepted a patent, brings himself within the rules that if the claim to a combination be restricted to specified elements, all must be regarded as material, and that limitations imposed by the inventor, especially such as were introduced into an application after it had been persistently rejected, must be strictly construed against the inventor and looked upon as disclaimers. The patentee is thereafter estopped to claim the benefit of his rejected claim or such a construction of his amended claim as would be equivalent thereto.[30]

In *Hellmich v. Hellman*,[31] two taxpayers sued to recover additional income taxes assessed against them after they, as stockholders of a business, received payouts when the corporation was dissolved. The issue was whether the amounts distributed to the stockholders out of the earnings and profits accumulated by the corporation were to be treated under the relevant statute as "dividends" exempt from the normal tax, or as payments made by the corporation in exchange for its stock, which were taxable "as other gains or profits." The Court, speaking through Sanford, concluded that

> when section 201(a) and section 201(c) are read together, under the long-established rule that the intention of the lawmaker is to be

deduced from a view of every material part of the statute, we think it clear that the general definition of a dividend in section 201(a) was not intended to apply to distributions made to stockholders in the liquidation of a corporation, but that it was intended that such distributions should be governed by section 201(c), which, dealing specifically with such liquidation provided that the amounts distributed should "be treated as payments in exchange for stock" and that any gain realized thereby should be taxed to the stockholders "as other gains or profits." This brings the two sections into entire harmony, and gives to each its natural meaning and due effect.[32]

In a decision superseded by the Declaratory Judgments Act,[33] *Liberty Warehouse Company v. Grannis*,[34] Sanford addressed a Kentucky law providing that parties before a general jurisdiction court of the state could petition for declaratory judgments announcing the rights of parties without requiring performance by anyone. A Kentucky corporation operating a loose-leaf tobacco warehouse filed a petition seeking a declaratory judgment from a federal district court of its rights under the terms of a Kentucky law regulating the sale of leaf tobacco at public auction. Sanford adhered to precedent and ruled that the federal court did not have jurisdiction to make such a declaration; he stated that jurisdiction under Article III extends only to "cases" and "controversies" and "does not extend to the determination of abstract questions or issues framed for the purpose of invoking the advice of the court without real parties or a real case."[35]

In *Sovereign Camp Woodmen of the World v. O'Neill*,[36] the defendants allegedly entered into an agreement and conspiracy to embarrass and attempt to ruin the Woodmen of the World Society. The action had been dismissed by the district court on the ground that the requisite jurisdictional amount was not present. The Supreme Court, speaking through Sanford, held that "[a] conspiracy to prosecute, by concert of action, numerous baseless claims against the same person for the wrongful purpose of harassing and ruining him, partakes of the nature of a fraudulent conspiracy; and in a suit to enjoin them from being separately prosecuted, it must likewise be deemed to tie together such several claims as one claim for jurisdictional purposes, making their aggregate amount the value of the matter in controversy."[37] The Court concluded "that, on the face of the bill, the District Court had jurisdiction of the suit by reason of the diversity of citizenship and the amount in controversy."[38]

The government sought in *United States v. State Investment Company*[39] to establish legal title to a large strip of land claimed as part of public lands. A "quiet title" action ensued against the defendant company that also claimed the land so that the court could determine the rightful owner. The company based its claim to the land on the Mora Grant, a community grant made by the Republic of Mexico in 1835. The location of the west boundary of the Mora Grant, known as "the Estillero," controlled the issue, and the question before the Court was whether the strip of land at issue was within the grant. The company contended that the west boundary had been "established by stones marked by [a US Surveyor] and by the natural objects called for in the survey."[40] The government argued that the boundary was "more than three miles farther east," as established by a later survey.[41] The district court concluded that the calls for natural objects and permanent monuments on the ground controlled the determination of the boundary. The government was found to have conveyed the land lying to the east of the boundary and had no title to it. The Circuit Court of Appeals concurred. Sanford, for the Court, affirmed "[t]he general rule ... that in matters of boundaries[,] calls for natural objects and fixed monuments control those for distances[,] [a]nd calls for courses likewise prevail over those for distances."[42] In view of these principles and finding no ground for exception, the Court affirmed the lower court decision that the boundary line was in the location claimed by the company.

Sanford was the author of *Oklahoma v. Texas*[43] involving the location of the true boundary line between those two states. After extensive analysis of the surveys submitted, Sanford, who received surveying training as an undergraduate at the University of Tennessee, disregarded the arguments of the parties and determined that the boundary was the line of the true 100th meridian extending north from its intersection with the south bank of the South Fork of Red River to its intersection with the parallel of 36 degrees 30 minutes. He ordered that this line should be accurately located and marked by a commissioner or commissioners appointed by the Court.[44] An order granting a motion in this case, dated February 24, 1930, was the last time Sanford ever spoke for the Court prior to his sudden death.[45]

In another boundary matter, *New Mexico v. Texas*,[46] New Mexico, which became a state in 1912, filed an action against its neighbor to settle a controversy concerning the location of the channel of the Rio Grande in 1850, at which time both parties agreed that the river marked the proper boundary between the two states. New Mexico claimed that a marker mentioned in an 1859 survey, which had disappeared, was improperly relocated in 1911. The disputed distance was about four miles. Both parties filed exceptions to the report of a special master. As the plaintiff, New Mexico bore the burden of proving that the special master's report was erroneous. Writing for the Court, Sanford held that "the testimony of the witnesses as to their recollection of the old river is far from satisfactory, and does not, in view of the other evidence in the case, sustain the burden of proof resting upon New Mexico.... [A]ccording to the greater weight of the evidence, the river, in 1850 ... ran southwardly ... as shown by certain of the surveys, patents and maps relied on by Texas...."[47] In discussing changes to the river course since 1850, which had resulted from accretion, Sanford observed that New Mexico "explicitly declared in its Constitution that its boundary ran [between parallels of 32 degrees and 31 degrees 47 minutes following the main channel of the Rio Grande] as it existed on the ninth day of September, [1850]. ... This was confirmed by the United States by admitting New Mexico as a State with the line thus described as its boundary; and Texas has also affirmed the same by its pleadings in this cause.... New Mexico, manifestly, cannot now question this limitation of its boundary or assert a claim to any land lying east of the line thus limited."[48] Sanford concluded that the boundary line between New Mexico and Texas ran in the middle of the channel of the Rio Grande as it was in 1850, as determined by "The Salazar-Diaz Survey of 1852, the Texas surveys of 1849 and 1860, the maps of the surveys made in 1852-1855 for the Joint Boundary Commissions, and the Clark map of 1859."[49] New Mexico's less precise witness testimony about the river's location in 1850 was discredited. To this day, the land claimed by New Mexico is a corner of Texas separated from the rest of the state by the Rio Grande.

In *Pendergast v. New York Telephone Company*,[50] the defendant public utility commission conducted a hearing and entered an order setting a temporary maximum rate that the plaintiff telephone company was allowed to charge for its services. The company thereafter brought an action asserting that the rates were confiscatory in nature and, therefore, should not be enforced. The district court entered an injunction restraining enforcement of the rate restriction until the commission could conduct a final hearing on the rate. Speaking through Sanford, the Court held that the telephone company's lawsuit was not premature; the company was not required to wait until the final hearing before filing an action in the district court. The commission's order constituted a final legislative act and, therefore, the company was entitled to injunctive relief until the rate-making process was completed.[51] The fact that the commission entered temporary rates did not deprive the company of its right to relief in the district court.

In cases concerning presidential power, the Taft Court usually resolved separation of power questions in favor of the executive.[52] One of the most important procedural opinions decided by the Court was *Okanogan Indians, et al. v. United States ("The Pocket Veto Case")*,[53] in which the Court, in an opinion authored by Sanford, clarified the rules by which a President could use the power of a pocket veto, a question that had remained open for 140 years.[54]

Article I, section 7 of the Constitution provides that if a president does not return a proposed bill to Congress within ten days, the proposal shall become law "in like manner as if he had signed it." In the case before the Court, Congress had passed a bill allowing certain Indian tribes to sue for damages for the loss of their tribal land. When the bill went to President Calvin Coolidge, he neither signed it nor vetoed it. Congress adjourned its session before the expiration of ten calendar days (Sunday excepted) after the bill had been presented to the president.[55] The determinative issue was whether the pocket veto clause applied only to final adjournments at the end of a Congress, or whether it also applied to adjournments at the end of a session of Congress. It was urged that an adjournment of the first session of the Congress does not prevent the president from returning the bill because the legislative existence of the Congress is not terminated, and the bill may be returned to an agent of the House in which the bill originated.[56]

Sanford held that the clause applied to adjournments at the end of a session as well as at the end of a Congress. He wrote that the Article I reference to ten days was ten calendar, not legislative, days; he noted, however, that if Congress is not in session for the full ten days after sending a bill to the president, the bill does not become law if the president does not sign it. Instead, it is conclusively vetoed because Congress cannot attempt to re-pass the unsigned bill.[57] Sanford observed that "when the adjournment of Congress prevents the return of a bill within the allotted time, the failure of the bill to become a law cannot properly be ascribed to the disapproval of the President—who presumably would have returned it before the adjournment if there had been sufficient time in which to complete his consideration and take action—but is attributable solely to the action of Congress in adjourning before the time allowed the President for returning the bill had expired."[58] In this case, the Court approved a liberal interpretation of the president's power of the pocket veto by allowing bills to be vetoed by not returning them to Congress during adjournments, as well as at the end of a congressional term.[59]

Federal Legislation

Sanford interpreted the Constitution in a flexible manner that allowed the federal government to address national problems. He was sympathetic to federal legislation and gave the national government the benefit of the doubt "if it could present a plausible case for enhanced federal regulation under existing national powers."[60] He recognized the need for a strong national government to protect individuals against abusive state governments, and his record was one of upholding federal power against the so-called rights of states.[61] This generalization is borne out by his position on a wide variety of subjects. Sanford upheld the greatly increased regulatory power of the Interstate Commerce Commission under the Transportation Act of 1920.[62] He believed that federal control over interstate power lines should be broadened[63] and that the right of the City of Chicago to divert water from Lake Michigan for drainage purposes should be curtailed.[64] Recognizing how effectively the federal government could address issues of national scope, Sanford believed in expanding the constitutional range of congressional power and upheld the quarantine activities of the Department of Agriculture.[65] He voted to sustain federal regulation of grain elevators and stockyards against both substantive due process and Tenth Amendment challenges.[66] Further, he defended activities of federal entities against state attempts to tax them.[67] Sanford generally believed that the Court should not interfere with legislative initiatives,[68] and he "was considerably more flexible" than Van Devanter, Butler, Sutherland, and McReynolds "on some aspects of governmental regulation."[69]

Admiralty

One aspect of national law in which Sanford wrote opinions was admiralty. Examples of Sanford's rulings in admiralty cases involving the Merchant Marine Act of 1920 include *Pacific S. S. Company v. Peterson*[70] and *Lindgren v. United States*.[71] In *Peterson*, the seaman was injured due to "the negligence of the mate of the vessel." Once the ship docked, the seaman was taken to a hospital "for maintenance and cure" and given his wages.[72] The company contended that the seaman had been fully compensated and could not bring an action under the amended provision of the Merchant Marine Act that gave "to seaman injured through negligence the rights given to railway employees by the Employers' Liability Act...."[73] Sanford reviewed prior general maritime law and concluded that "the right under the new rule to compensatory damages for injuries caused by negligence is not an alternative of the right under the old rule to maintenance, cure and wages...."[74] He noted "that the right of a seaman to receive his wages to the end of the voyage and to be cured at the ship's expense" was "grounded solely upon the benefit which the ship derives from his service" and has "no regard to the question whether his injury has been caused by the fault of others or by mere accident."[75] Sanford held that "claims for maintenance, cure and wages, and for indemnity for injuries occasioned by unseaworthiness, may be demanded and recovered in the same proceeding," and "that a recovery in one proceeding for wages and maintenance does not preclude the recovery in a subsequent proceeding of indemnity for injuries resulting from unseaworthiness."[76] Sanford further found that "there is no inconsistency between the right to recover compensatory damages under the new rule for injuries caused by negligence and the right to recover maintenance, cure and wages under the old rules," as "the adoption of one is [not] a repudiation or negation of the other."[77] "In short, the right to maintenance, cure and wages, implied in law as a contractual obligation arising out of the nature of the employment, is independent of the right to indemnity or compensatory damages for an injury caused by negligence."[78]

In *Lindgren* Sanford determined:

> By the Merchant Marine Act ... the prior maritime law was modified by giving to personal representatives of seamen whose death had resulted from personal injuries, the right to maintain an action for damages in accordance with the provisions of the Federal Employers' Liability Act. It is plain that the Merchant Marine Act is one of general application intended to bring about the uniformity in the exercise of admiralty jurisdiction required by the Constitution, and necessarily supersedes the application of the death statutes of the several States.[79]

Sanford noted that prior to the adoption of the Merchant Marine Act, the general maritime law had not authorized any recovery of damages or indemnity for the death of a seaman,[80] as state law was regarded as determinative of employer liability in such cases.[81] After exhaustive review of prior law, Sanford concluded "that the Merchant Marine Act—adopted by Congress in the exercise of its paramount authority in reference to the maritime law and incorporating in that law the provisions of the Federal Employers' Liability Act—establishes a modification of the prior maritime law ... supersed[ing] the operation of all state statutes dealing with that subject."[82] These decisions reflect his respect for precedent and preference for uniform laws.

Prohibition

The Eighteenth Amendment, which prohibited the "manufacture, sale, or transportation of intoxicating liquors within ... the United States ... for beverage purposes,"[83] was "the most radical political and social experiment of our day." The Taft Court decided a number of cases relating to Prohibition, all of which supported efforts to enforce it.[84] This support for Prohibition was somewhat surprising because most of the Court was opposed to the expansion of the national administrative state, "particularly in contexts in which the national government sought to displace local police power."[85]

Sanford "displayed a marked zeal for prohibition enforcement" and on occasion was willing to go to greater limits than the other justices in upholding the validity of acts of prohibition agents.[86] For example, he voted with the majority in *Carroll v. United States*,[87] holding that the Fourth Amendment did not prohibit the police from stopping and searching an automobile on the public highway without a warrant if the vehicle was believed to contain liquor.[88] The Court held that an "exception" existed allowing warrantless searches of cars based upon probable cause to believe contraband is present. The "mobility" of the vehicle created the "exigent circumstances" justifying the warrantless search.[89] The *Carroll* decision has been described as "condon[ing] a more reprehensible practice than that exercised by British officials in Colonial times."[90] Sanford also stood with the majority in *Olmstead v. United States*,[91] a controversial five-to-four decision upholding the legality of evidence obtained by tapping the private telephone wires of a bootlegging ring.[92] The Court held that electronic interception of oral communications was not a search or seizure and that wire-tapping was not subject to the Fourth Amendment. One scholar described this vigorous support of Prohibition as a fusion of a conservative belief in social control with an embrace of legal positivism.[93] Opposition to the Eighteenth Amendment was interpreted as resistance to the legal order itself.[94] For Sanford, along with Taft and Van Devanter, "'judicial conservatism' [became] a policy of respect for positive law in the context of what was surely the most controversial and momentous issue of their time."[95]

Sanford's background suggests that he was predisposed to favor the policy of Prohibition. Temperance forces had been active in his hometown of Knoxville as early as 1872, circulating petitions in favor of a law to restrict the sale of "spiritous and vinous liquors."[96] By 1907, when closure of saloons was achieved by referendum, Knoxville had 113 saloons, concentrated mainly on Central Avenue, Gay Street, and Market Square.[97] The 100 block of South Central alone had about ten competing saloons.[98] Partial prohibition had become law in Tennessee in 1909, whereas national Prohibition did not go into effect until 1920.[99] Sanford and his father clearly supported temperance, as demonstrated by the plans to ban alcohol in the community developed by the Lenoir City Company. The newspaper in which Sanford's family held an interest, *The Knoxville Journal and Tribune*, was a staunch supporter of Prohibition legislation as well.[100]

In *James Everard's Breweries v. Day*,[101] the issue was whether a section of the Supplemental Prohibition Act of 1921[102] was constitutional, insofar as it prevented physicians from prescribing intoxicating malt liquors for medicinal purposes. The plaintiffs asserted that the prohibition on prescribing or using intoxicating malt liquors for medicinal purposes was neither an appropriate nor reasonable exercise of the power conferred upon Congress by the Eighteenth Amendment. The plaintiffs also argued that the ban infringed upon the legislative power of the states in matters affecting the public health. For the Court, Sanford observed: "The opportunity to manufacture, sell and prescribe intoxicating malt liquors for 'medicinal purposes' opens many doors to clandestine traffic in them as beverages under the guise of medicines...."[103] According to Sanford, Congress had determined that intoxicating malt liquors possessed no substantial and essential medicinal properties that justified their use for medicinal purposes. He noted that neither beer nor any other malt liquor was listed as a medicinal remedy in the United States Pharmacopeia and that alcoholic beverages were not generally recognized as medicinal agents.[104] He concluded: "A provision ... which tends to diminish the opportunity for clandestine traffic ... has a reasonable relation to its enforcement."[105] The section was, therefore, constitutional.

One court scholar observed that "the movement in favor of federal control of matters formerly within the police power of the states reached a peak with the adoption of the Eighteenth Amendment."[106] Another observer concluded that "Sanford's opinion was ruthlessly nationalistic in the sense of favoring federal power over state power." Sanford found that if Prohibition "is within the authority delegated to Congress by the Eighteenth Amendment, its validity is not impaired by reason of any power reserved to the States. . . ." He observed: "If the act is within the power confided to Congress, the Tenth Amendment, by its very terms, has no application, since it only reserves to the States 'powers not delegated to the United States by the Constitution.'"[107] Sanford held that Congress had the power to achieve the purposes of the Eighteenth Amendment by "any means, appearing to it most eligible and appropriate, which are adapted to the end to be accomplished and consistent with the letter and spirit of the Constitution."[108] Journalists reported that the Court "certified as to the perpetual airtightness of the Eighteenth Amendment, pointing out that congress can do just about anything it wants to under that amendment, even to the abuse of the power it grants."[109] Taft regarded the *Everard's Breweries* case as "pretty important."[110]

Another Prohibition case in which Sanford voiced an expansive view of congressional powers was *Ma-King Products Company v. Blair*.[111] The petitioner, in accordance with the National Prohibition Act, applied to the Commissioner of Internal Revenue for a permit to operate a plant for denaturing alcohol. The commissioner, however, denied the application. Speaking for the Court, Sanford concluded:

> It is clear that the Act does not impose on the Commissioner the mere ministerial duty of issuing a permit to any one making an application on the prescribed form, but, on the contrary, places upon him, as the administrative officer directly charged with the enforcement of the law, a responsibility in the matter of granting the privilege of dealing in liquor for nonbeverage purposes, which requires him to refuse a permit to one who is not a suitable person to be entrusted, in a relation of such confidence, with the possession of liquor susceptible of division to beverage uses.
>
> The dominant purpose of the Act is to prevent the use of intoxicating liquor as a beverage, and all its provisions are to be liberally construed to that end. It does not provide that the Commissioner shall issue a liquor permit, but merely that he may do so. It specifically requires the application to show "the qualification of the applicant," and authorizes the Commissioner to prescribe, "the facts to be set forth therein." These provisions, as well as the purpose of the Act,

are entirely inconsistent with any intention on the part of Congress that the Commissioner should perform the merely perfunctory duty of granting a permit, to any and every applicant, without reference to his qualification and fitness; and they necessarily imply that, in order to prevent violations of the Act he shall, before granting a permit, determine, in the exercise of his sound discretion, whether the applicant is a fit person to be entrusted with such a privilege.[112]

Antitrust

Another aspect of Sanford's progressive predilections appears in his rulings in antitrust matters. Sanford favored strict adherence to antitrust laws,[113] perhaps because he had been influenced by his time spent as an antitrust prosecutor with the Department of Justice. He was said to support the enforcement of the antitrust laws "even more faithfully than old trustbuster Taft himself."[114] He joined with Taft and McReynolds in dissenting from the majority opinions in *Maple Flooring Manufacturers' Association v. United States*[115] and *Cement Manufacturers Protective Association v. United States*,[116] actions to enjoin specified activities of trade associations. In the former, the majority took the view that specified activities of trade associations in collecting and distributing trade information did not violate the antitrust act because there was no evidence that the information had a "necessary tendency to cause direct and undue restraint of competition" prohibited by the Sherman Act.[117] The majority held that the Sherman Act was neither intended to "inhibit the intelligent conduct of business operations nor . . . suppress such influences as might affect operations of interstate commerce through the application of the individual intelligence of those engaged in commerce."[118] Sanford dissented upon the ground that the cases fell "substantially within the rules" of *United States v. American Linseed Oil Co.*[119] and *American Column & Lumber Company v. United States*.[120] In *American Linseed*, a unanimous Court had determined that the gathering of information under the guise of "intelligent competition" had a tendency to suppress competition.[121] Urging rigorous application of *American Linseed*, Justice McReynolds, Sanford's former Department of Justice colleague, argued in a dissenting opinion that the cases at issue "disclose carefully developed plans to cut down normal competition in interstate trade and commerce."[122] Sanford's former law partner, Special Assistant to the Attorney General James A. Fowler, argued for the government in both cases.

Consistent with his support for vigorous antitrust enforcement, Sanford joined Taft's unanimous opinion in the second *Coronado Coal* case, *Coronado Coal Company v. United Mine Workers of America*.[123] The case grew out of the efforts of the United Mine Workers to unionize southern coal mines to protect wage levels for union miners in other parts of the country. The owners of Coronado Coal sought to change the company's labor force from union to nonunion miners and to shut down its mines in preparation for reopening on an open-shop basis. When the mines reopened, the union members went on strike and engaged in violent protests that eventually destroyed mine property and equipment. The Taft Court found that the violence on the part of the union members was aimed at stopping the interstate shipment of nonunion coal and constituted a conspiracy in restraint of trade. The decision reversed a lower court ruling holding that the United Mine Workers could not be sued under the Sherman Act and increased "the potentialities of the Sherman law as a weapon against unions."[124] The Court determined that there was substantial evidence that the local union's actions "were undertaken with the intent to prevent interstate shipment of coal that would compete with union coal in neighboring states."[125] In the Court's view, therefore, the union could be held liable under the Sherman Act.[126] When unlawful activities are intended to "restrain or control the supply entering and moving in interstate commerce ... their action is a direct violation of the Anti-Trust Act."[127] Thus, Sanford joined the other members of the Taft Court in applying the antitrust laws more aggressively to labor unions than to the corporations that were the primary intended targets of the legislation. A year before, when faced with a nonviolent local union strike in *United Leather Workers International Union, Local Lodge or Union No. 66 v. Herkert & Meisel Trunk Company*,[128] Sanford had joined the majority in holding that the union activity was beyond the reach of the Sherman Act.[129] With his concurrence in *Coronado*, however, the Court held, for the first time, that unions were subject to suit under the Sherman Act.[130]

In *Bedford Cut Stone Company v. Journeymen Stone Cutters' Association*,[131] Sanford was among the majority upholding a ruling against the union for boycotting the company.[132] A number of union stone cutters refused to work on limestone cut by workers employed by Bedford Cut Stone, a nonunion company. Although this particular strike appeared to have limited effect because of its local character, the Court concluded that the strike unduly burdened the stream of interstate commerce and violated antitrust laws. Over and above the attempt to bring about a "change of conduct on the part of [Bedford Cut Stone] in respect of employment of union members in Indiana,"[133] the Court found that the strike was directed against the use of the company's products in other states, with the "plain design of suppressing or narrowing the interstate market."[134] At conference, the vote had been five-to-four. To prevent such a split, Taft put pressure on Sanford and Stone to vote with the majority. Reluctantly, the two finally agreed.[135] Taft wrote to his brother that "while Sanford and Stone concur in our opinion, they do it grudgingly."[136] This case illustrated the Taft Court's use of antitrust laws as a weapon against the labor movement. As one scholar has noted:

> There was obvious incongruity between the narrow view of interstate commerce taken in cases such as *E.C. Knight*[[137]] and *Hammer v. Dagenhart*[[138]] and the Taft Court's opinion in *Bedford* where no distinction between local and national effects on commerce was noted. Many trade restrictions resulting from industry action "would be tolerated by the Court under the rule of reason." At the same time, the Court would disregard its rule of reason "when asked to apply it to the clearly reasonable activities of a labor union." Minimal local activity thus became interstate commerce when the Court felt the need to immunize a manufacturer from interference by a labor union.[139]

In *Eastman Kodak Company v. Southern Photo Materials Company*,[140] it was alleged that Eastman Kodak had unlawfully conspired to monopolize the interstate trade in the United States in photographic materials and supplies. Southern Photo Materials Company alleged that Eastman Kodak had monopolized the greater part of such interstate trade by acquiring control of competing companies engaged in manufacturing such materials, along with the businesses and stock houses of these dealers. Eastman Kodak unsuccessfully attempted to purchase Southern's business and then refused to sell its goods to Southern at discounted dealer prices. Faced with paying retail prices, Southern could no longer compete. Eastman Kodak defended on the ground that Southern could not prove its damages. Sanford found a jury question supported by the evidence of Eastman Kodak's refusal to sell to Southern for the purpose to monopolize.[141] He noted that "a defendant whose wrongful conduct has rendered difficult the ascertainment of the precise damages suffered by the plaintiff, is not entitled to complain that they cannot be measured with the same exactness and precision as would otherwise be possible."¹⁴² The jury verdict in favor of Southern was affirmed.

Statutory Construction

A significant aspect of Sanford's approach to the law was his treatment of statutes. The first case in which Sanford spoke for the Court, *Baltimore & Ohio Railroad Company v. United States*,¹⁴³ decided on March 19, 1923, illustrates Sanford's approach to statutory construction. The railroad asked for judgment for certain "extraordinary expenses," which it claimed to have incurred in constructing a branch railroad to an ordnance depot under "an informal or implied agreement" with the War Department for reimbursement for such expenses pursuant to the Dent Act.¹⁴⁴ Construing the plain language of the Dent Act, Sanford found no proof that there was any "agreement, express or implied" for the payment of the expenses the railroad incurred in expediting the building of the branch line. In dismissing the petition, he observed:

> [T]he mere fact that, on the urgent insistence of the officers of the [War] Department that the construction of the railroad be hastened so as to handle construction materials for the Depot and other freight (necessarily yielding revenue to the railroad), the company, on its own determination, substituted the cost plan of construction for the unit-price plan, without any notice to the Department of its intention so to do or of the increased expenses that would result, does not, in the absence of any intimation that it would look to the United States for reimbursement . . . or of any suggestion by the Department that such reimbursement would be made, afford any substantial basis upon which an agreement for the payment of such expenses can be implied.¹⁴⁵

Sanford also authored a related opinion, *Baltimore & Ohio Railroad Company v. United States*.¹⁴⁶ In that case, the railroad had leased piers to the government to allow shipment of war supplies overseas. When a fire broke out and the National Guard was sent to the area, the railroad quartered the soldiers in a train car set up as a temporary barracks. The railroad later requested compensation under the Dent Act for constructing the housing. In rejecting the railroad's claim, the Court held that the railroad failed to establish that the officials connected with the work had any authority to order the construction of a barracks and that no express or implied agreement existed. Sanford observed that the railroad could not recover expenses because it provided the services voluntarily, without mentioning compensation, and because it wished to provide for the troops that guarded its property. In Sanford's words:

> The "implied agreement" contemplated by the Dent Act as the basis of compensation is not an agreement "implied in law," more aptly termed a constructive or quasi contract, where, by fiction of law, a promise is imputed to perform a legal duty, as to repay money obtained by fraud or duress, but an agreement "implied in fact," founded upon a meeting of minds, which, although not embodied in an express contract, is inferred, as a fact, from conduct of the parties showing, in the light of the surrounding circumstances, their tacit understanding.[147]

Because the Dent Act authorized payment of war-related expenditures only if they were based on an express or implied agreement entered into with an officer or agent acting under the authority of the President or the Secretary of War, both of these decisions are good examples of Sanford's strict construction of statutes. Justice Brandeis later cited Sanford's *Baltimore & Ohio* opinions in interpreting the Dent Act.[148]

Sperry Oil & Gas Company v. Chisholm[149] involved oil and gas leases on tribal land. Chisholm, who was half Cherokee, brought suit, along with his wife, to cancel a supplemental instrument that modified an existing lease upon Chisholm's "homestead" and "surplus" allotments of tribal lands because it was not executed or joined in by his wife. The lower courts determined that the extension lease executed by Chisholm was void under the provisions of the Constitution and the laws of Oklahoma because his wife did not join in or consent to it. Carefully distinguishing between the "homestead" allotment and the "surplus" allotment,

Sanford, who had experience with tribal matters from his time in the Department of Justice, observed that Oklahoma law had no application to the extension lease on the tribal "homestead" of thirty acres: "The authority thus given by the Act of Congress to an Indian of the half-blood to make an oil and gas lease upon his restricted 'homestead' allotment, with the approval of the Secretary of the Interior, cannot be limited or contravened by the provision of the Oklahoma law. . . ."[150] According to Sanford, "the extension lease executed by Chisholm in 1914, which was made under the regulations of the Secretary of the Interior and was approved by him as to the 'homestead' allotment of thirty acres, must be held to be valid as to such allotment."[151] Sanford noted, however, that "[a]s to the fifty acres of the 'surplus' allotment, also included in the extension lease, a different question is presented." When the extension lease was executed there was no limitation under the Acts of Congress upon Chisholm's right to alienate, encumber or lease the tract. Like the property of non-Indian citizens, it had become in all respects subject to his control, under the laws of the state. Because his wife did not join in the execution of the extension lease, there was nothing which estopped her from asserting its invalidity under the provisions of the Oklahoma statute.[152]

Another example of Sanford's careful statutory construction is found in *Madera Sugar Pine Company v. Industrial Accident Commission of State of California*,[153] involving the constitutionality of California's Workmen's Compensation Act. The company contended that the act, requiring it to make compensation for the death of employees to their non-resident alien dependents without fault of the company, deprived the company of property without due process in violation of the Fourteenth Amendment. In finding that the statute was not in conflict with the Fourteenth Amendment, Sanford, on behalf of the Court, held that the law was designed to benefit all employees and did not provide less protection if the beneficiaries lived abroad.[154] This decision likewise demonstrated Sanford's sympathy for laws that enhanced the public welfare.

A Federal Employers' Liability Act case, *Davis v. Wolfe*,[155] involved a train conductor who was injured on the job when thrown from a train car because of a defective grab iron. The conductor sought damages under Section 4 of the Safety Appliance Act, which stated that "until otherwise ordered by the Interstate Commerce Commission, it shall be unlawful to use on any railroad engaged in interstate commerce any car 'not provided with secure grab irons or handholds in the ends and sides ... for greater security to men in coupling and uncoupling cars.'"[156] Sanford, for the Court, examined four prior cases and concluded:

> The rule clearly deducible ... is that, on the one hand, an employee cannot recover under the Safety Appliance Act if the failure to comply with its requirements is not a proximate cause of the accident which results in his injury, but merely creates an incidental condition or situation in which the accident, otherwise caused, results in such injury; and, on the other hand, he can recover if the failure to comply with the requirements of the Act is a proximate cause of the accident, resulting in injury to him while in the discharge of his duty, although not engaged in an operation in which the safety appliances are specifically designed to furnish him protection.[157]

After a careful examination of prior precedent, Sanford held: "It results that in the present case, as there was substantial evidence tending to show that the defective condition of the grab iron required by Section 4 of the Safety Appliance Act was a proximate cause of the accident resulting in injury to Wolfe while in the discharge of his duty as a conductor, the case was properly submitted to the jury under the Act; and the issues having been determined by the jury in his favor the judgment of the trial court was in that behalf properly affirmed."[158]

Pro-Government

In *Rindge Company v. Los Angeles County*,[159] the issue involved the acquisition of land along the Pacific Ocean for construction of public highways. Sanford concluded that the taking of the land was a taking for a public use authorized by the laws of California. In an opinion reflecting a liberal, "cultured" viewpoint, he wrote:

> Public uses are not limited, in the modern view, to matters of mere business necessity and ordinary convenience, but may extend to matters of public health, recreation and enjoyment.... [A] road need not be for a purpose of business to create a public exigency; air, exercise and recreation are important to the general health and welfare;

pleasure travel may be accommodated as well as business travel; and highways may be condemned to places of pleasing natural scenery.[160]

In a pro-government ruling, Sanford concluded that "the property of the ranch owners has been taken for highways constituting a public use authorized by law, and upon a public necessity for the taking duly established, and that they have not been deprived of their property in violation of the Fourteenth Amendment."[161]

R.E. Sheehan Co. v. Shuler[162] involved the constitutionality of two recent amendments to the New York Workmen's Compensation Law. These provisions required that when an injury caused the death of an employee leaving no beneficiaries, the employer or other insurance carrier must pay the state treasurer the sum of $500 for each of two special funds. The companies contended that the subdivisions conflicted with the Fourteenth Amendment because the awards made thereunder deprived them of their property without due process and denied them the equal protection of the laws. Sanford, speaking for the Court, determined that "the State acted within its power, and neither arbitrarily nor unreasonably, in providing that a portion of the compensation to injured employees ... should be made from public funds established ... by payments from employers whose own employees leave no beneficiaries."[163] He further provided that the provisions did not conflict with the equal protection clause, as all employers alike became subject to the requirements of the law.[164]

In *White River Lumber Company v. State of Arkansas ex rel. Applegate*,[165] a state statute authorized the collection of back taxes on lands which, through inadequate assessment, had escaped their just burden of taxation. The statute was limited to the recovery of such additional taxes on lands of corporations and did not extend to the recovery of additional taxes on the lands of natural persons.[166] The company alleged that the law "was repugnant to the due process and equal protection clauses of the Fourteenth Amendment." Sanford distinguished *Quaker City Cab Company v. Pennsylvania*,[167] which invalidated a Pennsylvania tax that applied only to receipts of cab companies operated by corporations, from this case by stating that in affirming the judgment of the Arkansas Supreme Court, no back tax was involved. Quoting from his opinion in *Whitney v. California*,[168] Sanford observed that a policy does not violate the equal protection clause "merely because it is not all-embracing.... A State may properly direct its legislation against what it deems an existing evil without covering the whole field of possible abuses."[169] The statute must be presumed to target "an evil where experience shows it to be most felt, and to be deemed by the legislature coextensive with the practical need."[170] Such a law is not to be invalidated "merely because other instances may be suggested to which also it might have been applied,"[171] and the classification is not open to objection unless it is "so lacking in any adequate or reasonable basis as to preclude the assumption that it was made in the exercise of legislative judgment and discretion."[172]

Bass, Ratcliff & Gretton, Ltd. v. State Tax Commission[173] involved a British brewery that manufactured and sold most of its ale in England, but did import some of its product into the United States, where it was sold through branch offices in New York and Chicago. The brewery was assessed a franchise tax by the New York Tax Commission for its ale sales in the state. The company paid the tax but filed suit seeking a refund, arguing that the tax was not based on any net income made in the United States but on income made outside of the United States. Furthermore, the company asserted that the tax deprived it of its property in violation of the due process clause of the Fourteenth Amendment and imposed a burden upon its foreign commerce in violation of the commerce clause of the Constitution. In authoring the majority opinion upholding the assessment against the business, Sanford wrote:

> [I]n the present case we are of the opinion that as the Company carried on the unitary business of manufacturing and selling ale, in which its profits were earned by a series of transactions beginning with the manufacture in England and ending in sales in New York and other places—the process of manufacturing resulting in no profits until it ends in sales—the State was justified in attributing to New York a just proportion of the profits earned by the Company from such unitary business.[174]

Furthermore, Sanford stated:

> We think that the Court of Appeals rightly held that the tax imposed for the carrying on of the business in New York is not invalid merely because in the preceding year the business conducted in New York may have yielded no net income. There is no sufficient reason why a foreign corporation desiring to continue the carrying on of business in the State for another year—from which it expects to derive a benefit—

should be relieved of a privilege tax because it did not happen to have made any profit during the preceding year.[175]

In *United States v. River Rouge Improvement Company*,[176] a case arising under the Rivers and Harbors Act,[177] the United States filed five petitions for the condemnation of numerous parcels of riparian[178] land needed for improvement of Michigan's Rouge River. After a jury trial, seventy-three awards of compensation were made to property owners.[179] The government sought review of fifteen judgments, arguing that the jury instructions were erroneous in reference to the extent and measure of the benefits to be considered as compensation and damages[180] to the remainder of parcels not condemned.[181] Speaking for the Supreme Court, Sanford found that the trial court's instructions resulted in prejudicial error:

> It is well settled that in the absence of a controlling local law otherwise limiting the rights of a riparian owner upon a navigable river, he has, in addition to the rights common to the public, a property right, incident to his ownership of the bank, of access from the front of his land to the navigable part of the stream, and when not forbidden by public law may construct landings, wharves or piers for this purpose. . . .
>
> This right of a riparian owner, it is true, is subordinate to the public right of navigation, and subject to the general rules and regulations imposed for the protection of such public right. And it is of no avail against the exercise of the absolute power of Congress over the improvement of navigable rivers, but must suffer the consequences of the improvement of navigation, if Congress determines that its continuance is detrimental to the public interest in the navigation of the river.[182]

Sanford ruled that while the jury instructions recognized the right of the United States to the deduction for the special benefits, they erroneously minimized the nature and extent of such benefits.[183] This led the jury to a lower estimate of the benefits than would have been made under the proper charge. He concluded:

> [W]e find that . . . the jury were left to determine the amount of the benefits to be deducted on the theory that a riparian owner on the

> improved river would have merely such uncertain and contingent "privileges" of access to the navigable stream and of constructing docks fronting on the harbor line, as the Government, in the exercise of an absolute control over the navigation of the river, might see fit to allow him, instead of being instructed that he would have a right to such access and the construction and maintenance of such docks until taken away by the Government in the due exercise of its power of control over navigation.... [T]here was nothing in the evidence indicating any probability that the Government would at any time abrogate or curtail [the rights of the riparian owners].[184]

In cases involving the power of the states to enforce order and impose restraint on private rights—the "police power"—Sanford's pro-government mindset was most evident.[185] One of the most important Taft Court state police power cases was the zoning ordinance matter of *Village of Euclid v. Ambler Realty Company*.[186] After the Village of Euclid enacted a comprehensive zoning ordinance, the property owner asserted that the ordinance would restrict the use of the land so as to "confiscate and destroy a great part of its value."[187] In a liberal ruling, the Taft Court upheld the local zoning ordinance against Ambler Realty's claim that it was deprived of property without due process. The Court saw Euclid's reasons for enacting its zoning regulations as "sufficiently cogent" to preclude finding the provisions "arbitrary and unreasonable, having no substantial relation to the public health, safety, morals, or general welfare."[188] Sanford voted with the majority, upholding the local residential zoning ordinance against a substantive due process challenge.[189] In this case, the Court discarded its "usual conservative constitutional activism and put forward the modern doctrine of judicial restraint in zoning cases."[190] The Court noted that if the validity of the legislative classification for zoning purposes was fairly debatable, the legislative judgment must be allowed to control.[191]

Pro-Business

Sanford was, as noted earlier, thought to have been conservative in economic matters. That would imply a pro-business inclination, and there are a number of cases in which that view can be seen. *Williams v. Great Southern Lumber Com-*

pany[192] involved an action brought to recover damages for the alleged unlawful killing of the plaintiff's husband, who was the president of the local labor union. The complaint alleged that a conspiracy had been formed between the company, its officers, agents, and others to harm Mr. Williams and destroy organized labor in the locality. The widow asserted that her husband was killed by a mob composed of these conspirators acting within the scope of their employment. The company contended that Mr. Williams' death occurred when a posse of paid and volunteer policemen attempted to arrest three other men.[193] Speaking through Sanford, the Court held that the judgment for the widow must be reversed because "[t]he errors in the exclusion and admission of evidence directly affected the substantial rights of the company."[194]

In *Federal Trade Commission v. Raymond Brothers-Clark Company*,[195] under review was an order of the Federal Trade Commission (FTC) requiring the defendant to desist from a method of competition. Sanford found that the case disclosed no elements of monopoly or oppression. He observed that a retail dealer "has the unquestioned right to stop dealing with a wholesaler for reasons satisfactory to himself."[196] Concluding that the company's conduct was not unlawful, Sanford acknowledged:

> A different case would of course be presented if the Raymond Company had combined and agreed with other wholesale dealers that none would trade with any manufacturer who sold to other wholesale dealers competing with themselves, or to retail dealers competing with their customers. An act lawful when done by one may become wrongful when done by many acting in concert, taking on the form of a conspiracy which may be prohibited if the result be hurtful to the public or to the individual against whom the concerted action is directed.[197]

In a pro-business decision, Sanford concluded that the defendant exercised its lawful right in withdrawing its trade from the other company.[198] The opinion restricted the power of the FTC to declare business practices "unfair methods of competition."[199]

In *Federal Trade Commission v. Eastman Kodak Company*,[200] the FTC contended that Eastman Kodak had engaged in acts constituting unfair methods of competition in the manufacture and sale of positive cinematograph films in interstate and foreign commerce and ordered the company, in part, to sell and convey three laboratories. Sanford, writing for the Court, determined that the FTC, pursuant to the applicable statute, "had no authority to require the Company divest itself of the ownership of the laboratories which it had acquired prior to any action by the Commission."[201] He noted: "If the ownership or maintenance of these laboratories has produced any unlawful status, the remedy must be administered by the Courts in appropriate proceedings."[202]

Sanford also joined Taft's opinion in *Charles Wolff Packing Company v. Court of Industrial Relations*,[203] holding that a Kansas statute imposing a comprehensive system of labor regulations in certain industries violated the Fourteenth Amendment.[204] In *Wolff Packing*, the company challenged the statute's constitutionality as well as the authority of the industrial court to compel the aggregate increase of wages amounting to $400 per week. The company contended that the act was in conflict with the provision of the Fourteenth Amendment forbidding any state to deprive any person of liberty or property without due process of law. The majority agreed and held that the act deprived the company of its property and liberty of contract.[205]

Substantive Due Process

The Fourteenth Amendment provides, in part, that no state shall "deprive any person of life, liberty, or property, without due process of law."[206] Substantive due process prohibits the government from infringing on fundamental constitutional liberties. The nature and scope of the liberty to be protected is not specified in the amendment and must be determined by the Court.[207] Over the years, the Court had "gradually coupled vested rights to the due process clause, so that due process came to be a substantive limitation upon the power of a state to regulate private property in the interests of the public welfare." The Taft Court majority "tended to equat[e] vested rights with economic individualism and property rights."[208] Under the Court's substantive due process analysis, if the goal of a statute was "reasonable," if the means employed were "reasonable," and there were no "unreasonable" limitations upon the freedom of contract or another private vested right, the statute was found to be a constitutional exercise of the police power of the state.[209] Substantive due process analysis "required the Court to evaluate questions of social and economic policy," giving the Court "an almost legislative control over national policy." The use of substantive due process "depended upon the economic and social attitudes of the majority for any particular case."[210]

Sanford's strongest stance on substantive due process was his dissent in the infamous case, *Adkins v. Children's Hospital of D.C.*[211] The issue before the Court in *Adkins* was the constitutionality of an act of Congress fixing minimum wages for working women and children in Washington, D.C. The purpose of the act was "to protect the women and minors of the District from conditions detrimental to their health and morals, resulting from wages which are inadequate to maintain decent standards of living."[212] This type of legislation epitomized the reforms of the Progressive era. There were two challenges brought to the legislation: one by a hospital that was paying wages below the statutory minimum; the other by a female elevator operator who, it was alleged, would lose her low-paying job if her employer were forced to comply with the act.[213] The statute was attacked as violating "the freedom of contract included within the guarantees of the due process clause of the Fifth Amendment."[214] Turning the clock back to 1905 and *Lochner v. New York*,[215] the majority of the Court in *Adkins* concluded that the minimum wage law for women and children unconstitutionally invaded the liberty of contract. Using a property rights approach, the majority held "minimum wage legislation to be an unconstitutional infringement on the liberty of employees to negotiate employment contracts."[216] Sutherland wrote: "It cannot be shown that well paid women safeguard their morals more carefully than those who are poorly paid. Morality rests upon other considerations than wages; and there is, certainly, no such prevalent connection between the two as to justify a broad attempt to adjust the latter with reference to the former."[217] According to Sutherland, "the inquiry in respect of the income necessary to preserve health and morals ... must be answered for each individual considered by herself and not by a general formula prescribed by a statutory bureau."[218] Sanford joined in Taft's dissenting opinion.[219]

The news media of the day observed that it would be difficult for the American people to accept the *Adkins* decision because of the "striking division of opinion among Four Justices who were all named by the same President." News reports noted the difference between the "corporation lawyers" and the judges:

> Chief Justice Taft and Associate Justice Sanford had had long judicial experience before they became members of the Supreme Court....

Both Chief Justice Taft and Associate Justice Sanford affirmed the validity of the Minimum-Wage Law, along with Associate Justice Holmes, who had achieved a national reputation as a Judge in Massachusetts long before he was appointed to the United States Supreme Court.

The two other Justices appointed by Mr. Harding helped declare the act of Congress unconstitutional, and one of them wrote the opinion of the court. Neither of these Associate Justices, Mr. Sutherland and Mr. Butler, had previous judicial experience. Both of them were successful corporation lawyers with conservative views on all modern economic questions, and it was their interpretation of the Constitution that prevailed in deciding the minimum-wage case.

This implies no reflection on their intellectual integrity or their honesty of purpose. It is a significant fact, nevertheless, that of the Four Justices who were appointed by Mr. Harding, the two who had previously been corporation lawyers should have denied the power of Congress to enact a minimum-wage law for women in the District of Columbia and the two who had been Judges should have held that Congress had full power under the Constitution to enact that legislation.[220]

By 1925, five of the sitting justices believed that the *Adkins* case had been wrongly decided, and the precedent survived only because the justices continued to recognize it as a matter of *stare decisis*.[221] After Sanford's death, *Adkins* was overturned in 1937 in *West Coast Hotel Company v. Parrish*.[222]

Sanford's record reveals that he was not a rigid and inflexible opponent of substantive due process. He joined the Court's opinions in *Meyer v. Nebraska*,[223] *Pierce v. Society of the Sisters*,[224] and *Farrington v. Tokushige*.[225] In *Meyer*, a Nebraska school teacher was arrested for teaching the German language in violation of a state law prohibiting such instruction.[226] The Court ruled that an act forbidding instruction in or of any language other than English violated the due process clause of the Fourteenth Amendment, infringing on Meyer's right to work and the parents' right to determine the course of their children's education.[227] In *Pierce*, the Court ruled that Oregon's Compulsory Education Law "unreasonably interferes with the liberty of parents and guardians to direct the upbringing and education of children."²²⁸ In *Farrington*, the Court affirmed the invalidation of a Hawaii law requiring permits for operating foreign language schools, finding that "[e]nforcement ... would deprive parents of fair opportunity to procure for their children instruction which they think important and we cannot say is harmful."²²⁹ These were the "first tentative steps to expand the Fourteenth Amendment's due process clause to personal rights other than liberty of contract."²³⁰ This trilogy of cases shielded Catholics and immigrants from school regulations requiring children to attend public schools if their parents wanted to send them to private schools. The cases also recognized important non-economic, substantive liberties under the Fourteenth Amendment's due process clause.

Public Interest

Closely related to those cases in which Sanford's position was pro-government were those in which the question of action in the public interest arose. The majority on the Taft Court carefully distinguished between ordinary property and property in the "narrow category of having been 'affected with a public interest.'"²³¹ Sanford was partial to the public interest. In *Tyson & Bro. - United Theatre Ticket Offices, Inc. v. Banton*,²³² the plaintiff was a licensed ticket broker who regularly resold tickets for admission to places of entertainment. New York passed a statute that imposed restrictions on ticket scalping, providing that "the price of or charge for admission to theaters, places of amusement or entertainment, or other places where public exhibitions, games, contests or performances are held, is a matter affected with a public interest."²³³ The statute also prohibited "the resale of any ticket or other evidence of the right of entry to any theater, etc., at a price in excess of fifty cents in advance of the price printed on the face of such ticket or other evidence of the right of entry."²³⁴

The majority of the Court held that a theater ticket brokerage was not a "business affected with a public interest" and that substantive due process prohibited government price regulation in that field.²³⁵ The Court, in an opinion written by Justice Sutherland, reasoned that "[t]he right of the owner to fix a price at which his property shall be sold or used is an inherent attribute of the property itself, and, as such, within the protection of the Due Process of Law clauses of the Fifth and Fourteenth Amendments."[236] The majority opinion further held that there was no public interest involved because "[a] business or property, in order to be affected with a public interest, must be such or be so employed as to justify the conclusion that it has been *devoted* to a public use and its use thereby, in effect *granted* to the public."[237] Thus, the Court determined that the government lacked the authority to regulate the resale price of theater tickets.

Sanford wrote a short dissent supporting the state's right to regulate theater ticket brokers, contending that there is nothing in the Constitution prohibiting the type of regulation attempted by the State of New York.[238] Sanford observed that the ticket brokers "acquire an absolute control of the desirable seats in the theaters, by which they deprive the public of access to the theaters themselves for the purpose of buying such tickets at the regular prices" and thus "are enabled to exact an extortionate advance in prices for the sale of such tickets to the public."[239] Sanford declared that "the business of the ticket brokers, who stand in 'the very gateway' between the theaters and the public, depriving the public of access to the theaters for the purchase of desirable seats at the regular prices, and exacting toll from patrons of the theaters desiring to purchase such seats, has become clothed with a public interest and is subject to regulation by the Legislature...."[240]

One year later, in *Ribnik v. McBride*,[241] Sanford specially concurred in the majority opinion that struck down a similar law to the one in *Tyson*. In *Ribnik*, the Court held that employment agencies were not "businesses affected with a public interest" and that governmental regulation of their fees violated substantive due process.[242] The majority determined that substantive due process barred price regulation in all but a few industries, such as public utilities and rail transportation.[243] The decision excluded most businesses from the public interest category and made them exempt from price regulation.[244] Sanford probably concurred only because *Tyson* was controlling authority,[245] and he had the utmost respect for judicial precedent. He frequently deferred to prior decisions even when they resolved questions of law in ways with which he had initially disagreed.[246]

In a decision favoring public interests over private ones, Sanford defined for the Court the term "alien seamen" in *United States v. New York & Cuba Mail S.S. Company*.[247] A seaman from Chile was found by immigration officials to be afflicted with a venereal disease and was placed at the Public Health Service hospital on Ellis Island for treatment. The steamship company refused to pay the hospital expenses, and the United States brought suit. The issue before the Court was "whether the term 'alien seamen,' as used in the Act, means seamen who are aliens, as the Government contends, or seamen on foreign vessels, as the Steamship Company contends: that is, whether in applying the Act the test is the citizenship of the seaman or the nationality of the vessel."[248] Sanford noted: "We think the term 'alien seamen' is not to be construed as meaning seamen on foreign vessels."[249] He determined that "[i]t is clear that the term 'alien seamen' as used in the Act means 'seamen who are aliens.'... The Act does not qualify this term by any reference to the nationality of the vessels...."[250] Sanford concluded that if seamen "are found to be diseased when brought into an American port, the vessel, whether American or foreign, may lawfully be required to bear the expenses of their medical treatment."[251]

Rights of Blacks and Other Minorities

Sanford's positions in cases involving the constitutional rights of blacks and other minorities were typical of those of legal thinkers of his time period.[252] As the Civil War generation was ceasing to have a dominant position in public affairs, an acceptance of white southerners' racial categorizations had become more prevalent. The Republican legacy of liberation stemming from the Civil War had faded.[253] At the turn of the century, the *Boston Evening Transcript* observed that the southern way was "now the policy of the Administration of the very party which carried the country into and through a Civil War to free the slave."[254] As posed by Justice Harlan in his dissent in *Berea College v. Kentucky*: "Have we become so inoculated with prejudice of race that an American government, professedly based on the principle of freedom, and charged with the protection of all citizens alike, can make distinctions between such citizens in the matter of their voluntary meeting for innocent purposes simply because of their respective races?"[255]

At the time Taft became chief justice in 1921, "blacks in the South remained segregated and stigmatized by Jim Crow laws; disenfranchised by invidiously administered literacy tests, white primaries, and poll taxes; and victimized by a criminal process from whose juries and other positions of power they were routinely excluded."[256] Taft openly contended that black suffrage had been a failure and expressed the opinion that literacy restrictions were a positive requirement.[257] Holmes had a general record in opposition to the rights of blacks in constitutional cases.[258] McReynolds "found ample play for considerations of practical expediency in the constitutional law of racial separation."[259] Across the country, American attitudes became "Southernized."[260]

Sanford's record in this area is mixed. He did not join the Court until after *Moore v. Dempsey*[261] was argued; therefore, he did not participate in that six-to-two holding that the conviction of black defendants in a trial dominated by a mob deprived them of due process. The case was one of the earliest rulings to protect the civil rights of blacks.[262] Sanford did join the Court's unanimous opinion in *Nixon v. Herndon*,[263] holding that a 1923 Texas statute prohibiting blacks from voting in the Democratic primary violated the equal protection clause of the Fourteenth Amendment. In that case, the statute provided that "in no event shall a negro be eligible to participate in a Democratic party primary election held in the State of Texas."[264] The Court, speaking through Holmes, held that "it seems to us hard to imagine a more direct and obvious infringement of the Fourteenth [Amendment]."[265]

At the same time, however, Sanford concurred in the Court's decision upholding segregated public education in *Gong Lum v. Rice*[266] under the separate but equal doctrine.[267] In *Gong Lum*, a child of Chinese descent was not allowed to attend the school of her choice because she was not a member of the Caucasian race.[268] The Court, speaking through Taft, found that the child was not denied equal protection of the laws when she was "classed among the colored races and furnished facilities for education equal to that offered to all...."[269] The Court did not address whether the "equal facilities" were, in fact, equal.[270] A description of a Mississippi "colored school" of the period was as follows: "There were no desks. The children sat on wooden benches.... Some of the children were atrociously filthy and ragged.... [T]he range of ages in the three or four approximate grades was between four and eighteen.... The teacher was very methodical as to ritual, and absolutely without intellectual method.... I did not see any blackboard work. There was a very small piece of blackboard of some description in one corner of the room...."[271] In view of Sanford's desire to improve education in the South, his silence in a case like this one from a southern state over which he was the circuit justice gives one pause.[272] None of the justices, however, voted to invalidate racially segregated education. The Court took for granted the authority of the state to segregate public schools. One legal scholar has observed that the opinion in *Gong Lum* provided "a snapshot of the Supreme Court's late nineteenth and early twentieth century constitutional jurisprudence of race relations at the apogee of its influence."[273] This commentator noted that the justices deciding *Gong Lum* "considered the case an 'easy' example of a state's police power trumping private rights, whether based on the Due Process or Equal Protection Clauses."[274] As noted by Professor G. Edward White, the justices "treated classifications based on race as presumptively reasonable rather than presumptively suspect because they believed that race and skin color were proxies for a host of salient differences among humans. They also either took states at face value when they asserted that facilities provided whites and non-whites were 'separate but equal,' or, if they suspected they were not, were disinclined to probe further. They understood the 'reasonableness' of segregating whites and non-whites because they thought racial differences were meaningful."[275] Clearly, most whites during the time frame of the Taft Court were disinclined to give meaningful review to the segregationist policies in existence.

A controversial opinion involving race authored by Sanford was *Corrigan v. Buckley*,[276] which upheld restrictive covenants banning the sale of real property to racial minorities. The case attracted wide attention because a decision in favor of the black purchaser would have impacted the laws in many states. Under the facts of this case, several neighbors entered into an agreement to prevent blacks from moving into their neighborhood. The case was set in the District of Columbia, over which, at that time, the Supreme Court's jurisdiction was limited to matters raising "substantial" federal claims.

Previously, the Court had struck down a city ordinance mandating residential segregation in *Buchanan v. Warley*.[277] In that case, the Court observed that "[t]he right which the ordinance annulled was the civil right of a white man to dispose of his property if he saw fit to do so to a person of color and of a colored person to make such disposition to a white person."[278] Substantive due process was employed to hold that the law violated the property rights of blacks.[279] The Court reversed the state court ruling declaring: "[T]he Fourteenth Amendment of the Constitution prevent[s] state interference with property rights except by due process of law." [280]

Even earlier, however, in the *Civil Rights Cases*,[281] the Supreme Court ruled that racial discrimination by private persons could not be penalized by Congress. In *Corrigan*, Sanford relied on the rule of the *Civil Rights Cases* to conclude that the prohibitions of the Fourteenth Amendment "have reference to State action exclusively, and not to any action of private individuals."[282] He found that the

Fourteenth Amendment did not prohibit the "wrongful acts of individuals, unsupported by state authority in the shape of laws, customs, or judicial or executive proceedings."[283] Sanford observed: "It is State action of a particular character that is prohibited. Individual invasion of individual rights is not the subject-matter of the Amendment."[284] Sanford opined that neither the Fifth, Thirteenth, nor Fourteenth Amendments was applicable and that "[i]t is obvious that none of these amendments prohibited private individuals from entering into contracts respecting the control and disposition of their own property; and there is no color[able basis] whatever for the contention that they rendered the indenture void...."[285] Accordingly, the Court held that judicial enforcement did not make the government responsible for a privately imposed, racially restrictive covenant. The Court found no substantial constitutional question and dismissed the case for lack of jurisdiction.

Critics observed that the Court had closed its eyes to the fact that such covenants were enforced by courts, which inescapably involved state action. Twenty-two years later, in *Shelley v. Kraemer*,[286] the Court still found that racial covenants per se did not violate the Constitution due to lack of state action.[287] However, because the state "made available ... the full coercive power of government to deny [property rights] on the grounds of race or color" through the state's courts, the enforcement of the covenant violated the equal protection clause.[288]

In an extremely harsh view of the *Corrigan* decision, one analyst has blamed it for "legitimiz[ing] racial restrictive covenants" that "contributed to the solidification of the black ghetto in many northern cities."[289] One commentator described *Corrigan* as "a cowardly legal moment."[290] Any harmful results clearly were not intended by Sanford, who had the reputation of considering carefully the rights of blacks.[291] For example, future Supreme Court Justice Hugo Black, while a practicing attorney, persuaded Sanford to place the case of *Lewis v. Roberts*[292] on the Supreme Court's docket in forma pauperis. Henry Lewis was a black convict who had been injured while working in the mines due to the negligence of the mining company. A lower court awarded Lewis $4,000, but the mining company declared bankruptcy before paying the judgment. When Black filed a claim on behalf of Lewis, the federal district court ruled that the mining company was liable only for debts owed to those with whom it had contracts, not to a convict with whom it had no written contract. Upon hearing the case, including Black's argument on behalf of Lewis, the Court ruled in favor of Lewis. Sanford, certainly recalling the Coal Creek Rebellion, delivered the decision.[293]

Sanford also joined a unanimous Court in *Harmon v. Tyler*,²⁹⁴ declaring invalid an ordinance that forbade any black to establish a home on any property in a white community or any white person to establish a home in a black community, "except on the written consent of a majority of the persons of the opposite race inhabiting such community or portion of the city to be affected."²⁹⁵ The Court, relying on the authority of *Buchanan v. Warley*,²⁹⁶ found that the state law violated the Fourteenth Amendment by interfering with the property rights of both blacks and whites. Sanford's decisions in these cases, while not thoroughly enlightened, are not completely benighted, and reflect his adherence to strict interpretation and respect for precedent.

Rights of Individuals

As he was during his time as a district court judge, Sanford was relatively sensitive to the rights of individuals. Like Theodore Roosevelt, the man who named him to the Department of Justice and the United States District Court for the Eastern and Middle Districts of Tennessee, Sanford was "interested primarily in human welfare rather than property."²⁹⁷ In *United States v. Manzi*,²⁹⁸ he dissented from a McReynolds opinion denying citizenship to the widow of a deceased alien because her request was not filed in a timely manner. Mr. Manzi died two months after filing his declaration of intention to become a US Citizen. In order for the widow to obtain the statutory benefit of his declaration, she was required to file her petition for naturalization not less than two or more than seven years after the deceased husband's declaration of intention.²⁹⁹ Manzi's widow waited more than seven years. Sanford disagreed with the majority's strict enforcement of the time limit.

Another case quite emblematic of Sanford's concern for the rights of individuals was the *Schwimmer* naturalization case. Perhaps influenced by the fact that his mother's family had been persecuted for their religious beliefs,³⁰⁰ Sanford dissented from the denial of American citizenship to Rosika Schwimmer, a pacifist who would not promise to bear arms in the nation's defense as required by the Naturalization Act of June 29, 1906. In *United States v. Schwimmer*,³⁰¹ the defendant testified that she "fully believed in our form of government"³⁰² and that her "'past work proves that I have always served democratic ideals."³⁰³ She refused to take up arms, however, arguing that she could fight in other ways.³⁰⁴

The Court, in an opinion penned by Justice Butler, denied citizenship due to Schwimmer's opposition to the forcible defense of the nation.[305]

Sanford's dissent cited with approval the reasoning set out in the Seventh Circuit's opinion in the case:

> We do not have before us the case of a male applicant for admission who is able to bear arms and is within the usual conscription age, but the case of a woman fifty years of age.
>
> Women are considered incapable of bearing arms. Male persons of the age of appellant have not been compelled to do so. [Schwimmer], if admitted cannot by any present law of the United States be compelled to bear arms. Judging by all the conscription acts of which we have knowledge, she never will be required to do so[.] . . .
>
> In other words, there is put to her a[] hypothetical question what would she do under circumstances that never have occurred and probably never will occur. . . . A petitioner's rights are not to be determined by putting conundrums to her.
>
> The views of appellant relied upon to support the denial of her application have no substantial relation to the inquiry authorized by the statute. They were immaterial to that inquiry and do not furnish sufficient basis for the decree.[306]

Sanford's choice to not join the majority opinion in *Schwimmer* was recalled after his passing: "In the current comments on his judicial career, it is commonly stated that he was one of the 'conservatives' of the Supreme Court. Yet he broke away from the 'conservatives' and acted with the 'liberals' in a case that attracted national attention because of the moral issue of human rights and privileges involved."[307] Among Sanford's papers are some penciled-out sections in a 1910 speech reflecting his views of the Supreme Court's role, a view supporting his dissent in *Schwimmer*: "[I]t is invested with higher prerogatives than any court of ancient or modern times; its jurisdiction extends over the sovereign States and the sovereign Nation itself, as well as over the weakest of its citizens; it may annul alike the statutes of the States or of the Nation, if they exceed the limitations of the Constitution, the supreme law of which it is the defender and the living voice." He further described the Court as "administering justice between the nation, the State, the citizen and the stranger within our gates, with equal and exact regard for the rights of each."[308] As noted by an authority on the Taft Court, its members understood themselves as a common law court "authorized to articulate the deepest experiences and values of the American people. This authority transcended the distinction between federal and state power...."[309]

At the time of his death, which came shortly after the *Schwimmer* decision, *The New York Times* hailed Sanford as a "Champion of Individual Rights." Recognizing Sanford's reputation as a district court judge, the paper noted, "On questions of more individual character he was a staunch champion of the rights of the individual, and in his service on the bench there were many incidents to illustrate his zeal to protect the rights of an individual in his court, particularly when an individual appeared defenseless."[310]

Viewed through a modern lens, a low point of Sanford's time on the Taft Court came in 1927 with the case of *Buck v. Bell*.[311] After the decision, Carrie Buck was sterilized in light of the Court's validation of a Virginia law mandating the surgery for people who had been declared "socially inadequate." In a case now considered one of the most infamous in Supreme Court history, the Court approved the police power of a state to erase the parental opportunities of its "unfit" citizens. For the Court, Holmes wrote: "It is better for all the world, if instead of waiting to execute degenerate offspring for crime, or to let them starve for their imbecility, society can prevent those who are manifestly unfit from continuing their kind." Carrie Buck, a "low-grade moron," along with her mother and Carrie's "illegitimate" infant, fit Holmes's category of the "manifestly unfit." According to Holmes: "Three generations of imbeciles are enough."[312] Sanford joined in the decision.

During the time frame of the Taft Court, eugenics theory found considerable intellectual acceptance. It stated that "defects—criminality, poverty, illegitimacy, and the like—were passed down from people like Buck to their children."[313] Negative eugenics—the idea that those with maladies deemed hereditary should be prevented from having children—had a wide following in the United States. One report defined the "socially inadequate" as the following:

> (1) feeble-minded; (2) insane (including the psychopathic); (3) criminalistic (including the delinquent and wayward); (4) epileptic; (5) inebriate (including drug-habitúes); (6) diseased (including the tuberculous, the syphilitic, the leprous, and others with chronic,

infectious and legally segregable diseases); (7) blind (including those with seriously impaired vision); (8) deaf (including those with seriously impaired hearing); (9) deformed (including the crippled); and (10) dependent (including orphans, ne'er-do-wells, the homeless, tramps and paupers).[314]

Chief Justice Taft, President Wilson, President Theodore Roosevelt, Justice Holmes, and Thomas Edison were eugenics enthusiasts. Another supporter was John Harvey Kellogg, the founder of the Battle Creek Sanitarium, where Sanford's mother had been a patient, and the Race Betterment Foundation.[315] Eugenics was supported by the Carnegie Institution, the Rockefeller Foundation, and researchers at leading US universities. By 1925, twenty-three of the forty-eight states in the Union at that time had passed at least one eugenics-based sterilization law.[316] By 1940, some 36,000 Americans had been sterilized.[317] In Germany, the American eugenics program was much admired. In fact, the National Socialists in Germany adopted it in its totality, not only sterilizing hundreds of thousands but euthanizing those identified as unworthy of life.[318] At the Nuremberg trials, Nazi defendants cited *Buck v. Bell* in their defense.[319]

It is ironic that Sanford, who left the State of Tennessee and its university's board of trustees at the height of the anti-evolution movement, found himself seated on the United States Supreme Court in time to hear *Buck v. Bell*. As a trustee, he had tried to avoid taking a position on the religiously-charged evolution debate. As a justice, however, he was forced to cast a vote on an issue that had enormous moral and religious implications. The eugenics movement coincided chronologically with the anti-evolution crusade, whose proponents vehemently opposed eugenics, but was more successful. At the time of the Tennessee legislature's consideration of the anti-evolution bill, evangelist Billy Sunday repeatedly linked eugenics with teaching evolution. William Jennings Bryan decried eugenics as "brutal."[320] In his closing arguments in the *Scopes* trial, as part of his attack on evolutionary theory, Bryan expressly denounced Albert Edward Wiggam's book, *The New Decalogue of Science*[321] and the eugenic ideas that it promoted.[322] According to Wiggam,

> nearly all the happiness and nearly all the misery of the world are due, not to environment, but to heredity; ... that it is, in the large statistical run of things, not the slums which make slum people, but

slum people who make the slums; that primarily it is not the church which makes people good, but good people who make the church; that godly people are largely born and not made, that if you want church members you will have to give nature a chance to produce them; that if you want artists, poets, philosophers, skilled workmen and great statesmen you will also have to give nature a chance to breed them.[323]

Eugenists gained many adherents by warning that Americans were allowing their collective biological inheritance to degenerate.[324] Dr. Walter E. Fernald told the Massachusetts Medical Society in 1912:

The past few years have witnessed a striking awakening of professional and popular consciousness of the wide-spread prevalence of feeblemindedness and its influence as a source of wretchedness to the patient himself and to his family, and as a causative factor in the production of crime, prostitution, pauperism, illegitimacy, intemperance, and other complex social diseases. . . . The feebleminded are a parasitic, predatory class, never capable of self-support or of managing their own affairs. . . . They cause unutterable sorrow at home and are a menace and danger to the community. . . . Feebleminded women are almost invariably immoral and if at large usually become carriers of venereal disease or give birth to children who are as defective as themselves. . . . Every feebleminded person, especially the high-grade imbecile, is a potential criminal needing only the proper environment and opportunity for the development and expression of his criminal tendencies.[325]

Eventually thirty-five states enacted laws to compel the sexual segregation and sterilization of "certain persons viewed as eugenically unfit, particularly the mentally ill and retarded, habitual criminals, and epileptics."[326] As offensive as these sentiments sound to modern ears, they were widely accepted when *Buck v. Bell* was decided. As noted by one academic, Sanford and the "rights libertarians" of the Court—McReynolds, Sutherland, and Van Devanter—"should have dissented in *Buck*, but did not."[327] Why did they remain silent? "Because outside the areas of labor and property rights and occasional forays such as *Meyer v. Nebraska* and *Pierce v. Society of the Sisters*, the libertarians followed the standard doctrine of the day—rights were subject to the police power."[328] Sanford's concurrence in *Buck v. Bell*, while deplorable to us now, is perhaps more understandable in light of the historical context of the decision.

Tenure of Office Act

Sanford was one of the six justices to rule the Tenure of Office Act unconstitutional. In March 1867, the act was passed by both houses of Congress, vetoed by President Andrew Johnson, and then passed again by the necessary two-thirds margin. It provided: (1) Any official appointed with the advice and consent of the Senate would require similar consent for dismissal; and (2) Presidential cabinet members were to hold their positions for a full term unless removed by the Senate. President Johnson ignored the act and fired Secretary of War Edwin M. Stanton. The 1868 impeachment of President Johnson, himself an East Tennessean like Sanford, was based in part on Johnson's attempt to ignore the act. The case before the Taft Court, *Myers v. United States*,[329] was filed by the estate of an Oregon postmaster fired by President Wilson. Myers's widow sought protection under the same act used by Stanton when he was fired by Johnson in 1868. She sought to recover her husband's salary from the time of his removal to the end of his regular four-year term, claiming that Wilson had no power to remove *Myers* without the consent of the Senate. The Taft Court majority, however, held that the act was unconstitutional, asserting that Congress may not restrict the power of the president to remove executive officials.[330] Taft considered the *Myers* case a test of loyalty to the American system of government and believed that the president's power to remove officials he appointed was plenary.[331]

Teapot Dome

Some of the last matters heard by Sanford concerned government corruption in the very presidential administration that made him a member of the United States Supreme Court. The misconduct known as "Teapot Dome" has been described as "the most serious scandal in the country's history prior to the Watergate affair of the Nixon administration in the 1970s."[332]

During the presidency of Theodore Roosevelt, the US Navy aspired to be capable of sailing all over the globe. Ships at that time were fueled by coal, requiring the building of coal-fueling stations around the world. During the Taft administration, ships began the conversion to more efficient petroleum for greater range. When concerns arose about the availability of oil for the Navy's use, Congress set aside "naval petroleum reserves" that could not be drilled unless a national emergency required it. One of the three naval petroleum reserves was at a place in Wyoming known for an unusual rock formation resembling a teapot—Teapot Dome.[333]

Oilmen coveted the naval reserves, and oil money was funneled into the 1920 presidential election and the Harding administration to secure access. Harry M. Daugherty, Harding's campaign manager in the 1920 presidential race, cleverly positioned Harding as the compromise candidate at the national convention and convinced party powers that Harding was a viable option. Oilmen helped facilitate Harding's nomination with money in expectation of influence.[334] Harding won the election by a large margin.

After Senator Albert B. Fall was appointed Harding's Secretary of the Interior, he convinced Secretary of the Navy Edwin Denby to support transferring authority over the reserves from the Department of the Navy to the Department of the Interior. Less than three months after the president took office, Harding signed an executive order to shift the control of the reserves. Fall then allowed the Navy's oil reserves to be secretly leased to millionaire oil industry pioneers Edward L. Doheny of Pan-American Petroleum and Transport Company and Harry F. Sinclair of Mammoth Oil Company.[335] Fall gave Doheny and Sinclair reserves worth roughly $100,000,000 in return for $409,000 in cash and bonds.[336]

Not long after President Harding's death, Gifford Pinchot, President Roosevelt's Forest Service Chief and the father of modern environmentalism, forced a Senate investigation into the leases.[337] Harding's successor, President Coolidge, signed into law a joint resolution authorizing special counsel to institute suit to cancel the oil leases and to prosecute those involved.[338] During the investigation, Senator Thomas Walsh of Montana,[339] leading the Senate Public Lands and Surveys Committee's review, told the special prosecutors:

> [M]ake no mistake about it, the people we are after are friends of the Attorney General. Harry Daugherty has had a hand in every dirty piece of business which has come out of the Harding administration.

> There is every reason to believe that, at the very least, Daugherty is one of the men who knows the whole sordid story of the oil leases—and there is enough evidence to warrant the suspicion that he himself might have profited from them. In addition, the Department of Justice and its Bureau of Investigation are hand picked by Daugherty and rotten to the core.[340]

Eventually, a Senate committee was formed to investigate Daugherty's failure to prosecute, among others, the cases arising from the Teapot Dome scandal and numerous charges of illegality, graft, and influence peddling in the Department of Justice.[341] Daugherty, facing ever-increasing pressure, resigned on March 28, 1924. It is hard to review the activities of the Harding administration and not come to the conclusion that Harry M. Daugherty, the man probably most responsible for Sanford's attainment of a seat on the Supreme Court, was aware of, and a participant in, at least some of what it was his job to prevent, eradicate, and adjudicate.[342]

Despite Walsh's efforts, Daugherty was not convicted of a crime during the Teapot Dome investigation. The contracts on the naval oil assets, however, were overturned. The California leases were found void and ordered canceled in 1925. The US Supreme Court affirmed this determination on February 28, 1927.[343] As to Teapot Dome in Wyoming, the Court held, in an opinion authored by Justice Butler, that the lease and contracts should be declared void because of the conspiracy between Fall and Sinclair.[344] Paradoxically, both Sinclair and Doheny were acquitted of conspiring to defraud the government. After Sinclair refused to respond to questions put to him by the Senate, however, the Supreme Court affirmed his conviction for contempt of Congress.[345] The Court held that Congress has the power to conduct investigations and compel witnesses to testify. Sinclair was also found in contempt of court for having the jury at his first trial shadowed by detectives.[346] Doheny was on trial at the time of Sanford's death.[347]

The matter addressed in *McGrain v. Daugherty*[348] was related to the review of Daugherty's administration of the Department of Justice. During the investigation of the attorney general, his brother, Mally S. Daugherty, was subpoenaed but refused to appear before the Senate committee. A warrant commanding Mally to be brought before the committee was issued. A federal district court in Cincinnati concluded that the Senate had exceeded its powers under the Constitution in requiring a private citizen to testify before its investigative committee concerning the Teapot Dome scandal. The Supreme Court, with Van Devanter writing for the Court, held that (1) the investigation was ordered for a legitimate object; (2) the witness wrongfully refused to appear and testify before the committee and was lawfully attached; (3) the Senate was entitled to have him give testimony pertinent to the inquiry, either at its bar or before the committee; and (4) the district court erred in discharging him from custody under the attachment. Procedurally, the Senate committee investigations of President Harding's administration stand as a landmark in the use of congressional powers.[349] Congress has regularly used this power since the decision. The ruling in *McGrain v. Daugherty* firmly established the power of Congress to conduct investigations, even without a specifically stated legislative purpose, and to gather information by requiring private citizens to testify. The investigative powers set out in the decision were utilized during the McCarthy, Watergate, and Iran-Contra hearings.[350]

When Time Permitted

During Sanford's time on the Court, he rarely found time for relaxation. It was well known in Washington, however, that "the large quantities of the latest fiction which passed from the Library of Congress to the Sanford residence were for the Justice himself."[351] Additionally, Sanford, along with McReynolds and Butler, were the golfers on the Supreme Court.[352] At an earlier point in his career, Sanford observed that in the pursuit of golf, "the lawyer gains added strength and zest of life and energy for his work." He suggested only partly in jest that two hours a day should be spent playing golf.[353] His secretary from his time on the district court bench recalled that Sanford "was intensely interested in golf, his only recreation. Judge Sanford had some two hundred golf clubs at home, and would always bring a new club or two to the office each morning."[354] In a 1923 speech to the Tennessee Bar Association, Sanford noted that "[t]he President defeated me pretty badly the other day. Justice McReynolds felt very badly about that and he has taken me under his wing and promised to show me just how he plays, so that next time I may be more successful, if I have that sort of contest."[355] An article written by family friend William Rule observed that "[g]olf is [Sanford's] sole recreation and he is as serious and as intense in playing the game as he is in weighing the important cases that come to him for adjudication."[356] Even articles regarding Sanford's death mentioned his enthusiasm for golf when his duties would permit him to play.[357]

There was another enjoyment for Sanford in Washington: lunch. He frequently dropped into the Senate restaurant for lunch during court recesses and took great pleasure in meeting the senators and others who gathered there.[358] He also enjoyed dining at a little cafeteria almost within the shadow of the Capitol's dome, "The Ugly Duckling," and when Sanford found the time to leave his work, he would walk across the street to experience a little taste of home: stuffed egg salad prepared by Mrs. Hugh Fred, a "Lady from Tennessee."[359]

CHAPTER ELEVEN

Gitlow v. New York

> *For present purposes we may and do assume that freedom of speech and of the press—which are protected by the First Amendment from abridgment by Congress—are among the fundamental personal rights and "liberties" protected by the due process clause of the Fourteenth Amendment from impairment by the States.*[1]
> —*Gitlow v. People of State of New York*, 268 U.S. 652 (1925)

Sanford's greatest impact on American law came in the area of civil liberties. The statement quoted above is generally recognized as the beginning of the process of incorporating the guarantees of the Bill of Rights[2] and making them applicable to the states through the Fourteenth Amendment's due process clause. Sanford's pronouncement in *Gitlow v. New York* "would prove of monumental significance as a judicial tool in the years to come."[3] After *Gitlow*, "it became difficult for the Court to avoid making the rest of the provisions of the First Amendment applicable to the states, and it began the process of selective incorporation of the rest of the provisions of the first eight amendments."[4] The period after *Gitlow* "involved a decisive shift towards the nationalization of the constitutional protections of the individual against overbearing local governmental action, a step that the court had repeatedly refused to take in the past."[5]

The initial Constitution of the United States, ratified in 1788, did not contain a bill of rights. The Constitution's supporters, the Federalists, desired a strong central government to manage the debts incurred by the country following the American Revolution. Opponents of a strong central government, the Anti-Federalists, feared that centralized power in a strong national government would lead to overreaching and oppression. They preferred instead that power remain in the hands of the individual states. As a condition of their support for the new Constitution, which they had opposed, the Anti-Federalists demanded protection of individual rights. Accordingly, a bill of rights was proposed by the Congress in 1789 and ratified by the states in 1791. The new central government was to have limited powers clearly delegated to it, and the guarantees of the Bill of Rights originally were applied only at the federal level and were understood to be restrictions of the powers of the national government. They did not explicitly restrict the powers of state and local governments.[6] "No delegation of power to the national government involved the power to invade basic individual liberties."[7] To protect individual rights, the Founders looked to the states to provide guarantees and any judicial enforcement.[8]

James Madison, the primary author of the Bill of Rights, believed that prohibitions on the national government needed to be extended to the states because "that majority will, exercised most dangerously at the state and local levels, presented a greater threat to liberty than any act of the national legislature."[9] He did not trust the states to police themselves. The records of the first Congress reveal that "Mr. Madison conceived this to be the most valuable amendment on the whole list [of amendments that constituted the Bill of Rights]; if there was any reason to restrain the government of the United States from infringing upon these essential rights, it was equally necessary that they should be secured against the state governments."[10] As he worked to garner support for the Bill of Rights, however, Madison found that states' rights advocates were opposed to applying the prohibitions to the states. The defeat in the Senate of his proposed amendment requiring states to respect speech, press, conscience, and juries clearly reveals that the First Amendment was initially intended to prohibit only the federal government from restricting speech.[11] This understanding of the applicability of the rights in the Bill of Rights was confirmed in 1833 in *Barron v. Baltimore*.[12] Speaking for a unanimous Court, Chief Justice John Marshall held that the rights in the Bill of Rights were not applicable to exercises of power by state and local governments but were applicable only as restraints on the powers of the national government.[13] He observed that the Constitution's amendments "contain no expression indicating an intention to apply them to the state governments. This court cannot so apply them."[14]

Once ratified, the Bill of Rights played "a remarkably small role during the Antebellum era." In 1845, Justice John Catron of Tennessee reaffirmed the principle of *Barron* in *Permoli v. New Orleans*,[15] when he dismissed the case for lack of jurisdiction: "The [federal] Constitution makes no provision for protecting the citizens of the respective states in their religious liberties; this is left to the state constitutions and laws; nor is there any inhibition imposed by the Constitution of the United States in this respect on the states."[16] Americans were required to rely upon their state constitutions and state bills of rights for the protection of basic political and civil liberties.[17]

Supported by the *Barron* decision, which held that the Bill of Rights applied only to the federal government, the southern states suppressed speech and regulated press coverage on the question of slavery. The decision also left those states free to deny procedural and substantive rights to blacks.[18] Ultimately, the Civil War made it clear that the objectives of the Founders had been frustrated, as the southern states that seceded destroyed the "more perfect Union."[19] Thus, the history out of which the Fourteenth Amendment grew was that of slavery, sectional conflict, secession by the South, victory by the North, abolition of slavery, and the problem of the status of the newly freed blacks and the rebellious southern states.[20] Only after the Civil War "dramatized the need to limit abusive states" would a "distinctively modern view" of the Bill of Rights more in line with the view of James Madison eventually emerge.[21]

When the Founders first gathered in 1787, the issue of slavery was front and center. On the southern plantations, crops such as tobacco, rice, and cotton could only be grown profitably with slave labor, and the planters were zealous to protect slavery from interference by the national government. Accordingly, the southern states declared that they would join the new Republic only if slavery was protected.[22] Among the concessions made by the Founders to the South was that for each slave, the state would receive credit for three-fifths of a free citizen for purposes of taxation and representation in Congress.[23] In electoral voting, therefore, one hundred slaves counted as sixty persons.[24] The Constitution also denied Congress the power to prohibit the slave trade for twenty years and included a fugitive slave clause in Article 4, section 2, which stipulated that "No Person held to Service or Labour in one state, under the Laws thereof, escaping into another, shall in consequence of any Law or Regulation therein, be discharged from such service or Labour, but shall be delivered up on Claim of the Party to whom such Service or Labour may be due."[25] Thus, while not explicitly permitting or prohibiting slavery, the Constitution implicitly accepted it as an institution. As the years passed, it became clear that the United States was being ruled by "the slave interest" or "the Slave Power," as the protected constitutional privilege allowed the South to shape national policy to its will. Additionally, because the federal government was deemed to have limited powers, the slave states were able to impose strict control over their populations.[26]

The Democratic Party, especially dominated by the slave interests, prevented the introduction of any new ideas from the North.[27] "[E]xtremely repressive laws to prop up slavery" were enacted, "censoring abolitionist speech and press, suppressing anti-slavery preachers, implementing dragnet searches of suspected fugitive slaves and slave-sympathizers, imposing savagely cruel punishments on runaway slaves and their allies, and violating virtually every right mentioned" in the federal Bill of Rights.[28] Republicans could not compete for southern votes because the slave states did not permit freedom of speech, press, or assembly to any group criticizing or questioning the slave system. Southern postmasters removed from the incoming mail and then destroyed any newspapers or books critical of slavery.[29] Northerners bitterly resented the idea that one part of the country had been allowed to opt out of the American system of free elections and free debate.[30]

Although milestones in the history of democracy and freedom, the framing of the Constitution in 1787 and the addition of the Bill of Rights two years came at a cost: the guarantees the Founders provided for slavery spawned the Slave Power and the Civil War. In the view of the Republicans in the postwar Congress, especially the Radical Republicans who were committed to equal treatment and enfranchisement of the freedmen, the Constitution had allowed the South to set up a racial caste system and a political oligarchy that stifled internal debate.[31] Even after losing the war, southerners apparently believed that their power to regulate the local black population, short of actual re-enslavement, was undiminished. The South's old conservative political and social regimes, led by former Confederates, soon became re-established. As early as 1865, southern legislatures began passing Black Codes, a legal system designed to keep the freed slaves in "their proper place" on the plantations and laboring for their old masters.[32] These measures were designed to undermine the Emancipation Proclamation and the Thirteenth Amendment by denying to blacks many important individual liberties secured to whites.[33] A new generation of founders committed themselves to repairing the Constitution's flaws.[34] Ironically, it was the year of Sanford's birth, 1865, that the Thirty-ninth Congress began reshaping the Constitution with the Fourteenth Amendment.

The election of 1864 had given the Republicans a sizeable majority in both the Senate and in the House.[35] When the predominantly Republican Congress reconvened in December 1865 and again in December 1866, the Republicans "hammered out a compromise program designed to create a different system of politics in the post-war South."[36] Virtually all the Republicans who spoke on the subject believed that the guarantees in the federal Bill of Rights limited or should limit the powers of the states as well as the central government.[37] For example, Congressman John Bingham, an Ohio lawyer and the primary framer of the Fourteenth Amendment, believed that the original Bill of Rights already applied directly to the states and that *Barron v. Baltimore* had been wrongly decided.[38] Senator Jacob M. Howard of Michigan noted that the purpose of the Fourteenth Amendment was to protect various privileges and immunities guaranteed by the Constitution against interference by the states, including "the personal rights guaranteed and secured by the first eight amendments of the Constitution.... The great object of the first section of this amendment is, therefore, to restrain the power of the states and compel them at all times to respect these great fundamental guarantees."[39] According to leading Republicans, therefore, "the [Fourteenth] amendment was simply declaratory of existing constitutional law, properly understood...."[40] Contrary to *Barron v. Baltimore*, some believed "that states could not deprive persons of due process. Still, they wrote this limitation into the Fourteenth Amendment. Finally, leading Republicans believed that no state could abridge the privileges and immunities of citizens of the United States—including those privileges and immunities secured by the Bill of Rights. This idea also was written into the Fourteenth Amendment."[41]

Accordingly, the Fourteenth Amendment, added in 1868, was directed at imposing restrictions on the powers of the state and local governments. Section 1 provided: "All persons born or naturalized in the United States, and subject to the jurisdiction thereof, are citizens of the United States and of the State wherein they reside. No State shall make or enforce any law which shall abridge the privileges or immunities of citizens of the United States; nor shall any State deprive any person of life, liberty, or property, without due process of law; nor deny to any person within its jurisdiction the equal protection of the laws."

The Fourteenth Amendment was the second of three Reconstruction Amendments. The Thirteenth Amendment (1865) abolished slavery, and the Fifteenth Amendment (1870) prohibited racial discrimination in voting. The clauses of the Fourteenth Amendment could be interpreted separately or in isolation.

Before the Fourteenth Amendment's intended purpose could be realized, the disputed presidential election of 1876 impacted the nation. Democratic New York Governor Samuel J. Tilden defeated Republican Ohio Governor Rutherford B. Hayes in the popular vote and received undisputed electoral votes amounting to one short of a majority. Returns from several states were in dispute.[42] After a series of negotiations and compromises, the Republican Party became willing to strike a bargain with the white South. Under the terms of the Compromise of 1877, an informal and unwritten deal, the Democrats agreed to accept the Republican presidential electors and allowed Hayes to become president. In return for securing the presidency and retaining control over most federal jobs and spending, Republicans agreed to withdraw federal troops from the South and end enforcement of laws protecting freed slaves and former Unionists.[43] With the departure of the army, Republican governments in the South collapsed when blacks were prevented from voting. Jim Crow segregation laws and other forms of discrimination increased. The nation—the North as well as the South—turned away from the plight of freed persons.[44] The Supreme Court gave the Fourteenth Amendment a narrow reading and essentially held the Reconstruction Amendments in disdain. As noted by Professor Bryan H. Wildenthal,

> "[f]or a brief shining moment during and after the Civil War, protection of Blacks had been associated with the cause of the Union. By the mid-1870s protection of Blacks seemed to disrupt national unity, and the commitment to protection of their rights faded away as quickly as it had come." Something similar took place with regard to incorporation. Born in the epic debates of the 1860s, it enjoyed a brief heyday in the early 1870s. . . . But it got caught up in the general retrenchment of federal power associated with the end of Reconstruction. . . . For a conservative Court, zealous in defense of

private property and corporate rights, but indifferent or hostile to individual liberty in the broader sense, incorporation was a bother. ... The moment did not last.[45]

The Supreme Court eventually would fundamentally alter the pre-Civil War understanding that the Bill of Rights restricted only the powers of the national government. Incrementally, through the due process clause of the Fourteenth Amendment, the Court made most of the Bill of Rights applicable as restrictions of the powers of the state and local governments as well.[46] The first attempt at incorporation, however, involved the privileges and immunities clause rather than the due process clause.[47]

In the *Slaughterhouse Cases*,[48] decided in 1873, the Court considered whether the privileges and immunities clause made the Bill of Rights applicable to the states. Under the facts of the case, the legislature of Louisiana granted a single corporation the exclusive right to maintain slaughterhouses within an area that included the City of New Orleans.[49] The plaintiffs, an association of butchers, argued that the act granted a monopoly for twenty-five years to the corporation and negatively impacted their livelihoods. Justice Samuel Freeman Miller, speaking for the Court, concluded that the Fourteenth Amendment was not intended to modify profoundly the nature of the federal system as it had existed prior to the Civil War.[50] To Miller, neither the framers of the amendment nor the legislatures of the states which ratified the amendment intended "to bring within the power of Congress the entire domain of civil rights heretofore belonging exclusively to the states."[51] The Court declared that it simply could not possibly have been the intention of the framers of the Fourteenth Amendment to "fetter and degrade the State governments by subjecting them to the control of Congress."[52] In other words, "the most basic rights of the individual had state law and state constitutions as their source, notwithstanding the addition of the Fourteenth Amendment to the Constitution, and ... the privileges and immunities clause guaranteed only a very narrow spectrum of relatively unimportant rights against deprivation by the states."[53] According to one historian, the Court's view of the privileges and immunities clause was that "it created a new class of national rights so small that [Justice Miller] had to describe it to prove it existed: the right to visit the nation's capital, the right to run for national office, the right to have access to seaports and to ensure federal protection at sea."[54] Miller declared that the most important rights of the individual derived from state citizenship and were not among the rights of United States citizenship protected by the privileges and immunities clause.[55] A contrary result, in his view, would "radically chang[e] the whole theory of the relations of the state and federal governments to each other and of both these governments to the people."[56] Only Justice Joseph Bradley argued that the Fourteenth Amendment required the application of the Bill of Rights or similar fundamental rights to the states.[57] As noted by Wildenthal, the case was "most ill-suited ... to address the incorporation issue" as it "did not turn on whether the Fourteenth Amendment incorporated any of the specific privileges or immunities set forth in the Bill of Rights."[58] The right the butchers claimed—their right to pursue their livelihood, their "right of free labor"—does not appear in the Bill of Rights.[59] The case came to represent the "evisceration" of the privileges and immunities clause.[60]

Next, proponents of incorporation argued that the Fourteenth Amendment's due process clause should be interpreted to apply the protections of the Bill of Rights to the states. The phrase "due process of law" was not new to the Constitution, as the Fifth Amendment limits the federal government with parallel language: "nor [shall any person] be deprived of life, liberty, or property, without due process of law...."[61] In a series of decisions between 1870 and 1900, however, the Court held that the Fourteenth Amendment's due process clause did not require the states to provide a jury trial in civil cases involving more than $20, to indict criminal defendants by grand juries, or to afford criminal defendants jury trials, despite the provisions of the Seventh, Fifth, and Sixth Amendments of the Bill of Rights imposing these requirements on the national government.[62]

In 1884, in *Hurtado v. California*,[63] the State of California had convicted Hurtado upon an information filed by a prosecutor and examined by a magistrate but not a grand jury. On appeal to the US Supreme Court, Hurtado argued that the due process clause of the Fourteenth Amendment required indictment by a grand jury in a state capital murder case. The Court determined, however, that no right "specifically guaranteed in the Bill of Rights could apply to the states via the due process clause of the Fourteenth Amendment."[64] Decisions of such ilk elicited strong dissenting opinions from Justice John Marshall Harlan, who argued that the purpose of the Fourteenth Amendment had been to make all of the rights in the Bill of Rights applicable as restrictions of the powers of state and local governments: "I go further and hold that the privileges of free speech and a free press, belonging to every citizen of the United States, constitute essential parts of every man's liberty, and are protected against violation by that clause of the Fourteenth Amendment forbidding a state to deprive any person of his liberty without due process of law."[65]

The reasoning of the *Hurtado* Court was "eventually undermined" by "[p]ressure by business interests." Until 1890, the issue of "due process" was viewed as a procedural limitation of government. "Business interests ... now began to argue that their economic and property rights deserved more than fair governmental procedures under the due process clause."[66] The principles of Social Darwinism—"that the economy ought to be ruled by an aristocracy of wealth, that poverty is inevitable and is in part the fault of the poor themselves, and that the role of the government ought to be confined to that of policeman"—were "widely accepted by intellectuals as well as businessmen."[67] The Court adopted these ideas. Instead of interpreting the due process clause to protect individuals against the powers of the state and local governments, the Court began to hold that it protected businesses against government regulation.[68]

During the 1890s, the Court of Chief Justice Melville Fuller, a railroad lawyer from Chicago, believed in the superiority of private enterprise. On March 24, 1890, the era of protecting businesses from government regulation—"substantive due process"—began after the Fuller Court in *Chicago, Milwaukee & St. Paul Railway Co. v. Minnesota*[69] endorsed the view that "the Due Process Clause of the Fifth and the Fourteenth Amendments gives federal courts the power to review the substance of legislation, not just the procedures it establishes." The Court held that a law prescribing railroad rates denied the businessmen their right to due process.[70] Throughout the 1890s, the Fuller Court "accepted the argument that various provisions of the Constitution [included] the moral and economic principle of *laissez faire* and that government could not interfere with the free market's distribution of economic wealth and power."[71]

During Fuller's twenty-two-year tenure as chief justice the country saw massive changes:

> The passing of the frontier, the rise of an interstate industrialism, the shift from a rural to an urban distribution of population, the breakdown of nineteenth-century capitalism and the efforts to construct in its stead a twentieth-century capitalism, the breakthrough[s] in science and technology, the change in the society of nations brought about by global wars and the dialectic of totalitarianism—the

constitutional posture of the American people had to be readjusted in response to each of these.[72]

From the depression of the 1870s onward, intellectuals and policymakers in the United States, fearful of the rising tide of strikes and political protests, had worried that the country would adopt "socialistic" measures to resolve this unrest.[73] In the 1890s, commentators feared that workers were moving toward socialism or even revolution. Apocalyptic forecasts abounded, with one newspaper predicting "fire and sword will devastate the country."[74] The assassination of President William McKinley in 1901 by a self-professed anarchist caused public alarm and anger to run high. Many frightened Americans equated anarchists with all labor unions, all radical European immigrants, and the entire political left.[75] The prevailing view in race relations was that white supremacy and racial segregation was "in the nature of things."[76] In the South, the "chalk line of Jim Crow[77] was drawn across virtually every area of public contact."[78] At this time in the Court's history, anti-incorporation was the Court's controlling view, as "[p]olitics and public opinion had turned decisively against the Reconstruction commitment to equal protection."[79]

In 1897, the Court took the first step to extend the protections guaranteed in the Bill of Rights to state and local governments. In *Chicago, Burlington & Quincy Railroad Company v. Chicago*,[80] the Court upheld the railroad's argument that forcing it to sell its property at the demand of the state legislature violated the due process clause of the Fifth Amendment as applied by the Fourteenth Amendment.[81] In the opinion, the Court, speaking through Justice Harlan, held that "a judgment of a state court, even if it be authorized by statute, whereby private property is taken for the State or under its direction for public use, without compensation made or secured to the owner, is, upon principle and authority, wanting in the due process of law required by the Fourteenth Amendment of the Constitution of the United States. . . ."[82] The Court determined that states "were indeed bound by the principle of just compensation laid down in the Fifth Amendment."[83] Harlan noted: "In determining what is due process of law, regard must be had to substance, not to form."[84] Thus the Court held for the first time that a right in the Bill of Rights was also a right protected against state action by the due process clause of the Fourteenth Amendment. Until this case, the Court had consistently refused to find that any of the rights in the Bill of Rights could be applied as restrictions on state power through the Fourteenth Amendment.[85]

The case did not, however, use reasoning based on the incorporation theory.[86] The Court's "well-known and overriding concern during this era with economic liberty and the defense of business and property interests," as opposed to rights of individuals, obviously explains this decision.[87]

In the 1907 case of *Patterson v. Colorado*,[88] the majority, with Justice Holmes writing for the Court, dismissed a newspaper publisher's challenge to a Colorado Supreme Court decision convicting him of criminal contempt for criticizing a ruling of the court.[89] The appeal was not based on the First or Fourteenth Amendment. Holmes assumed for the sake of argument that the First Amendment applied:[90] "We leave undecided the question whether there is to be found in the 14th Amendment a prohibition similar to that in the 1st." Upon considering the facts before him, Holmes found that even if the First Amendment applied to the state, Patterson had no case. Justice Harlan expressed his belief that "the privileges of free speech and a free press, belonging to every citizen of the United States, constitute essential parts of every man's liberty, and are protected against violation by the clause of the 14th Amendment forbidding a state to deprive any person of his liberty without due process of law."[91]

Before the Court in 1908, in *Twining v. New Jersey*,[92] came the contention that the right against self-incrimination was among those rights protected from invasion by the states. Justice Moody, writing for the Court, acknowledged that the *Chicago, Burlington & Quincy Railroad Company* holding gave support to arguments that the due process clause protected rights *like* those in the Bill of Rights. He admitted that prior Courts had given "much less effect to the Fourteenth Amendment than some of the public men active in framing it intended,"[93] and conceded that the "view [that the Fourteenth Amendment nationalizes the Bill of Rights] has been, at different times, expressed by justices of this Court . . . and was undoubtedly . . . entertained by some of those who framed [it]."[94] Asserting that "the rights in the Bill of Rights did not apply to the states exactly as they applied to the national government,"[95] he agreed that "it is possible that some of the personal rights safeguarded by the first eight Amendments against national action may also be safeguarded against state action, because a denial of them would be a denial of due process of law." According to Moody, of importance is not that "those rights are enumerated in the first eight Amendments, but . . . that they are included in the conception of due process of law."[96] He stated that the test of whether a right was protected by due process was this: "Is it a fundamental principle of liberty and justice which inheres in the very idea of free government and is the inalienable right of a citizen of such a government?"[97] Although the Court determined that the right against self-incrimination was "universal in American law," the Court held that it was "not fundamental in due process of law, nor an essential part of it."[98] Thus, the *Twining* Court relied on the reasoning of *Hurtado* and similar cases to hold that the Bill of Rights did not directly apply to the states via the due process clause. It instead indicated that rights similar to those in the Bill of Rights might be guaranteed by the due process clause because they were thought to be inherent in the terms liberty and due process of law.[99] Justice Harlan, in dissent, stated: "At the close of the late Civil War . . . the question arose whether provision should not be made by constitutional amendments to secure against attack by the States the rights, privileges, and immunities which, by the original Amendments, had been placed beyond the power of the United States or any Federal agency to impair or destroy. . . . The privileges and immunities mentioned in the original Amendments and universally regarded as our heritage of liberty from the common law, were thus secured [by the Fourteenth Amendment] to every citizen of the United States and placed beyond assault by any government, Federal or state. . . ."[100]

During the early twentieth century, state and federal authorities reacted to political unrest with repressive laws. In the late 1910s and 1920s, "the majority of Americans and of the Supreme Court justices believed that some speech and publications could be so dangerous as to deserve suppression and the jailing and censure of offending speakers and authors."[101] In response to the so-called "Red Scare" following the 1917 Russian Revolution, most states passed sedition laws criminalizing the promotion of revolution.[102] During President Wilson's tenure, a number of questionable laws were passed and many citizens were imprisoned in the interest of "national security."[103] In "[e]xamining the tenor of the times . . . 'no group of Americans was more hostile to free speech claims . . . than the judiciary, and no judgments were more hostile than [those of] the justices on the United States Supreme Court.'"[104]

The First World War brought a series of cases to the Court involving denial of First Amendment protection to radical or anti-war speech. In 1919, in *Schenk v. United States*[105] and *Abrams v. United States*,[106] the Court ruled on the constitutionality of those questionable laws. In *Schenk*, the Court, speaking through Justice Holmes, articulated the "clear and present danger" doctrine. Holmes noted that speech was not protected if "the words are used in such circumstances and are of such a nature as to create a clear and present danger that they will bring about the substantive evils that Congress has a right to prevent."[107] He also stated that "the most stringent protection of free speech would not protect a man in falsely shouting fire in a theatre and causing a panic."[108] That same year in *Abrams*, Holmes dissented in a case utilizing the clear and present danger test. The defendants in *Abrams*, avowed socialists and revolutionaries, were convicted of conspiracy to violate the Espionage Act by distributing circulars intended to provoke and encourage resistance to the United States and the war effort.[109] Holmes clarified that not all anti-government speech presented a clear and present danger: "It is only the present danger of immediate evil or an intent to bring it about that warrants Congress in setting a limit to the expression of opinion."[110]

The following year, in another war-related case, *Gilbert v. Minnesota*,[111] the Court considered a state law that declared it a misdemeanor for any person to teach or advocate that citizens should not aid or assist the United States in prosecuting and carrying on war with the nation's enemies. Gilbert argued that the statute was "obnoxious to the 'inherent right of free speech.'"[112] Justice McKenna, writing for the Court, stated: "[W]ithout so deciding or considering the freedom asserted as guaranteed or secured either by the Constitution of the United States or by the Constitution of the state, we pass immediately to the contention, and for the purposes of this case may concede it—that is, concede that the asserted freedom is natural and inherent, but it is not absolute; it is subject to restriction and limitation."[113] As Justice Holmes had done in *Patterson*, Justice McKenna side-stepped the question of whether the Fourteenth Amendment made the First Amendment applicable to the states.

Before President Harding's administration became embroiled in scandal, presidential pardons cleared the jails of most of World War I's political prisoners. The pardons resolved individual cases, but the statutes under which these prisoners had been convicted remained on the books. In peacetime especially, these laws created great tension with the First Amendment right of free speech. Throughout the Taft Court era, the justices were called upon to balance both state and national police powers against individual rights.

As late as 1922, the Supreme Court declared that "neither the Fourteenth Amendment nor any other provision of the Constitution of the United States imposes upon the states any restrictions about 'freedom of speech.'"[114] *Prudential Insurance Company v. Cheek*[115] was authored by Justice Pitney, whom Sanford replaced.[116] Pitney wrote that "the Constitution of the United States imposes upon the states no obligation to confer upon those within their jurisdiction either the right of free speech or the right of silence."[117]

It was against this backdrop that Sanford, an avid historian and son of a New England Unionist, sparked the long overdue process of incorporation of the First Amendment protections of speech and press to the states in *Gitlow v. New York*.[118] In *Gitlow*, the Court considered New York's conviction of Benjamin Gitlow, who had published a pamphlet called the *Left Wing Manifesto*, advocating the establishment of socialism by "class action ... in any form."[119] Gitlow, an ex-assemblyman from the Bronx, was one of the founders of the American Communist Party. His 1919 arrest and trial were part of a New York version of the better-known Palmer raids.[120] After bombings and violence in 1919, "Palmer raids," ordered by Attorney General A. Mitchell Palmer, were conducted by the US Department of Justice in 1919 and 1920 to round up foreign anarchists, communists, and radical leftists.[121]

Gitlow was charged with three counts of violating New York's Criminal Anarchy Act, which prohibited advocating the overthrow of the government by force. The act defined criminal anarchy as "the doctrine that organized government should be overthrown by force or violence, or by assassination of the executive head or of any of the executive officials of government, or by any unlawful means." The act provided that any person, who by "word of mouth or writing advocates, advises or teaches the duty, necessity or propriety" of criminal anarchism, or who "[p]rints, publishes, edits, issues or knowingly circulates, sells, distributes or publicly displays any book, paper, document, or written or printed matter in any form" advocating criminal anarchy, was guilty of a felony.[122] According to the indictment, Gitlow had violated the act because:

> He "feloniously advocated, advised, and taught ... the necessity and propriety of overthrowing and overturning organized government by force."
>
> He printed *The Revolutionary Age*, which urged the overthrow of the government.
>
> He was an "evil-disposed, and pernicious person ... of most wicked and turbulent disposition[]."[123]

At trial, Gitlow argued that the *Manifesto* was not a revolutionary call for violence and that because there was no resulting action flowing from the *Man-*

ifesto's publication, the statute penalized utterances without any propensity to incite concrete action. He was not charged with the commission of any overt illegal act or with conspiracy to commit an illegal act, nor was it claimed that he advocated that anyone else go out and commit an overt act. Essentially, he was charged with advocating ideas that, if enough people agreed with them, might lead to illegalities at some point in the future.[124] Gitlow, inspired by the Russian Revolution, envisioned a Soviet America, and his writings and speeches were intended to bring that about.[125] In the view of the State of New York, however, the ideas he communicated were enough to constitute a crime. According to the State, whether the words were actually likely to persuade anyone to do anything illegal was beside the point.[126] Gitlow was convicted and sentenced to five to ten years at hard labor.[127]

On appeal to the Supreme Court, Gitlow argued that the Fourteenth Amendment extended to protect his First Amendment rights against state as well as federal action. New York asserted that "[t]he First Amendment was purely a limitation on the power of Congress and that limitation has not been extended to the states by the Fourteenth [A]mendment."[128] The New York statute that criminalized Gitlow's speech was perceived to be beyond the reach of the First Amendment. Express constitutional protection for free speech could come only from the state constitution.

The Court heard arguments twice in *Gitlow* and handed down its decision in the case on June 8, 1925. In order to establish the Court's jurisdiction and to allow the Court "to find that New York's Criminal Anarchy statute, as applied, was not so unreasonable as to deprive Gitlow of his liberty without due process of law,"[129] Sanford's most famous words as a Supreme Court justice were uttered:[130] "For present purposes, we may and do assume that freedom of speech and of the press which are protected by the First Amendment from abridgment by Congress are among the fundamental personal rights and 'liberties' protected by the due process clause of the Fourteenth Amendment from impairment by the States."[131]

For civil libertarians, "the declaration of incorporation . . . provided one victory" but "the majority opinion provided none at all."[132] In reviewing Gitlow's conviction, the Supreme Court applied the "bad tendency" test, which was then dominant in federal First Amendment analysis.[133] This test allowed punishment of speech if (1) the speaker intended to encourage conduct that the government may ban and (2) the speech had any tendency to produce such conduct.[134] In a seven-to-two ruling explicitly endorsing the "bad tendency" principle—"that speakers are responsible for the reasonable, probable outcome of their words, irrespective of how likely it is that those words will create an overt criminal act"—a majority of the Supreme Court agreed with the position of the State of New York.[135]

Sanford's opinion for the majority upheld the conviction because, in the Court's view, states should be free to prosecute citizens who advocate violent overthrow of the government. The "bad tendency" of such speech placed it outside the First Amendment's protections. According to Sanford's opinion, "[t]he State cannot reasonably be required to measure the danger from every such utterance in the nice balance of a jeweler's scale. A single revolutionary spark may kindle a fire that, smoldering for a time, may burst into a sweeping and destructive conflagration."[136] Earlier decisions, Sanford observed, had established that freedom of speech is not absolute.[137] It "does not deprive a State of the primary and essential right of self preservation."[138] Sanford further noted that "utterances inciting to the overthrow of organized government by unlawful means, present a sufficient danger of substantive evil to bring their punishment within the range of legislative discretion."[139] That was what the statute under consideration in *Gitlow* forbade: By punishing one who "advocates ... the duty, necessity or propriety of overthrowing ... organized government by force or violence," the state had penalized only "the advocacy of action," not "the utterance or publication of abstract 'doctrine' or academic discussion having no quality of incitement to any concrete action."[140] In language revealing the tenor of the time period, Sanford held that Gitlow had participated in the publication and circulation of the document and that "such utterances, by their very nature, involve danger to the public peace and to the security of the State."[141]

As noted by Professor Marc Lendler, "the reason *Gitlow* is still widely cited and discussed" is because Sanford's jurisdictional statement "is generally regarded as the beginning of the incorporation of the Bill of Rights."[142] In *Twining*, Justice Moody "had suggested that some fundamental rights might be contained in the notion of due process" applicable to the states but that "these rights would be 'of such a nature' that they were included in the concept of due process; they should not be taken from the Bill of Rights."[143] As observed by Lendler, in *Gitlow*, Sanford specifically "announce[d] that the First Amendment [did] apply"[144] as the source of "the rights protected from state action."[145] The incorporation aspect of *Gitlow* became its most important legacy.[146] With Sanford's words, the Supreme

Court took a major step down the road of nationalizing the Bill of Rights.[147] *Gitlow* was "the first major, and the only important liberal-activist free speech case in the entire Taft era of Supreme Court history."[148] As noted by Milton R. Konvitz, the Court made no effort to give reasons for the proposition and spoke

> as if no one had ever questioned it or could possibly do so. The only attempt by Justice Sanford to deal with precedents was a reference to a case decided by the Court only three years before, in which the Court said that "neither the Fourteenth Amendment nor any other provision of the Constitution of the United States imposes upon the States any restrictions about 'freedom of speech' or the 'liberty of silence.'" Justice Sanford characterized this passage in the earlier case as an "incidental statement" (which it was) that was not "determinative" of the question before the Court in *Gitlow*.[149]

As noted by Ronald K. L. Collins and Sam Chaltain, the "good news was that the Court had assumed that the free-speech provision of the First Amendment applied to the states. Though not a formal victory, it was a symbolic one." The *Gitlow* decision came to be viewed as "a constitutional milestone" hailed as the first case in which the Court applied the First Amendment to the states.[150]

Konvitz described Sanford's statement as "a revolutionary break with the past."[151] He opined that the *Gitlow* Court "thus took one broad, breathtaking leap, making a decision that was to have the most significant consequences for constitutional development and for the American people and its institutions."[152] As observed by Konvitz, "[w]hat dissenting Justices had urged upon the Court for years now became the position of the entire Court."[153] The historian Galloway called Sanford's enunciation a "'throw-away' line without any serious analysis or explanation that became one of the most important 'asides' in Supreme Court history."[154] A detractor, John Denton Carter, contended that Sanford "no doubt unwittingly" made the declaration that "laid the foundation for a later revolutionary reconstruction of constitutional law."[155] Whatever the reason for the pronouncement, the *Gitlow* opinion ushered in "a decisive shift towards the nationalization of the constitutional protections of the individual against overbearing local governmental action."[156]

The papers of Sanford and the other justices reveal "that the Court as a whole did not at any point in the process address itself to the problem of the relation between the federal courts and state governments, did not discuss it, and did not evince any particular awareness that the problem was involved." It appears that "a major constitutional shift was effected without a coherent discussion of its merits."[157] Sanford left only one clue about why he accepted the assumption of incorporation in *Gitlow*. A comment of Sanford's from his Department of Justice tenure reveals his thoughts on the applicability of the Bill of Rights to the states. Upon receiving a request that an inmate be transferred from the United States prison at Leavenworth, Kansas, to Minot, North Dakota, for the purpose of giving testimony in a state court proceeding, Sanford observed: "While there is no authority for it, it seems to me that if a person charged with a crime in a state court is desirous of obtaining the testimony of a federal prisoner in his behalf, it is not a matter of judicial comity for the federal court to grant the writ but a matter of law and necessity. Otherwise, what becomes of the provision of the Sixth Article that in all criminal prosecutions the accused shall have compulsory process for obtaining witnesses in his favor?"[158] The comment demonstrates Sanford's belief that the Sixth Amendment's guarantee of compulsory process to ensure witnesses in one's favor should apply to the states.

The *New Republic* noted that a "profit and loss account of the *Gitlow* case shows one new gain, the possibility of federal protection against state suppression. A more liberal Court may prevent a checker-board nation, with ultraconservative states into which moderately radical Americans come at peril of imprisonment for sedition."[159] Charles Warren, a constitutional scholar of the day, observed:

> This most recent development may well awaken serious thought as to whether there is not danger that the "liberty" of the States is being unduly sacrificed to this new conception of "liberty" of the individual.... If the doctrine of the case is carried to its logical and inevitable conclusion, every one of the rights contained in the Bill of Rights ought to be and must be included within the definition of "liberty," and must be guaranteed by the Fourteenth Amendment against deprivation by a State "without due process of law."[160]

Warren's critical article in the *Harvard Law Review* predicted "that *Gitlow* was but the beginning of a process that would make all of the restrictions of the Bill of Rights applicable to the states."[161] Pointing out that Sanford's statement for the Court reversed fifty years of contrary decisions,[162] Warren felt that the assumption amounted to a "major and unwarranted shift in the American constitutional scheme of things" that "unduly sacrificed to this new conception of 'liberty' of the individual" the "liberty" of the states.[163] To the contrary, James Parker Hall responded that he did not think the implications of the *Gitlow* assumption would give rise to much change.[164] Surprisingly, "these two articles were the only commentary in law reviews in the period 1925 to 1930 that seriously discussed the issue of incorporation broached by *Gitlow*."[165] Because the Court upheld the conviction, the immediate impact of the *Gitlow* ruling was muted. Several years would pass before the *Gitlow* pronouncement would result in any major doctrinal change by which the Fourteenth Amendment incorporated other rights.[166]

In two decisions to follow, Sanford again addressed issues of the First Amendment's protection of speech.[167] In both cases the Court held that although due process protected freedom of expression, the freedom must be narrowly construed.[168]

In *Whitney v. California*,[169] Charlotte Anita Whitney was a member of the Oakland, California, branch of the Socialist Party and a delegate to its 1919 national convention. A split occurred between a radical group and the old-line socialists. Thereafter, the Oakland delegates allied with the radical group, which later formed the Communist Labor Party of America (CLP). The party's platform included a statement that its purpose was "to create ... a unified revolutionary working class movement" with the goal of overthrowing "capitalist rule."[170] Whitney participated in organizing the CLP of California (CLPC), and a plank she wrote for its platform "urged workers who are possessed of the right of franchise to cast their votes for the ... Communist Labor Party."[171] Her comrades, however, rejected her plank and included a statement of intent to organize general strikes in which the workers would seize power by violent means. Despite the fact that Whitney argued against the proposals for seizing power by force, she was charged with violating California's Criminal Syndicalism Act after she attended the Oakland convention. The act prohibited a person from knowingly becoming a member of any organization advocating "Criminal Syndicalism."[172]

Whitney testified that "it was not her intention that the CLPC should be an instrument of terrorism or violence."[173] The State of California contended, however, that the CLPC was created to teach criminal syndicalism and, as a member of the CLPC, Whitney had participated in the crime. Lawyers for Whitney contended that the California Criminal Syndicalism Act was "repugnant to the due process clause as a restraint on the rights of free speech, assembly and association."[174] There was "no argument about the appropriateness of the Court hearing a speech-rights case based on state law."[175] Sanford rejected Whitney's contention on the ground that it was a reasonable exercise of the state's police powers to view the statute as punishing only those who join and further the aims of associations whose purpose was to "advocate, teach, or aid and abet the commission of crimes or unlawful acts of force, violence, or terrorism as a means of accomplishing industrial or political changes."[176] Although Sanford did not repeat the *Gitlow* stipulation, he held that although "freedom of speech and assembly are part of the liberty protected by the due-process clause of the Fourteenth Amendment, that liberty is not absolute; it is subject to reasonable restraints by the legislature. . . ."[177] He concluded that Whitney's conviction did not infringe on any right of free speech, assembly, or association and did not violate the due process or equal protection clauses. The State "in the exercise of its police power may punish those who abuse [their rights to freedom of speech] by utterances inimical to the public welfare, tending to incite crime, disturb the public peace, or endanger the foundations of organized government and threaten its overthrow by unlawful means."[178]

In Justice Brandeis's celebrated concurring opinion, he noted: "Despite arguments to the contrary which had seemed to me persuasive, *it is settled* that the due process clause of the Fourteenth Amendment applies to matters of substantive law as well as to matters of procedure. Thus all fundamental rights comprised within the term liberty are protected by the Federal Constitution from invasion by the States. The right of free speech, the right to teach, and the right of assembly are, of course, fundamental rights. . . . These may not be denied or abridged. . . ."[179] Brandeis argued that "freedom of utterance has a special place in a democratic government" and that "[f]ree exchange of ideas relating to public policy is the means by which legitimate political and social change is brought about in a democracy."[180] Discussion and assembly can be limited by the state only in extreme circumstances, and it is always "open to Americans to challenge the law abridging free speech and assembly by showing that there was no emergency justifying it."[181] Because the state had presented evidence of the existence of an emergency and Whitney's counsel had not argued to the contrary, Brandeis felt compelled to concur in Sanford's opinion.[182] Whitney had neither contended that the California statute as applied to her was void because there was no clear and present danger of a serious evil, nor had she requested that the question of the existence of such conditions be passed upon by the trial court or a jury. With other evidence tending to establish a conspiracy to commit present serious crimes, Brandeis, joined by Holmes, felt that the Court was without power to disturb the state court's judgment.[183]

Although Sanford's majority opinion in *Whitney* was overruled in 1969 in *Brandenburg v. Ohio*,[184] the late Judge Robert Bork argued that the *Brandenburg* Court should have adopted "the stricter criteria in Justice Sanford's majority opinions in *Gitlow* and *Whitney*."[185] The *Brandenburg* holding requires both that a speaker must intend violence to occur and that the violence actually does occur. In *Brandenburg*, the Court assumed greater responsibility on the part of the adults who are the receivers of the speech in question.[186] During the Taft Court era, in contrast, the justices took a paternalistic approach to those who read or heard the subversive message. It seemed "as if the Supreme Court assumed that the pamphlets" would bring "immediate, powerful, uniform, and direct effects on anyone who read them."[187]

In *Fiske v. Kansas*,[188] Sanford, again speaking for the Court, showed a little liberal activism, upholding a defense invoking the Fourteenth Amendment to guarantee the federal right of free speech against a state criminal anarchy statute.[189] Harold B. Fiske, a twenty-six-year-old organizer, had been arrested and charged with violating Kansas's Criminal Syndicalism Act for soliciting people to become members of the Industrial Workers of the World (IWW), a group advocating that workers take possession of the means of production and abolish the wage system. Fiske was accused of distributing the preamble to the radical labor union's constitution:

> That the working class and the employing class have nothing in common, and that there can be no peace so long as hunger and want are found among millions of working people and the few who make up the employing class have all the good things of life. . . . Between these two classes a struggle must go on until the workers of the world organize as a class, take possession of the earth and the machinery of production and abolish the wage system. . . . Instead of the conservative motto, "A fair day's wages for a fair day's work," we must inscribe on our banner the revolutionary watchword, "Abolition

of the wage system." By organizing industrially we are forming the structure of the new society within the shell of the old.

At the time of his arrest, Fiske was described as "a regular walking roll top desk, his pockets serving for pigeon holes" for the abundance of IWW literature he was carrying.[190]

The Kansas statute provided: "Any person who, by word of mouth, or writing, advocates, affirmatively suggests or teaches the duty, necessity, propriety or expediency of crime, criminal syndicalism, or sabotage . . . is guilty of a felony. . . ."[191] The only evidence introduced by the prosecution indicating that Fiske had advocated force or violence as a means of political or industrial change was the IWW's constitutional preamble. The Kansas Supreme Court noted that the preamble, on its face, did not advocate violence, but the court determined that the jury could have properly found that Fiske, while explaining it to recruits, conveyed "the sinister meaning attributed to it by the state."[192]

Although Fiske argued that his prosecution by the State of Kansas violated his First Amendment right to freedom of speech, the arguments by Fiske's counsel touched only briefly on whether the Fourteenth Amendment guaranteed freedom of speech in a state prosecution, as both sides treated the assumption in *Gitlow* as settled law. The Fiske brief noted toward the end: "We assume from the decision in *Gitlow v. New York* . . . that freedom of speech and of the press are among the fundamental personal rights and liberties protected by the due process clause of the Fourteenth Amendment from impairment by the states, and therefore have not discussed this question at length."[193]

Sanford's opinion for the Court acknowledged that the defendant's view was correct. He observed:

> There is no suggestion in the preamble that the industrial organization of workers as a class for the purpose of getting possession of the machinery of production and abolishing the wage system, was to be accomplished by any other than lawful methods; nothing advocating the overthrow of the existing industrial or political conditions by force, violence or unlawful means. And standing alone, as it did in this case, there was nothing which warranted the court or jury in ascribing to this language, either as an inference of law or fact, "the sinister meaning attributed to it by the state. . . ."[194]

Sanford found that the evidence did not fit the prohibition of the statute. The result was that the Syndicalism Act had been applied to sustain the conviction of the defendant "without any charge or evidence that the organization in which he secured members advocated any crime, violence or other unlawful acts or methods as a means of effecting industrial or political changes or revolution."[195] Thus applied, the act was "an arbitrary and unreasonable exercise of the police power of the states, unwarrantably infringing the liberty of the defendant in violation of the due process clause of the Fourteenth Amendment."[196] *Fiske* revealed that Sanford was not "emotionally committed to denying rights to radicals."[197]

Zechariah Chafee, Jr. contended that the *Fiske* case made the *Gitlow* assumption a reality.[198] In grasping the significance of *Fiske*, Chafee observed that "the Supreme Court for the first time made freedom of speech mean something."[199] He argued that the Court would not have heard the *Fiske* case had not the speech issue been involved.[200] Agreeing with Chafee, Henry Abraham asserted that the Court "confirmed unanimously the nationalization of freedom of speech in the case of *Fiske v. Kansas*."[201] The case marked the first time the Court overturned a state law on the grounds that it violated the First and Fourteenth Amendments to the Constitution by denying an individual his freedom of speech.[202]

Sanford accordingly opened the door to a new era in the constitutional law of civil liberties. In the unanimous decision in *Grosjean v. American Press Company*, Justice Sutherland, Sanford's former colleague, stated: "That freedom of speech and of the press are rights of the same fundamental character [as the right of the accused to the aid of counsel in a criminal prosecution] safeguarded by the due process clause of the Fourteenth Amendment against abridgement by state legislation, has likewise been settled by a series of decisions of this Court beginning with *Gitlow v. New York*. . . ."[203] Another colleague, Justice Stone, commented in a note to Justice Felix Frankfurter: "Free speech was held to be guaranteed by the Fourteenth Amendment in *Fiske v. Kansas* by a unanimous Court, Sanford writing. . . ."[204] Other cases followed, holding more rights guaranteed by the Bill of Rights applicable to the states through the due process clause of the Fourteenth Amendment.[205] Taft's successor as chief justice, Charles Evans Hughes, wrote two opinions for the Court that firmly established in American constitutional law the rule "that freedom of speech and of the press were protected from state interference by the due-process clause of the Fourteenth Amendment." In *Stromberg v. California*,[206] Hughes wrote:

"It has been determined that the conception of liberty under the due process clause of the Fourteenth Amendment embraces the right of free speech. The right is not an absolute one, and the state in the exercise of its police power may punish the abuse of this freedom."[207] In *Near v. Minnesota*,[208] the Court, speaking again through Hughes, incorporated the free press provision of the First Amendment: "It is no longer open to doubt that the liberty of the press and of speech is safeguarded by the due process clause of the Fourteenth Amendment from invasion by state action."[209]

In 1937, the selective incorporation doctrine was fashioned by Justice Benjamin Cardozo in *Palko v. Connecticut*,[210] whereby some, but not necessarily all, Bill of Rights provisions would be extended to the states on a selective or piecemeal basis. *Gitlow* has been cited as precedent in *Griswold v. Connecticut*,[211] which recognized the constitutional right to privacy, and *McDonald v. City of Chicago*,[212] which incorporated the right to bear arms.[213] Sanford's *Gitlow* opinion was one of the earliest steps taken in a line of thinking that would be used to profoundly alter the American legal landscape in the hands of Chief Justice Earl Warren and Justices Hugo Black, William O. Douglas, William J. Brennan, Jr., and Thurgood Marshall.[214] Indeed, the selective incorporation doctrine has been used to conclude that practically all of the protections of the Bill of Rights were incorporated into the Fourteenth Amendment and are applicable to the states.[215] "Of the twenty-four separate privileges and immunities that may be parsed from the first eight amendments, eighteen have been applied in substance to the states."[216]

The incorporation doctrine has been a source of controversy in succeeding courts and political administrations.[217] The idea that the framers of the Fourteenth Amendment intended guarantees of the Bill of Rights to limit state action is rejected by many scholars.[218] In the 1980s, the incorporation doctrine gained national attention when then-Attorney General Edwin Meese and others criticized the doctrine as inconsistent with the intent of the original Framers of the Constitution.[219] All efforts to do away with the doctrine, however, have been unsuccessful, and it survives as Sanford's most vital legal legacy.

 CHAPTER TWELVE

Forgotten

*Time, like an ever rolling stream,
bears all who breathe away;
they fly forgotten, as a dream
dies at the opening day.*
　　　　　— "O God, Our Help in Ages Past," verse 5

In the spring of 1970 during the confirmation hearing for the appointment of Judge G. Harrold Carswell to the United States Supreme Court, Senator Thomas F. Eagleton of Missouri cited Sanford as an example of mediocrity on the Court: "I realize that men of limited capacity have served on the Court in the past.... For every Oliver Wendell Holmes, we can dredge up an Edward T. Sanford."[1] Then-Senate Minority Leader Howard H. Baker, Jr., of Tennessee challenged Eagleton's assertion and termed the statements about Sanford "inappropriate." Baker called Sanford a "competent jurist," observing that to compare him to Holmes was unfair because the latter was pre-eminent among justices.[2] Indeed, justices like Holmes, Brandeis, and Taft overshadowed Sanford.[3] In contrast to these men, Sanford is essentially consigned to oblivion, even in his hometown, where once he was the community's "most illustrious son."[4] A Knoxville attorney remarked several years ago that it struck him as "quite astounding we could have somebody from this region . . . go on to the high court and then . . . be almost forgotten."[5] Even his death was obscured by the fact that he died on the same day as Taft.[6]

Sanford's death on March 8, 1930, was a great shock to his colleagues.[7] On the day Sanford passed away, Justice Van Devanter described him as "a very kindly man, actuated by the best of motives," who "found it difficult to think ill of any one."[8] In describing Sanford to another judge, Van Devanter observed: "Few have so kindly a spirit. . . . His death came so suddenly and unexpectedly that it is difficult to think he is gone."[9] The week after Sanford's death, in open court, Justice Holmes addressed the irony of Taft's and Sanford's dying on the same day:

> On Saturday, just as we were expecting him at a conference of the Justices, we were informed that our brother, Mr. Justice Sanford, had become unconscious pending a slight operation. Five minutes later we received word that he was dead. Thus suddenly the light of a faithful worker who was born also to charm went out. Afterwards came the news that the late Chief Justice had found relief from his hopeless illness in death. Such events must be accepted in silent awe.[10]

Across Washington, the nation's leaders expressed their regret at the untimely passing of Sanford. Senator George W. Norris of Nebraska, chairman of the Judiciary Committee, exclaimed: "I knew Justice Sanford personally. I had great respect for him as a jurist. I never questioned his conscientiousness or his ability. Like thousands of other citizens who have come into contact with him, I deeply mourn his untimely taking off."[11] Senator George H. Moses of New Hampshire, president pro tempore of the Senate, remarked: "Mr. Justice Sanford was one of the ablest men who have recently been named to the Supreme Court bench. His New England education combined with his Southern birth and training gave him a national aspect upon the problems which came before the court and the decisions which he wrote and rendered will long stand as an epitome of the quality which should and does inhere in our greatest tribunal."[12]

Tennesseans particularly were saddened. US Senator William E. Brock from Chattanooga noted as follows:

> I am both grieved and shocked to have just learned of the passing away of Mr. Justice Sanford, one of Tennessee's most distinguished and beloved sons. A kinder and more noble character never lived; a man who was loved and admired and respected by all who came in contact with him, and to know him as we knew him back home was to love him as we loved him. The example of his life has contributed much in making this a better world in which to live and those of us who were privileged to know him intimately have been greatly benefited by contact with this noble character whose memory we will love and cherish forever. The highest court of our nation has lost one of its most distinguished members, the State of Tennessee has lost one of her most beloved and outstanding sons, and the nation has lost one of its most able jurists.[13]

US Representative Cordell Hull of Tennessee observed: "Justice Sanford was a real lawyer and ranked as an outstanding member of the Supreme Court. He possessed a remarkable personality, which made him one of the most popular men, both socially and in the legal profession, that Tennessee has produced during my time."[14] US Representative J. Will Taylor from LaFollette, Tennessee recalled:

> In my early years at the bar I had the privilege to be associated with Sanford in a rather remote capacity in the practice of law, and I have never come in contact with a finer character. His private life was unblemished, and his public career uniformly characterized by the highest quality of zeal and fidelity to public duty.
>
> His untimely death on almost the threshold of a brilliant career on the greatest tribunal in the world is a distinctive national calamity.[15]

In Knoxville, Sanford's hometown, Knox County Bar Association president Charles H. Smith scheduled a meeting to pass formal resolutions of regret for "the most honored member of the Knox County Bar." In describing Sanford's record, the group noted the "great pride that it was made" and the "still greater sorrow that it is ended."[16] The former postmaster and custodian of the federal courthouse recalled Sanford fondly: "Mild-mannered, kind, considerate . . . [h]e was the finest character I honestly believe I ever knew."[17] William Frierson, former US solicitor general and mayor of Chattanooga, declared: "[W]e in Tennessee, where he grew to manhood, practiced law, and later presided over the District Court, honor the man we knew as Ed Sanford. We would hold him in affectionate and admiring memory if he had never held official position."[18]

The staff of the *Tennessee Law Review* "express[ed] its deep regret at the untimely passing of Justice Sanford," noting:

> The distinct loss suffered by the nation in the recent death of Edward Terry Sanford, Associate Justice of the United States Supreme Court, is felt with peculiar keenness in Tennessee, his native state, and in Knoxville, his late home. This loss is reflected deeply at the University of Tennessee, which as his Alma Mater contributed to his rise, and which later shared in the bounty of his ability when, as an alumnus, he became a member of the faculty of the Law College and thereafter served on the Board of Trustees. . . . He was always greatly interested in the development of the University and eager to promote its welfare. . . .[19]

The *Harvard Law Review* reflected on Sanford's passing as follows: "Judge Sanford was a sound, if not a brilliant, lawyer. His great reputation as a district judge was due to his high character, his ripe judgment, his sound sense, and his tact. On the Supreme Court he was a conservative influence, not seeking to brush out new paths, but keeping to the old ways and following established authority."[20]

After Sanford's death, the members of the Bar of the Supreme Court met and adopted resolutions commemorating his life and service. A paragraph from those proceedings described his character and work ethic as follows:

> He served this court with great distinction from the time of his qualification until his untimely death on the 8th day of March, 1930, at the early age of sixty-four. He had a personality of unusual charm and was a most gifted speaker. He was a lover of literature and the arts, was widely read and deeply experienced in law and jurisprudence. He had ardent patriotism and a high sense of public duty. His work

upon the Supreme Court was thorough, conscientious and exacting and had the high commendation of his associates and the Bar. His death is his country's loss, and is mourned by the great circle of his admiring friends and associates both upon the Bench and at the Bar.[21]

Attorney General William D. Mitchell related that Sanford "was in every sense a man of the highest culture. But, above all, his dominant traits of character were kindliness and affection for his fellowmen." Chief Justice Charles Evans Hughes observed: "He met every responsibility with integrity of motive and singleness of purpose and he discharged every trust with complete fidelity."[22]

In a column in the *Milwaukee Sentinel* shortly after Sanford's passing, an editor likewise described the jurist's "useful life, rounded out by fine and meritorious service in the nation's highest tribunal." The writer stressed that, "amid his pressing official and professional duties," Sanford "found time for public spirited service," and that "his loss will be deeply felt by the government he served so well."[23] *The New York Times* observed:

> It has been said of Mr. Sanford that while he was perhaps not a great Judge, he was a most useful member of the Supreme Court. His service on that tribunal had not been long enough to build up a high reputation in the public estimate or in the opinion of his profession, but all lawyers who knew anything of his work have spoken in warm praise of his industry, his devotion to duty, his fair-mindedness and his readiness to pour all his powers into the work of the Supreme Court. A man of refined manners, of high education, of ample private means, he set an example of willingness to spend and be spent in the public service which ought to shame many citizens indifferent to their civic obligations, while being a wholesome reminder and stimulus to young men coming forward at the bar and in politics. Judge Sanford's death, cut off as he was in what seemed to be the height of his usefulness, is a grievous loss, not only to the Supreme Court, but to American public life.[24]

Sanford died after only seven years on the Court, a period many consider too short for a clear judicial philosophy to be discerned. Because of his brief service on the Taft Court, where most of the justices "felt presumptively obligated to join" opinions rather than dissent, "even if they disagreed with their content,"[25] Sanford received a rating of "average" in a survey of Supreme Court justices published in the late 1970s.[26] Historian Paul Finkelman declared that Sanford "fell far short" as a Supreme Court justice.[27] Constitutional law scholar Henry J. Abraham described Sanford's time on the Court as "seven years of average but not unimportant Court service."[28]

According to historian Harold M. Hollingsworth, "Sanford was far from a great Supreme Court justice, but, unlike McReynolds, he was a credit to Tennessee and the Court."[29] Compared to some of his contemporaries on the Court, Sanford appears in a positive light. Sanford's colleague Willis Van Devanter wrote a lower proportion of majority opinions than any other Taft Court justice. During that time frame, Van Devanter wrote fewer than 100 (six percent) of the Taft Court's majority opinions.[30] The justice whom Sanford replaced, Mahlon Pitney, was described by Taft, the president who appointed him, as a "weak member" of the Court to whom he could "not assign cases."[31] Pierce Butler, elevated to the Court shortly before Sanford, is rated as a "distinct failure" by most Court observers, who describe him as "aggressive, domineering and stubborn." His "reactionary reading of the Constitution" is recounted as "second only to that of McReynolds."[32] As noted by Abraham, McReynolds "deservedly earned the all but unanimous condemnation of the Court experts, who have rated him at the top of their brief list of failures."[33]

Professor Michael Ariens opines that in addition to Sanford's short period on the Court, his reputation may have suffered historically because (1) he is not easy to "peg" or pigeonhole; (2) his opinions often concern matters of statutory interpretation; and (3) he was on a Court with three justices who have been the subject of many literary and academic portraits—Taft, Holmes, and Brandeis—and he suffers by comparison.[34] This seems a fair and accurate assessment. Indeed, "short tenure naturally tends to depress rankings," and typically "so-called 'liberal' justices are more highly ranked than ... so called 'conservative' justices."[35] Highly rated Brandeis and Holmes "are revered" for their "judicial activism" in contrast to Sanford's more moderate judicial mindset.[36] That only a small archive of his papers and correspondence has survived greatly hinders attempts to rehabilitate Sanford's reputation.

Sanford's goal throughout his lifetime was to be of good service to his country and fellow man. As a lawyer, he suggested improvements to the legal system and raised the standards of the profession. He unofficially recognized that the

Sixth Amendment's compulsory process provision should extend to the states during his time with the Department of Justice, approximately sixty years before the Supreme Court recognized it. As a judge, Sanford initiated the process of applying most of the Bill of Rights to the states. In his life and his work, he brought all of his background and experiences to model much of what he once said about Justice Lurton: "[H]e was an ideal judge; a model of the presiding officer of a Court, courteous and patient in hearing, cordial and sincere in both his personal and official relations, he exemplified in an unusual degree, the qualities of a judge demanded by the ancient Visigothic Code, when it declared that he should be quick of perception, firm of purpose, clear in judgment, no respector of persons, and assiduous in the performance of his duties. . . ."[37]

By the mid-1920s, however, Sanford's views on Prohibition, censorship, and other repressions were held in contempt by intellectuals. Based on the influences of his family and environment, Sanford was not a "modern" thinker in the terms of the times.[38] The values that meant so much to him and that he represented were melting away.[39] As noted by Frederick Lewis Allen, public opinion was changing. "Spartan idealism was collapsing. People were tired of girding up their loins to serve noble causes. They were tired of making the United States a land fit for heroes to live in."[40] Back in his hometown of Knoxville, the prosperous city developed in large part by his father was likewise changing. Odette Keun, a Belgian writer who spent the summer in Knoxville six years after Sanford's death described the city as "corrosive . . . one of the ugliest, dirtiest, stuffiest, most unsanitary towns in the United States."[41]

One must pause to ponder what Taft's exit from the Court would have meant for Sanford's jurisprudence if he had lived. Because Sanford seemed to feel indebted to Taft for his seat on the Court, perhaps he did not always utter his opinions openly for fear of being branded as a radical and disappointing his benefactor. If Sanford had lived and had served on the Court when one-third of the nation's workforce was jobless, industry was all but paralyzed, farmers were desperate, and most of the banks were shuttered,[42] would he have joined the "Four Horsemen" (McReynolds, Sutherland, Butler, and Van Devanter) in their attempts to invalidate New Deal agendas, or would he have adopted the progressive views of the Roosevelt administration and voted to uphold programs vital to the welfare of the general public and the nation's recovery? Would he, like his replacement, Owen Roberts, have switched his allegiance from the conservative bloc of justices and begun voting in support of New Deal legislation? To preserve the nation and the Court, he undoubtedly would have supported the progressive course. Sanford had demonstrated a belief in increased regulatory power and had voted to uphold federal power over the rights of the states. He believed that the Court should not interfere with legislative initiatives and was "considerably more flexible" than Justices Van Devanter, Butler, Sutherland, and McReynolds on government regulation.[43] As a district judge, he had been a greater friend of labor than his Supreme Court record would suggest. "[H]e had a deep appreciation for the struggles of those who labored for a living," and it had been "no easy matter for employers to secure injunctions from him in labor disputes."[44] Most importantly, Sanford demonstrated sympathy for laws that enhanced the public welfare.

As regards his judicial reputation, Sanford never desired to blaze new paths when he gained a seat on the Court. A good summary of Sanford was provided by his law partner and friend, James A. Fowler:

> [H]e did not believe that the Constitution was intended to be a cast iron corset or a rope of sand, but by sensible interpretation it should be adjusted to new conditions as they arise in the progress of civilization. He was neither a reactionary nor a radical, but was one of the large majority of Justices of that great judicial body who from generation to generation have occupied consistently the middle of the road. And the force thus wielded has guided our Nation along a safe path; and has caused that body to be regarded as the key of the arch which supports and insures the preservation of our Republic.[45]

Sanford's legacy should be applauded. He was an accomplished attorney and a distinguished jurist who rekindled a meaningful constitutional principle that has become commonplace.[46] Sanford, a man so well known in Tennessee that he was considered gubernatorial material, was an advocate for his hometown, his state, and his universities. He served as a teacher and was a booster for improving education across the South. Sanford was active in civic organizations and was readily available to give a speech at any occasion on any topic. He was a ready patriot "who placed his love for his fellow men and his duty to his country above all earthly things."[47] Clearly, Sanford always was determined to do his "best to make the world a little easier for those who have not been so favored. . . ."[48] A friend, Charles N. Burch, described Sanford's fidelity to duty as like that of the "Roman soldier who met his death at Pompeii when that city was submerged by the eruption of Vesuvius. He did not fly from his post of duty but remained where duty bade him stay, and nineteen centuries later his remains were found standing erect, sword in hand, and his face towards Rome."[49] It is time for Sanford to emerge from obscurity. "Few lives have been more fully lived than his in all ambitions that were dreamed for it, or, in the full earnestness and honor with which high trusts were met and borne."[50]

APPENDIX

Sanford's Decisions

US Supreme Court

American National Co. v. U.S., 274 U.S. 99, 47 S.Ct. 520 (1927)
Arnold v. U.S. for use of W.B. Guimarin & Co., 263 U.S. 427, 44 S.Ct. 144 (1923)
Atlantic Coast Line R. Co. v. Davis, 279 U.S. 34, 49 S.Ct. 210 (1929)
Atlantic Coast Line R. Co. v. Driggers, 279 U.S. 787, 49 S.Ct. 490 (1929)
Baltimore & O.R. Co. v. U.S., 261 U.S. 385, 43 S.Ct. 384 (1923)
Baltimore & O.R. Co. v. U.S., 261 U.S. 592, 58 Ct. Cl. 709 (1923)
Bass, Ratcliff & Gretton v. State Tax Commission, 266 U.S. 271, 45 S.Ct. 82 (1924)
Begg v. City of New York, 262 U.S. 196, 43 S.Ct. 513 (1923)
Botany Worsted Mills v. U.S., 278 U.S. 282, 49 S.Ct. 129 (1929)
Brosnan v. Brosnan, 263 U.S. 345, 44 S.Ct. 117 (1923)
Buzynski v. Luckenbach S.S. Co., 277 U.S. 226, 48 S.Ct. 440 (1928)
Canute S.S. v. Pittsburgh & West Virginia Coal Co., 263 U.S. 244, 44 S.Ct. 67 (1923)
Chamberlain Machine Works v. U.S., 270 U.S. 347, 46 S.Ct. 225 (1926)
Citizens' Savings Bank & Trust Co. v. Sexton, 264 U.S. 310, 44 S.Ct. 338 (1924)
City of New Brunswick v. U.S., 276 U.S. 547, 48 S.Ct. 371 (1928)
Commercial Credit Co. v. U.S., 276 U.S. 226, 48 S.Ct. 232 (1928)
Corrigan v. Buckley, 271 U.S. 323, 46 S.Ct. 521 (1926)
Danciger v. Smith, 276 U.S. 542, 48 S.Ct. 344 (1928)
Davis v. L.L. Cohen & Co., 268 U.S. 638, 45 S.Ct. 633 (1925)
Davis v. Willigord, 271 U.S. 484, 46 S.Ct. 547 (1926)
Davis v. Wolfe, 263 U.S. 239, 44 S.Ct. 64 (1923)
District of Columbia v. Thompson, 281 U.S. 25, 50 S.Ct. 172 (1930)
Eastman Kodak Co. of New York v. Southern Photo Materials Co., 273 U.S. 359, 47 S.Ct. 400 (1927)
Endicott-Johnson Corporation v. Encyclopedia Press, 266 U.S. 285, 45 S.Ct. 61 (1924)
Endicott-Johnson Corporation v. Smith, 266 U.S. 291, 45 S.Ct. 63 (1924)

Engel v. Davenport, 271 U.S. 33, 46 S.Ct. 410 (1926)
Federal Trade Commission v. Eastman Kodak Co., 274 U.S. 619, 47 S.Ct. 688 (1927)
Fidelity & Deposit Co. v. Tafoya, 270 US. 426, 46 S.Ct. 331 (1926)
Fiske v. State of Kansas, 274 U.S. 380, 47 S.Ct. 655 (1927)
Fleischmann Const. Co. v. U.S., to Use of Forsberg, 270 U.S. 349, 46 S.Ct. 284 (1926)
F.T.C. v. Raymond Bros.-Clark Co., 263 U.S. 565, 44 S.Ct. 162 (1924)
Gerdes v. Lustgarten, 266 U.S. 321, 45 S.Ct. 107 (1924)
Gitlow v. People of State of New York, 268 U.S. 652, 45 S.Ct. 625 (1925)
Goodyear Tire & Rubber Co. v. U.S., 276 U.S. 287, 66 Ct. Cl. 764 (1928)
Gorham Mfg. Co. v. State Tax Commission of New York, 266 U.S. 265, 45 S.Ct. 80 (1924)
Grant v. A.B. Leach & Co., 280 U.S. 351, 50 S.Ct. 107 (1930)
Graves v. State of Minn., 272 U.S. 425, 47 S.Ct. 122 (1926)
Grayson v. Harris, 279 U.S. 300, 49 S.Ct. 306 (1929)
Gulf, M. & N.R. Co. v. Wells, 275 U.S. 455, 48 S.Ct. 151 (1928)
Harrison v. Chamberlin, 271 U.S. 191, 46 S.Ct. 467 (1926)
Hay v. May Department Stores, Co., 271 U.S. 318, 46 S.Ct. 498 (1926)
Hecht v. Malley, 265 U.S. 144, 44 S.Ct. 462 (1924)
Hellmich v. Hellman, 276 U.S. 233, 48 S.Ct. 244 (1928)
Herbring v. Lee, 280 U.S. 111, 50 S.Ct. 49 (1929)
Hodges v. Snyder, 261 U.S. 600, 43 S.Ct. 435 (1923)
Horowitz v. U.S., 267 U.S. 458, 45 S.Ct. 344 (1925)
I.T.S. Rubber Co. v. Essex Rubber Co., 272 U.S. 429, 47 S.Ct. 136 (1926)
Jackson v. The Archimedes, 275 U.S. 463, 48 S.Ct. 164 (1928)
James Everard's Breweries v. Day, 265 U.S. 545, 44 S.Ct. 628 (1924)
Kunhardt & Co. v. U.S., 266 U.S. 537, 45 S.Ct. 158 (1925)
Lederer v. McGarvey, 271 U.S. 342, 46 S.Ct. 534 (1926)
Lee v. Osceola & Little River Road Imp. Dist. No. 1 of Mississippi County, Ark., 268 U.S. 643, 45 S.Ct. 620 (1925)
Leiter v. U.S., 271 U.S. 204, 46 S.Ct. 477 (1926)
Lewis v. Roberts, 267 U.S. 467, 45 S.Ct. 357 (1925)
Lewis v. U.S., 279 U.S. 63, 49 S.Ct. 257 (1929)
Liberty Nat. Bank of Roanoke, Va. v. Bear, 265 U.S. 365, 44 S.Ct. 499 (1924)
Liberty Nat. Bank of Roanoke, Va. v. Bear, 276 U.S. 215, 48 S.Ct. 252 (1928)
Liberty Warehouse Co. v. Grannis, 273 U.S. 70, 47 S.Ct. 282 (1927)
Lindgren v. U.S., 281 U.S. 38, 50 S.Ct. 207 (1930)

L. Richardson & Co. v. U.S., 266 U.S. 541, 60 S.Ct. 1024 (1925)
Madera Sugar Pine Co. v. Industrial Accidental Commission of State of California, 262 U.S. 499, 43 S.Ct. 604 (1923)
Maguire & Co. v. U.S., 273 U.S. 67, 47 S.Ct. 274 (1927)
Ma-King Products Co. v. Blair, 271 U.S. 479, 46 S.Ct. 544 (1926)
Maryland Cas. Co. v. Jones, 279 U.S. 792, 49 S.Ct. 484 (1929)
McCarthy v. Arndstein, 262 U.S. 355, 43 S.Ct. 562 (1923)
McCaughn v. Ludington, 268 U.S. 106, 45 S.Ct. 423 (1925)
McCoy v. Shaw, 277 U.S. 302, 48 S.Ct. 519 (1928)
McDonald v. Maxwell, 274 U.S. 91, 47 S.Ct. 497 (1927)
McGregor v. Hogan, 263 U.S. 234, 44 S.Ct. 50 (1923)
McMaster v. Gould, 276 U.S. 284, 48 S.Ct. 299 (1928)
Meek v. Centre County Banking Co., 264 U.S. 499, 44 S.Ct. 366 (1924)
Meek v. Centre County Banking Co., 268 U.S. 426, 45 S.Ct. 560 (1925)
Mellon v. Arkansas Land & Lumber Co., 275 U.S. 460, 48 S.Ct. 150 (1928)
Mellon v. O'Neil, 275 U.S. 212, 48 S.Ct. 62 (1927)
Milheim v. Moffat Tunnel Improvement Dist., 262 U.S. 710, 43 S.Ct. 694 (1923)
Minneapolis, St. P. & S.S.M. Ry. Co. v. Goneau, 269 U.S. 406, 46 S.Ct. 129 (1926)
Morimura, Arai & Co. v. Taback, 279 U.S. 24, 49 S.Ct. 212 (1929)
Myers v. International Trust Co., 273 U.S. 380, 47 S.Ct. 372 (1927)
National Leather Co. v. Commonwealth of Massachusetts, 277 U.S. 413, 48 S.Ct. 534 (1928)
New York State Rys. v. Shuler, 265 U.S. 379, 44 S.Ct. 551 (1924)
Okanogan, Methow, San Poelis (or San Poil), Nespelem, Colville, and Lake Indian Tribes or Bands of State of Washington v. U.S., 279 U.S. 655, 49 S.Ct. 463 (1929)
Pacific S.S. Co. v. Peterson, 278 U.S. 130, 49 S.Ct. 75 (1928)
Pearson v. U.S., 267 U.S. 423, 45 S.Ct. 240 (1925)
Pendergast v. New York Telephone Co., 262 U.S. 43, 43 S.Ct. 466 (1923)
People of New York ex rel. Rosevale Realty Co. v. Kleinert, 268 U.S. 646, 45 S.Ct. 618 (1925)
People of State of New York ex rel. Doyle v. Atwell, 261 U.S. 590, 43 S.Ct. 410 (1923)
Perkins-Campbell Co. v. U.S., 264 U.S. 213, 44 S.Ct. 237 (1924)
Price v. Magnolia Petroleum Co., 267 U.S. 415, 45 S.Ct. 312 (1925)
Public Utilities Commission of R.I. v. Attleboro Steam & Elec. Co., 273 U.S. 83, 47 S.Ct. 294 (1927)

Quon Quon Poy v. Johnson, 273 U.S. 352, 47 S.CT. 346 (1927)
R.E. Sheehan Co. v. Shuler, 265 U.S. 371, 44 S.Ct. 548 (1924)
Rindge Co. v. Los Angeles County, 262 U.S. 700, 43 S.Ct. 689 (1923)
Roche v. McDonald, 275 U.S. 449, 48 S.Ct. 142 (1928)
Sanitary Refrigerator Co. v. Winters, 280 U.S. 30, 50 S.Ct. 9 (1929)
Scott v. Paisley, 271 U.S. 632, 46 S.Ct. 591 (1926)
Seaboard Rice Milling Co. v. Chicago, R.I. & P. Ry. Co., 270 U.S. 363, 46 S.Ct. 247 (1926)
Smith v. Apple, 264 U.S. 274, 44 S.Ct. 311 (1924)
Southern Pac. Co. v. Haglund, 277 U.S. 304, 48 S.Ct. 510 (1928)
Southern Pac. Co. v. U.S., 268 U.S. 263, 45 S.Ct. 500 (1925)
Sovereign Camp, W.O.W. v. O'Neill, 266 U.S. 292, 45 S.Ct. 49 (1924)
Sperry Oil & Gas Co. v. Chisholm, 264 U.S. 488, 44 S.Ct. 372 (1924)
St. Cloud Public Service Co. v. City of St. Cloud, 265 U.S. 352, 44 S.Ct. 492 (1924)
State of New Mexico v. State of Texas, 276 U.S. 557, 48 S.Ct. 437 (1928)
State of New Mexico v. State of Texas, 276 U.S. 558, 48 S.Ct. 344 (1928)
State of N.M. v. State of Colo., 267 U.S. 30, 45 S.Ct. 202 (1925)
State of N.M. v. State of Tex., 275 U.S. 279, 48 S.Ct. 126 (1927)
State of Okl. v. State of Texas, 272 U.S. 21, 47 S.Ct. 9 (1926)
State of Oklahoma v. State of Texas, 281 U.S. 689, 50 S.Ct. 227 (1930)
Stephenson v. Kirtley, 269 U.S. 163, 46 S.Ct. 50 (1925)
Taylor v. Voss, 271 U.S. 176, 46 S.Ct. 461 (1926)
The President Arthur, 279 U.S. 564, 49 S.Ct. 420 (1929)
Thomson Spot Welder Co. v. Ford Motor Co., 265 U.S. 445, 44 S.Ct. 533 (1924)
U.S. Fidelity & Guaranty Co. v. Guenther, 281 U.S. 34, 50 S.Ct. 165 (1930)
U.S. Shipping Board Emergency Fleet Corp. v. Rosenberg Bros. & Co., 276 U.S. 202, 48 S.Ct. 256 (1928)
U.S. v. Carver, 278 U.S. 2294, 49 S.Ct. 100 (1929)
U.S. v. Cohn, 270 U.S. 339, 46 S.Ct. 251 (1926)
U.S. v. Flannery, 268 U.S. 98, 45 S.Ct. 420 (1925)
U.S. v. Goldman, 277 U.S. 229, 48 S.Ct. 486 (1928)
U.S. v. International Harvester Co., 274 U.S. 693, 47 S.Ct. 748 (1927)
U.S. v. Kaufman, 267 U.S. 408, 45 S.Ct. 322 (1925)
U.S. v. Morrow, 266 U.S. 531, 45 S.Ct. 173 (1925)
U.S. v. New York & Cuba Mail S.S. Co., 269 U.S. 304, 46 S.Ct. 114 (1925)
U.S. v. River Rouge Improvement Co., 269 U.S. 411, 46 S.Ct. 144 (1926)

U.S. v. State Inv. Co., 264 U.S. 206, 44 S.Ct. 289 (1924)
U.S. v. Valante, 264 U.S. 563, 44 S.Ct. 411 (1924)
U.S. v. Zerbey, 271 U.S. 332, 46 S.Ct. 532 (1926)
Western Pac. R. Co. v. U.S., 268 U.S. 271, 45 S.Ct. 503 (1925)
White River Lumber Co. v. State of Arkansas ex rel. Applegate, 279 U.S. 692, 49 S.Ct. 457 (1929)
Whitney v. California, 274 U.S. 357, 47 S.Ct. 641 (1927)
Willcuts v. Milton Dairy Co., 275 U.S. 215, 48 S.Ct. 71 (1927)
Williams v. Great Southern Lumber Co., 277 U.S. 19, 48 S.Ct. 417 (1928)
Wong Tai v. U.S., 273 U.S. 77, 47 S.Ct. 300 (1927)
Work v. State of Louisiana, 269 U.S. 250, 46 S.Ct. 92 (1925)

Lower Court Decisions

District Court

Allen v. Sewanee Fuel & Iron Co., 268 F. 219 (1917)
American Bank Protection Co. v. City Nat. Bank of Johnson City, 203 F. 715 (1913)
American Confectionery Co. v. North British & Mercantile Ins. Co., 199 F. 195 (1912)
American Trust Co. v. American Cent Life Ins Co., 5 F.2d 69 (1922)
Ausbrooks v. Western Union Telegraph Co., 282 F. 733 (1921)
Buck v. Felder, 196 F. 419 (1911)
Buck v. Felder, 208 F. 474 (1912)
Bucyrus Co. v. McArthur, 219 F. 266 (1914)
Card v. Standard Coal & Coke Co., 202 F. 351 (1912)
Cauffiel v. Lawrence, 256 F. 714 (1919)
City of Knoxville v. Southern Paving Const. Co., 220 F. 236 (1914)
Coca-Cola Co. v. Nashville Syrup Co., 200 F. 153 (1912)
Coca-Cola Co. v. Nashville Syrup Co., 200 F. 157 (1912)
Commercial Trust Co. v. Chattanooga Ry. & Light Co., 281 F. 856 (1921)
Cumberland Tel. & Tel. Co. v. Railroad and Public Utilities Com'n of Tennessee, 287 F. 406, 1921 WL 49602 (1921)
Duckworth v. Appostalis, 208 F. 936 (1913)
Ex parte Fuston, 253 F. 90 (1918)
Goodrich-Lockhart Co. v. Sears, 270 F. 971 (1919)
Helm v. Zarecor, 213 F. 648 (1913)

In re American Lime Co., 201 F. 433 (1912)
In re Boyd, 228 F. 1003 (1915)
In re Capital Sec. Co., 251 F. 927 (1918)
In re Condemnation Suits by U.S., 234 F. 443 (1916)
In re Crisp, 239 F. 419 (1917)
In re Day, 176 F. 377 (1909)
In re Dayton Coal & Iron Co., 239 F. 737 (1916)
In re Dayton Coal & Iron Co., 291 F. 390 (1922)
In re Ginsburg, 208 F. 160 (1913)
In re Globe Laundry, 198 F. 365 (1912)
In re Harris & Bacherig, 214 F. 482 (1913)
In re Jones, 209 F. 717 (1913)
In re Kennedy Tailoring Co., 175 F. 871 (1909)
In re Lenoir-Cross & Co., 226 F. 227 (1915)
In re M.F. Rourke Co., 209 F. 877 (1913)
In re Moore, 173 F. 679 (1909)
In re Nashville Laundry Co., 240 F. 795 (1917)
In re North Star Ice & Coal Co., 242 F. 301 (1918)
In re Nuckols, 201 F. 437 (1912)
In re Patterson Lumber Co., 247 F. 578 (1918)
In re Pullian, 171 F. 595 (1909)
In re Southern Pharmaceutical Co., 286 F. 148 (1921)
In re Standard Oak Veneer Co., 173 F. 103 (1909)
In re Subpoenas Duces Tecum, 248 F. 137 (1916)
In re T.C. Burnett & Co., 201 F. 162 (1912)
In re Tennessee River Coal Co., 206 F. 802 (1912)
J H Day Co. v. Mountain City Mill Co., 225 F. 622 (1915)
J H Day Co. v. Mountain City Mill Co., 257 F. 561 (1918)
Jones v. Casey-Hedges Co., 213 F. 43 (1913)
Menees v. Matthews, 197 F. 633 (1912)
Mercantile Trust Co. v. Tennessee Cent. R. Co., 291 F. 462 (1921)
Mercantile Trust Co. v. Tennessee Cent. R. Co., 286 F. 425 (1922)
Muskegon Boiler Works v. Tennessee Valley Iron & R. Co., 274 F. 836 (1921)
Patton v. Cincinnati, N.O. & T.P. Ry., 208 F. 29 (1913)
Randolph v. Craig, 267 F. 993, 1 A.F.T.R. 1242 (1920)
Reich v. Tennessee Copper Co., 209 F. 880 (1913)

Sharp v. Bonham, 213 F. 660 (1913)
Shelton v. Southern Ry. Co., 255 F. 182 (1918)
Slater v. Illinois Cent. R. Co., 209 F. 480 (1911)
U.S. for use of Brading-Marshall Lumber Co. v. Wells, 203 F. 146 (1913)
U.S. v. Forty Barrels and Twenty Kegs of Coca-Cola, 191 F. 431 (1911)
U.S. v. Nashville, C. & St. L. Ry., 217 F. 254 (1914)
U.S. v. One Cadillac Eight Auto., 255 F. 173 (1918)
U.S. v. One Cheverolet Automobile, 267 F. 1021 (1920)
U.S. v. Smith, 240 F. 756 (1917)
U.S. v. Southern Ry. Co., 285 F. 766 (1921)
U.S. v. Taylor, 284 F. 489 (1921)
U.S. v. Traynor, 173 F. 114 (1909)
U.S. v. Wilson, 266 F. 712 (1920)
Vestal v. Ducktown Sulphur, Copper & Iron Co., 210 F. 375 (1911)
Western Union Telegraph Co. v. Lousiville & N.R. Co., 201 F. 932 (1912)
Western Union Telegraph Co. v. Lousiville & N.R. Co., 208 F. 581 (1913)

Circuit Court

American Bank Protection Co. v. City Nat. Bank of Johnson City, Tenn., 181 F. 375 (1909)
Baltimore & O.S.W.R. Co. v. U.S., 242 F. 420, 155 C.C.A. 196 (1917)
Benoist v. Smith, 191 F. 514 (1911)
Brady v. Bernard & Kittinger, 170 F. 576, 95 C.C.A. 656 (1909)
Brennan v. Tillinghast, 201 F. 609, 120 C.C.A. 37 (1913)
Brown v. Cumberland Tel. & Tel. Co., 181 F. 246 (1909)
Buckeye Cotton Oil Co. v. Sloan, 250 F. 712, 163 C.C.A. 44 (1918)
Cain v. Southern Ry. Co., 199 F. 211 (1911)
Chicago, R.I. & P. Ry. Co. v. Barrett, 190 F. 118, 111 C.C.A. 158 (1911)
City of Memphis v. St. Louis & S.F.R. Co., 183 F. 529, 106 C.C.A. 75 (1910)
D'Arcy v. Jackson Cushion Spring Co., 212 F. 889, 129 C.C.A. 409 (1914)
D'Arcy v. Sheffield Car Co., 213 F. 483, 130 C.C.A. 83 (1914)
Dewey v. Sewanee Fuel & Iron Co., 191 F. 450 (1910)
Dilbert v. Wernicke, 214 F. 673, 131 C.C.A. 109 (1914)
Etowah Light & Power Co. v. Yancey, 197 F. 845 (1911)
General Inv. Co. v. Lake Shore & M.S.Ry. Co., 250 F. 160, 162 C.C.A. 296 (1918)
Grand Rapids Show Case Co. v. Baker, 216 F. 341, 132 C.C.A. 485 (1914)

Gray v. Louisville & N.R. Co., 197 F. 874 (1912)
Gruetter v. Cumberland Tel. & Tel. Co., 181 F. 248 (1909)
Hamilton Iron & Steel Co. v. Groveland Min. Co., 233 F. 388, 147 C.C.A. 324 (1916)
Hicks v. Crawford Coal & Iron Co., 190 F. 334 (1911)
In re Wolf, 188 F. 519 (1911)
Jackson Cushion Spring Co. v. D'Arcy, 181 F. 340, 104 C.C.A. 170 (1910)
Jackson Skift & Novelty Co. v. Rosenbaum, 225 F. 531, 140 C.C.A. 515 (1915)
Kimmerle v. Farr, 189 F. 295, 111 C.C.A. 27 (1911)
Ladew v. Tennessee Copper Co., 179 F. 245 (1910)
Lewis v. Cincinnati, N.O. & T.P. Ry. Co., 192 F. 654 (1910)
Lillie v. Dennert, 232 F. 104, 146 C.C.A. 296 (1916)
Lyle v. National Home for Disabled Volunteer Soldiers, 170 F. 842 (1909)
McEldowney v. Card, 193 F. 475 (1911)
Melton v. Pensacola Bank & Trust Co., 190 F. 126, 111, C.C.A. 166 (1911)
Nelson v. City of Murfreesboro, 179 F. 905 (1909)
Pennsylvania Co. v. Fanger, 231 F. 851, 146 C.C.A. 47 (1916)
Pensacola State Bank v. Thornberry, 226 F. 611, 141 C.C.A. 367 (1915)
Postal Cable Tel. Co. v. Cumberland Tel. & Tel. Co., 177 F. 726, (1910)
Pullman Co. v. Tamble, 173 F. 200 (1909)
Rowe v. Hill, 215 F. 518, 132 C.C.A. 30 (1914)
Rowe v. Kidd, 259 F. 127, 170 C.C.A. 195 (1919)
Sheffield Car Co. v. D'Arcy, 194 F. 686, 116 C.C.A. 322 (1912)
Stephens v. Smartt, 172 F. 466 (1909)
Stevenson v. Tennessee Copper Co., 193 F. 268 (1911)
T.B. Townsend Brick & Contracting Co. v. Central Trust Co. of New York, 187 F. 63, 109 C.C.A. 381 (1911)
The W.H. Gilbert, 232 F. 457, 146 C.C.A. 505 (1916)
U.S. v. Dillin, 168 F. 813, 94 C.C.A. 337 (1909)
Welch v. Cincinnati, N. O. & T. P. Ry. Co., 177 F. 760 (1908)
Winters v. Baltimore & O.R. Co., 177 F. 44, 16 Ohio F. Dec. 485 (1910)

NOTES

CHAPTER 1

1. Tom W. Campbell, *Four Score Forgotten Men: Sketches of the Justices of the U.S. Supreme Court* (Little Rock, Ark.: Pioneer Publ'g Co. 1950), at 353, 357.
2. *The Evening Tribune* (San Diego, Cal.) (Mar. 8, 1930) at 1. The dentist's name is listed as "J. Borden Crane" in some accounts. *See* "Death Claims Justice Sanford On Same Day as Taft, Late Chief," *The Reading (*Pa.*) Eagle* (Mar. 9, 1930) at 4.
3. "Death Takes High Justice: Sanford Succumbed Suddenly Saturday," *The Florence (*S.Car.*) Times-News* (Mar. 9, 1930) at 12; "Justice Sanford Victim of Sudden Death At Capital," *The Kingsport (*Tenn.*) Times* (Mar. 9, 1930) at 4.
4. "Judge Sanford of US Supreme Court is Dead: Expires After Collapse in Dentist's Chair," *The Chicago Sunday Tribune* (Mar. 9, 1930) at A2.
5. "Justice Sanford Victim of Sudden Death At Capital," *The Kingsport (*Tenn.*) Times* (Mar. 9, 1930) at 4; "Final Tribute To Justice Sanford," *The Altoona (*Pa.*) Mirror* (Mar. 10, 1930) at 1; *The Evening Tribune* (San Diego, Cal.) (Mar. 8, 1930) at 1.
6. Campbell, *Four Score Forgotten Men*, at 357.
7. *Id.*
8. "Justice Sanford Dies Following Collapse," *The Palm Beach (*Fla.*) Daily News* (Mar. 8, 1930) at 19.
9. "Judge Sanford of High Court Died Suddenly," *The Huntsville (*Ala.*) Daily Times* (Mar. 9, 1930) at 1.
10. "Knoxville Jurist Stricken Fatally In Dentist's Chair; End Follows At Home," *The Knoxville News-Sentinel* (Mar. 8, 1930) at 1.
11. *Time* (Mar. 17, 1930); NNDB, tracking the entire world, http://www.nndb.com/people/1869/000180329/; *see* "Kidney Failure: What to Expect," National Kidney and Urologic Diseases Information Clearinghouse, National Institute of Diabetes and Digestive and Kidney Diseases, http://www.niddk.nih.gov/healthinformation/health-topics/kidney-disease/kidney-failure-what-to-expect/Documents/kidney_failure_what_to_Expect_508.pdf .
12. "What Uremic Poisoning Is and the Ways to Get Relief," *The Sacramento (*Cal.*) Union* (Dec. 30, 1921) at 10.
13. "Sanford, Jurist on High Court, Dies at Capital," *The Springfield (*Mass.*) Republican* (Mar. 9, 1930) at 1.
14. "Judge Sanford of US Supreme Court is Dead: Expires After Collapse in Dentist's Chair," *The Chicago Sunday Tribune* (Mar. 9, 1930) at A2.
15. "Judge Sanford Dies Suddenly," *The Seattle Daily Times* (Mar. 9, 1930) at 4.
16. "Sudden Death Makes Vacant Seat on Bench," *The Riverside (*Cal.*) Daily Press* (Mar. 8, 1930) at 1; "Knoxville Jurist Stricken Fatally In Dentist's Chair; End Follows At Home," *The Knoxville News-Sentinel* (Mar. 8, 1930) at 1.
17. "Final Tribute To Justice Sanford," *The Altoona* (Pa.) *Mirror* (Mar. 10, 1930) at 1.
18. Letter from Willis Van Devanter to Mrs. Francis E. Warren (Mar. 17, 1930), Willis Van Devanter Papers, Box 15, Letter Book 42; Manuscript Division Library of Congress, Washington, D.C. ("Van Devanter Papers").

19. Letter from Willis Van Devanter to John C. Pollock (Mar. 8, 1930), Van Devanter Papers.

20. "Sanford Is Buried In City of His Birth," *The New York Times* (Mar. 11, 1930) at 22. Anna Magee (Mrs. George Milne Cameron) lived in Kirkland Lake, Ontario, Canada. *Id.*

21. "Judge Sanford of High Court Died Suddenly," *The Huntsville (Ala.) Daily Times* (Mar. 9, 1930) at 1. Mary died at the age of ninety-one and is buried in Knoxville's Old Gray Cemetery. See "Mrs. F.A. Ault Dies at 91," *The Knoxville News-Sentinel* (Dec. 1, 1970) at 24.

22. "Judge Sanford of High Court Died Suddenly," *The Huntsville (Ala.) Daily Times* (Mar. 9, 1930) at 1. Alfred was on a trip to Egypt when he received word of his brother's passing. "Society," *The Evening Star* (Washington, D.C.) (Mar. 14, 1930) at 18. "Justice Sanford Victim of Sudden Death at Capital," *The Kingsport (Tenn.) Times* (Mar. 9, 1930) at 4.

23. Emma attended the East Tennessee Female Institute and later graduated from Brooklyn Heights College in Brooklyn, New York. "Mrs. Robinson Dies In Canada," *The Knoxville News-Sentinel* (Feb. 3, 1940) at 10. She initially married a cousin with the same name as her father–Edward Jackson Sanford. His father was Senator William F. Sanford of the Canadian Parliament. "Society," *The Knoxville Journal* (Feb. 14, 1892) at 2. She had one child, Constance Phyllis Sanford, born in 1893, who married Wylie Hart of Toronto. Carlton E. Sanford, *Thomas Sanford, The Emigrant to New England* (Rutland, Vt.: The Tuttle Co. Printers 1911) at 256. After her first husband passed away in 1897, Emma subsequently married George L. Robinson. Prominent in charity work, she died in 1940 at age seventy-one and is buried in Mount Pleasant Cemetery in Toronto, Ontario, Canada. David Babelay, *They Trusted and Were Delivered: The French-Swiss of Knoxville, Tennessee*, Vol. 1 (Knoxville, Tenn.: Vaud-Tennessee Publisher 1988) at 52.

24. Sidney H. Asch, *The Supreme Court and Its Great Justices* (Arco 1976) at 86.

25. Kenneth Jost, *The Supreme Court A-Z* (Thousand Oaks, Cal.: CQ Press 2012) at 443.

26. OYEZ, US Supreme Court Media, http://www.oyez.org/justices/edward_t_sanford/.

27. Alpheus Thomas Mason, *The Supreme Court from Taft to Burger* (Baton Rouge, La.: Louisiana State Univ. Press 1980) (3rd ed rev.) at 70 (quoting Henry F. Pringle, *The Life and Times of William Howard Taft*, 2, [Hamden, Conn.: Archon Books 1964; reprint: American Political Biography Press May 1, 1998] at 1043–44).

28. "Ex President Taft Dies at Capital Succumbing to Many Weeks' Illness, Five Hours After Justice Sanford," *The New York Times* (Mar. 9, 1930) at 1.

29. Sanford, Louise's oldest brother, stood in for his deceased father at her wedding to give her away. "Knoxville Wedding of Interest in Nashville," *The Nashville (Tenn.) American* (Nov. 6, 1909) at 5. Before her 1909 marriage to Fisher, a Democratic lawyer from Memphis, Louise's chief interest was the Knoxville YWCA. She was an active supporter of women's suffrage. John William Leonard, ed., *Women's Who's Who of America: A Biographical Dictionary of Contemporary Women of the U.S. and Canada, 1914–1915* (New York: American Commonwealth Co. 1914) at 292. Fisher previously was a member of the Tennessee State Senate from 1913–14 and US attorney for the Western District of Tennessee from 1914–17. He served as a US representative from 1917–31. Stanley A. Cook, "Path to the High Bench; The Pre-Supreme Court Career of Justice Edward Terry Sanford" (Ph.D. diss., Univ. of Tennessee 1977) at 6. Louise and her husband both are buried at Knoxville's Old Gray Cemetery. *Id.* at 9 n8.

30. President Taft initially appointed Hughes to the Supreme Court in 1910. Hughes stepped down from the Court when he ran for president in 1916 against Woodrow Wilson. He was narrowly defeated in a close race that many called prematurely in his favor. When Taft stepped down from the Court in 1929, President Herbert Hoover appointed Hughes to succeed Taft as chief justice. Campbell, *Four Score Forgotten Men*, at 14–15.

31. Allen E. Ragan, "Mr. Justice Sanford," 15 *East Tennessee Historical Soc'y Publ'ns* (1943) at 87 (McReynolds and Stone); Campbell, *Four Score Forgotten Men*, at 357 (McReynolds, Butler, and Stone); "In Memoriam," 281 U.S. v (1929) ("A committee of the Court, consisting of the Chief Justice, Mr. Justice McReynolds, Mr. Justice Butler, and Mr. Justice Stone, has gone to Tennessee for the services over the late Mr. Justice Sanford....").

32. Judge Hicks, born in Clinton, Tennessee, had replaced Sanford as a district court judge in 1923 and was appointed to the Sixth Circuit Court of Appeals in 1928. Harry Phillips, *History of the Sixth Circuit: A Bicentennial Project* (The Bicentennial Comm'n of the Judicial Conf. of the U.S. 1976) at 144.

33. *The Brooklyn Daily Eagle* (Mar. 10, 1930) at 3.

34. "Sanford Is Buried In City of His Birth," *The New York Times* (Mar. 11, 1930) at 22.

35. "Knoxville Pays Last Honor to E.T. Sanford," *The Dallas Morning News* (Mar. 11, 1930) at 1; "Justice Sanford Is Laid To Rest," *The Macon (Ga.) Telegraph* (Mar. 11, 1930) at 1.

36. Edward T. Sanford Papers, MPA.0303. Univ. of Tennessee Libraries, Knoxville, Special Collections, ("Sanford Papers").

37. "Sanford Is Buried in City of His Birth," *The New York Times* (Mar. 11, 1930) at 22; "Justice Sanford Dies Following Collapse," *The Palm Beach (Fla.) Daily News* (Mar. 8, 1930) at 19. Edward Sanford Metcalfe was born July 25, 1915.

38. "Rites To Be Held In Tennessee Hills," *The San Francisco Chronicle* (Mar. 10, 1930) at 2.

39. "Sanford Monument Put Up In Greenwood," *The Knoxville News-Sentinel* (Sept. 3, 1940) at 8.

CHAPTER 2

1. Oliver Perry Temple, Knoxville Industrial Ass'n Address of 1869 (Knoxville, Tenn.: T. Haws & Co. 1869).

2. Paul M. Gaston, *The New South Creed: A Study in Southern Mythmaking* (Baton Rouge, La.: Louisiana State Univ. Press 1970) at 87–88.

3. McClung Historical Collection, Lawson McGhee Library, Knoxville, Tennessee. Anna and John Adrian died of measles. Elisa Buffat, *Memoirs and Diary of Elisa Buffat (née) Bolli* (Spring Place, Tenn.: 1916) at 65. Sources found in the author's research indicate that Louis Chavannes lived about seven months (Jan. 1, 1868 to July 1868) after his birth in 1868. An obituary in *The Knoxville Daily Chronicle* related that George William died at age five months and nineteen days with pneumonia. *The Knoxville Daily Chronicle* (Mar. 8, 1872) at 4. All four children are buried in Old Gray Cemetery in Knoxville.

4. Edward T. Sanford, *Blount College and the University of Tennessee: A Historical Address delivered before the Alumni Association and members of the University of Tennessee, June 12, 1894* (Knoxville: Univ. of Tennessee 1894) at 5.

5. M. Lee Smith, "Tennessee's Postbellum Political History: Voting Patterns and Party Identification," in *Tennessee Government and Politics: Democracy In The Volunteer State*, John R. Vile & Mark Byrnes, eds. (Nashville, Tenn.: Vanderbilt Univ. Press 1998) at 1.

6. "What Caused the War?," Tennessee 4 Me, http://www.tn4me.org/article.cfm/a_id/1/minor_id/1/major_id/5/era_id/5.

7. "Slavery," http://www.tn4me.org/minor_cat.cfm/62/major_id/21/era_id/4.

8. Stanley J. Folmsbee, Robert E. Corlew & Enoch L. Mitchell, *History of Tennessee*, Vol. I (New York: Lewis Historical Publ'g Co. 1960) at 469, 476; Patricia E. Brake, *Justice in the Valley: A Bicentennial Perspective of the United States District Court for the Eastern District of Tennessee*

(Franklin, Tenn.: Hillsboro Press 1998) at 25. Until 1830, East Tennessee had been the major center for antislavery activities in the United States as a result of the influence of Presbyterianism. Richard B. Drake, "Slavery and Anti-Slavery in Appalachia," in *Appalachians and Race: The Mountain South from Slavery to Segregation*, John C. Inscoe, ed. (Lexington, Ky.: Univ. of Kentucky Press 2001) at 22. Samuel Carrick, the first president of Blount College, which later became the University of Tennessee, helped spark the abolitionist movement in the United States. *Perceptions of Appalachian Students about Post-Secondary Education* (ProQuest 2008) at 39.

9. Joseph H. Cartwright, *The Triumph of Jim Crow: Tennessee Race Relations in the 1880s* (Knoxville, Tenn.: Univ. of Tennessee Press 1976) at 3–4.

10. *Id.* at 4. *See* Chase C. Mooney, "The Question of Slavery and the Free Negro in the Tennessee Constitutional Convention of 1834," 12 *Journal of S. History* (Nov. 1946) at 487–509.

11. Cartwright, *The Triumph of Jim Crow*, at 3.

12. Larry H. Whiteaker, "Civil War," *Tennessee Encyclopedia of History and Culture*, https://tennesseeencyclopedia.net/entry.php?rec=265.

13. William J. MacArthur, Jr., "Charles McClung McGhee, Southern Financier" (Ph.D. diss., Univ. of Tennessee 1975) at 19.

14. "A Divided State," Tennessee 4 Me, http://www.tn4me.org/minor_cat.cfm/minor_id/1/major_id/5/era_id/5.

15. Folmsbee, et al., *History of Tennessee*, Vol. 2 at 27.

16. Folmsbee, et al., *History of Tennessee*, Vol. 1 at 315.

17. Folmsbee, et al., *History of Tennessee*, Vol. 2 at 26–27. Many experts contend that if Bell, with his influence, personality, and popularity, had dared to make the fight for the Union made by Tennessee Senator Andrew Johnson or future Tennessee governor William G. Brownlow, the result of the secession agitation in Tennessee might have been very different. James Welch Patton, *Unionism and Reconstruction in Tennessee, 1860–1869* (Chapel Hill, N. Car.: The Univ. of N. Carolina Press 1934) at 17.

18. Robert Tracy McKenzie, *Lincolnites and Rebels: A Divided Town in the American Civil War* (New York: Oxford Univ. Press 2006) at 45.

19. The Republican Party was formed in September 1854 in Worcester, Massachusetts. A.J. Langguth, *After Lincoln: How the North Won the Civil War and Lost the Peace* (New York: Simon & Schuster 2014) at 9. Lincoln did not carry any states outside of the North. Brake, *Justice in the Valley*, at 31–32.

20. Brake, *Justice in the Valley*, at 32; Folmsbee, et al., *History of Tennessee*, Vol. 2, at 28.

21. W. Bruce Wheeler, "Knoxville, Tennessee," *Tennessee Encyclopedia of History and Culture*, https://tennesseeencyclopedia.net/entry.php?rec=745.

22. McKenzie, *Lincolnites and Rebels*, at 5 (The population was 4,400); Betsy Beeler Creekmore, *Knoxville* (Knoxville, Tenn.: E. Tennessee Historical Soc'y 1991) at 69 (The population was 5,300).

23. McKenzie, *Lincolnites and Rebels*, at 6.

24. James Madison, *Federalist* No. 45 (Jan. 26, 1788).

25. The master theorist of "state sovereignty" was South Carolina's John C. Calhoun, who insisted that the Constitution had been a "compact" between state governments, one that could be dissolved whenever a state or its people saw fit. Garrett Epps, *Democracy Reborn: The Fourteenth Amendment and the Fight for Equal Rights in Post-Civil War America* (New York: Henry Holt and Co. 2006) at 49.

26. McKenzie, *Lincolnites and Rebels*, at 71.

27. Creekmore, *Knoxville,* at 69. Knox County's total population was around 22,800 at this time. Statewide, in the February 1861 vote, 69,675 voted against secession compared to 57,789 in support. *Id.*

28. Gordon B. McKinney, *Southern Mountain Republicans, 1865–1900: Politics and the Appalachian Community* (Knoxville, Tenn.: Univ. of Tennessee Press 1998) at 17.

29. Albert Chavannes, "Saunders' Raid," *East Tennessee Sketches* (Knoxville, Tenn.: 1900) at 77–88.

30. Folmsbee, et al., *History of Tennessee*, Vol. 2, at 32–33.

31. McKenzie, *Lincolnites and Rebels*, at 70.

32. "Tennessee," http://www.econlib.org.

33. Whiteaker, "Civil War," *Tennessee Encyclopedia of History and Culture,* https://tennesseeencyclopedia.net/entry.php?rec=265.

34. James Walter Fertig, *The Secession and Reconstruction of Tennessee* (Chicago: Univ. Of Chicago Press 1898) at 27.

35. Dean Newman, "Chronology of Knoxville," *The Knoxville Journal* (June 8, 1861) at 11.

36. Brake, *Justice in the Valley*, at 34. The East Tennessee vote was approximately 33,000 to 14,000. Whiteaker, "Civil War," *Tennessee Encyclopedia of History and Culture,* https://tennesseeencyclopedia.net/entry.php?rec=265. The Tennessee counties in which a majority voted to remain in the Union were Anderson, Bledsoe, Blount, Bradley, Campbell, Carroll, Carter, Claiborne, Cocke, Fentress, Grainger, Greene, Hamilton, Hancock, Hardin, Hawkins, Henderson, Jefferson, Johnson, Knox, Marion, McMinn, Morgan, Roane, Scott, Sevier, Washington, and Weakley, along with Decatur, Macon, and Wayne in the west. *The Daily Nashville Patriot* (June 25, 1861) at 3.

37. McKinney, *Southern Mountain Republicans*, at 17.

38. *Journal of the Congress of the Confederate States of America*, 1861–1865, Vol. I (Washington, D.C.: Library of Congress) at 272; Brake, *Justice in the Valley,* at 32; Fertig, *The Secession and Reconstruction of Tennessee* at 11.

39. Creekmore, *Knoxville*, at 71.

40. William Edward Hardy, *"Farewell to all Radicals:' Redeeming Tennessee, 1869–1870"* (Ph.D. diss., Univ. of Tennessee 2013) at 8.

41. *Id.*

42. Eric Foner, *Reconstruction: America's Unfinished Revolution, 1863–1877* (New York: Harper & Row, Publishers 1988) at 44.

43. Lucas P. Kelley, "A Divided State in a Divided Nation: An Exploration of East Tennessee's Support of the Union in the Secession Crisis of 1860–1861," 84 *The Journal of E. Tennessee History* (2012) at 14.

44. *Brownlow's Knoxville Whig and Rebel Ventilator* (Nov. 11, 1863).

45. Kelley, "A Divided State in a Divided Nation," at 14–15. *See* Oliver P. Temple & Mary Boyce Temple, eds., "Judge John Baxter," *Notable Men of Tennessee, From 1833 to 1875: Their Times and Their Contemporaries* (New York: Cosmopolitan Press 1912) at 66–74; McKenzie, *Lincolnites and Rebels*, at 36—37, 49, 56—58, 106—08, 135—37, 145; Oliver P. Temple, *East Tennessee and the Civil War* (Johnson City, Tenn.: Overmountain Press 1995) at 156–57, 172–73, 194–97, 234–35, and 437–41; Thomas Alexander, "Strange Bedfellows: The Interlocking Careers of T.A.R. Nelson, Andrew Johnson, and W.G. (Parson) Brownlow," 24 *E. Tennessee Historical Soc'y Publ'ns* (1952) at 68–91; Temple, et al., "Judge Connally F. Trigg," *Notable Men of Tennessee*, at 208–12.

46. Patton, *Unionism and Reconstruction in Tennessee*, at 44.

47. Jim Stokley & Jeff D. Johnson, eds., *An Encyclopedia of East Tennessee* (Oak Ridge, Tenn.: Children's Museum of Oak Ridge 1981) at 268–69.

48. The ET&G ran from Dalton, Georgia to Blair's Ferry (later Loudon), Tennessee, until funds became available to build a railroad bridge across the Tennessee River. John Benhart, Jr., *Appalachian Aspirations: The Geography of Urbanization and Development in the Upper Tennessee River Valley* (Knoxville, Tenn.: Univ. of Tennessee Press 2007) at 24. The extension to Knoxville was completed around June 1855. *Id.* at 25. The ET&V arrived in Knoxville a year later. Jack Neely, *Market Square: A History of the Most Democratic Place on Earth* (Knoxville, Tenn.: Market Sq. Dist. Ass'n 2009) at 18.

49. MacArthur, "Charles McClung McGhee," at 20 (citing James W. Holland, "The East Tennessee and Georgia Railroad, 1836–1860," 3 *E. Tennessee Historical Soc'y Publ'ns* (1931) 89–107, and Holland, "The Building of the East Tennessee and Virginia Railroad," *id.*, No. 4 (1932) 83–101).

50. Benhart, *Appalachian Aspirations*, at 25. Following the secession of Virginia, Confederate President Jefferson Davis officially transferred the Confederacy's capital to Richmond from Montgomery, Alabama, on May 29, 1861. *The New York Times* (Apr. 24, 1861) at 4.

51. William Bruce Wheeler, *Knoxville, Tennessee: A Mountain City in the New South* (2nd ed.) (Knoxville, Tenn.: Univ. of Tennessee Press 2005) at 5.

52. Charles F. Bryan, "'Tories' Amidst Rebels: Confederate Occupation of East Tennessee, 1861–63," 75 *The Journal of E. Tennessee History* (2003) at 43.

53. McKenzie, *Lincolnites and Rebels*, at 12; Digby Gordon Seymour, *Divided Loyalties: Fort Sanders and the Civil War in East Tennessee* (Nashville, Tenn.: Williams Prtg. Co. 1990) (rev. ed.) at 4 (earlier printings, Knoxville, Tenn: Univ. of Tennessee Press 1963; Knoxville, Tenn.: E. Tennessee Historical Soc'y 1982).

54. Folmsbee, et al., *History of Tennessee*, Vol. I at 335; Mark Banker, *Appalachians All: East Tennesseans and the Elusive History of an American Region* (Knoxville, Tenn.: Univ. of Tennessee Press 2010) at 61.

55. Lucile Deaderick, ed., *Heart of the Valley: A History of Knoxville, Tennessee* (Knoxville, Tenn.: E. Tennessee Historical Soc'y 1976) at 17.

56. Stanley J. Folmsbee, "Sectionalism and Internal Improvements in Tennessee, 1796–1845" (Knoxville, Tenn.: E. Tennessee Historical Soc'y 1939) at 83–86.

57. Creekmore, *Knoxville*, at 89.

58. McKinney, *Southern Mountain Republicans*, at 13 (quoting *The Knoxville Whig* [May 18, 1861]).

59. E. Merton Coulter, *William G. Brownlow: Fighting Parson of the Southern Highlands* (Knoxville, Tenn.: Univ. of Tennessee Press 1999) at 135–40.

60. *Id.* at 40. When once asked by Confederate General Gideon J. Pillow to become the chaplain of the General's regiment, Brownlow reportedly replied: "When I shall have made up my mind to go to Hell, I will cut my throat, and go direct, and not travel round by way of the Southern Confederacy." *Id.* at 143–44.

61. Seymour, *Divided Loyalties*, at 36.

62. Folmsbee, et al., *History of Tennessee*, Vol. 2 at 92.

63. William C. Harris, "East Tennessee's Civil War Refugees and the Impact of the War on Civilians," 75 *The Journal of E. Tennessee History* (2003) at 64.

64. Seymour, *Divided Loyalties*, at 7.

65. Donald Davidson, *The Tennessee, The New River: Civil War to TVA*, Vol. 2 (Nashville, Tenn.: J.S. Sanders & Co. 1992 ed.) at 114.

66. Carl H. Moneyhon, *Republicanism in Reconstruction Texas* (Austin, Texas: 1980) at 18; H.R. 30, pt. 3:14, pt. 1:115, 39th Cong., 1st Sess.

67. McKenzie, *Lincolnites and Rebels*, at 145.

68. Temple, et al., *Notable Men of Tennessee*, at 45.

69. Seymour, *Divided Loyalties*, at 274–75 (citing J.G. Randall & David Donald, *The Civil War and Reconstruction* (Boston: D.C. Heath 1961) at 477–88).

70. Langguth, *After Lincoln*, at 20.

71. Fertig, *The Secession and Reconstruction of Tennessee*, at 11. After the Union capture of Nashville early in February 1862, Lincoln appointed Senator Andrew Johnson as Tennessee's military governor.

72. Union forces bore names relating to the rivers near which they originally operated. The Confederate forces carried names denoting the state or locality in which they principally fought. Folmsbee, et al., *History of Tennessee*, Vol. 2 at 55.

73. McKenzie, *Lincolnites and Rebels*, at 7.

74. Terry Family Papers, MS 482, Sterling Memorial Library, Yale Univ., New Haven, Connecticut ("Terry Family Papers").

75. Thomas W. Humes, *The Loyal Mountaineers of Tennessee* (Knoxville, Tenn.: Ogden & Brothers Co. 1888) (reprinted, Johnson City, Tenn.: The Overmountain Press 1998) at 357 (Narrative by Edward J. Sanford).

76. *Id.*

77. *Id.* at 358–63.

78. Letter from Edward J. Sanford to Isadore Lee Wright Terry (Oct. 20, 1862), Terry Family Papers.

79. Letter from Edward J. Sanford to Adrian Terry (Aug. 9, 1862), Terry Family Papers.

80. John Allison, ed., *Notable Men of Tennessee: Personal and Genealogical, with Portraits*, Vol. 1 (S. Historical Ass'n 1905) at 222; "U.S. Justice Edward Sanford," *Tennessee History Classroom*, http://www.tennesseehistory.com/class/Sanford.htm; Seymour, *Divided Loyalties*, at 203 n.2.

81. Creekmore, *Knoxville*, at 82.

82. McKenzie, *Lincolnites and Rebels*, at 172. This was one of only a handful of such decrees Lincoln made during the war. Years later, E.J. provided historian Oliver Perry Temple with an account of the battle for Temple's book, *East Tennessee and the Civil War*, at 492–93. Nearly 40,000 soldiers fought over Knoxville in the fall of 1863. McKenzie, *Lincolnites and Rebels*, at 6. In 1890, at a reunion of veterans from both sides, E.J. hosted a grand reception at his home. "Elegant Reception at the Home of Col. E.J. Sanford," *The Knoxville Journal* (Oct. 10, 1890) at 1.

83. McKenzie, *Lincolnites and Rebels*, at 175.

84. *Id.* at 175–76.

85. Creekmore, *Knoxville*, at 84.

86. James B. Campbell, "East Tennessee During Federal Occupation, 1863–1865," 19 *E. Tennessee Historical Soc'y Publ'ns* (1947) at 73.

87. Robert Booker, "Concerns During Civil War Included Health, Education," *The Knoxville News-Sentinel* (May 19, 2015) at 5 (quoting *Brownlow's Knoxville Whig* [January 30, 1864]).

88. Temple, *East Tennessee and The Civil War*, at 513.

89. Buffat, *Memoirs*, at 65; Connecticut Hale Cemetery Inscriptions and Newspaper Notices, 1629–1934, Ancestry.com at 70.

90. Charles F. Bryan, Jr., "The Civil War in East Tennessee: A Social, Political, and Economic Study" (Ph. D. diss., Univ. of Tennessee 1978) at 139–40.

91. Banker, *Appalachians All*, at 69.

92. Harris, "East Tennessee's Civil War Refugees and the Impact of the War on Civilians," at 62.

93. McKenzie, *Lincolnites and Rebels*, at 6.

94. Davidson, *The Tennessee*, at 116.

95. Campbell, "East Tennessee During Federal Occupation, 1863–1865," at 70–71; Whiteaker, "Civil War," *Tennessee Encyclopedia of History and Culture*, https://tennesseeencyclopedia.net/entry.php?rec=265.

96. James Bernard Campbell, "Some Social and Economic Phases of Reconstruction in East Tennessee, 1864–1869" (Master's thesis, Univ. of Tennessee 1946) at 13.

97. *Id.*

98. Gregory Scott Hicks, "Rebuilding a Community: Prosperity and Peace in Post-Civil War Knoxville, Tennessee, 1865–1870" (Master's thesis, Univ. of Tennessee 2008) at 1.

99. Daniel E. Sutherland, ed., *A Very Violent Rebel: The Civil War Diary of Ellen Renshaw House* (Knoxville, Tenn.: Univ. of Tennessee Press 1996) at 180–86, 195.

100. Amy McRary, "Retribution, Regrowth Mark Post-war Knoxville," *The Knoxville News-Sentinel* (Apr. 11, 2015) at 1.

101. Stephen V. Ash, *Past Times: A Daybook of Knoxville History* (Knoxville, Tenn.: The Knoxville News-Sentinel 1991) at 39.

102. Banker, *Appalachians All*, at 84.

103. Campbell, "East Tennessee During Federal Occupation," at 74, 85.

104. William Rule, George Frederick Mellen & John Wooldridge, eds., *Standard History of Knoxville, Tennessee* (Chicago: Lewis Publ'g Co. 1900; reprinted by Kessinger Books 2010) at 137.

105. Campbell, "East Tennessee During Federal Occupation," at 85.

106. *Id.* at 91.

107. *Id.* at 89 (citing *The Knoxville Free Press*, (Aug. 22, 1867, and Nov. 5, 1867)).

108. *Id.* (citing *The Knoxville Free Press*, (Sept. 1, 1867)).

109. *Id.*

110. Rule, et al., *Standard History of Knoxville, Tennessee*, at 106–07.

111. "Our Fire Laddies," *The Knoxville Journal* (Apr. 26, 1891) at 1.

112. "History of Fire Department-City of Knoxville," http://www.knoxvilletn.gov/government/city_departments_offices/fire_department/history_of_fire_department.

113. William J. MacArthur, Jr., *Knoxville: Crossroads of the New South* (Knoxville, Tenn.: E. Tennessee Historical Soc'y 1982) at 60.

114. Campbell, "Some Social and Economic Phases," at 41 (citing *The Knoxville Whig* [June 10, 1867, and Sept. 30, 1869]). Macadam was a type of road construction. A layer of small broken stone was compacted into a solid mass on a roadbed. "Macadamize," http://Merriam-Webster.com/dictionary/macadamize.

115. John Fleming, *The Knoxville Press and Herald* (Oct. 24, 1868).

116. William J. MacArthur Jr., *Knoxville: Crossroads of the New South* (Knoxville, Tenn.: E. Tennessee Historical Soc'y 1982) at 54.

117. Campbell, "East Tennessee During Federal Occupation," at 91 (citing *The Knoxville Free Press* [Sept. 4, 1867]).

118. Jack Neely, *Knoxville's Secret History* (Knoxville, Tenn.: Scruffy City Publ'g 1995) at 156.

119. Jack Neely, *Knoxville: This Obscure Prismatic City* (Charleston, S.Car.: The History Press 2009) at 25.

120. Knoxville-Knox Cnty. Metro. Planning Comm'n Docs. 1994, at E-14.
121. Wheeler, *Knoxville, Tennessee: A Mountain City in the New South*, at 17.
122. *Goodspeed's History of Hamilton, Knox and Shelby Counties of Tennessee* (Nashville, Tenn.: The Goodspeed Publ'g Co. 1887) reprint (Nashville, Tenn.: Charles and Randy Elder Booksellers 1974) at 851.
123. Jack Neely, "Westwood History to 1931," http:/Knoxheritage.org/westwood/history-of-westwood/ (Apr. 4, 2014).
124. Banker, *Appalachians All*, at 88–89.
125. Knoxville-Knox Cnty. Metro. Planning Comm'n Docs. 1994, at E-25; Neely, *This Obscure Prismatic City*, at 52.
126. Neely, *Knoxville: This Obscure Prismatic City*, at 52.
127. Knoxville-Knox Cnty. Metro. Planning Comm'n Docs. 1994, at E-25.
128. *Id.* at E-23.
129. Kathleen A. Johnston, "The City of Tomorrow With the Spirit of the Past: Bankrolling the Industrial Development of Knoxville, Tennessee, 1875–1907" (Master's thesis, Univ. of Tennessee 1994) at 6–7.
130. "The New South Booming," *The New York Times* (Jan. 23, 1887) at 3.
131. Neely, *Knoxville's Secret History*, at 156.
132. Campbell, "East Tennessee During Federal Occupation," at 89 (quoting *The Knoxville Whig* [Mar. 11, 1868]). Charles McClung McGhee, a friend of Sanford's father, owned a pork packing house on Gay Street, the main street of downtown Knoxville, and it was not uncommon for hogs to be driven down that main thoroughfare on their way to his business. William J. MacArthur, Jr., *Knoxville's History: An Interpretation* (Knoxville, Tenn.: E. Tennessee Historical Soc'y 1978) at 33.
133. Jack Neely, "Knoxville's 'Old City,'" http://oldcityknoxville.org/history/.
134. MacArthur, *Knoxville's History: An Interpretation*, at 35.
135. *Id.* at 38.
136. Campbell, "East Tennessee During Federal Occupation," at 88 (quoting *The Knoxville Press and Herald* [Dec. 1, 1868]).
137. MacArthur, *Knoxville's History: An Interpretation*, at 36.
138. Fertig, *The Secession and Reconstruction of Tennessee*, at 11.
139. Epps, *Democracy Reborn*, at 22.
140. *Id.* at 22–23.
141. Foner, *Reconstruction*, at 44; Davidson, *The Tennessee*, at 118.
142. Davidson, *The Tennessee*, at 118.
143. Acts, 34th Tenn. Gen. Assembly, 1st Sess., at 39 (1865).
144. Campbell, "Some Social and Economic Phases of Reconstruction in East Tennessee," at 32.
145. Davidson, *The Tennessee*, at 119.
146. Phillip Langsdon, *Tennessee: A Political History* (Franklin, Tenn.: Hillsboro Press 2000) at 175–78.
147. A. F. Gilman, "The Origin of the Republican Party" (Wisconsin: A. F. Gilman 1914).
148. McKinney, *Southern Mountain Republicans*, at 12.
149. *Id.* at 21.
150. *Id.* at 28–29.
151. Patton, *Unionism and Reconstruction in Tennessee*, at 87.
152. Folmsbee, et al., *History of Tennessee*, Vol. 2 at 98.

153. William E. Hardy, "The Margins of William Brownlow's Words: New Perspectives on the End of Radical Reconstruction in Tennessee," 84 *The Journal of E. Tennessee History* (2012) at 80.

154. Epps, *Democracy Reborn*, at 223.

155. MacArthur, "Charles McClung McGhee," at 22.

156. Cartwright, *The Triumph of Jim Crow*, at 9.

157. Hicks, "Rebuilding a Community," at 3. "The Radical Republicans believed that blacks were entitled to the same political rights and opportunities as whites. They also believed that Confederate leaders should be punished for their roles in Civil War." "Radical Reconstruction," www.ushistory.org/us/35b.asp.

158. "Radical Republicans," http://www.tn4me.org/article.cfm/a_id/42/minor_id/10/major_id/6/era_id/5. Ratification by the necessary number of states was accomplished on July 28, 1868.

159. Patton, *Unionism and Reconstruction in Tennessee*, at 215–16.

160. Epps, *Democracy Reborn*, at 246.

161. Patton, *Unionism and Reconstruction in Tennessee*, at 223–24 (quoting *The Nashville Daily Press and Times* (July 2, 1866)).

162. Brake, *Justice in the Valley*, at 49.

163. Patton, *Unionism and Reconstruction in Tennessee*, at 224–25; Lee Seifert Greene, David E. Grubbs & Victor C. Hobday, *Government in Tennessee* (3rd ed.) (Knoxville, Tenn.: Univ. of Tennessee Press 1975) at 17.

164. Brake, *Justice in the Valley*, at 49.

165. Governor William G. Brownlow Papers, 1865–69, Tenn. State Library and Archives http://idserver.utk.edu/?id=200700000001899.

166. Banker, *Appalachians All*, at 84.

167. McKenzie, *Lincolnites and Rebels*, at 216–17.

168. Davidson, *The Tennessee*, at 122.

169. *Id.* at 121 (citing Buffat, *Memoirs*, at 79).

170. Wheeler, *Knoxville, Tennessee: A Mountain City in the New South*, at 6; MacArthur, *Knoxville's History: An Interpretation*, at 27.

171. Knoxville–Knox Cnty. Metro. Planning Comm'n Docs. 1994, at E-17.

172. MacArthur, "Charles McClung McGhee," at 23.

173. Foner, *Reconstruction*, at 301.

174. Benhart, *Appalachian Aspirations*, at 10.

175. Cartwright, *The Triumph of Jim Crow*, at 10.

176. *Id.* at 30.

177. *Id.*

178. Hardy, "Farewell to all Radicals," at 80.

179. *Id.* at 10 (quoting "Message to the Senate and House of Representatives," Jan. 23, 1867, in Robert H. White, Stephen V. Ash & Wayne C. Moore, eds., *Messages of the Governors of Tennessee* (Nashville, Tenn.: Tenn. Historical Comm'n. 1952–Current) 5:546).

180. Hardy, "Farewell to all Radicals," at 10.

181. Cartwright, *The Triumph of Jim Crow*, at 12.

182. *Id.* at 13.

183. Hardy, "Farewell to all Radicals," at 11.

184. Cartwright, *The Triumph of Jim Crow*, at 13.

185. *The Knoxville Press and Messenger* (Feb. 24, 1869).

186. McKinney, *Southern Mountain Republicans*, at 37.

187. LeRoy P. Graf, Ralph W. Haskins & Paul H. Bergeron, eds., *The Papers of Andrew Johnson* (Knoxville, Tenn.: Univ. of Tennessee Press 1967–2000) 15:565–75, 579–83, 594–614.

188. Hardy, "Farewell to all Radicals," at 96.

189. Langsdon, *Tennessee: A Political History*, at 190.

190. McKinney, *Southern Mountain Republicans*, at 38.

191. Hardy, "Farewell to all Radicals," at 196 (citing Pub. Acts, 36th Tenn. Gen. Assembly, 1st Sess. [1869–70], chaps. 2, 17, at 3–4, 19–20; Tenn. Gen. Assembly, H. J., 36th Gen. Assembly, 1st Sess. [1869–70] at 36, 41).

192. C. Vann Woodward, *Origins of the New South, 1877–1913* (Baton Rouge, La.: Louisiana State Univ. Press 1974) at 55 (quoting Philip M. Hamer, ed., *Tennessee: A History, 1673–1932* (New York: American Historical Soc'y, Inc. 1933) Vol. 2, at 676).

193. MacArthur, *Knoxville's History: An Interpretation*, at 28.

194. Nat'l Reg. Hist. Places, § E, at 29. Blacks currently comprise approximately seventeen percent of the population of Knoxville. Seventy-four percent of the city's residents are white. http://www.city-data.com.

195. Epps, *Democracy Reborn*, at 223.

196. MacArthur, *Knoxville's History: An Interpretation*, at 28.

197. *Id.*

198. Folmsbee, et al., *History of Tennessee*, Vol. 2 at 108 (quoting Maj. Gen. Clinton Fisk, Assistant Commander of Freedmen's Bureau for Kentucky and Tennessee).

199. Whitelaw Reid, *After the War: A Southern Tour, May 1, 1865 to May 1, 1866* (C. Vann Woodward, ed.) (New York 1966) at 351–52, quoted in Jason M. Yeatts, "That We May Think Right, Vote Right, and Do Right: Knoxville's Black Community, 1865–1867," 82 *The Journal of E. Tennessee History* (2010) at 76.

200. Bryan, Jr., "The Civil War in East Tennessee," at 299, 343.

201. Robert Booker, "Knoxville lagged on segregation laws," *The Knoxville News-Sentinel* (Sept. 22, 2015) at 5.

202. *Id.*

203. Yeatts, "That We May Think Right, Vote Right, and Do Right," at 85.

204. Hicks, "Rebuilding a Community," at 3, 6.

205. Hardy, "Farewell to all Radicals," at 67.

206. Cartwright, *The Triumph of Jim Crow*, at 11; "Getting a Fair Share," Tennessee 4 Me http://www.tn4me.org/minor_cat.cfm/minor_id/56/major_id/20/era_id/6.

207. A federal circuit court declared the applicable state law unconstitutional in 1880. Woodward, *Origins of the New South*, at 211 n.20.

208. Booker, "Knoxville lagged on segregation laws," *The Knoxville News-Sentinel* (Sept. 22, 2015) at 5. The law left the two races unsegregated in second-class coaches. Woodward, *Origins of the New South*, at 211 n.20 (citing Stanley J. Folmsbee, "The Origin of the First 'Jim Crow' Law," 15 *Journal of S. History* [1949], at 235–47).

209. Booker, "Knoxville lagged on segregation laws," *The Knoxville News-Sentinel* (Sept. 22, 2015) at 5.

210. Matthew Lakin, "'A Dark Night': The Knoxville Race Riot of 1919," 72 *The Journal of E. Tennessee History* (2000) at 1.

211. Woodward, *Origins of the New South*, at 211.

212. Cartwright, *The Triumph of Jim Crow*, at 177–78.

213. MacArthur, *Knoxville's History: An Interpretation*, at 41.

214. Booker, "Concerns during Civil War included health, education," *The Knoxville News-Sentinel* (May 19, 2015) at 5 (quoting *The Army Mail Bag,* [May 30, 1864]).

215. Amy McRary, "Laura Ann Cansler Was Knoxville's first African-American Teacher," *The Knoxville News-Sentinel* (Dec. 29, 2012).

216. http://www.knoxvillecollege.edu/about-knoxville-college/brief-history/.

217. Nat'l Reg. Hist. Places, § E, at 30.

218. *Id.*; Rule, et al., *Standard History*, at 407.

219. Nat'l Reg. Hist. Places, § E, at 30.

220. *Id.*; MacArthur, *Knoxville's History: An Interpretation*, at 41.

221. Robert Booker, "First Black Politicos met with Hostility," *The Knoxville News-Sentinel* (Nov. 8, 2011) at B3.

222. Nat'l Reg. Hist. Places, § E, at 30; Amy McRary, "Cal Johnson Went From Slavery to successful businessman," *The Knoxville News-Sentinel* (Dec. 29, 2012); Foner, *Reconstruction*, at 356.

223. Booker, "First Black Politicos met with Hostility," *The Knoxville News-Sentinel* (Nov. 8, 2011) at B3.

224. Campbell, "Some Social and Economic Phases of Reconstruction in East Tennessee," at 105. The US Supreme Court has defined a floterial district as a "legislative district which includes within its boundaries several separate districts or political subdivisions which independently would not be entitled to additional representation but whose conglomerate population entitles the area to another seat in the particular legislative body being apportioned." *Davis v. Mann*, 377 U.S. 678, 686 n.2 (1964). In other words, a floterial district "lays over" or "floats above" several distinct districts. By combining several underrepresented districts and providing them collectively with one or more floterial representatives ("Floaters"), such districts are designed to reduce underrepresentation. Gary Moncrief & Robert Joula, "When the Courts Don't Compute: Mathematics and Floterial Districts in Legislative Reapportionment Cases," 4 *Journal of Law & Politics* 737 (1987–1988) at 738.

225. Cartwright, *The Triumph of Jim Crow*, at 182.

226. Michael J. McDonald & William Bruce Wheeler, *Knoxville, Tennessee: Continuity and Change in an Appalachian City* (Knoxville, Tenn.: Univ. of Tennessee Press 1983) at 27.

227. "Just The Beginning Foundation: William Hastie," http://www.jtb.org/index.php?src=directory&view=biographies&srctype=detail&refno=9.

228. John Anthony Maltese, *The Selling of Supreme Court Nominees* (Baltimore, Md.: Johns Hopkins Univ. Press 1998) at 126. Kennedy reportedly passed over Hastie because he was thought to be too conservative. *Id.* That Kennedy gave serious consideration to appointing Hastie "represented the first time in American history that an African American was an actual contender for the Supreme Court." Sheldon Goldman, *Picking Federal Judges: Lower Court Selection from Roosevelt Through Reagan* (New Haven, Conn.: Yale Univ. Press 1999) at 184–85.

229. Woodward, *Origins of the New South*, at 211.

230. Nat'l Reg. Hist. Places, § E, at 30.

231. MacArthur, *Knoxville's History: An Interpretation*, at 42.

232. Knoxville-Knox Cnty. Metro. Planning Comm'n Docs. 1994, at 28–31.

233. W.T. Jordan, "The Freedmen's Bureau in Tennessee," 11 *E. Tennessee Historical Soc'y Publ'ns* (1939) at 60.

234. Yeatts, "That We May Think Right, Vote Right, and Do Right," at 99–100.

235. Roger D. Posey, "The Anti-Alcohol City: Social, Economic, and Political Aspects of Knoxville, Tennessee, 1870–1907" (Master's thesis, Univ. of Tennessee 1982) at 95; Davidson, *The Tennessee*, at 123.

236. Lakin, "A Dark Night," at 1.

237. Lakin, "A Dark Night," at 2–3 (citing doc. from Charles W. Cansler to Tennessee Governor Tom C. Rye, Feb. 1918).

238. Russ Manning & Sondra Jamieson, *Historic Knoxville and Knox County: City Center, Neighborhoods, and Parks* (Norris, Tenn.: Laurel Place 1990) at 38–39.

239. Letter from David W. Kuhn to Andrew W. Mellon (Jan. 6, 1923) Dep't of Justice Records, Nat'l Archives, College Park, Md.

CHAPTER 3

1. "US Justice Edward Sanford," *Tennessee History Classroom,* http://www.tennesseehistory.com/class/Sanford.htm.

2. MacArthur, Jr., *Knoxville's History: An Interpretation*, at 45.

3. "Lenoir City: The Pet of the Great E.T.V. and G.R.R.," *The State Chronicle* (Raleigh, N. Car.) (July 24, 1890) at 3.

4. Allison, *Notable Men of Tennessee*, at 221; *see* William Rule, "The New Supreme Court Justice," *The New York Times* (Feb. 4, 1923) at 4.

5. Karin A. Shapiro, *A New South Rebellion: The Battle Against Convict Labor in the Tennessee Coalfields 1871–1896* (Chapel Hill, N. Car.: Univ. of N. Carolina Press 1998) at 25; E.J. was a candidate for mayor of Knoxville in 1874. "City Items," *The Republican Banner* (Nashville, Tenn.) (Jan. 16, 1874) at 4. .

6. Cook, "Path to the High Bench," at 7.

7. Allison, *Notable Men of Tennessee*, at 222.

8. Cook, "Path to the High Bench," at 11, 16.

9. Ragan, "Mr. Justice Sanford," at 74.

10. "The New South Booming," *The New York Times* (Jan. 23, 1887) at 3.

11. Allison, *Notable Men of Tennessee*, at 223.

12. Tennessee ratified the Fourteenth Amendment in 1866 and was thereafter readmitted to the Union by Congress that same year, thus avoiding Reconstruction. The remaining ten states of the former Confederacy were subjected to the Military Reconstruction Act of 1867, legislation that divided those states into five military districts, each commanded by a Union general and occupied by federal troops. Brake, *Justice in the Valley*, at 49; *See* Lee Seifert Greene, David E. Grubbs, & Victor C. Hobday, *Government in Tennessee* (3rd ed.) (Knoxville, Tenn.: Univ. of Tennessee Press 1975), at 17.

13. Paul K. Conkin, *Peabody College: From A Frontier Academy to the Frontiers of Teaching and Learning* (Nashville, Tenn.: Vanderbilt Univ. Press 2002) at 94.

14. Mary U. Rothrock, ed., *The French Broad-Holston Country: A History of Knox County, Tennessee* (Knoxville, Tenn.: E. Tennessee Historical Soc'y 1972) at 479–80; MacArthur, "Charles McClung McGhee," at 69.

15. Letter from Edward Jackson Sanford to Mrs. Adrian Terry (Oct. 20, 1862), Terry Family Papers.

16. *Proceedings of the Bar and Officers of the Supreme Court of the United States in Memory of Edward T. Sanford, December 13, 1931,* at 8 (remarks of Chauncey G. Parker).

17. Ash, *Past Times*, at 76. Elijah Embree Hoss was an ordained minister in the Methodist Episcopal Church (1870) and served as a pastor in Knoxville until 1872. He later taught ecclesiastical history at Vanderbilt University from 1885 to 1890. Hoss was ordained a bishop in 1902. "Finding Aid for the E.E. Hoss Address Regarding John Sevier," MS.0148 Univ. of Tennessee Libraries, Special Collections.

18. *Proceedings of the Bar and Officers of the Supreme Court*, at 8.

19. "Standard History of Knoxville," http://Files.usgwarchives.net/tn/knox/history/1900/standard/municipa5gms.txt.

20. Mrs. J.A. Dunn, "Seen and Heard," *The Knoxville News-Sentinel* (Oct. 2, 1932) at 4. Prince Street is now Market Street.

21. "Strolling," *The Knoxville News-Sentinel* (Oct. 1, 1941) at 21.

22. *Id*.

23. Lucy Templeton, "Long-Time Resident of Knoxville Tells Something About City Half Century Ago," *The Knoxville News-Sentinel* (Oct. 26, 1947) at 36; "Horsepower Back In the Gay Nineties," *The Knoxville News-Sentinel* (July 13, 1930) at G3, 19.

24. "Adrian Terry," United States, Civil War Soldier Records and Profiles, 1861–65. Terry received a B.A. and Ph. B. in Civil Engineering from Yale University in 1854. Class of 1854, *Decennial Record*, Yale Univ. (1899) at 228.

25. Terry Family Papers; Charles Wesley Smiley, ed., *Catalogue of the Psi Upsilon Fraternity*, Yale Univ. (New York: Baker & Godwin, Printers 1879) at 80.

26. Terry Family Papers.

27. Babelay, *They Trusted and Were Delivered*, Vol. 1 at 25.

28. 1870 United States Federal Census, Census Place: Knoxville Ward 6, Knox, Tenn: Roll: M593-1541; Page 425A; Image: 687: Family History Library Film: 553040.

29. "Soda Fount Marked 'Red Letter' Day," *The Knoxville News-Sentinel* (July 5, 1936) at 69.

30. *The Knoxville Daily Chronicle* (Jun. 10, 1873) at 4. A velocipede was an early kind of bicycle, http://dictionary.reference.com.

31. "Bold Stealing," *The Knoxville Daily Chronicle* (Apr. 1, 1873) at 4.

32. "Mr. Borches' Splendid Purchase," *The Knoxville Journal* (Dec. 25, 1888) at 4.

33. William C. Ross, *A Scrapbook For My Grandchildren* (New York: G.P. Putnam's Sons 1941) at 29.

34. "Will Be a Great Game: The Lawyers of the City Have Challenged the Doctors," *The Knoxville Journal* (Sept. 4, 1892) at 10.

35. John H.A. Maguire, "The Supreme Court Justice From Knoxville: The Politics of the Appointment of Justice Edward Terry Sanford" (Master's thesis, Univ. of Tennessee 1990) at 19; Charles A. Noone, "Edward Terry Sanford: Gentleman, Scholar, Lawyer, Jurist," 43 *Commercial Law Journal* 34 (1938).

36. James A. Fowler, "Mr. Justice Edward Terry Sanford," 17 *American Bar Ass'n Journal* 229 (Apr. 1931).

37. Folmsbee, et al., *History of Tennessee*, Vol. 1 at 440–41.

38. Davidson, *The Tennessee*, at 140.

39. Folmsbee, et al., *History of* Tennessee, Vol. 1 at 441.

40. Campbell, "Some Social and Economic Phases of Reconstruction in East Tennessee," at 86; Hardy, "Farewell to all Radicals," at 139.

41. Hardy, "Farewell to all Radicals," at 197.

42. Woodward, *Origins of the New South*, at 63 (quoting Charles W. Dabney, *Universal Education in the South* [Chapel Hill, N. Car.: Univ. of N. Carolina 1936] at 302–5).

43. Knoxville-Knox Cnty. Metro. Planning Comm'n Docs. 1994, at E-30; Rule, et al., *Standard History of Knoxville*, at 402. A law had been passed by the legislature in 1854 authorizing counties to levy taxes to help pay for education. Langsdon, *Tennessee: A Political History*, at 129.

44. *The Knoxville Daily Chronicle* (May 21, 1872); Ash, *Past Times*, at 79.

45. Sanford, *Blount College and the University of Tennessee*, at 20. Nationally, by 1870, only two percent of Americans over seventeen years old had completed high school. Rebecca Edwards, *New Spirits: Americans In the Gilded Age, 1865–1905* (New York: Oxford Univ. Press 2006) at 116.

46. Ash, *Past Times*, at 140; Sanford, *Blount College and the University of Tennessee*, at 44; Hicks, "Rebuilding A Community," at 6; "Our History, The University of Tennessee," http://www.utk.edu; Jack Neely, "The University of Tennessee: The Trip to the Hill," *The Knoxville Mercury* (Aug. 20, 2015). Sanford's brother Hugh was educated at University (Baker-Himel) School in Knoxville, which was established in 1889. *See Harvard College Class of 1900, Secretary's Report* IV (Cambridge, Mass.: Harvard Univ. Press).

47. "Adolph S. Ochs Dead at 77; Publisher of *Times* Since 1896," *The New York Times* (Apr. 19, 1935) at 1.

48. Rule, et al., *Standard History of Knoxville, Tennessee*, at 389.

49. 1870 United States Federal Census, Census Place: Knoxville Ward 6, Knox, Tenn.: Roll: M593–1541; Page 425A, Image 687: Family History Library Film: 553040. Lending support to this conjecture is the fact Georgiana married the summer that Sanford turned eleven and entered preparatory school. Georgiana married Rev. Charles Wallace Kelley on July 11, 1876, in Redding Ridge, Connecticut. Rebecca Donaldson Beach, *The Reverend John Beach and his descendants: together with historical and biographical sketches and the ancestry and descendants of John Sanford, of Redding, Connecticut* (Ulan Press 2012) (orig. printed New Haven, Conn.: The Tuttle, Morehouse & Taylor Press 1898). Additionally, a "Mrs. Richardson" and her assistants appear to have taught in a chapel behind St. John's church, and an "Ed Sanford" was remembered among the children there. Lucy Templeton, "A Country Calendar," *The Knoxville News-Sentinel* (Nov. 14, 1931) at 4.

50. Allison, *Notable Men of Tennessee*, at 222.

51. *Id.* at 222–23; Rule, et al., *Standard History of Knoxville, Tennessee*, at 405–06; Davidson, *The Tennessee*, at 139. To be fair, "it was easier to wring blood from a turnip than get taxes for schools out of a moneyless population." Davidson, *The Tennessee*, at 139.

52. Neely, *Market Square*, at 38. Rule served as Knoxville's mayor in 1873 and 1898.

53. Robert L. Taylor, Jr., "The New South Mind of a Mountain Editor: William Rule, 1877–1898," 47 *E. Tennessee Historical Soc'y Publ'ns* (1975) at 102; "Editor Will Spend 85th Birthday at Office Desk," *The Atlanta Constitution* (May 10, 1924) at 10.

54. McKinney, *Southern Mountain Republicans*, at 79.

55. George W. Ochs, "History of Journalism in East Tennessee," in *E. Tennessee Historical and Biographical* (Chattanooga, Tenn.: A.D. Smith & Co. 1983) at 164.

56. Rule, "The New Supreme Court Justice," *The New York Times* (Feb. 4, 1923) at 4; Ragan, "Mr. Justice Sanford," at 75.

57. "U.S. Justice Edward Sanford," *Tennessee History Classroom*, http://www.tennesseehistory.com/class/Sanford.htm.

58. J. A. Dunn, "Seen and Heard," *The Knoxville Journal* (Mar. 11, 1930).

59. Cook, "Path to the High Bench," at v.

60. Maguire, "The Supreme Court Justice From Knoxville," at 16.

61. *Tennessee Encyclopedia of History and Culture*, http://tennesseeencyclopedia.net/entry.php?rec=1170; Cook, "Path to the High Bench," at 8 n.7, 10; Attorney Sam E. Young interview, Sept. 29, 1973, in Knoxville; Fowler, "Mr. Justice Edward Terry Sanford," at 229.

62. Timothy L. Hall, *Supreme Court Justices: A Biographical Dictionary* (New York: Info base Publ'g 2001) at 288.

63. Babelay, *They Trusted and Were Delivered*, Vol. 1 at 48; Alfred Buffat, *Reminiscences of Alfred Buffat* (Spring Place, Tenn.: 1908) at 20. Adrien was "the spiritual leader" of the French-speaking Swiss in the Knoxville area, and "everyone came to him with questions about how to accomplish all the things that needed to be done to establish homes or set up businesses." Nancy P. Brummett, *The Journey of Elisa* (Colorado Springs, Colo.: Cook Commc'ns 2000) at 41. According to Buffat, it was with Anna's "means that Mr. Chavannes helped his fellow-countrymen." Buffat, *Reminiscences*, at 53.

64. Anna Chavannes, *Journal of Anna Chavannes* (May 9–July 14, 1848), MS 917.3, McClung Historical Collection (1930), http://cmdc.knoxlib.org/cdm/fullbrowser/collection/p15136coll4/id/1645/rv/compoundobject/cpd/1721. Three children died in their infancy: Louisa (1838), Amelie (1843–1844), and Louis (1846).

65. David Babelay, "Swiss Settlers, Knoxville," *The Tennessee Encyclopedia of History and Culture* (Nashville, Tenn.: Tenn. History Soc'y 1998).

66. Brummett, *The Journey of Elisa*, at 19–20; A. Christopher Smith, "J.N. Darby in Switzerland at the Crossroads of Brethren History and European Evangelism," *Christian Brethren Review* (1983) biblicalstudies.org.uk at 76–77; "A Swiss Family Turns to Knoxville," *The Knoxville News-Sentinel* (May 10, 1931) at 23.

67. Chavannes, *Journal of Anna Chavannes*, http://cmdc.knoxlib.org/cdm/fullbrowser/collection/p15136coll4/id/1645/rv/compoundobject/cpd/1721; Babelay, *They Trusted and Were Delivered*, Vol. 1 at 1, 7. The Chavannes had fled France into Switzerland due to persecution for their Protestant beliefs. Babelay, They Trusted, and Were Delivered, Vol. 1 at 47.

68. New York, Passenger Lists, 1820–1957, Year: 1848, Arrival: New York, New York; Microfilm Serial: M237, 1820–1897; Microfilm Roll: Roll 073; Line 1; List Number: 552; Page Number 3.

69. Babelay, *They Trusted and Were Delivered*, Vol. 1 at 52.

70. Chavannes, *Journal of Anna Chavannes* (May 9–July 14, 1848).

71. Babelay, *They Trusted and Were Delivered*, Vol. 1 at 9.

72. "Mr. Borches' Splendid Purchase," *The Knoxville Journal* (Dec. 25, 1888) at 4; Babelay, *They Trusted and Were Delivered* (Vol. 1) at 25. Cowan had passed away in 1871. The house was listed as 816 Hill Avenue in the *U.S. City Directories, 1822–1989*, at 262.

73. Jeff Johnson, "Maplehurst Park," *An Encyclopedia of East Tennessee* (Oak Ridge, Tenn.: Children's Museum of Oak Ridge 1981) at 312.

74. Jack Neely, "Paradise Found Out?" *Metro Pulse* (Knoxville, Tenn.) (May 29, 2003) at 10–11.

75. "Society Welcomes Sanfords," *The Washington Post* (Feb. 18, 1907) at 7; *The Cincinnati Enquirer* (June 1, 1913) at 5.

76. Edward O. Frantz, *The Door of Hope: Republican Presidents and the First Southern Strategy, 1877–1933* (Gainesville, Fla.: Univ. Press of Florida 2011) at 57.

77. "Gov. McKinley Honored," *The Knoxville Journal* (Sept. 18, 1895) at 1.

78. "Maplehurst Windows Gaze Into Past," *The Knoxville New-Sentinel* (Nov. 27, 1934) at 11. The McKinleys had lost two young daughters to cholera and scarlet fever. Karl Rove, *The Triumph of William McKinley: Why the Election of 1896 Still Matters* (New York: Simon & Schuster 2015) at 29, 30.

79. "President Roosevelt to be Knoxville's Guest," *The Knoxville Sentinel* (Sept. 8, 1902) at 1.

80. "Edward Sanford Mansion (Maplehurst)," in Special Collections Online, Univ. of Tennessee Libraries, Item #3874, http://kiva.lib.utk.edu/spc/items/show/3874.

81. Neely, "Paradise Found Out?" *Metro Pulse* (Knoxville, Tenn.) (May 29, 2003) at 10–11.

82. *Id.*

83. Babelay, *They Trusted and Were Delivered*, Vol. 1 at 25, 48, 49, 50–51; "Mme. Chavannes' Diary," *The Knoxville News-Sentinel* (July 6, 1930) at 23.

84. "A Good Lady Gone," *The Knoxville Journal* (Sept. 26, 1891) at 8.

85. *Id.*

86. Letter from C.P.J. Mooney to Warren G. Harding (Jan. 6, 1923) Dep't of Justice Records, Nat'l Archives, College Park, Md.

87. Babelay, *They Trusted and Were Delivered*, Vol. 1 at 80; Brummett, *The Journey of Elisa*, at 41.

88. Chavannes, *Journal of Anna Chavannes*, at 39; Babelay, *They Trusted and Were Delivered*, Vol. 1 at 80.

89. Brummett, *The Journey of Elisa*, at 41.

90. Buffat, *Memoirs*, at 82.

91. Rule, et al., *Standard History of Knoxville*, at 543–44. The orphanage was organized in 1875. *Id.* The current church building was built in 1892. St. John's was the church home of James Agee, Frances Hodgson Burnett, Clarence Brown, and Joseph Wood Krutch. Knox Heritage, "Saint John's Episcopal Church," http://knoxheritage.org.

92. James David Robenalt, *The Harding Affair: Love and Espionage During the Great War* (New York: Palgrave MacMillan 2009) at 16.

93. "Death of Mrs. E.J. Sanford," *The Knoxville Journal* (Oct. 3, 1895) at 5.

94. Babelay, *They Trusted and Were Delivered*, Vol. 1 at 49; Adrien "suffered from a nervous affection and a disease of the throat." Buffat, *Reminiscences*, at 20.

95. *Id.*

96. Letter from J.D. Connel to Warren G. Harding (Dec. 26, 1922), Dep't of Justice Records, Nat'l Archives, College Park, Md. The socialist writings and speeches of her brother Albert likewise probably influenced the opinion of the author of the letter.

97. Babelay, *They Trusted and Were Delivered*, Vol. 1 at 81.

98. Sanford, *Blount College and the University of Tennessee*, at 80–81.

99. Maguire, "The Supreme Court Justice From Knoxville," at 20 (citing *Catalogue of the Officers and Students of East Tennessee University 1876–1877*). In *To Foster Knowledge*, the authors noted: ("[L]oss of students" at East Tennessee University "had occurred mainly in the Preparatory Department, a loss caused by the establishment and increased patronage of a public high school in Knoxville."). James Riley Montgomery, Stanley J. Folmsbee & Lee Seifert Greene, *To Foster Knowledge: A History of the University of Tennessee 1794–1970* (Knoxville, Tenn.: Univ. of Tennessee Press 1984) at 90.

100. Jim Tumblin, "Edward Terry Sanford (1865–1930)," *The Shopper News* (Knoxville, Tenn.) (May 13, 2015) at A-2.

101. *Id.*

102. Maguire, "The Supreme Court Justice From Knoxville," at 20 (citing Preparatory Dep't, Academic Records, Vol. 6, 1876–77, Univ. of Tennessee Archives).

103. Ch. XVIII of the *Acts of the 1st Sess. of the Gen. Assembly of the Territory of the United States of America South of the River Ohio*, at 89; Stanley Folmsbee & Lucile Deaderick, "The Founding of Knoxville, Tenn.," 13 *E. Tennessee Historical Soc'y Publ'ns* (1941) at 3–20.

104. Montgomery, et al., *To Foster Knowledge*, at 96; Newman, *Knoxville Chronology*, at 16 (Mar. 11, 1879).

105. Milton Klein, "Prominent Alumni: Part III," in *Volunteer Moments: Vignettes of the History of the University Tennessee, 1794–1994* (1996), http://trace.tennessee.edu/utk_libarcvol/1/; Cook, "Path to the High Bench," at 12; Maguire, "The Supreme Court Justice From Knoxville," at 20.

106. Cook, "Path to the High Bench," at 8.

107. In 1892, Sanford served as a pallbearer at the funeral of Humes. "Rev. Thomas W. Humes," *The Knoxville Journal* (Jan. 19, 1892) at 5.

108. Allison, *Notable Men of Tennessee*, at 222; Fred A. Bailey, "Oliver Perry Temple and the Struggle for Tennessee's Agricultural College," 36 *Tennessee Historical Quarterly* (1977), at 45. The Morrill Act allocated federal land to states for teaching "agricultural and mechanical" subjects and military training. *Id.*

109. Montgomery, et al., *To Foster Knowledge*, at 75; 1 *The University of Tennessee Record*, No. 5 (Knoxville, Tenn.: Univ. of Tenn. Press (1898)) at 221 (relating that the funds were "attained through the heroic efforts of Knoxville's esteemed public citizen and benefactor, Hon. E.J. Sanford").

110. Aaron D. Purcell, *University of Tennessee* (Charleston, S. Car.: Arcadia Publ'g 2007) at 35.

111. Rule, et al., *Standard History of Knoxville*, at 361–62; Tumblin, "Edward Terry Sanford (1865–1930)," *The Shopper News* (Knoxville, Tenn.) (May 13, 2015) at A-2.

112. Cook, "Path to the High Bench," at 8 n.5; Sanford, *Blount College and the University of Tennessee*, at 67.

113. 6 *The University of Tennessee Record*, No. 2 (Knoxville, Tenn.: Univ. of Tennessee Press Feb. 1903) at 70. E.J. also served as president of the board of trustees of the Tennessee Medical College in Knoxville. "They Bid Good-Bye," *The Knoxville Journal* (Mar. 20, 1891) at 8.

114. *University of Tennessee and State Agricultural and Mechanical College Catalogue, 1882–83* (Knoxville, Tenn.: T. Haws, Book and Job Printer 1883) at 16. Maguire, "The Supreme Court Justice From Knoxville," at 21.

115. *Id.*; *The Knoxville Daily Chronicle* (June 9, 1881) at 1 ("Students distinguished on their entire course of study for the year.").

116. *Catalogue of the Officers and Students of the University of Tennessee, 1881–82* (Knoxville, Tenn.: T. Haws, Book and Job Printer 1882). The annual cost of books and tuition was about $150 per year. *Id.* at 34; Maguire, "The Supreme Court Justice From Knoxville," at 21.

117. Cook, "Path to the High Bench," at 13.

118. Maguire, "The Supreme Court Justice From Knoxville," at 22.

119. "Other Commencements," *The Baltimore Sun* (June 21, 1883) at 4; Lewis L. Laska, "Mr. Justice Sanford and the Fourteenth Amendment," 33 *Tennessee Historical Quarterly*, No. 2 (1974) at 212; Cook, "Path to the High Bench," at 13; Klein, "Prominent Alumni: Part III," in *Volunteer Moments*, http://trace.tennessee.edu/utk_libarcvol/1/; *Tennessee Encyclopedia of History and Culture*, http://tennesseeencyclopedia.net/entry.php?rec=1170; Aaron D. Purcell, *University of*

Tennessee (Charleston, S.Car.: Arcadia Publ'g 2007) at 46; Fowler, "Mr. Justice Edward Terry Sanford," at 229.

120. "University of Tennessee," *The Daily American* (Nashville, Tenn.) ((June 21, 1883) at 1; "Other Commencements," *The Baltimore Sun* (Jun. 21, 1883) at 4 (six other bachelor degrees were awarded); Cook, "Path to the High Bench," at 12; Fowler, "Mr. Justice Edward Terry Sanford," at. 229; Klein, "Prominent Alumni: Part III," in *Volunteer Moments,* http://trace.tennessee.edu/utk_libarcvol/1/; John W. Falconnier, "Sanford, Junior Member of U.S. Court," *The Knoxville Sentinel* (Jan. 25, 1923) at 12.

121. Sanford, *Blount College and the University of Tennessee,* at 81.

122. Purcell, *University of Tennessee,* at 56.

123. Sanford, *Blount College and the University of Tennessee,* at 23.

124. Cook, "Path to the High Bench," at 38–39 (letter from Howell E. Jackson to Edward T. Sanford (Jan. 22, 1883)). Jackson was a US Senator from Tennessee from March 4, 1881, until April 14, 1886, at which time he was appointed to the Sixth Circuit Court of Appeals by President Grover Cleveland. He was the first to preside over a session of the US Circuit Court of Appeals for the Sixth Circuit at Cincinnati. Campbell, *Four Score Forgotten Men,* at 296. Jackson was later appointed to the US Supreme Court by President Benjamin Harrison on February 2, 1893. *Id.* at 295.

125. Montgomery, et al., *To Foster Knowledge,* at 148 (quoting Sanford, *Blount College,* at 78); Michael Dennis, *Lessons in Progress: State Universities and Progressivism in the New South, 1880–1920* (Urbana, Ill.: Univ. of Illinois Press 2001) at 96.

126. Edwards, *New Spirits: Americans In the Gilded Age,* at 13.

127. *Id.* at 75.

128. *Id.* at 118.

129. Klein, "Prominent Alumni: Part III," in *Volunteer Moments,* http://trace.tennessee.edu/utk_libarcvol/1/; Cook, "Path to the High Bench," at 49; *Tennessee Encyclopedia of History and Culture,* http://tennesseeencyclopedia.net/entry.php?rec=1170/; Sanford Papers. Another date mentioned is 1916. Laska states that Sanford taught until 1921. Lewis L. Laska, "Mr. Justice Sanford and the Fourteenth Amendment," 33 *Tennessee Historical Quarterly,* No. 2 (1974) at 215. *See also* "Edward Terry Sanford," 4 *Journal Nat'l Ass'n Referees Bankruptcy* 91 (Apr. 1930).

130. Laska, "Mr. Justice Sanford and the Fourteenth Amendment," at 215; Rule, et al., *Standard History of Knoxville,* at 384; 16 *The University of Tennessee Record,* No. 4 (1913) at 11. *See The University of Tennessee Register* (Knoxville, Tenn.: Univ. of Tennessee Press) (Terms 1897–98 through 1915–16).

131. Rule, et al., *Standard History of Knoxville,* at 383; *see* 1 *The University of Tennessee Record,* No. 1 (1898) at 99.

132. 6 *The University of Tennessee Record,* No. 2 (1903) at 126. "We take pleasure in recognizing valuable additions to our library received lately from ... E.T. Sanford, Esq." 5 *The University of Tennessee Record,* No. 1 (1902) at 219.

133. Letters of transmittal in the Gift Correspondence File of the Univ. of Tennessee Library's Special Collections Branch; Cook, "Path to the High Bench," at 51.

134. *University of Tennessee and State Agricultural and Mechanical College Catalogue, 1882–83,* at 42.

135. "Invitations Issued," *The Knoxville Journal* (June 12, 1891) at 4; "On the Hill," *The Knoxville Journal* (Apr. 7, 1895) at 8.

136. "Five two-week courses," *The Comet* (Johnson City, Tenn.) (Dec. 24, 1908) at 3.

137. Klein, "Prominent Alumni: Part III," in *Volunteer Moments*, http://trace.tennessee.edu/utk_libarcvol/1/; "U.S. Justice Edward Sanford," *Tennessee History Classroom*, http://www.tennesseehistory.com/class/Sanford.htm; From 1906 until 1909, Sanford served as vice president for East Tennessee. Cook, "Path to the High Bench," at 50; Maguire, "The Supreme Court Justice From Knoxville," at 34.

138. "U.S. Justice Edward Sanford," *Tennessee History Classroom*, http://www.tennesseehistory.com/class/Sanford.htm.

139. *Id.*; Klein, "Prominent Alumni: Part III," in *Volunteer Moments*, http://trace.tennessee.edu/utk_libarcvol/1/.

140. Klein, "Prominent Alumni: Part III," in *Volunteer Moments*, http://trace.tennessee.edu/utk_libarcvol/1/; "U.S. Justice Edward Sanford," *Tennessee History Classroom*, http://www.tennesseehistory.com/class/Sanford.htm; Sanford, *Blount College and the University of Tennessee*.

141. "J. Sterling Morton," *Encyclopaedia Britannica* (online), https://www.britannica.com/biography/J-Sterling-Morton.

142. Neal O'Steen, *Tennessee Partners: The University of Tennessee and Its Alumni Association* (Knoxville, Tenn.: Univ. of Tennessee Nat'l Alumni Ass'n 1986) at 47.

143. Charles William Dabney Papers, 1715–1945, at the University of North Carolina contain private correspondence between the two relating to the possibility of Dabney's becoming Secretary of Agriculture under President Woodrow Wilson. Charles William Dabney Papers (1412), S. Historical Collection, The Wilson Library, Univ. of N. Carolina at Chapel Hill ("Dabney Papers").

144. 3 *Phi Kappa Phi Journal*, No. 1 (1923) at 42.

145. 6 *The University of Tennessee Record*, No. 2, at 261.

146. *Id.*

147. 1 *The University of Tennessee Record*, No. 1, at 12; Klein, "Prominent Alumni: Part III," in *Volunteer Moments*, http://trace.tennessee.edu/utk_libarcvol/1/; Harry Phillips, *History of the Sixth Circuit: A Bicentennial Project* (The Bicentennial Comm'n of the Judicial Conf. of the U.S. 1976) at 68–69; *University of Tennessee Board of Trustees' Minutes*, IV, at 137, 141. He also served for a period on the College of Liberal Arts Committee. *University of Tennessee Register, 1919–20*, at 6. See "Edward Terry Sanford," 8 *Tennessee Law Rev.* 189–90 (1930); Cook, "Path to the High Bench," at 44, 47; Maguire, "The Supreme Court Justice From Knoxville," at 32.

148. Cook, "Path to the High Bench," at 8.

149. *See* James R. Montgomery, "Threshold of a New Day, the University of Tennessee, 1919–1946," 74 *The University of Tennessee Record*, No. 6 (1971) at 94; Purcell, *University of Tennessee*, at 46.

150. Laska, "Mr. Justice Sanford and the Fourteenth Amendment," at 211. James Montgomery, "The Volunteer State Forges Its University," 69 *The University of Tennessee Record*, No. 6 (1966) at 117–19.

151. "Federal Judgeship for Hon. E.T. Sanford," *The Knoxville Journal and Tribune* (May 15, 1908) at 1; Cook, "Path to the High Bench," at 44.

152. Milton Klein, "Brown Ayres: Twelfth President, 1904–1919," in *Volunteer Moments*, http://trace.tennessee.edu/utk_libarcvol/1/.

153. Maguire, "The Supreme Court Justice From Knoxville," at 33 (citing Montgomery, "Volunteer State," at 117–19 and "Threshold of a New Day," at 94); O'Steen, *Tennessee Partners*, at 63.

154. Montgomery, "The Volunteer State Forges Its University," at 69, 119–26.

155. "Lens of Friendship Turned upon Mr. Justice Sanford," *The Knoxville Journal and Tribune* (Feb. 17, 1923) at 11.

156. Purcell, *University of Tennessee*, at 52; *University of Tennessee Register, 1919–20*, at 6; "Edward Terry Sanford," 8 *Tennessee Law Rev.* 189–90 (1930); Klein, "Prominent Alumni: Part III," in *Volunteer Moments*, http://trace.tennessee.edu/utk_libarcvol/1/; Cook, "Path to the High Bench," at 47; Maguire, "The Supreme Court Justice From Knoxville," at 32.

157. Cook, "Path to the High Bench," at 47. The association is a nonprofit group of 179 law schools. Its mission is "to uphold and advance excellence in legal education." The association was founded in 1900 "to elevate the standards of legal education in an era when it was still possible to become a lawyer through apprenticeship or self-study as Abraham Lincoln did." "Association of American Law Schools," http://www.aals.org.

158. Milton Klein, "John R. Neal: An Extraordinary Law Professor," in *Volunteer Moments*, http://trace.tennessee.edu/utk_libarcvol/1/. Neal also wrote the charter for the Highlander Folk School, then located in Monteagle, Tennessee. *Id.*

159. James D. Hoskins, "The University of Tennessee College of Law," 16 *Tennessee Law Rev.* 679, 679 (1941).

160. Klein, "Brown Ayres: Twelfth President, 1904–1919," in *Volunteer Moments*, http://trace.tennessee.edu/utk_libarcvol/1/.

161. Charles W. Kent of the University of Virginia also reportedly declined an offer. "Declined Appointment," *The Weekly Economist* (Elizabeth City, N. Car.) (July 22, 1904) at 4; "Dr. Kent Will Not Leave Virginia," *The Times Dispatch* (Richmond, Va.) (July 21, 1904) at 5.

162. Elizabeth A. Davis and Betsey Creekmore, "Ayres, not Ayers: Tale of a Troubling Transposition," *Tennessee Alumnus* (Jan. 31, 2011) at 1.

163. "University of Tennessee Alumni Address" (June 16, 1903), Sanford Papers.

164. O'Steen, *Tennessee Partners*, at 45.

165. *Id.*

166. *Id.*

167. Cook, "Path to the High Bench," at 48.

168. Board of Trustees Minutes, VII, at 337.

169. 26 *The University of Tennessee Record*, No. 4 (1923) at 66.

170. 2 *Tennessee Law Rev.* No. 4 (May 1924) at 32–33.

171. *Id.* at 31, 33.

172. Letter from Phi Alpha Delta Executive Office to Sanford Chapter, Phi Alpha Delta, University of Tennessee College of Law (Jan. 29, 2016) (Change of chapter's name to Edward T. Sanford Chapter took effect immediately).

173. "Academic Freedom Fight in Southern University," *Riverside* (Cal.) *Daily Press* (July 12, 1923) at 1; "University Squabble Passed On To Board," *Seattle Daily Times* (July 12, 1923) at 19.

174. "Trustees Will Hear University Dispute," *The Trenton* (N.J.) *Evening Times* (July 12, 1923) at 10.

175. Later investigations by the American Association of University Professors ("AAUP") concluded that Sprowls' view on evolution was not the controlling reason for letting him go. The AAUP, however, "disapproved of Morgan's interference in Sprowls's decision to assign a text on evolution." Edward J. Larson, *Summer For The Gods: The Scopes Trial and America's Continuing Debate Over Science and Religion* (New York: Basic Books 1997) at 79; "Report on the University of Tennessee," *Bulletin of the Amer. Ass'n of Univ. Professors* 10 (1924) at 56–63, 213–59.

176. John T. Lambert, "Sprowls Story of Evolution Fight," *The New Orleans States* (June 2, 1925) at 8.

177. Sanford's resignation came almost five months to the day after his appointment to the US Supreme Court. During that time, he apparently neither tendered his resignation, nor was he asked to resign.

178. Frederick Lewis Allen, *Only Yesterday: An Informal History of the 1920s* (New York: Perennial Classics 2000) at 169.

179. Lambert, "Sprowls Story of Evolution Fight," *The New Orleans States* (June 2, 1925) at 8.

180. Butler Act, House Bill No. 185 (Jan. 21, 1925), signed into law Mar. 21, 1925, 49 Tenn. Code Ann. §1922.

181. Allen, *Only Yesterday*, at 174.

182. John W. Butler, quoted in "Dayton's Amazing Trial," *The Literary Digest* 86 (July 25, 1925) at 7.

183. Lambert, "Sprowls Story of Evolution Fight," *The New Orleans States* (June 2, 1925) at 8.

184. Larson, *Summer For The Gods*, at 57.

185. Maguire, "The Supreme Court Justice From Knoxville," at 22.

186. *The Nashville Tennessean* (Apr. 14, 1909) at 4.

187. *Harvard College, Class of 1885, Secretary's Report Fiftieth Ann.* (Cambridge, Mass.: Harvard Univ. Press 1935) at 207.

188. Fowler, "Mr. Justice Edward Terry Sanford," at 229; Cook, "Path to the High Bench," at 13, 16; Maguire, "The Supreme Court Justice From Knoxville," at 22. See *Harvard College, Class of 1885, Baccalaureate Sermon, Class Day Oration, et al.* (Cambridge, Mass.: William H. Wheeler 1885) at 15, 17; Klein, "Prominent Alumni: Part III," in *Volunteer Moments*, http://trace.tennessee.edu/utk_libarcvol/1/; Phillips, *History of the Sixth Circuit*, at 68–69; "Harvard Commencement," *The Boston Journal* (June 24, 1885) at 1; "Class Day At Harvard," *The New York Tribune* (June 20, 1885) at 5.

189. Editorial, *The Nashville Tennessean* (Mar. 10, 1930) at 4.

190. See Laska, "Mr. Justice Sanford and the Fourteenth Amendment," at 211.

191. Rehnquist was awarded a B.A., M.A., and J.D. from Stanford, along with a M.A. from Harvard.

192. Cook, "Path to the High Bench," at 14 (citing *Harvard College, Class of 1885, Baccalaureate Sermon, Class Day Oration, et al.*, at 15, 17).

193. *Id.* at 14–15 (citing *Harvard College, Class of 1885, Baccalaureate Sermon, Class Day Oration, et al.*, at 19, 20).

194. Fowler, "Mr. Justice Edward Terry Sanford," at 229; Kermit L. Hall, "Sanford, Edward Terry," *The Oxford Companion to the Supreme Court of the United States* (2005); Encyclopedia.com, 16 Jul. 2010, http://www.encyclopedia.com; Cook, "Path to the High Bench," at 16; Maguire, "The Supreme Court Justice From Knoxville," at 22; *Harvard College, Class of 1885 Secretary's Report*, No. 2 (Cambridge Mass.: Harvard Univ. Press 1888–89) at 46.

195. Phillips, *History of the Sixth Circuit*, at 68–69; Maguire, "The Supreme Court Justice From Knoxville," at 22; *Catalogue of the Legal Fraternity of Phi Delta Phi*, 7th ed., Geo. A. Katzenberger, ed. (Ann Arbor, Mich.: The Inland Press 1897) at 254.

196. *Harvard College, Class of 1885, Secretary's Report Twenty-fifty Anniversary* (Cambridge, Mass.: Harvard Univ. Press 1910) at 105.

197. Cook, "Path to the High Bench," at 16 n.27.

198. *Proceedings of the Bar and Officers of the Supreme Court of the United States*, at 8.
199. Cook, "Path to the High Bench," at 16; Noone, "Edward Terry Sanford: Gentleman, Scholar, Lawyer, Jurist," at 34; *Harvard College, Class of 1885 Secretary's Report*, No. 2 at 46.
200. "The South at Harvard," *The Courier Journal* (Louisville, Ky.) (Mar. 18, 1894) at 19.
201. "Fair Harvard's Oarsmen," *The New York Times* (Oct. 12, 1884) at 9.
202. *The Harvard University Register* (Boston: Alfred Mudge & Son 1899) at 112.
203. Bruce A. Kimball, *The Inception of Modern Professional Education: C.C. Langdell, 1826–1906* (Chapel Hill, N. Car.: Univ. of N. Carolina Press 2009) at 242.
204. *Id.*
205. Choate Chapter 1889.
206. Albert Chandler, ed., *The Brief: A Quarterly Magazine of the Law* (Lancaster, Pa.: New Era Publ'g Co. 1909) at 145.
207. "Phi Beta Kappa," *The Cambridge Tribune* (July 2, 1910) at 5; *Proceedings of the Bar and Officers of the Supreme Court of the United States*, at 45; Noone, "Edward Terry Sanford: Gentleman, Scholar, Lawyer, Jurist," at 35.
208. *Proceedings of the Bar and Officers of the Supreme Court of the United States*, at 45; Noone, "Edward Terry Sanford: Gentleman, Scholar, Lawyer, Jurist," at 35.
209. "Phi Beta Kappa," https://phibetakappa.utk.edu/history.php.
210. Certificate dated March 10, 1929, Sanford Papers.
211. *Harvard College, Class of 1885, Secretary's Report*, No. 2 at 46; "Edward Terry Sanford," *Tennessee Encyclopedia of History and Culture*, http://tennesseeencyclopedia.net/entry.php?rec=1170.
212. 43 *Harvard Law Rev.* 926, No. 6 (Apr. 1930).
213. *Id.*
214. Melvin I. Urofsky, "Louis D. Brandeis: His Days at Harvard Law School," *Experience*, No. 2 (2010) at 13.
215. Melvin I. Urofsky, *Louis D. Brandeis: A Life* (New York: Pantheon Books 2009) at 25. The first member of the US Supreme Court to receive an actual law degree (Harvard 1832) was Benjamin Robbins Curtis, appointed to the Court in 1851. Henry Julian Abraham, *Justices, Presidents, and Senators: A History of United States Supreme Court Appointments from Washington to Bush II* (Lanham: Rowman & Littlefield Publishers Inc. 2007) at 49.
216. Jack M. Ferren, *Salt of the Earth-Conscience of the Court: The Story of Justice Wiley Rutledge* (Chapel Hill, N. Car.: Univ. of N. Carolina Press 2004) at 45.
217. *Id.*
218. Duncan Maysilles, *Ducktown Smoke: The Fight Over One of the South's Greatest Environmental Disasters* (Chapel Hill, N. Car.: Univ. of N. Carolina Press 2011) at 107.
219. *Id.* at 46–47; "The Socratic Method," https://www.law.uchicago.edu/socratic-method.
220. "Harvard Names Prominent Men on Visiting Boards," *The Sunday Herald* (Boston) (Oct. 21, 1923) at 8.
221. Cook, "Path to the High Bench," at 54.
222. "Sanford Head of Harvard Alumni," *The Boston Herald* (Oct. 11, 1923) at 3.
223. *Id.* at 55; Letter from Harvard President A. Lawrence Lowell to Edward T. Sanford (Feb. 26, 1924), Sanford Papers.
224. *Harvard College, Class of 1885, Secretary's Report Fiftieth Anniversary* (1935) at 212.
225. Harvard Commencement Speech, Justice Edward T. Sanford (June 19, 1924).

226. *Harvard College, Class of 1885, Baccalaureate Sermon, Class Day Oration, et al.*, at 19, 20. See "The Parable of the Talents," Matthew 25:14–30 New King James Version (NKJV).

227. 4 *The University of Cincinnati Record*, No. 9 (Univ. of Cincinnati Press June 1908) at 74.

228. *Id.* at 45.

CHAPTER 4

1. Cook, "Path to the High Bench," at 18; Sanford Papers.

2. "U.S. Justice Edward Sanford," *Tennessee History Classroom*, http://www.tennesseehistory.com/class/Sanford.htm; Maguire, "The Supreme Court Justice From Knoxville," at 24; Klein, "Prominent Alumni: Part III," in *Volunteer Moments,* http://trace.tennessee.edu/utk_libarcvol/1/.

3. L.B. McFarland, "Resolution on the death of Wm. C. Folkes," 9 *Proceedings of the Annual Session of the Bar Association of Tennessee, Tennessee Bar Ass'n* (1890) at 72–74; Joshua William Caldwell, *Sketches of the Bench and Bar of Tennessee* (Knoxville, Tenn.: Ogden Bros. & Co., Printers 1898) at 367. The first Battle of Manassas (known as Bull Run to Unionists) was fought on July 21, 1861, near Manassas, Virginia. The first major battle of the Civil War, it was a victory for the Confederates. Peter Luebke, "First Battle of Manassas," *Encyclopedia Virginia*, Virginia Foundation for the Humanities (Dec. 6, 2012), http://www.EncyclopediaVirginia.org/Manassas_First_Battle_of. The Battle of Malvern Hill was fought on July 1, 1862, in Henrico County, Virginia. It is considered a Confederate defeat, but Union General George B. McClellan's Peninsula Campaign was halted as a result. Michael P. Gabriel, "Battle of Malvern Hill," *Encyclopedia Virginia,* Virginia Foundation for the Humanities (Apr. 5, 2011), http://www.EncyclopediaVirginia.org/Malvern_Hill_Battle_of.

4. Paul Kens, "Horace Harmon Lurton," *The Supreme Court Justices: A Biographical Dictionary,* M. Urofsky, ed. (Routledge Publisher 1994) at 287.

5. Phillips, *History of the Sixth Circuit,* at 64; Campbell, *Four Score Forgotten Men,* at 319.

6. Letter from Horace Lurton to Edward T. Sanford (May 20, 1908), Sanford Papers.

7. "Edward T. Sanford, Address to the Tennessee Bar Association Annual Meeting (June 1923)," Sanford Papers.

8. Donald F. Anderson, "Building National Consensus: The Career of William Howard Taft," 68 *U. Cin. L. Rev.* 323 (Winter 2000) at 334 (citing James F. Watts, Jr., "Horace H. Lurton," in Leon Friedman & Fred L. Israel, eds., 3 *The Justices of the United States Supreme Court, 1789–1969, Their Lives and Major Opinions* (New York: R.R. Bowker Co. 1969) at 1848–49, 1853, 1854–55).

9. Kens, "Horace Harmon Lurton," at 287, 288.

10. Edwards, *New Spirits,* at 4.

11. "Gilded Age," America's Story from America's Library, http://americaslibrary.govjb/gilded/jb-gilded-subj.html.

12. Robert Douglas Lukens, "Portraits of Progress in New South Appalachia: Three Expositions in Knoxville, Tennessee, 1910–1913" (Master's thesis, Univ. of Tennessee 1996) at 7.

13. *Harvard College, Class of 1885, Secretary's Report,* No. 3 (1892) at 53.

14. Fowler, "Mr. Justice Edward Terry Sanford," at 229; Rule, et al., *Standard History of Knoxville,* at 496; "The Flat Gap Horror," 47 *The Tennessee Genealogical Mag.*, No. 3 (Fall 2000) at 7.

15. Rule, et al., *Standard History of Knoxville,* at 496; Caldwell, *Sketches of the Bench and Bar,* at 326.

16. Will T. Hale, 4 *History of Tennessee and Tennesseans: The Leaders and Representative Men in Commerce, Industry and Modern Activities* (Chicago: Lewis Publ'g Co. 1913) at 1411; Rule, et al., *Standard History of Knoxville*, at 499.

17. Caldwell, *Sketches of the Bench and Bar*, at 377–78.

18. Hale, *History of Tennessee and Tennesseans*, at 1411.

19. Caldwell, *Sketches of the Bench and Bar*, at 378. Thornburgh was a delegate to several Republican National Conventions. James Alexander Fowler Papers, MPA.0304, Univ. of Tennessee Libraries, Knoxville, Special Collections ("Fowler Papers"); Rothrock, *The French Broad-Holston Country*, at 397.

20. Fowler, "Mr. Justice Edward Terry Sanford," at 229; Cook, "Path to the High Bench," at 18.

21. Caldwell, *Sketches of the Bench and Bar*, at 326; "The Flat Gap Horror," at 3.

22. "The Flat Gap Horror," at 4–5. *See* Rule, et al., *Standard History of Knoxville*, at 293–94; Fowler Papers.

23. "The New Law Firm," The *Knoxville Journal* (Sep. 3, 1889) at 4.

24. Klein, "Prominent Alumni: Part III," in *Volunteer Moments,* http://trace.tennessee.edu/utk_libarcvol/1/; Maguire, "The Supreme Court Justice From Knoxville," at 27; Fowler, "Mr. Justice Edward Terry Sanford," at 229.

25. Fowler, "Mr. Justice Edward Terry Sanford," at 229.

26. Maguire, "The Supreme Court Justice From Knoxville," at 26.

27. The Hattie House Hotel, located at the corner of Gay Street and Clinch Avenue, opened on June 1, 1880. It was remodeled in 1894 as the Imperial Hotel. After it burned down in 1916, it was replaced by the Farragut Hotel in 1919. Imperial Hotel, "Special Collections Online," http://kiva.lib.utk.edu/spc/items/show/3860. Another source states the man damaged the poolroom with firecrackers. Robert P. Williams, *The Knoxville News-Sentinel* (Dec. 23, 1945) at 17.

28. "Jurist's First Case Recalled," *The Knoxville News-Sentinel* (Mar. 8, 1930) at 10.

29. Ragan, "Mr. Justice Sanford," at 75.

30. Noone, "Edward Terry Sanford," at 34.

31. Sometimes spelled "Luckey."

32. Cook, "Path to the High Bench," at 19, n.41; "Maj. C.E. Lucky Passes Away," *The Knoxville Journal and Tribune* (Jan. 24, 1922) at 7.

33. Hale, *History of Tennessee and Tennesseans*, at 1468–69.

34. Fowler, "Mr. Justice Edward Terry Sanford," at 299.

35. Andrew Morrison, *Knoxville, Tennessee 1891* (The Engelhardt Series: Amer. Cities, Vol. 25) (Charles A. Reeves, Jr., 2002) at 42. By 1903, the firm of Lucky, Sanford, and Fowler was located in the Empire Building. *Progressive Knoxville 1903: The Metropolis of East Tennessee,* http://cmdc.knoxlib.org/cdm/compoundobject/collection/p15136coll4/id/3330.

36. "Marietta & North Georgia Railroad," http://railga.com/mnga.html.

37. Maysilles, *Ducktown Smoke*, at 104.

38. Manning & Jamieson, *Historic Knoxville*, at 32.

39. William G. Thomas, *Lawyering for the Railroad: Business, Law, and Power in the New South* (Baton Rouge, La.: Louisiana State Univ. Press 1999) at xiii, 2, 7.

40. *Harvard College, Class of 1885, Secretary's Report,* No. 3, at 54.

41. "Verdict for the Company. The Case of Mrs. Peck before Judge Key at Chattanooga," *The Knoxville Journal* (May 29, 1894) at 5.

42. Rule, et al., *Standard History of Knoxville*, at 254; Hale, *History of Tennessee and Tennesseans*, at 1408–09.

43. MacArthur, "Charles McClung McGhee," at 218. The estimates of the total acreage vary per source.

44. Rule, et al., *Standard History of Knoxville*, at 242.

45. MacArthur, *Knoxville's History: An Interpretation*, at 42 (McGhee's mother's grandfather was General White, and her father was McClung). The present location of the Masonic Temple in Knoxville at 505 Locust Street was originally the home of McGhee, built about 1872. Manning & Jamieson, *Historic Knoxville*, at 46.

46. Hale, *History of Tennessee and Tennesseans*, at 1473.

47. *Id.* at 1474; Banker, *Appalachians All*, at 98.

48. *See* MacArthur, "Charles McClung McGhee," at 13 (citing *The Athens* [Tenn.] *Post*) (July 5, 1861) (cited in Reba Bayless Boyer, *Monroe County, Tennessee Records*, II (S. History Press 1983) at 185).

49. Shapiro, *A New South Rebellion*, at 25 (quoting letter from E.J. Sanford to C.M. McGhee (Oct. 10, 1891), Charles M. McGhee Papers, McClung Historical Collection, Lawson McGhee Library, Knoxville, Tenn.) ("McGhee Papers").

50. Shapiro, *A New South Rebellion*, at 25, 34, 213, 230, 232.

51. Allison, *Notable Men of Tennessee*, at 222, 223; Rule, et al., *Standard History of Knoxville*, at 210, 286.

52. Creekmore, *Knoxville*, at 95.

53. Hicks, "Rebuilding A Community," at 26. During the 1982 World's Fair, the company's 1870s-era nail factory was renovated for use as an event center. The building, known now as the Foundry, has been listed on the National Register of Historic Places. J. S. Rabun, Nat'l Reg. of Hist. Places Registration Form for Knoxville Iron Foundry Complex-Nail Factory and Warehouse, Oct. 6, 1980.

54. Hicks, "Rebuilding A Community," at 27.

55. Banker, *Appalachians All*, at 92; Allison, *Notable Men of Tennessee*, at 222.

56. Perry C. Cotham, *Toil, Turmoil & Triumph: A Portrait of the Tennessee Labor Movement* (Franklin, Tenn.: Hillsboro Press 1995) at 57.

57. *Id.*

58. "Southern Railway Knoxville History," http://www.jreb.org/ns/index.php?topic=6971.0;wap2.

59. MacArthur, "Charles McClung McGhee," at 24.

60. *Id.* at 25. *See* Riley Oakey Biggs, "Development of Railroad Transportation in East Tennessee During the Reconstruction Period" (Master's thesis, Univ. of Tennessee 1934) at 65.

61. MacArthur, "Charles McClung McGhee, at 27.

62. The state's issues with railroad debt were settled in 1883 by the "50–3" funding act–the railroad bonds were scaled to 50 percent and the interest reduced to three percent. Johnston, "The City of Tomorrow with the Spirit of the Past," at 11 (citing Edward C. Duggins, "The Background for Regulation of Railroads in Tennessee," [Master's thesis, Univ. of Tennessee 1939]).

63. MacArthur, "Charles McClung McGhee," at 45–46.

64. Thomas, *Lawyering for the Railroad*, at 4.

65. MacArthur, "Charles McClung McGhee," at 52–53.

66. *Id.* at 46, 61; *The Knoxville Daily Chronicle* (Sept. 14, 1871) at 2.
67. MacArthur, "Charles McClung McGhee," at 62.
68. *Id.* at 61.
69. "The Knoxville and Ohio Railroad," *The Knoxville* (Tenn.) *Weekly Chronicle* (Nov. 15, 1871) at 5; Henry Hall, ed., "Edward J. Sanford," *America's Successful Men of Affairs: An Encyclopedia of Contemporaneous Biography*, Vol. 2 (New York: The New York Tribune 1896) at 680.
70. Henry E. Colton, *The East Tennessee, Virginia and Georgia Railway System: Its Resources* (E. Tenn., Va. & Ga. Railway Sys. 1890) at 68.
71. "With the Railroaders," *The Knoxville Journal* (Dec. 24, 1893) at 6. In 1897, however, the Tennessee Supreme Court held that the K&O's exemption from ad valorem taxes did not include an exemption from the imposition of a privilege tax. *Knoxville & O.R. Co. v. Harris*, 43 S.W. 115 (Tenn. 1897).
72. Rule, et al., *Standard History of Knoxville*, at 282; MacArthur, *Knoxville's History: An Interpretation*, at 43; MacArthur, "Charles McClung McGhee," at 20 (citing James W. Holland, "The East Tennessee and Georgia Railroad," at 89–107; Holland, "The Building of the East Tennessee and Virginia Railroad," at 83–101).
73. Hall, "Edward J. Sanford," at 680; MacArthur, "Charles McClung McGhee," at 104.
74. MacArthur, "Charles McClung McGhee," at 63–64; Rule, et al., *Standard History of Knoxville, Tennessee*, at 286; *The News and Observer* (Raleigh, N. Car.) (Nov. 15, 1883) at 1 (E.J. Sanford elected to board of directors of ETV&G). In 1891, E.J. and McGhee were listed on the board of directors of ETV&G. "History of Knoxville: Chapter 14: Transportation," http://knoxcotn.org/old_site/history/rule/chap14.html.
75. MacArthur, "Charles McClung McGhee," at 118.
76. Colton, *The East Tennessee, Virginia and Georgia*, at 11.
77. MacArthur, "Charles McClung McGhee," at 119.
78. *Id.* at 120 (Letters from C.M. McGhee to E.J. Sanford (June 13, 1887; June 16, 1887), and letters from E.J. Sanford to C.M. McGhee (June 13, 1887; August 24, 1888; August 28, 1888; October 17, 1888) McGhee Papers; "The Rogersville Road Sold: Mr. Aiken Sells His Interest to Mr. E.J. Sanford," *The Knoxville Journal* (Oct. 21, 1888) at 1. This article lists the price as $150,000.
79. Letter from C.M. McGhee to E.J. Sanford (Oct. 18, 1888), McGhee Papers; *see* Hall, "Edward J. Sanford," at 680.
80. Letter from C.M. McGhee to E.J. Sanford (Oct. 27, 1888), McGhee Papers.
81. "Railway Extensions Proposed," *The Knoxville Journal* (Mar. 16, 1889) at 1; 45 *The Commercial & Financial Chronicle and Hunt's Merchant Magazine* (New York: William B. Dana. Co. 1887) at 857.
82. Letter from E.J. Sanford to C.M. McGhee (July 20, 1889), McGhee Papers; "Tennessee and Ohio: Mr. Sanford Sells His Road to Gen. Samuel Thomas, President of the East Tennessee System," *The Knoxville Journal* (July 21, 1889) at 1.
83. MacArthur, "Charles McClung McGhee," at 121, 122.
84. "History of Knoxville: Chapter 14: Transportation," http://knoxcotn.org/ old_site/history /rule/chap14.html.
85. Rule, et al., *Standard History of Knoxville*, at 286–87.
86. "Gone To New Orleans," *The Knoxville Journal* (Apr. 7, 1894) at 3 (Representative of Central Trust Company of New York).
87. "The Sale Confirmed," *The Knoxville Journal* (July 15, 1894) at 6.

88. David G. Savage, "From the Gilded Age to the Great Depression," *Guide to the U.S. Supreme Court*, Vol. 1 (5th ed.) (Washington, D.C.: CQ Press 2010) at 35.

89. William J. Cooper, Jr. & Thomas E. Terrill, *The American South: A History*, Vol. II (New York: McGraw Hill 2002) at 505.

90. Thomas, *Lawyering for the Railroad*, at 100–02.

91. Cooper & Terrill, *The American South*, at 457.

92. 42 S.W. 693 (Tenn. Ch. App. 1897).

93. *Heck v. McEwen*, 80 Tenn. 97 (1883).

94. MacArthur, "Charles McClung McGhee," at 219; *Cullen*, 42 S.W. at 693. Cullen and Newman had attempted to secure 6,250 shares of Wiley stock and other property held by the Wiley estate. MacArthur, "Charles McClung McGhee," at 221.

95. MacArthur, "Charles McClung McGhee," at 219.

96. 42 S.W. at 693.

97. *Id.* at 695. All the interests of Wiley were purchased for $150,000, including 5,100 shares of Poplar Creek Coal and Iron. MacArthur, "Charles McClung McGhee," at 222.

98. The land grants in Anderson, Campbell, and Morgan counties in Tennessee were held by three corporations: Coal Creek Mining and Manufacturing Company, Poplar Creek Coal and Iron Company, and Tennessee Mining and Manufacturing Company. Presentation by Barry Thacker, P.E., at the joint ASCETSPE Engineering Society Meeting (Feb. 22, 2000), http://www.coalcreekaml.com/BKTASCEpresentation.htm. E.J. served as president of Poplar Creek Coal and Iron Company as well as Coal Creek Mining and Manufacturing Company. Allison, *Notable Men of Tennessee*, at 223; Rule, et al., *Standard History of Knoxville*, at 242.

99. "Mining Company Sued," *The Atlanta Constitution* (Feb. 26, 1897) at 2; "An Accounting Demanded," *The Courier-Journal* (Louisville, Ky.) (Feb. 26, 1897) at 7; "Cullen and Newman Begin Action Against the Coal Creek Corporation," *The Atlanta Constitution* (Feb. 26, 1897) at 2.

100. *Ultra vires* is a Latin term meaning "beyond powers." "*Ultra vires*," Legal Dictionary, dictionary.law.com.

101. MacArthur, "Charles McClung McGhee," at 219.

102. *Id.* at 218.

103. *Cullen*, 42 S.W. at 698.

104. J.P. Morgan pieced the Southern Railway together out of twenty-six different foreclosures, primarily the bankruptcies of the Richmond and Danville and the ETV&G. "Southern Railway Knoxville History," http://www.jreb.org/ns/index.php?topic=6971.0;wap2. Morgan's investors gained access to coal, iron, cotton, tobacco, lumber, sulphur, turpentine, and Florida fruit. Edwards, *New Spirits*, at 273.

105. MacArthur, "Charles McClung McGhee," at 140.

106. MacArthur, *Knoxville's History: An Interpretation*, at 43.

107. MacArthur, "Charles McClung McGhee," at 141–42.

108. "Black Diamond Railroad," *The Wilmington* (N. C.) *Morning Star* (Nov. 30, 1898) at 4.

109. MacArthur, "Charles McClung McGhee," at 142 (citing *The Knoxville Journal* [June 10, 1895] at 5).

110. *Id.* at 143. It does appear that "English capitalists" and "people in the Carolinas" were anxious to get a direct line to Knoxville because of the high coal rates. *The Knoxville Journal and Tribune* (Nov. 4, 1899).

111. MacArthur, "Charles McClung McGhee," at 143; *The Knoxville Journal* (June 10, 1895) at 5.

112. Allison, *Notable Men of Tennessee*, at 223.

113. MacArthur, "Charles McClung McGhee" (Letter from E.J. Sanford to C.M. McGhee (July 22, 1895), McGhee Papers).
114. *Id.* (Letter from E.J. Sanford to C.M. McGhee (July 22, 1895), McGhee Papers).
115. *Id.* at 144 (citing *The Knoxville Journal and Tribune* (March 10, 1902)).
116. "They're On To Boone," *The Keowee Courier* (Pickens, S.Car.) (Mar. 12, 1902) at 1.
117. "Envy As An Investment," *The Knoxville Daily Journal* (Apr. 2, 1893) at 2.
118. Letter from E.J. Sanford to C.M. McGhee (Sep. 15, 1894) in MacArthur, "Charles McClung McGhee," at 245.
119. Ronald R. Allen, *Knoxville in the Gay Nineties* (Knoxville, Tenn.: 2011) at 32; "Railroad News Notes," *The Knoxville Journal* (Feb. 2, 1891) at 3.
120. "Society," *The Knoxville Journal* (Jan. 3, 1892) at 2. The "Emma" mentioned is perhaps Sanford's sister instead of his mother.
121. Cooper & Terrill, *The American South*, at 456.
122. Edward J. Renehan, Jr., *Dark Genius of Wall Street: The Misunderstood Life of Jay Gould, King of the Robber Barons* (New York: Basic Books 2005) at iii.
123. "Jay Gould," *Encyclopaedia Britannica* (online), https://www.britannica.com/biography/Jay-Gould.
124. Cook, "Path to the High Bench," at 73 (citing Hamer, *Tennessee, A History*, at 698–99; Fowler Papers. Prior to joining Sanford's firm, Fowler was retained by the state to assist the attorney general of the Second District in the prosecution of the rioters at Coal Creek. "Trials Begin To-day," *The Knoxville Journal* (Aug. 24, 1892) at 1. Labor supporters later made efforts to block Fowler's access to political positions.
125. Cotham, *Toil, Turmoil & Triumph*, at 55.
126. *Id.* at 56.
127. Shapiro, *A New South Rebellion*, at 54.
128. The 1870 Tennessee Constitution prohibited the state legislature from granting money to corporations. The revision was adopted in response to the actions of Brownlow's legislature, which issued bonds pouring millions of dollars into the railroads. Langsdon, *Tennessee: A Political History*, at 193.
129. Folmsbee, et al., *History of Tennessee*, Vol. 2 at 164; Cotham, *Toil, Turmoil & Triumph*, at 58.
130. Folmsbee, et al., *History of Tennessee*, Vol. 2 at 165.
131. "A History of Tennessee," *Tennessee Blue Book, 2011–2012* (Nashville, Tenn.: Secretary of State) at 506.
132. Shapiro, *A New South Rebellion*, at 53.
133. http://www.coalcreekaml.com/Legacy.htm.
134. Shapiro, *A New South Rebellion*, at 4–17, 39–49, 63.
135. "The Investigating Committee," *The Daily American* (Nashville) (Feb. 28, 1885) at 4. (Testimony of E.J. Sanford).
136. Augusta Grove Bell, *Circling Windrock Mountain: Two Hundred Years in Appalachia* (Knoxville, Tenn.: Univ. of Tennessee Press 1998) at 179.
137. Shapiro, *A New South Rebellion*, at 6.
138. Rule, et al., *Standard History of Knoxville*, at 208–10. Convict labor continued to be used until Tennessee ended convict leasing in 1896. *Id.*
139. Shapiro, *A New South Rebellion*, at 147–48 (Letter from E.J. Sanford to C.M. McGhee (Nov. 14, 1891), McGhee Papers).

140. Cotham, *Toil, Turmoil & Triumph*, at 66; Allison, *Notable Men of Tennessee*, at 223. E.J. also was president of the Poplar Creek Coal and Iron Company, which owned a large tract of land it leased on royalty to operating companies. *Id.* at 223; Rule, et al., *Standard History of Knoxville*, at 242. Charles McClung McGhee, E.J.'s friend and business associate, had served in the state legislature when the convict leases were approved. Rebecca Hunt Moulder, "Convicts As Capital: Thomas O'Conner and the Leases of the Tennessee Penitentiary System, 1871–1883," 48 *E. Tennessee Historical Soc'y Publ'ns* (1976) at 48. In regard to McGhee's presence in the legislature, a newspaper charged that E.J.'s faction of the Republican party had bribed the incumbent candidate with $1,000 to leave the race to McGhee. MacArthur, "Charles McClung McGhee," at 70.

141. Bell, *Circling Windrock Mountain*, at 182. Purportedly, one of the convicts put on the train was Henry Baker, formerly a member of outlaw Jesse James's gang, who had been caught and sentenced to ten years hard labor at the Knoxville Iron Company's mine at Coal Creek. As the train was headed to Knoxville, Baker jumped off. He changed his name to Tom Stanley and began a new life. Maurice Stanley, *Sorrows End* (Fairview, N. Car.: Bright Mountain Books, 2009); http://www.coalcreekaml.com/JesseJamesConnection.htm.

142. Shapiro, *A New South Rebellion*, at 75–102.

143. Pete Daniel, "The Tennessee Convict War," 34 *Tennessee Historical Quarterly*, No. 3 (Fall 1975) at 273–92.

144. Cotham, *Toil, Turmoil & Triumph*, at 62–72; http://www.coalcreekaml.com/Legacy2.htm.

145. Bell, *Circling Windrock Mountain*, at 189 (quoting *The Knoxville Journal* in A.C. Hutson, Jr., "The Overthrow of the Convict Lease System in Tennessee," 8 *E. Tennessee Historical Soc'y Publ'ns*. [1936] at 100).

146. Roger L. Hart, *Redeemers, Bourbons, and Populists* (Baton Rouge, La.: Louisiana State Univ. 1975) at 175.

147. Shapiro, *A New South Rebellion*, at 128 (Letter from Edward J. Sanford to Charles M. McGhee (Nov. 14, 1891), McGhee Papers).

148. *Id.* at 147. The Knights of Labor was the major labor organization in the United States during the time period. Cooper & Terrill, *The American South*, at 496.

149. Cotham, *Toil, Turmoil & Triumph*, at 56–80; James B. Jones, "Convict Lease Wars," in Carroll Van West, ed., *Tennessee Encyclopedia of History and Culture* (Nashville, Tenn.: Tennessee Historical Soc'y 2002).

150. Cotham, *Toil, Turmoil & Triumph*, at 56–80.

151. http://www.coalcreekaml.com/Legacy2.htm.

152. "The Fraterville Mine Disaster of 1902," *The History Blog*, http://www.thehistoryblog.com/archives/16817. Only 184 were identified. *Id.* The bodies of 30 itinerant miners were unclaimed and were buried next to the railroad spur line. The youngest miner killed was twelve years old. *Id.*; Tennessee4Me-Read about a mine tragedy in Anderson County, http://www.tn4me.org/letters5apage.cfm/sa_id/109/era_id/6/major_id/20/minor_id/59/a_id/153.

153. *The Knoxville Journal and Tribune* (May 19–20, 1902).

154. Allen R. Coggins, "Fraterville Mine Disaster," *Tennessee Encyclopedia of History and Culture*, http://tennesseeencyclopedia.net/entry.php?rec=511.

155. *The Knoxville Journal and Tribune* (May 19–20, 1902).

156. *Id.* (May 19–20, 1902).

157. *Id.* (May 19–20, 1902).

158. "Black damp" is mostly nitrogen with a small percentage of carbon dioxide. The gas is heavier than air. Flames will not burn in it, and humans cannot breathe it and survive. "Black damp," https://www.merriam-webster.com/dictionary/black%20damp.

159. "Interview with Inspector Shiflett," *The Knoxville Journal and Tribune* (May 19, 1902).

160. "Fraterville Mine Disaster," http://www.coalcreekaml.com/Legacy4.htm.

161. "The Fraterville Mine Disaster of 1902," *The History Blog*, http://www.thehistoryblog.com/archives/16817.

162. Oil wick lamps with open flames were hooked into the hats of the miners. *Id.*

163. Coggins, "Fraterville Mine Disaster," http://tennesseeencyclopedia.net/entry.php?rec=511; "The Fraterville Mine Disaster of 1902," *The History Blog*, http://www.thehistoryblog.com/archives/16817.

164. Manning & Jamieson, *Historic Knoxville*, at 82. Camp's residence in Knoxville is the current home of television station WATE. *Id.*

165. "The Fraterville Mine Disaster of 1902, *The History Blog*, http://thehistoryblog/com/archives/16817.

166. Bell, *Circling Windrock Mountain*, at 198.

167. 82 S.W. 1131 (Tenn. 1904).

168. 98 S.W. 178 (Tenn. 1906).

169. Donald F. Paine, "Chasing Widows: Unethical Solicitation of Clients," 40 *Tennessee Bar Journal* 25 (Feb. 2004).

170. Rule, et al., *Standard History of Knoxville*, at 335–36.

171. Deaderick, ed., *Heart of the Valley*, at 597. Sanford was still a part owner of the *The Knoxville Journal and Tribune* at the time he joined the Department of Justice. "Edward T. Sanford To Succeed McReynolds as Assistant Attorney General," *The Evening Star* (Washington, D.C.) (Dec. 28, 1906) at 3.

172. "Disaster's Red Wave," *The Chicago Live Stock World* (May 20, 1902) at 4.

173. Rule, et al., *Standard History of Knoxville*, at 218.

174. Deaderick, ed., *Heart of the Valley*, at 597; Alfred is buried in Highland Memorial Cemetery in Knoxville. Thomas W. Herringshaw, *Herringshaw's American blue-book of biography* (Chicago: Am. Publishers' Ass'n 1915) at 671. Along with his father, Alfred was a member of the Cumberland Club. Additionally, Alfred was a member of the Cherokee Country Club. *Id.*

175. "Boosts Alfred Sanford for Governor of Tennessee," *The Atlanta Constitution* (Apr. 19, 1918) at 8; "Tennessee's Governorship," *The Atlanta Constitution* (Apr. 19, 1918) at 8.

176. See "Alfred F. Sanford Dies in Fall from Hospital Window," *The Knoxville Journal* (May 23, 1946) at 1; "Largest U.S. Arboretum Was Sanford's Hobby," *The Knoxville Journal* (May 24, 1946) at 24.

177. "Eastern Route of Dixie Highway Across Tennessee and Kentucky Ready for Dedication by This Fall," *The Atlanta Constitution* (Feb. 20, 1916) at E4.

178. Tammy Ingram, *Dixie Highway: Road Building and the Making of the Modern South, 1900–1930* (Chapel Hill, N. Car.: Univ. of N. Carolina Press 2014) at 43.

179. *Id.* at 44.

180. "Alfred F. Sanford 71-Year-Old Capitalist, Dies in Fall From Philadelphia Hospital Window," *The Knoxville News-Sentinel* (May 23, 1946) at 1, 10.

181. Fowler, "Mr. Justice Edward Terry Sanford," at 229; Cook, "Path to the High Bench," at 20.

182. MacArthur, *Knoxville's History: An Interpretation*, at 45.

183. Rothrock, *The French Broad-Holston Country*, at 398–99; Cook, "Path to the High Bench," at 20; Milton Klein, "Lawrence D. Tyson, Philanthropist," in *Volunteer Moments*, http://trace.tennessee.edu/utk_libarcvol/1/.

184. Fowler, "Mr. Justice Edward Terry Sanford," at 229.

185. "Dixie Water Co.," *The Knoxville Journal* (July 17, 1895) at 5.

186. James King Crook, *The Mineral Waters of the United States and Their Therapeutic Uses* (New York: Lea Bros. & Co. 1899) at 435.

187. Cook, "Path to the High Bench," at 20; Maguire, "The Supreme Court Justice From Knoxville," at 29.

188. Klein, "Lawrence D. Tyson" in *Volunteer Moments*, http://trace.tennessee.edu/utk_libarcvol/1/; Maguire, "The Supreme Court Justice From Knoxville," at 28.

189. Letter from Edward T. Sanford to Woodrow Wilson (Mar. 20, 1916), Woodrow Wilson Papers, Manuscript Division, Library of Congress, Washington, D.C. ("Wilson Papers").

190. Klein, "Lawrence D. Tyson: Philanthropist," in *Volunteer Moments*, http://trace.tennessee.edu/utk_libarcvol/1/; MacArthur, *Knoxville's History: An Interpretation*, at 45. In 1920, Tyson unsuccessfully sought the Democratic nomination for vice president. Lukens, "Portraits of Progress in New South Appalachia," at 36–37.

191. Fowler, "Mr. Justice Edward Terry Sanford," at 229; Cook, "Path to the High Bench," at 20 n.43.

192. Fowler Papers.

193. Langsdon, *Tennessee: A Political History*, at 232. Democrats dominated most statewide elections during this period because of their ascendancy in the two pro-Confederate grand divisions, Middle and West Tennessee. *Id.*

194. Donald Paine, "The Trials of Lawyer James E. Fulton for Murdering Lawyer Sam Parker," 39 *Tennessee Bar Journal* No. 12 (Dec. 2003); Donald Paine Collection of State of Tennessee v. Fulton, MS. 2732. The Special Collections Library of the Univ. of Tennessee, Knoxville.

195. *See Pearne v. Coal Creek Mining & Manuf. Co.*, 18 S.W. 402 (Tenn. 1891); Cook, "Path to the High Bench," at 20; Maguire, "The Supreme Court Justice From Knoxville," at 29.

196. Maguire, "The Supreme Court Justice From Knoxville," at 29.

197. "Statement of James A. Fowler," Fowler Papers.

198. "U.S. Justice Edward Sanford," Tennessee History Classroom, http://www.tennesseehistory.com/class/Sanford.htm; Cook, "Path to the High Bench," at 20.

199. Maguire, "The Supreme Court Justice From Knoxville," at 26.

200. Cook, "Path to the High Bench," at 20.

201. Fowler, "Mr. Justice Edward Terry Sanford," at 229.

202. Cook, "Path to the High Bench," at 20.

203. Chancery courts are trial courts in which judges—called Chancellors—decide cases without a jury. Similarly, appellate courts decide appeals from cases decided in trial courts, but hear no new evidence and employ no juries.

204. Noone, "Edward Terry Sanford," at 35.

205. Fowler, "Mr. Justice Edward Terry Sanford," at 229.

206. "Question of Freight Rates," *The Morning Times* (Washington, D.C.) (Mar. 11, 1896) at 8; "Express Rates on Peaches," *The Evening Star* (Washington, D.C.) at 5.

207. *The New York Times* (Apr. 22, 1902) at 11. Sanford was admitted to practice before the US Supreme Court on March 7, 1901. "Legal Record," *The Washington Post* (Mar. 7, 1901) at 9.

208. 183 U.S. 13 (1901).

209. *Knoxville Iron Co.*, 183 U.S. at 18.

210. Daniel, "The Tennessee Convict War," at 273–92.

211. 53 S.W. 955, 956 (Tenn. 1899).

212. *Id.* at 955.

213. *Knoxville Iron Co.*, 183 U.S., at 20–21.

214. *Id.* at 19.

215. John Vile, "Knoxville Iron Company v. Harbison," *Tennessee Encyclopedia of History and Culture* (2002), https://tennesseeencyclopedia.net/entry.php?rec=749.

216. 83 S.W. 667 (Tenn. 1904).

217. *Id.*, at 668.

218. Cook, "Path to the High Bench," at 20 n. 48 (citing Fowler Papers).

219. *Id.*; *Maloney*, 83 S.W. at 674.

220. Cook, "Path to the High Bench," at 20 n. 48 (citing Fowler Papers).

221. Cook, "Path to the High Bench," at 19.

222. Passport Application (April 1, 1921).

223. "Society," *The Knoxville Journal* (Oct. 20, 1889) at 3. "Society," *The Knoxville Journal* (Nov. 24, 1889) at 2. *See also* "New Year's 1890, Society," *The Knoxville Journal* (Jan. 5, 1890) at 7; "Circus Party, Society," *The Knoxville Journal* (Sept. 7, 1890) at 11; "Debutante Reception, Society," *The Knoxville Journal* (Oct. 26, 1890) at 10.

224. Cook, "Path to the High Bench," at 19.

225. "Pocket Money," *The Cincinnati Enquirer* (Jan. 7, 1891) at 4; "Brilliant Wedding," *The Knoxville Journal* (Jan. 7, 1891) at 8.

226. "A Notable Event," *The Knoxville Journal* (Apr. 8, 1888) at 2. Woodruff bought the lot for another church known at that time as Second Baptist Church on North Broad. "The Corner Stone," *The Knoxville Journal* (Sept. 29, 1889) at 7. Lutie remained a practicing Baptist. She attended the Calvary Baptist Church while living in Washington, D.C. "New Member of U.S. Supreme Court Not Rated Stranger Here," *The Evening Star* (Washington, D.C.) (Feb. 4, 1923) at 32.

227. "Brilliant Wedding," *The Knoxville Journal* (Jan. 7, 1891) at 8. Ushers included Lutie's brother Wallace, John McGhee, Arthur Mead, and Frank McClung. Sanford's sister Emma, Katie Pumphrey, and Lutie's sisters Daisy and Pauline served as maids of honor. Sanford's best man was John Brown.

228. *Id.*

229. *Id.*

230. "Pocket Money," *The Cincinnati Enquirer* (Jan. 7, 1891) at 4.

231. *Id.*; *see also* "Society," *The Knoxville Journal* (Jan. 11, 1891) at 10.

232. "The Sanford Reception," *The Knoxville Journal* (Jan. 30, 1891) at 8.

233. "A Little Story Related," *The Knoxville Journal* (July 17, 1891) at 2.

234. Jim Tumblin, "Walking 'through the friendly years': Captain W.W. Woodruff," *The Shopper News* (Knoxville, Tenn.) (Jan. 10, 2011) at A-7.

235. Deaderick, ed., *Heart of the Valley*, at 45; Maguire, "The Supreme Court Justice From Knoxville," at 12.

236. McDonald & Wheeler, *Knoxville, Tennessee*, at 18.
237. "W.W. Woodruff Passes Away," *The Knoxville News-Sentinel* (Jan. 31, 1926) at 1.
238. MacArthur, *Knoxville's History: An Interpretation*, at 33.
239. Manning & Jamieson, *Historic Knoxville*, at 71.
240. "The Victorious Reds," *The Knoxville Journal* (Sept. 8, 1889) at 12.
241. Maguire, "The Supreme Court Justice From Knoxville," at 12; "Captain Woodruff Celebrates His 84th Birthday," *The Knoxville News-Sentinel* (Mar. 28, 1924). Carson-Newman College is located in Jefferson City, Tennessee, approximately forty miles northeast of Knoxville.
242. "Legislative," *The Knoxville Journal* (Oct. 19, 1888) at 1.
243. "The Standard Coal and Coke Company's New Directory," *The Knoxville Journal* (Sept. 30, 1888) at 1.
244. "Change of Officers," *The Knoxville Journal* (Jan. 20, 1889) at 4.
245. "Legislative," *The Knoxville Journal* (May 15, 1888) at 1; "On to Chicago," *The Knoxville Journal* (June 16, 1888) at 1.
246. *The Knoxville Journal* (June 17, 1891) at 2.
247. "Woodruff Speaks," *The Knoxville Journal* (July 23, 1891) at 1.
248. "His First Speech," *The Knoxville Journal* (July 21, 1891) at 8.
249. "A Good Record," *The Knoxville Journal* (Aug. 4, 1891) at 5.
250. "Houk's Majority," *The Knoxville Journal* (Aug. 10, 1891) at 1; McKinney, *Southern Mountain Republicans*, at 146.
251. "Theater Artist Limned Faces of Knoxville Beauties on Curtain Before Opera House Stage," *The Knoxville News-Sentinel* (July 5, 1936) at 47.
252. "Knoxville Lawn Tennis Club," *The Knoxville Journal* (Apr. 15, 1888) at 1.
253. "An Enjoyable Reception," *The Knoxville Journal* (Apr. 28, 1888) at 5.
254. *The Courier-Journal* (Louisville, Ky.) (June 22, 1902) at 13; "Ayers Inducted Into His Office," *The Atlanta Constitution* (Apr. 26, 1905) at 5.
255. "Society," *The Knoxville Journal* (Nov. 6, 1892) at 2.
256. "Charmed with Knoxville," *The Knoxville Journal* (June 1, 1895) at 8.
257. "Gov. McKinley Honored," *The Knoxville Journal* (Sept. 18, 1895) at 1.
258. Lukens, "Portraits of Progress in New South Appalachia," at 9.
259. "New Member of U.S. Supreme Court Not Rated Stranger Here," *The Evening Star* (Washington, D.C.) (Feb. 4, 1923) at 32.
260. *The Courier-Journal* (Louisville, Ky.) (Oct. 12, 1902) at 18.
261. Hale, *History of Tennessee and Tennesseans*, at 1409.
262. 10 *The American Monthly Magazine*, No. 2 (Washington, D.C.: Nat'l Soc'y DAR Feb. 1897) at 160. Katherine Sherrill "Bonnie Kate" Sevier was the second wife of John Sevier, who served as the first governor of Tennessee. *DAR Chapter Biography*, http://www.tndar.org/~bonny kate/bonnykatebio.htm.
263. 10 *The American Monthly Magazine*, No. 2, at 160.
264. 11 *The American Monthly Magazine*, No. 3 (Sep. 1897) at 278.
265. *The Asheville* (N.Car.) *Gazette-News* (Oct. 1, 1913) at 5.
266. "Knoxville Society," *The Courier-Journal* (Louisville, Ky.) (Jun. 23, 1901) at 15. Lutie's mother, an Ohioan, married Woodruff on November 28, 1865, in Frankfort, Kentucky. *Brownlow's Knoxville Whig and Rebel Ventilator* (Knoxville, Tennessee) (Dec. 6, 1865) at 3. She was nineteen when Lutie was born. Mrs. Woodruff was active with the "ladies of Knoxville." "Ladies Meeting," *The Knoxville Journal* (May 14, 1889) at 4.

267. "Memorial Association to Make Request of Congress," *The Nashville Tennessean* (Nov. 23, 1919) at 21.
268. "Health Center, By Healing the Sick, Makes Dependent Families Self-Supporting," *The Knoxville News-Sentinel* (Dec. 22, 1922) at 4.
269. "Society," *The Knoxville Journal* (Oct. 1, 1893) at 10.
270. "The First Fair of Its Kind: Knoxville's 1913 National Conservation Exposition," http://www.easttnhistory.org/exhibits/first-fair-its-kind.
271. This fact was acknowledged in the *Federation Bulletin: A Magazine for the Woman of ToDay*, a publication of the General Federation of Women's Clubs. 6 *Federation Bulletin: A Magazine for the Woman of To-Day*, No. 1 (Boston, Oct. 1908) at 80. *See also* Gifford Pinchot, Don Carlos Ellis & Julia Clifford Lathrop, *The First Exposition of Conservation and Its Builders: An Official History of the National Conservation Exposition, held at Knoxville, Tenn. in 1913 and of Its Forerunners, The Appalachia Expositions of 1910–11*, W.M. Goodman, ed., (Knoxville, Tenn.: Knoxville Lithographing Co. 1914) at 47.
272. "Work of Women at the Appalachian Exposition," *The Knoxville Sentinel* (July 20, 1910) at 9.
273. Lukens, "Portraits of Progress in New South Appalachia," at 31.
274. Becky French Brewer & Douglas Stuart McDaniel, *Park City* (Charleston, S.Car.: Arcadia Publ'g 2005) at 41; Conkin, *Peabody College*, at 206; MacArthur, *Knoxville's History: An Interpretation*, at 49–50; Jack Neely, "A Fair to Remember: Knoxville's National Conservation Exposition of 1913, *Metro Pulse* (Knoxville, Tenn.) (Nov. 11, 2009); Lukens, "Portraits of Progress in New South Appalachia," at 40.
275. Lukens, "Portraits of Progress in New South Appalachia," at 41.
276. Neely, "A Fair to Remember: Knoxville's National Conservation Exposition of 1913," *Metro Pulse* (Knoxville, Tenn.) (Nov. 11, 2009).
277. MacArthur, *Knoxville's History: An Interpretation*, at 50.
278. "President Taft Is The Guest of Knoxville To-Day," *The Evening Chronicle* (Charlotte, N. C.) (Nov. 11, 1911) at 1.
279. Neely, "A Fair to Remember: Knoxville's National Conservation Exposition of 1913," *Metro Pulse* (Knoxville, Tenn.) (Nov. 11, 2009).
280. Pinchot, et al., *The First Exposition of Conservation and Its Builders*, at 10–13.
281. "The First Fair of Its Kind: Knoxville's 1913 National Conservation Exposition," http://www.easttnhistory.org/exhibits/first-fair-its-kind. The first-day attendance was 33,280.
282. Neely, "A Fair to Remember: Knoxville's National Conservation Exposition of 1913," *Metro Pulse* (Knoxville, Tenn.) (Nov. 11, 2009).
283. Pinchot, et al., *The First Exposition of Conservation and Its Builders*, at 89.
284. *Id.*
285. *The Cincinnati Enquirer* (Oct. 5, 1913) at 6.
286. "Women At Work," *The Gastonia* (N. Car.) *Gazette* (May 30, 1913) at 7. Mrs. Van Deventer's husband was clerk of the District Court for the Eastern District of Tennessee during Sanford's time on that bench. Van Deventer eventually served as an aide to the State Department and as an associate of Secretary of State Cordell Hull of Tennessee. His nephew married the grandmother of the current Tennessee Governor, Bill Haslam. Coury Turczyn, "The Full Story of the Waterwheel on Lyons Bend," *Metro Pulse* (Knoxville, Tenn.) (Jan. 3, 2011). Lowry, born in Greeneville, Tennessee, was a well-known banker from Atlanta. He was a former president of the American Bankers Association and the Atlanta Chamber of

Commerce. "Robert James Lowry," *Journal of the Am. Bankers Ass'n*, Vol. 2 (July 1918–June 1919) (New York: Fred Farnsworth 1919) at 423. Wright was the president of the exposition. "President Will Open Conservation Exposition," *The Herald Democrat* (Leadville, Col.) (Aug. 31, 1913) at 5; "Women At Work," *Gastonia* (N. Car.) *Gazette* (May 30, 1913) at 7.

287. "Justice Lurton Dies At Seashore," *The New York Times* (July 13, 1914) at 1.

288. Lukens, "Portraits of Progress in New South Appalachia," at 61 ("Women Meet in Debate Unique in Annals of Public Speaking," *The Knoxville Journal and Tribune* (Oct. 17, 1913) at 10).

289. John W. Leonard, ed., *Women's Who's Who of America: A Biographical Dictionary of Contemporary Women of the U.S. and Canada, 1914–1915* (New York: Am. Commonwealth Co. 1914).

290. 31 *Proceedings of the Annual Session of the Bar Association of Tennessee*, 1912, at 72–73.

291. Larson, *Summer For the Gods*, at 37–38.

292. "At Lenoir City: Mr. Edward T. Sanford Made an Impressive Speech," *The Knoxville Journal* (Oct. 29, 1896) at 4.

293. Ferren, *Salt of the Earth*, at 19.

294. *Id.* Rutledge thereafter attended nearby Maryville College in Maryville, Tennessee, and once wrote, "I, of course, owe more to Maryville College than I do perhaps to any of the other educational institutions which I attended." *Id.* at 27.

295. "World War I," *Tennessee 4 Me*, http://www.tn4me.org/minor_cat.cfm/era_id/6/major_id/30/minor_id/92.

296. Sanford Papers.

297. "Knox County, Tennessee in World War I," http://knoxcotn.org/old_site/military/wwi/book/libertyloans.html; Reese T. Amis, ed., *Knox County in the World War, 1917, 1918, 1919* (Knoxville, Tenn: Knoxville Lithographing Co. 1919) at 420. Lutie listed as "in charge" of this phase of the work. *Id.*

298. *Id.;* Ash, *Past Times*, at 93. Lutie's early education was at the Old Bell House, according to her childhood friend Patty Boyd. "Lasting Friendship," *The Knoxville News-Sentinel* (Oct. 5, 1945) at 17. She was also a graduate of the Ogontz School for Young Ladies in Pennsylvania. *The Knoxville News-Sentinel* (July 5, 1936) at 41.

299. "Knox County, Tennessee, in the World War," at 416.

300. Letter from Arthur C. Denison to Harry M. Daugherty (Jan. 4, 1923), Dep't of Justice Records, RG 60, Nat'l Archives, College Park, Md.

301. "Social Activities," *The Boston Herald* (May 9, 1929) at 21.

302. "Society" *The Evening Star* (Washington, D.C.) (Jan. 27, 1928) at 185; "Society," *The Evening Star* (Washington, D.C.) (Apr. 25, 1929) at 18; "President Greets Diplomatic Corps," *The Evening Star* (Washington, D.C.) (Nov. 16, 1928) at 7.

303. "Society," *The Evening Star* (Washington, D.C.) (May 16, 1928) at 19.

304. "Spanish Fiesta Program Promises to Be Colorful," *The Evening Star* (Washington, D.C.) (Feb. 27, 1927) at 50; "Monticello Ball to Be Gala Party Tonight," *The Evening Star* (Washington, D.C.) (Feb. 21, 1925) at 8.

305. *Proceedings of the Bar and Officers of the Supreme Court of the United States*, at 13–14.

306. Noone, "Edward Terry Sanford," at 37.

307. "Judge Sanford's Will Is Filed For Probate," *The Huntsville* (Ala.) *Daily Times* (Mar. 13, 1930) at 1; "Sanford Estate Is Left to Wife," *The Kingsport* (Tenn.) *Times* (Mar. 13, 1930) at 6.

308. "Estate of Sanford Valued at $265,000," *The Billings* (Mont.) *Gazette* (Mar. 30, 1930) at 6; "Mrs. Sanford," *Daily Herald* (Biloxi, Miss.) (Jun 5, 1929) at 10; "Will Summer At Nantucket," *The Boston Herald* (May 23, 1929) at 16. Sanford's will provided that if Lutie should die before he

did, or both should die together, the Metropolitan National Bank of Washington, the executor, should hold the remaining estate in trust. Income from the trust would have gone to his daughter Anna Magee and his grandson, Edward Sanford Metcalfe, with the former receiving two-thirds. "Estate of Justice Sanford Is Left to His Widow," *The Sioux City (Iowa) Journal* (Mar. 14, 1930) at 1. Chicot County is the southeasternmost county in Arkansas. It is bounded by Louisiana to the south and the Mississippi River to the east. The county is known for its cotton production. "The Encyclopedia of Arkansas History & Culture; Chicot County," http://www.encyclopediaofarkansas.net/encyclopedia/entry-detail.aspx?entryID=753&media=print.

309. The house in Nantucket was a charming old cottage on the cliff overlooking the harbor. It adjoined the house owned by Hugh Sanford. *The Knoxville News-Sentinel* (Dec. 16, 1928) at 33. *See* correspondence with Edward Sanford, great nephew of Sanford, June 18, 2015. Over the years, the heirs of Sanford's siblings have donated sizeable acreage of island property to the Nantucket Conservation Foundation. *See* Land Donors, Nantucket Conservation Foundation, https://www.nantucketconservation.org. Several members of the family returned to their roots, as the English ancestors of the Sanfords, Thomas Sanford of Essex County, England, arrived in Massachusetts around 1632. Sanford, *Thomas Sanford, the Emigrant to New England*, at 67, 71.

310. *Proceedings of the Bar and Officers of the Supreme Court of the United States*, at 24.

311. "Personal," *The Knoxville News-Sentinel* (May 13, 1930) at 8; "Society," *The Evening Star* (Washington, D.C.) (June 15, 1930) at 50.

312. "Society," *The Evening Star* (Washington, D.C.) (Sept. 16, 1930) at 19.

313. "Mrs. Edward Sanford," *The Knoxville News-Sentinel* (Apr. 9, 1937) at 13.

314. She left her estate to her daughter and grandson, Edward Sanford Metcalfe. "Edward Metcalf[e] Receives Bequest From Mrs. Sanford," *The Knoxville News-Sentinel* (Aug. 14, 1939) at 1; "Legacy Embarrasses Young Bank Clerk," *The Knoxville New-Sentinel* (Aug. 16, 1939) at 14.

315. "Widow of Justice Sanford Expires," *The Kingsport* (Tenn.) *Times* (July 6, 1939) at 13; "Justice Sanford's Widow Dies in Toronto, Canada," *The Evening Star* (Washington, D.C.) (July 7, 1939) at 18.

316. "Mrs. Edward T. Sanford," *The Knoxville News-Sentinel* (July 7, 1939) at 8. Anna Magee was unable to attend the services in Knoxville because she suffered a mild heart attack just before the funeral train reached Detroit, Michigan. "Stricken On Way To Funeral Here," *The Knoxville News-Sentinel* (July 9, 1939) at 5.

317. NNDB, http://www.nndb.com/people/869/000180329/.

318. *Harvard College, Class of 1885, Secretary's Report* No. 3, at 54; Listed as 720 Hill Avenue in the *U.S. City Directories, 1822–1989*, at 262. The Knoxville Women's Club eventually acquired the two-story brick building for use as a clubhouse at the cost of $35,000. *The Knoxville News-Sentinel* (Sept. 5, 1956) at 22.

319. Ronald R. Allen, *Knoxville in the Gay Nineties* (Knoxville, Tenn.: 2011) at 57; 1900 Census, Knoxville Ward 2.

320. "Society," *The Daily Journal and Tribune* (Knoxville, Tenn.) (Oct. 25, 1891) at 2.

321. "Society," *The Knoxville Journal* (Feb. 7, 1892) at 2.

322. "Society," *The Knoxville Journal* (Mar. 19, 1893) at 10.

323. Neely, "Paradise Found Out? *Metro Pulse* (Knoxville, Tenn.) (May 29, 2003); Jack Neely, "Knoxville's Halloween History," *Knoxville* (Tenn.) *Mercury* (Oct. 29, 2015) at 5, http://www.knoxmercury.com/2015/10/29/knoxvilles-halloween-history/.

324. *The Washington Post* (Sept. 26, 1908) at 7. They probably were attending Ogontz as their mother had.

325. The 1900 Census listed two black servants at the home: Jessie Harris, 23, and Lula Noa, 23. By the 1910 United States Federal Census, Lutie's mother had passed away on October 17, 1905, at the age of 58. 1910 Census, Knoxville Ward 10.

326. *The Bourbon News* (Paris, Ky.) (Dec. 15, 1914) at 10.

327. "Notes From Nashville," *The Courier-Journal* (Louisville, Ky.) at 15. Until 1916, Massachusetts Institute of Technology (M.I.T.) was known as "Boston Tech." Samuel C. Prescott, *When M.I.T. Was "Boston Tech," 1861–1916* (Cambridge, Mass.: Technology Press 1954).

328. *The Bourbon News* (Paris, Ky.) (Oct. 30, 1914) at 4; *The Bourbon News* (Paris, Ky.) (Nov. 17, 1914) at 2. Metcalfe's father was J.G. Metcalfe, formerly general manager of the L&N. "When Some One Cares," *The Lexington* (Ky.) *Herald* (Sept. 13, 1914) at 1.

329. "Matrimonial, Sanford—Metcalfe," *The Bourbon News* (Paris, Ky.) (Nov. 17, 1914) at 2.

330. *Id.*

331. Eclampsia is the development of seizures in a woman with severe preeclampsia, which is high blood pressure and protein in the urine during pregnancy. MedicineNet.com http://www.medicinenet.com/pregnancy_preeclampsia_and_ eclampsia/article.html#what_are _preeclampsia_and _eclampsia.

332. *"New Member of U.S. Supreme Court Not Rated Stranger Here," The Evening Star* (Washington, D.C.) (Feb. 4, 1923) at 32.

333. Telephone Interview with Lutie Metcalfe Culver (Sanford's great-granddaughter) (Apr. 21, 2015); "Paris News," *The Lexington* (Ky.) *Herald* (Mar. 10, 1930) at 11.

334. 1920 Census, Knoxville Ward 10, Roll: T625_1749; Page 14A.

335. "Paris News," *The Lexington* (Ky.) *Herald* (Mar. 10, 1930) at 11; *The Lexington* (Ky.) *Herald* (Mar. 22, 1930) at 6.

336. "Elizabeth Smith Becomes a Bride," *The New York Times* (Nov. 6, 1938) at 54.

337. "Edward Metcalf[e] Receives Bequest From Mrs. Sanford," *The Knoxville News-Sentinel* (Aug. 14, 1939) at 1; "Legacy Embarrasses Young Bank Clerk," *The Knoxville News-Sentinel* (Aug. 16, 1939) at 14.

338. "Metcalfe, Frances Hill Arnold," *The Knoxville News-Sentinel* (June 22, 2009) at 9.

339. Telephone Interview with Lutie Metcalfe Culver (Apr. 21, 2015); Babelay, *They Trusted and Were Delivered*, at 98.

340. After his presidency, William Howard Taft served as the chairman of the Central Committee of the American Red Cross."Red Cross Preparedness," *The American Red Cross Magazine*, No. 1 (Jan. 1916) at 14; Gould, Lewis L., "Taft, William Howard," *American National Biography Online*, http://www.anb.org/articles/06/06-00642.html. He assisted Sanford with Anna Magee's application to serve in France with the Red Cross during World War I. Letter from William H. Taft to Edward T. Sanford (May 29, 1918), and Letter from Edward T. Sanford to William H. Taft (June 1, 1918) Taft Papers; Maguire, "The Supreme Court Justice From Knoxville," at 68. Records indicate that Anna Magee performed "1,600 hours or 12 months of volunteer work." "Knox County in the World War," at 414, http://www.knoxcotn.org/old_site /military/wwi/book/redcross4.html.

341. Lutie was a close friend of Anna Stothoff Magee of New York, serving as an attendant in Ms. Magee's wedding to D.A. Boissevain of Amsterdam. "A Swell Wedding," *The Knoxville Journal* (Dec. 16, 1889) at 5. Ms. Magee's father was General George Magee, president of the Fall Brook Railway Company and prominently identified with the Vanderbilt interests. *Id.* Ms. Magee visited Lutie in Knoxville on several occasions. She died in Paris in 1894. "Glenfeld Historical News Archive," http://fallbrookrailway.com/glenfeld/glenfeld_news.html at 3–4.

342. Nat'l Archives and Records Admin., Marriage Reports in State Dep't Decimal Files, 1910–1949, RG 59 File #133/1383; US Passport Applications, 1795–1925, Dec. 18, 1919, Cert. # 150771 (Anna Magee Sanford); "Sanford-Cameron," *The Chattanooga News* (Dec. 9, 1919) at 6.

343. *See* "Palm Beach Notes," *The Palm Beach* (Fla.) *Post* (Mar. 28, 1933) at 5.

344. "Tea Party Honors Mrs. Edward Sanford," *The Knoxville News-Sentinel* (Mar. 30, 1937) at 10.

345. Jessie MacTaggart, "Anna Cameron Adores Television," 8 *The Ottawa Citizen* (Ottawa, Ontario, Canada) *Weekend Magazine*, No. 18 (May 2, 1958).

346. "Anna Cameron Values Time Spent Alone," *The Ottawa Journal* (Ottawa, Ontario, Canada) (Feb. 6, 1960) at 4.

347. "Canadian Beauty Loves Acting and Live Audience," *The Brandon Sun* (Brandon, Manitoba, Canada) (Feb. 20, 1963) at 1.

348. "Actress, former CBC-TV host Anna Cameron dies," *The Chronicle Herald* (Halifax, Nova Scotia, Canada) (Jan. 14, 2014), http://thechronicleherald.ca/artslife/1179572-actress-former-cbc-tv-host-anna-cameron-dies.

CHAPTER 5

1. Molly Millsaps, Johnston & Millsaps Advertising, Knoxville (1986).
2. Sanford, *Blount College*, at 78.
3. *Id.*
4. Laska, "Mr. Justice Sanford and the Fourteenth Amendment," at 211.
5. "Edward Terry Sanford," *The Knoxville News-Sentinel* (Mar. 9, 1930) at 22.
6. *Tennessee Encyclopedia of History and Culture,* http://tennesseeencyclopedia.net/entry.php?rec=1170.
7. Noone, "Edward Terry Sanford," at 35.
8. "Tribute to Henry W. Grady," *The Knoxville Journal* (Jan. 2, 1890) at 5.
9. "Arrangements Completed," *The Knoxville Journal* (Jan. 12, 1890) at 7. Sanford gave "one of his neat speeches" at a baseball game. *The Knoxville Journal* (May 19, 1890) at 8.
10. A.W. Harlan, ed., 6 *The Dental Review: Devoted to the Advancement of Dentistry* (Chicago: H.D. Justi & Son 1892) at 337; "Grist of Doctors," *The Knoxville Journal* (Mar. 18, 1892) at 1.
11. "For the Public Good," *The Knoxville Journal* (Apr. 1, 1894) at 4.
12. "Primeval Tennessee," *The Knoxville Journal* (Mar. 22, 1895) at 8.
13. *Id.*
14. "Will Storm the Town," *The Knoxville Journal* (May 31, 1865) at 1; "This the Town," *The Knoxville Journal* (June 1, 1895) at 1.
15. "Guests of Southerners," *The New York Times* (June 5, 1895) at 16.
16. "Happy Fourth! Knoxville Celebrates the Day in Style," *The Knoxville Journal* (July 5, 1895) at 1.
17. Sanford's speeches on citizenship always ended in this manner.
18. "Gov. McKinley Honored," *The Knoxville Journal* (Sep. 18, 1895) at 1.
19. "Elizabethan Era," *The Knoxville Journal* (Apr. 4, 1896) at 2.
20. *The Knoxville Journal* (Oct. 5, 1896) at 4. These clubs were organized in support of the candidacy for the presidency of William McKinley and his running mate, Garret A. Hobart.
21. Karl Rove, *The Triumph of William McKinley: Why the Election of 1896 Still Matters* (New York: Simon & Schuster Paperbacks 2015) at 12, 15–17.
22. *Id.* at 41.

23. "Edward [T.] Sanford, Esq. Entertained with Matchless Eloquence North Knoxville Republicans," *The Knoxville Journal* (Oct. 13, 1896) at 5.

24. "Eloquent Speech," *The Knoxville Journal* (Sept. 18, 1896) at 5.

25. *Id.* Sanford's father was likewise delivering speeches on this topic: "Plea For Sound Money," *The Knoxville Journal* (May 5, 1895) at 11; "Finances Discussed," *The Knoxville Journal* (May 4, 1895) at 4.

26. Laska, "Mr. Justice Sanford and the Fourteenth Amendment," at 215. The actual anniversary date for the state was June 1, 1896. The fair opened a year late due to financial problems. James Clark McReynolds, a prominent attorney admitted to practice before the Sixth Circuit Court of Appeals at its special session in Nashville during the Centennial Exposition, would be Sanford's future colleague in the Department of Justice and on the Supreme Court. McReynolds was administered the oath before Justice John Marshall Harlan (Circuit Justice) and Judges William H. Taft and Horace Lurton. Phillips, *History of the Sixth Circuit*, at 11. Accordingly, on May 27, 1897, one justice of the Supreme Court of the United States (Harlan), a future chief justice (Taft), and two future associate justices (Lurton and McReynolds) were together in the courtroom of the old Custom House in Nashville. *Id.*; Harry Phillips, "Tennessee Sixth Circuit," 33 *Tennessee Historical Quarterly* 22 (1974) at 28.

27. "Dr. Eliot Cheered," *The Boston Herald* (Feb. 26, 1900) at 5.

28. "Dewey at Knoxville," *The Times-Picayune* (New Orleans) (May 15, 1900) at 9.

29. "Exercises at Knoxville," *The Atlanta Constitution* (May 31, 1901) at 4.

30. *The Courier Journal* (Louisville, Ky.)(Feb. 6, 1902) at 2. "Winfield Scott Schley-Spanish American War," http://www.spanamwar.com.

31. "Ambassador Bryce Pays a High Tribute to Pilgrim Fathers," *The Washington* (D.C.) *Herald* (Nov. 22, 1907) at 3.

32. Cook, "Path to the High Bench," at 56; "Historical Notes and News," 4 *Tennessee Historical Magazine*, (June 1918) at 149–51.

33. "Legion Meeting Shows Success of Organization," *The Nashville Tennessean* (Oct. 25, 1919) at 1.

34. Larson, *Summer For The Gods*, at 40.

35. "Sanford Talks On Citizenship," *The Nashville Tennessean* (June 12, 1922) at 5.

36. *Id.*

37. "Judge Sanford Scores Knoxville School," *The Nashville Tennessean* (Dec. 7, 1921) at 14.

38. Ragan, "Mr. Justice Sanford," at 77.

39. "Optimists Told People of World Shell Shocked," *The Atlanta Constitution* (June 15, 1923) at 22. He spoke to the Optimists again on April 14, 1928. Sanford Papers.

40. Marjorie C. Wilcox, "A History of the Grand Rapids Bar Association, February 1902 to February 1977," federalcourthistoricalwdmi.org. at 9.

41. "Los Angeles Boy First in Contest of School Orators," *The New York Times* (June. 5, 1926) at 1.

42. "Summary of Proceedings of the Tennessee Bar Association" (held at Nashville, May 26–28, 1902), *Annual Report of the American Bar Association* (Saratoga Springs, New York 1902); Laska, "Mr. Justice Sanford and the Fourteenth Amendment," at 211, 215. Sanford delivered a speech on this topic to the Irving Club in Knoxville in October 1893. "Irving Club Meeting," *The Knoxville Journal* (Oct. 8, 1893) at 2. Among Sanford's papers are the notes for a speech on this topic given at Grant University in Athens, Tennessee, in 1904. 34 *Annual Catalogue of Grant*

University (1900) at 10. In 1886, the Methodist Episcopal Church, North, founded Chattanooga University. Three years after it opened, Methodist officials merged the school with Grant Memorial University in Athens, which had been East Tennessee Wesleyan University, renaming the school U.S. Grant University, with Chattanooga and Athens branches. The decision to honor Grant was "an effort to secure financial support for the deeply indebted Southern college from Northern states and benefactors. . . ." "Tennessee Wesleyan College," http://tenneseeencyclopedia.net/entry.php?rec=1364. In 1907, the Chattanooga campus was renamed the University of Chattanooga. Steve Cox, "The History of the Library at the University of Tennessee, Chattanooga," Tennessee Library Ass'n, http://www.tnla.org/?384. The Athens branch became the Athens School of the University of Chattanooga. In 1925, the Athens School split from the University of Chattanooga and became Tennessee Wesleyan College, a junior college. It began awarding bachelor's degrees in 1957. In 1969, the University of Chattanooga merged into the University of Tennessee system. *Id.* Sanford's undated notes reveal that he also visited places like Mobile, Alabama, and Cincinnati, Ohio, to deliver speeches. His papers show presentations ranging from an oration at a boys' school to a farewell address to the French Ambassador. Sanford Papers.

43. 26 *Proceedings of the Annual Session of the Bar Association of Tennessee* (1907) at 32.

44. Ragan, "Mr. Justice Sanford," at 75.

45. Edward T. Sanford, *The Constitutional Convention of Tennessee of 1796* (Nashville, Tenn.: Marshall & Bruce Co. Printers and Stationers 1896) (reprinted from 15 *Proceedings of the Annual Session of the Bar Association of Tennessee* (1896)); Laska, "Mr. Justice Sanford and the Fourteenth Amendment," at 215. Tennessee's first constitution gave voting rights to all free males, including free blacks.

46. "U.S. Justice Edward Sanford," Tennessee History Classroom, http://www.tennesseehistory.com/class/sanford.htm; Cook, "Path to the High Bench," at 56, 57; Maguire, "The Supreme Court Justice From Knoxville," at 34.

47. Mrs. John T. More, "Tennessee Historical Society," *Tennessee Historical Quarterly* III (Sept. 1944) at 224–25.

48. 20 *Harvard Graduates' Magazine* (Boston, Mass.: The Harvard Graduates' Magazine Ass'n 1911–12) at 159.

49. J.B. Henneman, "Recent Tennessee History by Tennesseans," 4 *The Sewanee Rev.*, No. 4 (Aug. 1896) at 460.

50. Hall, "Edward Jackson Sanford," *America's Successful Men of Affairs*, at 680.

51. "Sanford, Edward Terry," Who's Who In TN, http://tngenweb.org/whos-who/sanford-edward-terry/.

52. Frederic S. Nathan, *Centurions In Public Service: Particularly as Presidents, Supreme Court Justices & Cabinet Members* (Dalton, Mass.: The Studley Press, Inc. 2010) at 9, 15, 16–17, 20, 26. The sitting Supreme Court justices were Taft, Stone, and Sanford. Other Supreme Court justices who belonged to the Century Club included Charles Evans Hughes, Benjamin Cardozo, John Marshall Harlan, Potter Stewart, William J. Brennan, and Lewis F. Powell, Jr. *Id.* at 17.

53. Other political figures included Wendell L. Willkie; Adlai Stevenson; George McGovern; George W. Wickersham; Henry Stimston; Andrew Mellon; Dean Acheson; John Foster Dulles; Dean Rusk; Henry Kissinger; W. Michael Blumenthal; Joseph Califano, Jr.; Cyrus R. Vance, and Caspar W. Weinberger. *Id.* at 26–31.

54. "All Male Club in Washington Ends Policy Against Women," *The New York Times*, June 19, 1988. at 20.

55. Britt Peterson, "Private Social Clubs Try to Delay Their Doom," *The Washingtonian* (Apr. 29, 2015), http://www.washingtonian.com/2015/04/29/private-social-clubs-are-doomed/.

56. "Justice Sanford Described As A Liberal Conservative," *The Evening Star* (Washington, D.C.) (Feb. 12, 1923) at 8.

57. Drew Pearson & Robert S. Allen, *The Nine Old Men* (New York: Doubleday, Doran and Company, Inc. 1936) at 31.

58. "Wade Cooper Heads Southern Society," *The Daily Times* (Wilson, N.C.) (Jul. 22, 1924) at 6. The Southern Society became increasingly popular during Wilson's presidency. "South Rests Easy In Social Saddle," *The Carroll* (Iowa) *Herald* (Oct. 21, 1914) at 9.

59. *Proceedings of the Bar and Officers of the Supreme Court of the United States*, at 45; Newman, *Knoxville Chronology*, at 17; Cook, "Path to the High Bench," at 57; Irving Club Collection, 1861–2012 (MS. 3649), http://libguides.utk.edu.

60. Newman, *Chronology of Knoxville*, at 17.

61. "Society," *The Knoxville Journal* (June 1, 1890) at 14.

62. Letter from S.B. Dow to Warren G. Harding (Dec. 29, 1922) Dep't of Justice Records, RG 60, Nat'l Archives, College Park, Md.; Hall, "Edward Jackson Sanford," *America's Successful Men of Affairs*, at 679–80. Depew was a chieftain in Cornelius Vanderbilt's railway system. A prominent Republican, he also served as president of the New York Central Railroad System and was New York's senator from 1899 to 1911. "Depew, Chauncey Mitchell (1834–1928)," http://bioguide.congress.gov. A favorite on the banquet circuit, Depew viewed the South as "the Bonanza of the future," with "vast forests untouched" and "enormous veins of coal and iron." Cooper & Terrill, *The American South*, at 458.

63. "For the Charity Ball," *The Knoxville Journal* (Dec. 24, 1893) at 4.

64. "Cumberland Club," *The Knoxville Journal* (Dec. 19, 1894) at 4.

65. *See* http://www.elks.org.

66. "The Elks Birthday," *The Knoxville News-Sentinel* (Oct. 14, 1940) at 4.

67. "Justice E.T. Sanford Dies," *The Prescott* (Ariz.) *Evening Courier* (Mar. 8, 1930) at 7; "Sanford Descendant of Pioneer Builders In East Tennessee," *The Knoxville News-Sentinel* (Mar. 8, 1930) at 10.

68. James C. Leonhart, *The Fabulous Octogenarian* (Baltimore, Md.: Redwood House, Inc. 1962) at 277; "Building Good Citizens," http://www.valleydistrictcivitan.com/civitan-international.

69. "Moonlight Excursion," *The Knoxville Journal* (Jul. 9, 1895) at 8.

70. Cook, "Path to the High Bench," at 58.

71. "Golf Pairings," *The Knoxville News-Sentinel* (Aug. 8, 1922) at 5.

72. "Justice Sanford To Address Kiwanians," *The Knoxville News-Sentinel* (July 18, 1923) at 1.

73. "Always the Victor," *The Knoxville Journal* (Oct. 9, 1892) at 10.

74. Edward T. Sanford, Address to Tennessee Bar Ass'n (June 1923). Sanford was admitted to the Bar in September 1888 while still at Harvard. The TBA's records indicate that Sanford joined in 1891. *See* 10 *Proceedings of the Annual Session of the Bar Association of Tennessee* (1891) at 251. He was an honorary member of the Alabama Bar Association. "Edward T. Sanford," *The Aberdeen* (S.D.) *Daily News* (Feb. 1, 1923) at 4; "Sanford Descendant of Pioneer Builders In East Tennessee," *The Knoxville News-Sentinel* (Mar. 8, 1930) at 10.

75. 14 *Proceedings of the Annual Session of the Bar Association of Tennessee* (1895) at 7; Cook, "Path to the High Bench," at 24.

76. Sanford, "The Constitutional Convention of 1796," in 15 *Proceedings of the Annual Session of the Bar Association of Tennessee* (1896) at 92; "Tennessee Lawyers Discuss," *The Atlanta Constitution* (July 31, 1896) at 2.

77. 17 *Proceedings of the Annual Session of the Bar Association of Tennessee* (1898) at 7

78. 15 *Proceedings of the Bar Association of Tennessee* (1896) at 6–7; Cook, "Path to the High Bench," at 25.

79. Cook, "Path to the High Bench," at 27.

80. 15 *Proceedings of the Annual Session of the Bar Association of Tennessee* (1893) at 24.

81. 23 *Proceedings of the Annual Session of the Bar Association of Tennessee* (1904) at 6, 13, 109. Additionally, Sanford was chosen to be a delegate to the Universal Congress of Lawyers and Jurists scheduled for St. Louis, Missouri. Cook, "Path to the High Bench," at 27–29.

82. Edward T. Sanford, "The Promotion of Uniformity of Legislation in the United States," 23 *Proceedings of the Annual Session of the Bar Association of Tennesse,* (1904) at 115–133.

83. Cook, "Path to the High Bench," at 30.

84. "Mountain Lawyers of All Tennessee," *Janesville* (Wis.) *Daily Gazette* (Aug. 8, 1905) at 1.

85. 32 *Proceedings of the Annual Meeting of the Bar Association of Tennessee* (1913) at 228.

86. *Id.* He served on the Committee for Legal Education and Admission to the Bar for the 1920–22 terms. *Proceedings of the Annual Meeting of the Bar Association of Tennessee* (Vols. 39, 40, 41), Nashville, Tenn. (July 14 & 15, 1920), Knoxville (June 7 & 8, 1921), and Memphis, Tenn. (May 30 & 31, 1922).

87. "U.S. Justice Edward Sanford," Tennessee History Classroom," http://www.tennesseehistory.com/class/sanford.htm.

88. 24 *Proceedings of the Annual Session of the Bar Association of Tennessee* (1905), at 87–88.

89. *The Tennessean* (Nashville) (May 27, 1911) at 1, 7.

90. Cook, "Path to the High Bench," at 33.

91. Speech to the Tennessee Bar Association (May 26, 1911) (draft), Sanford Papers.

92. Cook, "Path to the High Bench," at 34.

93. 32 *Proceedings of the Annual Session of the Bar Association of Tennessee* (June 25 & 26, 1913) at Memphis at 14; 24 *Proceedings of the Annual Session of the Bar Association of Tennessee* (1905–06) at 186; Allison, *Notable Men of Tennessee*, at 288; "Edward Terry Sanford," 4 *Journal Nat'l Ass'n Referees Bankruptcy* 91 (April 1930); Cook, "Path to the High Bench," at 34.

94. Maguire, "The Supreme Court Justice From Knoxville," at 34.

95. *Official Report of the Universal Congress of Lawyers and Jurists* (St. Louis, Mo.: Executive Committee 1905).

96. *American Bar Ass'n Journal* (July 1970) at 604.

97. *Id.*

98. 36 *Report of the Annual Meeting of the American Bar Association* (Baltimore, Md.: Lord Baltimore Press 1911) at 131; 37 *Report of the Annual Meeting of the American Bar Association* (Baltimore, Md: Lord Baltimore Press 1912) at 557.

99. 24 *Proceedings of the Annual Session of the Bar Association of Tennessee* (1905) held at Lookout Mountain, Tenn. at 28. This committee assignment is again listed in 1910.

100. "Change All Courts," *The Washington* (D.C.) *Post* (Aug. 27, 1908) at 4.

101. 32 *Report of the Annual Meeting of the American Bar Association* (1909) at 585–609.

102. *Report of the Annual Meeting of the American Bar Association* (1910) at 615–51.

103. *Id.* at 123. A draft of "The Establishment of the Federal Judicial System" can be found in his papers, Sanford Papers.

104. *Who's Who in Tennessee* (Memphis Tenn.: Paul & Douglass Co., Pubs. 1911).

105. 33 *Report of the Annual Meeting of the American Bar Association* (1910) at 156.

106. *Proceedings of the Bar and Officers of the Supreme Court of the United States* at 12.

107. John W. Green, "Some Judges of the United States District Court of Tennessee (1878–1939)," 18 *Tennessee Law Rev.* 227 (1943–45) at 238.

108. Noone, "Edward Terry Sanford," at 35; Laska, "Mr. Justice Sanford and the Fourteenth Amendment," at 211.

109. "Reception and Banquet by Lord Mayor and City Corporation," 10 *American Bar Ass'n Journal* 581 (1924) at 582.

110. Noone, "Edward Terry Sanford," at 35.

111. "American Lawyers See Mussolini," *The New York Times* (Aug. 14, 1924) at 2.

112. "Mussolini Receives American Lawyers," *The Washington* (D.C.) *Post* (Aug. 14, 1924) at 3.

113. "Bar Association Meets In Memphis," *The Kingsport* (Tenn.) *Times* (Oct. 13, 1929) at 1.

114. Cook, "Path to the High Bench," at 38.

115. Ragan, "Mr. Justice Sanford," at 76.

116. "U.S. Justice Edward Sanford," Tennessee History Classroom, http://www:tennesseehistory.com/class/sanford.htm.

117. Sanford, *Blount College*, at 77.

118. *Annual Report of the State Superintendent of Public Instruction of Tennessee*, Dep't of Public Instruction (1905) at 230.

119. *The Knoxville Journal* (June 12, 1890) at 1.

120. Cook, "Path to the High Bench," at 57.

121. *Proceedings of the Conference for Education in the South* (6th Sess.), Richmond, Va., (April 22–25, 1903) at 134.

122. *Southern Education Board Records*, 1898–925, blogs.lib.unc.edu/afam/index.Southern-Education-Boardrecords-1898–1925/ ("Southern Education Board Records").

123. Milton Klein, "Charles W. Dabney: Eleventh President, 1887–1904" in *Volunteer Moments*, http://trace.tennessee.edu/utk_libarcvol/1. Dabney sent agents into the South to study the conditions of state schools. Southern Education Board Records.

124. Milton Klein, *Volunteer Moments*, http://trace.tennessee.edu/utk_libarcvol/1.

125. Aaron D. Purcell, "'The Greatest Event Since the Civil War': Progressivism and the Summer School of the South at the University of Tennessee," 76 *Journal of E. Tennessee History* (2004) at 1.

126. James R. Montgomery, "The Summer School of the South," 22 *Tennessee Historical Quarterly*, No. 4 (Dec. 1963) at 372–73.

127. Klein, "Charles W. Dabney: Eleventh President, 1887–1904" in *Volunteer Moments*, http://trace.tennessee.edu/utk_libarcvol/1/

128. Dennis, *Lessons In Progress*, at 101; Montgomery, "The Summer School of the South," at 361.

129. Langsdon, *Tennessee: A Political History*, at 269.

130. Klein, "Charles W. Dabney: Eleventh President, 1887–1904," in *Volunteer Moments*, http://trace.tennessee.edu/utk_libarcvol/1.

131. Purcell, "The Greatest Event Since the Civil War," at 16.

132. *Id.*

133. Montgomery, et al., *To Foster Knowledge*, at 152.

134. Dennis, *Lessons In Progress*, at 103; Letter from William H. Baldwin to Edward T. Sanford (Jan. 13, 1902); Letter from Edward T. Sanford to William H. Baldwin (Jan. 22, 1902) Charles W. Dabney Papers.

135. Klein, "Charles W. Dabney: Eleventh President, 1887–1904," in *Volunteer Moments*, http://trace.tennessee.edu/utk_libracvol/1.

136. Purcell, "The Greatest Event Since the Civil War," at 21–22.

137. Montgomery, "The Summer School of the South," at 378 (citing *Board of Trustees Minutes* Aug. 4, 1908).

138. *Id.* at 378–80.

139. The offering of a summer session at Peabody ironically led to a decrease in attendance at the Summer School of the South at the University of Tennessee. Montgomery, "The Summer School of the South," at 380.

140. Conkin, *Peabody College*, at 115; "Great Future For George Peabody College Predicted," *The Nashville Tennessean* (May 18, 1913) at 67.

141. Laska, "Mr. Justice Sanford and the Fourteenth Amendment," at 211; Cook, "Path to the High Bench," at 51; Phillips, *History of the Sixth Circuit*, at 68. "U.S. Justice Edward Sanford," Tennessee History Classroom, http://www.tennesseehistory.com/class/Sanford.htm, *Tennessee Encyclopedia of History and Culture,* http://tennesseeencyclopedia.net./entry.php?rec=1170.

142. "Justice Edward T. Sanford," *Peabody Reflector and Alumni News* (Mar. 1930) at 37; Cook, "Path to the High Bench," at 51 n. 105; Conkin, *Peabody College*, at 177.

143. "Teachers' College In South," *The New York Times* (Oct. 13, 1912) at x13.

144. Conkin, *Peabody College*, at 177.

145. *Id.* at 104. The fund was "vigorously opposed" to integration. Foner, *Reconstruction*, at 366–67.

146. Conkin, *Peabody College*, at 103.

147. Hayes also was president of the board of trustees of the John F. Slater Fund for the Education of Freedmen. John H. Stanfield, II, "The John F. Slater Fund," in *Historical Foundations of Black Reflective Sociology* (Walnut Creek, Cal.: Left Coast Press 2011) at 69. The work of the Slater Fund was vital to the improvement of black education in Tennessee. Lester C. Lamon, *Black Tennesseans, 1900–1930* (Knoxville, Tenn.: Univ. of Tennessee Press 1977) at 86.

148. Conkin, *Peabody College*, at 103, 105.

149. *Id.* at 176; "Peabody School Chartered," *The Watchman and Southron* (Sumter, S. C.) (Oct. 6, 1909) at 2.

150. Conkin, *Peabody College*, at 176.

151. *Id.* at 192.

152. Cook, "Path to the High Bench," at 51–54.

153. Sanford Papers.

154. *Harvard College, Class of 1885, Class Day Oration*, at 26.

155. Peabody College Commencement (June 1916), Sanford Papers.

156. Conkin, Peabody College, at 209, 232–33.

157. Cook, "Path to the High Bench," at 52–53 (citing Peabody College Commencement [June 1917], Sanford Papers).

158. *Id.* at 53.

159. *Id.* at 53–54 (citing Peabody College Commencement (June 1920), Sanford Papers).

160. *Id.* at 54 (citing Peabody College Commencement (June 1920), Sanford Papers).

161. Sanford Papers.

162. Edwards, *New Spirits*, at 88.

163. Warren G. Harding, Address Accepting the Republican Nomination (June. 12, 1920), The American Presidency Project, http://www.presidency.ucsb.edu.

164. Edwards, *New Spirits*, at 119.

165. Sanford Papers.

166. *Id.*

167. Cook, "Path to the High Bench," at 38.

168. Ragan, "Mr. Justice Sanford," at 75.

169. Fowler Papers.

170. Frantz, *The Door of Hope*, at 61.

171. Campbell, *Four Score Forgotten Men*, at 353.

172. *The Nashville* (Tenn.) *American* (Apr. 8, 1904) at 3.

173. "Gov. McKinley Honored," *The Knoxville Journal* (Sept. 18, 1895) at 1; "The President's Tour," *Warrenton* (N.C.) *Gazette* (Apr. 24, 1891) at 1; "To See the President," *The Knoxville Journal and Tribune* (Sept. 7, 1902) at 4; "President Roosevelt to be Knoxville's Guest," *The Knoxville Sentinel* (Sept. 8, 1902) at 1.

174. McKinney, *Southern Mountain Republicans*, at 79–80.

175. *Id.* at 82. Houk's political ally was Oliver P. Temple, who secured the position of postmaster over Rule. *Id.* at 84–85.

176. *Id.* at 86.

177. *Id.* at 146–50.

178. *Id.* at 145, 150.

179. Langsdon, *Tennessee: A Political History*, at 220.

180. Hart, *Redeemers, Bourbons & Populists*, at 107.

181. Eligible crops included cotton, tobacco, wheat, corn, oats, barley, rye, rice, wool, and sugar. Edward L. Ayers, *The Promise of the New South: Life After Reconstruction* (New York: Oxford Univ. Press, Inc. 2007) at 239.

182. "Populism & Farmers," Tennessee 4 Me, http://www.tn4me.org/article.cfm/a_id/138/minor_id/56/major_id/20/era_id/6.

183. Cooper & Terrill, *The American South*, at 457.

184. Frantz, *The Door of Hope*, at 67–68; Hart, *Redeemers, Bourbons & Populists*, at 113.

185. Shapiro, *A New South Rebellion*, at 8. Buchanan's battle for the Democratic nomination went on for twenty-six ballots and lasted six days. Langsdon, *Tennessee: A Political History*, at 220.

186. Woodward, *Origins of the New South*, at 203.

187. The Seventeenth Amendment became law in 1913. It established the popular election of senators by the voters of the states.

188. "King Isham G. Harris," *The Knoxville Journal* (Jan. 23, 1895) at 1.

189. "Col. E.J. Sanford," *The Knoxville Journal* (Jan. 23, 1895) at 2.

190. *The Atlanta Constitution* (Feb. 20, 1897) at 6.

191. "Sanford Descendant of Pioneer Builders In East Tennessee," *The Knoxville News-Sentinel* (Mar. 8, 1930) at 10.

192. *The Columbia* (Tenn.) *Herald* (Apr. 20, 1900) at 4. Langsdon, *Tennessee: A Political History*, at 235. Governor McMillin was reelected. *Id.* at 237.

193. Langsdon, *Tennessee: A Political History*, at 232.

194. *The New York Tribune* (Mar. 7, 1902) at 12; "A Meeting of Republicans," *The Atlanta Constitution* (Mar. 7, 1902) at 2.

195. Cook, "Path to the High Bench," at 41; *The Gainesville* (Fla.) *Star* (Mar. 18, 1904) at 2; *The Gaffney Ledger* (S.C.) (Mar. 11, 1904) at 3.

196. Cook, "Path to the High Bench," at 41 (citing Fowler Papers).

197. "Bitterly Fighting," *The Cincinnati Enquirer* (Mar. 31, 1904) at 3.

198. Cook, "Path to the High Bench," at 41. Langsdon, *Tennessee: A Political History*, at 226, 239.

199. *The Courier-Journal* (Louisville, Ky.) (Mar. 14, 1904) at 3.

200. Frazier resigned as governor the following year to become US senator in March 1905. John Isaac Cox, Democratic speaker of the senate, became the state's governor. In 1906, Democrat Malcolm R. Patterson assumed the governor's chair after defeating Republican Henry Clay Evans. Langsdon, *Tennessee: A Political History*, at 239, 241, 242, 247.

201. Cook, "Path to the High Bench," at 41 n.83; "Federal Judgeship for Hon. E.T. Sanford," *The Knoxville Journal and Tribune*, May 15, 1908, at 1; "Political Notes and Hotel Gossip," *The Nashville* (Tenn.) *American* (June. 24, 1906) at 24.

202. Letter from Edward T. Sanford to Joseph G. Cannon, Sept. 29, 1905, RG 233: Records of the US House of Representatives, 1789–2015. Nat'l Archives 6788621, Washington, D.C.

203. "Politics and Politicians," *The Kingston* (N.Y.) *Daily Freeman*, Vol. 34 (Jan. 30, 1908) at 6.

204. "Taft Back of Plan to Win Tennessee," *The Washington* (D.C.) *Times* (June 9, 1910) at 8.

205. Langsdon, *Tennessee: A Political History*, at 266.

206. "U.S. Justice Edward Sanford," *Tennessee History Classroom*, http://www.tennesseehistory.com/class/Sanford.htm.

207. *Proceedings of the Twenty-ninth Annual Convention of the Tennessee Bankers' Association*, held in Knoxville, May, 1919.

208. Sanford Papers.

209. *Id.*

210. Pringle, *The Life and Times of William Howard Taft*, Vol. 2, at 928–36.

211. *Id. See* "A Great American Statesman," 37 *The World's Work* 612 (1919) at 612.

212. Pringle, *The Life and Times of William Howard Taft*, Vol. 2, at 928–36.

213. Robert C. Post, "Mr. Taft Becomes Chief Justice," 76 *Univ. Cincinnati Law Rev.* 761 (2008) at 769–70.

214. James N. Giglio, *H.M. Daugherty and the Politics of Expediency* (Kent, Ohio; Kent State Univ. Press 1978) at 34.

215. Klein, "Presidential Visit," in *Volunteer Moments*, http://trace.tennessee.edu/utk_libarcvol/1.

216. Allen, *Only Yesterday*, at 21.

217. Peter G. Renstrom, *The Taft Court: Justices, Rulings, and Legacy* (Santa Barbara, Calif.: ABC-CLIO 2003) at 13 ("There ensued a prevailing nationalistic anti-European sentiment.").

218. Willis Fletcher Johnson, *The Life of Warren G. Harding* (Philadelphia: John C. Winston Co. 1923) at 73–74.

219. "United War Work," a speech given at Madisonville, Tennessee (Nov. 1, 1918), Sanford Papers; "Sanford Descendant of Pioneer Builders In East Tennessee," *The Knoxville News-Sentinel* (Mar. 8, 1930) at 10.

220. "Proceedings in Memory of Mr. Justice Sanford," 285 U.S. xxxvii (1931).

221. Benhart, *Appalachian Aspirations*, at 77.

222. *Id.* at 74.

223. *Id.* at 74–76, 116–17; Kate Clabough, *Lenoir City* (Charleston, S.C.:, Arcadia Publ'g 2009) at 18. E.J. was one of the organizers of the re-founded Young Men's Christian Association in Knoxville in 1865. Allison, *Notable Men of Tennessee*, at 222. The Knoxville YMCA had been one of the nation's first when it was first founded in the early 1850s. Neely, *Market Square*, at 51. The YMCA "was an activist organization, preaching against alcohol consumption and also racial injustice." *Id.*

224. Benhart, *Appalachian Aspirations*, at 78; *see* "Lenoir City: The Pet of the Great E.T.V. and G.R.R.," *The State Chronicle* (Raleigh, N. C.) (July 24, 1890) at 3.

225. Benhart, *Appalachian Aspirations*, at 78. During the Civil War, Union General Ambrose Burnside was very impressed with Lenoir Station and offered to purchase the property from the Lenoir family. Clabough, *Lenoir City*, at 13.

226. Benhart, *Appalachian Aspirations*, at 78.

227. *Id.*

228. *Id.* at 85.

229. Edward Alsworth Ross, "Prohibition as the Sociologist Sees It," 142 *Harper's Magazine* 186 (1921) at 188. Lenoir City's temperance policy was reminiscent of the founding of Harriman, Tennessee, in 1890. There a wealthy real estate developer from New York, Frederick Gates, wanted to create an industrial city where alcohol was forbidden. Several thousands of acres of land in Roane County were purchased. In February 1890, three hundred lots were sold with deeds stipulating that the use of the site to manufacture, store, or sell liquor would render the deed null and void and that the property would revert to the land company. W. Calvin Dickinson, "Temperance Movement," *Tennessee Encyclopedia of History and Culture*, http://tennesseeencyclopedia.net/entry.php?rec=1302. Harriman never achieved the success envisioned by its developers. *Id.* Likewise, Cardiff, Tennessee, advertised in 1890 as "the Richest and Most Inexhaustible Coal and Iron Region in the South," was a failed project. Woodward, *Origins of the New South*, at 138

230. *East Tennessee: Historical and Biographical* (reprint) (LaCrosse, Wis.: Brookhaven Press 2001) at 429, orig. (Chattanooga, Tenn.: A.D. Smith & Co. 1893).

231. Benhart, *Appalachian Aspirations*, at 116.

232. Cooper & Terrill, *The American South*, at 487.

233. Edwards, *New Spirits*, at 85.

234. *Id.*

235. Benhart, *Appalachian Aspirations*, at 116–17. E.J. had a connection to another East Tennessee community. In 1884, the Knoxville Woolen Mills purchased the Hiwassee Manufacturing Company in the vicinity of Riceville in McMinn County. The company continued to operate until 1902, the year of E.J.'s death. The mill was important to the economic growth and development of McMinn County, and a smaller community developed around the mill known as "Sanfordville" in honor of E.J. The small town later moved nearly two miles to adjoin the Southern Railway line and the Lee Highway and became known as "Sanford." McClatchey-Gettys Farm, Nat. Reg. of Hist. Places Inventory–Nomination Form, US Dep't of the Interior, Item #8 (1982) at 2.

236. Rule, et al., *Standard History of Knoxville* at 131.

237. "Chamber of Commerce: Some Spicy Remarks Concerning Knoxville's Water Supply," *The Knoxville Journal* (Aug. 20, 1890) at 8.

238. Rule, et al., *Standard History of Knoxville* at 114.

239. "Chamber of Commerce," *The Knoxville Journal* (May 13, 1891) at 5.

240. Maguire, "The Supreme Court Justice From Knoxville," at 34; *Proceedings of the Bar and Officers of the Supreme Court of the United States*, at 45.

241. *The Knoxville Journal and Tribune* (Apr. 15, 1902) at 8.

242. "Knoxville General Hospital," Special Collections online, https://kiva.lib.utk.edu/spc.

243. Rule, et al., *Standard History of Knoxville,* at 542; Jack Neely, "Lawson McGhee," *Metro Pulse* (Knoxville, Tenn.) (July 29, 2004).

244. "U.S. Justice Edward Sanford," Tennessee History Classroom, http://tennesseehistory.com/class/Sanford.htm; Maguire, "The Supreme Court Justice From Knoxville," at 34. McGhee's daughter had died shortly after childbirth, as had Sanford's daughter Dorothy. McArthur, "Charles McClung McGhee," at 266.

245. Rule, et al., *Standard History of Knoxville* at 389.

246. "East Tennessee Female Institute," Special Collections online, https://kiva.lib.utk.edu/spc.

247. "Seniors Banqueted," *The Knoxville Journal* (May 31, 1895) at 5.

248. Cook, "Path to the High Bench," at 57.

249. 30 *Proceedings of the National Wholesale Druggists' Association in New Orleans, La.* (Nov. 1904) (Indianapolis, Ind.: Am. Printing Co. 1905) at 465.

250. Hiram Chamberlain, who originally established the business with Albers, had decided to retire. His brother William remained. Hiram was known for his progressive ideas on race. Jack Neely, "The Arby's Building, By Any Other Name," *Metro Pulse* (Knoxville, Tenn.) (Apr. 4, 2012) at 3; "Business Change," *The Knoxville Weekly Chronicle* (Jun. 5, 1872) at 8. Albers was a former Union Navy man from Cincinnati who spent much of the war in Confederate prisoner-of-war camps. Neely, "The Arby's Building, By Any Other Name," at 3.

251. In 1864, with his associate, Dr. O.F. Hill, E.J. organized the drug firm of E.J. Sanford and Company. "U.S. Justice Edward Sanford," *Tennessee History Classroom*, http://tennesseehistory.com/class/Sanford.htm; Allison, *Notable Men of Tennessee*, at 222. Dr. Hill retired in 1872.

252. The upper floor of the basement was used for the manufacture of extracts and proprietary medicines and for storage purposes. The other floor was for the stock of drugs, druggists' sundries, patent medicines, and proprietary articles, along with ready-mixed and dry paints. Six traveling salesmen, then called "drummers," were employed to be on the road in Virginia, West Virginia, North Carolina, Kentucky, and Alabama, as well as in Tennessee. Morrison, *Knoxville, Tennessee*, at 83.

253. Allison, *Notable Men of Tennessee*, at 221.

254. *Id.*

255. Mark Pendergrast, *For God, Country & Coca-Cola: The Definitive History of the Great American Soft Drink and the Company That Makes It* (2nd ed.) (New York: Basic Books 2000) at 9; Edwards, *New Spirits*, at 13.

256. Pendergrast, *For God, Country & Coca-Cola*, at 10.

257. Cooper & Terrill, *The American South*, at 465.

258. Edmund Cody Burnett, "Big Creek's Response To the Coming of the Railroad: Old Buncombe Promotes the Better Life In the Rural Community," 21 *Agricultural History* (July 1947) at 129–48.

259. Amy Geisel, "Walker Drug to Buy Knoxville Family Business Albers Inc., Will Keep Employees, Programs Here," *The Knoxville News-Sentinel* (July 8, 1994) at c-7.

260. "Looking Backward," *The Knoxville News-Sentinel* (Jan. 13, 1928) at 4.

261. Lawrence D. Tyson, *President's Report, Knoxville Woolen Mills* (Jan. 1905) (Knoxville, Tenn.: S.B. Newman & Co. 1905) at 1–4.

262. Morrison, *Knoxville, Tennessee*, at 100.

263. Rule, et al., *Standard History of Knoxville*, at 216; Allison, *Notable Men of Tennessee*, at 222.

264. Banker, *Appalachians All*, at 88–89.

265. Maguire, "The Supreme Court Justice From Knoxville," at 9.

266. *Id.*

267. McDonald & Wheeler, *Knoxville, Tennessee*, at 10–11.

268. "A Strong Company," *The Knoxville Journal* (May 4, 1888) at 1.

269. McDonald & Wheeler, *Knoxville, Tennessee*, at 11.

270. *Id.*

271. *Id.*

272. MacArthur, *Knoxville's History: An Interpretation*, at 48 (citing William J. Oliver); Wheeler, *Knoxville, Tennessee*, at 30.

273. McDonald & Wheeler, *Knoxville, Tennessee*, at 35.

274. MacArthur, *Knoxville's History: An Interpretation*, at 49.

275. Wheeler, *Knoxville, Tennessee*, at 30.

276. *Id.*; Rule, et al., *Standard History of Knoxville*, at 131.

277. Ben Morton, president of the wholesale grocery firm, H.T. Hackney Company, and Mayor of Knoxville from 1923 to 1927, developed other business interests, including banking, flour milling, and automobile dealerships. He was married to Pauline Woodruff, another one of Lutie Sanford's sisters. MacArthur, *Knoxville's History: An Interpretation*, at 51; Maguire, "The Supreme Court Justice From Knoxville," at 13.

278. Deaderick, *Heart of the Valley*, at 597–98.

279. Bell, *Circling Windrock Mountain*, at 251.

280. Deaderick, *Heart of the Valley*, at 597–98; John William Leonard, ed., *Who's Who in Finance and Banking: 1920–1922* (New York: Joseph & Sefton 1922) at 598; *Harvard College, Class of 1900, Secretary's Report*, No. 5., at 406. See "Hugh W. Sanford, Industrialist and Financier, Dies," *The Knoxville News-Sentinel* (Nov. 15, 1961) at 1.

281. "Services Held for Hugh W. Sanford," *The Knoxville News-Sentinel* (Nov. 16, 1961) at 40.

282. MacArthur, *Knoxville's History: An Interpretation*, at 51. Maguire, "The Supreme Court Justice From Knoxville," at 13.

283. MacArthur, *Knoxville's History: An Interpretation*, at 51, 52.

284. See Ross, *A Scrapbook for My Grandchildren*, at 52–53. Ross was identified as a pallbearer at Sanford's funeral. "Body of Sanford Goes to Tennessee," *The Washington Post* (Mar. 10, 1930) at 3.

285. Wheeler, *Knoxville, Tennessee*, at 31, 33.

286. Fowler Papers.

287. MacArthur, *Knoxville's History: An Interpretation*, at 60.

288. Lukens, "Portraits of Progress," at 11.

289. *Id.* at 12.

290. Albert Chavannes published the world's first sociological journal, "The Sociologist." See "Honored After Death," *The Kingsport* (Tenn.) *Times-News* (Dec. 12, 1965) at 35. He was the grandfather of a future mayor of Knoxville, Ed Chavannes, who succeeded Cas Walker in 1946. Deaderick, *Heart of the Valley*, at 627.

291. Francine C. Cary, "Albert Chavannes and the Future Commonwealth: The Utopian Novelist as Social Critic," 48 *E. Tennessee Historical Soc'y Publ'ns* (1976) at 77, 80.

292. "The Populite Meeting," *The Knoxville Journal* (Sept. 10, 1892) at 5. *See* Cecile Chavannes, "Canvassing the District," *East Tennessee Sketches* (Knoxville, Tenn. 1900) at 1.

293. "Farmer Wrote First Works on Sociology," *The Kingsport* (Tenn.) *Times-News* (July 4, 1954) at 19.

294. In addition to his shrewd business sense, Sanford's father was known for his outspoken views. Additionally, if E.J. felt unjustly treated, he was strongly inclined to retaliate. His motto was "Never forget a friend, and never let an enemy forget you." Fowler Papers. Albert Chavannes died in 1903, a year after E.J.

295. *Harvard College, Class of 1885, Baccalaureate Sermon, Class Day Oration, et al.*, at 19, 20.

CHAPTER 6

1. Burton, *Taft, Holmes, and the 1920s Court*, at 53.
2. Edwards, *New Spirits*, at 44.
3. R.W. Apple, Jr., "The Case or the Monopolistic Railroadmen," *Quarrels That Have Shaped The Constitution*, John A. Garraty, ed. (New York: Harper & Row, Publishers 1987 (rev. ed.)) at 175.
4. Burton, *Taft, Holmes, and the 1920s Court*, at 53; Pendergrast, *For God, Country & Coca-Cola*, at 108.
5. Langsdon, *Tennessee: A Political History*, at 239.
6. Anderson, "Building National Consensus," at 329 (citing Edmund Morris, *The Rise of Theodore Roosevelt* 2 (New York: Coward, McCann & Geoghegan 1979)).
7. Paul Finkelman, ed., *The Supreme Court: Controversies, Cases, and Characters from John Jay to John Roberts* (4 vols.) (ABC-CLIO 2014) at 579; Brake, *Justice in the Valley*, at 70.
8. John Hendrickson, "Governing by the Founders' Constitution, The Presidency of Warren G. Harding," Policy Study No. 08–9, Public Interest Institute (Dec. 2008) at 6–7; Theodore Roosevelt, "New Nationalism Speech," 1910. American socialism also grew as one reaction to the rapid expansion of industry in the late nineteenth century, but it was dwarfed by Populism and Progressivism, both of which found their way into the two major political parties. Marc Lendler, *Gitlow v. New York: Every Idea an Incitement* (Lawrence, Kan.: Univ. Press of Kansas 2012) at 5–6.
9. John A. Garraty, *Teddy Roosevelt: American Rough Rider* (New York: Sterling Publ'g Co., Inc. 2007) at 11–13.
10. Noone, "Edward Terry Sanford" at 35.
11. Klein, Prominent Alumni: Part III, in *Volunteer Moments*, http://trace.tennessee.edu/utk_libarcvol/1.
12. "Government Starts New Antitrust Suit; Special Counsel Engaged to Fight Fertilizer Combine," *The New York Times* (Apr. 22, 1906) at 9.
13. Fowler, "Mr. Justice Edward Terry Sanford," at 230; "Government Starts New Anti-Trust Suit; Special Counsel Engaged to Fight Fertilizer Combine," *The New York Times* (Apr. 22, 1906) at 9.
14. Fowler Papers. Because Tennessee was not a Republican stronghold, Roosevelt appointed certain state Democrats to federal positions to win over as many Democrats as possible before the 1904 election. *Id.*
15. Langsdon, *Tennessee: A Political History*, at 239.
16. *Id.*
17. Fowler Papers.
18. Cook, "Path to the High Bench," at 61–62; Fowler Papers.

19. *United States v. Virginia-Carolina Chem. Co.*, 163 F. 66, 71 (July 3, 1908).
20. *The Atlanta Constitution* (Apr. 22, 1906).
21. "A Huge Enterprise," *The American Fertilizer* (Vols. 12–13) (Ware Bros. 1900) at 14.
22. "*See* A Combine In Fertilizers," *The Minneapolis Journal* (Apr. 22, 1906) at 1.
23. Fowler, "Mr. Justice Edward Terry Sanford," at 230; Maguire, "The Supreme Court Justice From Knoxville," at 36; "Sees A Combine In Fertilizers," *The Minneapolis Journal* (Apr. 22, 1906) at 1.
24. "Government Starts New Anti-Trust Suit," *The New York Times* (Apr. 22, 1906) at 9.
25. 5 *Cotton Trade Journal* (1905) at 14; "As Regarding The 'Fertilizer Trust,'" *The Charlotte* (N. C.) *News* (Apr. 25, 1906) at 6.
26. U.S. Department of Justice, *Annual Report of the Attorney-General of the United States for the Year 1906* (Washington, D.C.: Gov. Printing Office 1906) at 9, in Cook, "Path to the High Bench," at 60; Klein, "Prominent Alumni: Part III," in *Volunteer Moments,* http://trace.tennessee.edu/utk_libarcvol/1/; Maguire, "The Supreme Court Justice From Knoxville," at 37. But *see United States v. Virginia-Carolina Chem. Co.*, 163 F. 66 (Cir. Ct. M.D. Tenn. July 3, 1908) (finding the indictment invalid and holding that "Attorney General of the United States was not authorized by law to confer upon the special assistants to the district attorney the right to conduct investigations before the grand jury, as was done in this case, and that [Mr.] Sanford . . . [was] improperly before the grand jury. . . ." *Id.* at 75).
27. 5 *Cotton Trade Journal* (1905) at 14.
28. Sandra Day O'Connor, *Out of Order: Stories From the History of the Supreme Court* (New York: Random House 2013) at 135. Roosevelt's support of reform was heavily influenced by his admiration of things as they were. In this sense he was more a conservative than a progressive. Garraty, *Teddy Roosevelt: American Rough Rider,* at 79.
29. Letter from James C. McReynolds to Attorney General Charles Bonaparte (Jan. 19, 1909), Arthur J. Morris Law Library, Special Collections Univ. of Virginia, Charlottesville, http://archives.law.virginia.edu/records/mss/85–1/digital/9099, ("McReynolds Papers").
30. Harold M. Hollingsworth, "Tennessee and the Supreme Court of the United States," 47 *E. Tennessee Historical Soc'y Pub'ns* (1975) at 12; 13 *Vanderbilt Univ. Quarterly* (Nashville, Tenn.: Vanderbilt Univ. 1913) at 206.
31. Woodward, *Origins of the New South,* at 309 (citing Meyer Jacobstein, *The Tobacco Industry in the United States* (New York: Columbia Univ. Press 1907) at 116, 117–23, 136).
32. McReynolds Papers.
33. *Id.*
34. *See* Letter From Charles J. Bonaparte to James C. McReynolds (Jan. 19, 1909), McReynolds Papers; Michael Allan Wolf, "James Clark McReynolds," in Melvin L. Urofsky, ed., *The Supreme Court Justices: A Biographical Dictionary* (New York: Garland Publ'g 1994) at 297.
35. His resignation was submitted to Sanford's former law partner, James A. Fowler, serving at that time as acting attorney general. Letter from James A. Fowler to James C. McReynolds, (Dec. 1, 1911), McReynolds Papers. Fowler had succeeded Sanford as assistant attorney general upon Sanford's appointment as a federal district court judge.
36. Russell Fowler, "Tennesseans on the United States Supreme Court," *Tenn. Bar Ass'n Journal* (Aug. 2014), http://www.tba.org/journal/tennesseans-on-the-united-states-supreme-court at 3.
37. O'Connor, *Out of Order,* at 135.
38. Phillips, *History of the Sixth Circuit,* at 64.

39. *Id.*
40. Alpheus Thomas Mason, *William Howard Taft: Chief Justice* (New York: Simon and Schuster 1964) at 164.
41. *Rules and Regulations Governing the Department of State* (1907) (Washington, D.C.: Gov't Printing Office 1907) at 5.
42. Cook, "Path to the High Bench," at 62 n.6.
43. James W. Ely & Theodore Brown, Jr., eas., *A History of the Tennessee Supreme Court*, (Knoxville, Tenn.: Univ. of Tennessee Press 2002) at 157.
44. *See* File of Edward T. Sanford, RG 60, Dep't of Justice Records, Nat'l Archives, College Park, Md.
45. Bonaparte served as attorney general from 1906 to 1909. Fowler's memoirs describe a special bond between Sanford and Bonaparte resulting from the former's role in reviving a Harvard fraternity that Bonaparte had helped organize. Cook, "Path to the High Bench," at 69 (citing Fowler Papers).
46. "Sanford, the Exact Type," *The Knoxville Journal and Tribune* (Jan. 3, 1907) at 3; "Sanford First Given U.S. Post by Roosevelt," *The Knoxville News-Sentinel* (Mar. 9, 1930) at A-6; "Justice Sanford Occupies Unique Position In Eyes of Tennesseans, Says New York World Biographer," *The Knoxville Sentinel* (May 6, 1923).
47. Maguire, "The Supreme Court Justice From Knoxville," at 40.
48. "Edward T. Sanford Is Nominated for Office," *The Knoxville Sentinel* (Jan. 3, 1907) at 9; "Edward T. Sanford Confirmed By Senate," *The Times Dispatch* (Richmond, Va.) (Jan. 10, 1907) 3; *see* U.S. Congress, Senate, *Journal of the Executive Proceedings*, 59th Cong., 2d Sess., 1907, xxxvii, 89–108.
49. Phillips, *History of the Sixth Circuit*, at 68.
50. Noone, "Edward Terry Sanford," *at* 35 (quoting Attorney General Mitchell).
51. 13 Stat. 510; Foner, *Reconstruction*, at 69.
52. "Reimbursement of Depositors of Freedman's Savings and Trust Company," H. Rpt. 1282, pt. 1 (May 6, 1910) at 13.
53. *Id.*
54. "The Freedman's Savings Bank: Good Intentions Were Not Enough: A Noble Experiment Goes Awry," http://www.occ.treas.gov/about/what-we-do/history/freedman-savings-bank.html.
55. The Treasury Annex on Pennsylvania Avenue was built on the site of the bank. "The Freedman's Bank: A Historic Place in the Financial Empowerment of African Americans," https://www.treasury.gov/connect/blog/pages/freedmans-savings-bank.aspx.
56. Langguth, *After Lincoln*, at 319.
57. "Reimbursement of Depositors of Freedman's Savings and Trust Company," at 15–16.
58. "The Freedman's Bank Bill," *The Washington* (D.C.) *Bee* (Dec. 11, 1915) at 1.
59. Cook, "Path to the High Bench," at 63.
60. "Hon. E.T. Sanford Named To Succeed Judge Clark," *The Nashville Tennessean* (May 15, 1908) at 1.
61. 206 U.S. 194 (1907).
62. 206 U.S. at 197.
63. 209 U.S. 337 (1908).
64. 209 U.S. at 339.
65. 206 U.S. 224 (1907).

66. 206 U.S. at 226.

67. "Rate Law Not Valid," *The French Broad Hustler* (N.C.)(July 25, 1907) at 7; "Conference In Secret By Glenn and Sanford at Raleigh, N.C. Today," *The Washington* (D.C.) *Times* (July 25, 1907) at 1; "Gov. Glenn Stands Firm," *The Baltimore Sun* (July 26, 1907) at 1. The 1906 Hepburn Act had strengthened the Interstate Commerce Commission by giving it the right to set railroad rates, subject to court review. Edwards, *New Spirits*, at 267.

68. Albert Nelson Marquis, ed. *Who's Who in America: A Biographical Dictionary of Notable Living Men and Women of the United States* (Chicago: A.N. Marquis & Co. 1912) at 814.

69. Woodward, *Origins of the New South*, at 382.

70. *Id.* (quoting Robert W. Winston, "The Passenger Rate War in North Carolina," in 6 *S. Atlantic Quarterly* (1907) at 346).

71. "Newspaper Specials," *The Wall Street Journal* (July 25, 1907) at 2; *The Commoner* (Lincoln, Neb.) (Aug. 2, 1907) at 9.

72. "Bank and Quotation Section," 85 *The Commercial & Financial Chronicle*, No. 2197 (New York, Aug. 3, 1907) at 1–2.

73. *The Commoner* (Lincoln, Neb.) (Aug. 2, 1907) at 9.

74. Woodward, *Origins of the New South*, at 382; Ingram, *Dixie Highway*, at 94.

75. 207 U.S. 564 (1908).

76. John Shurts, *Indian Reserved Water Rights: The Winters Doctrine In Its Social and Legal Context, 1880s-1930s* (Norman, Ok.: Univ. of Ok. Press 2000) at 3.

77. 207 U.S. at 577.

78. Shurts, *Indian Reserved Water Rights*, at 4.

79. Kennith E. Foster, "The Winters Doctrine: Historical Perspective and Future Applications of Reserved Water Rights in Arizona," 16 *Ground Water*, No. 3 (May/June 1978) at 186–87.

80. Cook, "Path to the High Bench," at 64 (citing Sanford Papers).

81. 268 U.S. 652 (1925).

82. 388 U.S. 14 (1967).

83. *See* Justice Harlan's dissents in *Hurtado v. California*, 110 U.S. 516 (1884); *Maxwell v. Dow*, 176 U.S. 581 (1900); *Twining v. New Jersey*, 211 U.S. 78 (1908).

84. 110 U.S. 516 (1884); Linda C.A. Przybyszewski, "John Marshall Harlan," in Melvin L. Urofsky, ed., *The Supreme Court Justices: A Biographical Dictionary* (New York: Garland Publ'g 1994) at 209.

85. 109 U.S. 3 (1883).

86. 163 U.S. 537 (1896).

87. *Plessy*, 163 U.S. at 559.

88. *Id.* at 560. Przybyszewski, "John Marshall Harlan," at 205–06.

89. Przybyszewski, "John Marshall Harlan," at 206.

90. *United States v. Shipp*, 203 U.S. 563 (1906).

91. *United States v. Shipp*, 214 U.S. 386 (1909); Douglas O. Linder, "The Trial of Joseph Shipp," Famous American Trials Website, Univ. of Missouri—Kansas City School of Law, http://www.law.umkc.edu/faculty/ projects/ftrials/shipp/sanford.html; Michael Webb, "God Bless You All—I Am Innocent: Sheriff Joseph Shipp, Chattanooga and the Lynching of Ed Johnson," in *Trial and Triumph, Essays in African American History*, Carroll Van West, ed. (Knoxville, Tenn.: Univ. of Tennessee Press 2001).

92. Mark Curriden, "A Supreme Case of Contempt," *ABA Journal* (June 2, 2009), http://www.abajournal.com/magazine/article/a_supreme_case_of_contempt at 1–2.

93. Judge McReynolds (no relation to Justice James C. McReynolds) remained on the bench of the Criminal Court for Hamilton County until 1921, when he was elected to the United States Congress from the Third Congressional District of Tennessee. He served in Congress until his death in 1939. Mark Curriden & Leroy Phillips, Jr., *Contempt of Court* (New York: Anchor Books 2001) at 342.

94. Curriden, "A Supreme Case of Contempt," at 2.

95. In 1906, Tennessee was one of the few states in the country that guaranteed a court-appointed lawyer to any person facing the death penalty. Curriden & Phillips, *Contempt of Court*, at 60.

96. *Id.* at 63.

97. Shepherd resigned from a circuit judgeship, stating that he "loved the battle too much" to spend his life "sitting high on a bench in a cheap robe...." *Id.* at 64; Sam D. Elliott, "The Colorful Career of Judge Lewis Shepherd," *The Times Free Press* (Chattanooga) (Apr. 20, 2014) at 45.

98. Elliott, "The Colorful Career of Judge Lewis Shepherd," *The Times Free Press* (Chattanooga) (Apr. 20, 2014) at 45.

99. Curriden, "A Supreme Case of Contempt," at 4.

100. Linder, "The Trial of Joseph Shipp et al.: An Account," at 4.

101. 214 U.S. 386, 407–08; http://www.famous-trials.com/sheriffshipp/1105-thomastells (citing W.G.M. Thomas interview with *The Chattanooga Times* (Feb. 10, 1906)).

102. Douglas O. Linder, "The Lynching of Ed Johnson," Famous American Trials Website, Univ. of Mo. -Kansas City School of Law, http://law2.umkc.edu/faculty/projects/ftrials/shipp/trialaccount.html at 5; Curriden & Phillips, *Contempt of Court*, at 144.

103. Curriden & Phillips, *Contempt of Court*, at 145.

104. Linder, "The Lynching of Ed Johnson," http://law2.umkc.edu/faculty/projects/ftrials/shipp/trialaccount.html at 5–6; Curriden & Phillips, *Contempt of Court*, at 150.

105. Linder, "The Lynching of Ed Johnson," http://law2.umkc.edu/faculty/projects/ftrials shipp/trialaccount.html at 6.

106. "Day of Doom Is Very Near," *The Chattanooga Times* (Mar. 18, 1906) at http://www.famous-trials.com/sheriffshipp/1087-dayofdoom.

107. Clark, a Democrat, had been appointed by President Grover Cleveland. Leonard, *Who's Who in America*, at 270; Phillips, *History of the Sixth Circuit*, at 122.

108. Linder, "The Lynching of Ed Johnson," http://law2.umkc.edu/faculty/projects/ftrials/shipp/trialaccount.html at 6–7; "Judge Clark Stays Johnson Execution," *The Chattanooga Times* (Mar. 12, 1906) at http://famous-trials.com/sheriffshipp/1088-johnsonexecution. The hearing was not concluded until midnight.

109. Linder, "The Lynching of Ed Johnson," http://law2.umkc.edu/faculty/projects/ftrials/shipp/trialaccount.html at 6–7.

110. Curriden & Phillips, *Contempt of Court*, at 170.

111. *Id.* at 348. Of course, because of the lynching, Parden never got the opportunity to argue the case. *Id.* The key constitutional question of federalism—the application of the Bill of Rights and the Fourteenth Amendment to state criminal courts—was rendered moot when the Johnson appeal was abated by the youth's death. *See Johnson v. Tennessee*, 214 U.S. 485 (1909).

112. Emmanuel Molyneaux Hewlett, a prominent black attorney in Washington, sponsored Parden's admission to the Supreme Court. Wendy Brown-Scott, "Important Lessons From History," 8 *Buffalo Human Rights L. Rev.* 147, 151 (2002).

113. Linder, "The Lynching of Ed Johnson," http://law2.umkc.edu/faculty/projects/ftrials/shipp/trialaccount.html at 7.

114. "The right of the people to be secure in their persons, houses, papers, and effects, against unreasonable searches and seizures, shall not be violated, and no Warrants shall issue, but upon probable cause, supported by Oath or affirmation, and particularly describing the place to be searched, and the persons or things to be seized."

115. "No person shall be held to answer for a capital, or otherwise infamous crime, unless on a presentment or indictment of a Grand Jury, except in cases arising in the land or naval forces, or in the Militia, when in actual service in time of War or public danger; nor shall any person be subject for the same offense to be twice put in jeopardy of life or limb; nor shall be compelled in any criminal case to be a witness against himself, nor be deprived of life, liberty, or property, without due process of law; nor shall private property be taken for public use, without just compensation."

116. "In all criminal prosecutions, the accused shall enjoy the right to a speedy and public trial, by an impartial jury of the State and district wherein the crime shall have been committed, which district shall have been previously ascertained by law, and to be informed of the nature and cause of the accusation; to be confronted with the witnesses against him; to have compulsory process for obtaining witnesses in his favor, and to have the Assistance of Counsel for his defense."

117. Linder, "The Lynching of Ed Johnson," http://law2.umkc.edu/faculty/projects/ftrials/shipp/trialaccount.html at 7–8.

118. *See* 214 U.S. at 412; Curriden & Phillips, *Contempt of Court*, at 196.

119. "Justice Harlan Allows Appeal of Ed Johnson," *The Chattanooga Times* (Mar. 19, 1906) at http://www.famous-trials.com/sheriffshipp/1095-newsharlam.

120. "God Bless You All—I Am Innocent," *The Chattanooga Times* (Mar. 20, 1906) at http://www.famous-trials.com/sheriffshipp/1092-newsgodbless.

121. *Id.*

122. Brake, *Justice in the Valley*, at 56.

123. *Id.*

124. Linder, "The Lynching of Ed Johnson," http://law2.umkc.edu/faculty/projects/ftrials/shipp/trialaccount.html at 8–9; Curriden & Phillips, *Contempt of Court*, at 213–14.

125. Curriden & Phillips, *Contempt of Court*, at 221.

126. "The Shipp Case: A Chronology," UMKC School of Law, http://law2.umkc.edu/faculty/projects/ftrials/shipp/chronology.html; Meredith Hindley, "Chattanooga versus the Supreme Court: The Strange Case of Ed Johnson," 35 *HUMANITIES*, No. 6 (Nov./Dec. 2014) at https://www.neh.gov/humanities/2014/novemberdecember/feature/Chattanooga-versus-the-supreme-court.

127. Linder, "The Lynching of Ed Johnson," http://law2.umkc.edu/faculty/projects/ftrials/shipp/trialaccount.html at 9–10.

128. "The Shipp Case: A Chronology," UMKC School of Law, http://law2.umkc.edu/faculty/projects/ftrials/shipp/chronology.html.

129. Brown-Scott, "Important Lessons From History," at 161; Curriden, "A Supreme Case of Contempt," at 1.

130. 203 U.S. 563 (1906).

131. Linder, "The Lynching of Ed Johnson," http://law2.umkc.edu/faculty/projects/ftrials/shipp/trialaccount.html at 10–11.

132. Curriden & Phillips, *Contempt of Court*, at 283. The Court determined that it was not a party in any sense that would create a conflict of interest because Shipp's actions were not a threat to the justices personally but only to their ruling and the authority of the Court. Because the justices were not "interested parties" in any sense that would affect their competence with regard to the case, the prosecution was allowed to proceed.

133. Linder, "The Lynching of Ed Johnson," http://law2.umkc.edu/faculty/projects/ftrials/shipp/trialaccount.html at 11; "Lynching Case Evidence," *The Washington Post* (June 3, 1907) at 9.

134. Linder, "The Lynching of Ed Johnson," http://www.law.umkc.edu/faculty/projects/ftrials/shipp/sanford.html.

135. "The Shipp Case: A Chronology," UMKC School of Law, http://law2.umkc.edu/faculty/projects/ftrials/shipp/chronology.html.

136. *Id.*

137. Elliott, "The Colorful Career of Judge Lewis Shepherd," *The Times Free Press* (Chattanooga) (Apr. 20, 2014) at 45.

138. "Sheriff Shipp's Case Will Be Re-Opened," *The Nashville Tennessean* (Mar. 19, 1908) at 8.

139. Curriden & Phillips, *Contempt of Court*, at 310; "Witnesses Missing," *The Nashville American* (Feb. 16, 1907) at 7.

140. "The Shipp Case: A Chronology," UMKC School of Law, Linder, http://law2.umkc.edu/faculty/projects/ftrials/shipp/chronology.html.

141. *Id.*

142. *Id.*

143. *Id.*

144. 214 U.S. at 423.

145. Brake, *Justice in the Valley*, at 56.

146. Linder, "The Lynching of Ed Johnson," http://law2.umkc.edu/faculty/projects/ftrials/shipp/trialaccount.html at 13–14. Justices Harlan, Holmes, Brewer, and Day joined Chief Justice Fuller's majority decision. Justices Peckham, White, and McKenna voted to acquit all defendants. Justice Moody, the former attorney general, did not participate.

147. *Id.* at 14.

148. Curriden & Phillips, *Contempt of Court*, at 349. Hutchins had earlier served in the 45th Tennessee General Assembly (18871888), representing Hamilton County. In 1887, he had introduced House Bill No. 447 to "regulate convict labor, a system that has replaced slave labor in the South." H. B. 447, 45th Tenn. General Assembly, 1st Sess. (1887). His bill, had it been considered and adopted, might have prevented an earlier event in Sanford's life, the Coal Creek Rebellion.

149. Linder, "The Lynching of Ed Johnson," http://law2.umkc.edu/faculty/projects/ftrials/shipp/trialaccount.html at 14. When he died in 1925, Shipp was buried in Forest Hills Cemetery, the site of Nevada Taylor's rape. "The Shipp Case: A Chronology," UMKC School of Law, http://law2.umkc.edu/faculty/projects/ftrials/shipp/chronology.html.

150. Law Library-American Law and Legal Information, "*et al. United States v. Shipp*: 1907–09—An Arrest Is Made, A Near Lynching And A Trial, A Guilty Verdict And Lynching, A Long Road to Justice," Vol. 1, *Great American Trials*, http://www.encyclopedia.com/.

151. "A Landmark in Habeas Corpus and Criminal Contempt," Legal History Blog (June 24, 2009), http://legalhistoryblog.blogspot.com/2009/06/landmark-in-habeas-corpus-and-criminal.html.

152. Fowler, "Mr. Justice Edward Terry Sanford," at 230.
153. *Id.*
154. "E.T. Sanford May be Made Assistant to Attorney General," *The New York Tribune* (Feb. 2, 1908) at 11. Newspapers reported that Sanford was slated to succeed Milton D. Purdy, the assistant to the attorney general. "Promotion For Sanford," *The Courier-Journal* (Louisville, Ky.) (Feb. 3, 1908) at 1.
155. Verton M. Queener, "The East Tennessee Republican Party, 1900–1914," 22 *E. Tennessee Historical Soc'y Publ'ns* 94 (1950) at 112.
156. Creekmore, *Knoxville*, at 101.
157. Cook, "Path to the High Bench," at 11. Sanford had a "major and visible" role in the visit. *Id.* at 40; "To See the President," *The Knoxville Journal and Tribune* (Sept. 7, 1902) at 4; "President Roosevelt to be Knoxville's Guest," *The Knoxville Sentinel* (Sept. 8, 1902) at 1; "President Roosevelt's Visit Successful in Spite of Rain," *The Knoxville Sentinel* (Sept. 9, 1902) at 8; Queener, "The East Tennessee Republican Party," at 112.
158. David Burner, "Edward Terry Sanford," *The Justices of the United States Supreme Court, 1789–1969: Their Lives and Major Opinions*, Vol. 3, Leon Friedman and Fred L. Israel, eds. (New York: Chelsea House Publishers 1969) at 2203. Drawing support from blacks in agricultural (and secessionist) Middle and West Tennessee and poor whites in industrial (and Unionist) East Tennessee, the Republican Party was a strong minority party throughout the 1880s. Shapiro, *A New South Rebellion*, at 123.
159. "Col E.J. Sanford," *The Knoxville Journal* (June 17, 1896) at 1; E.J. also served as a Tennessee delegate to the GOP National Convention of 1880. Stanley J. Folmsbee & Marguerite B. Hamer, eds., "The Presidential Election of 1896 As Reflected in the Correspondence of Charles McClung McGhee," 22 *E. Tennessee Historical Soc'y Publ'ns* 158 (1950) at 160; Cook, "Path to the High Bench," at 8.
160. *Id.*
161. Allison, *Notable Men of Tennessee*, at 222; Cook, "Path to the High Bench," at 11. Queener described the Sanfords as Knoxville's "richest family." Queener, "The East Tennessee Republican Party, 1900–1914," at 112.
162. Cook, "Path to the High Bench," at 40.
163. "Knoxville: Preparing To Receive President Roosevelt," *The Courier-Journal* (Louisville, Ky.) (Sept. 3, 1902) at 5.
164. Maguire, "The Supreme Court Justice From Knoxville," at 39.
165. Fowler, "Mr. Justice Edward Terry Sanford," at 230.

CHAPTER 7

1. Letter from Charles W. Dabney to Theodore Roosevelt (Jan. 30, 1903), Manuscript Division, Library of Congress, Washington, D.C.; Theodore Roosevelt Papers, http://www.theodorerooseveltcenter.org/research/Digital-Library/Record.aspx?libID=o40261 ("Roosevelt Papers").
2. Letter from Theodore Roosevelt to Charles W. Dabney (Feb. 2, 1903), Roosevelt Papers.
3. Phillips, *History of the Sixth Circuit*, at 21.
4. Cook, "Path to the High Bench," at 69.
5. *Id.* at 70.
6. "Lead Prosecutor in the Shipp Case," http://www.famous-trials.com/sheriffshipp/1066-sanford; Cook, "Path to the High Bench," at 70. The National Archives contain the handwritten note signed "H." Dep't of Justice Records, RG 60, Nat'l Archives, College Park, Md.

7. Langsdon, *Tennessee: A Political History*, at 245.

8. Cook, "Path to the High Bench," at 70 (citing E.E. Patton, "How Judge Edward Terry Sanford Became a Member of the United States Supreme Court" (Univ. of Tenn. Library, Special Collections) at 2; Fowler Papers.

9. *The Courier-Journal* (Louisville, Ky.) (Feb. 18, 1903) at 8.

10. Langsdon, *Tennessee: A Political History*, at 226–32.

11. Letter from William Howard Taft to Horace H. Lurton (Apr. 13, 1908), Horace H. Lurton Papers, Manuscript Division, Box 1, Folder 3 "Alphabetical Correspondence P-W, 1875–1914," Library of Congress, Washington, D.C. ("Lurton Papers").

12. Letter from William Howard Taft to Horace Lurton (Mar. 30, 1908), Lurton Papers.

13. *Id.*

14. Maguire, "The Supreme Court Justice From Knoxville," at 45.

15. *Id.* at 45–46.

16. Fowler Papers.

17. "Proceedings in Memory of Mr. Justice Sanford," 285 U.S. xxxvii (1931). Frierson was mayor of Chattanooga when Ed Johnson was hanged from the Walnut Street Bridge. Frierson's legal mentor was Lewis Shepherd, who served as one of Ed Johnson's defense attorneys. Frierson later served as assistant attorney general and solicitor general in President Woodrow Wilson's administration. "1901–1905 William Little Frierson," http://Chattanooga.gov.

18. Fowler, "Mr. Justice Edward Terry Sanford," at 230 ("[T]he President was ready to appoint him at any time he might express a willingness to accept the position."); Klein, "Prominent Alumni: Part III," in *Volunteer Moments,* http://trace.tennessee.edu/utk_libarcvol/1/; Cook, "Path to the High Bench," at 70.

19. "Edward T. Sanford Nominated to be Federal Judge," *The Evening Star* (Washington, D.C.) (May 14, 1908) at 2.

20. Noone, "Edward Terry Sanford," at 36; Cook, "Path to the High Bench," at 71.

21. Cook, "Path to the High Bench," at 71. While on the bench, Sanford observed an almost monastic seclusion. He refused to associate socially with members of the bar so that he might avoid criticism of favoritism or partiality. Ragan, "Mr. Justice Sanford," at 77.

22. Maguire, "The Supreme Court Justice From Knoxville," at 43.

23. "Justice E.T. Sanford, U.S. Supreme Court, Honored By Bar Here," *The Nashville Tennessean* (Feb. 14, 1923) at 1, 2.

24. "Proceedings in Memory of Mr. Justice Sanford," 285 U.S. xxxvii (1931).

25. Letter from Edward T. Sanford to William Frierson (June 2, 1920), Records of the US District Court for the Eastern District of Tennessee (21.45.1, 21.45.2) and Middle District of Tennessee (21.45.3, 21.45.4), Atlanta, Ga. ("District Court Files").

26. Fowler Papers; Patton, "How Judge Edward Terry Sanford Became a Member of the United States Supreme Court," at 3.

27. Maguire, "The Supreme Court Justice From Knoxville," at 45.

28. Fowler Papers. According to Fowler, Roosevelt asked him to make a commitment that he would not be antagonistic toward labor. Fowler felt that this request was inappropriate and remained silent. *Id.*

29. Maguire, "The Supreme Court Justice From Knoxville," at 44. To succeed Sanford at the Department of Justice, President Roosevelt selected Fowler, who went on to serve under five Presidents: Theodore Roosevelt, William H. Taft, Woodrow Wilson, Warren G. Harding, and Calvin Coolidge. After his federal career ended, Fowler was elected to Knoxville's city council

and served as mayor from 1927 to 1929. He received the Republican nomination for the United States Senate in 1928 but was defeated in the general election by Memphis Democrat Kenneth McKellar, close friend and political mentor of US Representative Hubert Fisher, Sanford's brother-in-law. Deaderick, *Heart of the Valley*, at 523–524; Ray Hill, "A Feudin' Son of Tennessee: Kenneth McKellar, Chapter 9," *Knoxfocus.com* (July 22, 2012). Fowler also served as a member of the University of Tennessee board of trustees with Sanford and was president of the board of trustees for his alma mater, Tennessee Wesleyan College. Fowler's legal work was referenced in the case sustaining the constitutionality of the Tennessee Valley Authority Act, *Ashwander v. TVA*, 297 U.S. 288 (1936). "James A. Fowler, Ex-U.S. Attorney," *The New York Times* (Nov. 19, 1955) at 17. Fowler passed away in 1955. *Id.*

30. "Federal Judge Named," *Palestine* (Tex.) *Daily Herald* (May 14, 1908) at 6. Roosevelt nominated Sanford on May 14, 1908. He was confirmed by the Senate on May 18, 1908. US Congress, Senate, 60th Cong., 1st. Sess., May 18, 1908, 38 *Journal of the Executive Proceedings*, at 405. He received his commission the same day.

31. "Edward T. Sanford Nominated to be Federal Judge," *The Evening Star* (Washington, D.C.) (May 14, 1908) at 2. Sanford resigned as assistant attorney general effective at the close of business on June 16, 1908. Memorandum, Charles Bonaparte, Attorney General (June 15, 1908), District Court Files.

32. Fowler, "Mr. Justice Edward Terry Sanford," at 230.

33. Judith A. Baer, "Edward Douglass White," in *The Supreme Court Justices: A Biographical Dictionary*, Melvin I. Urofsky, ed. (New York: Garland Publ'g 1994) at 525.

34. *Id.*

35. Sanford Papers.

37. "Judge Sanford Is Installed," *The Knoxville Sentinel* (June 17, 1908) at 10; "Judge Sanford Sworn In Nashville," *The Knoxville Journal and Tribune* (June 18, 1908) at 8; *Deut.* 1:16–17 (KJV).

38. Edward T. Sanford, Address to the Tennessee Bar Association Annual Meeting (June 1923); Sanford Papers.

39. Letter from Horace Lurton to Edward T. Sanford (May 20, 1908), Sanford Papers. Lurton's son-in-law, Horace Van Deventer, was clerk for the Eastern District during Sanford's entire judgeship. Cook, "Path to the High Bench," at 125, 172.

40. Letter from Horace Lurton to Edward T. Sanford (May 20, 1908), Sanford Papers.

41. "United States Circuit and District Courts in Tennessee," H. Rpt. 1860 (Jan. 15, 1909) at 1–2.

42. *Id.*

43. *Id.*

44. *Id.* Sanford further related that "[t]he intervals between the different terms of court at the same places are not now always equally divided into two periods of six months." *Id.* At the time Sanford was elevated to the district court, a reporter noted that Tennessee congressmen were continuing the push for another federal judgeship in Tennessee. "Hon. E.T. Sanford Named To Succeed Judge Clark," *The Nashville Tennessean* (May 15, 1908) at 1.

45. Klein, Prominent Alumni: Part III, in *Volunteer Moments,* http://trace.tennessee.edu/utk_libarcvol/1.

46. Ragan, "Mr. Justice Sanford," at 77.

47. Laska, "Mr. Justice Sanford and the Fourteenth Amendment," at 217.

48. *Id.*

49. Fowler, "Mr. Justice Edward Terry Sanford," at 230–31.

50. Laska, "Mr. Justice Sanford and the Fourteenth Amendment," at 218.

51. Fowler, "Mr. Justice Edward Terry Sanford," at 231. John W. Warrington of Ohio replaced Ohioan John K. Richards in 1909. In 1910, Loyal Edwin Knappen from Michigan was chosen to assume the seat vacated by Lurton. Arthur Carter Denison from Michigan was nominated by Taft to take the seat of Henry F. Severens in 1911. Phillips, *History of the Sixth Circuit*, at 21.

52. "All Want Sanford," *The Cincinnati Enquirer* (Dec. 19, 1909) at 5.

53. "At the White House," *The New York Tribune* (Jan. 6, 1910) at 6. Both senators were former Democratic governors of the state.

54. "Sanford For Judge," *The Evening Star* (Washington, D.C.) (Jan. 4, 1910) at 2.

55. Fowler, "Mr. Justice Edward Terry Sanford," at 231. Once President Wilson took office, it was not expected that a Republican would be considered. *Id.*

56. *Utica* (N.Y.) *Herald-Dispatch* (Nov. 4, 1909) at 2.

57. Cook, "Path to the High Bench," at 123.

58. Letter from Edward T. Sanford to Jacob M. Dickinson (Aug. 30, 1909), William H. Taft Papers, Manuscript Division, Library of Congress, Washington, D.C. ("Taft Papers"). Dickinson sent a letter to Taft to inform him of Sanford's change of heart. *Id.* The judge nominated by Taft to the Court of Customs Appeals—William Hunt, a district court judge from Montana—called the position "boring work." Shurts, *Indian Reserved Water Rights*, at 160.

59. Letter from Horace Lurton to Edward T. Sanford (Sept. 24, 1909), Sanford Papers.

60. "Plea Made for Another District Judge in Tennessee," *The Nashville Tennessean* (July 3, 1916) at 2. Tennessee had ninety-six counties until 1919, when James County, originally created from a small portion of Bradley County and the eastern third of Hamilton County in 1871, went bankrupt and was annexed into Hamilton County. Ooltewah was the county seat of James County. "James County, Tennessee, Tennessee's Lost County, www.hctgs.org/James_County _main.htm.

61. 1 Stat. 73 (Sept. 24, 1789).

62. "Historical Background," United States District Court for the Middle District of Tennessee, http://www.tnmd.uscourts.gov/historical_background_0.

63. *See* Federal Judicial Center, "Courts of the Federal Judiciary: U.S. Circuit Courts and the Federal Judiciary," http://www.fjc.gov/history/courts/u.s.-circuit-courts-and-federal-judiciary.

64. 1 Stat. 496 (Jan. 31, 1797); Susan Navarro Smelcer, "Supreme Court Justices: Demographic Characteristics, Professional Experience, and Legal Education, 1789–2010" (Congressional Research Service 2010) at 16.

65. Smelcer, "Supreme Court Justices," at 15–16.

66. *Id.* at 16.

67. *Id.* (citing Federal Judicial Center, "Courts of the Federal Judiciary: U.S. Circuit Courts and the Federal Judiciary").

68. 42 Stat. 837 (Sept. 14, 1922); Brake, *Justice in the Valley*, at xi, 3, 12, 24, 49; Phillips, *History of the Sixth Circuit*, at 33–34.

69. "Edward Terry Sanford,' http://www.fjc.gov/history/judges/Sanford-edward-terry.

70. *Proceedings of the Bar and Officers of the Supreme Court of the United States* ("Resolution Adopted by the Knox County Bar Ass'n") at 44; "Edward Terry Sanford," 4 *Journal Nat'l Ass'n Referees Bankr.* at 91.

71. "Wildcat Still Numerous: Federal Court Cookeville Docket Heaviest in History," *The Nashville Tennessean* (Nov. 8, 1919) at 7; "Plea Made For Another District Judge in Tennessee,"

The Nashville Tennessean (July 3, 1916) at 2. Sanford was "never ... able to hold court [in Winchester, Tennessee] because of his docket and his inability to give the time required to the courts" at the other locations. *Hearings Before the Committee On the Judiciary, House of Representatives, Sixty-Sixth Congress, Second Session on Tennessee-S.661*, Dec. 9, 1919 (Washington: Government Printing Office 1920) at 5.

72. "Edward Terry Sanford," 4 *Journal Nat'l Ass'n Referees Bankr.* at 91.

73. *Proceedings of the Bar and Officers of the Supreme Court of the United States*, ("Resolution Adopted by the Knox County Bar Ass'n") at 44.

74. 28 U.S.C. § 292(a).

75. Ragan, "Mr. Justice Sanford," at 77.

76. John B. Owens, "The Clerk, The Thief, His Life as a Baker: Ashton Embry and the Supreme Court Leak Scandal," 27 *Journal of Supreme Court History* 14 (Mar. 2002) at 15.

77. *The Tampa Tribune* (June. 9, 1912) at 12.

78. Owens, "The Clerk, The Thief, His Life as a Baker," at 15; *See* Stenographer Files for Judge Edward T. Sanford, RG 60, Stack Area 230, Nat'l Archives, College Park, Md.

79. Owens, "The Clerk, The Thief, His Life as a Baker," at 15 (quoting letter from Ashton F. Embry to a Mr. Sorinborger) (June 28, 1908), Appointment Papers for Departmental Positions, RG 60, Stack Area 230, Nat'l Archives College Park, Md.

80. *Id.*

81. Clare Cushman, "Fountain Pens and Typewriters: Supreme Court Stenographers and Law Clerks, 1910–1940," 41 *Journal of Supreme Court History* (Mar. 2016), http://onlinelibrary.wiley.com/doi/10.1111/jsch.12092/full at 16; Owens, "The Clerk, The Thief, His Life As a Baker," at 15. While serving in that position with Justice McKenna, Embry became embroiled in a scandal involving his purported role in leaking information on Supreme Court decisions. Prosecutors alleged that the information was used to speculate on the stock market. John B. Owens, "The Clerk, the Thief, His Life as a Baker: Ashton Embry and the Supreme Court Leak Scandal of 1919," 95 *Northwestern Univ. Law Rev.* 271, No. 1 (2000) at 271–308; Todd L. Peppers, *Courtiers of the Marble Palace: The Rise and Influence of the Supreme Court Law Clerk* (Stanford, Cal.: Stanford Univ. Press 2006) at 60. *See also* "Alleged 'Leaks' in Supreme Court," *The New York Times* (Dec. 16, 1919) at 1; "'Leak' Rumor Probed," *The Washington* (D.C.) *Post* (Dec. 16, 1919) at 5. Newspaper reporters described "an amazing conspiracy to interfere with the orderly processes of the supreme court of the United States by obtaining advance information regarding decisions and making use of the information for speculative purposes on Wall Street." "Indict Four for Fraud On Court," *The Salt Lake Telegram* (Apr. 1, 1920) at 1. Embry and three others were charged in indictments with conspiracy to defraud the United States of its right of secrecy surrounding opinions of the Supreme Court prior to public announcement of the Court's decision. The grand jury report cited Embry as furnishing a "tip" on the Court's decision in *United States v. Southern Pacific Company*, whereby the other defendants were able to sell "short" five hundred shares of Southern Pacific stock at a profit of $1,412.50. "Four Indicted for High Court Leak," *The Alton* (Ill.) *Evening Telegraph* (Apr. 1, 1920) at 1. The indictment was sustained in the court of appeals. "Indictment Is Sustained in U.S. Court 'Leak' Case," *The Pittsburgh* (Pa.) *Post-Gazette* (July. 28, 1921) at 1. An appeal to the United States Supreme Court was denied. Ultimately, Embry never faced trial, and the charges were dismissed. The case was weak from the start because the government's informant was unreliable. In addition, insider trading was not yet illegal and uncertainty existed about whether Embry's conduct constituted a crime. Counsel for Embry contended that while his action showed "reprehensible conduct, a

deplorable and regrettable lack of regard for the proprieties and ethics," he had not committed a felony. "Supreme Court Leak Gamble Case Argued," *The Rockford* (Ill.) *Republic* (June 10, 1921) at 18. So, while "leaking a Court opinion early violated the Court's customs," it did not violate any statute. "Ashton's Ashes," *Law.com* (Aug. 13, 2001), http://www.truthinjustice.org/sc-shiftdp .htm. One of the investigators on the case was J. Edgar Hoover, the future head of the Federal Bureau of Investigation. *Id.*

82. *Tennessee Encyclopedia of History and Culture*, http://tennesseeencyclopedia.net/entry .php?rec=1170; http://www.law.umkc.edu/faculty/projects/ftrials/shipp/sanford.html.

83. Ragan, "Mr. Justice Sanford," at 77.

84. *Id.* He served unostentatiously but in a manner that won him respect and esteem. *Id.*

85. "Former Secretary Recalls Sanford's Intimate Traits," *The Knoxville Journal* (Mar. 9, 1930) at 7-A.

86. Noone, "Edward Terry Sanford" at 37.

87. *Id.* at 36–37 (quoting Arthur C. Dore). After Sanford was elevated to the Supreme Court, Dore served as secretary for Judge George C. Taylor in the Eastern District of Tennessee.

88. Laska, "Mr. Justice Sanford and the Fourteenth Amendment," at 217 (quoting "A Consideration of Some of Mr. Justice Sanford's Opinions as Federal District Judge," 1 *New York Law Rev.* 1 No. 4 (Apr. 1923) at 187).

89. Cook, "Path to the High Bench," at 104.

90. Green, "Some Judges of the United States District Courts of Tennessee (1878–1939)," at 236.

91. Cook, "Path to the High Bench," at 105 n.81.

92. Ragan, "Mr. Justice Sanford," at 77. He was deliberate and unemotional. *Id.*

93. *Id.*

94. Fowler, "Mr. Justice Edward Terry Sanford," at 230. Knoxville attorney John W. Green observed that he "never knew a more conscientious, careful, and painstaking judge than Judge Sanford." Green, "Some Judges of the United States District Courts of Tennessee (1878–1939)," at 236.

95. Fowler, "Mr. Justice Edward Terry Sanford," at 230.

96. *Id.*

97. *Id.*

98. Ragan, "Mr. Justice Sanford," at 77.

99. Laska, "Mr. Justice Sanford and the Fourteenth Amendment," at 217; David Burner, "Edward Terry Sanford," in *The Justices of the United States Supreme Court, 1789–1969: Their Lives and Major Opinions*, Vol. 3, Leon Friedman & Fred L. Israel, eds. (New York: Chelsea House Publishers 1969) at 2204.

100. Cook, "Path to the High Bench," at 119.

101. "Mountaineer Given Help By Sanford," *The Knoxville News-Sentinel* (Mar. 9, 1930) at A-6.

102. *Proceedings of the Bar and Officers of the Supreme Court of the United States*, at 22–23 (remarks of Charles N. Burch).

103. Cook, "Path to the High Bench," at 84.

104. *The Nashville Tennessean* (Oct. 2, 1913) at 8.

105. *Id.*

106. Noone, "Edward Terry Sanford," at 37. Sanford also "was extremely particular for the welfare of jurors and witnesses and insisted [that] a high degree of courtesy and consideration for others should be maintained in his court." *Proceedings of the Bar and Officers of the Supreme*

Court of the United States, at 22. He was "helpful and kind" to "youthful and inexperienced practitioners." *Id.*

107. Noone, "Edward Terry Sanford," at 36–37 (1938) (quoting A.C. Dore). Noone was a member of the Chattanooga Bar. "Justice Sanford's Death Casts Shadow Over Knoxville," *The Knoxville Journal* (Mar. 9, 1930) at 7-A.

108. George F. Milton, Jr., "Sanford-Neither Radical Nor Reactionary," *The Outlook* (Feb. 14, 1923) at 299–300.

109. *The Chattanooga Times* (Nov. 21, 1922) at 4.

110. "He Aimed For the Senate, But Landed in the Supreme Court," *Current Opinion* (Apr. 23, 1923) at 411. The article's title refers to an alleged discussion between Sanford and a University of Tennessee classmate, Dana Harmon, over whether a certain measure should be enacted into law. Sanford purportedly declared, "And when I go to the United States Senate I'll introduce and pass it." Harmon replied, "Yes, and by the eternal, I'll veto it." Cook, "Path to the High Bench," at 62.

111. Fowler Papers.

112. Cook, "Path to the High Bench," at 107 (Cook's interviews with Sanford's nephews, Alfred F. Sanford and Hugh W. Sanford, Jr. (1974)).

113. *Id.* at 107 n.88.

114. *Id.* at 107.

115. Laska, "Mr. Justice Sanford and the Fourteenth Amendment," at 217; Cook, "Path to the High Bench," at 101.

116. Laska, "Mr. Justice Sanford and the Fourteenth Amendment," at 217.

117. Edward T. Sanford, Address to the Tennessee Bar Association Annual Meeting (June 1923), Sanford Papers.

118. Laska, "Mr. Justice Sanford and the Fourteenth Amendment," at 217.

119. Ragan, "Mr. Justice Sanford," at 77.

120. *Id.* (quoting George F. Milton, Jr., "The New Justice from Tennessee," *The Independent* (Feb. 17, 1923) at 117). *See* "Justice Sanford Described As a Liberal Conservative," *The Evening Star* (Washington, D.C.) (Feb. 12, 1923) at 8. Cook opined that Sanford generally deferred to regulatory authorities and closely adhered to statutory language and congressional intent. Cook, "Path to the High Bench," at 113.

121. Cook, "Path to the High Bench," at 119.

122. *Id.* at 116.

123. 287 F. 406 (M.D. Tenn. 1921).

124. 177 F. 726 (Cir. Ct. M.D. Tenn. 1910).

125. "Postal Wins A Suit," *The New York Times* (Apr. 2, 1910); "Injunction For Postal Telegraph," *The Nashville Tennessean* (Apr. 2, 1910) at 3.

126. 191 F. 431 (E.D. Tenn. 1911).

127. James Harvey Young, "Three Southern Food and Drug Cases," 49 *Journal of S. History* (Feb. 1903) at 5.

128. "The Great Coca Cola Trial," (Part 1) *Providentia* (Oct. 31, 2010), http://drvitelli.typepad.com/providentia/20/7/05/the-great-coca-cola-trial.html at 2; Pendergrast, *For God, Country & Coca-Cola*, at 26.

129. Brake, *Justice in the Valley*, at 73–74.

130. *Id.* at 74.

131. "The Great Coca Cola Trial," (Part 1) at 2. By comparison, an 8-oz. cup of coffee (black) has 95 milligrams of caffeine. An 8.3 oz. Red Bull contains 76 milligrams of caffeine. "Five Common Caffeine Myths Busted," http://abcnews.go.com/GMA/coffee-myths-busted-caffeine/story?id=5552790 (Aug. 11, 2008).

132. Pendergrast, *For God, Country & Coca-Cola*, at 108–09.

133. "The Great Coca Cola Trial," (Part 1) at 2. Dr. Wiley was recognized as "the father of the Pure Food and Drug Act of 1906, universally known as "Dr. Wiley's Law." Pendergrast, *For God, Country & Coca-Cola* at 111; Oscar E. Anderson, Jr., *The Health of a Nation: Harvey W. Wiley and the Fight for Pure Food* (Chicago: Univ. of Chicago Press 1958) at 1–15, 67.

134. *The Great Coca Cola Trial," (Part 1) at 2.*

135. Young, "Three Southern Food and Drug Cases," at 10.

136. *Id.*

137. Brake, *Justice in the Valley*, at 75.

138. Earnest Sutherland Bates, *The Story of the Supreme Court* (Fred B. Rothman & Co. 1982) at 270–71.

139. Pendergrast, *For God, Country & Coca-Cola*, at 117.

140. Roger M. Grace, "High Court Rules on Seizure of Coca-Cola as Contraband," *Metropolitan News-Enterprise* (Los Angeles, Cal.)(Feb. 9, 2006) at 11.

141. Pendergrast, *For God, Country & Coca-Cola*, at 117.

142. Brake, *Justice in the Valley*, at 76.

143. Pendergrast, *For God, Country & Coca-Cola*, at 116–17; Brake, *Justice in the Valley*, at 72–73.

144. Pendergrast, *For God, Country & Coca-Cola*, at 118.

145. *Id.*

146. 191 F. at 439; Grace, "High Court Rules on Seizure of Coca-Cola as Contraband," at 11 (quoting *The Atlanta Constitution* (April 8, 1911, and April 9, 1911)). In a 1912 case, Sanford found that the Coca-Cola Company had "shown a valid trade-mark in the words 'Coca-Cola.'" *Coca-Cola Co. v. Nashville Syrup Co.*, 200 F. 153, 155 (D.C. Tenn. 1912).

147. 191 F. at 438; Pendergrast, *For God, Country & Coca-Cola*, at 119.

148. 191 F. at 438.

149. Grace, "High Court Rules on Seizure of Coca-Cola as Contraband," at 11 (quoting *The Atlanta Constitution* (Apr. 8, 1911 and Apr. 9, 1911)).

150. 215 F. 535 (6th Cir. 1914).

151. 241 U.S. 265 (1916).

152. Pendergrast, *For God, Country & Coca-Cola*, at 121.

153. *Id.*

154. *Id.*

155. Young, "Three Southern Food and Drug Cases," at 18.

156. Mary Frances Berry, *My Face Is Black Is True: Callie House and the Struggle for Ex-Slave Reparations* (New York: Vintage Press 2005) at 4.

157. Mary F. Berry, "Reparations for Freedmen, 1890–1916: Fraudulent Practices or Justice Deferred?" Vol. 57, No. 3, *Journal of Negro History* (July 1972) at 223.

158. *Id.*

159. "Pensions For Freedmen, Etc.," 56th Cong. 1st Sess., S. Rpt. No. 75 (Jan. 16, 1900).

160. Berry, "Reparations For Freedmen," at 225.

161. *Id.* at 226.

162. *Id.* at 228; "'Slave Pension' Scheme Exposed," *The Nashville Tennessean* (Aug. 4, 1916) at 3.

163. Berry, "Reparations For Freedmen," at 228.

164. *Id.* at 228–29.

165. *Id.* at 229 (citing No. 521, U.S. Dist. Ct., M. D. Tenn. 1916).

166. "Aunt Callie, Head of Ex-Slave Relief Body, Ready for Trial," *The Nashville Tennessean* (Oct. 9, 1917) at 4; "Aunt Callie Was Whole Cheese In Ex-Slave Pension Body," *The Nashville Tennessean* (Oct. 10, 1917) at 5.

167. Berry, *My Face Is Black Is True*, at 195.

168. "Callie House Gets One-Year Sentence," *The Nashville Tennessean* (Oct. 13, 1917) at 11.

169. Berry, *My Face Is Black Is True*, at 195–96.

170. *The Nashville Tennessean* (Apr. 14, 1909) at 4.

171. Berry, *My Face Is Black Is True*, at 196.

172. *Id.* at 199

173. "Reimbursement of Depositors of Freedman's Savings and Trust Company," H. Rpt. 1282, pt. 1 (May 6, 1910) at 14.

174. Berry, *My Face Is Black Is True*, at 203; "Callie House Gets One-Year Sentence," *The Nashville Tennessean* (Oct. 13, 1917) at 11.

175. Berry, *My Face Is Black Is True*, at 183.

176. Fisher was married to Sanford's sister Louise.

177. "Stern Court Will Mete Out Justice," *The Nashville Tennessean* (Apr. 7, 1911) at 9.

178. *Id.*; "Negro Pension Attorney Sent to Federal Prison for Forging Money Order," *The Nashville Tennessean* (Apr. 13, 1911) at 5.

179. *Id.*

180. *Id.*

181. James O. Nall, *The Tobacco Night Riders of Kentucky and Tennessee: 1905—1909* (Nashville, Tenn.: McClanahan Publ'g House 1991) (Louisville, Ky.: Standard Press 1939) at 104–19.

182. *Id.*

183. "Witness Tells Alleged Secrets of Night Riders," *The Nashville Tennessean* (Oct. 28, 1911) at 12; "New Decision In Robertson Co. Night Rider Case," *The Nashville Tennessean* (Apr. 19, 1912) at 16; *Menees v. Matthews*, 197 F. 633 (M.D. Tenn. 1912).

184. Rick Gregory, "Beliefs of Their Fathers: Violence, Religion, and the Black Patch War, 1904–1914," *Border States: Journal of the Kentucky-Tennessee American Studies Ass'n*, No. 9 (1993), https://spider.georgetowncollege.edu/htallant/border/bs9/gregory.htm.

185. Rick Gregory, "The Black Patch War," *Tennessee Encyclopedia of History and Culture*, https://tennesseeencyclopedia.net/entry.php?rec=95.

186. Christopher Waldrep, *Night Riders: Defending Community in the Black Patch, 1890–1915* (Durham, N.C.: Duke Univ. Press 1993) at 85.

187. Bill Cunningham, *On Bended Knees: The True Story of the Night Rider Tobacco War in Kentucky and Tennessee* (Nashville, Tenn.: McClanahan Publ'g House 1983) at 93.

188. "Tobacco Raisers Made Defendants," *The Nashville Tennessean* (July 16, 1910) at 3.

189. Cunningham, *On Bended Knees*, at 92, 188; "Witness Tells Alleged Secrets of Night Riders," *The Nashville Tennessean* (Oct. 28, 1911) at 12.

190. "Argument For New Trial," *The Galveston* (Tex.) *Daily News* (Dec. 3, 1911) at 9; "Plaintiff In Night Rider Case Awarded $15,000.00 Damages," *The Nashville Tennessean* (Nov. 4, 1911) at 1.

191. "New Decision In Robertson Co. Night Rider Case," *The Nashville Tennessean* (Apr. 19, 1912) at 16; Donald Paine, "The Black Patch Tobacco War Trials," 42 *Tennessee Bar Journal* 24

(Sept. 2006). Prior to the *Menees* trial, on July 10, 1907, Special Assistant Attorney General James C. McReynolds filed on behalf of the Department of Justice a lawsuit charging James B. Duke and twenty-eight of his associates with violating the Sherman Antitrust Act of 1890 with the tobacco monopoly. Duke is now best remembered for endowing Duke University and the first rate medical facility at the school. Prior to Duke's death, an extensive search ensued for the first professor of medicine. The physician finally selected was an infectious disease specialist at Johns Hopkins with two degrees from Harvard. He had previously served ten years at the Rockefeller Institute for Medical Research, where he had been a member of an elite research team that discovered the cause of infantile paralysis. His name was Dr. Harold L. Amoss, son of David Amoss, a Kentucky physician and the Night Rider leader. Cunningham, *On Bended Knees*, at 91–92, 211–13.

192. "Fight On 'Jim Crow' Cars," *The Washington* (D.C.) *Herald* (Jan. 22, 1911) at 4.

193. Thomas, *Lawyering for the Railroad*, at 129.

194. Ayers, *The Promise of the New South*, at 17.

195. Thomas, *Lawyering for the Railroad*, at 137.

196. "Fight On 'Jim Crow' Cars," *The Washington* (D.C.) *Herald* (Jan. 22, 1911) at 4; "Jim Crow Cars Put Under Ban," *The Atlanta Constitution* (Jan. 22, 1911) at 3.

197. "Jim Crow Cars Put Under Ban," *The Atlanta Constitution* (Jan. 22, 1911) at 3.

198. "Must Be No Discrimination," *The New York Age* (Feb. 2, 1911); "Editorial," *The Chicago Defender* (Apr. 22, 1911) at 3.

199. "Judge David McKendree Key," United States District Court for the Middle Dist. of Tennessee, http://www.fjc.gov/history/judges/key-david-mckendree.

200. Cartwright, *The Triumph of Jim Crow*, at 166.

201. *Id.* at 167.

202. *Id.* (quoting David M. Key, "The Legal and Political Status of the Negro," 4 *Proceedings of the Annual Session of the Bar Association of Tennessee* (Nashville 1885) at 188–95).

203. James B. Jones, Jr., "The Baroness and the Lieutenant: Love and Espionage in War-Time Chattanooga, 1917–1918," *Every Day in Tennessee History*, http://www.netowne.com/historical/tennessee/baroness.htm at 1; "Prosperity, Depression, and War, 1921 to 1945," Robert H. Zieger, ed., *Encyclopedia of U.S. Political History*, Vol. 5 (Washington, D.C.: CQ Press 2010) at 66–67.

204. Her father was German-American Wilhelm Pickhardt, a New York millionaire. Robenalt, *The Harding Affair*, at 10.

205. Opened in 1904, Fort Oglethorpe saw many soldiers pass through during World War I, including John J. Pershing and Dwight Eisenhower. The fort was closed in 1946. "Remembering Fort Oglethorpe," *The Chattanoogan.com*, http://www.chattanoogan.com/2003/7/10/38548/Remembering-Fort-Oglethorpe.aspx.

206. Jones, "The Baroness and the Lieutenant, at 2.

207. *Id.* at 2, 6, 7.

208. "Baroness Zollner Held Without Bail," *The Atlanta Constitution* (Dec. 25, 1917) at 2; "No Bail For Baroness," *The Washington* (D.C.) *Post* (Dec. 25, 1917) at 3.

209. Robenalt, *The Harding Affair*, at 162.

210. *Id.*

211. *Id.* at 233–34.

212. *Id.* at 234–35.

213. "Habeas Corpus Filed By Baroness Zollner," *The Nashville Tennessean* (Jan. 3, 1918) at 5.

214. Jones, "The Baroness and the Lieutenant, at 8–9.

215. *Id.* at 9.

216. Robenalt, *The Harding Affair*, at 309; "Baroness Zollner Is Granted Freedom," *The Atlanta Constitution* (Jan. 18, 1918) at 12; "Zollner Released On Bail In Knoxville," *The Nashville Tennessean* (Jan. 18, 1918) at 8.

217. Robenalt, *The Harding Affair*, at 333.

218. "Oil Stories and Histories: Scandal: A Short History of the Teapot Dome Affair," http://oilstorieshistories.blogspot.com/2005/09/scandal-short-history-of-teapot-dome.html?m=1 at 6.

219. "Slander Conviction Won For Red Cross," *The Washington* (D.C.) *Herald* (Sept. 26, 1918) at 2.

220. *Id.*

221. "Holy Roller Guilty of Opposing the Draft," *The Atlanta Constitution* (June. 26, 1918) at 9; "Holy Roller Convicted of Resisting War Work," *The Washington* (D.C.) *Herald* (July. 8, 1918) at 4.

222. The act ostensibly was directed at keeping innocent young women from being lured into prostitution. Ch. 395, 36 Stat. 825 (June 25, 1910), codified as 18 U.S.C. §§ 2421–2424.

223. "Fred Toney, Diamond Star, Freed By Jury In Army Draft Case," *The Nashville Tennessean* (Jan. 5, 1919) at 1.

224. "Fred Toney Pleads Guilty to White Slave Charge; Sentenced," *The Nashville Tennessean* (Jan. 1, 1919) at 12.

225. *The Nashville Tennessean* (Feb. 2, 1913) at 17; "Smoke Cases Continued," *The Nashville Tennessean* (Nov. 20, 1912) at 8.

226. "Trial of Celebrated Case at Chattanooga," *The Nashville Tennessean* (Nov. 13, 1913) at 9; "Depositions At Athens," *The Nashville Tennessean* (Feb. 2, 1913) at 17; "Costly Copper Fumes," *The Cincinnati Enquirer* (Dec. 13, 1913) at 20; "Judgment Against Ducktown Company," *The Nashville Tennessean* (Dec. 13, 1913) at 9. *See Ladew v. Tenn. Copper Co.*, 179 F. 245 (Cir. Ct., W.D. Tenn. 1910); *George Peabody Wetmore v. Ducktown Sulphur, Copper & Iron Co.*, 218 U.S. 369 (1910); *Ladew v. Tenn. Copper Co.*, 218 U.S. 357 (1910).

227. Maysilles, *Ducktown Smoke*, at 3.

228. *Id.*

229. *Id.* (quoting Grady Clay, "Copper-Basin Cover-Up," 73 *Landscape Architecture*, No. 4 (1983): 49–55, 94.).

230. Maysilles, *Ducktown Smoke*, at 4.

231. "Must Release Captured Cars," *The Nashville Tennessean* (Dec. 27, 1918) at 4; *United States v. One Cadillac Eight Automobile*, 255 F. 173, 175 (M.D. Tenn. 1918).

232. "Must Release Captured Cars," *The Nashville Tennessean* (Dec. 27, 1918) at 4.

233. 41 Stat. 315.

234. Brake, *Justice in the Valley*, at 466.

235. *Id.* at 58.

236. "Moonshine Industry Shows Rapid Growth in Southern States," *The Dallas Express* (Dec. 20, 1919) at 6.

237. *Id.*

238. Allen, *Only Yesterday*, at 214.

239. Richard F. Hamm, *Shaping the Eighteenth Amendment: Temperance Reform, Legal Culture, and the Polity, 1880–1920* (Chapel Hill, N.C.: Univ. of N. Carolina Press 1995) at 240.

240. Allen, *Only Yesterday*, at 18.

241. The official name for the Volstead Act was the National Prohibition Act, ch. 85, 41 Stat. 305 (1919).

242. 253 U.S. 350 (1920).

243. Ch. 740, 49 Stat. 872 (1935); Allen, *Only Yesterday*, at 86.

244. David H. Burton, *Taft, Holmes, and the 1920s Court: An Appraisal* (Madison, N.J.: Fairleigh Dickinson Univ. Press 1998) at 117.

245. Brake, *Justice in the Valley*, at 83. The law at first meant little in Knoxville, where alcohol sales had been banned since 1907. Neely, *Knoxville's Secret History*, at 126. The 1907 ban was essentially ignored and not enforced, however, as the city saw more liquor sold after the ban than before it. Matt Lakin, "Crusade & Crash: Twenties Brought Corruption, Cleanup, Calamity," *The Knoxville News-Sentinel* (Mar. 25, 2012). In 1909, the State of Tennessee banned the manufacture, sale, and consumption of alcohol. "Prohibition," http://www.tn4me.org/article.cfm/a_id/144/minor_id/58/major_id/20/era_id/6.

246. "Whisky Laws Not Openly Violated," *The Nashville Tennessean* (Mar. 10, 1914) at 12.

247. "Liquor Sales Increase At 'Alarming' Rate; Tennessee Judge Announces More Drastic Policy in Dealing With Prohibition Violators," *The Evening Star* (Washington, D.C.) (Nov. 9, 1920) at 12. Sanford's distinction here seems to be that the moonshiner takes great risk to make the liquor but the bootlegger greedily profits by selling it

248. "Judge Advises Men Not to Buy Liquor," *The Camden* (Tenn.) *Chronicle* (May 13, 1921) at 1.

249. Robert Post, "Federalism, Positive Law, and the Emergence of the American Administrative State: Prohibition In the Taft Court Era," 48 *William and Mary Law Rev.* 1, 9 (Oct. 2006) (quoting H.L. Mencken, "Editorial," 1 *Am. Mercury* 161, 161 (1924)).

250. Ross, *A Scrapbook for My Grandchildren*, at 27. To "raise the very old Harry" means to "carry on," have a "high old time." *Dialect Notes*, Vol. 1 (Norwood, Mass.: The American Dialect Soc'y 1896) at 399.

251. "Plea Made For Another District Judge in Tennessee," *The Nashville Tennessean* (July 3, 1916) at 2.

252. *Id.* The condemnation cases were brought pursuant to the Weeks Law of March 1, 1911, ch. 186, 36 Stat. 961.

253. "Plea Made For Another District Judge in Tennessee," *The Nashville Tennessean* (July 3, 1916) at 2.

254. *Id.* When Tennessean and US Senator John K. Shields was mentioned as a potential candidate to replace Justice Day on the Supreme Court, some of President Harding's Senate friends encouraged the nomination. Tennessee Republican governor Alfred Taylor sent word to Harding that a Republican senator might be named if Shields was named to the Court. Taft, however, was vehemently opposed to Shields: "He is one of the narrowest, meanest men from a partisan standpoint that I know. His evasion and obstruction to the creation of a new Judge in Middle Tennessee, when it is so badly needed there, because he did not want a Republican appointed, was unworthy of a Senator and unworthy of a man as familiar as he was with the necessity for the creation of another judgeship." Letter from William H. Taft to Jacob M. Dickinson (Nov. 2, 1922), Taft Papers.

255. Cook, "Path to the High Bench," at 109.

256. Letter from Edward T. Sanford to John W. Warrington, Senior Circuit Judge (Apr. 3, 1914), District Court Files.

257. Letter from Edward T. Sanford to John McCall (Apr. 3, 1916), District Court Files.

258. "Plea Made for Another District Judge in Tennessee," *The Nashville Tennessean* (July 3, 1916) at 2.

259. Letter from Edward T. Sanford to John W. Warrington, Senior Circuit Judge (Feb. 18, 1918), District Court Files.

260. Letters from Edward T. Sanford to Loyal E. Knappen, Senior Circuit Judge (Feb. 20, 1920 & June 10, 1920), District Court Files.

261. "New Judgeship For State Urged," *The Nashville Tennessean* (Dec. 10, 1919) at A3.

262. *Hearings Before the Committee On the Judiciary, House of Representatives, Sixty-Sixth Congress, Second Session on Tennessee-S.661, December 9, 1919*, at 11–12. Yet another congressman noted that Sanford "frequently holds night sessions" in the Middle District at Nashville. *Id.* at 12.

263. *Id.*

264. *Id.*

265. Cook, "Path to the High Bench," at 30, 108.

266. Letter from William H. Taft to Arthur Denison (Jan. 8, 1923), Taft Papers.

267. Letter from Arthur Denison to William H. Taft (Jan. 11, 1923), Taft Papers.

268. *Proceedings of the Bar and Officers of the Supreme Court of the United States*, at 11.

269. Telegram, Congressman W.F. Clouse to Edward T. Sanford (June 24, 1922), District Court Files.

270. Cook, "Path to the High Bench;" District Court Files.

271. 280 F. 5 (1922).

272. 256 U.S. 450 (1921).

273. "Sanford Ends 15-Year Career As U.S. Judge," *The Pittsburg* (Kan.) *Sun* (Jan. 31, 1923) at 1; "Judge Sanford Closes Court," *Journal and Tribune* (Knoxville, Tenn.) (Jan. 31, 1923) at 5.

274. Noone, "Edward Terry Sanford," *at* 35 (quoting Attorney General Mitchell).

CHAPTER 8

1. Fred L. Israel, "Mahlon Pitney," in *The Justices of the United States Supreme Court, 1789–1969, Their Lives and Major Opinions*, 3 (New York: Chelsea House Publishers 1969 & 2009); Cook, "Path to the High Bench," at 135–36. President Harding signed the Pitney legislation on December 16, 1922. *Id.* In 1965, when President Lyndon Johnson named Abe Fortas to the High Court, Tennessee could claim six justices. Hollingsworth, "Tennessee and the Supreme Court of the United States," at 5.

2. Campbell, *Four Score Forgotten Men*, at 345–46.

3. *Id.* at 348.

4. *The Supreme Court and Its Work* (Washington, D.C.: Congressional Quarterly Inc. 1981) at 156–57.

5. David P. Currie, "The Constitution in the Supreme Court," 1986 *Duke Law Journal* 65 (Feb. 1986) at 65 n.2.

6. Harding, like Sanford, was born in 1865.

7. Abraham, *Justices, Presidents, and Senators* (1999) at 139.

8. Mason, *William Howard Taft: Chief Justice*, at 173.

9. Renstrom, *The Taft Court*, at 30–31.

10. Russell W. Galloway, Jr., "The Taft Court (1921–29)," 25 *Santa Clara Law Rev.* 1 (1985), http://digitalcommons.law.scu.edu/lawreview/vol25/iss1/1 at 2.

11. Warren G. Harding, "Return to Normalcy: May 14, 1920," TeachingAmericanHistory.org., http://www.teachingamericanhistory.org/library/document/return-to-normalcy

12. Renstrom, *The Taft Court*, at xi. The country also was rushing into "the Roaring Twenties," a period of permissiveness, greed, and change. Laton McCartney, *The Teapot Dome Scandal: How Big Oil Bought the Harding White House and Tried to Steal the Country* (New York: Random House 2009) at 8.

13. Allen, *Only Yesterday*, at 36.

14. Hendrickson, "Governing by the Founders' Constitution," at 5.

15. *Id.* at 3.

16. Renstrom, *The Taft Court*, at 12.

17. William Allen White, *Masks in a Pageant* (New York: The MacMillan Co. 1928) at 410.

18. "Warren G. Harding," *Biography.com*, http://www.biography.com/people/warren-g-harding-9328336 at 2.

19. *Id.*

20. "Warren G. Harding," http://www.biography.com/people/warren-g-harding-9328336#early-political-career.

21. "Warren G. Harding," http://www.biography.com/people/warren-g-harding-9328336#presidential-bid.

22. Hendrickson, "Governing by the Founders' Constitution," at 10; Lewis L. Gould, *Grand Old Party: A History of the Republicans* (New York: Random House 2003) at 222–26.

23. Abraham, *Justices, Presidents, and Senators* (1999) at 139.

24. *Id.* (as quoted in Arthur M. Schlesinger, Jr., *The Age of Roosevelt: The Crisis of the Old Order, 1919–1933* (Boston: Houghton Mifflin 1957) at 50–51).

25. Abraham, *Justices, Presidents, and Senators* (1999) at 139 (quoting Schlesinger, *The Age of Roosevelt*, at 51).

26. Finkelman, *The Supreme Court*, at 582.

27. Giglio, *H.M. Daugherty & the Politics of Expediency*, at 53.

28. Renstrom, *The Taft Court*, at 13.

29. Francis Russell, *In the Shadow of Blooming Grove: Warren G. Harding in His Times* (New York: McGraw-Hill Book Co. 1968) at 246.

30. *Id.* at xv. It was always Daugherty who sought out Harding. *Id.* at 241.

31. *Id.* at 308–10.

32. *Id.* at 334, 337.

33. *Id.* at 334, 337 n.6.

34. "Southern Men Urged," *The Arkansas Gazette* (Little Rock) (Nov. 18, 1920) at 1.

35. Kevin C. Murphy, "Uphill All the Way: The Fortunes of Progressivism, 1919–1929" (Ph.d diss. Columbia Univ. 2013) at 361.

36. Renstrom, *The Taft Court*, at 13.

37. Murphy, "Uphill All the Way," at 362–63

38. *Id.*

39. "The Chief Justice—A Mistaken Appointment," Vol. 113, No. 2923, *The Nation* (July 13, 1921) at 32.

40. Giglio, *H.M. Daugherty and the Politics of Expediency*, at 131.

41. *Id.*

42. Bates, *The Story of the Supreme Court*, at 262.

43. Hollingsworth, "Tennessee and the Supreme Court of the United States," at 13.

44. Klein, "Prominent Alumni: Part III," in *Volunteer Moments*, http://trace.tennessee.edu/utk_libarcvol/1/; "Tennessean Urged For Supreme Court," *The Atlanta Constitution* (Jun. 9, 1921) at 3; "Judge Sanford's Name Presented," *The Charlotte* (N. C.) *News* (Nov. 21, 1922) at 1.

45. Cook, "Path to the High Bench," at 128; 40 *Proceedings of the Annual Session of the Bar Ass'n of Tennessee* (1921) at 50–55.

46. "Resolution for Consideration and Nomination of Judge Edward Sanford as Justice of the United States Supreme Court, with Discussion," 40 *Proceedings of the Annual Session of the Bar Ass'n of Tennessee* (1921) at 50–55.

47. *Id.* Judge Wilson served on the Tennessee Court of Chancery Appeals.

48. Fowler, "Mr. Justice Edward Terry Sanford," at 232.

49. *Id.*

50. "Justice To The South," *The Atlanta Constitution* (Dec. 28, 1922).

51. Cook, "Path to the High Bench," at 140.

52. Telegram to Warren G. Harding from Austin Peay (Jan. 5, 1923), Dep't of Justice Records, Nat'l Archives, College Park, Md.

53. Letter to Warren G. Harding from Ben W. Hooper (Nov. 21, 1922), Dep't of Justice Records, Nat'l Archives, College Park, Md.

54. Letter to Warren G. Harding from Augustus E. Willson (Nov. 21, 1922) and Letter to Warren G. Harding from Edwin P. Morrow (Dec. 22, 1922), Dep't of Justice Records, Nat'l Archives, College Park, Md.

55. Letter to Harry M. Daugherty from the justices of the Tennessee Supreme Court (Jan. 22, 1923), Dep't of Justice Records, Nat'l Archives, College Park, Md.

56. *The Knoxville News-Sentinel* (Dec. 6, 1922) at 2.

57. Senate Resolution No. 6, Jan. 8, 1923, Pub. Acts of Tennessee, 1923.

58. Letter from William R. Day to Harry M. Daugherty (Dec. 28, 1922), File of Edward T. Sanford, RG 60, Dep't of Justice Records, Nat'l Archives, College Park, Md.

59. Letter from Loyal E. Knappen to Harry M. Daugherty (Jan. 2, 1923), File of Edward T. Sanford, RG 60, Dep't of Justice Records, Nat'l Archives, College Park, Md.

60. "Chief Justice Lauds Sanford," *The Chattanooga Times* (Oct. 7, 1921).

61. Ochs, seven years older than Sanford, grew up in Knoxville and learned the newspaper business from Sanford family friend William Rule. "Adolph S. Ochs Dead at 77; Publisher of Times Since 1896" *The New York Times* (Apr. 9, 1935) at 4.

62. Letter from Charles D. Hilles to William H. Taft (Feb. 9, 1923), Taft Papers.

63. Telegram to Warren G. Harding (Jan. 4, 1923), Dep't of Justice Records, Nat'l Archives, College Park, Md.

64. *Proceedings of the Bar and Officers of the Supreme Court of the United States*, at 11.

65. Cook, "Path to the High Bench," at 141 (interview with Adrian S. Fisher, Washington, D.C., Sept. 2, 1973). Adrian Sanford Fisher, the son of Hubert and Louise, served as a law clerk to US Supreme Court Justices Louis D. Brandeis and Felix Frankfurter and was a dean of Georgetown University Law School. Adrian was the first deputy director of the United States Arms Control and Disarmament Agency, appointed by President John F. Kennedy in 1961, the year it was formed. He was the leading arms control negotiator of the 1963 Limited Test Ban Treaty, which barred nuclear testing in the atmosphere, outer space, and underwater. He also was involved with the 1968 Treaty for the Nonproliferation of Nuclear Weapons.

Earlier in his career, Adrian had served as a technical advisor to the American judges at the Nuremberg trials in 1945 and 1946. "Obituary, Adrian S. Fisher," *The New York Times* (Mar. 19, 1983) at 28. Sadly, the Fisher family was struck by tragedy in the 1990s, when the wife of Hubert Fisher III was murdered by killers seeking payment for the drug debt of their son, Hubert Adrian. Marilyn Sadler, "A Murder in Central Gardens, Parts I and II, *Memphis City Magazine* (Oct. 1, 2007 and Nov. 1, 2007); David J. Krajicek, "Murder in Memphis," *The New York Daily News* (Apr. 13, 2008).

66. McReynolds was appointed assistant attorney general of the United States in 1903 by Theodore Roosevelt, and later served as attorney general under President Woodrow Wilson. In 1914, Wilson appointed him to the Supreme Court to fill the vacancy created by Justice Lurton's death. Phillips, *History of the Sixth Circuit*, at 64–65. Ray Stannard Baker in *Woodrow Wilson, Life and Letters* (8 Vols.) (New York: Greenwood Publ'g Group 1968), Vol. 6 at 113, reported that President Wilson viewed the appointment of McReynolds as a "great mistake."

67. Daniel S. McHargue, "Sectional Representation on the Supreme Court," 35 *Marquette Law Rev.*, No. 1 (1951) at 20 (citing "The New Justices of the Supreme Court," *Virginia Law Register* 9 n.s. at 127 (June 1923)).

68. Fowler, "Mr. Justice Edward Terry Sanford," at 230. Hollingsworth, "Tennessee and the Supreme Court of the United States," at 12; Wolf, "James Clark McReynolds," *The Supreme Court Justices*, at 297.

69. Sanford's brother-in-law, Hubert F. Fisher, a former star football player at Princeton and the University of Tennessee's head football coach from 1902 to 1903, at the time a Democratic congressman from Memphis, worked with Senator McKellar to gain support for Sanford. Newell Sanders also wrote to the president on behalf of Sanford. Letter to Warren G. Harding from Newell Sanders (Nov. 20, 1922), Dep't of Justice Records, Nat'l Archives, College Park, Md.

70. Letter from William H. Taft to Edward T. Sanford, Sanford Papers.

71. Telegram from William H. Taft to Edward T. Sanford, Sanford Papers.

72. *Congressional Record*, 67th Cong., 4th Sess., Jan. 29, 1923 at 2677; Renstrom, *The Taft Court*, at 33.

73. Letter from Willis Van Devanter to Edward T. Sanford (Jan. 30, 1923), Van Devanter Papers.

74. "Sanford Takes Oath As Justice," *The Knoxville Sentinel* (Feb. 5, 1923) at 4; "Judge Sanford Takes Oath of Office," *The Riverside* (Cal.) *Daily Press* (Feb. 5, 1923) at 1.

75. "Sanford Is Sworn By Justice Taft," *The Evening Tribune* (San Diego) (Feb. 19, 1923) at 17.

76. "Tendered by the Bar, Not Bartenders," *The Evening Telegraph* (Alton, Ill.) (Feb. 14, 1923) at 9.

77. Bates, *The Story of the Supreme Court*, at 262.

78. "Sanford Is Named For Supreme Court," *The Joplin* (Mo.) *Globe* (Jan. 25, 1923) at 1.

79. Anderson was a judge on the First Circuit Court of Appeals who disapproved of the treatment of dissidents during the Red Scare of 1919–20. "Criticizes Judge Anderson," *The New York Times* (Feb. 18, 1921) at 3.

80. Landis was a federal judge in the Northern District of Illinois who became the first commissioner of baseball. Bruce Watson, "The judge who ruled baseball," 31 *Smithsonian*, No. 7 (Oct. 2000) at 120–32; John T. McCutcheon, "Kenesaw Mountain Landis, Judge," *Appleton's Magazine* (Dec. 1907) at 418–27.

81. Ragan, "Mr. Justice Sanford," at 79 (quoting George F. Milton, Jr., "Sanford—Neither Radical Nor Reactionary," *The Outlook* (Feb. 14, 1923) at 298).

82. Milton "Sanford—Neither Radical Nor Reactionary," at 298–99. Milton became publisher and editor of *The Chattanooga News* upon his father's death in 1924; James A. Hodges, "George Fort Milton and the Art of History," 18 *The History Teacher*, No. 2 (Feb. 1984) at 252.

83. "Justice Sanford Described As a Liberal Conservative," *The Evening Star* (Washington, D.C.) (Feb. 12, 1923) at 8.

84. Anderson, "Building National Consensus," at 342.

85. "Selection of Justice Sanford Is a Well Deserved Promotion," *The Harrisburg* (Pa.) *Telegraph* (Feb. 5, 1923) at 8 (quoting *The Nashville* (Tenn.) *Banner*); Ragan, "Mr. Justice Sanford," at 79.

86. "Promotion of Judges," *The Springfield* (Mass.) *Republican* (Jan. 14, 1923) at 13.

87. Russell, *In the Shadow of Blooming Grove*, at 259.

88. *Id.* at 259, 264.

89. Laska, "Mr. Justice Sanford and the Fourteenth Amendment," at 216.

90. "U.S. Justice Edward Sanford," *Tennessee History Classroom*, http://www.tennesseehistory.com/class/Sanford.htm.

91. Fowler, "Mr. Justice Edward Terry Sanford," at 232; Hollingsworth, "Tennessee and the Supreme Court of the United States," at 13. Tennessee Republicans also believed that they deserved recognition for occasionally electing Republican governors and consistently sending Republican members to Congress. Further, East Tennesseans reliably elected Republicans to the state legislature. Charles S. Bullock & Mark J. Rozell, eds., *The New Politics of the Old South: An Introduction to Southern Politics* (New York: Rowman & Littlefield Publishers 2013) at 183.

92. Senate Resolution No. 6, House Resolution No. 10, January 8, 1923, Public Acts of Tennessee 1923, at 455–56.

93. Maguire, "The Supreme Court Justice From Knoxville," at 64 n.195.

94. Hollingsworth, "Tennessee and the Supreme Court of the United States," at 13; *Chicago Sunday Tribune* (Mar. 9, 1930), part A1, at 2.

95. *See* "Taft Supports Sanford," *The New York Times* (Jan. 6, 1923) at 3; "A Fitting Appointment," *The New York Times* (Jan. 7, 1923) at E4.

96. OYEZ, US Supreme Court Media, http://www.oyez.org/justices/edward_t_sanford/. Some contend that Sanford's work in support of America's entrance into the League of Nations after World War I made a favorable impression on Taft and Daugherty. This was probably Sanford's last political activity. Cook, "Path to the High Bench," at 42. Kermit L. Hall, ed "Edward Terry Sanford," *Oxford Companion to the U.S. Supreme Court*, (New York: Oxford Univ. Press 2005).

97. Fowler, "Mr. Justice Edward Terry Sanford," at 232.

98. Langsdon, *Tennessee: A Political History*, at 253.

99. Ragan, "Mr. Justice Sanford," at 78.

100. Cook, "Path to the High Bench," at 162 (letter from William H. Taft to Henry W. Taft (Jan. 16, 1923), Taft Papers).

101. *Id.* at 165 (letter from William H. Taft to Charles D. Hilles (Jan. 14, 1923), Taft Papers). Fowler also personally wrote the president on Sanford's behalf. Letter from James A. Fowler to Warren G. Harding (Nov. 15, 1922). File of Edward T. Sanford, RG 60, Dep't of Justice Records, Nat'l Archives, College Park, Md.

102. Letter from Charles D. Hilles to William H. Taft (Jan. 18, 1923), Taft Papers.

103. Letter from Charles D. Hilles to William H. Taft (Dec. 20, 1922), Taft Papers. Hilles did not explain why he distrusted Fowler.

104. Letter From William H. Taft to Warren G. Harding (Dec. 4, 1922), Warren G. Harding Papers, Manuscript Division, Library of Congress, Washington, D.C. ("Harding Papers"); Letter from William H. Taft to Warren G. Harding (Dec. 14, 1922) and letter from Charles D. Hilles to William H. Taft (Dec. 2, 1922), Taft Papers.

105. Cook, "Path to the High Bench," at 146–47 (citing Fowler Papers).

106. Letter from Harry M. Daugherty to James A. Fowler (June 18, 1932), Fowler Papers.

107. *Id.* Ironically, Sanford had penned a letter to President Harding urging the selection of Fowler as attorney general. Letter from Edward T. Sanford to Warren G. Harding (Feb. 5, 1921), District Court Records.

108. Walter F. Murphy, "In His Own Image: Mr. Chief Justice Taft and The Supreme Court Appointments," Vol. 1961, *The Supreme Court Review*, Phillip Kurland, ed. (Chicago: Univ. of Chicago 1961), at 179 (letter from William H. Taft to Warren G. Harding (Dec. 13, 1922)).

109. Murphy, "In His Own Image," at 180 (letter from William H. Taft to Charles D. Hilles (Dec. 19, 1922)). Taft felt somewhat indebted to Daugherty because of the latter's efforts on his behalf in the 1912 presidential election. Daugherty also had just worked closely with Taft to get the 1922 judicial bill passed. Giglio, *H.M. Daugherty and the Politics of Expediency*, at 132.

110. Murphy, "In His Own Image," at 181 (letter from William H. Taft to Charles D. Hilles (Dec. 31, 1922)).

111. *Id.* at 182 (letter from William H. Taft to Henry Taft (Jan. 16, 1923)). The Pennsylvania chief justice was Robert Von Moschzisker.

112. William G. Ross, *A Muted Fury: Populists, Progressives, and Labor Unions Confront the Courts, 1890–1937* (Princeton, N.J.: Princeton Univ. Press 1994) at 216 (letter from William H. Taft to Henry W. Taft (Jan. 16, 1923), Taft Papers). Daugherty was "the astute manipulator." Russell, *The Shadow of Blooming Grove*, at 109.

113. Abraham, *Justices, Presidents, and Senators*, at 144.

114. Anderson, "Building National Consensus," at 343.

115. Ross, *A Muted Fury*, at 216 (citing *The Nation* (Feb. 7, 1923) at 137). Cushman states that Sanford was "persistently moderate." Barry Cushman, "Edward Terry Sanford," *The Supreme Court Justices: A Biographical Dictionary*, Melvin I. Urofsky, ed. (New York: Garland Publ'g Co. 1994) at 396.

116. Ross, *A Muted Fury*, at 216 (citing Milton, "Sanford—Neither Radical nor Reactionary," at 299).

117. Abraham, *Justices, Presidents, and Senators*, at 140.

118. Russell, *In the Shadow of Blooming Grove*, at xv.

119. It appears that Sanford once was instrumental in the selection of Taft for a position. According to a reporter, Taft and another individual were deadlocked for the nomination for president of the ABA at the 1913 convention. One member of the nominating committee, a Harvard law professor, was absent. Sanford went to the professor's room, woke him up, and escorted him to the meeting to cast the deciding vote for Taft. Cole E. Morgan, "Many Mentioned for U.S. District Judge," *The Knoxville Sentinel* (Jan. 7, 1923) sec 2 at 1.

120. Walter F. Murphy, "Marshaling the Court: Leadership, Bargaining and the Judicial Process," 29 *Univ. of Chicago Law Rev.*, No. 4 (Summer 1962) at 649.

121. Murphy, "In His Own Image," at 183 (letter from Edward T. Sanford to William H. Taft (Jan. 30, 1923)).

122. *Id.* at 183 n.105.

123. Hollingsworth, "Tennessee and the Supreme Court of the United States," at 14 (quoting Jerome P. Frank, "Appointment of Justices: Prestige, Principles, and Politics," http://www.repository.law.indiana.edu/facpub/1856; *see* Daniel S. McHargue, "Appointments to the Supreme Court of the United States: The Factors That Have Affected Appointments (1789–1932)" (Thesis, Univ. of California, Los Angeles 1949); Robert Scigliano, *The Supreme Court and the Presidency* (New York: The Free Press 1971) at 88). See also Abraham, *Justices, Presidents, and Senators*, at 144.

124. Nathan, *Centurions In Public Service*, at 89.

125. George Martin, *CCB: The Life and Century of Charles C. Burlingham, New York's First Citizen, 1858–1959* (New York: Hill and Wang 2005) at 89–90. Burlingham initially gained recognition as an admiralty lawyer defending the White Star Line against claims arising out of the sinking of the Titanic. *Id.*

126. Nathan, *Centurions In Public Service*, at 94.

127. Letter from Charles C. Burlingham to William H. Taft (Dec. 4, 1922), Taft Papers.

128. Letter from William H. Taft to Arthur C. Denison (Jan. 8, 1923), Taft Papers.

129. Maguire, "The Supreme Court Justice From Knoxville" at 62 (quoting letter from William H. Taft to Charles C. Burlingham (Jan. 16, 1923), Taft Papers).

130. *Id.* at 63 (quoting letter from William H. Taft to Charles C. Burlingham (Jan. 16, 1923), Taft Papers); Murphy, "In His Own Image," at 182.

131. Jeffrey A. Segal & Harold J. Spaeth, *The Supreme Court and the Attitudinal Model Revisited* (Cambridge Univ. Press 2002) at 183.

132. As noted by Harold M. Hollingsworth, "[j]ustices, like other men, go to Washington because of politics, and politics in the United States is fundamentally State and local rather than national." Hollingsworth, "Tennessee and the Supreme Court of the United States," at 3. Historically, some tradition of public service has been displayed by justices named to the Court, the sole exception being George Shiras, Jr., who served from 1892 to 1903. Abraham, *Justices, Presidents, and Senators*, at 98.

133. Maguire, "The Supreme Court Justice From Knoxville," at iii.

134. Letter from J.D. Connel to Warren G. Harding (Dec. 26, 1922), RG 60, General Records of the Dep't of Justice Records, Nat'l Archives, College Park, Md.

135. Author of letter used periods.

136. Letter from J.D. Connel to Warren G. Harding (Dec. 27, 1922), RG 60, General Records of the Dep't of Justice, Nat'l Archives, College Park, Md.

137. *Id.*

138. "W.J. Oliver Arrested; Shell Plant Seized," *The New York Times* (Oct. 5, 1918) at 17.

139. Maguire, "The Supreme Court Justice From Knoxville," at 21 (citing Fowler Papers).

140. *Id.* at 30.

141. Sanford continued his involvement in coal mining after E.J.'s death. He and Fowler were listed as incorporators of two coal company ventures in late 1906 ("Camp Creek Coal Co., Knoxville, Tenn." and "Harness Coal Company, Knoxville, Tenn."). See 8 *Fuel Magazine: The Coal Operators National Weekly*, No. 1 (Chicago: Nov. 6, 1906). In another investment, Sanford, Lucky, Fowler, William Slattery, and Samuel Warfield incorporated the Lenoir Car Works, with $100,000 capital, to manufacture railroad cars. 74 *American Manufacturer Steel and Iron*, No. 24

(Pittsburgh, Pa.: Nat'l Iron and Steel Publ'g Co. 1904) at 757; 51 *Engineering News*, (McGraw-Hill Publ'g Co. 1904) at 467. The same group of men were involved in the receivership of the Southern Car & Foundry Company. 95 *The Iron and Machinery World* (Chicago 1904) at 30. It was purchased by the Southern Railway in 1905. Lenoir Car Works was once the largest employer in Loudon County, Tennessee. Joe Spence, "Lenoir Car Works," *Tennessee Encyclopedia of History and Culture,* https://tennesseeencyclopedia.net/entry.php?rec=779.

142. Cook, "Path to the High Bench," at 21 n.47 (citing Fowler Papers).

143. Will Book, Vol. 4, Knox County, Tenn. Archives at 114–118. The will named William P. Chamberlain as guardian of Louise Sanford, E.J.'s youngest child.

144. *Id.*

145. "The Nation's Highest Tribunal," *The Omaha World-Herald* (Mar. 2, 1930) at 21.

146. Fowler Papers.

147. Letter from E.J. Sanford to C.M. McGhee (Dec. 5, 1893) in McArthur, "Charles McClung McGhee," at 266.

148. "Ambitions Fulfilled," *The San Francisco Chronicle* (Feb. 25, 1923) at 2.

CHAPTER 9

1. Mason, "Chief Justice Taft at the Helm," at 367.

2. Robert C. Post, "William Howard Taft," *The Supreme Court Justices: A Biographical Dictionary*, Melvin I. Urofsky, ed. (New York: Garland Publ'g, Inc. 1994) at 457; Post, "Mr. Taft Becomes Chief Justice," 76 *Univ. Cincinnati Law Rev.* 761 (2008).

3. Both positions were courtesy of President Benjamin Harrison.

4. Anderson, "Building National Consensus," at 326.

5. Post, "Mr. Taft Becomes Chief Justice," at 761.

6. In Taft's single term as president, he appointed six justices: Horace Lurton, Chief Justice Edward Douglass White, Willis Van Devanter, Mahlon Pitney, Joseph Rucker Lamar, and Charles Evans Hughes. Taft chose his nominees with little care for their party affiliation. Three of his six appointees were Democrats, although all three were conservative Southern Democrats. The Taft appointees were all men of integrity personally known to Taft, and with the exception of Charles Evans Hughes, all had previous judicial experience. Most important to Taft, however, were the political values of those he nominated. He sought ideological conservatives who would protect property rights and minimize regulatory initiatives of both the federal and state governments. Renstrom, *The Taft Court*, at 26–27; *see* Abraham, *Justices, Presidents, and Senators*, at 125.

7. Phillips, *History of the Sixth Circuit*, at 67. Taft served as president of the Lincoln Memorial Commission and dedicated the monument as chief justice in 1922. Lewis L. Gould, "Taft, William Howard," *American National Biography Online,* http://www.anb.org.

8. Post, "William Howard Taft," at 460; Renstrom, *The Taft Court*, at 75.

9. Anderson, "Building National Consensus," at 332 (citing William Howard Taft, *Present Day Problems: A Collection of Addresses Delivered on Various Occasions* (Books for Libraries Press 1967) at 218).

10. Burton, *Taft, Holmes, and the 1920s Court*, at 89.

11. Mason, *The Supreme Court from Taft to Burger*, at 55.

12. Galloway, "The Taft Court (1921–29)," 25 *Santa Clara Law Rev.* 1 (1985), http://digitalcommons.law.scu.edu/lawreview/vol25/iss1/1 at 34.

13. Burton, *Taft, Holmes, and the 1920s Court*, at 45.

14. *Id.*
15. *Id.* at 41.
16. Post, "Mr. Taft Becomes Chief Justice," at 765.
17. Burton, *Taft, Holmes, and the 1920s Court*, at 88.
18. Post, "Mr. Taft Becomes Chief Justice," at 765.
19. Burton, *Taft, Holmes, and the 1920s Court*, at 88–89.
20. *Id.* at 86.
21. Burton, *Taft, Holmes, and the 1920s Court*, at 75.
22. *Id.* at 92.
23. David H. Burton, ed., *William Howard Taft: Essential Writings and Addresses* (Fairleigh Dickinson Univ. Press 2009) at 31.
24. Mason, *The Supreme Court from Taft to Burger*, at 66.
25. *Id.* at 48.
26. Post, "Mr. Taft Becomes Chief Justice," at 765.
27. Anderson, "Building National Consensus," at 332.
28. Renstrom, *The Taft Court*, at 77.
29. Post, "William Howard Taft," at 457; *see Truax v. Corrigan*, 257 U.S. 312 (1921); *American Steel Foundries v. Tri-City Cent. Trades Council*, 257 U.S. 184 (1921).
30. Galloway, "The Taft Court (1921–1930)," 25 *Santa Clara Law Rev.* 1 (1985), http://digitalcommons.law.scu.edu/lawreview/vol25/iss1/1; *Encyclopedia of the American Constitution*, Leonard W. Levy & Kenneth L. Karst, eds., Vol. 6 (2nd ed.) (Detroit: Macmillan Reference USA 2000) at 2638.
31. *See Bedford Cut Stone Co. v. Journeymen Stone Cutters' Ass'n*, 274 U.S. 37 (1927); *Coronado Coal Co. v. United Mine Workers*, 268 U.S. 295 (1925); Galloway, "The Taft Court (1921–29)," 25 *Santa Clara Law Rev.* 1 (1985), http://digitalcommons.law.scu.edu/lawreview/vol25/iss1/1 at 47.
32. Letter from William H. Taft to Horace Taft (May 7, 1927) (quoted in 2 Pringle, *The Life and Times of William Howard Taft*, at 967).
33. Post, "William Howard Taft," at 460.
34. McCartney, *The Teapot Dome Scandal*, at 157.
35. Galloway, "The Taft Court (1921–29)," 25 *Santa Clara Law Rev.* 1 (1985), http://digitalcommons.law.scu.edu/lawreview/vol25/iss1/1 at 45.
36. Renstrom, *The Taft Court*, at xii.
37. Galloway, "The Taft Court (1921–29)," at 8, 25 *Santa Clara Law Rev.* 1 (1985), http://digitalcommons.law.scu.edu/lawreview/vol25/iss1/1 at 46.
38. Renstrom, *The Taft Court*, at xii. There was a distinct anti-labor bias on the part of the Taft Court majority. *Id.*
39. Robert H. Zieger, ed., "Prosperity, Depression, and War, 1921 to 1945," Vol. 5, *Encyclopedia of U.S. Political History* (Washington, D.C.: CQ Press 2010) at 331.
40. Currie, "The Constitution in the Supreme Court," at 65; *see* Ray A. Brown, "Due Process of Law, Police Power, and the Supreme Court," 40 *Harvard Law Rev.* 943, 944 (1927) ("[I]n the six years since 1920 the Supreme Court has declared social and economic legislation unconstitutional under the due process clauses of either the Fifth or the Fourteenth Amendment in more cases than in the entire fifty-two previous years...."). *See Bluefield Waterworks & Improvement Co. v. Public Serv. Comm'n*, 262 U.S. 679 (1923); *Charles Wolff Packing Co. v. Court of Indust. Relations*, 262 U.S. 522 (1923); *Jay Burns Baking Co. v. Bryan*, 264

U.S. 504 (1924); *Pacific Gas & Elec. Co. v. City of San Francisco*, 265 U.S. 403 (1924). Article 1, Section 8, Clause 3 of the Constitution gives Congress the power "to regulate commerce with foreign nations, and among the several states, and with the Indian tribes." Congress uses the commerce clause to justify exercising legislative power over the activities of states and their citizens. The "dormant" commerce clause refers to the prohibition, implied in the commerce clause, against state legislation that discriminates against or excessively burdens interstate commerce. "Commerce Clause," https://www.law.cornell.edu/wex/commerce_clause. The due process clause and the dormant commerce clause were used to strike down state efforts to regulate industry, with the Court asserting that government action was illegally encroaching on interstate commerce. Galloway, "The Taft Court (1921–29)," at 8, 25 *Santa Clara Law Rev.* 1 (1985), http://digitalcommons.law.scu.edu/lawreview/vol25/iss1/1 at 46. *See Lemke v. Homer Farmers Elevator Co.*, 258 U.S. 65 (1922); *Pennsylvania v. West Virginia*, 262 U.S. 553 (1923); *Davis v. Farmer's Coop. Equity Co.*, 262 U.S. 312 (1923); *Texas Transport & Terminal Co. v. City of New Orleans*, 264 U.S. 150 (1924). The equal protection clause was used to strike down state efforts to regulate the economy and was also emptied of all significance as a defender of minority rights. *Kentucky Fin. Corp. v. Paramount Auto Exch. Corp.*, 262 U.S. 544 (1923).

41. Mason, *The Supreme Court from Taft to Burger*, at 70.

42. 72 *Congressional Record* (1930) at 3566.

43. Anderson, "Building National Consensus," at 330.

44. *Id.*

45. Mason, *The Supreme Court from Taft to Burger*, at 64–66 ("I am quite anxious, as I am sure we all are, that the continuity and weight of our opinions on important questions of law should not be broken any more than we can help by dissents.") (quoting letter from William H. Taft to Harlan F. Stone (Jan. 26, 1927), Box 76, Harlan F. Stone Papers, Manuscript Division, Library of Congress, Washington, D.C. ("Stone Papers")).

46. Letter from William H. Taft to John H. Clarke (Feb. 10, 1922), John H. Clarke Papers, Manuscript Division, Library of Congress, Washington, D.C. ("Clarke Papers").

47. Mason, *The Supreme Court from Taft to Burger*, at 69.

48. Barry Cushman, "Inside The Taft Court: Lessons From the Docket Books," Vol. 2015, No. 1, *The Supreme Court Review* (Univ. of Chicago Press Journals 2016), http://ssrn.com/abstract=2797442 at 13 (citing Robert C. Post, "The Supreme Court Opinions As Institutional Practice: Dissent, Legal Scholarship and Decision Making in the Taft Court," 85 *Minnesota Law Rev.* 1267 (2001) at 1310–11, 1356; Mason, *William Howard Taft*, at 198; Alpheus T. Mason, "The Chief Justice of the United States: *Primus Inter Pares*," 17 *Journal Public Law* (Emory Law School 1968) at 31–32).

49. Post, "The Supreme Court Opinion as Institutional Practice," http://escholarship.org/uc/item/62t1b008 at 12 n.55.

50. Lisa L. Milord, *The Development of the ABA Judicial Code* 137 (ABA 1992) (Canon 19, Canons of Judicial Ethics (1924)).

51. Mason, "Chief Justice Taft at the Helm," at 384 (quoting letter from William H. Taft to R.A. Taft (Dec. 26, 1926)).

52. *Id.* at 384 (quoting letter from William H. Taft to C.P. Taft, II (Nov. 1, 1925)).

53. Renstrom, *The Taft Court*, at 86.

54. Cushman, "Inside the Taft Court," at 14.

55. *Id.*

56. Post, "The Supreme Court Opinion as Institutional Practice," http://escholarship.org/uc/item/62t1b008, at 47.

57. Post, "The Supreme Court Opinions as Institutional Practice," 85 *Minnesota Law Rev.* at 1293 n.83.

58. Mason, "Chief Justice Taft at the Helm," at 373.

59. Burton, *Taft, Holmes, and the 1920s Court*, at 121.

60. O'Connor, *Out of Order*, at 134.

61. Wolf, "James Clark McReynolds," at 297–298; Hollingsworth, "Tennessee and the Supreme Court of the United States," at 20 ("I am not always to be found when there is a Hebrew abroad. Therefore, my 'inability' to attend must not surprise you."); *see* Abraham, *Justices, Presidents, and Senators*, at 134.

62. Abraham, *Justices, Presidents, and Senators*, at 134.

63. Hollingsworth, "Tennessee and the Supreme Court of the United States," at 19 (quoted in Mason, *William Howard Taft*, at 215–16).

64. *Id.* at 19–20; Mason, *William Howard Taft*, at 165–67 (letter from John H. Clarke to Woodrow Wilson (Sept. 9, 1922)).

65. Abraham, *Justices, Presidents, and Senators*, at 134.

66. O'Connor, *Out of Order*, at 135.

67. *Id.*

68. Pringle, *The Life and Times of William Howard Taft*, at 952.

69. Anderson, "Building National Consensus," at 344.

70. Philippa Strum, "Louis Dembitz Brandeis," in *Supreme Court Justices: A Biographical Dictionary*, Melvin I. Urofsky, ed. (New York: Garland Publ'g, Inc. 1994) at 39.

71. 285 U.S. 262 (1932).

72. Strum, "Louis Dembitz Brandeis," at 41.

73. Clare Cushman, "The 'Lost' Clerks of the White Court Era," *Journal of Supreme Court History Soc'y* (Mar. 4, 2015) at 30 (citing 41 Stat. 686–87 (May 29, 1920)), http://ssrn.com/abstract=2573926; Peppers, *Courtiers of the Marble Palace*, at 83.

74. Renstrom, *The Taft Court*, at 36.

75. Post, "The Supreme Court Opinion as Institutional Practice," http://escholarship.org/uc/item/62t1b008 at 10.

76. *Id.* at 11 n.50 (Letter from William H. Taft to Thomas W. Swan (May 17, 1924), Taft Papers).

77. *Id.* at 11.

78. Cushman, "The 'Lost' Clerks," at 30–31; Peppers, *Courtiers of the Marble Palace*, at 83.

79. Cushman, "The 'Lost' Clerks," at 46, 51; *see* "William Loney Dead," *The Washington* (D.C.) *Post and Times Herald* (Dec. 11, 1956) at sec. B.

80. "William Loney Dead," *The Washington* (D.C.) *Post and Times Herald* (Dec. 11, 1956) at sec. B. When Sanford died unexpectedly in 1930, Loney attempted to remain with the Court. He worked for Sanford's replacement, Owen J. Roberts, for a short period but was unsuccessful in getting a permanent position with the justice. He eventually returned to the Department of Justice. Cushman, "The 'Lost' Clerks," at 47–48; Peppers, *Courtiers of the Marble Palace*, at 95, 252; Chester A. Newland, "Personal Assistants to Supreme Court Justices: The Law Clerks," 40 *Oregon Law Rev* 299 (June 1961) at 303.

81. Letter from Edward T. Sanford to William H. Taft (Sept. 8, 1925), Taft Papers.

82. Letter from William H. Taft to O.W. Holmes (May 3, 1927), The John G. Palfrey Collection of Oliver Wendell Holmes, Jr. Papers, General Correspondence, Box 22, Folder 26, Historical and Special Collections, Harvard Law School Library, Cambridge, Mass. ("Holmes Papers").

83. Anderson, "Building National Consensus," at 339.

84. Melvin I. Urofsky, "The Brandeis-Frankfurter Conversations," 1985 *The Supreme Court Review* (1985) at 312.

85. *Id.* at 316.

86. Post, "The Supreme Court Opinions as Institutional Practice," at 1334 n.203; Urofsky, "The Brandeis-Frankfurter Conversations," at 336.

87. Post, "The Supreme Court Opinions as Institutional Practice," at 1302 n.112. However, even Holmes received criticism from Brandeis. Holmes was said to "[g]o[ ] off sometimes in construing statutes because he doesn't understand or appreciate facts" and "leaves more loopholes for rehearing petitions than anyone else." Urofsky, "The Brandeis-Frankfurter Conversations," at 307.

88. Post, "The Supreme Court Opinion as Institutional Practice," http://escholarship.org/uc/item/62t1b008 at 47 n.199.

89. Felix Frankfurter & James M. Landis, "The Business of the Supreme Court at October Term, 1929," 44 *Harvard Law Rev.* 1 (Nov. 1930); Burton, *Taft, Holmes, and the 1920s Court*, at 120–21.

90. "Governance & the Judicial Conference," http://uscourts.gov; *see* 42 Stat. 837 (1922).

91. The Judicial Conference does the following: (1) comprehensively surveys business conditions in the courts of the United States; (2) plans assignments of judges to or from courts of appeals or district courts, where necessary; (3) submits suggestions to the various courts that promote uniform management procedures and the expeditious conduct of court business; (4) exercises statutory authority for the review of circuit council conduct and disability orders filed pursuant to the applicable authority; and (5) continuously studies the operation and effect of the general rules of practice and procedure in the federal courts, as prescribed by the Supreme Court pursuant to law. The Judicial Conference also supervises the director of the Administrative Office of the U.S. Courts–the administrative officer of the courts of the United States under 28 U.S.C. § 604. "Governance & the Judicial Conference," http://uscourts.gov.

92. Post, "William Howard Taft," at 458.

93. 43 Stat. 936 (1925), 28 U.S.C. §§ 3443–50 (1926); "U.S. Justice Edward Sanford," *Tennessee History Classroom*, http://www.tennesseehistory.com/class/Sanford.htm.

94. Galloway, The Taft Court (1921–29), 25 *Santa Clara Law Rev.* 1 (1985), http://digitalcommons.law.scu.edu/lawreview/vol25/iss1/1 at 21.

95. Post, "The Supreme Court Opinion As Institutional Practice," http://escholarship.org/uc/item/62t1b008 at 5 n.23.

96. Post, "William Howard Taft," at 458.

97. O'Connor, *Out of Order*, at 77.

98. Peter Fish, "Judiciary Act of 1925," in Kermit L. Hall, et al., eds., *The Oxford Companion to the Supreme Court of the United States* 477 (New York: Oxford Univ. Press 1992).

99. Burton, ed., *William Howard Taft*, at 29; Peppers, *Courtiers of the Marble Palace*, at 41.

100. Loren B. Beth, *John Marshall Harlan: The Last Whig Justice* (Lexington, Ky.: Univ. of Kentucky Press 1992) at 142.

101. Charles Moore, *Washington Past and Present* (New York: The Century Co. 1929) at 126.

102. Alexander M. Bickel, *The Judiciary and Responsible Government, 1910–21*, Vol. 9 (New York: Macmillan 1984) at 81.

103. "Humor Sits with the Supreme Court," *The New York Times* (Jan. 16, 1927) at 11, sec. 4. When a fire broke out in the Capitol a couple of months prior to Sanford's death, "water leaked down" into Sanford's office. Sanford "hastily spread a tarpaulin over his office desk and papers." "The Congress: Fire No. 2," *Time Magazine* (Jan. 13, 1930).

104. Cushman, "The 'Lost' Clerks," at 46, 51; *see* "William Loney Dead," *The Washington Post and Times Herald* (Dec. 11, 1956) at sec. B.

105. *See* letter from William H. Taft to Senator Reed Smoot (July 3, 1925), Taft Papers.

106. Post, "William Howard Taft," at 460.

107. Phillips, *History of the Sixth Circuit*, at 67.

108. Mason, "Chief Justice Taft at the Helm," at 383 (quoting letter from William H. Taft to Edward T. Sanford (July 4, 1929)).

109. Galloway, "The Taft Court (1921–29)," 25 *Santa Clara Law Rev.* 1 (1985), http://digitalcommons.law.scu.edu/lawreview/vol25/iss1/1 at 34.

110. Mason, *The Supreme Court from Taft to Burger*, at 67.

CHAPTER 10

1. O'Connor, *Out of Order*, at 126–27.

2. Klein, "Prominent Alumni: Part III," in *Volunteer Moments*, http://trace.tennessee.edu/utk_libarcvol/1/; Hall, *Supreme Court Justices*, at 287.

3. Cushman, "Edward Terry Sanford," at 395.

4. Noone, "Edward Terry Sanford," at 38. In what had to be a difficult moment for the perfectionist Sanford, after he submitted one of his early opinions for approval, Justice Holmes advised him as follows: "[Notwithstanding] the effective and powerful example of Brandeis to the contrary I don't think opinions should be written in the form of essays with notes—they are theoretically spoken." Sheldon M. Novick, "Justice Holmes and the Art of Biography," 33 *William & Mary Law Rev.* 1219 (Summer 1992) (Letter from Oliver W. Holmes to Edward T. Sanford (Jan. 1, 1925), http://scholarship.law.wm.edu/wmlr/vol33/iss4/6.

5. Galloway, "The Taft Court," at 21.

6. Noone, "Edward Terry Sanford," at 38.

7. *Id.*

8. Ragan, "Mr. Justice Sanford," at 77, 87.

9. Galloway, "The Taft Court," at 1. Such policies opposed governmental interference in economic affairs beyond the minimum necessary for the maintenance of peace and property rights. "*Laissez-faire*," http://dictionary.reference.com/browse/laissez-faire.

10. *The Brooklyn Daily Eagle* (June 3, 1925) at 1.

11. Hollingsworth, "Tennessee and the Supreme Court of the United States," at 20 (quoting Mason, *Taft: Chief Justice*, at 163–64, 296).

12. Ragan, "Mr. Justice Sanford," at 77, 87; *see* Laska, "Mr. Justice Sanford and the Fourteenth Amendment," at 219.

13. Post, "Federalism, Positive Law, and the Emergence of the American Administrative State," at 2.

14. Abraham, *Justices, Presidents, and Senators*, at 145.

15. Laska, "Mr. Justice Sanford and the Fourteenth Amendment," at 233.

16. Galloway, "The Taft Court," at 18.
17. *Id.* at 32.
18. "Keeping The Court Balanced," *The Decatur* (Ill.) *Herald* (Feb. 7, 1923) at 6.
19. Galloway, "The Taft Court," at 32 (Letter from William H. Taft to Helen Manning (June 11, 1923), quoted in Pringle, *The Life and Times of William Howard Taft*, at 971).
20. *Id.* (Letter from William H. Taft to James R. Angell (Dec. 2, 1926), quoted in Pringle, *The Life and Times of William Howard Taft*, at 971).
21. Felix Frankfurter, "The Supreme Court in the Mirror of Justices," 105 *Univ. of Pennsylvania Law Rev.*, No. 6, 781 (Apr. 1957) at 788.
22. Urofsky, "The Brandeis-Frankfurter Conversations," at 310.
23. *Tennessee Encyclopedia of History and Culture*, http://tennesseeencyclopedia.net/entry.php?rec=1170. E.g., *Public Utils. Comm'n. v. Attleboro Steam & Elec. Co.*, 273 U.S. 83 (1927); *United States v. Flannery*, 268 U.S. 98 (1925).
24. *See Meek v. Centre Cnty. Banking Co.*, 264 U.S. 499 (1924) & 268 U.S. 426 (1925); *Harrison v. Chamberlin*, 271 U.S. 191 (1926); *Taylor v. Voss*, 271 U.S. 176 (1926).
25. Ragan, "Mr. Justice Sanford," at 77; Cushman, "Edward Terry Sanford," at 395.
26. Campbell, *Four Score Forgotten Men*, at 354.
27. "Justice Scalia: Hardest Decision 'Probably a Patent Case,'" www.ipwatchdog.com/2012/07/25/justice-scalia-hardest-decision-probably-a-patent-case/id=26743/. Scalia referred to patent matters as "the dullest case[s] imaginable." *Id.*
28. 272 U.S. 429 (1926).
29. *Id.* at 444.
30. 272 U.S. at 443–44 (internal citations omitted).
31. 276 U.S. 233 (1928).
32. *Id.* at 237 (internal citations omitted).
33. 28 U.S.C. §§ 2201–02.
34. 273 U.S. 70 (1927).
35. *Id.* at 74.
36. 266 U.S. 292 (1924).
37. *Id.* at 297–98.
38. *Id.*
39. 264 U.S. 206 (1924).
40. *Id.* at 210.
41. *Id.*
42. *Id.* at 211–12 (internal citations omitted).
43. 272 U.S. 21 (1926). This action was an original jurisdiction case, as it involved a suit between two states. U.S. Const., Article III, section 2.
44. 272 U.S. at 49; Campbell, *Four Score Forgotten Men*, at 356.
45. Campbell, *Four Score Forgotten Men*, at 356.
46. 275 U.S. 279 (1927).
47. *Id.* at 300.
48. *Id.* at 302.
49. *Id.* at 303; *see* John H. McNeely, "New Mexico v. Texas," *Handbook of Texas Online*, http://www.tshaonline.org/handbook/online/articles/jrn01; "Survey To Be Made Soon of Texas-N.M Boundary," *El Paso Herald* (Dec. 6, 1927).
50. 262 U.S. 43 (1923).

51. *Id.* at 48–49.

52. Finkelman, ed., *The Supreme Court: Controversies, Cases, and Characters From John Jay to John Roberts*, at 594; "Pocket Vetos Valid, Supreme Court Rules," *The News-Herald* (Franklin, Pa.) (May 28, 1929).

53. 279 U.S. 655 (1929).

54. Barry Cushman, "Edward Terry Sanford," *American National Biography*, John A. Garraty, ed. (New York: Oxford Univ. Press 1999); *Tennessee Encyclopedia of History and Culture*, http://tennesseeencyclopedia.net; Ragan, "Mr. Justice Sanford," at 80–81.

55. Each Congress "is elected for a two-year term of office" comprised of two regular annual sessions. An annual session "ends with an adjournment sine die." Richard S. Beth & Jessica Tollestrup, "Sessions, Adjournments, and Recesses of Congress," *Congressional Research Service* (Feb. 27, 2013) at I, 9, 10.

56. 279 U.S. 674.

57. Renstrom, *The Taft Court*, at 199.

58. 279 U.S. at 678–79.

59. Klein, "Prominent Alumni: Part III" in "Volunteer Moments, http://trace.tennessee.edu/utk_libarcvol/1.

60. Anderson, "Building National Consensus," at 340.

61. *Id.*; Ragan, "Mr. Justice Sanford," at 86.

62. Esch-Cummins Act, Pub. L. 66–152, 41 Stat. 456 (approved Feb. 28, 1920). The law returned railroads to private operation after World War I. *Id.* President Wilson had nationalized them in December 1917. Presidential Proclamation 1419, Dec. 26, 1917, under authority of the Army Appropriation Act, 39 Stat. 45 (Aug. 29, 1916).

63. *Public Util. Comm'n v. Attleboro Steam & Elec. Co.*, 273 U.S. 83 (1927) (authored by Sanford).

64. *Wisconsin v. Illinois*, 278 U.S. 367 (1929) (authored by Taft).

65. *Thornton v. United States*, 271 U.S. 414 (1926) (authored by Taft); Robert Post, "Federalism in the Taft Court Era: Can It Be 'Revived'?" 51 *Duke Law Journal* 1513 (2002), at 1537.

66. *Chicago Board of Trade v. Olsen*, 262 U.S. 1 (1923) and *Tagg Bros. & Moorhead v. United States*, 280 U.S. 420 (1930). In *Board of Trade*, upholding the Grain Futures Act of 1922, 38 Stat. 803 (1922), Taft wrote that "it is primarily for Congress to consider and decide the fact of the danger and meet it. This Court will certainly not substitute its judgment for that of Congress in such a matter unless the relation of the subject to interstate commerce and its effect upon it are clearly non-existent." 262 U.S. at 38; Post, "William Howard Taft," *The Supreme Court Justices*, at 460. In *Tagg Bros.*, the Court upheld federal regulation of fees charged by commission salesmen working in major stockyards under the Packers and Stockyards Act of 1921. Cushman, "Inside the Taft Court: Lessons From the Docket Books," http://ssrn.com/abstract=2797442 at 23.

67. Ragan, "Mr. Justice Sanford," at 86.

68. Hall, *Supreme Court Justices*, at 289.

69. Abraham, *Justices, Presidents, and Senators*, at 144; Cushman, "Edward Terry Sanford," at 395.

70. 278 U.S. 130 (1928).

71. 281 U.S. 38 (1930).

72. 278 U.S. at 133.

73. *Id.* at 134.

74. *Id.* at 136–137.
75. *Id.* at 137–38.
76. *Id.* at 137.
77. *Id.* at 138.
78. *Id.*
79. 281 U.S. at 44.
80. *Id.* at 43.
81. *Id.* at 47.
82. *Id.* at 46–47 (quoting *N. Coal & Dock Co. v. Strand*, 278 U.S. 142, 147 (1928)).
83. U.S. Const., Amend. XVIII, sec. 1.
84. Renstrom, *The Taft Court*, at 9.
85. Post, "Federalism, Positive Law, and the Emergence of the American Administrative State," at 1. "Prohibition represented the greatest expansion of federal regulatory authority since Reconstruction. It caused a major crisis in the theory and practice of American federalism, as the national government, which lacked the courts or police necessary for implementing the Eighteenth Amendment, sought to conscript state judicial and law enforcement resources." *Id.*
86. Ragan, "Mr. Justice Sanford," at 81. According to Taft biographer Robert Post, the Taft Court's support for Prohibition came from an unlikely alliance between two liberal justices—Holmes and Brandeis—and three conservative justices—Taft, Van Devanter, and Sanford. Conservatives McReynolds, Sutherland, and Butler were adamantly opposed to Prohibition. Post, "Federalism, Positive Law, and the Emergence of the American Administrative State," at 1.
87. 267 U.S. 132 (1925).
88. *Id.* at 149. In *Carroll*, Taft completely reinterpreted Fourth Amendment jurisprudence so as to enable effective supervision of illegal vehicular liquor traffic. Post, "William Howard Taft," *The Supreme Court Justices*, at 462.
89. Galloway, "The Taft Court," at 20 ("*Carroll* illustrates the law-and-order conservatism of the Taft Court.").
90. Forrest R. Black, "A Critique of the *Carroll* Case," 29 *Columbia Law Rev.* 1068 (1929) at 1098.
91. 277 U.S. 438 (1928).
92. Ragan, "Mr. Justice Sanford," at 81. *Olmstead* was overruled by the Supreme Court in *Katz v. United States*, 389 U.S. 347 (1967).
93. Post, "Federalism, Positive Law, and the Emergence of the American Administrative State," at 3.
94. *Id.* at 9.
95. *Id.* at 102.
96. *The Knoxville Daily Chronicle* (Dec. 22, 1872).
97. Posey, "The Anti-Alcohol City," at 64–65, 94. These three thoroughfares were the busiest in downtown Knoxville.
98. Neely, "Knoxville's 'Old City,'" http://oldcityknoxville.org/history/.
99. "The Saloon and Anarchy: Prohibition in Tennessee," www.sos.tn.gov/products/tsla/saloon-and-anarchy-prohibition-tennessee.
100. Posey, "The Anti-Alcohol City," at 65–66; *The Knoxville Journal and Tribune* (Feb. 11, 1907).
101. 265 U.S. 545 (1924).
102. 42 Stat. 222, sec. 2.

103. 265 U.S. at 561.
104. *Id.* at 562.
105. *Id.* at 561.
106. Edward A. Harriman, "The Twilight of the States," 16 *American Bar Association Journal* 128, 130 (1930).
107. 265 U.S. at 558 (citations omitted); *see* Post, "Federalism, Positive Law, and the Emergence of the American Administrative State," at 18.
108. 265 U.S. at 559.
109. "Wets Lose In Supreme Court," *The Palestine* (Ill.) *Enterprise* (June 13, 1924) at 10.
110. Post, "Federalism, Positive Law, and the Emergence of the American Administrative State," at 91 n.196 (Letter from William H. Taft to Charles P. Taft, II (Mar. 9, 1924)).
111. 271 U.S. 479 (1926).
112. *Id.* at 482.
113. *Tennessee Encyclopedia of History and Culture,* http://tennesseeencyclopedia.net/entry.php?rec=1170.
114. Abraham, *Justices, Presidents, and Senators*, at 144.
115. 268 U.S. 563 (1925).
116. 268 U.S. 588 (1925).
117. *Maple Flooring*, 268 U.S. at 578.
118. *Id.* at 583.
119. 262 U.S. 371 (1923).
120. 257 U.S. 377 (1921).
121. 262 U.S. at 388–89.
122. *Maple Flooring*, 268 U.S. at 585.
123. 268 U.S. 295 (1925).
124. Galloway, "The Taft Court," at 21–22.
125. Cushman, "Inside the Taft Court," at 36.
126. Finkelman, *The Supreme Court: Controversies, Cases, and Characters from John Jay to John Roberts*, at 608.
127. 268 U.S. at 310.
128. 265 U.S. 457 (1924).
129. Cushman, "Edward Terry Sanford," at 395.
130. Galloway, "The Taft Court," at 47.
131. 274 U.S. 37 (1927).
132. Renstrom, *The Taft Court*, at 86.
133. 274 U.S. at 47.
134. *Id.*
135. Mason, *The Supreme Court from Taft to Warren*, at 61; Mason, "Chief Justice Taft at the Helm," at 399 (letter from William H. Taft to Edward T. Sanford (Jan. 24, 1927)).
136. Letter from William H. Taft to Robert A. Taft (Apr. 10, 1927) (quoted in Alpheus Thomas Mason, *Harlan Fiske Stone: Pillar of the Law* (New York: Viking Press, 1956), at 259).
137. *United States v. E.C. Knight*, 156 U.S. 1 (1895). The *Knight* decision held that commercial activities inherently local in nature fell outside of "interstate commerce" and beyond the scope of the Sherman Antitrust Act, thus diminishing federal power to regulate economic activity. The case was overruled in 1937 by *N.L.R.B. v. Jones & Laughlin Steel Corp.*, 301 U.S. 1 (1937).

138. 247 U.S. 251 (1918). The decision held void the Keating-Owen Child Labor Law of 1916 that prohibited shipment of articles manufactured by child labor in interstate commerce. Pub. L. No. 64-249, 39 Stat. 675 (1916).

139. Finkelman, *The Supreme Court: Controversies, Cases, and Characters from John Jay to John Roberts*, at 608.

140. 273 U.S. 359 (1927).

141. *Id.* at 375.

142. *Id.* at 379; "Declares Dealers May Sue Eastman," *The New York Times* (July 24, 1927).

143. 261 U.S. 385 (1923).

144. 40 Stat. 1272 (1919). The act authorized payment of expenditures connected with prosecution of war if based on an express or implied agreement entered into with an officer or agent acting under the authority of the president or the secretary of war.

145. 261 U.S. at 386.

146. 261 U.S. 592 (1923) (decided on April 9).

147. *Id.* at 597; Campbell, *Four Score Forgotten Men*, at 354.

148. *Merritt v. United States*, 267 U.S. 338 (1925); *Jacob Reed's Sons v. United States*, 273 U.S. 200 (1927).

149. 264 U.S. 488 (1924).

150. *Id.* at 494.

151. *Id.* at 497.

152. *Id.* at 497–98 (internal citations omitted).

153. 262 U.S. 499 (1923).

154. *Id.* at 503–04.

155. 263 U.S. 239 (1923).

156. Act of Mar. 2, 1893, 27 Stat. 531, recodified as amended, 49 U.S.C. § 20302.

157. 263 U.S. at 243.

158. *Id.* at 244.

159. 262 U.S. 700 (1923).

160. *Id.* at 707–08 (internal citation omitted).

161. *Id.* at 710.

162. 265 U.S. 371 (1924).

163. *Id.* at 378.

164. *Id.*

165. 279 U.S. 692 (1929).

166. *Id.* at 695.

167. 277 U.S. 389 (1928).

168. 274 U.S. 357 (1927). *See* Chapter 11.

169. 279 U.S. at 696. Chief Justice Taft and Justices Van Devanter and Butler dissented.

170. *Id.*

171. *Id.*

172. *Id.* at 697.

173. 266 U.S. 271 (1924).

174. *Id.* at 282.

175. *Id.* at 284.

176. 269 U.S. 411 (1926).

177. Ch. 425, sec. 9, 30 Stat. 1151, 33 U.S.C. § 407.

178. Of, relating to, or situated on the bank of a river or other body of water. "Riparian," http://dictionary reference.com.

179. 269 U.S. at 413.

180. *Id.* at 414.

181. *Id.*

182. *Id.* at 418–19 (internal citations omitted).

183. *Id.* at 416.

184. *Id.* at 420.

185. Randy E. Barnett, "The Proper Scope of the Police Power," 79 *Notre Dame Law Rev.* 429 (2004) at 429.

186. 272 U.S. 365 (1926).

187. *Id.* at 384.

188. *Id.* at 394–95. The Court has never considered a case seeking to overturn *Euclid*.

189. Cushman, "Edward Terry Sanford," at 395.

190. Galloway, "The Taft Court," at 26.

191. 272 U.S. at 388.

192. 277 U.S. 19 (1928).

193. *Id.* at 24.

194. *Id.* at 26.

195. 263 U.S. 565 (1924).

196. *Id.* at 573.

197. *Id.* (citations omitted).

198. 263 U.S. at 574.

199. Galloway, "The Taft Court," at 15.

200. 274 U.S. 619 (1927).

201. *Id.* at 625. *See also United States v. International Harvester Co.*, 274 U.S. 698 (1927), in which the Government alleged that the company had engaged in a combination or alliance restraining and monopolizing interstate trade and commerce in harvesting machines and other agricultural implements in violation of the Sherman Antitrust Act. A consent decree was entered. Sanford determined that the company had shown compliance with the decree's requirements. He specifically noted: "We conclude that not only has the International Company complied with the specific requirements of the consent decree but that competitive conditions have been established in the interstate trade in harvesting machinery, bringing about 'a situation in harmony with law.'" 274 U.S. at 710; "High Court Upholds Harvester Company," *The New York Times* (June 7, 1927) at 17.

202. 274 U.S. at 625.

203. 262 U.S. 522 (1923).

204. Cushman, "Edward Terry Sanford," at 395; Taft articulated a constitutional distinction between ordinary property, which was entitled to full constitutional protection, and property affected with a public interest, which could be subjected to extensive administrative control by the state. Post, "William Howard Taft," *The Supreme Court Justices*, at 461.

205. 262 U.S. at 544; *see* John R. Anthony, "Attitude of the Supreme Court Toward Liberty of Contract," 6 *Texas Law Rev.* 266 (1927–28).

206. US Const., Amend. XIV, sec. 1.

207. "Substantive Due Process," http://legaldictionary.thefreedictionary.com/substantive+due+process.
208. *Id.*
209. Robert J. Cynkar, "*Buck v. Bell:* 'Felt Necessities' v. Fundamental Values?" 81 *Columbia Law Rev.*, No. 7 (Nov. 1981) at 1445.
210. *Id.*
211. 261 U.S. 525 (1923).
212. *Id.* at 541–42.
213. *Id.* at 542–43; Michael Allan Wolf, "George Sutherland," in Melvin I. Urofsky, ed., *The Supreme Court Justices: A Biographical Dictionary* (New York: Garland Publ'g 1994) at 449.
214. 261 U.S. at 545; Wolf, "George Sutherland," at 449.
215. 198 U.S. 45 (1905).
216. Galloway, "The Taft Court," at 11.
217. 261 U.S. at 556.
218. *Id.*
219. *Id.* at 562.
220. "A One-Man Constitution," *The Decatur* (Ill.) *Herald* (Apr. 14, 1923) at 6.
221. Cushman, "Inside the Taft Court," at 4–5.
222. 300 U.S. 379 (1937).
223. 262 U.S. 390 (1923).
224. 268 U.S. 510 (1925).
225. 273 U.S. 284 (1927).
226. 262 U.S. at 396–97.
227. *Id.* at 400.
228. 268 U.S. at 534–35.
229. 273 U.S. at 298.
230. http://www.kevincmurphy.com/uatw-legacies-laws.html at 4.
231. Robert C. Post, "Chief Justice William Howard Taft and the Concept of Federalism" 9 *Constitutional Commentary* 199, Univ. of Minnesota Law (Summer 1992) at 220, http://hdl.handle.net/11299/166449; *see Chas. Wolff Packing Co. v. Court of Indus. Relations*, 262 U.S. 522, 535 (1923).
232. 273 U.S. 418 (1927).
233. *Id.* at 427.
234. *Id.*
235. *Id.* at 445; Galloway, "The Taft Court," at 27.
236. 273 U.S. at 429.
237. *Id.* at 434.
238. *Id.* at 454–55.
239. *Id.* at 455.
240. *Id.*
241. 277 U.S. 350 (1928).
242. Galloway, "The Taft Court," at 30.
243. *Id.* at 45–46.
244. *Id.* This ruling upended *Munn v. Illinois*, 94 U.S. 113 (1877), the seminal case holding that all businesses that affect the public *are* subject to price regulation. In *Nebbia v. New York*,

291 U.S. 502 (1934), the Court rejected *Ribnik* and other similar decisions of the Taft Court, and reinstated the *Munn* rule. Galloway, "The Taft Court," at 30 n.105.

245. *See* Burner, "Edward Terry Sanford, at 2207–08; Cushman, "Edward Terry Sanford," at 395.
246. Renstrom, *The Taft Court*, at 88.
247. 269 U.S. 304 (1925).
248. 269 U.S. at 310.
249. *Id.*
250. *Id.* at 310–11.
251. *Id.* at 313–14.
252. Cushman, "Edward Terry Sanford," at 395.
253. Frantz, *The Door of Hope*, at 13.
254. Woodward, *Origins of the New South*, at 324–25 (quoting *The Boston Evening Transcript* (Jan. 14, 1899)).
255. 211 U.S. 45, 69 (1908) (Harlan, J., dissenting).
256. Benno C. Schmidt, Jr., "Principle and Prejudice: The Supreme Court and Race in the Progressive Era," 82 *Columbia Law Rev.*, No. 3 (Apr. 1982) at 445.
257. Frantz, *The Door of Hope*, at 13.
258. Schmidt, "Principle and Prejudice," at 491.
259. *Id.* at 488.
260. Frantz, *The Door of Hope*, at 12.
261. 261 U.S. 86 (1923).
262. Galloway, "The Taft Court," at 12.
263. 273 U.S. 536 (1927).
264. *Id.* at 540.
265. *Id.* at 541.
266. 275 U.S. 78 (1927).
267. Cushman, "Edward Terry Sanford," at 395. Taft declared that the issue of the constitutionality of segregated state public schools was "within the power of the state legislatures to settle without the intervention of the federal courts under the federal constitution." Alfred H. Kelly, "The School Desegregation Case," *Quarrels That Have Shaped the Constitution*, John A. Garraty, ed. (New York: Harper & Row, Publishers 1987 (rev. ed.)) at 310.
268. 275 U.S. at 80.
269. *Id.* at 85.
270. G. Edward White, "The Lost Episode of *Gong Lum v. Rice*," 18 *Green Bag* 2d 191 (Winter 2015) at 203.
271. *Id.* at 199 n.18 (quoting Thomas Pearce Bailey, *Race Orthodoxy in the South: And Other Aspects of the Negro Question* (New York: The Neale Publ'g Co. 1914) at 274–76).
272. Virginia Van der Veer Hamilton, *Hugo Black: The Alabama Years* (Tuscaloosa, Ala: Univ. of Alabama Press 1982) at 111.
273. White, "The Lost Episode of *Gong Lum v. Rice*," at 192.
274. *Id. Gong Lum* was overruled in *Brown v. Bd. of Educ.*, 347 U.S. 483 (1954).
275. White, "The Lost Episode of *Gong Lum v. Rice*," at 203.
276. 271 U.S. 323 (1926).
277. 245 U.S. 60 (1917).
278. *Id.* at 81.

279. Brent Rubin, "*Buchanan v. Warley* and the Limits of Substantive Due Process as Antidiscrimination Law," 92 *Texas Law Rev.* 477, 478 (2013).

280. 245 U.S. at 82.

281. 109 U.S. 3 (1883).

282. 271 U.S. at 330.

283. *Civil Rights Cases*, 109 U.S. at 17; Clement E. Vose, *Caucasions Only: The Supreme Court, the NAACP, and the Restrictive Covenant Cases* (Berkeley: Univ. of California Press 1959) at 15.

284. 271 U.S. at 330.

285. *Id.* at 330–31.

286. 334 U.S. 1 (1948).

287. *Id.* at 13 (citing *Corrigan*, 271 U.S. at 330–31).

288. *Id.* at 1920. *See* Rubin, "*Buchanan v. Warley* and the Limits of Substantive Due Process as Antidiscrimination Law," at 497.

289. Davison M. Douglas, "*Corrigan v. Buckley*, 271 U.S. 323 (1926)," http://uscivilliberties.org/cases/3650-Corrigan-v-Buckley-271-US-323-1926.html.

290. Brian Gilmore, "Landmark Court Case Neglected," *South Bend* (Ind.) *Tribune*, (May 7, 2008).

291. *The Nashville Tennessean* (Apr. 14, 1909) at 4.

292. 267 U.S. 467 (1925).

293. *Lewis v. Roberts*, 267 U.S. 467 (1925); Hamilton, *Hugo Black: The Alabama Years*, at III–12.; Stephen Parks Strickland, ed., *Hugo Black and The Supreme Court: A Symposium* (Indianapolis, Ind.: Bobbs-Merrill Co. 1967) at xxiii–xxv.

294. 273 U.S. 668 (1927).

295. 158 La. 439, 441, 104 So. 200, 200 (1925); *see Shelley v. Kraemer*, 334 U.S. 1, 12 (1948).

296. 245 U.S. 60 (1917).

297. Theodore Roosevelt, "The New Nationalism in Social Justice and Popular Rule," 19 *The Works of Theodore Roosevelt* (New York: Charles Scribner's Sons 1925) at 24.

298. 276 U.S. 463 (1928).

299. *Id.* at 464.

300. Babelay, *They Trusted and Were Delivered*, Vol. 1 at 80. The Chavannes family, originally from Charmoisy, France, had fled into Switzerland due to persecution for their Protestant beliefs. *Id.* at 47. They left Switzerland in 1848 for the same reason. *Id.* at 1.

301. 279 U.S. 644 (1929).

302. *Id.*

303. *Id.*

304. *Id.* at 647–48.

305. *Id.* at 652–53.

306. 27 F.2d 742, 744 (7th Cir. 1928).

307. "When Justice Sanford Dissented," *The Coshocton* (Ohio) *Tribune* (Apr. 2, 1930) at 6.

308. Edward T. Sanford, "The Establishment of the Federal Judicial System," Sanford Papers.

309. Post, "Federalism in the Taft Court Era: Can It Be 'Revived'?," at 1514.

310. "Sanford Collapsed In Dentist's Office," *The New York Times* (Mar. 9, 1930) at 28.

311. 274 U.S. 200 (1927).

312. *Id.* at 207; Paul A. Lombardo, *Three Generations, No Imbeciles: Eugenics, the Supreme Court, and Buck v. Bell* (Baltimore, Md.: Johns Hopkins Univ. Press 2008) at ix, x. The passage

of time revealed that Carrie Buck's pregnancy was not caused by "immorality" on her part but resulted from rape at the hands of the nephew of her adoptive mother. Her commitment was an attempt to save the family's reputation. Paul A. Lombardo, "Three Generations, No Imbeciles: New Light on *Buck v. Bell*," 60 *New York Univ. Law Rev.* (1985) at 30–62. After her sterilization, Carrie Buck was an avid reader until her death in 1983. Her "feebleminded" daughter Vivian made the honor roll until her death from measles in 1932. *Id.*

313. Lombardo, *Three Generations, No Imbeciles: Eugenics*, at x.

314. Cynkar, "*Buck v. Bell*," at 1428 (quoting Harry Laughlin, *The Legal Status of Eugenical Sterilization* (Chicago: Municipal Court 1929) at 65).

315. Lombardo, *Three Generations, No Imbeciles: Eugenics*, at xii, 10, 26, 32.

316. Cynkar, "*Buck v. Bell*," at 1433.

317. "The Scourge of Soviet Science," *The Wall Street Journal* (June 18–19, 2016) at C7.

318. "Remembering the Victims of Nazi Eugenics," http://m.dw.com/en/remembering-the-victims-of-nazi-eugenics/a-16945569.

319. Brendan Wolfe, "*Buck v. Bell* (1927)," *Encyclopedia Virginia*, Virginia Foundation for the Humanities (Nov. 4, 2015), https://www.EncyclopediaVirginia.org/Buck_v_Bell_1027.

320. Lombardo, *Three Generations, No Imbeciles: Eugenics*, at 28.

321. Albert E. Wiggam, *The New Decalogue of Science* (Indianapolis, Ind.: Bobbs-Merrill 1922).

322. Larson, *Summer For the Gods*, at 27 n.64.

323. Wiggam, *The New Decalogue of Science*, at 42–43.

324. Cynkar, "*Buck v. Bell*," at 1424.

325. *Id.* at 1424–25 (quoting S. P. Davies, *Social Control of the Feebleminded: A Study of Social Programs and Attitudes In Relation to the Problems of Mental Deficiency* (New York: Nat'l Comm. For Mental Hygiene 1923) at 24).

326. Larson, *Summer For the Gods*, at 27.

327. Victoria Nourse, "*Buck v. Bell*: A Constitutional Tragedy From A Lost World," 39 *Pepperdine Law Rev.* 101, 113 (Dec. 2011).

328. *Id.*

329. 272 U.S. 52 (1926).

330. *Id.* at 176.

331. Mason, "*Chief Justice Taft at the Helm*," at 396. Taft spent a great deal of time and effort on this case and was very upset when Brandeis, Holmes, and McReynolds refused to join his opinion. He wrote: "McReynolds and Brandeis belong to a class of people that have no loyalty to the court and sacrifice almost everything to the gratification of their own publicity and wish to stir up dissatisfaction with the decision of the court, if they don't happen to agree with it." Letter from William H. Taft to Horace Taft (Oct. 27, 1926) (quoted in Pringle, *The Life and Times of William Howard Taft*, at 1023, 1024–25).

332. "The Teapot Dome Scandal," http://www/wyohistory.org/encyclopedia/teapot-dome-scandal.

333. *Id.* The other tracts of oil-bearing land were at Elk Hills and Buena Vista in California.

334. "Oil Stories and Histories: Scandal: A Short History of the Teapot Dome Affair," http://oilstorieshistories.blogspot.com/2005/09/scandal-short-history-of-teapot-dome.html at 5.

335. Morris Robert Werner and John Starr, *Teapot Dome* (New York: Viking Press 1959) at 42, 54–57, 84–86.

336. *Id.* at 86.

337. "Oil Stories and Histories: Scandal: A Short History of the Teapot Dome Affair," http://oilstorieshistories.blogspot.com/2005/09/scandal-short-history-of-teapot-dome.html at 1.

338. 65 Cong. Rec. 1728–1729 (1924); 43 Stat. chap. 16 (1924).

339. Walsh was one of the attorneys for the defendants in the *Winters* case, handled by Sanford on appeal when he served as assistant attorney general. Shurts, *Indian Reserved Water Rights*, at 160.

340. Werner & Starr, *Teapot Dome*, at 159.

341. 65 Cong. Rec. at 3410 (1924).

342. "Oil Stories and Histories: Scandal: A Short History of the Teapot Dome Affair," at 5.

343. *See Pan Amer. Petroleum and Transport Co. v. United States*, 273 U.S. 456, (1927) (per Butler, J.).

344. *See Mammoth Oil Company, The Sinclair Crude Oil Purchasing Company, and the Sinclair Pipe Co. v. United States*, 275 U.S. 13 (1927). Butler authored the opinion, which Sanford joined. *See also Sinclair v. United States*, 279 U.S. 749 (1929).

345. *Sinclair v. United States*, 279 U.S. 263 (1929).

346. Allen, *Only Yesterday*, at 120.

347. "Decrees Delay for Trial of Doheny," *The* (San Diego) *Evening Tribune* (Mar. 10, 1930) at 2.

348. 273 U.S. 135 (1927).

349. "Oil Stories and Histories: Scandal: A Short History of the Teapot Dome Affair," http://oilstorieshistories.blogspot.com/2005/09/scandal-short-history-of-teapot-dome.html at 2.

350. Daniel E. Brannen Jr., Richard Clay Hanes & Rebecca Valentine, "*McGrain v. Daugherty* (1927) *Supreme Court Drama: Cases That Changed America*," Lawrence W. Baker, ed. (2nd ed.) Vol. 5 (Detroit: UXL 2011) at 1038.

351. Ragan, "Mr. Justice Sanford," at 87.

352. *Id.*

353. Toast, Tennessee Bar Association (May 26, 1911), Sandford Papers.

354. Noone, "Edward Terry Sanford," at 37.

355. *Id.*

356. William Rule, "The New Supreme Court Justice," *The New York Times* (Feb. 4, 1923) at xx4.

357. "Final Tribute to Justice Sanford," *The Altoona* (Pa.) *Mirror* (Mar. 10, 1930) at 13.

358. "High Justice Sanford Dead in Capital," *The San Francisco Chronicle* (Mar. 9, 1930) at 70.

359. *The Oakland* (Cal.) *Tribune* (May 8, 1929) at 2.

CHAPTER 11

1. *Gitlow*, 268 U.S. at 666. In *Chicago, Burlington & Quincy R.R. Co. v. Chicago*, 166 U.S. 226 (1897), the Court held that the Fourteenth Amendment imposes on the states the same requirements as the Fifth Amendment eminent domain clause imposes on the federal government. The case did not, however, use reasoning based on the incorporation theory. Galloway, *The Taft Court* at 19 n.63.

2. Only the first eight Amendments specify and protect personal rights, liberties, privileges, and immunities. These first eight consitute the "Bill of Rights."

3. Abraham, *Justices, Presidents, and Senators*, at 145.

4. Klaus H. Heberle, "From *Gitlow* to *Near*: Judicial 'Amendment' by Absent-Minded Incrementalism," 34 *The Journal of Politics* (Univ. of Chicago Press May 1972) at 459.

5. *Id.* at 460 (citing *Slaughterhouse* Cases, 83 U.S. 394, 409–10; *Maxwell v. Dow*, 176 U.S. 581, 605; *Twining v. New Jersey*, 211 U.S. 78, 94–99, 113–14).

6. Joseph R. Marbach, Ellis Katz & Troy E. Smith, eds., *Federalism In America: An Encyclopedia*, Vol. 1: A-J (Westport, Conn.: Greenwood Press 2006) at 326; Archibald Cox, *The Court and the Constitution* (Boston: Houghton Mifflin Co. 1987) at 112.

7. Richard C. Cortner, *The Supreme Court and the Second Bill of Rights: The Fourteenth Amendment and the Nationalization of Civil Liberties* (Univ. of Wisconsin Press 1980) at 3.

8. Cox, *The Court and the Constitution*, at 111–12.

9. Ronald K.L. Collins & Sam Chaltain, *We Must Not Be Afraid To Be Free: Stories of Free Expression In America* (New York: Oxford Univ. Press 2001) at 21.

10. John J. Patrick, Richard M. Pious, & Donald A. Ritchie, *The Oxford Guide to the United States Government* (New York: Oxford Univ. Press 2001) at 316.

11. Lendler, *Gitlow v. New York*, at 94.

12. 32 U.S. 243 (1833).

13. *Id.* See also *Livingston v. Moore*, 32 U.S. 469 (1833).

14. *Barron*, 32 U.S. at 250.

15. 44 U.S. 589 (1845).

16. *Id.*; Cortner, *The Supreme Court and the Second Bill of Rights*, at 45.

17. Cortner, *The Supreme Court and the Second Bill of Rights*, at 5.

18. Curtis, *No State Shall Abridge: The Fourteenth Amendment and the Bill of Rights*, at 23.

19. Howard N. Meyer, *The Amendment That Refused To Die: Equality and Justice Deferred, A History of the Fourteenth Amendment* (Lanham, Md.: Madison Books 2000) at 39.

20. Curtis, *No State Shall Abridge*, at 26.

21. Akkil Reed Amar, "Hugo Black and the Hall of Fame," 53 *Ala. Law Rev.* 1221 (2002) at 1224.

22. Epps, *Democracy Reborn*, at 4–5.

23. U.S. Const., Art. 1, sec. 2, para. 3.

24. Langguth, *After Lincoln*, at 132.

25. Brake, *Justice in the Valley*, at 25. The Constitution recognized the "peculiar institution" as a matter for state control. Don E. Fehrenbacker, "The Dred Scott Case," *Quarrels That Have Shaped the Constitution*, John A. Garraty, ed. (New York: Harper & Row Publishers 1987) at 87.

26. Epps, *Democracy Reborn*, at 10.

27. *Id.*

28. Amar, "Hugo Black and the Hall of Fame," at 1225.

29. Curtis, *No State Shall Abridge*, at 31.

30. *Id.* at 52.

31. Radical Republican Senator Charles Sumner asserted that the people of Massachusetts "would see their state sink below the sea and become a sand bar rather than acknowledge a human being could be treated as property." Langguth, *After Lincoln*, at 17.

32. Epps, *Democracy Reborn*, at 83.

33. Curtis, *No State Shall Abridge*, at 35; Aremona G. Bennett, "Freedom: Personal Liberty and Private Law, Phantom Freedom, Official Acceptance of Violence to Personal Security and Subversion of Proprietary Rights and Ambition Following Emancipation, 1865–1912," 70 *Chicago-Kent Law Rev.* 439, 453–54 (1994).

34. Curtis, *No State Shall Abridge*, at 102, 220–21.

35. Langguth, *After Lincoln*, at 120.

36. Cooper & Terrill, *The American South*, at 379, 382. "A major factor in the northern Republicans' determination to create and implement their Reconstruction plan was their conviction that they had to protect what the Union had won in battle from a seemingly unbowed South. Republicans also felt compelled to do something to protect Unionists [like those in East Tennessee] and blacks in the South." *Id.* at 380.

37. Curtis, *No State Shall Abridge*, at 72.

38. Bryan H. Wildenthal, "The Lost Compromise: Reassessing the Early Understanding in Court and Congress on Incorporation of the Bill of Rights in the Fourteenth Amendment," 61 *Ohio State Law Journal* 1051, 1071 (2000); Curtis, *No State Shall Abridge*, at 72; *Cong. Globe*, 39th Cong., 1st sess. 1291 (1866). Bingham served as a prosecutor at the trial of the conspirators in the assassination of President Abraham Lincoln. Gerard N. Magliocea, *American Founding Son: John Bingham and the Invention of the Fourteenth Amendment* (New York: New York Univ. Press 2013).

39. Cortner, *The Supreme Court and the Second Bill of Rights*, at 5 (*Cong. Globe*, 39th Cong., 1st Sess. at 2765–66 (May 23, 1866)); *See*, for example, *Cong. Globe*, 39th Cong., 1st sess. 1120, 1270 (1866).

40. Curtis, *No State Shall Abridge*, at 91.

41. *Id.*

42. Foner, *Reconstruction*, at 575–76.

43. Epps, *Democracy Reborn*, at 262–63.

44. Brake, *Justice In The Valley*, at 54.

45. Bryan H. Wildenthal, "The Road to *Twining*: Reassessing the Disincorporation of the Bill of Rights," 61 *Ohio State Law Journal* 1457 (2000) at 1520 (quoting Curtis, *No State Shall Abridge*, at 180).

46. Marbach, et al., *Federalism In America*, at 327.

47. The phrase "privileges or immunities" had no settled meaning when the Fourteenth Amendment was adopted, and the words "are broad enough to protect almost any right to liberty, human dignity, privacy, or property that the Court might read into them in order to protect individual citizens against governmental action." Cox, *The Court and the Constitution*, at 112.

48. 83 U.S. 36 (1873).

49. *Id.* at 59.

50. Cortner, *The Supreme Court and the Second Bill of Rights*, at 7.

51. 83 U.S. at 77.

52. *Id.* at 78; Epps, *Democracy Reborn*, at 263.

53. Richard C. Cortner, "The Nationalization of the Bill of Rights: An Overview," American Political Science Ass'n and American Historical Ass'n (1985).

54. Lendler, *Gitlow v. New York*, at 95.

55. Cortner, *The Supreme Court and the Second Bill of Rights*, at 10.

56. 83 U.S. at 78.

57. *Id.* Chief Justice Chase and Associate Justices Field, Bradley, and Swayne dissented.

58. Wildenthal, "The Lost Compromise," at 1080.

59. *Id.* at 1081.

60. Bryan H. Wildenthal, *Nationalizing the Bill of Rights: The Rise, Fall, and Rise of the Fourteenth Amendment Incorporation Doctrine* (Book Manuscript, Intro, and Chs. 1 and 2, May 2006 Draft), http://ssrn.com/abstract=905621 at 11.

61. Jacob W. Landynski, "Due Process and the Concept of Ordered Liberty: 'A Screen of Words Expressing Will in the Service of Desire?'" 2 *Hofstra Law Rev.*, No. 1 (Winter 1974) at 3. As noted by Professor Landynski: "The phrase first appeared in 1354 in a statute of Edward III, which provided that no person should be subjected to punishment 'without being brought in answer by due process of law.' 28 Edw. III, c. 3. The language is believed to be derived from, and synonymous with, King John's promise in chapter 39 of Magna Carta that he would not 'go upon' or 'send upon' any 'freeman' except 'by the law of the land.'" *Id.*

62. *See Walker v. Sauvinet*, 92 U.S. 90 (1876); *Hurtado v. California*, 110 U.S. 516 (1884); *Maxwell v. Dow*, 176 U.S. 581 (1900).

63. 110 U.S. 516 (1884).

64. Cortner, "The Nationalization of the Bill of Rights," at 2.

65. Marbach, et al., *Federalism In America*, at 327. In a later Fourteenth Amendment case involving a jury composed of less than twelve persons, Harlan noted: "[I]t would seem that the protection of private property is of more consequence than the protection of the life and liberty of citizens." *Maxwell v. Dow*, 176 U.S. 581, 614 (1900) (Harlan, J., dissenting).

66. Cortner, *The Supreme Court and the Second Bill of Rights*, at 2.

67. Landynski, "Due Process and the Concept of Ordered Liberty," at 9 (citing Richard Hofstadter, *Social Darwinism in American Thought* (rev. ed. 1959)(Philadelphia: Univ. of Pennsylvania Press 1944)).

68. *Id.*

69. 134 U.S. 418 (1890).

70. *Id.* at 457 Savage, "From the Gilded Age to the Great Depression," at 36. The doctrine of economic substantive due process was later squarely endorsed in *Allgeyer v. Louisiana*, 165 U.S. 578 (1897).

71. Savage, "From the Gilded Age to the Great Depression," at 35 (quoting Michael Les Benedict, "History of the Court: Reconstruction, Federalism, and Economic Rights," in *The Oxford Companion to the Supreme Court of the United States*, ed. Kermit H. Hall, et al. (New York: Oxford Univ. Press 1992) at 388).

72. Savage, "From the Gilded Age to the Great Depression," at 35 (quoting William F. Swindler, *Court and Constitution in the Twentieth Century: The Old Legality, 1889–1932* (Indianapolis: Bobbs-Merrill 1964) at 1–2).

73. Edwards, *New Spirits*, at 256.

74. *Id.* at 257.

75. *Id.* at 267.

76. Savage, "From The Gilded Age to the Great Depression," at 35.

77. These laws purportedly were named after a dance tune, "Jump Jim Crow," that ridiculed blacks. "Jim Crow Laws," http://www.tn4me.org/minor_cat.cfm/minor_id/93/major_id/31/era_id/6.

78. Alan F. Westin, "The Case of the Prejudiced Doorkeeper," *Quarrels That Shaped the Constitution*, John A. Garraty, ed. (New York: Harper & Row Publishers 1987) at 155.

79. Schmidt, "Principle and Prejudice," at 466. In 1891 Congress had defeated the Lodge Bill, which would have broadened federal protection to blacks seeking to vote in federal elections. Three years later, Congress "wiped from the books virtually all the explicit Reconstruction statutory protections for black voting rights." *Id.*

80. 166 U.S. 226 (1897).

81. *Id.* at 241.
82. *Id.*
83. Amar, "Hugo Black and the Hall of Fame," at 1226–27.
84. 166 U.S. at 235.
85. This decision implicitly repudiated the reasoning in *Hurtado*. Cortner, *The Supreme Court and the Second Bill of Rights*, at 2.
86. Galloway, *The Taft Court*, at 19 n. 63.
87. Wildenthal, "The Road to *Twining*," at 1501–05.
88. 205 U.S. 454 (1907).
89. *Id.* at 458–59.
90. *Id.* at 462.
91. *Id.* at 465; Collins & Chaltain, *We Must Not Be Afraid to Be Free*, at 30–31.
92. 211 U.S. 78 (1908).
93. *Id.* at 96.
94. Wildenthal, *Nationalizing the Bill of Rights: The Rise, Fall, and Rise of the Fourteenth Amendment Incorporation Doctrine* (Book Manuscript, Intro and Chs. 1 and 2, May 2006 Draft), http://ssrn.com/abstract=905621 at 2.
95. Cortner, *The Supreme Court and the Second Bill of Rights*, at 3.
96. 211 U.S. at 99.
97. *Id.* at 97–106.
98. *Id.* at 110–14.
99. Cortner, *The Supreme Court and the Second Bill of Rights*, at 49.
100. 211 U.S. at 121–22 (Harlan, J., dissenting).
101. Thomas C. Mackey, "'They Are Positively Dangerous Men': The Lost Court Documents of Benjamin Gitlow and James Larkin Before the New York City Magistrates' Court, 1919," 69 *New York Univ. Law Rev.* (1994) at 423–24.
102. Renstrom, *The Taft Court*, at 8.
103. http://www.tennesseehistory.com/class/Sanford.htm.
104. *Free Speech on Trial: Communication Perspectives on Landmark Supreme Court Decisions*, Richard A. Parker, ed. (Tuscaloosa, Ala.: Univ. of Alabama Press 2003) at 21.
105. 249 U.S. 47 (1919).
106. 250 U.S. 616 (1919).
107. 249 U.S. at 52.
108. *Id.* The "clear and present danger test" became the standard by which to evaluate "dangerous" speech.
109. 250 U.S. at 617–19.
110. *Id.* at 628.
111. 254 U.S. 325 (1920).
112. *Id.* at 328.
113. *Id.* at 332.
114. *Prudential Ins. Co. v. Cheek*, 259 U.S. 530, 543 (1922); Epps, *Democracy Reborn*, at 267. Taft, Van Devanter, and McReynolds dissented.
115. 259 U.S. at 543.
116. 259 U.S. 530, 539, 543.
117. *Id.* at 538.

118. *Gitlow v. New York*, 268 U.S. 652, 666 (1925).

119. *Id.* at 655.

120. Lendler, *Gitlow v. New York*, at 1.

121. Encyclopedia Britannica, http://www.britannica.com. The raids led to the arrest of more than 6,000 persons. Renstrom, *The Taft Court,* at 8. Thousands of Russian immigrants, along with Communist Party and Communist Labor Party members, were hunted down. Many were detained in the reception room at Ellis Island. Collins & Chaltain, *We Must Not Be Afraid to Be Free,* at 23.

122. *Gitlow*, 268 U.S. 652; Brief for the State of New York, at 13–14.

123. This count was later withdrawn at the trial. Collins & Chaltain, *We Must Not Be Afraid to Be Free*, at 18, 25.

124. 268 U.S. at 655; Lendler, *Gitlow v. New York*, at 20.

125. Lendler, *Gitlow v. New York*, at 1–2. Sanford's uncle, Albert Chavannes, gained fame as a writer of utopian novels in which the economy is governed by socialist ideals, rather than capitalism, and morality is based on social scientific experimentation instead of religion. He became known as an early American sociologist, and he edited and published what was perhaps the first periodical devoted primarily to sociology, *The Sociologist*.

126. Lendler, *Gitlow v. New York*, at 2.

127. *Id.* at 47.

128. *Id.* at 111.

129. Heberle, "From *Gitlow* to *Near*," at 461.

130. Phillips, *History of the Sixth Circuit*, at 68–69.

131. *Gitlow*, 268 U.S. at 666.

132. Lendler, *Gitlow v. New York*, at 115.

133. Galloway, *The Taft Court*, at 19.

134. *Id.* at 19 n.64.

135. *Id.* at 1–2, 21, 92–93. Holmes, however, observed that "there was no present danger of an attempt to overthrow the government by force on the part of the admittedly small minority who shared the defendant's views." *Gitlow*, 268 U.S. at 673. Holmes's position had been enunciated in *Schenk v. United States*, 249 U.S. 47 (1919) and required that the danger be both "clear" and "present." *Id.* at 52.

136. *Gitlow*, 268 U.S. at 673.

137. *Id.* at 666–67. In support of this assertion, the Court cited, among others, *Fox v. Washington*, 236 U.S. 273, 277–78 (1915) (upholding punishment for expression interpreted to encourage indecent exposure); *Patterson v. Colorado,* 205 U.S. 454, 463 (1907) (upholding punishment for expression interfering with judicial proceeding); and several of the World War I cases, including *Schenk v. United States*, 249 U.S. 47, 52–53 (1919) (upholding punishment for encouraging draft resistance).

138. *Gitlow*, 268 U.S. at 669.

139. *Id.*

140. *Id.* at 664–65.

141. *Id.* at 669. The prosecution made no showing that Gitlow had created any serious danger. Brandeis and Holmes dissented, arguing that speech may not be punished absent a clear and present danger of some serious evil.

142. Lendler, *Gitlow v. New York*, at 113.

143. *Id.*

144. *Id.* at 114.
145. *Id.*
146. *Id.* at 125.
147. Marbach, et al., *Federalism in America*, at 328.
148. Galloway, "The Taft Court," at 19–20.
149. Milton R. Konvitz, *Fundamental Rights* (New Brunswick, NJ: Transaction Publishers 2001), at 66.
150. Collins & Chaltain, *We Must Not Be Afraid to Be Free*, at 33, 35.
151. Konvitz, *Fundamental Rights*, at 65.
152. *Id.*
153. *Id.*
154. Galloway, "The Taft Court," at 19.
155. John Denton Carter, *The Warren Court and the Constitution: A Critical Review of Judicial Activism* (Gretna, La.: Pelican Publ'g 1973) at 69.
156. Heberle, "From *Gitlow* to *Near,*" at 459.
157. *Id.* at 460.
158. Sanford Papers.
159. "The *Gitlow* Case," *The New Republic* (July 1, 1925) at 142.
160. Charles Warren, "The New Liberty Under the Fourteenth Amendment," 39 *Harvard Law Rev.* (Jan. 1926) at 431.
161. Heberle, "From *Gitlow* to *Near,*" at 478 (citing Warren, "The New Liberty Under the Fourteenth Amendment," 39 *Harvard Law Rev.* 431 (Jan. 1926)).
162. Lendler, *Gitlow v. New York*, at 125.
163. Collins & Chaltain, *We Must Not Be Afraid To Be Free*, at 33.
164. James P. Hall, "Comment on Recent Cases," 20 *Illinois Law Rev.* (Apr. 1926) at 809.
165. Heberle, "From *Gitlow* to *Near,*" at 478.
166. Renstrom, *The Taft Court*, at 206.
167. On the question of whether the Fourteenth Amendment made the principles of freedom of expression applicable to the state, Holmes stated: "The general principle of free speech ... must be taken to be included in the Fourteenth Amendment, in view of the scope that has been given to the word 'liberty' as there used...." *Gitlow*, 268 U.S. at 672.
168. Currie, "The Constitution in the Supreme Court," at 66.
169. 274 U.S. 357 (1927).
170. *Id.* at 363.
171. *Id.* at 365.
172. Syndicalism is a revolutionary doctrine by which workers seize control of the economy and the government by direct means. https://www.merriam-webster.com/dictionary/syndicalism.
173. 274 U.S. at 366.
174. Heberle, "From *Gitlow* to *Near,*" at 466.
175. Lendler, *Gitlow v. New York*, at 128.
176. 274 U.S. at 371.
177. Heberle, "From *Gitlow* to *Near,*" at 466–67.
178. 274 U.S. at 371.
179. *Id.* at 373 (emphasis added). The law of free speech known today grew out of the opinions of Justices Holmes and Brandeis.
180. Heberle, "From *Gitlow* to *Near,*" at 469.

181. 274 U.S. at 377.
182. Heberle, "From *Gitlow* to *Near*," at 469.
183. 274 U.S. at 372–80; Cushman, "Inside the Taft Court," at 39–40.
184. 395 U.S. 444, 448–49 (1969).
185. Robert Bork, "Neutral Principles and Some First Amendment Problems," 47 *Indiana Law Journal* 1, 23 (1971–72).
186. Parker, *Free Speech on Trial*, at 46.
187. *Id.* at 44.
188. 274 U.S. 380 (1927).
189. Galloway, "The Taft Court," at 26. This case was assigned originally to Van Devanter. Taft reassigned it to Sanford because of Van Devanter's ill health and because Sanford was working on other syndicalism cases. Mason, "Chief Justice Taft at the Helm," at 382.
190. Richard C. Cortner, "The Wobblies and *Fiske v. Kansas*: Victory Amid Disintegration," *Kansas History* 4 (Spring 1981) at 32.
191. 274 U.S. 382.
192. Cortner, "The Wobblies and *Fiske v. Kansas*: Victory Amid Disintegration," at 33 (quoting *Great Bend* [Kan.] *Tribune* [July 3, 1923]).
193. *Fiske v. Kansas*, Brief for Plaintiff in Error (1927) at 11.
194. 274 U.S. at 386.
195. *Id.* at 387.
196. *Id.*
197. Burner, "Edward Terry Sanford," in *The Justices of the United States Supreme Court, 1789–1969*, at 2207.
198. Zechariah Chafee, Jr., *Free Speech in the United States* (Cambridge: Harvard Univ. Press 1954) at 352.
199. Anthony D. Romero, "The First Amendment and Defense of the Unpopular," (Undelivered Speech, Amherst College [Mar. 29, 2004] at 3 [citing Zachariah Chafee]).
200. Heberle, "From *Gitlow* to *Near*," at 470 n.37.
201. Henry Abraham, *Freedom and the Court* (3rd ed.) (New York: Oxford Univ. Press 1977) at 62.
202. *Id.*
203. 297 U.S. 233, 244.
204. Heberle, "From *Gitlow* to *Near*, at 470 n.37 (letter from Harlan F. Stone to Felix Frankfurter), Frankfurter Papers, Manuscript Division, Library of Congress, Washington, D.C. ("Frankfurter Papers").
205. Renstrom, *The Taft Court*, at 206; *In re Oliver*, 333 U.S. 257 (1948) (Sixth Amendment right to public trial); *Wolf v. Colorado*, 338 U.S. 25 (1949) (Fourth Amendment); *Mapp v. Ohio*, 367 U.S. 643 (1961) (exclusionary rule); *Robinson v. California*, 370 U.S. 660 (1962) (Eighth Amendment right against cruel and unusual punishment); *Gideon v. Wainwright*, 372 U.S. 335 (1963) (Sixth Amendment right to counsel); *Malloy v. Hogan*, 378 U.S. 1 (1964) (Fifth Amendment right against compelled self-incrimination); *Pointer v. Texas*, 380 U.S. 400 (1965) (Sixth Amendment right to confront opposing witnesses); *Klopfer v. North Carolina*, 386 U.S. 213 (1967) (Sixth Amendment right to a speedy trial); *Washington v. Texas*, 388 U.S. 14 (1967) (Sixth Amendment right to compulsory process); *Duncan v. Louisiana*, 391 U.S. 145 (1968) (Sixth Amendment right to jury trial); *Benton v. Maryland*, 395 U.S. 784 (1969) (Fifth Amendment right against double jeopardy).

206. 283 U.S. 359 (1931).
207. *Id.* at 368. Hughes cited *Gitlow*, *Whitney*, and *Fiske*.
208. 283 U.S. 697 (1931).
209. *Id.* at 707.
210. 302 U.S. 319 (1937).
211. 381 U.S. 479 (1965).
212. 561 U.S. 742 (2010).
213. The Fifth Amendment right to an indictment by a grand jury and the Seventh Amendment right to a jury trial in civil lawsuits have not been incorporated.
214. http://www.dailykos.com.
215. Renstrom, *The Taft Court*, at 207; Phillips, *History of the Sixth Circuit*, at 69.
216. Wildenthal, "The Lost Compromise," at 1076–77.
217. "U.S. Justice Edward Sanford," Tennessee History Classroom, http://www.tennesseehistory.com/class/Sanford.htm.
218. Curtis, *No State Shall Abridge*, at 2.
219. "U.S. Justice Edward Sanford," Tennessee History Classroom, http://www.tennesseehistory.com/class/Sanford.htm.

CHAPTER 12

1. Lindsay Powell, "High Knox Jurist Called 'Mediocre,'" *The Knoxville News-Sentinel* (Mar. 25, 1970) at 1.
2. Cook, "Path to the High Bench," at 1.
3. Hall, *Supreme Court Justices*, at 289.
4. "Edward Terry Sanford," *The Knoxville News-Sentinel* (Mar. 9, 1930) at 22.
5. "A Justice Forgotten?" *Court Historical Soc'y Newsletter*, United States District Court for the Eastern District of Tennessee (Dec. 2004) (quoting Francis Lloyd, Esq.).
6. OYEZ, US Supreme Court Media, http://www.oyez.org/justices/edward_t_sanford/. Robert C. Post, in "Mr. Taft Becomes Chief Justice," 76 *Univ. Cincinnati Law Rev.* 761 (2008) noted that while "Taft's standing was never higher than at the moment of his demise . . . it has since sunk into deep oblivion, which suggests that judicial administration is not the platform on which to erect an enduring judicial reputation." *Id.* at 783. Post related that on Taft's retirement, *Time* magazine "ruthlessly encapsulate[d] his career with the pithy assessment: 'Outstanding decisions: none.'" *Id.* at 784.
7. "Justice Sanford Dies Following Collapse," *The Palm Beach* (Fla.) *Daily News* (Mar. 8, 1930) at 19. Sanford was succeeded on the Court by Owen Josephus Roberts, who, as a special United States attorney, had been assigned by President Calvin Coolidge to investigate the Teapot Dome scandal. Roberts successfully prosecuted and imprisoned President Warren G. Harding's Secretary of the Interior, Albert Fall. Kermit L. Hall, "Owen Josephus Roberts," in Melvin I. Urofsky, ed., *The Supreme Court Justices: A Biographical Dictionary* (New York: Garland Publ'g Co. 1994) at 383.
8. Letter from Willis Van Devanter to John C. Pollock (Mar. 8, 1930), Van Devanter Papers.
9. Letter from Willis Van Devanter to John C. Knox (Mar. 11, 1930), Van Devanter Papers.
10. Stephen Keyes Williams, 74 *Cases Argued and Decided in the Supreme Court of the United States* (Lawyers Co-operative Publ'g Co. 1929) at 1185; http://www.law.umkc.edu/faculty/projects/ftrials/shipp/sanford.html.
11. "Mourn Passing of Sanford," *The New York Times* (Mar. 9, 1930) at 28.

12. *Id.*

13. "Leaders Eulogize Justice Sanford," *The Evening Star* (Washington, D.C.) (Mar. 9, 1930) at 4.

14. "Mourn Passing of Sanford," *The New York Times* (Mar. 9, 1930) at 28.

15. "Leaders Eulogize Justice Sanford," *The Evening Star* (Washington, D.C.) (Mar. 9, 1930) at 4.

16. "Knoxville Is Shocked," *The Huntsville* (Ala.) *Daily Times* (Mar. 8, 1930); "Knoxville Bar Pays Tribute to Sanford," *The Washington Post* (Mar. 9, 1930) at M4. "Resolution Adopted by the Knox County Bar Association," *Proceedings of the Bar and Officers of the Supreme Court of the United States in Memory of Edward T. Sanford,* at 248.

17. "Jurist's First Case Recalled," *The Knoxville News-Sentinel* (Mar. 8, 1930) at 10.

18. "Proceedings in Memory of Mr. Justice Sanford," 285 U.S. xxxvii (1931).

19. "Edward Terry Sanford," 8 *Tennessee Law Rev.* 189–90 (1930); a portrait of Sanford was completed in 1925 by Knoxville artist Lloyd Branson and presented in 1927 to the University of Tennessee College of Law. "Book II Mar- Sept 1927," *College of Law Library History,* http://trace.tennessee.edu/utk_lawlibhist/14 at 18, 19; "Dedication of Tennessee Hall," 5 *Tennessee Law Rev.*, No. 4 (1927); "The Society's Archives," *Court Historical Soc'y Newsletter,* United States District Court for the Eastern District of Tennessee, Inc. (Feb. 2011) at 1. The portrait was later given to the United States District Court for the Eastern District of Tennessee, where it hung in the main courtroom until the court was moved to the Howard Baker, Jr., United States Courthouse. According to Don Ferguson, historian for the Historical Society for the United States District Court for the Eastern District of Tennessee, the portrait currently hangs in the historical suite at the courthouse.

20. 43 *Harvard Law Rev.*, No. 6 (Apr. 1930) at 926.

21. Green, "Some Judges of the United States District Court of Tennessee (1878–1939)," 18 *Tennessee Law Rev.* 227, 238 (1943–45).

22. "Taft and Sanford Eulogized," *The New York Times* (June 2, 1931) at 20.

23. "A Useful Life," *The Milwaukee Sentinel* (Mar. 14, 1930) at 4.

24. "Mr. Justice Sanford," *The New York Times* (Mar. 10, 1930) at 15.

25. Post, "The Supreme Court Opinion as Institutional Practice," at 7., http://escholarship.org/uc/item/62t1B008.

26. *Tennessee Encyclopedia of History and Culture* http://tennesseeencyclopedia.net. The average rating is given to those justices "usually well versed in legal craftsmanship and legal statesmanship" but who have failed to "put an indelible stamp on the law and to make their presence felt either in their own time or later." Albert P. Blaustein and Roy M. Mersky, *The First One Hundred Justices: Statistical Studies on the Supreme Court of the United States* (Hamden, Conn.: Archon Books 1978) at 51.

27. Finkelman, *The Supreme Court: Controversies, Cases, and Characters from John Jay to John Roberts,* at 586.

28. Abraham, *Justices, Presidents, and Senators* (1999), at 151.

29. Hollingsworth, "Tennessee and the Supreme Court of the United States," at 21. Hollingsworth stated that McReynolds' reputation is not one of which Tennesseans may be proud. *Id.* at 20.

30. Finkelman, *The Supreme Court,* at 586; Renstrom, *The Taft Court,* at 99.

31. Renstrom, *The Taft Court,* at 99, (quoting Mason, *William Howard Taft: Chief Justice,* at 213).

32. Finkelman, *The Supreme Court*, at 588.
33. Abraham, *Justices, Presidents, and Senators*, at 135.
34. Michael Ariens, http://www.michaelariens.com/conlaw/justices/sanford.htm.
35. William G. Ross, "The Ratings Game: Factors That Influence Judicial Reputation," 79 *Marquette Law Rev.* 401 (Winter 1996) at 406.
36. Ross at 405, 413; G. Edward White, "The Cannonization of Holmes and Brandeis: Epistemology and Judicial Reputations," 70 *New York Univ. Law Rev.* 576, 578–85 (1995).
37. "In Memoriam Horace Harmon Lurton," 34 *Proceedings of the Annual Meeting of the Bar Association of Tennessee* (1915) at 117–18.
38. Allen, *Only Yesterday*, at 203.
39. *Id.* at 206.
40. *Id.* at 216–17.
41. Neely, "A Fair to Remember," *Metro Pulse* (Knoxville, Tenn.) (Nov. 11, 2009).
42. William E. Leuchtenburg, "When Franklin Roosevelt Clashed With the Supreme Court—and Lost," *Smithsonian Magazine* (May 2005).
43. Abraham, *Justices, Presidents, and Senators*, at 144.
44. Ragan, "Mr. Justice Sanford," at 77.
45. Fowler, "Mr. Justice Edward Terry Sanford," at 233 (emphasis added.).
46. Hall, *Supreme Court Justices*, at 289.
47. "Resolution Adopted By The Knox County Bar Association," *Proceedings of the Bar and Officers of the Supreme Court of the United States in Memory of Edward T. Sanford*, at 248.
48. *Class of 1885, Harvard College, Baccalaureate Sermon, Class Day Oration, et al.*, at 20.
49. *Proceedings of the Bar and Officers of the Supreme Court*, at 25.
50. *Id.* at 14.

BIBLIOGRAPHY

MANUSCRIPTS

Governor William G. Brownlow Papers, 1865–69, Tennessee State Library and Archives, http://idserver.utk.edu/?id=200700000001899.
John H. Clarke Papers, Manuscript Division, Library of Congress, Washington, D.C.
Charles William Dabney Papers, 1715–1945 (1412), S. Historical Collection, The Wilson Library, Univ. of N. Carolina at Chapel Hill.
James Alexander Fowler Papers, MPA. 0304. Univ. of Tennessee Libraries, Knoxville, Special Collections.
Felix Frankfurter Papers, Manuscript Division, Library of Congress, Washington, D.C.
Warren G. Harding Papers, Manuscript Division, Library of Congress, Washington, D.C.
Horace H. Lurton Papers, Manuscript Division, Library of Congress, Washington, D.C.
McClung Historical Collection, Lawson McGhee Library, Knoxville, Tenn.
Charles M. McGhee Papers, McClung Historical Collection, Lawson McGhee Library, Knoxville, Tenn.
James Clark McReynolds Papers, Arthur J. Morris Law Library, Special Collections, Univ. of Virginia, Charlottesville, Va., http://archives.law.virginia.edu/records/mss/B5-1/digital/9099.
The John G. Palfrey Collection of Oliver Wendell Holmes, Jr., Papers, General Correspondence, Box 22, Folder 26, Historical and Special Collections, Harvard Law School Library, Cambridge, Mass.
Theodore Roosevelt Papers, Manuscript Division, Library of Congress. http://www.thetheodorerooseveltcenter.org/research/Digital-library/record.aspx?libID=0184080.
Edward T. Sanford Papers, MPA. 0303. Univ. of Tennessee Libraries, Knoxville, Special Collections.
Harlan F. Stone Papers, Manuscript Division, Library of Congress, Washington, D.C.
William H. Taft Papers, Manuscript Division, Library of Congress, Washington, D.C.
Terry Family Papers, MS 482, Sterling Memorial Library, Yale Univ., New Haven, Connecticut.
Willis Van Devanter Papers, Manuscript Division, Library of Congress, Washington, D.C.
Woodrow Wilson Papers, Manuscript Division, Library of Congress, Washington, D.C.
"Finding Aid for the E.E. Hoss Address Regarding John Sevier," MS 0148, Univ. of Tennessee Libraries, Special Collections.

GOVERNMENT DOCUMENTS AND STATISTICAL SOURCES

1 Stat. 496 (Jan. 31, 1797).
18 U.S.C. §§ 2421–24.
28 U.S.C. §292(a).
28 U.S.C. §§ 344–50 (1926).
30 Stat. 1151, Ch. 425, Sec. 9, 33 U.S.C. §407.
40 Stat. 1272 (1919).
42 Stat. 222, Sec. 2.
42 Stat 837 (Sept. 14, 1922).

43 Stat. 936 (1925).
49 Stat. 872, Ch. 740 (1935).
"1901–1905 William Little Frierson," Chattanooga.gov.
Act of Mar. 2,1893, 27 Stat. 531, recodified as amended, 49 U.S.C. §20302.
Butler Act, House Bill No. 185 (Jan. 21, 1925), signed into law Mar. 21, 1925, 49 Tenn. Code Ann. §1922.
City-Data.com.
Esch-Cummins Act, Pub. L. 66–152, 41 Stat 456 (approved Feb. 28, 1920).
Federal Judicial Center, "Courts of the Federal Judiciary: U.S. Circuit Courts and the Federal Judiciary," http://www.fjc.gov/public/home.nsf/hisc.
File of Edward T. Sanford, RG 60, Dep't of Justice Records, Nat'l Archives, College Park, Md.
"Governance & the Judicial Conference," http://uscourts.gov.
"Historical Background" United States District Court for the Middle District of Tennessee http://www.tnmd.uscourts.gov/historical_background_0.
Journal of the Congress of the Confederate States of America, 1861–65, I, (Washington, D.C. Library of Congress).
Keating-Owen Child Labor Law of 1916, Pub. L. No. 64–249, 39 Stat. 675 (1916).
Marriage Reports in State Dep't Decimal Files, 1910–1949.
National Prohibition Act, ch. 85, 41 Stat. 305 (1919).41 Stat. 315 (1919).
"Pensions for Freedmen, Etc.," 56th Cong. 1st Sess., Rep. No. 75 (Jan. 16, 1900).
Preparatory Dep't, Academic Records, 1876–77, Univ. of Tennessee Archives.
Presidential Proclamation 1419, Dec. 26, 1917, under authority of the Army Appropriation Act, 39 Stat. 45 (Aug. 29, 1916).
Pub. Acts, 34th Tenn. Gen. Assembly, 1st Sess. (1865).
Pub. Acts & H.J., 36th Tenn. Gen. Assembly, 1st Sess. (1869–70).
"Reimbursement of Depositors of Freedman's Savings and Trust Company," H. Rpt. 1282, pt. 1 (May 6, 1910).
Senate Resolution No. 6, House Resolution No. 10, Jan. 8, 1923, Pub. Acts of Tennessee, 1923.
"The Freedman's Bank: A Historic Place in the Financial Empowerment of African Americans," https://www.treasury.gov/connect/blog/pages/freedmans_savings_bank.aspx.
"United States Circuit and District Courts in Tennessee," H. Rpt. 1860 (Jan. 15, 1909).
United States Civil War Soldier Records and Profiles, 1961–1865.
United States Federal Census for Knoxville, Tenn. (1870, 1880, 1900, 1910, 1920).
U.S. City Directories, 1822–1989.
Cong. Globe, 39th Cong. 1st sess. 2765–66 (May 23, 1866).
Cong. Globe, 39th Cong. 1st sess. 1120, 1270 (1866).
Cong. Globe, 39th Cong., 1st. sess. 1291 (1866).
U.S. Passport Applications, 1795–1925.
Weeks Law of March 1, 1911, ch. 186, 36 Stat. 961 (Comp. St. 1913, Secs. 5174–5187).
Will of E.J. Sanford, Will Book, Vol. 4, Knox County, Tenn. Archives.

NEWSPAPERS

The Aberdeen (S.D.) *Daily News*
Alton (Ill.) *Evening Telegraph*
The Altoona (Pa.) *Mirror*
The Arkansas Gazette (Little Rock)
The Asheville Gazette-News
The Athens (Tenn.) *Post*
The Atlanta Constitution
The Baltimore Sun

The Billings (Mont.) *Gazette*
The Boston Herald
The Boston Journal
The Bourbon News (Paris, Ky.)
The Brandon Sun (Brandon, Manitoba, Canada)
The Brooklyn Daily Eagle
Brownlow's Knoxville Whig and Rebel Ventilator
The Cambridge Tribune
The Carroll (Iowa) *Herald*
The Charlotte (N. C.) *News*
The Chattanooga Times
The Chicago Defender
Chicago Live Stock World
The Chicago Tribune
The Chronicle Herald (Halifax, Nova Scotia, Canada)
The Cincinnati Enquirer
The Columbia Herald
The Comet (Johnson City, Tenn.)
The Commercial & Financial Chronicle
The Commoner (Lincoln, Neb.)
The Coshocton (Oh.) *Tribune*
The Courier-Journal (Louisville, Ky.)
The Daily American (Nashville)
The Daily Herald (Biloxi, Miss.)
The Daily Nashville (Tenn.) *Patriot*
The Daily Times (Wilson, N. C.)
The Dallas Express
The Dallas Morning News
The Decatur (Ill.) *Herald*
The El Paso Herald
The Evening Chronicle (Charlotte, N.C.)
The Evening Star (Washington, D.C.)
The Evening Telegraph (Alton, Ill.)
The Evening Tribune (San Diego, Cal.)
The Florence (S. C.) *Times-News*
The French Broad Hustler (N.C.)
The Gaffney Ledger (S. C.)
The Gainesville (Fla.) *Star*
The Galveston Daily News (Galveston, Tex.)
The Gastonia (N. C.) *Gazette*
The Harrisburg (Pa.) *Telegraph*
The Huntsville (Ala.) *Daily Times*
Janesville (Wis.) *Daily Gazette*

The Joplin (Mo.) *Globe*
The Kingsport (Tenn.) *Times*
The Kingsport (Tenn.) *Times-News*
The Kingston (N.Y.) *Daily Freeman*
The Knoxville Daily Chronicle
The Knoxville Daily Journal
The Knoxville Free Press
The Knoxville Journal
The Knoxville Journal and Tribune
The Knoxville Mercury
The Knoxville News-Sentinel
The Knoxville Free Press
The Knoxville Press and Herald
The Knoxville Press and Messenger
The Knoxville Sentinel
The Knoxville Weekly Chronicle
The Knoxville Whig
The Keowee Courier (Pickens, S. C.)
The Lexington (Ky.) *Herald*
The Macon (Ga.) *Telegraph*
Metro Pulse (Knoxville, Tenn.)
Metropolitan News-Enterprise (Los Angeles)
The Memphis Appeal
The Milwaukee Sentinel
The Minneapolis Journal
The Montreal Gazette
The Morning Times (Washington, D.C.)
The Nashville (Tenn.) *American*
The Nashville (Tenn.) *Daily Press and Times*
The Nashville Tennessean
The New Orleans States
The New York Age
The New York Daily Times
The New York Times
The New York Tribune
The News and Observer (Raleigh, N.C.)
The News-Herald (Franklin, Pa.)
The Oakland (Cal.) *Tribune*
The Omaha World-Herald
The Ottawa Citizen Weekend Magazine
The Ottawa Journal
The Palestine (Tex.) *Daily Herald*
The Palestine (Ill.) *Enterprise*
The Palm Beach (Fla.) *Daily News*
The Palm Beach (Fla.) *Post*

The Pittsburgh (Pa.) *Post-Gazette*
The Pittsburg (Ks.) *Sun*
The Prescott (Ariz.) *Evening Courier*
The Reading (Pa.) *Eagle*
The Republican Banner (Nashville, Tenn.)
The Riverside (Cal.) *Daily Press*
The Rockford (Ill.) *Republic*
The Sacramento (Cal.) *Union*
The Salt Lake Telegram
The San Francisco Chronicle
The Seattle Daily Times
The Shopper News (Knoxville, Tenn.)
The Sioux City (Iowa) *Journal*
The Springfield (Mass.) *Republican*
The State Chronicle (Raleigh, N. C.)
The Tampa Tribune

The Times Dispatch (Richmond, Va.)
The Times Free Press (Chattanooga)
The Times-Picayune (New Orleans)
The Trenton (N.J.) *Evening Times*
The Utica (N.Y.) *Herald-Dispatch*
The Wall Street Journal
The Warrenton (N. C.) *Gazette*
The Washington (D.C.) *Bee*
The Washington (D.C.) *Herald*
The Washington (D.C.) *Post*
The Washington (D.C.) *Times*
The Washington Post and Times Herald
The Washingtonian
The Watchman and Southron (Sumter, S.C.)
The Weekly Economist (Elizabeth City, N. C.)
The Wilmington (N.C.) *Morning Star*

BOOKS, ARTICLES, AND UNPUBLISHED WORKS

Abraham, Henry, *Freedom and the Court* (3rd. ed.) (New York: Oxford Univ. Press 1977).
Abraham, Henry Julian, *Justices, Presidents, and Senators: A History of the United States Supreme Court Appointments from Washington to Clinton* (Lanham, Md.: Rowman & Littlefield Publishers, Inc. 1999). . . . *to Bush II* (2007).
"A Consideration of Some of Mr. Justice Sanford's Opinions as Federal District Judge," 1 *New York Law Rev.* 186 (Apr. 1923).
"A Divided State," Tennessee 4 Me, http://www.tn4me.org/minor_cat.cfm/minor_id/1/major_id/5era-id/5.
"A Great American Statesman," 37 *World's Work* 612 (1919).
"A History of Tennessee," *Tennessee Blue Book*, 2011–12 (Nashville, Tenn.: Secretary of State).
"A Huge Enterprise," *The American Fertilizer* (Vols. 12–13) (Ware Bros. 1900).
"A Justice Forgotten?" *Court Historical Soc'y Newsletter*, United States District Court for the Eastern District of Tennessee, Inc. (Dec. 2004).
"A Landmark in Habeas Corpus and Criminal Contempt," Legal History Blog (June 24, 2009), http://legalhistoryblog.blogspot.com/2009/06/landmark-in-habeas-corpus-and-criminal.html.
Allison, John, ed., *Notable Men of Tennessee: Personal and Genealogical, with Portraits*, Vol. 1 (S. Historical Ass'n 1905).
Alexander, Thomas, "Strange Bedfellows: The Interlocking Careers of T.A.R. Nelson, Andrew Johnson, and W.G. (Parson) Brownlow," 24 *E. Tennessee Historical Soc'y Publ'ns* (1952): 68–91.
Allen, Frederick Lewis, *Only Yesterday: An Informal History of the 1920s* (New York: Perennial Classics 2000).
Allen, Ronald R., *Knoxville in the Gay Nineties* (Knoxville, Tenn.: 2011).
Amar, Akhil Reed, *The Bill of Rights: Creation and Reconstruction* (New Haven, Conn.: Yale Univ. Press 1998).
———, "Hugo Black and the Hall of Fame," 53 *Ala. Law Rev.* 1221 (2002).
American Bar Ass'n Journal, July 1970.

74 American Manufacturer Steel & Iron, No. 24 (Pittsburgh, Pa.: National Iron & Steel Publ'g Co. 1904).
10 *The American Monthly Magazine*, No. 2 (Washington, D.C.: Nat'l Soc'y DAR Feb. 1897).
11 *The American Monthly Magazine*, No. 3 (Washington, D.C.: Nat'l Soc'y DAR Sept. 1897).
Amis, Reese T., ed., *Knox County in the World War, 1917, 1918, 1919* (Knoxville: Knoxville Lithographing Co. 1919).
Anderson, Donald F., "Building National Consensus: The Career of William Howard Taft," 68 *Univ. Cincinnati Law Rev.* 323 (Winter 2000): 323–56.
Oscar E. Anderson, Jr., *The Health of a Nation: Harvey W. Wiley and the Fight for Pure Food* (Univ. of Chicago Press 1958).
34 Annual Catalogue of Grant University (1900).
Annual Report of the American Bar Ass'n, "Summary of Proceeding of Tennessee Bar Association" (held at Nashville May 26–28, 1902) (Saratoga Springs, New York: 1902).
Annual Report of the State Superintendent of Public Instruction of Tennessee, Dep't of Public Instruction (1905).
Anthony, John R., "Attitude of the Supreme Court Toward Liberty of Contract," 6 *Texas Law Rev.* 266 (1927–28).
Apple, Jr., R.W., "The Case of the Monopolistic Railroadmen," in *Quarrels That Have Shaped The Constitution*, John A. Garraty, ed. (New York: Harper & Row 1987 [rev. ed.]).
Ariens, Michael, http://www.michaelariens.com/conlaw/justices/sanford.htm.
Army *Mail Bag* (May 30, 1864).
Asch, Sidney H., *The Supreme Court and Its Great Justices* (Arco 1976).
Ash, Stephen V., *Past Times: A Daybook of Knoxville History* (*Knoxville News-Sentinel* 1991).
"Ashton's Ashes," *Law.com* (Aug. 13, 2001), www.truthinjustice.org/sc-shiftdp.htm.
"Association of American Law Schools," http://www.aals.org.
Ayers, Edward L., *The Promise of the New South: Life After Reconstruction* (New York: Oxford Univ. Press 2007).
Babelay, David, "Swiss Settlers, Knoxville," *The Tennessee Encyclopedia of History and Culture* (Nashville: Tennessee History Soc'y (1998)).
Babelay, David, *They Trusted and Were Delivered: The French-Swiss of Knoxville, Tennessee* (2 Vols.) (Knoxville: Vaud-Tennessee Publisher 1988).
Baer, Judith A., "Edward Douglass White," *The Supreme Court Justices: A Biographical Dictionary*, Melvin I. Urofsky, ed. (New York: Garland Publ'g 1994).
Bailey, Fred A., "Oliver Perry Temple and the Struggle for Tennessee's Agricultural College," 36 *Tennessee Historical Soc'y* 1977.
Bailey, Thomas Pearce, *Race Orthodoxy in the South: And Other Aspects of the Negro Question* (New York: The Neale Publ'g Co. 1914).
Baker, Ray Stannard, *Woodrow Wilson, Life and Letters* (8 Vols.) (New York: Greenwood Publ'g Group 1968) (Vol. 6).
"Bank and Quotation Section," 85 *The Commercial & Financial Chronicle*, No. 2197 (New York, Aug. 31, 1907).
Banker, Mark, *Appalachians All: East Tennesseans and the Elusive History of an American Region* (Knoxville: Univ. of Tennessee Press 2010).
Barnett, Randy E., "The Proper Scope of the Police Power," 79 *Notre Dame Law Rev.* 429–95 (2004)
Bates, Earnest Sutherland, *The Story of the Supreme Court* (Fred B. Rothman & Co. 1982).

Beach, Rebecca Donaldson, *The Reverend John Beach and his descendants: together with historical and biographical sketches and the ancestry and descendants of John Sanford, of Redding, Connecticut* (Ulan Press 2012, originally printed New Haven, Conn.: The Tuttle, Morehouse & Taylor Press 1898).

Bell, Augusta Grove, *Circling Windrock Mountain: Two Hundred Years in Appalachia* (Knoxville: Univ. of Tennessee Press 1998).

Benedict, Michael Les, "History of the Court: Reconstruction, Federalism, and Economic Rights," *The Oxford Companion to the Supreme Court of the United States*, ed., Kermit H. Hall, et al. (New York: Oxford Univ. Press 1992).

Benhart, John, Jr., *Appalachian Aspirations: The Geography of Urbanization and Development in the Upper Tennessee River Valley: 1865–1900* (Knoxville: Univ. of Tennessee Press 2007).

Bennett, Aremona G., "Freedom: Personal Liberty and Private Law, Phantom Freedom, Official Acceptance of Violence to Personal Security and Subversion of Proprietary Rights and Ambition Following Emancipation, 1865–1912," 70 *Chicago-Kent Law Rev.* 439 (1994).

Berry, Mary Frances, *My Face Is Black Is True: Callie House and the Struggle for Ex-Slave Reparations* (New York: Vintage Press 2005).

Berry, Mary F., "Reparations for Freedmen, 1890–1916: Fraudulent Practices or Justice Deferred?" Vol. 57, No. 3, *Journal of Negro History* (July 1972).

Beth, Loren B., *John Marshall Harlan: The Last Whig Justice* (Lexington: Univ. of Kentucky Press 1992).

Beth, Richard S. & Jessica Tollestrup, "Sessions Adjournments, and Recesses of Congress," *Congressional Research Service* (Feb. 27, 2013).

Bickel, A., *The Unpublished Opinions of Mr. Justice Brandeis* (1957).

Bickel, Alexander M., *The Judiciary and Responsible Government, 1910–21* (Vol. 9) (New York: Macmillan 1984).

Biggs, Riley Oakey, "Development of Railroad Transportation in East Tennessee During the Reconstruction Period," (Master's thesis, Univ. of Tennessee 1934).

"Big Idea: Rejuvenating Phi Beta Kappa Chapter," http://www.utk.edu/tntoday/2013/02/15/big-idea-phi-beta-kappa/.

Black, Forrest R., "A Critique of the *Carroll* Case," 29 *Columbia Law Rev.* 1068 (1929).

Blaustein, Albert P., & Roy M. Mersky, *The First One Hundred Justices: Statistical Studies on the Supreme Court of the United States* (Hamden, Conn.: Archon Books 1978).

Blaustein, Albert P., & Roy M. Mersky, "The Statistics." *The Justices of the United States Supreme Court, 1789–1969: Their Lives and Major Opinions*, Leon Friedman and Fred L. Israel, eds., Vol. 4, (New York: Chelsea House 1969).

"Book II Mar–Sept 1927," *College of Law Library History*, http://trace.tennessee.edu/utklaw libhist/14.

Booker, Robert, "Concerns During Civil War Included Health, Education," *The Knoxville News-Sentinel* (May 19, 2015).

Booker, Robert, "Knoxville Lagged on Segregation Laws," *The Knoxville News-Sentinel* (Sept. 22, 2015).

Booker, Robert, "First Black Politicos Met with Hostility," *The Knoxville News-Sentinel* (Nov. 8, 2011).

Bork, Robert, "Neutral Principles and Some First Amendment Problems," 47 *Indiana Law Journal* 1, 23 (1971–72).

Boyer, Reba Bayless, *Monroe County, Tennessee Records*, II (S. History Press 1983).

Brake, Patricia E., *Justice in the Valley: A Bicentennial Perspective of the United States District Court for the Eastern District of Tennessee* (Franklin, Tenn.: Hillsboro Press 1998).

Brannen, Daniel E., Jr., Richard Clay Hanes & Rebecca Valentine, "*McGrain v. Daugherty* (1927)" in *Supreme Court Drama: Cases That Changed America*, Lawrence W. Baker, ed. (2nd ed.) (Vol. 5) (Detroit: UXL 2011).

Brewer, Becky French, & Douglas Stuart McDaniel, *Park City* (Charleston, S. C.: Arcadia Publ'g 2005).

Brown, Ray A., "Due Process of Law, Police Power, and the Supreme Court," No. 7, 40 *Harvard Law Rev.* 943 (1927).

Brown-Scott, Wendy, "Important Lessons from History," 8 *Buffalo Human Rights L. Rev.* 147 (2002).

Brummett, Nancy P., *The Journey of Elisa* (Colorado Springs, Colo.: Cook Commc'ns 2000).

Bryan, Charles F., "'Tories' Amidst Rebels: Confederate Occupation of East Tennessee, 1861–63," 75 *The Journal of E. Tennessee History* (2003).

Bryan, Charles F., Jr., "The Civil War in East Tennessee: A Social, Political, and Economic Study" (Ph.D. diss., Univ. of Tennessee 1978).

Buffat, Alfred, *Reminiscences of Alfred Buffat* (Spring Place, Tenn.: 1908).

Buffat, Elisa, Memoirs and Diary of Elisa Buffat (neé) Bolli (Spring Place, Tenn.: 1916).

"Building Good Citizens," http://www.valleydistrictcivitan.com/civitan-international.

Bullock, Charles S., III, and Mark J. Rozell, eds., *The New Politics of the Old South: An Introduction to Southern Politics* (New York: Rowman & Littlefield Publishers 2013).

Burner, David. "Edward Terry Sanford," *The Justices of the United States Supreme Court, 1789–1969: Their Lives and Major Opinions*, Vol. 3, Leon Friedman & Fred L. Israel, eds. (New York: Chelsea House 1969).

Burnett, Edmund Cody, "Big Creek's Response to the Coming of the Railroad: Old Buncombe Promotes the Better Life in the Rural Community," 21 *Agricultural History* (July 1947).

Burton, David H., *Taft, Holmes, and the 1920s Court: An Appraisal* (Madison, N.J., Fairleigh Dickinson Univ. Press 1998).

Burton, David H., ed., *William Howard Taft: Essential Writings and Addresses* (Fairleigh Dickinson Univ. Press 2009).

Caldwell, Joshua William, *Sketches of the Bench and Bar of Tennessee* (Knoxville: Ogden Bros. & Co., Printers 1898).

Campbell, James B., "East Tennessee During Federal Occupation, 1863–1865," 19 *E. Tennessee Historical Soc'y Publ'ns* (1947): 64–80.

Campbell, James Bernard, "Some Social and Economic Phases of Reconstruction in East Tennessee, 1864–1869" (Master's thesis, Univ. of Tennessee 1946).

Campbell, Tom W., *Four Score Forgotten Men: Sketches of the Justices of the U.S. Supreme Court* (Little Rock, Ark.: Pioneer Publ'g Co. 1950).

Carter, John Denton, *The Warren Court and the Constitution: A Critical Review of Judicial Activism* (Gretna, La.: Pelican Publ'g 1973).

Cartwright, Joseph H., *The Triumph of Jim Crow: Tennessee Race Relations in the 1880s* (Knoxville: Univ. of Tennessee Press 1976).

Cary, Francine C., "Albert Chavannes and the Future Commonwealth: The Utopian Novelist as Social Critic." 48 *E. Tennessee Historical Soc'y Publ'ns* (1976).

Catalogue of the Legal Fraternity of Phi Delta Phi, 7th ed., Geo. A. Katzenberger, ed. (Ann Arbor, Mich.: The Inland Press 1897).

Catalogue of the Officers and Students of the University of Tennessee, 1881–82 (Knoxville: T. Haws, Book & Job Printer 1882).

Catalogue of the Psi Upsilon Fraternity, Yale Univ., Charles Wesley Smiley, ed. (New York: Baker & Godwin, Printers 1879).

Chafee, Zechariah, Jr., *Free Speech in the United States* (Cambridge: Harvard Univ. Press 1954).

Chandler, Edward, ed., *The Brief: A Quarterly Magazine of the Law* (Lancaster, Pa.: New Era Publ'g Co. 1909).

Chavannes, Anna, *Journal of Anna Chavannes* (May 9–July 14, 1848), MS 917.3, McClung Historical Collection (1930).

Chavannes, Albert, "Saunders' Raid," *East Tennessee Sketches* (Knoxville, Tenn.: 1900).

Chavannes, Cecile, "Canvassing the District," *East Tennessee Sketches* (Knoxville: 1900).

"The Chief Justice-A Mistaken Appointment," 113 *The Nation*, No. 2923 (July 13, 1921).

Clabough, Kate, *Lenoir City* (Charleston, S. C.: Arcadia Publ'g 2009).

Class of 1854, Decennial Record, Yale Univ. (1899).

Clay, Grady, "Copper-Basin Cover Up," 73 *Landscape Architecture*, No. 4 (1983): 49–55, 94.

Coggins, Allen R., "Fraterville Mine Disaster," *Tennessee Encyclopedia of History and Culture*, http://tennesseeencyclopedia.net/entry.php?rec=511.

Collins, Ronald K.L. & Sam Chaltain, *We Must Not Be Afraid to Be Free: Stories of Free Expression in America* (New York: Oxford Univ. Press 2011).

Colton, Henry E., *The East Tennessee, Virginia and Georgia Railway System: Its Resources* (E. Tenn., Va. & Ga. Railway Sys. 1890).

"Commerce Clause," https://www.law.cornell.edu/wex/commerce_clause.

45 *The Commercial & Financial Chronicle and Hunt's Merchant Magazine* (New York: William B. Dana Co. 1887).

Conkin, Paul K., *Peabody College: From A Frontier Academy to the Frontiers of Teaching and Learning* (Nashville, Tenn.: Vanderbilt Univ. Press 2002).

Connecticut Hale Cemetery Inscriptions and Newspaper Notices, 1629–34 (Ancestry.com).

Cook, Stanley A., "Path to the High Bench: The Pre-Supreme Court Career of Justice Edward Terry Sanford" (Ph.D. diss., Univ. of Tennessee 1977).

Cooper, William J., Jr., & Thomas E. Terrill, *The American South: A History* (Vol. 2) (New York: McGraw Hill 2002).

Cortner, Richard C., "The Nationalization of the Bill of Rights: An Overview," American Political Science Ass'n and American Historical Ass'n (1985).

Cortner, Richard C., *The Supreme Court and the Second Bill of Rights: The Fourteenth Amendment and the Nationalization of Civil Liberties* (Univ. of Wisconsin Press 1980).

Cortner, Richard C., "The Wobblies and *Fiske v. Kansas*: Victory Amid Disintegration," Kansas History 4 (Spring 1981).

Cotham, Perry C., *Toil, Turmoil & Triumph: A Portrait of the Tennessee Labor Movement* (Franklin, Tenn.: Hillsboro Press 1995).

5 *Cotton Trade Journal* (1905).

Coulter, E. Merton, *William G. Brownlow: Fighting Parson of the Southern Highlands* (Knoxville: Univ. of Tennessee Press 1999).

Cox, Archibald, *The Court and the Constitution* (Boston: Houghton Mifflin 1987).

Cox, Steve, "The History of the Library at the University of Tennessee, Chattanooga," Tennessee Library Ass'n, http://www.tnla.org/?384.

Creekmore, Betsy Beeler, *Knoxville* (Knoxville: E. Tennessee Historical Soc'y 1991).
Crook, James King, *The Mineral Waters of the United States and Their Therapeutic Uses* (New York: Lea Bros. & Co. 1899).
Cunningham, Bill, *On Bended Knees: The True Story of the Night Rider Tobacco War in Kentucky and Tennessee* (Nashville, Tenn.: McClanahan Publ'g House, Inc. 1983).
Curriden, Mark, "A Supreme Case of Contempt," *American Bar Ass'n Journal* (June 2, 2009) http://www.abajournal.com/magazine/article/a_supreme_case_of_contempt.
Curriden, Mark, "Contempt of Court: The Turn-of-the-Century Lynching that Launched 100 years of Federalism in the U.S. Courts," 62 *Texas Bar Journal, No. 10* (Nov. 1999) at 1022–26.
Curriden, Mark, & Leroy Phillips, Jr., *Contempt of Court* (New York: Anchor Books 2001).
Currie, David P., "The Constitution in the Supreme Court," 1986 *Duke Law Journal* 65 (Feb. 1986).
Curtis, Michael Kent, *No State Shall Abridge: The Fourteenth Amendment and the Bill of Rights* (Durham, N. Car.: Duke Univ. Press 1990).
Cushman, Barry, "Edward Terry Sanford," *The Supreme Court Justices: A Biographical Dictionary*, Melvin I. Urofsky, ed. (New York: Garland Publ'g Co. 1994).
Cushman, Barry, "Inside the Taft Court: Lessons from the Docket Books," Vol. 2015, No. 1 *The Supreme Court Rev.*, (Univ. of Chicago Press Journals 2016), http://ssrn.com/abstract=2797442.
Cushman, Barry, "Edward Terry Sanford," *American National Biography*, John A. Garraty, ed. (New York: Oxford Univ. Press 1999).
Cushman, Clare, "Fountain Pens and Typewriters: Supreme Court Stenographers and Law Clerks, 1910–1940," Vol. 41, Issue 1, *Journal of Supreme Court History* (Mar. 2016), http://onlinelibrary.wiley.com/doi/10.1111/jsch12092/full at 16.
Cushman, Clare, "The 'Lost' Clerks of the White Court Era," *Journal of Supreme Court History* (Mar. 4, 2015), Supreme Court Historical Society, http://ssrn.com/abstract=2573926.
Cynkar, Robert J., "*Buck v. Bell*: 'Felt Necessities' v. Fundamental Values?.," 81 *Columbia Law Rev.*, No. 7 (Nov. 1981).
Dabney, Charles W., *Universal Education in the South* (Chapel Hill: Univ. of N. Carolina 1936).
Daniel, Pete, "The Tennessee Convict War," 34 *Tennessee Historical Quarterly*, No. 3 (Fall 1975).
DAR Chapter Biography, http://www.tndar.org/~bonnykate/bonnykatebio.htm.
Davidson, Donald, *The Tennessee, The New River: Civil War to TVA*, Vol. 2 (Nashville, Tenn.: J.S. Sanders & Co. 1992 ed.).
Davies, S.P., *Social Control of the Feebleminded: A Study of Social Programs and Attitudes in Relation to the Problems of Mental Deficiency* (New York: Nat'l Comm. for Mental Hygiene 1923).
Davis, Elizabeth A., and Betsey Creekmore, "Ayres, not Ayers: Tale of a Troubling Transposition," *Tennessee Alumnus* (Jan. 31, 2011).
"Dayton's Amazing Trial," 86 *The Literary Digest* (July 24, 1925).
Deaderick, Lucile ed., *Heart of the Valley: A History of Knoxville, Tennessee* (Knoxville: E. Tennessee Historical Soc'y 1976).
"Dedication of Tennessee Hall," 5 *Tennessee Law Rev.* No. 4 (1927).
Dennis, Michael, *Lessons in Progress: State Universities and Progressivism in the New South, 1880–1920* (Urbana: Univ. of Illinois Press 2001).
"Depew, Chauncey Mitchell (1834–1928)," http://bioguide.congress.gov.

Dialect Notes, Vol. 1 (Norwood, Mass.: The American Dialect Soc'y 1896).
Dickinson, W. Calvin, "Temperance," *Tennessee Encyclopedia of History and Culture*, http://tennesseeencyclopedia.net/entry.php?rec=1302.
Douglas, Davison M., "Corrigan v. Buckley, 271 U.S. 323 (1926)," http://uscivilliberties.org/cases/3650-Corrigan-v-Buckley-271-us-323-1926.html.
Drake, Richard B., "Slavery and Anti Slavery in Appalachia," in *Appalachians and Race: The Mountain South from Slavery to Segregation*, John C. Inscoe, ed. (Lexington: Univ. of Kentucky Press 2001).
Duggins, Edward C., "The Background for Regulation of Railroads in Tennessee," (Master's thesis, Univ. of Tennessee 1939).
Dunn, Mrs. J.A., "Seen and Heard," *The Knoxville News-Sentinel* (Oct. 2, 1932).
"East Tennessee Female Institute," Special Collections Online, https://kiva.lib.utk.edu/spc.
East Tennessee: Historical and Biographical (reprint) (LaCrosse, Wis.: Brookhaven Press 2001) (orig. Chattanooga, Tenn.: A.D. Smith & Co. 1893).
"Edward Sanford Mansion (Maplehurst)," Special Collections Online, Univ. of Tennessee Libraries, Item #3874, http://kiva.lib.utk.edu/spc/items/show/3874.
"Edward Terry Sanford," 8 *Tennessee Law Rev.* 189–90 (1930).
"Edward Terry Sanford," 4 *Journal Nat'l Ass'n Referees Bankruptcy* 91 (Apr. 1930).
"Edward Terry Sanford," *Oxford Companion to the U.S. Supreme Court*, Kermit L. Hall, ed. (New York: Oxford Univ. Press 2005).
Edwards, Rebecca, *New Spirits: Americans In the Gilded Age, 1865–1905* (New York: Oxford Univ. Press 2006).
Elliott, Sam D., "The Colorful Career of Judge Lewis Shepherd," *Times Free Press* (Chattanooga) (Apr. 20, 2014).
Ely, James W. & Theodore Brown, Jr., eds., *A History of the Tennessee Supreme Court* (Knoxville: Univ. of Tennessee Press 2002).
"The Encyclopedia of Arkansas History & Culture: Chicot County," http://www.encyclopediaofarkansas.net/encyclopedia/entry-detail.aspx?entryID=7538media=print.
Encyclopedia of the American Constitution, Leonard W. Levy & Kenneth L. Karst, eds., Vol. 6 (2nd ed.) (Detroit: Macmillan Reference USA 2000).
51 Engineering News (McGraw-Hill 1904).
Epps, Garrett, *Democracy Reborn: The Fourteenth Amendment and the Fight for Equal Rights in Post-Civil War America* (New York: Henry Holt and Co. 2006).
Facts on File History Database Ctr., http://www.fofweb.com.
Falconnier, John W., "Sanford, Junior Member of U.S. Court," *The Knoxville Sentinel* (Jan. 25, 1923).
6 *Federation Bulletin: A Magazine for the Woman of To-Day*, No. 1 (Boston: Oct. 1908).
Federici, Michael P., "Progressivism," in *American Conservatism: An Encyclopedia*, Bruce Frohner, et al., eds. (Wilmington, Del.: ISI Books 2006).
Fehrenbacher, "The Dred Scott Case," *Quarrels That Have Shaped the Constitution*, John A. Garraty, ed. (New York: Harper & Row 1987).
Ferren, Jack M., *Salt of the Earth—Conscience of the Court: The Story of Justice Wiley Rutledge* (Chapel Hill, N.Car.: Univ. of N. Carolina Press 2004).
Fertig, James Walter, *The Secession and Reconstruction of Tennessee* (Chicago: Univ. of Chicago Press 1898).

Finkelman, Paul, ed., *The Supreme Court: Controversies, Cases, and Characters from John Jay to John Roberts* (4 vols.) (ABC-CLIO 2014).

"The First Fair of Its Kind: Knoxville's 1913 National Conservation Exposition," http://www.easttnhistory.org/exhibits/first-fair-its-kind.

Fish, Peter, "Judiciary Act of 1925," in Kermit L. Hall, et al., eds., *The Oxford Companion to the Supreme Court of the United States* (New York: Oxford Univ. Press 1992).

"Five Common Caffeine Myths Busted," http://abcnews.go.com/GMA/coffee-myths-busted-caffeine/story?id=5552790 (Aug. 11, 2008).

"The Flat Gap Horror," 47 *The Tennessee Genealogical Mag.*, No. 3 (Fall 2000).

Fleming, John, *The Knoxville Press and Herald* (Oct. 24, 1868).

Folmsbee, Stanley J., "The Origin of the First 'Jim Crow' Law," 15 *Journal of S. History* (1949).

Folmsbee, Stanley J., "Sectionalism and Internal Improvements in Tennessee, 1796–1845" (Knoxville: E. Tennessee Historical Soc'y 1939).

Folmsbee, Stanley J., Robert E. Corlew, & Enoch L. Mitchell, *History of Tennessee*, Vols. 1 & 2 (New York: Lewis Historical Publ'g Co. 1960).

Folmsbee, Stanley & Lucile Deaderick, "The Founding of Knoxville, Tenn." 13 *E. Tennessee Historical Soc'y Publ'ns* (1941).

Folmsbee, Stanley J. & Marguerite B. Hamer, eds., "The Presidential Election of 1896 as Reflected in the Correspondence of Charles McClung McGhee," 22 *E. Tennessee Historical Soc'y Publ'ns* (1950): 158–68.

Foner, Eric, *Reconstruction: America's Unfinished Revolution, 1863–1877* (New York: Harper & Row 1988).

Foster, Kenneth E., "The Winters Doctrine: Historical Perspective and Future Applications of Reserved Water Rights in Arizona," 16 *Ground Water*, No. 3 (May/June 1970).

Fowler, James A., "Mr. Justice Edward Terry Sanford." 17 *American Bar Ass'n Journal* 229 (Apr. 1931): 229–33.

Fowler, Russell, "Tennesseans on the United States Supreme Court," http://www.tba.org/journal/tennesseans-on-the-united-states-supreme-court.

Frank, Jerome P., "Appointment of Justices: Prestige, Principles, and Politics," http://www.repository.law.indiana.edu/facpub/1856.

Frankfurter, Felix & James M. Landis, "The Business of the Supreme Court at October Term, 1929," 44 *Harvard Law Rev.* 1 (Nov. 1930).

Frankfurter, Felix, "The Supreme Court in the Mirror of Justices," 105 *Univ. of Pennsylvania Law Rev.* No. 6, 781 (Apr. 1957).

Frantz, Edward O., *The Door of Hope: Republican Presidents and the First Southern Strategy, 1877–1933* (Gainesville, Fla.: Univ. Press of Florida 2011).

"The Fraterville Mine Disaster of 1902," The History Blog, http://www.thehistoryblog.com/archives/16917.

"Fraterville Mine Disaster," http://www.coalcreekaml.com/Legacy4.htm.

"The Freedman's Savings Bank: Good Intentions Were Not Enough: A Noble Experiment Goes Awry," http://www.occ.gov/about/what-we-do/history/freedman-savings-bank.html.

"The Freedman's Bank: A Historic Place in the Financial Empowerment of African Americans," https://www.treasury.gov/connect/blog/pages/freedmans-savings-bank.aspx.

Free Speech on Trial: Communication Perspectives on Landmark Supreme Court Decisions, Richard A. Parker, ed. (Tuscaloosa: Univ. of Alabama Press 2003).

Friedman, Leon, & Fred L. Israel, *The Justices of the United States Supreme Court, 1789–1969: Their Lives and Major Opinions* (New York: R.R. Bowker Co. 1969).
8 Fuel Magazine: The Coal Operators National Weekly, No. 1 (Chicago: Nov. 6, 1906).
Gabriel, Michael P., "Battle of Malvern Hill," *Encyclopedia Virginia*, Virginia Foundation for the Humanities (Apr. 5, 2011), http://www.EncyclopediaVirginia.org/Malvern_Hill_Battle_of.
Galloway, Russell W., Jr, "The Taft Court (1921–29)," 25 *Santa Clara Law Rev.* 1 (1985).
Garraty, John A., *Teddy Roosevelt: American Rough Rider* (New York: Sterling Publ'g Co., Inc. 2007).
Garraty, John A., ed., *Quarrels That Have Shaped the Constitution* (New York: Harper & Row 1987) (rev. ed.).
Geisel, Amy, "Walker Drug to Buy Knoxville Family Business Albers, Inc.," *The Knoxville News-Sentinel* (July 8, 1994).
Gaston, Paul M., *The New South Creed: A Study in Southern Mythmaking* (Baton Rouge: Louisiana State Univ. Press 1970).
"Getting a Fair Share," Tennessee4Me, http://www.tn4me.org/minor_cat.cfm/minor_id/56/major_id/20/era_id/6.
Giglio, James N., *H.M. Daugherty and the Politics of Expediency* (Kent State Univ. Press 1978).
"Gilded Age," America's Story from America's Library, http://americaslibrary.govjb/gilded/jb-gilded-subj.html.
Gilmore, Brian, "A Neglected Civil Rights Landmark Case," (Apr. 30, 2008), http://progressive.org/mp_gilmore043008.
"The Gitlow Case," *The New Republic* (July 1, 1925).
"Glenfeld Historical News Archive," http://fallbrookrailway.com/glenfeld/glenfeld_news.html.
Goldman, Sheldon, *Picking Federal Judges: Lower Court Selection from Roosevelt Through Reagan* (New Haven, Conn.: Yale Univ. Press 1999).
Goodspeed's History of Hamilton, Knox and Shelby Counties of Tennessee (Nashville: The Goodspeed Publ'g Co. 1887); reprint: (Nashville: Charles and Randy Elder Booksellers 1974).
Gould, Lewis L., *Grand Old Party: A History of the Republicans* (New York: Random House 2003).
Gould, Lewis L., "Taft, William Howard," *American National Biography Online*, http://www.anb.org/articles/06/06-00642.
Grace, Roger M., "High Court Rules on Seizure of Coca-Cola as Contraband," *Metropolitan News-Enterprise* (Los Angeles) (Feb. 9, 2006).
Graf, LeRoy P., Ralph W. Haskings & Paul H. Bergeron, eds., *The Papers of Andrew Johnson* (Knoxville: Univ. of Tennessee Press 1967–2000).
"The Great Coca Cola Trial" (Part 1) *Providentia* (Oct. 31, 2010), http://drvitelli/typepad.com/providentia/2010/10/the-great-coca-cola-trial.html.
Green, John W. "Judge Edward T. Sanford." *Law and Lawyers: Sketches of the Federal Judges of Tennessee, Sketches of the Attorney General of Tennessee, Legal Miscellany, Reminiscences by John W. Green* (Jackson, Tenn.: McCowat-Mercer Press 1950).
Green, John W. "Some Judges of the United States District Court of Tennessee (1878–1939)." 18 *Tennessee Law Rev.* 227 (1943–45): 227–41.
Greene, Lee Seifert, David E. Grubbs & Victor C. Hobday, *Government in Tennessee* (3d ed.) (Knoxville: Univ. of Tennessee Press 1975).

Gregory, Rick, "Beliefs of Their Fathers: Violence, Religion, and the Black Patch War, 1904–1914, Border States: *Journal of the Kentucky-Tennessee American Studies Ass'n*, No. 9 (1993), https://spider.georgetowncollege.edu/htallant/border/bs9/gregory.htm.

Gregory, Rick, "The Black Patch War," *Tennessee Encyclopedia of History and Culture*, https://tennesseeencyclopedia.net/entry.php?rec-95.

Hale, Will T., 4 *History of Tennessee and Tennesseans: The Leaders and Representative Men in Commerce, Industry and Modern Activities* (Chicago: Lewis Publ'g Co. 1913).

Hall, Henry, ed., "Edward J. Sanford," *America's Successful Men of Affairs: An Encyclopedia of Contemporaneous Biography* (Vol. 2) (New York: The New York Tribune 1896).

Hall, James P., "Comment on Recent Cases," 20 *Illinois Law Rev.* (Apr. 1926).

Hall, Kermit L., "Owen Josephus Roberts," in *The Supreme Court Justices: A Biographical Dictionary*, Melvin I. Urofsky, ed. (New York: Garland 1994).

Hall, Kermit L., "Sanford, Edward Terry," *The Oxford Companion to the Supreme Court of the United States*, 2005, *Encyclopedia.com* (16 Jul. 2010), http://www.encyclopedia.com.

Hall, Timothy L. *Supreme Court Justices: A Biographical Dictionary* (New York: Infobase Publ'g 2001).

"Halloween," *Knoxville Mercury* (Oct. 29, 2015).

Hamer, Philip M., ed., *Tennessee, A History, 1673–1932*, Vol. 2 (New York: American Historical Soc'y Inc. 1933).

Hamilton, Virginia Van der Veer, *Hugo Black: The Alabama Years* (Tuscaloosa: Univ. of Alabama Press 1982).

Hamm, Richard F., *Shaping the Eighteenth Amendment: Temperance Reform, Legal Culture, and the Polity, 1880–1920* (Chapel Hill: Univ. of N. Carolina Press 1995).

"Harding at the Crossroads," *The New Republic* (Jan. 12, 1921).

Harding, Warren G., Address Accepting the Republican Nomination (Jan. 12, 1920), The American Presidency Project, http://www.presidency.ucsb.edu.

Harding, Warren G., "Return to Normalcy: May 14, 1920," Teaching American History.org http://www.teachingamericanhistory.org/library/document/return-to-normalcy.

Hardy, William E., "The Margins of William Brownlow's Words: New Perspectives on the End of Radical Reconstruction in Tennessee," 84 *The Journal of E. Tennessee History* (2012): 78–86.

Hardy, William Edward, "'Farewell to all Radicals:' Redeeming Tennessee, 1869–1870" (Ph.D. diss., Univ. of Tennessee 2013).

Harlan, A. W., ed., 6 *The Dental Review: Devoted to the Advancement of Dentistry* (Chicago: H.D. Justi & Son 1892).

Harriman, Edward A., "The Twilight of the States," 16 *American Bar Ass'n Journal* 128 (1930).

Harris, William C., "East Tennessee's Civil War Refugees and the Impact of the War on Civilians," 75 *The Journal of E. Tennessee History* (2003): 62–75.

Hart, Roger L., *Redeemers, Bourbons, and Populists* (Baton Rouge: Louisiana State Univ. 1975).

Harvard College, Class of 1885, Secretary's Report, No. 2 (Cambridge, Mass.: Harvard Univ. Press 1888–89).

Harvard College, Class of 1885, Secretary's Report, No. 3 (Cambridge, Mass.: Harvard Univ. Press 1892).

Harvard College, Class of 1885, Secretary's Report, Twenty-fifth Ann. (Cambridge, Mass.: Harvard Univ. Press 1910).

Harvard College, Class of 1885, Secretary's Report, Fiftieth Ann. (Cambridge, Mass.: Harvard Univ. Press 1935).
Harvard College, Class of 1885, Baccalaureate Sermon, Class Day Oration, et al. (Cambridge, Mass.: William H. Wheeler 1885).
Harvard College, Class of 1900, Secretary's Report, No. 4 (Cambridge, Mass.: Harvard Univ. Press).
Harvard College, Class of 1900, Secretary's Report, No. 5 (Cambridge, Mass.: Harvard Univ. Press).
20 *Harvard Graduates' Magazine* (Boston: The Harvard Graduates' Magazine Ass'n 1911–12).
43 *Harvard Law Rev.* 926 (Apr. 1930).
25 *Harvard Univ. Register* (Boston: Alfred Mudge & Son 1899).
"He Aimed for the Senate, But Landed in the Supreme Court," *Current Opinion* (Apr. 23, 1923):411–12.
Heberle, Klaus H., "From *Gitlow* to *Near*: Judicial 'Amendment' by Absent-Minded Incrementalism," 34 *The Journal of Politics* (Univ. of Chicago Press May 1972).
Hendrickson, John "Governing by the Founders' Constitution: The Presidency of Warren G. Harding," Policy Study No. 08–9, Public Interest Inst. (Dec. 2008).
Henneman, J.B., "Recent Tennessee History by Tennesseans," 4 *The Sewanee Rev.*, No. 4 (Aug. 1896).
Herringshaw, Thomas W., *Herringshaw's American blue-book of biography* (Chicago: Am. Publishers' Ass'n 1915).
Hicks, Gregory Scott, "Rebuilding a Community: Prosperity and Peace in Post-Civil War Knoxville, Tennessee, 1865–1870" (Master's thesis, Univ. of Tennessee 2008).
Hill, Ray, "A Feudin' Son of Tennessee: Kenneth McKellar," Ch. 9, knoxfocus.com (July 22, 2012).
Hindley, Meredith, "Chattanooga Versus the Supreme Court: The Strange Case of Ed Johnson," 35 *Humanities*, No. 6 (Nov./Dec. 2014).
"Historical Notes and News," *Tennessee Historical Magazine*, IV (June 1918).
"History of Fire Department-City of Knoxville," http://knoxvilletn.gov/government/city_departments_offices/fire_department/history_of_fire_department.
"History of Knoxville: Chapter 14: Transportation," http://knoxcotnorg/old_site/history/rule/chap14.html.
History of Tennessee From the Earliest Time to the Present; Together with a Historical and a Biographical Sketch of the County of Knox and the City of Knoxville, Besides a Valuable Fund of Notes, Original Observations, Reminiscences Etc. (Nashville: The Goodspeed Publishing Co. 1887).
History of the Library at the University of Tennessee, Chattanooga, Tennessee Library Ass'n, http://www.tnla.org/?384.
Hodges, James A., "George Fort Milton and the Art of History," 18 *The History Teacher* No. 2 (Feb. 1984).
Hofstadter, R., *Social Darwinism in American Thought* (rev. ed. 1959).
Holland, James W., "The East Tennessee and Georgia Railroad, 1836–1860, 3 *E. Tennessee Historical Soc'y Publ'ns* (1931): 89–107.
Holland, James W., "The Building of the East Tennessee and Virginia Railroad," 4 *E. Tennessee Historical Soc'y Publ'ns* (1932): 83–101.

Hollingsworth, Harold M., "Tennessee and the Supreme Court of the United States," 47 *E. Tennessee Historical Soc'y Publ'ns* (1975).

Hoskins, James D. "The University of Tennessee College of Law," 16 *Tennessee Law Rev.* 679 (1941).

Howell, Alice, et al., ed., *Heart of the Valley: A History of Knoxville, Tennessee* (Knoxville: East Tennessee Historical Society 1976).

http://m.dailykos.com/story/2014/07/23/1316104/-Justice-of-the-Day-EDWARD-TERRY-SANFORD.

Humes, Thomas W., *The Loyal Mountaineers of Tennessee* (Knoxville: Ogden & Brothers Co. 1888) (reprinted: Johnson City, Tenn.: The Overmountain Press 1998).

Hutson, A.C., Jr., "The Overthrow of the Convict Lease System in Tennessee," 8 *E. Tennessee Historical Soc'y Publ'ns* (1936): 82–103.

Imperial Hotel, "Special Collections Online," http://kiva.lib.utk.edu/spc/items/show/3860.

Ingram, Tammy, *Dixie Highway: Road Building and the Making of the Modern South, 1900–1930* (Chapel Hill: Univ. of N. Carolina Press 2014).

"In Memoriam," 281 U.S. v (1929).

Inscoe, John C., ed., *Appalachians and Race: The Mountain South from Slavery and Anti Slavery in Appalachia* (Lexington: Univ. of Kentucky Press 2001).

95 *The Iron and Machinery World* (Chicago 1904).

Irving Club Collection, 1861–2012 (MS. 3649), http://libguides.utk.edu.

Israel, Fred L., "Mahlon Pitney," in *The Justices of the United States Supreme Court, 1789–1969, Their Lives and Major Opinions* 3 (New York: Chelsea House 1969 & 2009).

Jacobstein, Meyer, *The Tobacco Industry in the United States* (New York: Columbia Univ. Press 1907).

"Jay Gould," Encyclopedia Britannica (online), https://www.britannica.com/biography/Jay-Gould.

"Jim Crow Laws," http://www.tn4me.org/minor_cat.cfm/minor_id/93/major_id/31/era_id/6.

Johnson, Jeff, "Maplehurst Park," *An Encyclopedia of East Tennessee* (Oak Ridge, Tenn.: Children's Museum of Oak Ridge 1981).

Johnson, Rossiter, ed., *Twentieth Century Biographical Dictionary of Notable Americans* (Boston, Mass.: The Biographical Society 1904).

Johnson, Willis Fletcher, *The Life of Warren G. Harding* (Philadelphia: John C. Winston Co. 1923).

Johnston, Kathleen A., "The City of Tomorrow with the Spirit of the Past: Bankrolling the Industrial Development of Knoxville, Tennessee, 1875–1907" (Master's thesis, Univ. of Tennessee 1994).

Jones, James B., Jr., "The Baroness and the Lieutenant: Love and Espionage in War-Time Chattanooga, 1917–1918," *Every Day in Tennessee History*, http://www.netowne.com/historical/tennessee/baroness.htm.

Jones, James B., "Convict Lease Wars," *Tennessee Encyclopedia of History and Culture*, 2002.

Jordan, W.T., "The Freedmen's Bureau in Tennessee," 11 *E. Tennessee Historical Soc'y Publ'ns* (1939): 47–61.

Jost, Kenneth. *The Supreme Court A-Z* (Thousand Oaks, Cal.: CQ Press 2012).

Journal of the Congress of the Confederate States of America, 1861–1865, I. (Washington, D.C.: Library of Congress, Washington D.C.).

"Judge David McKendree Key," United States District Court for the Middle Dist. of Tennessee, http://www.fjc.gov/history/judges/key-david-mckendree.
"Just The Beginning Foundation: William Hastie," http:jtb.org/index.php?5ra=directory&view=biographies&srctype=detail&refno=9.
"Justice Edward T. Sanford," *Peabody Reflector and Alumni News* (Mar. 1930).
"Justice Scalia: Hardest Decision 'Probably a Patent Case,'" www.ipwatchdog.com/2012/07/25/justice-Scalia-hardest-decision-probably-a-patent-case/id=26743/.
Katzenberger, George A., ed., *Catalogue of the Legal Fraternity of Phi Delta Phi*, 7th ed. (Ann Arbor, Mich.: The Inland Press 1897).
Kelley, Lucas P., "A Divided State in a Divided Nation: An Exploration of East Tennessee's Support of the Union in the Secession Crisis of 1860–1861" (Knoxville: 84 *The Journal of East Tennessee History* (2012)): 3–22.
Kelly, Alfred H., "The School Desegregation Case," *Quarrels That Have Shaped the Constitution*, John A. Garraty, ed. (New York: Harper & Row 1987 (rev. ed.)).
Kens, Paul, "Horace Harmon Lurton," in M. Urofsky, ed., *The Supreme Court Justices: A Biographical Dictionary* (Routledge Publisher 1994).
Key, David M., "The Legal and Political Status of the Negro," 4 *Proceedings of the Annual Session of the Bar Association of Tennessee* (Nashville 1885).
"Kidney Failure: What to Expect," National Kidney and Urologic Diseases Information Clearinghouse, National Institute of Diabetes and Digestive and Kidney Diseases, www.niddk.nih.gov/healthinformation/health-topics/kidney-disease/kidney-failure-what-to-expect/Documents/kidney_failure_what_to_Expect_508.pdf.
Kimball, Bruce A., *The Inception of Modern Professional Education: C. C. Langdell, 1826–1906* (Chapel Hill: Univ. of N. Carolina Press 2009).
Klein, Milton, *Volunteer Moments: Vignettes of the History of the University of Tennessee, 1794–1994*, http://trace.tennessee.edu/utk_libarcvol/1:1–223.
Knox Heritage, "Saint Johns Episcopal Church," http://knoxheritage.org.
"Knoxville College," http://www.knoxvillecollege.edu/about-knoxville-college/brief-history/.
"Knoxville General Hospital," Special Collections Online, https://kiva.lib.utk.edu/spc.
Knoxville-Knox Cnty. Metropolitan Planning Commission Documents (1994).
"Knox County, Tennessee in World War I," http://knoxcotn.org/old_site/military/wwi/book/libertyloans.html & book/redcross4/html.
Konvitz, Milton R., *Fundamental Rights* (New Brunswick, NJ: Transaction Publishers 2001).
Krajicek, David J., "Murder in Memphis," *The New York Daily News* (April 13, 2008).
Lakin, Matt, "Crusade & Crash: Twenties Brought Corruption, Cleanup, Calamity," *The Knoxville News-Sentinel* (Mar. 25, 2012): 1–29.
Lakin, Matthew, "'A Dark Night': The Knoxville Race Riot of 1919," 72 *The Journal E. Tennessee History* (2000): 1–29.
Lambert, John T., "Sprowls Story of Evolution Fight," *The New Orleans States* (June 2, 1925).
Lamon, Lester C., *Black Tennesseans, 1900–1930* (Knoxville: Univ. of Tennessee Press 1977).
Land Donors, Nantucket Conservation Foundation, https://www.nantucketconservation.org.
Landynski, Jacob W., "Due Process and the Concept of Ordered Liberty: 'A Screen of Words Expressing Will in the Service of Desire?'" 2 *Hofstra Law Rev.*, No. 1 (Winter 1974).
Langguth, A.J., *After Lincoln: How the North Won the Civil War and Lost the Peace* (New York: Simon & Schuster 2014).

Langsdon, Phillip, *Tennessee: A Political History* (Franklin, Tenn.: Hillsboro Press 2000).
Larson, Edward J., *Summer For The Gods: The Scopes Trial and America's Continuing Debate Over Science and Religion* (New York: Basic Books 1997).
Laska, Lewis L., "Mr. Justice Sanford and the Fourteenth Amendment," 33 *Tennessee Historical Quarterly*, No. 2 (1974): 210–27.
Laughlin, Harry, *The Legal Status of Eugenical Sterilization* (Chicago: Municipal Court 1929).
Law Library—American Law and Legal Information, "et al. *United States v. Shipp*: 1907–09-An Arrest Is Made, A Near Lynching and a Trial, A Guilty Verdict and Lynching, A Long Road to Justice," 1 *Great American Trials*, http://lws.jrank.org/pages/2756/united-states-v-shipp-et-al-1907-09.html.
Lendler, Marc, *Gitlow v. New York: Every Idea an Incitement* (Lawrence: Univ. Press of Kansas 2012).
Leonard, John William, ed., *Who's Who in America* (Chicago: A.N. Marquis & Co. 1903).
Leonard, John William, ed., *Women's Who's Who of America: A Biographical Dictionary of Contemporary Women of the U.S. and Canada, 1914–1915* (New York: Am. Commonwealth Co. 1914).
Leonard, John William, ed., *Who's Who in Finance and Banking*: 1920–1922 (New York: Joseph & Sefton 1922).
Leonhart, James C., *The Fabulous Octogenarian* (Baltimore, Md.: Redwood House 1962).
Leuchtenburg, William E., "When Franklin Roosevelt Clashed with the Supreme Court-and Lost," *Smithsonian Magazine* (May 2005).
Linder, Douglas O., "The Lynching of Ed Johnson," Famous Trials Website, Univ. of Missouri-Kansas City School of Law, http://law2.umkc.edu/faculty/projects/ftrials/shipp/trial account.html.
Linder, Douglas O., "The Trial of Joseph Shipp," Famous American Trials, Univ. of Missouri-Kansas City School of Law, http://www.law.umkc.edu/faculty/projects/ftrials/shipp /sanford.html.
Lombardo, Paul A., *Three Generations, No Imbeciles: Eugenics, the Supreme Court, and Buck v. Bell* (Baltimore, Md.: Johns Hopkins Univ. Press 2008).
Lombardo, Paul A., "Three Generations, No Imbeciles: New Light on *Buck v. Bell*," 60 *New York Univ. Law Rev.* 30 (1985).
Luebke, Peter, "First Battle of Manassas," *Encyclopedia Virginia*, Virginia Foundation for the Humanities (Dec. 6, 2012), http://www.EncyclopediaVirginia.org/Manassas_First_Battle_of.
Lukens, Robert Douglas, "Portraits of Progress in New South Appalachia: Three Expositions in Knoxville, Tennessee, 1910–1913," (Master's thesis, Univ. of Tennessee 1996).
MacArthur, William, J., Jr., "Charles McClung McGhee, Southern Financier" (Ph.D. diss. Univ. of Tennessee 1975): 1–274.
MacArthur, William, J., Jr., *Knoxville: Crossroads of the New South* (Knoxville: E. Tennessee Historical Soc'y 1982).
MacArthur, William, J., Jr., "*Knoxville's History: An Interpretation*" (Knoxville: E. Tennessee Historical Soc'y 1978).
Mackey, Thomas C., "'They Are Positively Dangerous Men'" The Lost Court Documents of Benjamin Gitlow and James Larkin Before the New York City Magistrates' Court, 1919" 69 *New York Univ. Law Rev.* (1994): 421–36.
MacTaggart, Jessie, "Anna Cameron Adores Television," 8 *Ottawa Citizen Weekend Magazine*, No. 18 (May 2, 1958).

Madison, James, *Federalist* No. 45 (Jan. 26, 1788).
Magliocea, Gerard N., *American Founding Son: John Bingham and the Invention of the Fourteenth Amendment* (New York: New York Univ. Press 2013).
Maguire, John H.A., "The Supreme Court Justice from Knoxville: The Politics of the Appointment of Justice Edward Terry Sanford" (Master's thesis, Univ. of Tennessee 1990).
Maltese, John Anthony, *The Selling of Supreme Court Nominees* (Baltimore. Md.: Johns Hopkins Univ. Press 1998).
Manning, Russ & Sondra Jamieson, *Historic Knoxville and Knox County: City Center, Neighborhoods, and Parks* (Norris, Tenn.: Laurel Place 1990).
Marbach, Joseph R., Ellis Katz, and Troy E. Smith, eds., *Federalism in America: An Encyclopedia*, Vol. 1: A-J (Westport, Conn.: Greenwood Press 2006)
Marquis, Albert Nelson, ed., *Who's Who in America: A Biographical Dictionary of Notable Living Men and Women of the United States* (Chicago: A.N. Marquis & Co. 1912).
"Marietta & North Georgia Railroad," railga.com/mnga.html.
Martin, George, *CCB: The Life and Century of Charles C. Burlingham, New York's First Citizen, 1858–1959* (New York: Hill and Wang 2005).
Mason, Alpheus Thomas, "Chief Justice Taft at the Helm," 18 *Vanderbilt Law Rev.*, No. 2 (Mar. 1965).
Mason, Alpheus Thomas, "The Chief Justice of the United States: Primus Inter Pares," No. 1, 17 *Journal of Public Law* (Emory Law School 1968).
Mason, Alpheus Thomas, *Harlan Fiske Stone:* Pillar of the Law (New York: Viking Press 1956).
Mason, Alpheus Thomas, *William Howard Taft: Chief Justice* (New York: Simon and Schuster 1964).
Mason, Alpheus Thomas, *The Supreme Court from Taft to Burger* (Baton Rouge: Louisiana State Univ. Press 1980) (3rd ed. Rev.).
Maysilles, Duncan, *Ducktown Smoke: The Fight Over One of the South's Greatest Environmental Disasters* (Chapel Hill: Univ. of N. Carolina Press 2011).
McCartney, Laton, *The Tea Pot Dome Scandal: How Big Oil Bought the Harding White House and Tried to Steal the Country* (New York: Random House 2009).
McClatchey-Gettys Farm, Nat. Reg. of Historical Places Inventory-Nomination Form, US Dep't of the Interior (1982).
McCutcheon, John T., "Kenesaw Mountain Landis, Judge," *Appleton's Magazine* (Dec. 1907):418–427.
McDonald, Michael J., & William Bruce Wheeler, *Knoxville, Tennessee: Continuity and Change in an Appalachian City* (Knoxville: Univ. of Tennessee Press 1983).
McFarland, L.B., "Resolution on the Death of Wm. C. Folkes," 9 *Proceedings of the Annual Session of the Bar Association of Tennessee*, Tennessee Bar Ass'n (1890):72–74.
McHargue, Daniel S., "Sectional Representation on the Supreme Court," 35 *Marquette Law Rev.*, No. 1 (1951): 13–28.
McHargue, Daniel S., "Appointments to the Supreme Court of the United States: The Factors That Have Affected Appointments, (1989–1932)," (Thesis, Univ. of California, Los Angeles 1949).
McKenzie, Robert Tracy, *Lincolnites and Rebels: A Divided Town in the American Civil War* (New York: Oxford Univ. Press 2006).
McKinney, Gordon B., *Southern Mountain Republicans, 1865–1900: Politics and the Appalachian Community* (Knoxville: Univ. of Tennessee Press 1998).

McNeely, John H., "*New Mexico v. Texas,*" *Handbook of Texas Online,* http://www.tshaonline.org/handbook/online/articles/jrno1.
McRary, Amy, "Laura Ann Cansler Was Knoxville's First African-American Teacher," *The Knoxville News-Sentinel* (Dec. 29, 2012).
McRary, Amy, "Cal Johnson Went from Slavery to Successful Businessman," *The Knoxville New-Sentinel* (Dec. 29, 2012).
McRary, Amy, "Retribution, Regrowth Mark Post-war Knoxville," *The Knoxville News-Sentinel* (Apr. 11, 2015).
Mencken, H.L., "Editorial," 1 *Am. Mercury* 161 (1924).
Meyer, Howard N., *The Amendment That Refused to Die: Equality and Justice Deferred, A History of the Fourteenth Amendment* (Lanham, Md.: Madison Books 2000).
Milord, Lisa L., *The Development of the ABA Judicial Code* 137 (1992) (ABA 1992) (Canon 19, Canons of Judicial Ethics (1924)).
Milton, George F., Jr., "The New Justice from Tennessee," *The Independent* (Feb. 17, 1923): 117.
Milton, George F., Jr., "Sanford-Neither Radical nor Reactionary," *The Outlook* (Feb. 14, 1923): 298–300.
Moncrief, Gary & Robert Joula, "When the Courts Don't Compute: Mathematics and Floterial Districts in Legislative Reapportionment Cases," 4 *Journal of Law & Politics* 737 (1987–1988).
Moneyhon, Carl H., *Republicanism in Reconstruction Texas* (Austin, Texas: 1980).
Montgomery, James, "The Volunteer State Forges Its University," 69 *University of Tennessee Record*, No. 6 (Knoxville: Univ. of Tennessee 1966).
Montgomery, James R., "Threshold of a New Day, the University of Tennessee, 1919–1946," 74 *University of Tennessee Record*, No. 6 (Knoxville: Univ. of Tennessee 1971).
Montgomery, James R., "The Summer School of the South," 22 *Tennessee Historical Quarterly*, No. 4 (Dec. 1963): 361–81.
Montgomery, James Riley, Stanley J. Folmsbee & Lee Seifert Greene, *To Foster Knowledge: A History of the University of Tennessee, 1794–1970* (Knoxville: Univ. of Tennessee Press 1984).
Mooney, Chase C., "The Question of Slavery and the Free Negro in the Tennessee Constitutional Convention of 1834," 12 *Journal of S. History* (Nov. 1946): 487–509.
Moore, Charles, *Washington Past and Present* (New York: The Century Co. 1929).
More, Mrs. John T., "Tennessee Historical Society," *Tennessee Historical Quarterly*, III (Sept. 1944): 224–25.
Morgan, Cole E., "Many Mentioned for U.S. District Judge," *The Knoxville Sentinel* (Jan. 1923).
Morrison, Andrew, *Knoxville Tennessee 1891* (The Englehardt Series: Amer. Cities, Vol. 25) (Repro. 2002, Charles A. Reeves, Jr.).
Moulder, Rebecca Hunt, "Convicts as Capital: Thomas O'Conner and the Leases of the Tennessee Penitentiary System, 1871–1883," 48 *E. Tennessee Historical Soc'y Publ'ns* (1976): 40–70.
"Mr. Justice Sanford," 43 *Harvard Law Rev.* 926 (1930).
Murphy, Kevin C., "Uphill All the Way: The Fortunes of Progressivism, 1919–1929," http://www.kevincmurphy.com/uatw-politics-harding.html.
Murphy, Walter F. "In His Own Image: Mr. Chief Justice Taft and Supreme Court Appointments." Vol. 1961, *The Supreme Court Review*, Phillip Kurland, ed. (Chicago: Univ. of Chicago 1961).
Murphy, Walter F., "Marshaling the Court: Leadership, Bargaining and the Judicial Process," 29 *Univ. of Chicago Law Rev.*, No. 4 (Summer 1962).

Nall, James O., *The Tobacco Night Riders of Kentucky and Tennessee 1905–1909* (Nashville, Tenn.: McClanahan Publ'g House 1991) (orig. Louisville, Ky.: Standard Press 1939).

Nathan, Frederic S., *Centurions in Public Service: Particularly as Presidents, Supreme Court Justices & Cabinet Members* (Dalton, Mass.: The Studley Press, Inc. 2010).

Nat. Reg. Hist. Places sec. E.

Neely, Jack, "A Fair to Remember: Knoxville's National Conservation Exposition of 1913," *Metro Pulse* (Knoxville, Tenn.) (Nov. 11, 2009).

Neely, Jack, *Knoxville: This Obscure Prismatic City* (Charleston, S.Car.: The History Press 2009).

Neely, Jack, "Knoxville's Halloween History," *Knoxville Mercury* (Oct. 29, 2015).

Neely, Jack, "Knoxville's 'Old City,'" http://oldcityknoxville.org/history/.

Neely, Jack, *Knoxville's Secret History* (Knoxville, Tenn.: Scruffy City Publ' 1995).

Neely, Jack, "Lawson McGhee," *Metro Pulse* (Knoxville, Tenn.) (July 29, 2004).

Neely, Jack, *Market Square: A History of the Most Democratic Place on Earth* (Knoxville, Tenn.: Market Sq. Dist. Ass'n 2009).

Neely, Jack, "Paradise Found Out?" *Metro Pulse* (Knoxville, Tenn.) (May 29, 2003).

Neely, Jack, "The Arby's Building, By Any Other Name," *Metro Pulse* (Knoxville, Tenn.: Apr. 4, 2012).

Neely, Jack, "The University of Tennessee: The Trip to the Hill," *Knoxville Mercury* (Aug. 20, 2015).

Neely, Jack, "Westwood History to 1931," http:/Knoxheritage.org/westwood/history-of-westwood/ (April 4, 2014).

"The New Justices of the Supreme Court," *Virginia Law Register* 9 (June 1923).

Newland, Chester A., "Personal Assistants to Supreme Court Justices: The Law Clerks," 40 *Oregon Law Rev.* 299 (June 1961).

Newman, Dean, "Chronology of Knoxville," Knoxville Journal 1939 (June 8, 1861).

NNDB, tracking the entire world, http://www.nndb.com/people/1869/000180329/.

Noone, Charles A., "Edward Terry Sanford: Gentleman, Scholar, Lawyer, Jurist," 43 *Commercial Law Journal* 34 (1938).

Nourse, Victoria, "*Buck v. Bell*: A Constitutional Tragedy from A Lost World," 39 *Pepperdine Law Rev.* 101 (Dec. 2011).

Novick, Sheldon M., "Justice Holmes and the Art of Biography," 33 *William & Mary Law Rev.* 1219 (1992), http://scholarship.law.wm.edu/bum/r/vol33/iss4/6.

Ochs, George W., "*History of Journalism in East Tennessee*" East Tennessee: Historical and Biographical (Chattanooga, Tenn.: A.D. Smith & Co. 1893).

O'Connor, Sandra Day, *Out of Order: Stories from the History of the Supreme Court* (New York: Random House 2013).

Official Report of the Universal Congress of Lawyers and Jurists (St. Louis, Mo.: Exec. Comm. 1905).

"Oil Stories and Histories, Scandal: A Short History of the Teapot Dome Affair," http://oil storieshistories.blogspot.com/2005/09/scandal-short-history-of-teapot-dome.html?m=1.

O'Steen, Neal, *Tennessee Partners: The University of Tennessee and Its Alumni Organization* (Knoxville: Univ. of Tennessee Nat'l Alumni Ass'n 1986).

"Our History, The University of Tennessee," www.utk.edu.

Owens, John B., "The Clerk, The Thief, His Life as a Baker: Ashton Embry and the Supreme Court Leak Scandal," 27 *Journal of Supreme Court History* 14 (Mar. 2002): 14–44.

Owens, John B., "The Clerk, The Thief, His Life as a Baker: Ashton Embry and the Supreme Court Leak Scandal of 1919," 95 *Northwestern Univ. Law Rev.* 271 (2000): 271–308.

OYEZ, U.S. Supreme Court Media, http://www.oyez.org/justices/edward_t_sanford/.
Paine, Donald, "The Black Patch Tobacco War Trials," 42 *Tennessee Bar Journal* 24 (Sept. 2006).
Paine, Donald, "The Trials of Lawyer James E. Fulton for Murdering Lawyer Sam Parker," 39 *Tennessee Bar Journal*, No. 12 (Dec. 2003).
Paine, Donald F., "Chasing Windows: Unethical Solicitation of Clients," 40 *Tennessee Bar Journal* 25 (Feb. 2004).
Parker, Richard A., ed., *Free Speech on Trial: Communication Perspectives on Landmark Supreme Court Decisions* (Tuscaloosa: Univ. of Alabama Press 2003).
Patrick, John J., Richard M Pious & Donald A. Ritchie, *The Oxford Guide to the United States Government* (New York: Oxford Univ. Press 2001).
Patton, E.E., "How Judge Edward Terry Sanford Became a Member of the United States Supreme Court," (Univ. of Tennessee Library, Special Collections).
Patton, James Welch, *Unionism and Reconstruction in Tennessee, 1860–1869* (Chapel Hill: The Univ. of N. Carolina Press 1934).
Pearson, Drew, & Robert S. Allen, *The Nine Old Men* (New York: Doubleday, Doran and Co. 1936).
Pendergrast, Mark, *For God, Country & Coca-Cola: The Definitive History of the Great American Soft Drink and the Company That Makes It* (2d ed.) (New York: Basic Books 2000).
Peppers, Todd L., *Courtiers of the Marble Palace: The Rise and Influence of the Supreme Court Law Clerk* (Stanford, Cal.: Stanford Univ. Press 2006).
Perceptions of Appalachian Students About Post-Secondary Education (Pro Quest 2008).
Peterson, Britt, "Private Social Clubs Try to Delay Their Doom," *The Washingtonian* (Apr. 29, 2015).
"Phi Beta Kappa," https://phibetakappa.utk.edu/history.php.
3 *Phi Kappa Phi Journal*, Vol. 3, No. 1 (1923).
Phillips, Harry, *History of the Sixth Circuit: A Bicentennial Project* (The Bicentennial Comm'n of the Judicial Conf. of the U. S. 1976).
Phillips, Harry, "Tennessee Lawyers of National Prominence." *Tennessee Bar Journal* 17 (1981); 34–53.
Phillips, Harry, "Tennessee Sixth Circuit," 33 *Tennessee Historical Quarterly* 22 (1974).
Pinchot, Gifford, Don Carlos Ellis & Julia Gifford Lathrop, *The First Exposition of Conservation and its Builders: An Official History of the National Conservation Exposition, held at Knoxville, Tenn. in 1913 and of its Forerunners, The Appalachian Expositions of 1910–11*, W.M. Goodman, ed. (Knoxville: Knoxville Lithographing Co. 1914).
"Populism & Farmers," Tennessee4Me, http://www.tn4me.org/article.cfm/a_id/138/minor_id/56/major_id/20/era_id/6.
Posey, Roger D., "The Anti-Alcohol City: Social, Economic, and Political Aspects of Knoxville, Tennessee, 1870—1907" (Master's thesis, Univ. of Tennessee 1982).
Post, Robert, "Federalism, Positive Law, and the Emergence of the American Administrative State: Prohibition in the Taft Court Era," 48 *William and Mary Law Rev.* (Oct. 2006).
Post, Robert, "Federalism in the Taft Court Era: Can It Be 'Revived'?," 51 *Duke Law Journal* 1513 (2002).
Post, Robert, "Judicial Management and Judicial Disinterest: The Achievements and Perils of Chief Justice William Howard Taft," *1998 Journal of Supreme Court History* (Vol. 1).
Post, Robert C., "Chief Justice William Howard Taft and the Concept of Federalism: A Constitutional Commentary" (*Univ. of Minnesota Law*) (Summer 1992), http://hdl.handle.net/11299/166449.

Post, Robert C., "Mr. Taft Becomes Chief Justice," 76 *Univ. Cincinnati Law Rev.* 761 (2008).
Post, Robert C., "The Supreme Court Opinion as Institutional Practice: Dissent, Legal Scholarship, and Decision making in the Taft Court, 85 *Minnesota Law Rev.* 1267 (2001), http://escholarship.org/uc/item/62t1B008.
Post, Robert C., "William Howard Taft," *The Supreme Court Justices: A Biographical Dictionary*, Melvin I. Urofsky, ed. (New York: Garland Publ'g 1994).
Powell, Lindsay, "High Knox Jurist Called 'Mediocre,'" *The Knoxville News-Sentinel* (Mar. 25, 1970).
Prescott, Samuel C., *When M.I.T. Was "Boston Tech," 1861–1916* (Cambridge, Mass.: Technology Press 1954).
"Presidents of the Tennessee Bar Association," 36 *Tennessee Law Rev.* 219 (1968).
Pringle, Henry F., *The Life and Times of William Howard Taft*, 2 (Hamden, Conn.: Archon Books 1964) (reprint American Political Biography Press May 1, 1998).
"Proceedings in Memory of Mr. Justice Sanford," 285 U.S. xxxvii (1931).
Proceedings of the Bar and Officers of the Supreme Court of the United States in Memory of Edward T. Sanford, December 13, 1930 (Washington, D.C.: privately printed 1931).
Proceedings of the Annual Session of the Bar Ass' of Tennessee (1891) (1893) (1895) (1896) (1898) (1900) (1902) (1904) (1905) (1906) (1907) (1911) (1912) (1913) (1920) (1921) (1922).
30 *Proceedings of the National Wholesale Druggists' Ass'n, New Orleans, La.* (Nov. 1904) (Indianapolis, Ind.: Am. Printing Co. 1905).
Proceedings of the Conference for Education in the South (6th Sess.) (Richmond, Va. Apr. 22–25, 1903).
Proceedings of the Twenty-ninth Annual Convention of the Tennessee Bankers' Ass'n, held in Knoxville, May 1919.
Progressive Knoxville 1903: The Metropolis of East Tennessee, http://cmdc.knoxlib.org/cdm/ref/collection/p15136coll4/id/3330.
"Prohibition," http://www.tn4me.org/article.cfm/a_id/144/minor_id/58/major_id/20/era_id/6.
"Prosperity, Depression, and War, 1921 to 1945," *Encyclopedia of U.S. Political History*, Robert H. Zieger, ed., Vol. 5 (Washington, D.C.: CQ Press 2010).
Przybyszewski, Linda C.A., "John Marshall Harlan," in Melvin I. Urofsky, ed., *The Supreme Court Justices: A Biographical Dictionary* (New York: Garland Publ'g 1994).
Purcell, Aaron D., *University of Tennessee* (Charleston, S. Car.: Arcadia Publ'g 2007).
Purcell, Aaron D., "'The Greatest Event Since the Civil War:' Progressivism and the Summer School of the South at the University of Tennessee," 76 *Journal of E. Tennessee History* (2004): 1–28.
Queener, Verton M. "The East Tennessee Republican Party, 1900–1914," 22 *E. Tennessee Historical Soc'y Publ'ns* (1950): 94–127.
Rabun, J.S., National Register of Historic Places Registration Form for Knoxville Iron Foundry Complex-Nail Factory and Warehouse, Oct. 6, 1980.
"Radical Republicans," http://www.tn4me.org/article.cfm/a_id/42/minor_id/10/major_id/6/era_id/5.
"Radical Reconstruction," www.ushistory.org/us/35b.asp.
Ragan, Allen E., "Mr. Justice Sanford," 15 *E. Tennessee Historical Soc'y Publ'ns* (1943): 73–88.
Randall, J.G., & David Donald, *The Civil War and Reconstruction* (Boston: D.C. Heath 1961).
"Reception and Banquet by Lord Mayor and City Corporation," 10 *American Bar Ass'n Journal* 581 (1924).

"Red Cross Preparedness," 11 *The American Red Cross Magazione*, No 1 (Jan. 1916).
Reid, Whitelaw, *After the War: A Tour of the Southern States, 1865–1866*, C. Vann Woodward, ed. (New York: 1966).
"Reimbursement of Depositors of Freedman's Savings and Trust Company," H. Rpt. 1282, pt. 1 (May 6, 1910).
"Remembering Fort Oglethorpe," The Chattanoogan.com, http://www.chattanoogan.com/2003/7/10/38548/remembering-fort-oglethorpe.aspx
"Remembering the Victims of Nazi Eugenics," http://m.dw.com/en/remembering-the-victims-of-nazi-eugenics/a-16945569.
Renehan, Jr., Edward J., *Dark Genius of Wall Street: The Misunderstood Life of Jay Gould, King of the Robber Barons* (New York: Basic Books 2005).
Renstrom, Peter G., *The Taft Court: Justices, Rulings, and Legacy* (Santa Barbara, Calif.: ABC-CLIO 2003).
32 *Report of the Annual Meeting of the American Bar Ass'n* 585–609 (1909).
33 *Report of the Annual Meeting of the American Bar Ass'n* 123, 156 615–51 (1910).
36 *Report of the Annual Meeting of the American Bar Ass'n* 131 (1911).
43 *Report of the Annual Meeting of the American Bar Ass'n* (1923).
"Report on the University of Tennessee," *Bulletin of the Amer. Ass'n of Univ. Professors* 10 (1924).
"Resolution Adopted by the Knox County Bar Association," *Proceedings of the Bar and Officers of the Supreme Court of the United States in Memory of Edward T. Sanford*, December 13, 1930 (Washington, D.C.: privately printed 1931).
"Resolution for Consideration and Nomination of Judge Edward Sanford as Justice of the United States Supreme Court, with Discussion," 40 *Proceedings of the Annual Session of the Bar Ass'n of Tennessee* (1921).
Robenalt, James David, *The Harding Affair: Love and Espionage During the Great War* (New York: Palgrave MacMillan 2009).
"Robert James Lowry," 11 *Journal of the Am. Bankers Ass'n* at 423 (July 1918–June 1919) (New York: Fred Farnsworth 1919).
Romero, Anthony D., "The First Amendment and Defense of the Unpopular" (Undelivered Speech, Amherst College (Mar. 29, 2004).
Roosevelt, Theodore, "New Nationalism in Social Justice and Popular Rule," 19 *The Works of Theodore Roosevelt* (New York: Charles Scribner's Sons 1925).
Roosevelt, Theodore, "New Nationalism Speech," 1910.
Ross, Edward Alsworth, "Prohibition as the Sociologist Sees It," 142 *Harper's Magazine* 186, 188 (1921).
Ross, William C., *A Scrapbook for My Grandchildren* (New York: G.P. Putnam's Sons 1941).
Ross, William G., *A Muted Fury: Populists, Progressives, and Labor Unions Confront the Courts, 1890–1937* (Princeton, N.J.: Princeton Univ. Press 1994).
Ross, William G., "The Ratings Game: Factors That Influence Judicial Reputation," 9 *Marquette Law Rev.*, Issue 2, 401 (Winter 1996).
Rothrock, Mary U., ed., *The French Broad-Holston Country: A History of Knox County, Tennessee* (Knoxville: E. Tennessee Historical Soc'y 1972).
Rove, Karl, *The Triumph of William McKinley: Why the Election of 1896 Still Matters* (New York: Simon & Schuster 2015).
Rubin, Brent, "*Buchanan v. Warley* and the Limits of Substantive Due Process as Antidiscrimination Law," 92 *Texas Law Rev.* 477 (2013).

Rule, William, *The Loyalists of Tennessee in the Late War* (Cincinnati: H.C. Sherick & Co. 1887).
Rule, William, George Frederick Mellen & John Wooldridge, eds., *Standard History of Knoxville, Tennessee* (Chicago: Lewis Publ'g Co. 1900, reprinted by Kessinger Books 2010).
Rule, William, "The New Supreme Court Justice," *The New York Times* (Feb. 4, 1923).
Rules and Regulations Governing the Department of State (1907) (Washington, D.C.: Gov. Printing Office 1907).
Russell, Francis, *In the Shadow of Blooming Grove: Warren G. Harding in His Times* (New York: McGraw-Hill 1968).
Sadler, Marilyn, "A Murder in Central Gardens, Parts I & II," *Memphis City Magazine* (Oct. 1, 2007 and Nov. 1, 2007).
"The Saloon and Anarchy: Prohibition in Tennessee," http://www.tn.gov/tsla/exhibits/prohibition/temperance.htm.
Sanford, Carlton E., *Thomas Sanford, the Emigrant to New England* (Rutland, Vt.: The Tuttle Co. Printers 1911).
Sanford, Edward T., "The Promotion of Uniformity of Legislation in the United States," 23 *Proceedings of the Annual Session of the Tennessee Bar Ass'n of Tennessee* (1904).
Sanford, Edward T., *Blount College and the University of Tennessee: A Historical Address delivered before the Alumni Association and members of the University of Tennessee, June 12, 1894* (Knoxville: Univ. of Tennessee 1894).
Sanford, Edward T., *The Constitutional Convention of 1796* in 15 *Proceedings of the Annual Session of the Bar Association of Tennessee* (Nashville, Tenn.: Marshall & Bruce Co. Printers and Stationers 1896).
Sanford, Edward T., Address to the Tennessee Bar Association Annual Meeting (June 1923).
Sanford, Edward T., "The Establishment of the Federal Judicial System," Sanford Papers.
Sanford, Edward T., "United War Work," a speech given at Madisonville, Tennessee (Nov. 1, 1918), Sanford Papers.
"Sanford, Edward Terry," Who's Who in Tennessee, http://tngenweb.org/whos-who/sanford-edward-terry/.
Savage, David G., "From the Gilded Age to the Great Depression," *Guide to the U.S. Supreme Court*, Vol. 1 (5th ed.) (Washington, D.C.: CQ Press 2010).
"Scandal: A Short History of the Teapot Dome Affair," http://oilstorieshistories.blogspot.com/2005/09/scandal-short-history-of-teapot-dome.thml.
Schlesinger, Jr., Arthur M., *The Age of Roosevelt: The Crisis of the Old Order, 1919–1933* (Boston: Houghton Mifflin 1957).
Schmidt, Benno C., Jr., "Principle and Prejudice: The Supreme Court and Race in the Progressive Era," 82 *Columbia Law Rev.*, No. 3 (Apr. 1982).
Scigliano, Robert, *The Supreme Court and the Presidency* (New York: The Free Press 1971).
"The Scourge of Soviet Science," *The Wall Street Journal* (June 18–19, 2016).
Segal, Jeffrey A. & Harold J. Spaeth, *The Supreme Court and the Attitudinal Model Revisited* (Cambridge Univ. Press 2002).
Senate Resolution No. 6, House Resolution No. 10 Jan. 8, 1923, Public Acts of Tennessee, 1923.
Seymour, Digby Gordon, *Divided Loyalties: Fort Sanders and the Civil War in East Tennessee* (Knoxville: Univ. of Tennessee Press 1963) (rev. ed.) (Knoxville: E. Tennessee Historical Soc'y 1982; Nashville, Tenn.: Williams Printing Co. 1990).
Shapiro, Karin A., *A New South Rebellion: The Battle Against Convict Labor in the Tennessee Coalfields 1871–1896* (Chapel Hill: Univ. of N. Carolina Press 1998).

"The Shipp Case: A Chronology—UMKC School of Law, http://law2.umkc.edu/faculty/projects/ftrials/ship/chronology.html.

Shurts, John, *Indian Reserved Water Rights: The Winters Doctrine in Its Social and Legal Context, 1880s–1930s* (Norman: Univ. of Oklahoma Press 2000).

Smelcer, Susan Navarro, "Supreme Court Justices: Demographic Characteristics, Professional Experience and Legal Education, 1789–2010" (Congressional Research Service 2010).

Smith, A. Christopher, "J. N. Darby in Switzerland at the Crossroads of Brethren History and European Evangelism," *Christian Brethren Review* (1983), www.biblicalstudies.org.uk at 76–77.

Smith, M. Lee, "Tennessee's Postbellum Political History: Voting Patterns and Party Identification" in *Tennessee Government and Politics: Democracy in The Volunteer State*, John R. Vile & Mark Byrnes, eds. (Nashville, Tenn.: Vanderbilt Univ. Press 1998).

"The Society's Archives," *Court Historical Soc'y Newsletter*, United States District Court for the Eastern District of Tennessee, Inc. (Feb. 2011).

"The Socratic Method," https://www.law.uchicago.edu/socratic-method.

"Southern Railway Knoxville History," http://www.jreb.org/ns/index.php?topic=6971.0;wap2.

Southern Education Board Records, 1898–1925, blogs.lib.unc.edu/afam/index.southern-Education-Boardrecords-1898–1925/.

"Special Collections Online," http://kiva.lib.utk.edu/spc/items/show/3860.

Spence, Joe, "Lenoir Car Works," *Tennessee Encyclopedia of History*, https://tennesseeencyclopedianet/entry.php?rec=779.

Stanley, Maurice, *Sorrows End* (Fairview, N. C.: Bright Mountain Books 2009).

Stenographer Files for Judge Edward T. Sanford (Nat'l Archives, RG 60, Stack Area 230, Box 1116).

Stokely, Jim, and Jeff D. Johnson, eds., *An Encyclopedia of East Tennessee* (Oak Ridge, Tenn.: Children's Museum of Oak Ridge 1981).

Strickland, Stephen Parks, ed., *Hugo Black and The Supreme Court* (Indianapolis, Ind.: 1967).

Strum, Philippa, "Louis Dembitz Brandeis," in *Supreme Court Justices: A Biographical Dictionary*, Melvin I. Urofsky, ed. (New York, Garland Publ'g, Inc. 1994).

"Summary of Proceedings of the Tennessee Bar Association," (held at Nashville, May 26–28, 1902) *Annual Report of the American Bar Ass'n* (Saratoga Springs, New York, 1902)).

Swindler, William F., *Court and Constitution in the Twentieth Century: The Old Legality, 1889–1932* (Indianapolis: Bobbs-Merrill 1964).

The Supreme Court and Its Work (Washington, D.C.: Congressional Quarterly, Inc. 1981).

Sutherland, Daniel E., ed., *A Very Violent Rebel: The Civil War Diary of Ellen Renshaw House* (Knoxville: Univ. of Tennessee Press 1996).

Taft, William Howard, *Present Day Problems: A Collection of Addresses Delivered on Various Occasions* (Books for Libraries Press 1967).

Taylor, Robert L., Jr., "The New South Mind of a Mountain Editor: William Rule, 1877–1898," 47 *E. Tennessee Historical Soc'y Publ'ns* 1975.

"The Teapot Dome Scandal," http://www.wyohistory.org/encyclopedia/teapot-dome-scandal.

Temple, Oliver Perry, *East Tennessee and the Civil War* (Cincinnati: Robert Clark Co., 1899) (Reprinted Johnson City, Tenn.: Overmountain Press 1995).

Temple, Oliver Perry, Knoxville Industrial Ass'n Address of 1869 (Knoxville: T. Haws & Co. 1869).

Temple, Oliver P. & Mary Boyce Temple, eds., *Notable Men of Tennessee, From 1833 to 1875: Their Times and Their Contemporaries* (New York: The Cosmopolitan Press 1912).
Templeton, Lucy, "A Country Calendar," *The Knoxville News-Sentinel* (Nov. 14, 1931) at 4.
Templeton, Lucy, "Long-Time Resident of Knoxville Tells Something About City Half Century Ago," *The Knoxville News-Sentinel* (Oct. 26, 1947).*2 Tennessee Law Rev.* No. 4 (May 1924).
"Tennessee," http://www.econlib.org/library/YPOBooks/Lalor/llcy1022.html.
Tennessee Encyclopedia of History and Culture, http://tennesseeencyclopedia.net/entry.php?rec=1170.
Tennessee History Classroom, http://www.tennesseehistory.com/class/Sanford.htm.
"Tennessee Wesleyan College, http://tennesseeencyclopedia.net/entry.php?rec=1364.
Thacker, Barry, Presentation at ASCETSPE Engineering Soc'y Meeting (Feb. 22, 2000), http://www.coalcreekaml.com/BKTASCEpresent-ation.htm.
"The Chief Justice—A Mistaken Appointment," *The Nation* (July 13, 1921) (Vol. 113, No. 2923).
Thomas, William G., *Lawyering for the Railroad: Business, Law, and Power in the New South* (Baton Rouge: Louisiana State Univ. Press 1999).
Time (Mar. 17, 1930).
Time (Jan. 13, 1930).
TSLA, "This Honorable Body: African American Legislators in the 19th Century Tennessee," https://sos.tn.gov/products/tsla/honorable-body-african-american-legislators-19th-century-tennessee
Tumblin, Jim, "Edward Terry Sanford (1865–1930)" (*The Shopper News* (May 13, 2015))
Tumblin, Jim, "Walking 'Through the Friendly Years': Captain W. W. Woodruff," *The Shopper News* (Jan. 10, 2011).
Turczyn, Coury, "The Full Story of the Waterwheel on Lyons Bend," *Metro Pulse* (Knoxville, Tenn.) (Jan. 3, 2011).
Tyson, Lawrence D., *President's Report, Knoxville, Woolen Mills* (Jan. 1905) (Knoxville, Tenn.: S.B. Newman & Co. 1905).
4 University of Cincinnati Record No. 9 (Univ. of Cincinnati Press June 1908).
University of Tennessee Record, Vol. 1, No. 1 (Knoxville: Univ. of Tennessee Press 1898).
University of Tennessee Record, Vol. 1, No. 5 (Knoxville: Univ. of Tennessee Press 1898).
University of Tennessee Record, Vol. 5, No. 1 (Knoxville: Univ. of Tennessee Press 1902).
University of Tennessee Record, Vol. 6, No. 2, (Knoxville: Univ. of Tennessee Press Feb. 1903).
University of Tennessee Record, Vol. 16, No. 4 (Knoxville: Univ. of Tennessee Press 1913).
University of Tennessee Record, Vol. 26, No. 4 (Knoxville: Univ. of Tennessee Press 1923).
University of Tennessee Record, Vol. 69, No. 6 (Knoxville: Univ. of Tennessee Press Nov. 1966).
University of Tennessee Record, Vol. 74, No. 6 (Knoxville: Univ. of Tennessee Press 1971).
University of Tennessee Register, 1897–98, 1915–16, 1919–20 (Knoxville: Univ. of Tennessee Press).
University of Tennessee and State Agricultural and Mechanical College Catalogue, 1882–83 (Knoxville, Tenn.: T. Haws, Book and Job Printer 1883).
University of Tennessee Board of Trustees' Minutes, 4.
Urofsky, Melvin I., & David W. Levy, eds., *Letters of Louis D. Brandeis* (5 Vols.) (4) (Albany: State Univ. of New York Press 1971).
Urofsky, Melvin I., "Louis D. Brandeis: His Days at Harvard Law School," *Experience*, No. 2 (2010).
Urofsky, Melvin I, *Louis D. Brandeis: A Life* (New York: Pantheon Books 2009).
Urofsky, Melvin I., "The Brandeis-Frankfurter Conversations," *The Supreme Court Review* Vol. 1985 (1985).

"U.S. Justice Edward Sanford," Tennessee History Classroom, http://www.tennesseehistory.com/class/Sanford.htm.

U.S. City Directories, 1822–1989.

U.S. Congress, Senate, Journal of the Executive Proceedings, 59th Cong., 2d Sess., 1907, xxxvii, 89–108.

U.S. Department of Justice, *Annual Report of the Attorney-General of the United States for the Year 1906* (Washington, D.C.: Gov. Printing Office 1906).

13 Vanderbilt Univ. Quarterly (Nashville, Tenn.: Vanderbilt Univ. 1913).

Vile, John, "Knoxville Iron Company v. Harbison," *Tennessee Encyclopedia of History and Culture* 2002, https://tennesseeencyclopedia.net/entry.php?rec=749.

Vile, John R. & Mark Burns, eds., *Tennessee Government and Politics: Democracy in the Volunteer State* (Nashville, Tenn.: Vanderbilt Univ. Press 1998).

Vose, Clement E., *Caucasions Only: The Supreme Court, the NAACP, and the Restrictive Covenant Cases* (Berkeley: Univ. of California Press 1959).

Waldrep, Christopher, *Night Riders: Defending Community in the Black Patch, 1890–1915* (Durham: Duke Univ. Press 1993).

Warren, Charles, "The New Liberty Under the Fourteenth Amendment," 39 *Harvard Law Rev.* (Jan. 1926).

Warren G. Harding, Address Accepting the Republican Nomination (Jun. 12, 1920), The American Presidency Project, http://www.presidency.ucsb.edu.

"Warren G. Harding," Biography.com, http://www.biography.com/people/warren-g-harding-9328336.

Watson, Bruce, "The judge who ruled baseball," 31 *Smithsonian*, No. 7 (Oct. 2000).

Watts, James F., Jr., "Horace H. Lurton," in Leon Friedman & Fred L. Israel, eds., 3 *The Justices of the United States Supreme Court, 1789–1969, Their Lives and Major Opinions* (New York: R.R. Bowker Co. 1969).

Werner, Morris Robert, & John Starr, *Teapot Dome* (New York: Viking Press 1959).

Weisberger, "The Selective Incorporation Process and Judicial Activism."

Webb, Michael, "God Bless You All—I Am Innocent: Sheriff Joseph Shipp, Chattanooga and the Lynching of Ed Johnson," in *Trial and Triumph, Essays in African American History*, Carroll Van West, ed. (Knoxville: Univ. of Tennessee Press 2001).

Westin, Alan F., "The Case of the Prejudiced Doorkeeper," *Quarrels That Have Shaped the Constitution*, John A. Garraty, ed. (New York: Harper & Row Publishers 1987).

"What Caused the War?" Tennessee 4 Me, http://www.tn4me.org/article.cfm/a_id/1/minor_id/1/major_id/5/era_id/5.

Wheeler, W. Bruce, *"Knoxville*, Tennessee," *Tennessee Encyclopedia of History and Culture*, 2009, https://tennesseeencyclopedia.net/entry.php?rec=745.

Wheeler, William Bruce, *Knoxville, Tennessee: A Mountain City in the New South* (2nd ed.) (Knoxville: Univ. of Tennessee Press 2005).

White, G. Edward, "The Canonization of Holmes and Brandeis: Epistemology and Judicial Reputations," 70 *New York Univ. Law Rev.* 576 (1995).

White, G. Edward, "Oliver Wendell Holmes, Jr.," *The Supreme Court Justices: A Biographical Dictionary* (Melvin I. Urofsky, ed.) (New York: Garland Publ'g 1994).

White, G. Edward, "The Lost Episode of *Gong Lum v. Rice*," 18 *Green Bag* 2d 191 (Winter 2015): 191–205.

White, Robert H., Stephen V. Ash & Wayne C. Moore, eds., *Messages of the Governors of Tennessee* (Nashville: Tennessee Historical Comm'n 1952-current).

White, William Allen, *Masks in a Pageant* (New York: The MacMillan Co. 1928).
Whiteaker, Larry H., "Civil War," *Tennessee Encyclopedia of History and Culture,* https://tennesseeencyclopedia.net/entry.php?rec=265.
Wiecek, William M., "Synoptic of United States Supreme Court Decisions Affecting the Rights of African-Americans, 1873–1940," 4 *Barry Law Rev.* 21 (2003).
Wiggam, Albert E., *The New Decalogue of Science* (Indianapolis: Bobbs-Merrill 1922).
Wilcox, Marjorie C., "A History of the Grand Rapids Bar Association, February 1902, to February 1977," federalcourthistoricalwdmi.org.
Wildenthal, Bryan H., "The Lost Compromise: Reassessing the Early Understanding in Court and Congress on Incorporation of the Bill of rights in the Fourteenth Amendment," 61 *Ohio State Law Journal* 1051 (2000).
Wildenthal, Bryan H., "The Road to *Twining*: Reassessing the Disincorporation of the Bill of Rights," 61 *Ohio State Law Journal* 1457 (2000).
Wildenthal, Bryan H., "Nationalizing the Bill of Rights: The Rise, Fall, and Rise of the Fourteenth Amendment Incorporation Doctrine (Book Manuscript, Intro, and chs. 1 and 2, May 2006 Draft), http://ssrn.com/abstract=905621.
Williams, Stephen Keyes, 74 *Cases Argued and Decided in the Supreme Court of the United States* (Lawyers Co-operative Publ'g Co. 1929).
"Winfield Scott Schley-Spanish American War," http://www.spanamwar.com.
Winston, Robert W., "The Passenger Rate War in North Carolina," in 6 *S. Atlantic Quarterly* (1907).
Who's Who in Tennessee (Memphis, Tenn.: Paul & Douglass Co., Publishers 1911).
Wolf, Michael Allan, "James Clark McReynolds," in Melvin I. Urofsky, ed., *The Supreme Court Justices: A Biographical Dictionary* (New York: Garland Publ'g 1994).
Wolf, Michael Allan, "George Sutherland," in Melvin I. Urofsky, ed., *The Supreme Court Justices: A Biographical Dictionary* (New York: Garland Publ'g 1994).
Wolfe, Brendan, "*Buck v. Bell* (1927), *Encyclopedia Virginia*, Virginia Foundation for the Humanities (Nov. 4, 2015), http://www.EncyclopediaVirginia.org/Buck_v_Bell_1027.
Woodward, C. Vann, *Origins of the New South*, 1877–1913 (Baton Rouge: Louisiana State Univ. Press 1974).
"World War I," Tennessee4Me, http://www.tn4me.org/minor_cat.cfm/era_id/6/major_id/30/minor_id/92.
Yeatts, Jason M., "That We May Think Right, Vote Right, and Do Right: Knoxville's Black Community, 1865–1867," 82 *The Journal of E. Tennessee History* (2010): 76–100.
Young, James Harvey, "Three Southern Food and Drug Cases," 49 *Journal of S. History* (Feb. 1903).
Zieger, Robert H., ed., "Prosperity, Depression, and War, 1921 to 1945," in 5 *Encyclopedia of U.S. Political History* (Washington, D.C.: CQ Press 2010).

INDEX

AALS (Association of American Law Schools), 44, 343n157
AAUP (American Association University Professors), 343n175
ABA (American Bar Association), 98–101, 191, 192, 197, 229, 231
    Canons of Judicial Ethics, 229
    committee work, 99
    European trip (1924), 99–100
abolition, 7
abolitionists, 6, 7, 18, 326n8
Abrams v. US, 292
"ache in stomach," 32
Acheson, Dean, 363n53
Adkins v. Children's Hospital (dissent), 263–64
admiralty, 153, 239, 245–47
"affected with a public interest," 265–67
African Americans, 230, 334n228, 375n55
    See also blacks
agents, undercover Secret Service, 139
Aigle (Vaud, Switzerland), 35
Aiken, Horace M., 63
Alabama Bar Association, 364n74
Albers, Andrew Jackson (A.J.), 32, 119–20, 371n250
Albers Drug Company, 120
alcohol, 120, 161, 175–78, 248, 370n229, 391n245
    consumption and sales, 370n223, 389n245, 391n245
    denaturing, 249
    saloons, in Knoxville, 17
Allgeyer v. Louisiana, 418n70
Alumni and University orator (Tennessee), 42
Alumni Association (Tennessee), 42, 43, 46
Ambler Realty Co., Euclid v., 260
"America the Beautiful," reading, 90
American Association of University Professsors. *See* AAUP
American Bar Association. *See* ABA
American Column & Lumber Company, 250
American Communist Party, 294
American eugenics program, 274
American Linseed Oil Co., US v., 250
American Press Co., Grosjean v., 303
American Red Cross, 3, 87, 173, 360n340
    and Sanford's daughter, 87
    slander of, 173
American Tobacco Company, 168
    boycott of, 168
    "The Trust," 168
Americanism, 195
Amoss, David, 388–89n191
Amoss, Harold L., 388–89n191
Anderson, Henry, 198

Anderson County (TN), 60, 62, 64, 69, 117, 350n98, 352n152
Andrews, George, 57, 58
Andrews and Thornburgh law firm, 57
anti-evolution crusade, 47–49, 274
Anti-Federalists, 282
antitrust laws, 128, 228, 250–52
Appalachian Expositions, 82–84
appointment process, 188–206
Armour & Company, 127, 128
    Army Mail Bag, 24
    See also Fertilizer Trust
Arthur, Chester A., 94
    See also Century Association
Association of American Law Schools. *See* AALS.
Atlanta (GA), 10, 16, 17, 162, 164, 168, 196
Atlanta, Knoxville, and Northern Railroad (absorbed by Louisville and Nashville), 60
Ault, Frederick A., 3
Ault, Mary Sanford, 3, 32, 37, 119
    Austin School (Knoxville, TN), 25
    death, 324n21
    recalling William McKinley's visit, 37
Ayres, Brown, 45, 103, 104
Ayers, Howard, 45

Bachelor of Laws, 50, 53
Bachelor of Philosophy (Tennessee), 41
Bachelor's degree
    Harvard, 50
    Tennessee, 41, 53
Bachman, Nathan, 192
"bad tendency" test, 295–96
Baker, Abner, 14
Baker, Henry, 352n141
Baker, Jr., Howard H., 305
Baker, Sr., Howard H., 47
Baker-Himel, 122, 337n46
Baldwin, William H., 102
    See also Southern Education Board
Baltimore, Barron v., 282–83, 285
    See also Marshall, John
Baltimore & Ohio Railroad Company v. US, 253–54
Banton, Tyson & Bro. United Theatre Ticket Office, Inc. v., 265
bar exam, Tennessee, 55, 56–57
Barron v. Baltimore, 282–83, 285
Bass, Ratcliff & Gretton, Ltd. v. State Tax Comm'n, 258–59
Battle Creek Sanitarium, 38, 274
    See also Kellogg, John Harvey
Baxter, John, 10, 152
Beard, W.D., 129

455

Beard, William, 14
Bedford Cut Stone Co. v. Journeyman Stone Cutters' Ass'n, 251–52
Bell, Buck v., 273–76
Bell, John, 7, 326n17
　See also Constitutional Union Party
Belmont, August, 118
Berea College v. Kentucky, 267
Bill of Rights, 135, 195, 281–85, 287–88, 290–92, 296–98, 303–4, 311, 377n111, 415n2
Bingham, John, 285
Black, Hugo, 270, 304
Black Codes, 284–85
"Black Diamond Line," 66–67
　See also Ohio River, Jellico, Knoxville & Tidewater
Black Patch Tobacco War, 168, 169, 388–89n191
black population,
　Knoxville, 23–27, 333n194
　in south, 284
blacks
　advancement of by Brownlow, 19, 21
　discrimination against, 24, 267–71
　incarceration rates, 68
　poll tax, 24, 267
　schools for, 24–25
　Sanford's record, 267–71
　suffrage, 267
　suffrage in Tennessee, 21, 24
Blair, Ma-King Products Co. v., 249–50
Blount College (Knoxville, TN), 39, 41–42, 326n8
Blount College and the University of Tennessee, 34, 41
Blount County (TN), 12
Board of Trustees, University of Tennessee, 39–40, 44–49, 80, 101–3, 104, 308, 344n177, 382n29
　E.J.'s tenure, 39
　Law Department, 42, 44, 47–48, 146
　presidential vacancy committee, 44–45
　Sanford's tenure, 44, 46, 48, 344n177
Bolsheviks, 239
Bonaparte, Charles J., 129, 141, 142, 375n45
Boone, Albert E., 66–67
　See "Black Diamond Line"
bootleggers, 161, 391n247
Borah, William, 188
Borches, Jacob W., 33
Bork, Robert, 301
Boston, (KY), Union Army Camp, 12
Boy Scouts, 95
Bradley, Joseph, 288
Bradley County (TN), 383n60
Brandeis, Louis D., 184, 193–94, 216–17, 225, 230–31, 233, 239, 254, 300–301, 305, 310, 403n87, 404n4, 407n86, 414n331, 420n141, 421n179
　concurrence in *Whitney v. California*, 300
Brandenburg v. Ohio, 301
Branson, Lloyd, 424n19
Breckenridge, John C., 7
Brennan, William J., Jr., 304, 363n52
Briceville (TN), 69
Bristol (VA/TN), 10, 151

Brock, William E., 307
Brown, David, 25
Brownlow, Walter P., 111, 113, 114, 147
　domination of Tenn. Republican party, 114
Brownlow, William G., 10–11, 15, 17–23, 31, 34–35, 58, 62, 68, 110–11, 113–14, 142, 326n17
　election as governor, 18
　enemy of Andrew Johnson, 19
　federal patronage, 110
　militia and martial law, 22
　political organization in Knoxville, 110–11
　pro-Unionist, 10, 11
　punishment of former Confederates, 19
　state support of railroads, 21, 62, 348n62, 351n128
Brownlow's Knoxville Whig, 10, 13, 23, 35, 73
Brushy Mountain State Penitentiary, 70
　convicts mined coal at, 70
Bryan, William Jennings, 84, 274
　Sanford disagreed with, 84
Buchanan, John P., 63, 69–70, 111, 368n185
　populist, 69
　Tennessee Farmers Alliance, 69, 111
Buchanan v. Warley, 269, 271
Buck, Carrie, 273–76, 413–14n312
Buck v. Bell, 273–76
Buckley, Corrigan v., 269–70
Bulkley, Charles H., 64, 65
　See also Coal Creek Mining & Manufacturing & *Cullen v. Coal Creek*
Bullitt, Marshall, 198
Burch, Charles N., 86, 157, 313
Bureau of Chemistry (forerunner of Food & Drug Administration), 163
Burlingham, Charles C. (C.C.), 202, 203, 398n125
　See also Century Association
Burning Tree Club (Bethesda, MD), 94
Burnside, Ambrose, 12, 25, 31, 80, 370n225
　captured Knoxville, 31
　East Tennessee campaign, 80
　Fort Sanders, Battle of, 12–13
Burnside School, 25
Burr & Terry Lumber Mill, 32
Butler, John W., 49
　See also Butler Act
Butler, Pierce, 4, 93–94, 184, 194, 200–202, 216–17, 223, 229, 238–39, 245, 272, 278–79, 310–12, 325n31, 407n86, 415n344
　railroad attorney 184
Butler Act, 49, 344n180
　anti-evolution bill, 49

cadet corps (Univ. of Tennessee), 41
caffeine, Sanford's views on, 162–65, 387n131
Caldwell, Joshua William, 94
　See also Irving Club (Knoxville, TN)
Calhoun, John C., 326n25
California, Hurtado v., 135, 288, 289, 292
California, Stromberg, v., 303–4
California, Whitney v., 299–301
California Criminal Syndicalism Act, 299–300

Calvary Baptist Church (Washington, D.C.), 355n226
Cameron, Anna Magee Sanford, 3, 83, 86, 87–88, 173, 358–59n308, 359n314 and n316, 360n340
Cameron, Anna Sanford, 88
Cameron, Dorothy, 88
Cameron, George Milne, 87
Camp, Eldad Cicero, 72, 353n164
　See also Fraterville Mine Disaster
Camp, George M., 71
　See also Fraterville Mine Disaster
Camp Chase (OH), Union prison camp, 56
　See also Lurton, Horace Harmon
Campbell County (TN), 64, 350n98
Canada Improvement Co., 127
　See also Fertilizer Trust
Cansler, Charles W., 26
Cansler, Laura, 25
Capitol building (Washington, D.C.), 235, 402n103
Cardiff (TN), 370n229
Cardozo, Benjamin, 363n52
Carnegie group, 25, 274
Carrick, Samuel, 326n8
Carroll v. US, 247
Carson-Newman College, 80, 356n241
Carswell, Harrold O., 305
Catron, John, 183, 283
Cement Manufacturers Protective Ass'n v. US, (dissent), 250
Census
　(1870), 31, 34
　(1880), 32
　(1900), 360n325
　(1910), 153, 360n325
Centennial Address (Univ. of Tennessee), 42
Centennial Exposition (Nashville), 91, 362n26
Central Market Company, 121
Century Association, 94, 202, 363n52 and n53
Cerecedo Hermanos y Compania, US v., 132
Chamberlain, Hiram, 61, 371n250
Chamberlain, William P. (W.P.), 32, 119–20, 371n250, 399n143
　See also Knoxville Woolen Mills
Chamberlain & Albers Co., 119
　consolidated with E.J. Sanford & Co., 119
Chattanooga (TN), 26, 97, 99–111, 136–43, 147–48, 150, 154, 160, 163, 171, 192, 194, 197, 307, 363n42
　Bar, 386n107
　"bar tenders banquet," 194
　US Supreme Court trial, 140–41
　Walnut Street Bridge, 139
Chautaugua, 103
Chavannes, Anna F., 32, 36–37, 98–99, 210
Chavannes, Charles Adrien, 35–38, 74, 338n63, 339n94
Chavannes, Emile, 36
Chavannes, Leon, 36
Chavannes, Louis, 5, 325n3
Chavannes, Louisa Marie, 36
Chavannes, Marc Samuel Albert, 8, 36, 123–24, 210, 339n96, 372n290, 420n125
　Confederate citizen-guard, 8
　Populist, 124
　sociologist, 123, 372n290
　utopist, 123
Chavannes family, 36, 338n67, 413n300
　Bible, 37
　Confederate sympathizers, 8, 31, 36
　fled Switzerland, 36, 338n67, 413n300
　See also ship *Hector*
Cheek, Prudential Ins. Co. v., 293
Cherokee Country Club (Knoxville, TN), 80, 96, 353n174
Chevy Chase Club of Washington D.C., 94
Chi Delta Literary Society, 41
　See also Monthly Crescent
Chicago, Burlington & Quincy Railroad Co. v. Chicago, 290, 415n1
Chicago, Milwaukee & St. Paul Railway Co. v. Minnesota, 289
Chicot County (AK) 85, 358–59n308
Children's Hospital, Adkins v., (dissent), 263–64
Chilhowee Club of Knoxville, 95
Chisholm, Speery Oil & Gas Co. v., 254
Christopher Columbus Langdell, 52
　See also Harvard Law
Cincinnati, 11, 154, 174, 179, 278, 362–63n42
Cincinnati Reds, 174
　See also Toney, Fred
citizenship instruction, 92
Civil Rights Act (1866), 19
Civil Rights Cases, 135, 269
Civil War, 6, 14, 21, 23, 29, 31, 34, 39, 42, 56, 80, 90, 175, 267, 283–84, 287, 292
Civitan International, 95–96, 192
Clark, Charles Dickens, 127, 138, 141, 145, 147, 377n107
Clarke, Edmund, 42
Clarke, John H., 184, 229–30
Class Day oration (Harvard), 50, 53, 98, 105
Claxton, Philander Priestly, 102, 104
　US Commissioner of Education, appointment as, 102, 104
　See also Summer School of the South
"clear and present danger" doctrine, 292–93, 301, 419n108
clerk, stenographic, 154–55, 231–32
　compared to modern law clerk, 154
Cleveland, Grover, 84, 94, 105, 341n124, 377n107
　See also Century Association
CLP (Communist Labor Party), 299, 420n121
　See also Whitney v. California
CLPC (Communist Labor Party of California), 299–300
　See also Whitney v. California
Coal Creek (TN), 61–62, 64, 69–70, 81, 149, 351n124, 352n141
　Ingersoll v. Coal Creek Coal Company, 73
　Slover v. Coal Creek Coal Company, 72
　See also Fraterville mine disaster
Coal Creek Mining & Manufacturing Company, 59–61, 64–66, 68, 70, 72–73, 75–76, 117, 350n94, 97, and 98
　Cullen v., 64, 65, 66
　Pearne v., 75
　Sanford a director, 61, 70
　Sanford legal representation, 59

INDEX 457

Coal Creek Rebellion, 68–70, 149, 270, 351n124, 352n140 and n141, 379n148
coal industry, 16, 62, 66
   coal-fueling stations (US Navy), 277
   See also Knoxville Iron Company; labor
Coca-Cola, 162–65, 387n146
   Company, 163, 165, 387n146
   seizure of, 163, 387n146
cocaine, 120, 162–63
Collier, Maloney v., 78
Colorado, Patterson v., 291
Commencement Addresses at Peabody, 105–110
commerce, interstate, 250–52, 255, 400–401n40, 406n66, 408n137, 409n138
commerce clause, 258, 400–401n40
   dormant, 400–401n40
Commoner, the Great, 84
   See also Bryan, William Jennings
Communist Labor Party. *See* CLP.
Communist Labor Party of California. *See* CLPC.
Communist Party, 294, 420n121
Compromise of 1877, 286
Confederacy, 7, 8–10, 12, 34, 112, 189
   in East Tennessee, 8–14
Confederate Army, 10–11, 14, 17
   loss of Knoxville, 12
   See also Fort Sanders, Battle of
Confederate States of America, 7–9, 12, 189
   Tennessee became member, 9
Confederate sympathizers, 20, 36
Confederates, former, 19, 284
   voting privileges returned, 22
Conference on Education in the South, executive committee, 101
Connecticut, 8, 12, 29, 31–32, 337n49
Connecticut, Palko v., 304
Connel, J.D., 203, 205
conservatism, 121, 123
   in Knoxville, 121, 123
   judicial, 247–48
Conservatives, in Tennessee, 21–22
Consolidated Signet Society (Harvard), 51
Constitution Tennessee (1796), 6, 363n45
Constitution US, 93, 135, 142, 231, 282–87, 289–93, 297, 300, 303, 326n25, 400–401n40
Constitutional Convention of 1787 (federal), 93
Constitutional Convention of 1796 (Tennessee), 93
Constitutional Convention of 1834 (Tennessee), 6
Constitutional Union Party, 7
contempt of Congress, 278
convict labor, 69–70, 72, 351n138, 352n140
   denounced by W.W. Woodruff, 81
convict leasing, 68–70, 351n138, 352n140
Cookeville (TN), 154
Coolidge, Calvin, 85, 219, 244, 277, 381n29, 423n7
copper smelters, 174
Coronado Coal Co. v. United Mine Workers of America, 251
corporations, Progressives villification of, 126
Corrigan v. Buckley, 269–70

Cosmos Club (Washington, D.C.), 94
   See also National Geographic Society
"Could you do better than to put in Sanford?," 147
   See also Harlan, John Marshall
Court of Customs Appeals, 152–53, 383n58
covenants
   racial restrictive, 270
   See also *Corrigan v. Buckley*
Cowan, James Hervey, 36
   See also Maplehurst
Cowan, L.M., 120
   See also Knoxville Woolen Mills Co.
Cox, John Isaac, 136, 369n200
   See also *US v. Shipp*
Cox, W.M., 14
Crane, Arthur B., 1
Creswell, Robert, 25
Criminal Anarchy Act (NY), 294, 295
   See also *Gitlow v. New York*
Criminal Syndicalism, 299, 302
   Act (CA), 299–300
   See also *Whitney v. California*
Criminal Syndicalism (KS), 301–2
   See also *Fiske v. Kansas*
Cullen, Curtis, 65, 350n94
Cullen v. Coal Creek Mining & Manuf. Co., 64–66
Culver, Lutie Metcalfe, 87
Cumberland Club of Knoxville, 95, 353n174
Cumberland Telephone and Telegraph Co., Postal Cable Telegraph Co. v., 162
Cumberland Telephone and Telegraph Co. v. Railroad and Public Utilities Comm'n of Tennessee, 161–162
currency, silver-based, 84
Custom House in Knoxville, 110, 194, 209
Custom House Ring, 110–11

Dabney, Charles W., 43–45, 53, 101–3, 145–46, 342n143, 366n123
   recommended Sanford for seat on Sixth Circuit, 145–46
   support for schooling of blacks, 102
   "very dear friend of" Sanford's, 146
DAR (Daughters of the American Revolution), 81–82
   Bonny Kate Chapter, 81–82, 356n262
Dark Tobacco District Planters' Protection Association of Kentucky and Tennessee, 168
   urged members to boycott American Tobacco Co., 168
Darrow, Clarence, 44
   See also Scopes, John T., trial
Darwinian thinking, 92, 107
Daugherty, Harry M., 85, 116, 184, 186–88, 191–92, 196–200, 277–78, 393n30, 396n96, 397n109 and n112
Daugherty, Mally S., 278–79
Daugherty, McGrain v., 278
Davis v. Wolfe, 255
Day, William R., 145–46, 184, 192, 391n254
   Mixed Claims Commission, 184
Dayton (TN), 44, 48
Declaratory Judgments Act, 241

Democratic Redeemers, 24, 34
  public school law, 24
Democratic Solid South, 187
Democrats in Tennessee, 7–8, 11, 18, 21, 22, 34, 78, 110, 112–15
  split arose, 115
Denby, Edwin, 277
  See also Teapot Dome
Denison, Arthur Carter, 85, 179–80, 203, 383n51
Dent Act, 253–54
dentist, 1, 2
  See also Crane, Arthur B.
Department
  of Agriculture, 245
  of Interior, Bureau of Pensions, 166
  of Justice, 127—142, 145, 148–49, 152, 154, 166, 185, 192, 250, 278, 298
  of the Navy, 172, 277
Depew, Chauncey, 95, 364n62
depressions, 62, 64, 118, 290
Dewey, George, 91
Dickinson, Jacob, 152, 383n58
disputes, railway rate, 132
district court. *See* Eastern & Middle Districts of Tennessee.
Dixie Highway, 74
Dixie Water, 74–75
Doheny, Edward L., 277, 278
  See also Teapot Dome
Dore, Arthur C., 85, 155, 158–59, 279, 385n87
dormant commerce clause, 400–401n40
Douglas, Stephen, 7
Douglas, William O., 304
Douglass, Frederick, 24, 131
  in Knoxville, 24
Dow, S.B., 95
Ducktown (TN), 60, 174
  copper industry, 60, 174
  destructive fumes, 174
Ducktown Sulphur, Copper & Iron Co., 174
due process of law, 262, 265, 269, 286, 288–92, 295, 299–300, 303, 304, 400n40, 418n61
Duke, James Buchanan "Buck," 168, 388–89n191
  American Tobacco Co, 168
  Duke's monopoly, 168
  university endowed by Duke, 388–89n191
Dulles, John Foster, 363n53

E.J. Sanford & Co., 119, 371n251
  consolidated w/Chamberlain & Albers Co., 119
Eagleton, Thomas F., 305
East Tennessee, 6–7
East Tennessee, anti-secession sentiments, 10
East Tennessee, post-war, 14
  politics post-war, 17
  Republican stronghold, 18
East Tennessee, Virginia and Georgia Railroad (ETV&G), 49–50, 57, 61, 63–64, 66, 124, 350n104
  Criticism of by Albert Chavannes, 124
  E.J. on board of directors, 349n74
  obtained by the Southern Railway, 66
  Sanford and, 57, 64
East Tennessee and Georgia Railroad (ET&G), 10, 31, 328n48
East Tennessee and Virginia Railroad (ET&V), 10, 63, 328n48
East Tennessee Female Institute (Knoxville, TN), 119, 324n23
East Tennessee National Bank (Knoxville, TN), 59, 60, 73, 120, 205
  E.J. director and officer, 60, 205
  See also Woodruff, W.W.
East Tennessee News, The, 26
East Tennessee University (Knoxville, TN), 34, 38–40, 170, 339n99
  awarded Morrill Act funds, 40
  became University of Tennessee, 39
  condition after Civil War, 39
  E.J. at, 39, 40
  preparatory department, 39, 339n99
  Sanford at, 34, 39
  See also Morrill Act (1862)
East Tennessee Wesleyan (Athens, TN), 75, 362–63n42
Eastern & Middle Districts of Tennessee, 51, 53, 141, 147, 149, 154, 170
  backlog, 206
  crowded docket, 175
  House of Representatives, letter regarding, 150–51
  Sanford appointed, 149
Eastman Kodak Co., Federal Trade Commission v., 261
Eastman Kodak Company v. Southern Photo Materials Co., 252
eclampsia, 4, 87, 359n331
  See also Metcalfe, Dorothy Sanford
Edison, Thomas, 274
  See also eugenics
Eighteenth Amendment, 175–76, 247–49, 407n85
Eisenhower, Dwight D., 94, 389n205
  See also Century Association
Eliot, Charles W. (Harvard), 91, 146
Elks, 95
  Sanford First Exalted Ruler of Lodge No.160, 95
Emancipation Proclamation (1863), 12, 285
  Tennessee not mentioned, 12
Embry, Ashton Fox, 154–55, 384–85n81
Emerson, Ralph Waldo, 29, 43, 55
  alumni speech on, 43
Empire Building Corporation, 73, 122
equal protection clause, 257, 268–70, 300, 400–401n40
Esch-Cummins Act, 406n62
Espionage Act, 171–72, 293
ET&G. *See* East Tennessee and Georgia Railroad
ET&V. *See* East Tennessee and Virginia Railroad
ETV&G. *See* East Tennessee, Virginia and Georgia Railroad
Euclid v. Ambler Realty Co., 260
eugenics, 273, 274
  negative eugenics, 273
Evans, Henry Clay, 111, 369n200
evolution fight, 48, 343n175

INDEX 459

Fall, Albert, 277, 278, 423n7
　See also Teapot Dome
Farmers Alliance, 111
　in Tennessee, 69, 111
Farragut, David G., 91, 105
　See also George Peabody College for Teachers
Farragut Hotel, 347n27
　See also Hattie House and Imperial Hotel
Farrington v. Tokushige, 264–65
Federal Bureau of Investigation (FBI), 384–85n81
Federal Employers' Liability Act, 246–47, 255
federal judiciary, establishment of, 93, 99
federal patronage, 147
Federal Trade Commission (FTC), 261–62
Federal Trade Commission v. Eastman Kodak Co., 261
Federal Trade Commission v. Raymond Bros.–Clark Co., 261
federalism, 377n111, 407n85
Federalists, 282
Ferguson, Plessy v., 135
Fernald, Walter E., 275
　See also eugenics
Fertilizer Trust, 126–28, 130
　Canada Improvement Co., 127
　Sanford secured indictments, 128
Fifteenth Amendment, 20, 24, 286
Fifth Amendment, 263, 266, 288, 290, 415n1, 422n205, 423n213
First Amendment, 135, 281–82, 291–97, 299, 302–4
First Baptist Church (Knoxville, TN), 25, 79, 86
Fisher, Adrian Sanford, 394–95n65
Fisher, Hubert III, 394–95n65
Fisher, Hubert F., 3, 4, 167, 221, 324n29, 381–82n29, 388n176, 394–95n65, 395n69
　Sanford's brother-in-law, 167
Fisher, Louise Sanford, 3, 4, 33, 84, 221, 324n29, 388n176, 394–95n65, 399n143
Fiske, Harold B., 301–3
Fiske v. Kansas, 301–3
Folkes, William C., 55
Fort Belknap Indians, 133–34
　See also *Winters v. US*
　reservation, 133–34
Fort Oglethorpe (Chattanooga, TN), 171, 389n205
Fort Sanders, Battle of (Knoxville, TN), 12, 13, 31, 90
Fort Sumter, 8
Fortas, Abe, 392n1
Forty Barrels and Twenty Kegs of Coca-Cola, US v., 162
"Four Horsemen," 129, 311
"Four Minute Men," 85
　See also Liberty Bond drives
Fourteenth Amendment, 19–20, 135, 138, 255, 257–58, 262, 264–66, 268–71, 281, 283, 285–93, 295, 297–304, 335n12, 415n1, 417n47, 418n65, 421n167
　incorporation doctrine, 281, 295–96, 415n1
　selective incorporation, 281
　Tennessee's ratification of, 19, 335n12
Fourth Amendment, 247, 422n205
Fowler, James Alexander, 4, 33, 58, 75–76, 110, 113, 123, 127, 148–49, 151–52, 156, 160, 188, 190–91, 196–98, 207,
250, 312, 351n124, 374n35, 381n28, 381–82n29, 397n103
　and n107, 398–99n141
　law partner, 33
　Republican candidate for Tennessee governor, 75, 113
France, 36, 51, 87, 100, 173, 413n300
　Charmoisy, 36, 413n300
　Chavennes fled, 338n67, 413n300
　L'Ecole des Sciences Politiques, 51
　Le Havre, 36
　Palais de Justice, 99, 100
　Paris, 51, 99, 100
　study in, 51
Francis, William, 25
Frankfurter, Felix, 303
Fraterville Mine Disaster, 70–73, 351n152
Frazier, James Beriah, 113, 152, 369n200
Fred, Hugh Mrs., 280
　See also Ugly Duckling, The
free silver, 90–91
　See also Bryan, William Jennings
free speech, 293, 295, 300, 302–04, 421n167 and n179
　inherent right of, 293
　right of, 160, 293–94, 300–301, 304
Freedman's Savings and Trust Co., 130–31, 167
Freedmen's Bureau, 23–24
freedom of contract, 262–63
freight rates, 76, 132
French, Lizzie Crozier, 83
　See also Knoxville Equal Suffrage League
French Ambassador, 362–63n42
Frierson, William Little, 148–49, 308, 381n17
FTC. See Federal Trade Commission.
Fuller, Melville, 138, 289
Fulton, James E., 75, 354n194

Gammon, Isaac, 25
George Peabody College for Teachers, 104–5, 196, 167n139
　commencement exercises, 105–110
　Sanford as first president of the board of trustees, 104
　Sanford as founding member, 104
　Sanford as frequent graduation speaker, 105
Germany, 51, 84, 91, 171, 173, 274
　admired US eugenics program, 274
　German militarism, 92, 107
　study in, 51
gerrymandering, 22
Gibson, Henry R., 111
Gibson, Jeremiah, 141
　See also *US v. Shipp*
Gilbert v. Minnesota, 293
Gilded Age, 57, 64, 108
Gilded Age, The (novel by Mark Twain and Charles Dudley Warner), 57, 108
Gilman, Charlotte Perkins, 82
　See also Appalachian Exposition
Gitlow, Benjamin, 294
　Left Wing Manifesto, 294

Gitlow v. New York, 135, 281–304
   sparked incorporation process, 281, 296–97
Glenn, Nina Deaderick, 132
   Knoxville ties, 132
Glenn, Robert Brodnax, 132–33
Goat & Sheepskin Import Co. v. US, 132
Gong Lum v. Rice, 268–69
GOP (Grand Old Party), 19, 110
   See also Republicans
GOP National Conventions, 143, 380n159
Gould, Jay, 67, 123
Grady, Henry W., 5, 57, 90
   Sanford and E.J. believers in, 57, 90
   speech, New England Society of New York, 57
Grady Depot (GA) case, 60
Graham, J.I., 173–74
grand divisions of Tennessee, 6, 7
Grand Old Party (GOP). *See* GOP.
Grant, Ulysses S., 225
Grant University, 362–63n42
Gratz, Louis, 14
Great Britain, 100
Green, Grafton, 4, 192
Green, John W., 157
Greeneville (TN), 150–51, 154, 156, 173, 179, 357n286
Greenwood Cemetery (Knoxville, TN), 4, 86
Grosjean v. American Press Co., 303
Guild Hall (London, England), 99–100

H.T. Hackney Company, 122, 372n277
   See also Morton, Benjamin Andrew
Hale, Annie Riley, 83–84
   See also National Conservation Exposition
Hale, Nathan W., 114, 129, 147, 149
Hale-Sanders wing, 147
Hall, G. Stanley, 102
   See also Summer School of the South
Halloween, 86
Hamilton County (TN), 135, 138–39, 377n93, 379n148, 383n60
Hampden-Sydney Academy (Knoxville, TN), 34
Harbison, Samuel, 77
   See also *Knoxville Iron Co. v. Harbison*
Harding, J.W., 167–68
   "Doctor Harding," 167
Harding, Warren G., 95, 108, 116, 173, 183, 184–88, 190, 191–92, 196, 198–201, 203, 206, 226, 264, 277, 381n29, 391n254, 392n1, 393n30
   administration, 116, 207, 277–78, 279, 293
   affair, 173
   campaign manager, 186–87, 277
   election, 185–86, 277
   nomination, 186, 277
   Supreme Court appointees, 184
Harlan, John Marshall, 135, 138–39, 147, 267, 288, 290–92, 360, 362n26, 363n52, 379n146, 391n148, 380n6
   advocate for the total incorporation of Bill of Rights by Fourteenth Amendment, 135
   circuit justice on Ed Johnson case, 138
   last Whig justice, 135, 402

Harmon, Judson, 140
   See also *US v. Shipp*
Harmon v. Tyler, 271
Harriman (TN), 370n229
   See also Lenoir City Company
Harris, Isham, 8, 34, 112
Harris, Shadrick, 14
Harris, William J., 194
Harrison, Benjamin, 36, 110, 183, 341n124, 399n3
Hart, Constance Phyllis Sanford, 324n23
   See also Robinson, Emma Sanford
Harvard, 42–43, 49–53, 57, 98, 105, 122, 129, 180, 215, 364n74
   alumni speech (Chicago), 91
   association president, 52
   Class Day Orator (1885), 50, 53, 105
   Commencement speech, 53
   Committee on Alumni Relations, Sanford on, 52
   Consolidated Signet Society, 51
   degrees received, 50
   extracurricular activities, 51
   Literary Department, 49
   Historical Society, 51
   Phi Beta Kappa, 52
   Phi Beta Kappa rowing, 51
   Phi Beta Kappa Southern Club, 51
   travel to Europe after Harvard, 51
Harvard Law, 52, 55, 59, 79, 99, 146, 344, 364n74
   See also Langdell, Christopher Columbus
   degree received, 52
   during Sanford's time, 52
   honorary Doctor of Laws degree received, 52
   Phi Delta Phi, 51
   Pow Wow Law Club, 51
   Sanford Law Club, 52
   testimonial given in Sanford's honor, 52–53
Harvard Law Review, 52, 298, 308
   editor, 52
Harvard Law School Association, 52
Harvey v. Marble Co., 56
   bar exam question, 56
Hastie, William Henry, 25, 334n228
Hattie House (Knoxville, Tennessee), 59, 347n27
   case involving, 59
   See also Imperial Hotel
Hayes, Rutherford B., 105, 170, 286, 367n147
Heiskell, S.G., 67
   See Black Diamond Line
Henry E. Frankenburg Co. v. US, 132
Hepburn Act (1906), 133, 376n67
Herndon, Nixon v., 268
Herring, Mansfield, 158
Hewlett, Emmanuel Molyneaux, 377n112
   See also Johnson, Ed and Parden, Noah W.
Hicks, Xenophon, 4, 325n32
Highlander Folk School, 343n158
   See also Neal, John R.
Hill, O.F., 371n251
   See also E.J. Sanford & Co.
Hilles, Charles D., 192, 197–98, 199–200, 397n103
historian, 93–94, 294

INDEX   461

History of Tennessee class, Sanford taught, 42
Hiwassee Manufacturing Co., 370n235
  See also Sanford (TN) and Sanfordville (TN)
Hobart, Garret A., 361n20
  See also McKinley and Hobart Club
Holmes, Oliver Wendell, 1, 2, 140, 184, 194, 216–18, 225, 232, 239, 264, 268, 273–74, 291–93, 301, 305–6, 310, 403n87, 404n4, 407n86, 414n331, 420n135 and n141, 421n179
"Holy Roller preacher," 173–74
Hooper, Ben W., 73, 83, 115, 192
Hoover, Herbert, 85, 94, 324n30
Hoover, J. Edgar, 384–85n81
  See also Supreme Court Leak Scandal
Hoskins, James D., 44
Hoskins Library, 80
Hoss, Elijah Embree, (E.E.), 31, 336n17
Hough, Charles M., 198, 202–3
  See also Burlingham, Charles C. (C.C.)
Houk, John C., 81, 111
Houk, Leonidas, 110–11, 120, 367n175
House, Callie D., 165–67
House, Ellen Renshaw, 14
Howard, Jacob M., 285
  See also Fourteenth Amendment
Hoyt, Henry M., 140, 142, 232
Hughes, Charles Evans, 4, 100, 165, 223, 235, 237–38, 303–4, 309, 324n30, 325n31, 399n6
Hull, Cordell, 307, 357n286
Humes, Thomas W., 20, 39, 340n107
Hurtado v. California, 135, 288–89, 292, 419n85
Hutchins, Styles Linton, 137–38, 142, 379n148
  See also Parden, Noah W. and Johnson, Ed

Ickes, Harold, 187
immigration, Tennessee, 21, 112, 117, 121
Imperial Hotel, 166, 347n27
  See also Hattie House
incorporation, 286–88, 291, 294–96, 298–99, 304, 415n1
  anti-incorporation, 290
  selective, 304
  total, 135
Indian reserved water rights, 133–34
  See also Winters Doctrine
Indians, 133–34, 254–55
Industrial Accident Comm., Madera Sugar Pine Co. v., 255
Industrial Workers of the World. See IWW
Ingersoll v. Coal Creek Coal Co., 73
  lawyer solicitation, outlawed, 73
injunction, 157, 162, 174, 204, 228, 243, 312
"Intellectual Beverage and Temperance Drink," 162
Interstate Commerce Act (1887), 64
Interstate Commerce Commission (ICC), 76, 169–70, 245, 255, 376n67
interstate trade and commerce, 97, 250–52, 409n138, 410n201
intoxicating liquors, 176, 247–49
  transporting, 175
Irving Club (Knoxville, TN), 94–95, 362n42
  See also Caldwell, Joshua William

Italy, 100
  See also Mussolini, Benito
  side trip by ABA, 100
IWW (Industrial Workers of the World), 228, 301–2

Jackson, Andrew, 10
Jackson, Howell E., 41, 152, 183, 193, 341n124
  Sanford letter to, 41
Jacksonian party system, 7
James, Henry, 108
  "poison plant of the money-passion," 108
James County (TN), 383n60
  See also Ooltewah (TN)
James Everard's Breweries v. Day, 248–49
Jefferson Hall (Univ. of Tennessee), 104
  See also Summer School of the South
Jellico (TN), 62
"Jim Crow Case," 169–70
"Jim Crow" laws, 24, 169, 267, 286, 290, 333n208, 418n77
  interstate railroad opposition, 169
Johnson, Andrew H., 17–19, 22, 59, 276, 326n17
  military governor, 17–18, 329n71
Johnson, Cal, 25
Johnson, Ed, 135, 136, 139, 381n17
  as federal prisoner, 139
  attorneys, 136–37, 141–42
  lynching, 135
  See also *US v. Shipp*
Johnson, Hiram, 187–88
Johnson City (TN), 204, 319, 321
Jones, Cornelius, 167
  See also House, Callie D.
Jones, Howard, 141
  See also *US v. Shipp*
Jones, John Paul, 91
Journal and Tribune Company, 122
Journeyman Stone Cutters' Ass'n, Bedford Cut Stone Co. v., 251–52
Judges Act (1922), 233
Judicial Conference, 403n91
Judiciary Act (1789), 153–54
  concerning Tennessee, 153–54
Judiciary Act (1925), 233
"Jump Jim Crow," 418n77
Jurisprudence and Law Reform Committee, 97
  See also ABA
"justiciable mind," 194

K&K (Knoxville & Kentucky Railroad), 62–63
K&O (Knoxville & Ohio Railroad Co.), 62–66, 349n71
  inherited by Southern, 66
  sale to ETV&G, 63
  Sanford legal representative, 63
  stock, 62, 66–67
  stock shares owned by Knoxville and Knox County, acquisition of, 62, 66–67
Kansas, Fiske v., 301–3
Keating-Owen Child Labor Law, 409n138
Kefauver, Estes, 37
  See also Maplehurst

462 INDEX

Kellogg, John Harvey, 38, 274
  See also Battlecreek Sanitarium
Kellogg, Vernon, 92
  See also eugenics
Kennedy, John F., 25, 334n228, 394n65
Kent, Charles W., 343n161
Keun, Odette, 311
Key, David McKendree, 170
"Kid Curry," 17
  See also Logan, Harvey
Kidd, Benjamin, 92
  See also Kellogg, Vernon
Kings Mountain, Battle of, 90
Kirkland Lake, Ontario, Canada, 87–88, 324n20
Kissinger, Henry, 363n53
  See also Century Association
Kiwanis Club, 49, 96, 116
Knappen, Loyal Edwin, 192, 383n51
Knights of Labor, 70, 352n148
  See also Coal Creek Rebellion
  opposed by E.J., 70
Knox County (TN), 8, 9, 23, 25, 34
  as predominantly Unionist, 8
  blacks in, 23
  secession vote, 327n27 and 36
Knox County Bar Association, 307
Knox County Populite Central Club, 124
Knox County public schools, 34
Knoxville (TN), 3, 4, 7, 10–11, 13–17, 25, 57, 62, 66, 79, 85, 112, 116, 121–23, 137, 151, 154, 166, 197, 248, 311
  as manufacturing center, 16–17
  as pro-Union stronghold, 8, 23
  as Republican stronghold, 18
  as transportation hub, 10
  as Whig stronghold, 10
  as wholesale industry center, 16
  blacks in, 23–26, 333n194
  capture by Union Army, 12
  Chilhowee Park, 82
  Conservation Exposition of, 83–84
  continuous occupation during Civil War, 10, 14
  cow ordinance, 17
  expositions in, 82, 84, 197
  libraries, 16, 25
  "most illustrious son," 89
  political environment, 110
  post-war, 14, 15–16
  praised by Sanford in speech, 91
  pre-war prices, 14
  private schools, 34
  public education, blacks, 25
  public schools, 24, 33–35, 42, 49, 119
  racial disturbances and lynching, 23, 26–27
  saloons, 15, 17, 248
  segregation, 24, 25
  school board, 24, 35
  Sixth Ward, 31
  Summit Hill, 32, 209
  See also Knoxville streets
Knoxville, Cumberland Gap & Louisville Railroad, 58
  See also Andrews, George
  accident on, 58
Knoxville & Kentucky Railroad. *See* K&K.
Knoxville & Ohio Railroad Co. *See* K&O.
Knoxville Board of Education, 35, 80
Knoxville Brick Company (Powell Station, TN), 73
Knoxville Chamber of Commerce, 118
Knoxville Chronicle, The, 34–35
  consolidated with *Whig,* 35
  See also Rule, William
Knoxville College, 25
Knoxville Colored High School, 26
Knoxville Equal Suffrage League, 83–84
Knoxville Fall Carnival, 81
Knoxville Female Academy, 119
Knoxville General Hospital, 119
Knoxville Iron Company, 25, 61–62, 69–73, 77, 352n141
  coal consumption, 62
  coal orders, 77
  convict laborers, 69, 72
  Knoxville Iron Co. v. Harbison, 77
  Nail Factory and Warehouse, 348n53
Knoxville Journal, The, 35
  See also Rule, William
Knoxville Journal & Tribune, The, 73, 248, 353n171
  opened relief fund for Fraterville miners, 73
Knoxville Lawn Tennis Club, 81
Knoxville Office Company, 73, 122
Knoxville Public Library, 80, 119
  became Lawson McGhee Library, 119
Knoxville Race Riot (1919), 26–27
Knoxville Southern Railroad, 59
  represented by Sanford, 59
  See also M & NG
Knoxville Stove Works, 122
  became Knoxville Metal Products Co., 122
  See also Sanford, Hugh Wheeler
Knoxville Street Fair and Trade Carnival, 91
  Sanford praised city in speech, 91
Knoxville streets
  Academy Street, 31
  Central Avenue, 26, 248
  Clinch Avenue, 31, 82
  Commerce Street, 32–33
  Cumberland Avenue, 80, 87
  Gay Street, 24, 31, 33, 79–80, 85, 120, 213, 248, 331n132, 347n27
  Hill Avenue, 36, 86, 338, 358
  Locust Street, 82, 348n45
  Market Street, 15, 31, 336n20
  Prince Street, 15, 31–33, 59, 336
  Summit Hill Drive, 27
  Union Avenue, 15
  Vine Avenue, 27, 31
  West Cumberland Avenue, 205
  West Hill Avenue, 36, 205
Knoxville Water Company, 118, 121

Knoxville Woolen Mills Co., 30, 73, 75, 120–23, 370n235
    bankruptcy, 123
    description of, 120–121
    strikes, 123
    See also Ross, William Cary
Knoxville YMCA, 370n223
Knoxville YWCA, 324
Ku Klux Klan, 21–22, 24
    violence, 22

labor, 68–70, 126, 186, 195, 226–28, 312, 351n124, 380
    disputes, 69, 157, 227
    immigrant, 64, 290
    labor unions, 251–52, 290
    organized, 70, 227–28
    postwar unskilled, 21
    protest against Fowler, 149
laborers, local, 21, 25
    free (non-convict), 69–70
"Lady from Tennessee," 280
    See also Ugly Duckling, The and Fred, Hugh Mrs.
Lady Managers, 37
    See also St. John's Episcopal Church, orphanage
laissez faire, 289, 404n9
    individualism, 123
L&N (Louisville & Nashville Railroad Company), 60, 62, 87, 360n328
Langdell, Christopher Columbus, 52
    case study method, 52
    See also Harvard Law
Lausanne (Switzerland), 36, 51
Lausanne, Academy of, 36
law clerks, 231–32, 383
    modern, 154
Lawson McGhee Library, 51, 80, 119
"lawyers are born, not made," speech, 97–98
League of Nations, 115–16, 197, 395n96
    Republican opposition to League of Nations, 115–16
    speech by Sanford, 115
League to Enforce Peace, 115–16, 197
    Local Knox County chapter, 116
    Taft visit to Knoxville, 116
Left Wing Manifesto, 294–95
    See also Gitlow, Benjamin
legislation
    minimum wage, 263
    prohibition, 248–51
    social and moral, sympathetic to, 161
    special interest, 96
    uniform, 96
Lehmann, Frederick W., 154
Lenoir, William, 117
Lenoir Car Works, 398–99n141
Lenoir City (TN), 84, 117–18, 370n229
Lenoir City Company, 73, 116–18, 122, 248, 370n229
    incorporation, 118
    problems with debt, 118
    Sanford on board of directors, 118
    Sanford's firm served as general counsel, 118
    temperance policy, 117, 370n229
Lenoir family estate, 117, 368, 397
Lenoir Station, 370n225
Leroy-Beaulieu, Paul, 51
Lewis v. Roberts, 270
Lewis v. US, 180
liberties
    civil, 281, 283, 303
    personal, 226
Liberty Bond drives, 84–85, 115, 180
Liberty Loans, 84, 180
Library of Congress, 279
Lincoln, Abraham, 7–8, 11–13, 18–19, 39, 56, 326n19, 329n71 and n82, 343n157, 417n38
Lincoln Memorial Commission, 399n7
Lincoln's Inn (London, England), 99
    Harvard Law School dinner, 99
Lindsay, H.B., 147
Lions Clubs, 92
liquor, 118, 175, 177, 181, 247, 249, 370n229, 391n245 and n247
    distilling, 175
    malt, 248
Liquor Law Repeal and Enforcement Act (1933), 176
Littleton, Jesse M., 113–14
Lodge Bill, 418n79
Logan, Harvey, 17
    See also "Kid Curry"
London, England, 87, 99–100
Loney, William R., 232, 235, 402n80
Longstreet, James, 12
    See also Fort Sanders, Battle of
Longworth, Alice Roosevelt, 220
Lord Mayor's banquet, Guild Hall (London England), 99–100
Los Angeles Cnty., Rindge Co. v., 256–57
Loudon (TN), 328n48
Loudon County (TN), 173, 398–99n143
Louisiana, Allgeyer v., 418n70
Louisville & Nashville Railroad Company.
    See L&N.
Lowry, Robert J., 83, 357–58n286
Lucky, Cornelius E., 59, 61, 74, 84
Lucky, Julia S., 84
    See also Knoxville Equal Suffrage League
Lucky, Sanford & Fowler law firm, 75, 347n35
Lucky & Sanford law firm, 59, 64, 74
Lurton, Horace Harmon, 45, 55–57, 61, 83, 128–29, 146–47, 150–52, 183, 194, 197, 311, 362n26, 382n39, 383n51, 395n66, 399n6
    administered district court oath to Sanford, 150
    judicial philosophy, 57
    McReynold's replaced on Supreme Court, 395n66
    released by Lincoln from Union prison, 56
    Sixth Circuit Court of Appeals, 56
    son-in-law, Horace Van Deventer, 382n39
    Taft's first appointee to Supreme Court, 56
    Tennessee Sup. Ct., 55–56
lynching, 26, 135, 140–41

Madera Sugar Pine Co. v. Industrial Accident Comm., 255
Madison, James, 282–83
Madisonville (TN), 369n219
Magee, Anna Stothoff, 360n341
Magee, George, 360n341
Maher, James D., 141
  special commissioner, 141
  See also *US v. Shipp*
Ma-King Products Co. v. Blair, 249–50
"malady of the larynx, a," 36
  See also Chavannes, Charles Adrien
Malone, Thomas H., 192
Maloney v. Collier, 78
  Knox County Election Commission corruption, 78
Mammoth Oil Company, 277
  See also Teapot Dome
M&NG (Marietta & North Georgia Railway), 59–60
  See also Ducktown (TN)
Manhattan Club, 94
Mann Act, White Slave Traffic, 129, 174, 390n222
Manzi, US v., 271
Maple Flooring Manufacturers' Ass'n v. US, (dissent), 250
Maplehurst, 36–37, 79, 86, 90, 212, 338n72
  Benjamin Harrison, 36
  described, 36
  fire, 37
  Kappa Sigma fraternity house, 37
  Theodore Roosevelt, 36
  William McKinley, 36
  See also Estes Kefauver
Maples, Samuel R., 25
Marble Co., Harvey v., 56
Marble quarries, 16
Marietta & North Georgia Railway. See M&NG.
Market Square (Knoxville, TN), 15, 24–25, 248
Marshall, John, 282
  See also *Barron v. Baltimore*
Marshall, Thurgood, 304
Martin, William, 173
Maryville (TN), 24, 84, 358n294
Maryville College, 358n294
  See also Rutledge, Wiley Blount
Mason, Delia, 87
Massachusetts Medical Society, 275
  See also eugenics
Matthews, Menees v., 168, 388–89n191
  See also Black Patch Tobacco War
Maynard, Horace, 10–11, 110
McAlester, Sam, 171
McCall, E. John, 113, 179
McClung, Charles, 61
McClung, C.M., 120
McClung Historical Collection, 51
McEwen, William S., 64–65
McGhee, Charles M., 61–67, 71, 74, 117, 118, 119–20, 207, 331n132, 348n45, 349n74, 352n140, 371n244
  director, Coal Creek Mining & Manuf., 61, 65
  ETV&G, 61
  ETV&G board of directors, 349n74

K&K, 62
K&O, 62
library named for deceased daughter, 371n244
T&O, 63–64
University of Tennessee trustee, 61
McGhee, May Lawson, 61, 119, 371n244
  library named for, 61
  See also Lawson McGhee Library
"McGhee Invincibles," 61
McGrain v. Daugherty, 189, 278
McKellar, Kenneth D., 188, 382n29, 395n69
McKenna, Joseph, 134, 155, 184, 216, 225, 231, 293, 379n146, 384n81
McKinley, William, 36–37, 90, 105, 110, 111, 185, 226, 290, 339n78, 361n20
McKinley and Hobart Club, 90, 361n20
McKinney, Colin P., 192
McMillan, Alex, & Company, 37
  See also Maplehurst
McMillin, Benton, 113, 368n192
McMinn County (TN), 370n235
McReynolds, James Clark, 4, 47, 94, 125–29, 149, 183–84, 193, 216–17, 223, 225, 230, 238, 245, 250, 268, 275–76, 279, 310–11, 325n31, 362n26, 374n35, 388–89n191, 395n66, 401n61, 407n86, 414n331, 419n114
  bigoted views, 230
  federal nominations and appointments, 126–27, 129
  personality and reputation, 129, 230, 424n29
  University of Virginia School of Law, 47, 193
  Vanderbilt University, 47, 127, 193
McReynolds, Samuel D., 136–40, 377n93
  See also Johnson, Ed and *US v. Shipp*
measles, 13, 35, 325n3
  See also Sanford, Anna and Sanford, John Adrian
Meek, Daisy Woodruff, 86, 355n227
Meese, Edwin, 304
Memphis, 10, 17, 86, 100, 153, 167, 188, 321, 324n29
Menees, Thomas, 168–69, 212, 00, 388–89n191
  See also Black Patch Tobacco War
Menees v. Matthews trial, 168, 388n191
"Night Riders of the Black Patch," 168
Merchant Marine Act, 245–47
Merkert & Meisel Trunk Co., United Leather Workers International Union, Local Lodge or Union No. 66 v., 251
Metcalfe, Dorothy Sanford, 4, 83, 86–87, 371n244
Metcalfe, Edward Sanford, 4, 87, 325n37, 358–59n308, 359n314, 360n328
Metcalfe, Frances Hill Arnold, 87
Metcalfe, James Garrison, 87, 358n328
Methodist Episcopal Church, 363
Meyer v. Nebraska, 264–65, 275–76
Middle Tennessee, 6–7, 9, 17, 69, 127, 178
military reconstruction, 30
  in Tennessee, 19, 335n12
Military Reconstruction Act (1867), 335n12
Miller, Nathan, 198
Miller, Samuel Freeman, 287–88

INDEX 465

Milton, George Fort, 194, 396n82
miners, 68, 69, 70–73, 81
   bodies, 352n152
   convict, 70
   free, 69–70
Minnesota, Chicago, Milwaukee & St. Paul Railway Co. v., 289
Minnesota, Gilbert v., 293
Minnesota, Near v., 304
minorities, 267–71
"Minute Women," 85
   See also Liberty Bond drives
M.I.T. *See* "Boston Tech"
Mitchell, William D., 130, 181, 309
Mixed Claims Commission, 184
mob violence, 137–39
Mocha hair, 132
Moes, Charles F., 88
Moes, Shari Cameron, 88
   See also Cameron, Dorothy
"monkey legislature," 48
   See also "Slaughter of the PhDs"
Monkey Trial, 44, 48
   See also Scopes, John T. trial
monopolies, 123–24, 261, 287
Monroe County (TN), 37, 61
Monteagle (TN), 343n158
Monthly Crescent, 41
   See also Chi Delta Literary Society
Monticello Memorial Fund, 85
Moody, William, 127, 139, 291, 296, 379n146
moonshining, 158 176, 177, 391n247
moot court, 51
Morgan, Harcourt A., 4, 48, 49, 343n175
Morgan, John, 56
   "Morgan's Raiders," 56
Morgan, J.P., 105, 118, 350n104
Morgan, Junius Spencer, 105
Morgan County (TN), 64, 70, 350n98
Morrill Act (1862), 39–40, 340n108 and n109
Morrison, Hugh G., 192
Morrow, Edwin P., 192
Morton, Benjamin Andrew, 122, 372n277
   See also H.T. Hackney Co.
Morton, J. Sterling, 43
   founder, Arbor Day, 43
Morton, Pauline Woodruff, 122, 355n227, 372n277
   See also Morton, Benjamin Andrew
Moschzisker, Robert Von, 397n111
Moses, George H., 306
"most nondescript group of unimportant little people ever organized," 202
Mussolini, Benito, 100
Myers v. US, 276

Nantucket, 86–88, 359n309
Nashville (TN), 16–18, 49, 113, 128, 150, 154, 165, 166, 193
Nashville Bar Association, 148
Nation, Carrie, 128
National Conservation Commission, 83

National Conservation Exposition (1913) (Knoxville, TN), 82, 84, 357n281
National Ex-Slave Mutual Relief Bounty and Pension Assoc., 165–67
   See also House, Callie D.
National Fertilizer Works, 128
National Geographic Society, 94
   See also Cosmos Club (Washington, D.C.)
National Prohibition Act, 181, 249, 391n245
National Prohibition Cases, 176
National Protestant Church of Switzerland, 36
National Union Party, 18
National University School of Law, 154, 232
National War Labor Board, 226
Naturalization Act, 271
Naval Academy, 172
Navy's oil reserves, 277
Nazi defendants, 274
   cited *Buck v. Bell* as defense at Neuremburg, 274
Nazi eugenics, 413
Neal, John R., 44, 48, 343n158
   co-counsel with Clarence Darrow, 44
   defense of John T. Scopes, 44
   law student protest for, 48
   See also "Slaughter of the PhDs"
Near v. Minnesota, 304
Nebraska, Meyer v., 264–65, 275–76
Nelson, Thomas A.R., 10, 59
   Andrew Johnson's impeachment counsel, 59
   Tennessee Sup. Ct., 59
New Deal, 129, 311
New Decalogue of Science, The, 274
   See also Wiggam, Albert Edward
"New Federal Equity Rules," 97
New Jersey, Twining v., 291
New Mexico, 242–43, 318
New Mexico v. Texas, 242
New Orleans (LA), 10, 16–17
New Orleans, Permoli v., 283
"New South," 57, 81–84, 89, 119, 121, 195
   spokesman of, 90
New York, Gitlow v., 135, 281–304, 316, 420n135, n137, and n141, 421n167
New York City (NY), 10, 67, 88, 94, 193
New York Club, 94
New York Telephone Co., Pendergast v., 243
Newman, Charles S., 65, 350n94 and n97
Night Riders, 168, 388–89n191
   a/k/a Silent Brigade, 168, 388–89n191
   See also Dark Tobacco District Planters' Protection Association of Kentucky and Tennessee
Nineteenth Amendment, 186
Nixon v. Herndon, 268
normalcy, return to, 185, 391
   See also Harding, Warren G.
Norris, George W., 229, 306
North Carolina, 8, 45, 74, 117, 132–33, 174, 192, 371n252
   rate bill, 133
North Carolina Corp. Commission, 133
Northern Radicalism, 9

nostrums, 120, 185
Nova Scotia, 88
Nuremberg trials, 274, 394–95n65

Ochs, Adolph S., 34, 192, 394n61
   The New York Times publisher, 34
Ogden, Adele Chavannes, 36
Ogden, E.W., 73
Ogontz School for Young Ladies, 358n298, 359n324
Ohio, Brandenburg v., 301
Ohio Gang, 187
   See also Daugherty, Harry M.
Ohio River, Jellico, Knoxville, and Tidewater, 66
   See also Black Diamond Line
Okanogan Indians, et al. v. US, 244
   See also Pocket Veto Case
Oklahoma v. Texas, 242
Old Bell House, 358n298
Old Gray Cemetery (Knoxville, TN), 37, 324n21 and n29, 325n3
Oliver, William J., 121, 206
Oliver Manufacturing Company, W.J., 205, 206
Olmstead v. US, 247
"One Hundred Percent Club," 121
"one of the more prominent and personable Tennesseans of his time," 89
Ooltewah (TN), 383n60
   See also James County (TN)
Open Brethren, 36
   See also Chavannes Family
Optimist Club, 92–93, 192
Oregon's Compulsory Education Law, 264
owners, riparian, 259–60

Palais de Justice (Paris France), 99–100
Palko v. Connecticut, 304
Palmer, Mitchell A., 294
Palmer raids, 294, 420n121
Pan-American Petroleum, 277
   See also Teapot Dome
Parden, Noah W., 137–38, 142, 377n111 and n112
   appeal request heard by Justice John Marshall Harlan, 138
   See also Hutchins, Styles Linton and Johnson, Ed
Parker, Chauncey G., 31
Parker, Sam, 75
partial prohibition in Tennessee (1909), 248, 391n245
patent cases, 240
patent medicines, 120, 162, 164, 371n252
   post-Civil War, 120
Patterson, Malcolm R., 369n200
Patterson v. Colorado, 291
Peabody, George, 103, 105, 109
Peabody Education Fund, 104–5
Peabody Normal College, 104–5
Pearne v. Coal Creek Mining & Manuf. Co., 75
Peay, Austin, 46, 49, 191
Pemberton, John Styth, 162
   See also Coca-Cola

Pendergast v. New York Telephone Co., 243
Permoli v. New Orleans, 283
"Petition for Proclamation to Save East Tennessee Rebels," 20
Phi Alpha Delta, 47, 343n172
   legal fraternity, 47
   McReynolds chapter, 47
   Sanford chapter, 47, 343n172
Phi Beta Kappa, 52, 59
   Harvard, 52
   Vanderbilt, 52
Phi Delta Phi, 51
   Harvard, 52
   Vanderbilt, Malone chapter, 51
Phi Kappa Phi (Univ. of Tennessee), 43
   Sanford named alumnus member, 43
Phi Kappa Phi Journal, 43, 341
   Comment regarding Sanford, 43
Philadelphia (PA), 86–87
Phillips, Carrie, 173
   See also Zollner, Iona Wilhelmina
Pickhardt, Wilhelm, 389n 204
   See also Zollner, Iona Wilhelmina
Pierce v. Society of the Sisters, 264–65, 275–76
Pillow, Gideon J., 328n60
Pinchot, Gifford, 83, 277
   Chairman, Knoxville Conservation Exposition advisory board, 83
Pitney, Mahlon, 183, 293–94, 310, 392n1, 399n6
   succeeded by Sanford, 201
plantation aristocrats, 11
Plessy v. Ferguson, 135
Pocket Veto Case, 244
Pokeberry juice, selling, 120
police power, 19, 248, 260, 262, 273, 276, 293, 300, 303–4
   under Brownlow, 19
Poplar Creek Coal and Iron Company, 65, 73, 75, 350n97 and 98, 352n140
Populism, 373n8
Populists, 64, 124
Postal Cable Telegraph Co. v. Cumberland Telephone and Telegraph Co., 162
Pound, Cuthbert, 198
Powell Station (TN), 73
Powell, John Wesley, 94
   See also Cosmos Club
preeclampsia, 360n331
Presbyterianism, 325–26n8
presidential election of 1876, 286
   See also Hayes, Rutherford B. and Tilden, Samuel J.
privileges and immunities, 285–86, 287–88, 292, 304, 415n2, 417n47
   "evisceration" of, 288
Progressive Era, 126, 184, 263
Progressives, 126, 187, 200, 239
progressivism, 126, 184, 373n8
Prohibition, 82, 118, 161, 175–77, 180–81, 194, 247–49, 269, 282, 291, 303, 311, 391n245, 407n85 and n86
Prudential Ins. Co. v. Cheek, 293
Pure Food and Drug Act, 162–64

INDEX   467

Race
  relations, 23–27
  riots, 26, 227, 228
Race Betterment Foundation, 274
  See also Kellogg, John Harvey
racial segregation, 24
Radical Reconstruction, 22
  in Tennessee, 22–23, 30
Radical Republicans, 19, 21–22, 24, 30, 284, 332n157
  public school law, 24
railroad accident, 58
Railroad and Public Utilities Comm'n of Tennessee, Cumberland Telephone and Telegraph Co. v., 161–162
railroad lawyers, 60
railroads, 10
  abuses, 133
  arrival in East Tennessee, 10
  brought legal business, 60
  generator of economic growth, 16
  importance in Civil War, 10
  Populists view, 64
  post-war, 16
  Sanford's representation of, 60
  segregation on, 24
  southern, 170
  Tennessee debt, 348n62, 351n128
  viewed with suspicion, 64
railway rate dispute, 132–33
Raymond Bros.-Clark Co., Federal Trade Commission v., 261
R.E. Sheehan Co. v. Shuler, 257
Read Phosphate Co., 128
Rebel Conscript Law, 12
rebels, 19–20, 23, 326–30
Reconstruction, 19, 23, 30, 57, 286, 332n157, 335n12, 407n85, 417n36
  Amendments, 286
  in Tennessee, 31, 332n157
Red Scare, 292
Rehnquist, William, 50
Reid, Whitelaw, 23
Republican Party, 18, 80, 326n19
  retreated to East Tennessee, 31
Republican National Convention (1880), 143
Republican National Convention (1896), 142–43
Republican National Convention (1912), 185
Republican National Convention (1920), 186
Republican Party in Knox County and East Tennessee, 11, 18, 26, 110–11, 114
  benefitted from blacks, 26
Republican State Convention, 113
Republicans, 7, 22–23, 78, 110–11, 115–16, 285
  in Tennessee, 21–24, 110, 114, 396n91
  obstacles in state, 113
  Sanford speeches delivered on behalf of GOP presidential candidates, 110
Reservoir Street, 33
R.H. Sanson v. Southern Railway Co., 77
Rice, *Gong Lum v.*, 268–69
Richards, John K., 146, 383n51

Richmond and Danville, 350n104
"rights subject to police power," 275–76
Rindge Co. v. Los Angeles Cnty., 256–57
"River Lawn," 36
  See also Maplehurst
River Rouge Improvement Co., US v., 259
Rivers and Harbors Act, 259
Roadstrum, Victor N., 129
  See also Fertilizer Trust
Roane, Archibald, monument dedication, 91
Roane County (TN), 370n229
Roaring Twenties, 107
Roberts, Lewis v., 270
Roberts, Owen Josephus, 311, 402n80, 423n7
Robinson, Emma Sanford, 3, 32, 36, 324n23, 355n227
  death of, 324n23
Robinson's *Mind in the Making*, 48
Rockefeller, John D., 101
Rockefeller Educational Board, John D., 48
Rockefeller Foundation, 274
Rogers, William Perry, 53
Rogersville and Jefferson, 63
  sold to ET&V, 63
Roosevelt, Franklin D., 94, 129, 172, 187, 311
Roosevelt, Theodore, 36–37, 45, 82, 94, 102, 105, 110, 125–26, 129, 132–33, 139, 142, 143, 145–49, 172–73, 185, 226, 229, 271, 274, 276–77, 373n14, 374n28, 381n28 and n29, 382n30, 395n66
  antitrust policies, 126
  attended Appalachian Exposition, 82
  ordered investigation of Ed Johnson incident in Chattanooga, 139
  presidency, 126
Ross, William Cary, 33, 122–23, 177–78, 372n284
  See also Knoxville Woolen Mills
  childhood activities, 33
  Yale graduate, 122
Rotary Club, 49, 73, 96, 192
Rotary Golf Tournament, 96
Rule, William, 35, 73, 110, 129, 147, 279–80, 337n52, 394n61
  Custom House Ring's candidate, 110–11
  editor, *Journal & Tribune*, 73
  Sanford family friend, 35, 147
  support for Sanford, 129, 147
Russian Revolution (1917), 292, 295
Rutledge, Wiley Blount, 84, 358n294
  See also William Jennings Bryan

Safety Appliance Act, 255–56
Sanders, Newell, 4, 111, 114, 147, 149, 395n69
Sanders, William P., 8
Sanford (TN), 370n235
Sanford, Alfred Fanton, 3, 32, 51, 73–74, 122, 205, 206, 324n22, 353n174
  throat malady, 74
  See also *Journal and Tribune*
Sanford, Alfred F., II, 87
Sanford, Anna, 5, 12–13, 31, 35, 88, 325n3
  death of, 13, 325n3

Sanford, Chamberlain & Albers Co., 32, 73, 119–20, 371n252
   Sanford remained officer after father's death, 119
   Soda fountain, 32
Sanford, Edward Jackson (E.J.), 5, 12, 15–18, 21, 23, 26, 29–33, 35–36, 38, 40, 57–58, 60–62, 64, 66–67, 69–71, 73, 79–81, 86, 90, 94–95, 101, 107, 118–20, 122, 142–43, 145–46, 211, 301, 329n82, 335n5, 349n74, 350n98, 352n140, 353n174, 362n25, 370n223, 371n251, 373n294
   advocate of tax levy, 35
   agent for Morrill Act, 39, 340n109
   at Ft. Sanders, Battle of, 12
   Coal Creek Mining & Manuf. Co., president and director, 60–61, 65, 71
   convict labor, supporter of, 69–70
   death, 119, 124
   East Tennessee National Bank, officer and director, 60
   estate, 123, 207
   ETV&G director, 57, 63
   fled Knoxville during Civil War, 12, 31
   K&K, director, 62
   K&O, officer and director, 62, 112
   Knoxville Iron Company stockholder, director and officer, 61, 69
   Knoxville Woolen Mills, 75, 120
   Lenoir City Company 116–18
   "made a fortune selling Pokeberry juice," 120
   protectionist, 112
   public school advocate, 35
   ran for US Senator, 112–13
   Receptions for McKinley, Harrison, and Roosevelt, 110
   Reconstruction activities, 20
   "Sanfordville," 370n235
   sat on Univ. of Tennessee board of trustees with son, 44
   school board president, member, 35
   supporter of convict labor, 69
   T&O, 63
   temperance supporter, 248
   Unionist, 8
   will, 207
Sanford, Edward Terry, 1, 43, 74, 82–90, 121, 123, 141, 146, 148, 151, 215–17, 220–25, 232, 250, 275–76, 337n46, 340n107 and n115, 341n129, 342n147, 344n177, 355n207 and n227, 358n308, 359, 361n9, 362n39 and n42, 363n52, 364n74, 365n81 and n86, 371n244, 372n284, 374n26, 375n45, 380n154 and n157, 381n21, 382n31 and n44, 383n58, 383–84n71, 384n84, 385n94 and n106, 386n110 and n120, 392n262, 395n69, 396n97, 397n107, n115, and n119, 398n141, 404n4 and n103, 407n86, 410n201, 415n339, 422n189, 424n19
   advocate of international efforts to secure peace, 115
   appointment, 34, 192, 194–95, 199, 200, 311
   assistant attorney general, 53, 130, 152, 382n31, 415n339
   assistant to attorney general, 380n154
   Associate Justice, 216, 222–23, 264
   attorney, first job as, 57–59
   bad investments, 123, 205–7

   bar admission, 55, 364n74
   campaign speeches, 110, 185
   candidate for governor, 113
   civic involvement, 51
   Coal Creek director, 61, 65, 70–71
   conflicts of interest, 161, 380n21
   cosmopolitan outlook, 99
   courtroom management, 156–61, 166–67
   death, 2, 4, 36, 85–87, 123, 198, 238, 264, 278, 280, 306, 308, 311, 325n31, 402
   Department of Justice tenure, 142
   described as "one of the most prominent politicians in Tennessee," 113
   disliked criminal law practice, 59
   disposition, 76, 151, 173
   district court districts, 175–76
   district court docket, 167, 171
   district court nomination, 382n30
   district court secretary, 85
   education, 50
   family, 30, 68, 79, 87, 160–61, 380n161
   flaws, 35, 50, 151, 155
   fell behind with docket, 150, 179
   Fertilizer Trust, 126–28
   financial issues with law firm and debts, 123, 205, 207
   graduation speaker, 90, 105
   hobbies, 96, 279–80
   hometown, 5
   judicial philosophy, 161–62, 166–67, 238–39, 245, 311
   Knoxville, youth in, 15, 17, 27, 33
   legal reputation and legacy, 76, 135, 304, 312, 381n21
   Lenoir City Co., 248
   nomination, Supreme Court, 192–93, 196, 201
   nomination, gubernatorial, 113
   nostalgia for yesteryear, 92
   on Board of Trustees at University of Tennessee, 44, 53
   oratorical abilities, 43, 89–90
   portrait, 424n19
   prohibition, 161, 248
   political activities and ideals, 110–16, 126, 161–62, 200, 239
   pro bono legal work, 51
   public duty, high sense of, 116
   railroad work, 60
   railway rate dispute, 132
   "Republican standard bearer," 115
   sale of Hill Ave. property, 205, 359
   satellite of Taft, 3
   sensitive to the rights of individuals, 171
   smoker, 155
   sought appellate court position, 151
   special assistant to attorney general, 126
   speeches and themes, 43, 53, 90–95, 105–110, 230, 312
   spiritual development, 98
   support, enjoyed bipartisan, 191
   support for Southern education, 104
   supportive of women attaining rights, 42
   values, 50–51, 43, 106–8, 116, 171, 312
   will, 85–86, 358

Sanford, Edward Terry (cont'd)
   work habits, 141, 154–56, 230
   work load, 178, 193, 194–96, 232, 233, 235, 238
   World War I activities, 84–85, 107
Sanford, Emma Chavannes, 5, 12, 30–32, 35–38, 81, 98–99, 115, 211, 274
   Battle Creek Sanitarium, 38
   death of, 38
   Executive Board of Lady Managers St. John's, 37
   illness, 37–38
   personality, 37–38
   supporter of St. John's orphanage, 37, 115
Sanford, George William, 5, 32, 325n3
   death of, 32, 325n3
Sanford, Georgiana, 32, 34, 337n49
Sanford, Hugh Wheeler, 3, 32–33, 51, 86–87, 122, 161, 206, 337n46, 359n309
   business interests and patents, 73, 122
   director of Sanford, Chamberlain & Albers, 122
   Knoxville Stove Works (Knoxville Metal Products), 122
   Sanford-Day Iron Works, 73, 122
   served on Council of National Defense, 122
   served on War Industries Board, 122
Sanford, John Adrian, 5, 12, 13, 35, 325n3
   death of, 13, 325n3
Sanford, Kitty, 86
Sanford, Louis Chavannes, 5, 32, 325n3
   death of, 32, 325n3
Sanford, Lutie Mallory Woodruff, 2–4, 67, 79–87, 95–96, 122, 148, 198, 215, 220, 355n226 and n227, 356n266, 358n59, n297, n298, and n308, 359n314, 360n325 and n341, 372n277
   death of, 86, 359n314 and n316
   marriage, 79
   served in "minute women," 85
Sanford, Margaret Woodruff, 122
Sanford, Mary, 3
Sanford, Mrs. Alfred F., 86
Sanford, William F., 324n23
Sanford family, 212, 380n161
   one of the richest and most prominent, 30, 380n161
Sanford Law Club, 52
Sanford Realty Co., 73, 122
Sanford-Day Iron Works, 73, 122
Sanfordville (TN), 370n235
Say, Leon, 51
Scalia, Antonin, 240, 405n27
Schenk v. US, 292
Schley, Winfield Scott, 91
school education, public, 34, 104, 265, 268
   segregated, 268, 412n267
Schwimmer, Rosika, naturalization case, 271
Schwimmer, US v., 271–73
Scopes, John T., trial, 44, 48, 274
Scott, George S., 63
Scott, William B., Sr., 24
scrip, 78
secession, 5, 7–9, 17–18, 283, 326n17, 328n51
   East Tennessee vote on, 9
   ordinance of secession nullified, 18
   Tennessee vote on, 9
   Secessionists, 10
Second Creek (Knoxville, TN), 31, 61
   Knoxville Iron Company, 61
Sedition Acts, 171, 292
segregation, 24, 135, 169
segregation laws, 333
selective incorporation, 281, 304
Senate Chamber, former, 234
Senate Committee investigations, 279
Senate confirmation, 200
Senate Judiciary Committee, 178, 193, 231
Senate restaurant, 280
Senter, DeWitt C., 22
"separate but equal," 170, 269
Sermon on the Mount, 91–92, 107–108
Seventeenth Amendment, 368n187
Seventh Amendment, 423n213
Severens, Henry F., 383n51
Sevier, John, 90, 356n262
Sevier, Katherine Sherill "Bonnie Kate," 356n262
Sevier County (TN), 25, 35
Sevierville (TN), 84
Shelley v. Kraemer, 270
Shepherd, Lewis, 136, 138, 141, 377n97, 381n17
   former judge, 136
   See also Johnson, Ed
Sherman, William T., 80
Sherman Antitrust Act (1890), 125–26, 128, 227, 250–51, 389n191, 408n137, 410n201
   Fertilizer Trust, 126–28, 130
   Sanford's predilections, 250
   tobacco trust, 388–89n191
Shetals, Andrew, 32
Shetals, Cynthia, 32
Shetals, Emily, 32
Shields, John K., 83, 129–30, 391n254
ship *Hector*, 36
Shipp, Joseph, 135–36, 139–41, 379n149
   criminal contempt of the Supreme Court, 140
   Supreme Court acquired original jurisdiction, 140
Shipp, US v., 136–142, 166, 379n132, 379n146
Shope, William Krebs Beresford, 172
   See also Zollner, Iona Wilhelmina Shope
Shuler, R.E. Sheehan Co. v., 257
Silent Brigade, 168
   See also Dark Tobacco District Planters' Protection Association of Kentucky and Tennessee
Sinclair, Harry F., 277–78
   See also Teapot Dome
Sinclair, Upton, 163
   The Jungle, 163
Sixth Amendment, 140, 288, 311, 422n205
Sixth Amendment's guarantee, 134, 138, 298
Sixth Circuit Court of Appeals, 45, 56, 151–52, 154, 165, 179–81, 192, 226, 341n124, 362n26
   vacancies, 151–52
"Slaughter of the PhDs," 47
   See also Neal, John R.; Sprowls, Jesse W.
Slaughterhouse Cases, 287

slave holders, 9–10
Slave Pension, 386
"Slave Power," 18, 284
slave states, 6, 284
slavery, abolition of, 6, 7, 18, 283, 286
slaves, 6–8, 11–12, 18, 36, 43, 167, 267, 283
Slover v. Coal Creek Coal Co., 72
Smith, Alphonso C., 45
Smith, Charles H., 307
smoke cases, 174
    See also Ducktown (TN)
social Darwinism, 123, 289
socialism, 290, 294, 373n8
Socialist Party, 299
socialists, 10, 82, 231, 239, 293, 299
Society of Mayflower Descendants, 91
Society of the Sisters, Pierce v., 264–65, 275–76
Sociologist, The, 123, 368, 419n125
Sociologist,
    early American, 419n125
    See also Chavannes, Marc Samuel Albert
solicitor general position, 149
Solid South, 190
Sons of the American Revolution, 81
Sound Money Clubs, 90, 91, 362n25
Southern Car & Foundry Co., 398–99n141
Southern Education Board, 101–3
Southern Photo Materials Co., Eastman Kodak Company v., 252
Southern plantations, 283
Southern postmasters, 284
Southern public education goals, 101–2
Southern Railway Company, 64, 66–67, 76–77, 132–33, 200, 350n104, 370n235, 398–99n141
    R.H. Sanson v., 77
Southern Republicans, 187, 196
Southern Society of Washington, 94, 364n58
Southern Unionism, 23
Southern Whigs, 7
Southerners, 14, 18, 51, 64, 74, 165, 188, 190–91, 195, 284
Spanish-American War, 75, 91
Spaulding, John William, 171–72
    See also Zollner, Iona Wilhelmina
Speery Oil & Gas Co. v. Chisholm, 254
Sprowls, Jesse W., 48–49, 343n175
    See also "Slaughter of the PhDs"
Square Deal, 185
St. John's Episcopal Church, 4, 37, 337n49, 339n91
    orphanage, 37, 115, 339n91
St. Paul's Church (London, England), 87
Standard Coal & Coke Co, 80, 319
Standard Oil, 123
Standard Oil Trust, 125
stare decisis, 264
State Investment Co., US v., 242
State of Arkansas, White River Lumber Co. v., 257
State Tax Comm'n, Bass, Ratcliff & Gretton, Ltd. v., 258–59
States' Rights, 8, 189
statutory construction, 253–56

Staub's Opera House/Theater, 41, 81
    Sanford's graduation in, 41
Stevenson, Adlai, 363n53
Stevenson, Robert Louis, 90, 95
Stone, Harlan F., 4, 217, 223, 231, 252, 303, 325n31
strikes, 26
Stromberg v. California, 303–4
Stuart, George R., 164
substantive due process, 262–65, 289
    economic, 418n70
suffrage, 20, 83
    black, 20–21, 267
    women's, 41, 83–84, 186, 231, 324n29
Suhrie, Ambrose L., 102
Summer School of the South, 101–4, 367n139
    demise of, 102
    "greatest summer school the world has ever known," 112
Sumner, Charles, 416n31
Sunday, Billy, 49, 274
    revival meetings, 48–49
    See also Monkey Trial
Supplemental Prohibition Act (1921), 248
Supreme Court Bar, 238, 308
Supreme Court Building, new, 235
Supreme Court Leak Scandal, 383–84n81
Sutherland, George, 2, 93, 184, 194, 201, 202, 216–17, 225, 230, 235, 238, 245, 263, 265, 275–76, 303. 311–12, 407n86
    wife, 2
Swift Co., 128
    See also Fertilizer Trust
Swiss government, 36
    religious intolerance, 36
Switzerland
    Aigle, 35
    Lausanne, 51
syndicalism, 421n172, 422n189

Taft, Alphonso, 225
Taft, Henry W., 184, 197, 200
Taft, William H., 3–4, 45, 56, 82, 93–94, 102, 108, 115–16, 131, 147, 149, 151, 179, 183–85, 192–94, 196–98, 200–203, 216–17, 222, 225, 229, 231, 233, 235, 238–39, 247, 250, 267, 274, 276, 303, 306, 310–11, 324n30, 360n340, 362n26, 383n51, 391n254, 397n109, 399n6, 401n45, 407n86 and n88, 410n204, 412n267, 414n331, 419n114, 422n189, 423n6
    "Americanism as Compared to Bolshevism," 116
    attended second exposition, 82
    belief in teamwork, 229
    died same day as Sanford, 3
    dislike of dissents, 229
    dislike of footnotes, 229
    exit, 311
    fear of Communism, 228
    founder and president of League to Enforce Peace, 115
    funeral service, 4
    "inner club" at home on Sunday, 3, 4
    judicial philosophy, 226–230
    jurisprudence, 228

INDEX   471

Taft, William H. (*cont'd*)
  Knoxville visit (1920), 116
  leadership, 229
  legacy, 233–34
  pre-presidential career, 226
  role in obtaining Sanford's appointment, 4
  served on Sixth Circuit with Lurton, 56
  urged block of Brandeis appointment, 231
  Yale Law professor, 226
Taft Court, 216–19, 225, 228, 230, 232, 237–38, 251, 269, 273, 293, 297, 301, 309–10
  Distinct anti-labor bias, 400n38, 400–401n40, 404n9, 407n89
  use of antitrust laws, 252
T&O, 63–64
  sold to ETV&G, 64
Taylor, Alfred, 391n254
Taylor, George C., 383
Taylor, J. Will, 192, 307
Taylor, Nevada, 136, 379n149
  See also Johnson, Ed
Taylor, Robert L., 91
  Sanford gave address of welcome, 91
  urged Sanford's appointment to Sixth Circuit, 152
TBA (Tennessee Bar Association), 55–56, 93, 96–98, 101, 170, 188–89, 207, 279, 364n74, 365n81, n86, and n99
  president of the organization, 96
  Sanford joined, 364n74
  Sanford's bar exam story, 56
  Sanford's involvement decreased upon becoming judge, 97
  suggested upgrades to the profession, 96
  uniform laws, decried lack of, 96–97
TBA committees, 96, 365n86
TBA speech, 98
Teapot Dome, 276–79, 414n333, 423n7
temperance, 114, 128, 248
temperance policy, 117
Temple, Oliver Perry (O.P.), 8, 10, 58, 120, 329n82, 368n175
Tennessee, State of, 6
  debt, 68
  description of, 6
  military alliance with Confederacy, 8
  military rule, 17
  readmitted to Union, 19–20, 335n12
  slave state, 6
  Unionist convention (1865), 18
  US Supreme Court justices, 183
Tennessee Agricultural Commission, 16
Tennessee & Ohio (T&O). *See* T&O
Tennessee Board of Immigration, 21
Tennessee Coal, Iron, and Railroad Co., 61, 69
Tennessee Centennial Exposition, 91, 362n26
Tennessee Chemical Co., 128
Tennessee Congressional delegation, 179
  pushed for additional judgeship, 179
Tennessee Constitution, 182, 351n128
  (1796), 6, 363n45
  (1870) prohibited state funding to corporations, 351n128
  amended (1865), 18
  poll tax, 24
Tennessee Constitutional Convention,
  (1796), 93
  (1834), 6
Tennessee Copper Company, 174
Tennessee Farmers Alliance, 69, 111–12
Tennessee Fourth Infantry, 27
Tennessee Historical Society member, 93
Tennessee Law Review, 47, 308
  editor Howard H. Baker, Sr., 47
  observation, on Sanford, 47, 308
Tennessee Medical College (Knoxville, TN), 90, 340n113
  E.J. on board of trustees, 340n113
Tennessee Mining & Manufacturing Co., 350n98
Tennessee Redeemers, 34
Tennessee Republican Executive Committee, 147
Tennessee Republican Party, 114, 147
Tennessee Republicans, 21, 115, 143, 196, 396n91
Tennessee River, 33, 74, 117, 139, 328
Tennessee "school fund," 34
Tennessee State Baptist Convention, 80
Tennessee Supreme Court, 4, 45, 55–56, 58–59, 72–73, 77–78, 113, 129, 137, 146, 151, 192, 349n71
  Sanford as potential justice, 113
Tennessee Valley Authority Act, 381–82n29
Tennessee Wesleyan College, 361, 381–82n29
Tennessee's grand divisions, 6
Tennessee's "lost county," 383n60
  See also James County (TN)
Tennessee's military governor, 18
Tenth Amendment, 228, 245, 249
Tenure of Office Act, 276
Terry, Adrian, 32, 62, 336n24
  E.J.'s best friend, 32
  home, 32
  K&K, 62
  Sanford's godfather, 32
  Sanford named for, 32
  service in Union Army, 32, 62
Terry, Alfred Howe, 32
Texas, New Mexico v., 242
Texas, Oklahoma v., 242
Texas, Washington v., 422n205
Thirteenth Amendment, 18, 285–86
  Tennessee ratified, 18
Thompson, J. Lawn, 2
Thornburgh, Jacob Montgomery, 57–59, 110, 347n19
  death of, 59
Thornburgh & Sanford, law firm, 58
"Three generations of imbeciles," 273
  See also *Buck v. Bell*
"Three Musketeers," 121
ticket brokers, 266
ticket scalping, 239, 265
Tilden, Samuel J., 286
Titanic, 398n125
  See also Burlingham, Charles C. (C.C.)

472 INDEX

tobacco, 128, 168, 350n104, 368n181, 388–89n191
   belt, 168
   cases, 128
   industry, 168
   litigation, 128
   monopoly, 388–89n191
   prices, 168
Tobacco Trust, 128
   See also Duke, James Buchanan "Buck"
Tokushige, Farrington v., 264–65
Toney, Fred, 174
   Mann Act White Slave Traffic indictment, 174
   Selective Service Act charge, 174
trade, restraint of, 126, 128, 251
Transportation Act of 1920, 245
Traveler's Protective Association, 16, 120
Trigg, Connally F., 10
trust-busting, 126
trusts, 123–26, 128, 168, 227, 282, 309
Twain, Mark, 57, 108
Twining v. New Jersey, 291
Tyler, Harmon v., 271
Tyson, Lawrence D., 74–75, 120, 354n190
   law partner of Sanford's, 74
   Puerto Rico military governor, 75
   Spanish-American War, 75
   US senator, 75
Tyson & Bro. United Theatre Ticket Office, Inc. v. Banton, 265

Ugly Duckling, The, 280
   See also Fred, Hugh Mrs.
Uncle Wash, 167
Union Army, 10–11, 12, 14, 17, 32, 35, 72, 80
   capture of Knoxville, 12, 23
   Tennesseans in, 11
Union Army Camp at Boston, (KY), 12
Union occupation, 61
Union sympathizers, 35
Unionism and Reconstruction in East Tennessee, 18, 20, 31, 327n36
Unionists of East Tennessee, 8–11, 20, 31
United Leather Workers International Union, Local Lodge or Union No. 66 v. Merkert & Meisel Trunk Co., 251
United Mine Workers of America, Coronado Coal Co. v., 251
United Presbyterian Church, 25
United States Federal Census, 87, 360n325
Universal Congress of Lawyers and Jurists, 98, 365n81
University of Chattanooga, 362–63n42
University of Cincinnati, 43–45, 53, 103
University of Maine, 43
University of Tennessee, 20, 34, 37–45, 49, 52–53, 61, 63, 73–74, 80, 101–4, 145–46, 196, 308, 325–26n8, 340n116, 341n132, 342n147
   admission of women, 41
   alumni address, 342
   Alumni and University orator (1894), 42
   Alumni Association, member, 42, 43, 46, 82
   Alumni Association, president, 42
   center for education reform, 102

   Chattanooga, at, 362–63n42
   department of education, 102–3
   national prestige, 102
   obtained Woodruff mansion, 80
   preparatory department, 34, 339n99
   See also Board of Trustees, University of Tennessee; University of Tennessee, Sanford at
University of Tennessee, Sanford at, 39, 40–43, 46–47, 74, 103, 242
University of Tennessee College of Law, 44, 47, 424n19
   housed in former female academy, 119
   Law Department, 42
   law review, tribute, 47
   Sanford served as professor, 42, 308
   Tyson, received law degree from, 74
University of Tennessee Memorial Hospital, 119
University of Tennessee Record, 40, 43
University of Virginia, 193, 343n161
University of Virginia School of Law, 47, 193
University School (Baker-Himel), 122, 337n46
urbane, 200, 237
uremic poisoning, 2–3
US, Abrams v., 292
US, Baltimore & Ohio Railroad Company v., 253–54
US, Carroll v., 247
US, Cement Manufacturers Protective Ass'n v. (dissent), 250
US, Goat & Sheepskin Import Co. v., 132
US, Henry E. Frankenburg Co. v., 132
US, Lewis v., 180
US, Maple Flooring Manufacturers' Ass'n v. (dissent), 250
US, Myers v., 276
US, Okanogan Indians, et al. v., 244
US, Olmstead v., 247
US, Schenk v., 292
US, Winters v., 133
US Attorney for the Western District of Tennessee, 167
US Civil Service, women in, 42
US District court, 87
US District Judge, 91
US Supreme Court, 56, 77, 79, 84–85, 95, 116, 135, 141, 149, 165, 179–80, 183, 187–90, 231, 276, 278, 286, 292, 355n207
US v. American Linseed Oil Co., 250
US v. Cerecedo Hermanos y Compania, 132
US v. Forty Barrels and Twenty Kegs of Coca-Cola, 162
US v. Manzi, 271
US v. River Rouge Improvement Co., 259
US v. Schwimmer, (dissent) 271–73
US v. Shipp, 136–142, 166, 379n132, 379n146
US v. State Investment Co., 242
US v. Yuginovitch, 180
utopian novelist, 371, 420n125
utopian visions, 176

valedictory oration (1883), 41
Van Buren, Martin, 10, 183
Van Devanter, Willis, 3, 93–94, 184, 193, 216–17, 225, 229, 232–33, 238–39, 245, 247, 275–76, 279, 306, 310–12, 399n6, 407n86, 419n114, 422n189
   alarmed by Sanford's condition, 2
   Taft's closest ally, 239

Van Deventer, Horace, 83, 194, 357n286, 382n39
  Lurton's son-in-law, 53
Van Deventer, James, 120
Van Deventer, Mrs. Horace, 93, 357n286
  Lurton's daughter, 83
Vanderbilt Law School, 51, 193, 196
Vanderbilt University, 47, 105, 127, 193, 336n17
velocipede, 32, 336n30
veterans, black, 26
veto, pocket, 244
violence, racial, 23, 26
Virginia-Carolina Chemical Co., 127
Visigothic Code, 311
Volstead Act, 175–76, 180, 391n241
voters, black, 22
voting rights, black, 418n79

Walnut Street Bridge, 139, 381n17
  lynching of Ed Johnson, 139
Walsh, Thomas, 277, 278, 415n339
  See also Teapot Dome
War Industries Board, 122
War-time Prohibition Act, 175–76
Warren, Earl, 304
Warrington, John W., 383n51
Washington, Booker T., 26
Washington, D.C., 1, 3–4, 10, 46, 85, 91, 94, 141, 154, 165, 199
Washington Press Club, 90
Washington v. Texas, 135, 422n205
Weeks Law (1911), 391n252
West Tennessee, 6–8, 11–12, 18–19, 110, 354n193, 380n158
Whigs, 7, 10–11, 18
  See also Harlan, John Marshall
Whitaker, Matt, 138, 139–40
White, Edward Douglass, 149, 184, 196, 226, 399n6
  prediction about Sanford, 149
White, Hugh Lawson, 11
White, James, 61
white disfranchisement, 18–19, 21–22
White House, 19, 191
White River Lumber Co. v. State of Arkansas, 257
White Star Line, 398n125
  See also Burlingham, Charles C. (C.C.)
Whitney, Charlotte Anita, 299
Whitney v. California, 257, 299–301
Wickersham, George W., 363n53
Wiggam, Albert Edward, 274–75
  New Decalogue of Science, The 274
Wiley, Harvey Washington, 163, 387n133
  See also Coca-Cola
Wiley, Henry H., 64–65, 350n94 and n97
  See also Coal Creek Mining & Manuf. Co.
Williams, Alice, 166
Willson, Augustus E., 192
Wilson, Jimmie, 192
Wilson, S.F., 189
Wilson, W.B., 83

Wilson, Woodrow, 75, 83, 94, 106, 115–16, 129, 165, 173, 183, 185, 230, 231, 274, 276, 292, 324n30, 342n143, 381n17 and n29, 395n66, 406n62
  Sanford letter, 75
Wilsonian progressivism, 184
Winchester (TN), 383–84n71
Winters Doctrine, 134
  Indian water rights principle of protecting present and future Indian water needs, 134
Winters v. US, 133
wire-tapping, 247
Wobblies, 228
  See also IWW
Wolfe, Davis v., 255
Women, progress for, 42
Women's Christian Temperance Union, 82
Woodruff, Ella T. (Connelly), 79, 356n266, 360n325
Woodruff, William Wallace (W.W.), 20, 58, 60, 79–81, 87, 111, 120, 205, 355n226, 356n266
  allegation that he supported Sanford's family, 206
  denounced convict labor, 81
  East Tennessee National Bank, officer and director, 60
  mansion, 80, 205
  railroad accident, 58
  ran for Congress, 80–81
Woodruff heirs, 80
Woodruff house, 80, 87, 205, 214
World's Fair (Chicago), 82–83
World War I, 26, 53, 75, 84, 104, 106, 115, 122, 171, 173, 175, 180, 184, 197, 226–28, 292–93, 360n340, 389n205, 396n96
  post-war warnings by Sanford, 106–107
  post-World War I similar to post-Civil War, 108
  Sanford commencement speech on, 53, 106
World War I cases, 292, 420n137
Wright, T.A., 83, 357n286
W.W. Woodruff & Company, 80, 122
Wyoming, 74, 233, 277–78
Wyoming Territorial Supreme Court, 233

Yale, 87, 329, 334, 336n24
Yale graduate, 122
Yale Law School, 116, 226
  Taft professor at, 116, 231
Yale University, 336n24
Yardley, William F., 25
"ye ancient Games of Hallow E'en," 86
YMCA, 90, 95, 370n223
Young, J.B., 25
Young Ladies' Reception Committee, 83
Yuginovitch, US v., 180
YWCA (Knoxville), 324n29

Zollner, Iona Wilhelmina, Pickhardt Sutton, Shope, 171–73, 389n204
  father, Wilhelm Pickhardt, 389n204
  husband, German Army Captain, 171–172

www.ingramcontent.com/pod-product-compliance
Lightning Source LLC
Chambersburg PA
CBHW030441090526
44586CB00044B/444